The F

ENGLAND, WALES & IRELAND
& THE CHANNEL ISLANDS

1995

COLOUR SECTION

SELF-CATERING

THAMES VALLEY HOLIDAY HOMES

Two country holiday homes overlooking the Thames Valley

Overleigh sleeps 2-6 people. Underleigh sleeps 1-4 people. Both properties are fully equipped – central heating, colour TV, telephone, pretty gardens/orchard, plenty of parking. Situated in a picturesque village a short distance from the famous Cliveden Estate, within easy reach of London 25 miles and Windsor 10 miles.

Registered with Tourist Board.

For further information see classified entry under Wooburn Green, Bucks.

Send for free colour brochure: Mrs E.G. Griffin

MYOSOTIS, WIDMOOR, WOOBURN GREEN, BUCKS HP10 0JG

Tel: Bourne End (01628) 521594 Fax: 01628 850471

Tregurrian Hotel

*AA** ETB* ♛♛♛

LES ROUTIERS

Watergate Bay, Near Newquay
Cornwall TR8 4AB
Tel: St. Mawgan (01637) 860280

100 yards from this glorious sandy beach and spectacular Atlantic coastline. Peaceful position between Newquay and Padstow.

- **27 rooms with radio/listening, tea makers, heaters, most en suite – TV all rooms. Car park.**
- **Heated pool and sun patio, Games room, Solarium**
- **Licensed Bar, Sauna, Jacuzzi**
- **Family run, children welcome at reduced rates (some free offers off-season)**
- **Central for touring all of Cornwall**
- **Parties and coaches by arrangement**
- **Open Easter to November**
- **Spring and Autumn Breaks**
- **Dinner, Bed and Breakfast £144 to £230 (inclusive of VAT)**

Brochure from resident proprietors, Marian and Derrick Molloy.

Please note all advertisers
in this colour section
also have a full review
in the classified section
under the relevant county.

BOSSINEY HOUSE HOTEL

Tintagel
Cornwall PL34 0AX
Tel: 01840 770240
Fax: 01840 770501

Perched on the cliffs overlooking one of the finest stretches of National Trust coastline in Cornwall. ½ mile from Tintagel.

- ★ **19 bedrooms including family suite, pleasant sea or country views and nearly all en-suite.**
- ★ **Residents' lounge, TV lounge, spacious dining room & cocktail bar.**
- ★ **Renowned à la carte and table d'hôte menus.**
- ★ **2½ acres of lawns and gardens including putting green.**
- ★ **Scandinavian log chalet in the grounds with heated swimming pool, sauna and solarium.**
- ★ **Magnificent cliff walks and nearby facilities including surfing, horse riding, golf, squash, pony-trekking and fishing.**
- ★ **Reduced prices for longer stays. Dinner, bed and breakfast.**

AA ★★ RAC

For details and our colour brochure please contact resident proprietors C. & R. Savage, The Bossiney House Hotel

Enjoy a holiday by the sea in the heart of King Arthur's kingdom.

ETB ♛♛♛ APPROVED

BOARD

The CLIFF HOTEL, Crooklets Beach, Bude, Cornwall EX23 8NG
Telephone: 01288 353110

A small top-class hotel where quality matters; with indoor swimming and spa pool, solarium, all weather tennis court, putting green, par 3 chipping hole, children's play area (swing, see-saw). All weather bowling green. 200 yards from Crooklets Beach, adjoining National Trust cliffs and farms. All set in five acres of grounds. Bedrooms are ensuite with colour TV (video and Sky), radio, drinks facility, phone. Food is the chef-proprietor's first priority and he ensures that the choice and quality are second to none. Weekly half board from £200.

"This hotel is like an oasis in a desert". . . Mr. Peter Savill (ETB Inspector).

BOARD

Dalswinton Country House Hotel

AA ★★
ENGLISH TOURIST BOARD ♛♛♛

St. Mawgan, Near Newquay, Cornwall TR8 4EZ
Telephone: St. Mawgan (01637) 860385

- All rooms en suite
- Full central heating
- Colour TV in rooms
- Tea/coffee facilities
- Residential and Restaurant Licence
- 5 course Dinner – choice of menu
- Log fires in lounge and bar
- Heated swimming pool

OPEN ALL YEAR including CHRISTMAS & NEW YEAR

Approached by its own private 200 yard drive, The Dalswinton is an old Cornish house of immense character in 1½ acres of secluded grounds. Overlooking the beautiful valley of Lanherne with views to the sea. Ideally situated between Newquay and Padstow, reputed to be the finest coastline in Europe. The Hotel has been completely refurbished and offers superb cooking in a comfortable, friendly atmosphere. Excellent beaches and coves within one and a half miles with many picturesque coastal walks. Some of the best coarse fishing in Cornwall, two new golf courses plus horse riding are all available locally. Bed and Breakfast from £15.50 per night. Weekly from £95. Dinner, Bed and Breakfast from £137. Bargain Breaks available. Colour brochure on request.

SELF-CATERING

"Halwyn"

Manaccan, Helston, Cornwall
Mr & Mrs H. Donald
Tel. 01326 280359 or 565694

Delightful farmhouse and cottages in tranquil surroundings. Open all year.

Indoor swimming pool, sauna and solarium.

For full details see SELF CATERING SECTION – CORNWALL – HELSTON.

A REAL COUNTRY HOUSE HOTEL JUST OUTSIDE OF FALMOUTH

THE HOME

PENJERRICK, FALMOUTH

Telephone: Falmouth (STD 01326) 250427 and 250143

Situated in lovely unspoilt countryside, yet only 2½ miles from Falmouth.
Ideal for lovers of the country, yet within 18 minutes' walk of Maenporth Beach.

An Ashley Courtenay Highly Recommended Hotel

Our house, in its large garden, has lovely views over tree-clad countryside to Maenporth and the bay. Close to the Helford River with its beautiful walks and boating facilities. Ideal base for touring. Majority of bedrooms now completely refurbished with full ensuite facilities, TV and tea/coffee making facilities and heating. Our home is graciously furnished and carpeted to a high standard. All beds are modern divans. Central heating. Our elegant dining room has separate tables. Large lounge with colour TV. In addition there is a spacious sun lounge overlooking the garden.

★

TABLE LICENCE   GOOD ENCLOSED CAR PARK   BUS SERVICE

★

Mr & Mrs P. Tremayne have welcomed guests to their lovely house for the past 30 years

★

Dinner, Room and Breakfast from £130 per week, including 17.5% VAT.

Illustrated brochure from: Mrs. T. P. Tremayne

We are of a farming family and our visitors' book is blushingly complimentary over the home-cooked food and its presentation. This is our home and as such we welcome you to it and hope you will enjoy it as much as we do.

Also Self-Catering Furnished Farmhouse and Cottage at Constantine, Falmouth

BOARD

AA** RAC**

Rosemundy House Hotel

ETB

Telephone St. Agnes (01872) 552101

Rosemundy House is a delightful Georgian residence set in its own sheltered and attractive grounds in the village of St. Agnes and within a mile of Trevaunance Cove beach. Rosemundy is family owned and run and we take pride in the quality of food, service and accommodation we offer. St. Agnes is an unspoilt village on the north Cornish coast between St. Ives and Newquay and is an ideal centre for touring.

- Family-run Hotel
- Attractive licensed bar
- Good home cooking
- Colour TV lounge
- 43 ensuite bedrooms
- Colour TV in all bedrooms
- Tea/coffee making facilities in all bedrooms
- Large car park
- 45ft heated swimming pool
- Games room with table tennis, pool, snooker, darts, etc
- Badminton, Croquet, Putting
- Horse riding, golf, tennis, surfing, gliding, fishing nearby

Dinner, Bed and Breakfast from £140 to £235 per week (including VAT)
Bed and Breakfast from £115 to £210 per week (including VAT). We make no service charge.

Rosemundy House Hotel, Rosemundy, St. Agnes, Cornwall TR5 0UF

SELF-CATERING

- Superior S/C Apartments for 2 to 7
- Fully equipped, all electric, Col.TV.
- Own bath/shower and toilet
- Unrivalled views over Bay. Minutes from beach
- Free parking. Coin-op launderette
- Quiet peaceful location
- Well behaved pets welcome
- Low Season from £65 to £125; High from £160 to £340 depending on size of Apartment
- SAE for Brochure and Tariff
- English Tourist Board 2-4 keys Approved and Commended

Resident Proprietors: Norman & Margie Jenkins

PLAIDY BEACH HOLIDAY APARTMENTS
Dept FG, Plaidy, Looe, Cornwall PL13 1LG Telephone: 01503 262044

BOARD

Crantock Plains Farmhouse

1990, 1991 & 1992 WINNERS OF 'NEWQUAY IN BLOOM'

Relax in this charming character farmhouse in peaceful countryside and combine comfort, home cooking and personal service for an enjoyable holiday. Crantock Plains Farm is situated two and a half miles from Newquay and half a mile off the A3075 Newquay-Redruth road. Picturesque village of Crantock with Post Office, village stores, tea rooms, two pubs and beautiful sandy beach is nearby, as are riding stables and many sporting activities. Four doubles (one twin en-suite), two family rooms, one family en-suite. Ground floor bedrooms are available. Shower room; two toilets, bathroom; sittingroom; central heating, log fire. Electric blankets for chilly nights. Table licence. Home grown vegetables when available. No pets. Open all year. Please send SAE for brochure with details of prices. Non-smoking establishment. Tourist Board and H.A.S.S. Registered. Cream Tea Award.

Mr and Mrs Rowlands, Crantock Plains Farm, Near Newquay, Cornwall. Tel: Crantock (01637) 830253

SELF-CATERING

ST. MARGARET'S HOLIDAY PARK
Tel/Fax: (01726) 74283

Family owned and run holiday park, set in six acres of beautiful parkland and offering good quality accommodation of varying sizes, from detached bungalows sleeping up to eight persons to self contained chalets nestling amongst the trees and sleeping from two to five people. Two of the bungalows are suitable for disabled persons. All property is well equipped including colour TV and microwave ovens. Launderette and pay phone on park. St. Austell golf course is 400 yards away and the Polgooth shops and inn are conveniently near. Well controlled pets allowed. Special rates early/late season or for two persons. Open March to December. Terms and colour brochure from: **Mrs M. King, St. Margaret's Holiday Park, Polgooth, St. Austell, Cornwall PL26 7AX.**

SELF-CATERING

CORNWALL • LOOE

Holiday bungalow or hillside villa, both semi-detached with own access. Patio overlooking sea, patio furniture, lovely panoramic views. Picturesque, secluded south-facing suntrap valley – walk straight on to safe, sandy beach with rock pools to explore. Windsurfing, parascending, boat trips, all watersports, tennis, entertainment, indoor pool, restaurant, launderette, supermarket, beach tavern, fish and chip shop, club with entertainment, membership inclusive. Horse-riding nearby. NT and woodland walks. Teletext colour TV with remote and Sky channels, microwave, shower and bath, duvets and bedlinen supplied. Superior accommodation for 4/6 therefore no pets in accommodation or on beach. Highly recommended.

Mrs Colloff, 188 Lancaster Drive, Hornchurch, Essex RM12 5SL Tel: 01708 444866 Fax: 01708 709483

SELF-CATERING

CHARACTER COTTAGES AND PINE LODGES

Fringe of Lake District, National Park. 3 lodges peacefully situated in our grounds in picturesque hamlet. Views over farmland to Caldbeck Fells, 30 mins Lake Ullswater, Keswick or Gretna Green.

* 1/2/3 Bedrooms (sleep 2/7)
* Shower/bath, second WC in 3 bedroom properties
* Heaters in all properties
* Colour TVs
* Microwaves
* 3 cottages, 1 heavily beamed with wood burning stove
* Laundry
* Open all year, winter breaks
* Warm for your arrival
* Excellent quality throughout
* Direct dial telephones
* up to Highly Commended

Featured in Good Holiday Cottage Guide. Terms £135-£440. For details and brochure:

Mrs Ivinson (FHG), Green View, Welton, Near Dalston, Carlisle CA5 7ES
Telephone: 016974 76230 Fax: 016974 76523

BOARD

SUMMER HILL COUNTRY HOUSE

Hawkshead Hill, Ambleside, Cumbria LA22 0PP Tel: (015394) 36311

HIGHLY COMMENDED

Pleasantly situated in its own grounds, in the heart of England's Lake District. All bedrooms have ensuite facilities including colour TV, trouser press and hair dryer. Strictly non-smoking. Pets by arrangement. We are close to Tarn Hows (a well-known beauty spot and small lake) and are blessed with an abundance of wild life and country walks. B&B from £19-£22.

Contact Carol and Henry Rogers for brochure.

Patterdale Hall Estate

GLENRIDDING · PENRITH · CUMBRIA · CA11 0PJ
Telephone & Fax: Glenridding (017684) 82308 (24 hours)

In a magnificent mountain setting at the southern end of Ullswater, Patterdale Hall Estate is ideally situated for holidays and outdoor activities. Its spacious wooded grounds reach from the shores of the lake to the lower slopes of the Helvellyn range. The 300 acres contains a working hill farm, own private section of foreshore and 100 acres of private woodland and gardens. Sailing, fishing, canoeing, windsurfing and steamer trips on Ullswater, and the Estate makes an ideal base for touring the whole of the Lake District.

There are 16 self-catering units in various parts of the Estate including two Bothies awaiting grading and:

Three	Two	Six	Two	One
English Tourist Board COMMENDED (4 keys)	English Tourist Board APPROVED (3 keys)	English Tourist Board COMMENDED (1 key)	English Tourist Board COMMENDED (3 keys)	English Tourist Board COMMENDED (1 key)
Apartments	Cottages	Cedar Chalets	Pine Lodges	Dairy

Terms are from £112 to £381 per week including central heating and one tank of hot water per day. Other electricity metered. Linen hire available. Children welcome. Pets by arrangement in cottages. Colour TV in all units. Launderette on site. Patterdale Hall itself also offers accommodation for groups, with meals provided.

"Short Breaks" and special offers available. Telephone for detailed brochure.

ENGLISH TOURIST BOARD ACCESSIBLE

SELF-CATERING

BOARD

The Beaumont Hotel

Holly Road, Windermere, Cumbria LA23 2AF
Telephone: (015394) 47075

Opened Easter 1992, this elegant Victorian House Hotel lends itself to all the Grace & Charm of its time combined with all the comforts of today. Ideally situated for Windermere and Bowness and a perfect location for touring the Lakes. All 12 luxury bedrooms are ensuite with tea making facilities, TV and hairdryers. Some ground floor rooms.

Two Four-Poster rooms are available for that Special Occasion and a 'Romantic Presentation' of wine, chocolates, fruit and flowers may be ordered. The Beaumont has very quickly gained a reputation for quality and excellent value. Please ring for room availability. Standards are high, Breakfasts are hearty and the Hospitality is warm and sincere. Prices from £20. Private parking.

AA QQQQ Selected. RAC Highly Acclaimed. Highly Commended

SELF-CATERING

ETB 4 Keys Commended

SECLUDED COTTAGES FISHING, PETS WELCOME

Tranquil quality cottages overlooking two modest lakes amid Lakeland's beautiful Eden Valley countryside, only 30 minutes' drive equidistant from Ullswater, North Pennines, Hadrian's Wall and Scottish Borders. You will find beds freshly made up for your arrival, tranquillity and freedom in your surroundings, and good coarse and game fishing at hand. Accommodation is guaranteed clean, well equipped and maintained; laundry area; **PETS WELCOME.** Centrally located, exceptional wildlife and walking area. **NO SILLY RULES.** Relax and escape to **YOUR** home in the country – why settle for less! Telephone or SAE for details.

Crossfield Cottages, Kirkoswald, Penrith CA10 1EU. 7 day 8am-10pm Tel: 01768 896275 (Fax available) (Answering machine only 10pm-8am) 24 hour Brochure Line: 01768 898711 (manned most Saturdays).

BOARD

HAWKSMOOR

Lake Road, Windermere, Cumbria LA23 2EQ
Telephone: (015394) 42110

Situated mid-way between Bowness and Windermere, within easy walking distance of both villages and backed by woodland. All rooms have bath/shower and toilet ensuite, tea/coffee making facilities and colour television. Hawksmoor enjoys a reputation for good home cooking, personal service by the proprietors and has a superb private car park. Some ground floor rooms are available. *Please telephone for room availability or brochure.* November – mid-May, excluding Bank Holidays; Dinner, Bed & Breakfast from £70-£85 for 2/3 nights. Discounts for Sunday.

AA Selected
RAC Highly Commended

Highly Commended

BOARD

GLENCREE LAKE ROAD, WINDERMERE, CUMBRIA LA23 2EQ

A warm welcome to our elegantly furnished and decorated small Hotel will enhance your enjoyment of your stay in The Most Beautiful Corner of England.

* Lovely, spacious ensuite rooms; * Colour TV; * Tea/coffee Trays; * Comfortable beds – some kingsize; * A pretty woodland outlook from most rooms

A traditional English Breakfast cooked to perfection will fortify your exploration of Lakes & Fells.
QQQ Recommended by AA; Highly Acclaimed award by RAC and other prestigious guides.
Access/Visa. Call us now for reservation.
Tel: 015394 45822. Prop: Mrs Julie P. Butler.

BOARD

SANDOWN

Lake Road, Windermere, Cumbria LA23 2JF Tel: 015394 45275

Superb Bed and Breakfast accommodation. All rooms ensuite with colour TV and tea/coffee making facilities. Situated two minutes from Lake Windermere, shops and cafes. Many lovely walks. Open all year. Special out of season rates, also two-day Saturday/Sunday Breaks. From £18.00 to £27 per person excluding Bank Holidays. Well-behaved dogs welcome. Each room has own safe private car parking. SAE or telephone for further details.

Proprietors: Irene and George Eastwood

SELF-CATERING

WINDERMERE

10 minutes' walk from lake or village.
Open all year. 10 fully equipped spacious apartments sleep 2-6.
Pool, colour TV, central heating.
Terms £100-£370.

For brochure contact:
Bruce and Marsha Dodsworth, Birthwaite Edge, Birthwaite Road, Windermere LA23 1BS
Telephone: 015394 42861

See self catering section – Windermere, Cumbria

BOARD

Linda & Alan Bleasdale

Borwick Lodge

Outgate, Hawkshead, Ambleside, Cumbria LA22 0PU
Tel: Hawkshead (015394) 36332

Twice winners of the AWARD for "Accommodation of the Highest Standards of Comfort, Amenity and Hospitality". Delightful 17th century country house nestling in 3 acres of secluded gardens. Breathtaking panoramic lake and mountain views. Ideally situated. Close to Hawkshead village with good choice of restaurants and inns. Beautiful ensuite rooms with colour TV and tea-making facilities. King-size four-poster rooms. Prize-winning home-made breads. Tourist Board "Two Crown Highly Commended". Somewhere special in this most beautiful corner of England. Ample parking. NON-SMOKING THROUGHOUT. Bed and Breakfast from £18. May we send our brochure? *See Board Section – Ambleside, Cumbria.*

BOARD/SELF-CATERING/CARAVANS

Shallow Grange
Chelmorton
Nr. Buxton SK17 9SG

HIGHLY COMMENDED

Shallow Grange is situated in the heart of the Peak District set amidst beautiful open views. This working dairy farm has numerous unspoilt breathtaking walks, whilst Chatsworth, Haddon Hall, Bakewell and Buxton are all within a short drive. This 18th century farmhouse has recently been fully modernised without detracting from its original character, oak beams, inglenook fireplace, etc., are all complemented with antique furniture. All bedrooms are ensuite with tea/coffee making facilities and colour televisions. The house is fully centrally heated, double glazed and carpeted throughout. Fully licensed. Sorry, no pets. Holiday cottage sleeps 4. Deluxe Caravan Site.

Phone Christine Holland (01298 23578) for terms or brochure. Fax: 01298 78242.

For the widest choice of cottages in Devon …

. . . and the best value you'll find anywhere

Contact us now for a free copy of our guide to the 500 best value cottages around Devon's unspoilt National Trust Coast. Spring and Autumn breaks in delightful Exmoor farm cottages from only £65 to luxury beachside homes with swimming pools at over £650 p.w. in Summer. All are regularly inspected and guaranteed to offer first class value.

Free leisure guide and £75 worth of discount shopping vouchers with every booking. Cottages for sale details and free hotel accommodation also available.

North Devon Holiday Homes

19 Cross Street, Barnstaple, EX31 1BD
Tel: (01271) 76322 (24 hrs)

RADFORDS

DAWLISH

In beautiful unspoilt countryside not too far from the beach

Chosen by the independent 'Peaudouce Guide' to Hotels as the very best Hotel for Children that they visited.

FOR THE PERFECT FAMILY HOLIDAY

Come and relax at Radfords in one of our chintzy old world lounges, our comfortable bar or our six acres of lovely garden – or come and enjoy an active action-packed holiday swimming in our heated indoor pools, playing badminton outdoors or enjoying a game of table tennis or skittles or one of the many other games in our large indoor games room. Squash, indoor badminton, golf, tennis, fishing and horse riding are all available close by. We have our own solarium for that essential sun tan.

We have family bedrooms or two room family suites available, all with a private bathroom, to accommodate a total of about thirty families. All bedrooms have tea/coffee making facilities.

THE CHILDREN will love their special heated indoor pool, the outdoor playground, the freedom of our large gardens and the assorted ponies and dogs there are to talk to. In the evenings they can look forward to a swimming gala, live entertainment, a party and their own cartoon show etc. Playroom now available.

THE ADULTS can look forward to superb food lovingly cooked and served and the various entertainments we arrange for them – from skittle tournaments to live entertainers. We also have a fully equipped laundrette and an evening babysitter to help make your holiday as relaxing as possible. We have a playgroup several mornings a week. Mothers can bring babies and small children here with every confidence. Radfords has been featured on TV by Judith Chalmers and holds the Farm Holiday Guide Diploma.

MEMBER WEST COUNTRY TOURIST BOARD.

Please telephone or send for an illustrated brochure to:

Mr and Mrs T. C. Crump, MHCI

RADFORDS, DAWLISH, SOUTH DEVON EX7 0QN

(Dawlish 863322. STD 01626-863322)

BOARD

Raddicombe Lodge South Devon

Set in peaceful surroundings overlooking the sea and country, midway between the picturesque harbour towns of Brixham and Dartmouth. The Lodge has a charm and character all of its own, with pitched ceilings and lattice windows. Scrumptious traditional English Breakfast, well appointed bedrooms with tea making facilities and colour TV; ensuite rooms available. Ample parking. AA and RAC listed. Les Routiers Recommended. English Tourist Board 2 Crowns. Offering room and breakfast only. For prices see our classified entry.

Phone or write to Graham and Yvonne Glass, Raddicombe Lodge, 102 Kingswear Road, Brixham TQ5 0EX. Tel: (01803) 882125.

SELF-CATERING

Compton Pool Farm, South Devon

★ Heated indoor swimming pool ★ Children's play area ★ Fishing lakes ★ Tennis court ★ Games barn ★ Sauna ★ Family holidays ★ Farm animals ★ Lots to do

E.T.B.

Nestling in a sheltered sunny valley, surrounded by red Devon hills, the nine tastefully converted, comfortably furnished stone cottages are grouped around a central courtyard and fish pond. All cottages are attractively decorated and fully equipped. The farm is kept tidy and the gardens colourful. Torquay and the sea are nearby and Dartmoor is close at hand.

JOHN & CATHY SONGER, COMPTON POOL FARM, COMPTON, DEVON TQ3 1TA.
Tel: 01803 872241 Fax: 01803 874012

SELF-CATERING

ETB Commended and Highly Commended

SMYTHEN FARM COASTAL COTTAGES

MEMBER

The cottages are set in an area of natural beauty, with unspoilt views over the beautiful Sterridge Valley to the sea and the coast of Wales beyond. Heated swimming pool in a suntrap enclosure. Spacious lawns and gardens. Children's play area with treehouse, swings and slide. Garden furniture and barbecue. Games room. Laundry room. Pay phone. Central for sandy beaches and touring Exmoor. The village of Berrynarbor is just two miles, with stores, an inn and many quality eating places. The area is well blessed with tourist attractions, from surfing and fishing to golf and pony trekking.

For brochure and terms apply to: Mrs F. M. Irwin, Smythen House, Sterridge Valley, Berrynarbor, Ilfracombe, Devon EX34 9TB. Telephone: Combe Martin (01271) 883515

SELF-CATERING

EXMOOR NATIONAL PARK
NEAR LYNTON

Our fully self contained STONE BUILT clean and cosy bungalows are peacefully situated in a uniquely beautiful setting in 17 private acres of THE PARK. Wildlife abounds. An ideal base for exploring on foot, by horse or by car, the Moors and spectacular COASTLINE. The Market Towns and Tourist Attractions of North Devon and Somerset are easily accessible. ETB Registered. £120-£340 per week per bungalow.

Brochure with pleasure from resident proprietors Mr & Mrs Boyce, 'Dean Steep', Barbrook, Lynton, North Devon EX35 6JS. Telephone (01598) 753272

BOARD

INGLESIDE HOTEL
Lynton, North Devon EX35 6HW Tel: 01598 752223

Ingleside, a family run AA/RAC hotel in premier position. High standards of accommodation, food and wine assured. All rooms ensuite, colour TV, tea/ coffee makers. Safe car park in hotel grounds. Lynton is the perfect centre to enjoy the magnificent beauty of Exmoor's coast, cliffs, rivers and countryside, whether walking, strolling or motoring. Brochure with sample menus and information sheet of local and surrounding area gladly sent.

Mr & Mrs C. S. Horn. B&B from £22 p.d. (£140 p.w.) Dinner £12.

BOARD/SELF-CATERING

MAELCOMBE HOUSE

A small coastal working farm nestling beneath wooded cliffs overlooking Lannacombe Bay. Beach one minute from comfortable farmhouse which is nearly the most southerly in Devon. Choice of family, double or single rooms. Excellent food, much being produced on farm; freshly caught seafood is a speciality. Activities include fishing, tennis (new hard court), bathing, spectacular walking, exploring, climbing or just relaxing in the gardens. Prices from £104.50 per week for Bed & Breakfast or £149.50 for Bed, Breakfast & Evening Meal, with special reductions for children. Also two self-catering flats to sleep 6; limited camping facilities are provided. Telephone or write for colour brochure.

Mr and Mrs C. M. Davies, Maelcombe House, East Prawle, Near Kingsbridge, Devon TQ7 2DA (Chivelstone (01548) 511 300).

SELF-CATERING

West Ridge, Devon

Seaton EX12 2TA "West Ridge", Harepath Hill, Mrs E.P. Fox: Tel. & Fax: (Seaton [01297] 22398).

"West Ridge" bungalow stands on elevated ground above the small coastal town of Seaton. It has 1½ acres of lawns and gardens and enjoys wide panoramic views of the beautiful Axe Estuary and the sea. Close by are Axmouth, Beer and Branscombe. The Lyme Bay area is an excellent centre for touring, walking, sailing, fishing, golf, etc. This comfortably furnished accommodation (including the spacious kitchen/living room on the right of the picture) is ideally suited for 3 to 5 persons. A cot can be provided. Available March to October. £125 to £315 weekly (fuel charges included). Full gas c/h; Colour TV.

ETB 🔑🔑🔑 Commended. SAE for brochure.

BOARD

Hotel Fiesta

50 St. Mary Church Road, Torquay, Devon TQ1 3JE

An elegant neo-Georgian building in spacious grounds with large sunny garden. Good food and friendly atmosphere. All rooms have teamaking facilities, washbasins and central heating. Separate tables in diningroom. TV lounge, games room, pool table and children's play area. Within easy reach of beaches, shops and entertainment plus 18 hole golf course and a wide range of sporting facilities. Bed and Breakfast from £93 to £105 weekly; Dinner, Bed and Breakfast from £119 to £139 weekly. Daily rates on request. For colour brochure and tariff phone Mike and Verna James on **01803 292388**.

BOARD

Lindum Hotel

IDEAL CENTRAL SITUATION

A friendly, family-run Licensed Hotel, conveniently situated for beach, shops, theatre and harbour. Within 600 yards of Abbey Sands, Gardens and main shopping area. An established reputation for good food, first class service in a relaxed and friendly atmosphere. *20 bedrooms many with ensuite facilities; *Varied choice of menus; *Full central heating; *Some ground floor rooms; *Cocktail bar; *TV lounge and sun lounge; *All bedrooms with radio/intercom/child listening and tea making facilities; *Some rooms with colour TV; *Free car parking; *Special terms for party bookings. Convenient for new Conference and Leisure Centre. Bed and Breakfast from £15. Free Brochure/Tariff with pleasure.

Lindum Hotel, Abbey Road, Torquay TQ2 5NP Telephone: 01803 292795 AA RAC

GOOD FOOD, FIRST CLASS SERVICE AND EXCELLENT VALUE FOR MONEY

SELF-CATERING

Hemsford Country Holidays,
Hemsford, Littlehempston,
Totnes, Devon TQ9 6NE
Telephone: 01803 762637

HEMSFORD

'The Complete Country Holiday'

Hemsford is ideally situated in the heart of South Devon, with Torbay, Dartmoor and the excellent beaches of the South Hams only a short drive away. Our 16 comfortable and well-equipped cottages (one suitable for disabled guests) accommodate 2-10 people and are available all year and all have night store heating. Own riding stables, heated indoor pool, sauna, solarium, games room, licensed bar, two all-weather tennis courts, 9-hole approach golf and children's play area. **Terms £90 to £1062 per week.** Full colour brochure on request. Regret no pets.

SELF-CATERING

WEST PUSEHILL FARM COTTAGES

For the very best in self-catering

Our 11 cottages are idyllically situated in an area of "outstanding natural beauty" only one mile from Devon's Golden Coast. Each stone built cottage is equipped and furnished to a high standard. Varying in size, they accommodate 2-8 people. Suitable for holidays throughout the year. Prices from £103 – £562.

Facilities include: heated swimming pool, licensed restaurant and bar, sauna, solarium, children's play area, pets corner games room and laundry. For full colour brochure phone or write to *John and Gill Violet*

West Pusehill Farm, Westward Ho!, North Devon
Tel: Bideford (01237) 475638 or 474622

The Warmest WELCOME in the West!

FAMILY HOLIDAY PARK

Ever had too much to do?

- Stylish **DOLPHIN CLUB** & Entertainment Centre.
- Super Indoor Heated **NEPTUNE TROPICANA** Water Leisure complex - four Feature-packed Pools, Solarium, Sauna, spectator viewing.
- New **CRUISERS** adult Cocktail bar
- Children's **JOLLY ROGER** Club with Disco, Cinema & large Games Arcade.
- Short, level walk to safe sandy beach.
- Great ***Value - for - money*** prices
- **FREE** Electricity, Linen, Colour TV
- Welcome TV - great films, local attractions, and YOU having fun!
- 2 Shops • Cafe • 2 Takeaways
- Crazy Golf • Adventure Playground
- Laundrette • Baby Listening
- Hire Service with computer games
- Pets *Welcome* (at small charge)

You will at Welcome Family!

WELCOME FAMILY HOLIDAY PARK
DAWLISH WARREN
SOUTH DEVON EX7 0PH

RESERVATIONS	01626 862070
DIAL a BROCHURE	01626 888323

We look forward to making YOU feel Welcome!

SELF-CATERING

An Oasis of Tranquillity

Highly Commended

Nestling at the head of a valley, with magnificent views across Exmoor, yet only ten minutes from the beach. Watermill and stone barns in 8 acres of gardens and woodland, converted into 10 high quality cottages. Heated indoor swimming pool, sauna and fitness room.

Four posters, dishwashers, microwaves, central heating, wood stoves, home made meals, shop, laundry, children's playground, Bed linen and maid service inclusive. Open March to November. Prices from £160 to £750 per week. Short break holidays available off peak.

Wheel Farm Country Cottages,
Berrydown 12, Combe Martin, Devon EX34 0NT.

Tel: 01271-882100

BOARD/SELF-CATERING

LEWESDON FARM HOLIDAYS

STABLE & BARN COTTAGES
HOLIDAY CARE ACCESSIBLE CATEGORIES 1 & 2

A local stone barn conversion situated well back from B3162 in an area of outstanding natural beauty, close to Heritage Coast. Designed with disabled in mind, all on one level with open plan sittingroom/kitchen-diningroom. Two bedrooms in each cottage, all en suite, sleep four or six with optional bunk beds. Stable Cottage also has washer/dryer. Cot and high chair, linen and coal can all be supplied for a small fee. Logs free. Slot meter for electricity. Fresh eggs and milk to order.

BED & BREAKFAST can be arranged close by if required. **NON SMOKERS PLEASE.**

A superb location for walking or just relaxing and the ideal choice for that truly peaceful holiday.

Jack and Jackie Spooncer, Lewesdon Farm Holidays, Stoke Abbott, Beaminster, Dorset DT8 3JZ.
Telephone: (01308) 868270 ETB Commended

SELF-CATERING/CARAVANS

MANOR FARM HOLIDAY CENTRE
CHARMOUTH, BRIDPORT, DORSET

Situated in rural valley of outstanding natural beauty, Manor Farm has all the requisite amenities for an exciting yet carefree holiday. Shop, launderette, licensed bar with family room, swimming pool and children's pool, play area. Ten minutes' level walk to beach, safe for bathing and famous for its fossils. Golf, riding, tennis, fishing and boating all nearby. Accommodation in 3 bedroomed bungalow, 2 and 3 bedroomed houses and luxury caravans. All units sleep six, and are equipped with colour TV, fitted carpets and parking/garage.

SAE to Mr. R. B. Loosmore
or Telephone 01297-560226

BOARD

Cromwell House Hotel

Lulworth Cove, Wareham BH20 5RJ
Tel: 01929 400253/400332 Fax: 01929 400566

Catriona and Alistair Miller welcome guests to their comfortable family-run hotel, set in secluded gardens with spectacular sea views. Situated 200 yards from Lulworth Cove, with direct access to the Dorset Coastal Footpath. A heated swimming pool is available for guests' use from May to October. Accommodation is in 14 ensuite bedrooms, with TV, direct-dial telephone, radio, and tea/coffee making facilities; most have spectacular sea views. Restaurant, bar wine list.

AA ★★ RAC ★★

BOARD

MARSHWOOD MANOR

Commended

Near Bridport, Dorset DT6 5NS
Tel. Broadwindsor (01308) 868442

Comfort and informal atmosphere in 50 acres of the peaceful Marshwood Vale. Excellent food, home made bread, garden produce. Heated outdoor swimming pool. Open all year. Children and pets welcome AA listed.

For full details see
Board Section – 'Bridport', Dorset

BOARD

COTSWOLDS

COMMENDED

Mrs A. E. Hughes, Ham Hill Farm, Whittington, Cheltenham, Gloucestershire
Telephone 01242 584415

This 160-acre farm has a new farmhouse built in 1983 in true traditional Cotswold style, with beautiful views of the Cotswolds and only about two miles from the town of Cheltenham. All visitors will be made welcome and everything will be done to make their stay enjoyable. Leisure activities nearby – riding, golf, walking (Cotswold Way). Rooms available, one family, one single, one double and two twins, all with washbasins, TV, Teasmades. Three en-suite rooms, bathroom, two toilets; sittingroom and diningroom. Central heating. Open all year round. Children over seven years welcome. Bed and Breakfast from £16.50 per person, £17.50 ensuite. Singles £20. Brochures available. **No smoking.**

SELF-CATERING

FAIRHAVEN HOLIDAY COTTAGES

Derby House, 123 Watling Street, Gillingham, Kent ME7 2YY
Phone & Fax (01634) 570157 (24 hours)

Offering an extensive selection of personally inspected holiday homes, all shapes and sizes, situated in a variety of attractive locations . . . coast, countryside and town.

COTTAGES IN THE SOUTH OF ENGLAND & WALES

PUBLISHER'S NOTE

While every effort is made to ensure accuracy, we regret that FHG Publications cannot accept responsibility for errors, omissions or misrepresentation in our entries or any consequences thereof. Prices in particular should be checked because we go to press early. We will follow up complaints but cannot act as arbiters or agents for either party.

SELF-CATERING

HOLIDAY IN OUR ENGLISH COUNTRY GARDEN

2 ACRES IN RURAL NORFOLK WITH RIVER NEARBY.

10 select and spacious family-run bungalows and lovely country farmhouse. Peacefully set in 2 acres of delightful gardens with Games room. Heated pool. Children's play area. Fishing, Boating, Riding and Golf nearby. Only 50 yards from River Staithe with access to Broads and well situated for touring. Car essential.

Hedera House & Plantation Bungalows

For full details & colour brochure contact:
H. G. Delf, Thurne Cottage, The Staithe, Thurne, Norfolk NR29 3BU. Tel. (01692) 670242 or (01493) 844568.

NORFOLK

SELF-CATERING

Withy Grove Farm

Come and enjoy a relaxing and friendly holiday 'Down on the Farm' set in beautiful Somerset countryside. Peaceful rural setting adjoining River Huntspill, famed for its coarse fishing and close to Burnham-on-Sea and other beauty spots. Self-catering barns and cottages are tastefully converted, sleeping 4/6. Fully equipped with colour TV.

★ Heated Swimming Pool
★ Licensed Bar and Entertainment (*in high season*)
★ Games Room ★ Skittle Alley
★ Reasonable Rates

For more information please contact:
Mrs Wendy Baker, Withy Grove Farm, East Huntspill, Near Burnham-on-Sea, Somerset TA9 3NP. Telephone: (01278) 784471

CARAVANS

Oxenleaze Farm Caravans Wiveliscombe

AN INEXPENSIVE, SUPERB FAMILY HOLIDAY.

This exceptional site is set in the peace and tranquillity of the Devon/Somerset borders, close to Exmoor, renowned for its beautiful countryside. Eleven luxury and super luxury caravans stand in one acre on a working hill farm. Each has its own shower, flush toilet, hot and cold water, cooker, fridge, fire and colour television. Car essential, parking beside each van. The site, ideal for an 'away from it all' holiday, offers games room, children's play area, sandpit, swings, barbecue, indoor heated swimming pool, laundry and telephone. A fisherman's paradise for those keen on coarse angling – free fishing on beautiful one and a half acre pond stocked with large carp and tench. No closed season. Early bookings advised. Strictly no pets. Open Easter to October.

SAE for brochure to Richard and Marion Rottenbury, Oxenleaze Farm Caravans, Chipstable, Wiveliscombe, Somerset TA4 2QH. Telephone: Wiveliscombe (01984) 623427

British Graded Holiday Parks

BOARD

'LANGBER COUNTRY GUEST HOUSE'

Ingleton, 'Beauty Spot of the North', in the National Parks area. Renowned for waterfalls, glens, underground caves, magnificent scenery and Ingleboro' mountain – 2,373 ft. An excellent centre for touring Dales, Lakes and coast. 'Langber', a detached country house, is set amidst beautiful scenery with 57 acres of fields and gardens. There are three family, three double or twin and one single bedrooms, some ensuite. Central heating, comfortably furnished throughout. Fire precautions. Babysitting offered. Open all year except Christmas; AA and RAC listed. Tourist Board registered. Reductions for children under 13 sharing parents' room. Terms on application. S.A.E. please.

Mrs Mollie Bell, Langber Country Guest House, Ingleton, North Yorkshire LA6 3DT. Tel: (015242) 41587

BOARD

Ryedale House *Coach Road, Sleights, near Whitby YO22 5EQ (01947 810534). Mrs Pat Beale.*

Welcoming non-smoking Yorkshire house of charm and character at the foot of the moors, National Park and 'Heartbeat' country, 3½ miles from Whitby. Rich in history, magnificent scenery, picturesque harbours, cliffs, beaches, scenic railways, superb walking. 3 double/twin beautifully appointed bedrooms (some private facilities). Guests' lounge and diningroom (separate tables) with breathtaking views over Eskdale. Enjoy our large sun terrace and gardens, relax, we're ready to pamper you! Noted for delicious Yorkshire fare – extensive breakfast and snacks menus, picnics (traditional and vegetarian). Recommended local inns and restaurants. Parking, near public transport. Regret no pets. B&B £15.50 - £18 per person, min. 2 nights. Weekly reductions, special breaks Winter-Spring and October. Member Yorkshire & Humberside Tourist Board.

SELF-CATERING

KILLARNEY LAKELAND COTTAGES

Muckross, Killarney, Co. Kerry, Ireland

Superb complex of traditional and modern cottages situated on **O'SHEA'S** Farm on 12 acres of landscaped parkland on the edge of the Killarney National Park, providing an ideal base for touring in South-West Ireland.

- 2, 3 and 4 bedroomed cottages (sleep 4/8)
- Colour TV; multi-channel TV
- Dishwasher ❖ Direct Dial Telephones
- Laundry Service ❖ Full Central Heating
- Two tennis courts, games room and children's play equipment on site
- Available locally: Nature Walks, Golf, Fishing, Swimming Pool, Boating, Horse Riding, Hill Walking

IRISH TOURIST BOARD APPROVED

Telephone or Fax for colour brochure:

Tel: 00-353 6431538 Fax: 00-353 6434113

BOARD

Killarney Villa

A well-appointed establishment offering superior accommodation with comfortable public areas. QQQ – AA 1992.

Set in peaceful, rural, scenic surroundings with beautiful gardens, patio and pond – within minutes' drive of the town centre/Killarney Lake District, and two 18-hole golf courses. All bedrooms have private facilities, orthopaedic beds. Two guest lounges with Satellite TV and video; small library and two diningrooms. Private car park. Roof-top conservatory offering tea and coffee 7am-11pm. Real 'home from home' atmosphere exists here and Killarney Villa is highly recommended for overall excellence in accommodation, service and hygiene, ensuring that guests take away happy memories of their stay with us. **Registered with the Irish Tourist Board. AA Listed.**

Bed and full Irish Breakfast £14.50 per person sharing; £15 per person sharing during July/August. Special 1995 Holiday Packages available on request. See also black and white display advertisement.

P.J. and Rosaleen O'Sullivan, Killarney Villa, Waterford Road (N72), Killarney, Co. Kerry, Ireland. Telephone: 00 353 64 31878

CARAVANS

West's Holiday Park

Where relaxing comes as naturally as the surrounding beauty

• A perfect holiday location • Central to South West • In an area of outstanding natural beauty • Caravan holiday homes with showers for hire • Children's indoor swimming pool • Tennis • Fishing • Golf • Sandy beaches • On the Ring of Kerry • Killarney National Park/Gap of Dunloe/Caves/Dingle Peninsula/Fungi the Dolphin/Skellig Rocks/Glencar area etc • Outdoor pursuits

Terms from £90 per week. Also terms for Ferry and Accommodation.

Reservations/Brochure: Liam and Linda West, Killarney Road, Killorglin, Co. Kerry
Telephone: 00 353 66 61240 Fax: 00 353 66 61833

BOARD

Mrs. M. Jones

Lochmeyler Farm

DE LUXE

AA SELECTED

RAC HIGHLY ACCLAIMED

RAC Guest House of the Year 1993

Llandeloy, Pen-y-Cwm, near Solva, Haverfordwest, Dyfed SA62 6LL. Telephone: (01348) 837724

A 220 acre dairy farm centre St. David's Peninsula, four miles from Solva harbour, two miles coastal path. Luxury accommodation in 16th century farmhouse. 10 en-suite rooms, some four-poster beds. All bedrooms have TV, video with video library, tea-making facilities etc. Spacious diningroom where traditional farmhouse cooking or vegetarian meals are served – all prepared by proprietor using fresh farm produce. Children 10 years and over welcomed. B&B £20 per night; BB&ED from £30 per night. Credit Cards accepted. Guests provided with National Park pack of all walks and places of interest in area, also Ordnance Survey Map. PETS WELCOME FREE OF CHARGE!

SELF-CATERING

· MYDROILYN ·

Stone farm buildings, recently converted into 4 cottages, providing modern standard of comfort in traditional setting. Sleep 2/3 (terms £80-£160) or 4/8 (terms £140-£280). Gas, electricity, linen included. All have shower room; fully equipped kitchen; colour TV; shared laundry room; facilities for children. Secluded rural area, abundant with wildlife and flowers; 5 miles from sandy beaches, picturesque harbours of Cardigan Bay, National Trust coastal paths; breathtaking mountain scenery; birdwatching, fishing, pony trekking, steam railway nearby.

WTB and AA approved. Open Easter to October.

Gil & Mike Kearney, Blaenllanarth Holiday Cottages, Mydroilyn, Lampeter, Dyfed SA48 7RJ. Telephone: Lampeter (01570) 470374.

BOARD

Highland Grange Farm

Robeston Wathen, Narberth SA67 8EP
Telephone (01834) 860952

This lovely, modern family home is set in a location you will find hard to beat. An ideal base on the A40 for your holiday in central Pembrokeshire. Numerous amenities in the area, many way-marked walks, fishing; cycling; horse-riding arranged. Good farmhouse cooking, pleasant guest lounge, small library. Country Inn nearby also water mill and tea room. Finally, we wish it to be known that our house is a home where you will always be most welcome. Open all year. **WTB Welcome Host Certificate.**

BOARD

TYDDYN DU FARM

Gellilydan, Ffestiniog, Near Porthmadog LL41 4RB
Telephone and Fax: 01766 590281

WALES TOURIST BOARD
HIGHLY COMMENDED

This beautiful 17th century historic farmhouse is situated amidst spectacular scenery in the heart of Snowdonia National Park. It is an excellent central location base for the numerous attractions, beaches and walks of North Wales. The farmhouse has a relaxed homely atmosphere, charm and character with a massive stone inglenook fireplace, antique furniture, exposed beams and stonework. Superb private ground floor cottage suite, with solid fuel stove, sleeps up to four (meals served in farmhouse). All bedrooms have colour TV, beverage trays and most are ensuite. Payphone for guests' use. Candlelight dinners are served using fresh local produce, with home-made soups and buns. Vegetarians welcome. Packed lunches available. Breakfast menu with seven choices, plus porridge! Non-smoking areas in farmhouse. You are welcome to bottle feed pet lambs, collect the eggs, feed the ducks on our mill pond and fuss over Polly the pony. We are easy to find – 300 yards off the A470, near the village of Gellilydan. Open all year. Bed and Breakfast from £16-£19, Dinner £8.50, Weekly Dinner, Bed and Breakfast from £150.

Stamp for brochure please to Mrs P. Williams.

SELF-CATERING

BRYN BRAS CASTLE

LLANRUG, Nr. CAERNARFON, NORTH WALES LL55 4RE
Tel & Fax Llanberis (01286) 870210

This romantic neo-Romanesque Castle is set in the gentle Snowdonian foothills near north Wales' mountains, beaches, resorts and heritage. Built in 1830, on an earlier structure, the Regency castle reflects peace not war ... it stands in 32 acres of tranquil gardens, with views. Bryn Bras offers distinctive and individual apartments, for 2-4 persons within the castle, each having spacious rooms radiating comfort, warmth and tranquillity and providing freedom and independence. All highest grade.

Many inns and restaurants nearby. This welcoming castle, still a family home, particularly appeals to romantic couples.

Open all year including for Short Breaks.
BROCHURE SENT WITH PLEASURE.

HOLIDAY ACCOMMODATION
Classification Schemes in England, Scotland and Wales

The National Tourist Boards for England, Scotland and Wales have agreed a common 'Crown Classification' scheme for **serviced (Board)** accommodation. All establishments are inspected regularly and are given a classification indicating their level of facilities and services.

There are six grades ranging from 'Listed' to 'Five Crowns'. The higher the classification, the more facilities and services offered. Crown classification is a measure of *facilities* not *quality*. A common quality grading scheme grades the quality of establishments as 'Approved', 'Commended', 'Highly Commended' or 'Deluxe' according to the accommodation, welcome and service they provide.

For **Self-Catering**, holiday homes in England are awarded 'Keys' after inspection and can also be 'Approved', 'Commended', 'Highly Commended' or 'Deluxe' according to the facilities available. In Scotland the Crown scheme includes self-catering accommodation and Wales also has a voluntary inspection scheme for self-catering grading from '1 (Standard)' to '5 (Excellent)'.

Caravan and Camping Parks can participate in the British Holiday Parks grading scheme from 'Approved (✓)' to 'Excellent (✓✓✓✓✓)'. In addition, each National Tourist Board has an annual award for high-quality caravan accommodation: in England – Rose Awards; in Scotland – Thistle Commendations; in Wales – Dragon Awards.

When advertisers supply us with the information, FHG Publications show Crowns and other awards or gradings, including AA, RAC, Egon Ronay etc. We also award a small number of Farm Holiday Guide Diplomas every year, based on readers' recommendations.

Mrs Prosser is a Farm Holiday Guide Diploma winner

FRIENDLY FARMHOUSE HOSPITALITY

A warm welcome awaits you in our Cottages – Self-catering or Bed & Breakfast

Upper Genfford Guest House, Talgarth, Brecon LD3 0EN. Tel: Talgarth (01874) 711360

Each accommodates five to seven people. Cottages surrounded by scenic walking country, an area of outstanding natural beauty, rich in historic and archaeological interest. Ideal for exploring the Welsh Borders, Brecon Beacons and the Wye Valley. All kinds of tourist attractions. The cottages are beautifully furnished with fitted carpets throughout. Oak-beamed lounges, log fires, Calor gas heater, central heating, colour TV. Bedrooms en-suite. In Bed and Breakfast cottage – good, home produced food, home-made cakes, welcome cups of tea, a warm and friendly atmosphere. WEEKEND BREAKS available. Pets welcome. Linen on request. Terms – B&B from £14. SELF CATERING £90 to £150 per week.

AA Recommended QQQ. WTB Award. FHG Diplomas.
Please phone or write to **Mrs Bronwen Prosser** for further details.

RED HOUSE

Trefeglwys, Caersws, Montgomeryshire SY17 5PN
Tel: 01686 430285

A highly furnished, self-contained part of the farmhouse, situated on a mixed working family farm. With panoramic views, unspoilt scenery and the tranquillity of the Trannon Valley it makes an ideal, convenient base for touring mid-Wales attractions and recreational pursuits – Llanidloes 6 miles and Clywedog reservoir, Powys Castle and the coast all close at hand. A fully equipped kitchen plus washing machine, refurbished bathroom and tea served on arrival all ensure guests' comfort is the main priority and extras include log fire, oak beams, garden furniture, ample parking and wildlife, so come to Red House and enjoy a refreshing change. Bed linen included. Open all year. SAE for brochure. OS Map ref SN992 899.

When making enquiries please mention FHG Publications.

Please remember a stamped addressed envelope with enquiries.

BEACH BUNGALOW

OUR WORLD BY THE SEA

Executive Beach Bungalow, in its own grounds, quiet secluded cove, with your own beach, moments from your Patio door. Every comfort in an area of outstanding natural beauty. On flat coastal strip with sub-tropical plants confirming Gulf Stream mild climate. Tour beautiful Snowdonia, 'The Castles' and the famous Llyn Peninsula and beaches. Tastefully furnished by Parker Knoll. Modern split level lounge-dining room, overlooking lawn, beach and sea. 3 bedrooms, vanitory units. TV's and duvets; 1 & 2 Double & Single; 3 Single or double; 4 children's upstairs 4 singles; 2 Bathrooms en-suite. Teletext colour TV' video, compact disc tape and music centre, dishwasher, microwave, fridge, freezer, washing machine, tumble dryer, electric blankets, telephone and central heating, patio furniture, parking 5 cars. P.O. and shop handy. Safe bathing and water sports, sea/river fishing. Nearby Restaurants, Bar Snacks, take-aways and most leisure activities, including golf, rambling, pony trekking, three modern Leisure Centres. Featured by BBC and Wales Tourist Board (top grade 5 award). Come and inspect any time, between Caernarfon and Nefyn on A499 (Llyn Peninsula). Try a £49 Minibreak.

JAN	FEB	MARCH	APRIL	MAY	JUNE	JULY	AUG	SEPT	OCT	NOV	DEC
7... £89	4... £99	4...£149	1...£189	6...£219	3...£339	1...£429	5...£559	2...£429	7...£249	4...£169	2... £99
14... £79	11... £99	11...£159	8 GF.£199	13...£229	10...£349	8...£499	12...£559	9...£389	14...£229	11...£159	9... £99
21... £79	18...£109	18...£169	15 BH.£379	20...£259	17...£389	15...£529	19...£549	16...£369	21...£269	18...£129	16...£299
28... £89	25...£109	25...£179	22...£229	27 BH.£439	24...£399	22...£559	26 BH.£529	23...£329	28...£279	25...£119	23...£429
			29 BH.£219			29...£559		30...£289			30...£329

*Deposit ¼ of total. Minimum £50 p.w. & Insurance £3 nightly. Sleeps 10, over 5 persons £35 each per week. Free electric allowance £7. Central Heating 70° £35 weekly. (Dogs £5 nightly, 2 only. Never left alone). **Weekend, Midweek or Week Breaks phone 01286 660400.***

VILLA CHALET

Your own beach, moments from your lounge patio sliding door, overlooking lawn, beach and sea. Every comfort, Lounge dinette, exclusive 3 piece suite. Teletext colour TV, Electric fire, bed settee, 3 separate bedrooms. 1 Double, vanitory basin, en-suite to bathroom, electric blankets and heater. 2 Double, or 2 singles, two drop-down beds for children. 3 Single with drop-down bed. Blankets and pillows provided. Bring linen, towels or own duvet? Kitchen area. Microwave, electric hob & oven, fridge-freezer, slow cooker, kettle, toaster and Hoover. Bathroom, Sit-down shower-bath, wash basin, toilet. Well heated, patio furniture, much up market Dragon Award. **Featured by the BBC and Wales Tourist Board.** View any time. Try a £25 Minibreak.

MARCH	APRIL	MAY	JUNE	JULY	AUG	SEPT	OCT
18... £78	1... £98	6...£158	3...£248	1...£288	5...£338	2...£278	7...£118
25... £88	8 GF.£118	13...£168	10...£258	8...£298	12...£338	9...£238	14...£108
	15 BH.£178	20...£178	17...£268	15...£318	19...£338	16...£198	21...£178
	22...£128	27 BH.£328	24...£278	22...£338	26 BH.£318	23...£178	
	29 BH.£128			29...£338		30...£148	

WALES
It's magic

New 2 Bedroomed, Similar, Deduct £25 from above rates.** Deposit ¼ of total. Minimum £50 p.w. & Insurance £2 nightly. Sea view £3 nightly. Limited to 8, over 5 persons £21 each per week. (Dogs £3 nightly, 2 only. Never left alone). **Weekend, Midweek or Week Breaks phone 01286 660400.

BEACH HOLIDAY HOME

BEACH MODERN LUXURY HOLIDAY HOME (or Tourist Board approved caravan)

Your own beach, moments from your door. Top Grade 5 award. 6-berth B type, 2 bedrooms: 8 berth A type, 2 bedrooms limited to 6: 10 berth A type, 3 bedrooms limited to 8. Lounge, Kitchen, Dinette, Bedrooms, 1st, one Double; 2nd, some have a Single with a drop-down Bed, or 2 Singles to make a Double; 3rd, Single or Twins, some make a Double. Request on phone and on white booking form. In some a Double Bed Settee makes up in the Lounge/Dinette. Blankets and pillows provided. Bring linen and towels or own duvet? Bathroom, shower, wash basin, toilet. Well heated, remote control Colour TV, Fridge, Large Cooker, Electric Blanket, Kettle and Hoover. Featured by the BBC, Wales Tourist Board, and British Holiday Home Parks. **Superior Dragon Award Holiday Homes with heated Bedroom, £2 nightly.** View any time. Try a £12 minibreak.

MARCH				APRIL				MAY				JUNE			
Date	4-6 berth	4-8 berth	6-10 berth	Date	4-6 berth	4-8 berth	6-10 berth	Date	4-6 berth	4-8 berth	6-10 berth	Date	4-6 berth	4-8 berth	6-10 berth
18	£35	£38	£40	1	£37	£39	£42	6	£45	£55	£59	3	£69	£89	£99
25	£37	£39	£42	8GF	£45	£59	£65	13	£47	£57	£63	10	£79	£95	£105
				15BH	£55	£75	£85	20	£49	£69	£75	17	£85	£109	£115
				22	£39	£49	£51	27BH	£99	£135	£159	24	£95	£115	£125
				29MD	£45	£55	£59								

JULY				AUGUST				SEPTEMBER				OCTOBER			
Date	4-6 berth	4-8 berth	6-10 berth	Date	4-6 berth	4-8 berth	6-10 berth	Date	4-6 berth	4-8 berth	6-10 berth	Date	4-6 berth	4-8 berth	6-10 berth
1	£105	£125	£135	5	£159	£195	£209	2	£79	£99	£109	7	£35	£45	£47
8	£109	£135	£139	12	£159	£195	£209	9	£65	£79	£85	14	£35	£47	£49
15	£125	£149	£159	19	£159	£195	£209	16	£49	£65	£75	21	£45	£65	£69
22	£159	£189	£209	26BH	£129	£165	£179	23	£45	£55	£63				
29	£159	£195	£209					30	£39	£45	£53				

***12 foot wide super luxury holiday homes, 20% more spacious. Add £35 to above prices.** Deposit £33 p.w. & Insurance £1 nightly. Sea view £2 nightly. Twin bedded room £2 nightly. Microwave £1 nightly. Superior Dragon Award, with heated bedroom £2 nightly, latest model, recent model, up market model, double glazed model heated to 70°, special position, upgraded etc. £5 nightly each. Request quotation. Over 6 persons £3 per night each. Dogs £2 nightly.*

Weekend, Midweek or Week Breaks phone 01286 660400.

BEACH HOLIDAY, WEST POINT, THE BEACH, PONTLLYFNI, CAERNARFON, NORTH WALES, LL54 5ET

PERSONAL ATTENTION, BROCHURE & RESERVATIONS TEL. 01286 660400.

The Farm Holiday Guide to
HOLIDAYS
IN

ENGLAND, WALES & IRELAND

AND THE CHANNEL ISLANDS

Farms, guest houses and country hotels
Cottages, flats and chalets
Caravans and camping
Activity Holidays
Country Inns

FHG

Other FHG Publications

Recommended Short Break Holidays
Recommended Country Hotels of Britain
Recommended Wayside Inns of Britain
Pets Welcome!
Bed and Breakfast in Britain
The Golf Guide: Where to Play/Where to Stay
Farm Holiday Guide Scotland
Self-Catering & Furnished Holidays
Britain's Best Holidays
Guide to Caravan and Camping Holidays
Bed and Breakfast Stops
Children Welcome! Family Holiday Guide

ISBN 1 85055 182 0
Cover photograph: Mirror Syndication International.
Design by Edward Carden (Glasgow).

Typeset by RD Composition Ltd., Glasgow.
Printed and bound by Benham's Ltd., Colchester.

Distribution – **Book Trade**: WLM, 117 The Hollow, Littleover, Derby DE3 7BS (Tel: 01332 272020. Fax: 01332 774287).
News Trade: United Magazine Distribution Ltd, 16-28 Tabernacle Street, London EC2A 4BN (Tel: 0171-638 4666. Fax: 0171-638 4665).

Published by FHG Publications Ltd.,
Abbey Mill Business Centre, Seedhill, Paisley PA1 1TJ (0141-887 0428. Fax: 0141-889 7204).
A member of the U.N. Group.

US ISBN 1-55650-659-7
Distributed in the United States by
Hunter Publishing Inc., 300 Raritan Center Parkway CN94,
Edison, N.J., 08818, USA

FOREWORD

The Farm Holiday Guide to
Holidays in
ENGLAND, WALES
IRELAND & THE CHANNEL ISLANDS 1995

It's almost fifty years since the first edition of the *Farm Holiday Guide* appeared and it's not surprising that these fifty years have seen marked changes in the British holiday scene. Holidays abroad, mainly for the sun, are no longer a novelty – unlike the family holiday fortnight in July or August in a British seaside resort, which is now comparatively rare.

Fortunately less rare and showing much less of a decline over the years is our preference for direct booking and for freedom of choice to enjoy short breaks in the many attractive and accessible coast and country holiday destinations which Britain offers. You will find hundreds of such opportunities, with all kinds of accommodation choices, in this 48th edition of the *Farm Holiday Guide*. And if your preference is for the quieter resort, the farm or the country guest house . . . so much the better!

The following points will help you make the best use of *Farm Holiday Guide*.

ENQUIRIES AND BOOKINGS. Give full details of dates (with an alternative), numbers and any special requirements. Ask about any points in the holiday description which are not clear and make sure that prices and conditions are clearly explained. You should receive confirmation in writing and a receipt for any deposit or advance payment. If you book your holiday well in advance, especially self-catering, confirm your arrival details nearer the time. Some proprietors, especially for self-catering, request full payment in advance but a reasonable deposit is more normal.

CANCELLATIONS. A holiday booking is a form of contract with obligations on both sides. If you have to cancel, give as much notice as possible. The longer the notice the better the chance that your host can replace your booking and therefore refund any payments. If the proprietor cancels in such a way that causes serious inconvenience, he may have obligations to you which have not been properly honoured. Take advice if necessary from such organisations as the Citizen's Advice Bureau, Consumer's Association, Trading Standards Office, Local Tourist Office, etc., or your own solicitor.

COMPLAINTS. It's best if any problems can be sorted out at the start of your holiday. If the problem is not solved, you can contact the organisations mentioned above. You can also write to us. We will follow up the complaint with the advertiser – but we cannot act as intermediaries or accept responsibility for holiday arrangements.

FHG Publications Ltd. do not inspect accommodation and an entry in our guides does not imply a recommendation. However our advertisers have signed their agreement to work for the holidaymaker's best interests and as their customer, you have the right to expect appropriate attention and service.

HOLIDAY INSURANCE. It is possible to insure against holiday cancellation. Brokers and insurance companies can advise you about this.

Don't forget our **Farm Holiday Guide Diploma**. Every year we award a small number of Diplomas to holiday proprietors who have been specially recommended to us by readers. The names of our 1994 Diploma winners are listed in several places throughout this book and we will be happy to receive your recommendations for 1995.

You will also see our Voucher/Coupons for free or reduced rate entry to a range of popular holiday attractions if you turn a few pages forward. We hope that these will add to your holiday enjoyment.

We hope too that *Farm Holiday Guide* will bring you many happy holidays and you will mention the title when you make enquiries or bookings.

Peter Clark
Publishing Director

FHG

CONTENTS

FHG

CONTENTS

WALES

IRELAND

WALES

IRELAND

ENGLAND & WALES
COUNTIES

1 London
2 Avon
3 Bedfordshire
4 Berkshire
5 Buckinghamshire
6 Cambridgeshire
7 Cheshire
8 Cleveland
9 Cornwall
10 Cumbria
11 Derbyshire
12 Devon
13 Dorset
14 Durham
15 Essex
16 Gloucestershire
17 Hampshire
18 Hereford & Worcester
19 Hertfordshire
20 Humberside
21 Isle of Wight
22 Kent
23 Lancashire
24 Leicestershire
25 Lincolnshire
26 Manchester, Greater
27 Merseyside
28 Midlands, West
29 Norfolk
30 Northamptonshire
31 Northumberland
32 Nottinghamshire
33 Oxfordshire
34 Salop
35 Somerset
36 Staffordshire
37 Suffolk
38 Surrey
39 Sussex, East
40 Sussex, West
41 Tyne & Wear
42 Warwickshire
43 Wiltshire
44 Yorkshire, North
45 Yorkshire, South
46 Yorkshire, West

A Clwyd
B Dyfed
C Glamorgan, Mid
D Glamorgan, South
E Glamorgan, West
F Gwent
G Gwynedd
H Powys

FHG

READERS' OFFER 1995

VALID until end 1995

INTERNATIONAL HELICOPTER MUSEUM

Weston Airport, Locking Moor Road, Weston-super-Mare, Avon BS22 8PP Tel: 01934 635227

Admit **ONE CHILD FREE** with full paying adult

NOT TO BE USED IN CONJUNCTION WITH ANY OTHER OFFER

FHG

READERS' OFFER 1995

VALID during 1995 Season

Beale Park

Lower Basildon, Reading, Berkshire RG8 9NH Tel: (01734) 845172

Admit **ONE CHILD FREE** with an accompanying adult

NOT TO BE USED IN CONJUNCTION WITH ANY OTHER OFFER

FHG

READERS' OFFER 1995

VALID during 1995

Sacrewell Farm & Country Centre

Thornhaugh, Peterborough, Cambridgeshire PE8 6HJ Telephone: (01780) 782222

One **FREE** admission with each paid entry of similar age group (adult/child)

NOT TO BE USED IN CONJUNCTION WITH ANY OTHER OFFER

FHG

READERS' OFFER 1995

VALID during 1995 Season

Flambards Village Theme Park

Helston, Cornwall TR13 0GA Telephone: (01326) 574549

£1.00 OFF full admission price

NOT TO BE USED IN CONJUNCTION WITH ANY OTHER OFFER

FHG

READERS' OFFER 1995

VALID during 1995 Season

North Cornwall Museum and Gallery

The Clease, Camelford, Cornwall Telephone: (01840) 212954

One **FREE** adult entry with every paid adult entry

NOT TO BE USED IN CONJUNCTION WITH ANY OTHER OFFER

Britain's only dedicated helicopter museum with over 50 full-size exhibits, models, displays, restoration hangar, ride simulator. Cafeteria.

DIRECTIONS: A371 on east boundary of town; 5 mins from M5 Junction 21. Follow the 'propellor' road signs.

OPEN: 10am-6pm daily (4pm Nov to March). Closed Christmas, Boxing Day & New Year's Day.

FHG PUBLICATIONS, ABBEY MILL BUSINESS CENTRE, PAISLEY PA1 1TJ

Exotic birds, pets' corner, adventure playgrounds, river cruises etc, all set in acres of gardens, lakes and water meadows.

DIRECTIONS: on A329 one mile from Pangbourne.

OPEN: daily February 20th–December 23rd.

FHG PUBLICATIONS, ABBEY MILL BUSINESS CENTRE, PAISLEY PA1 1TJ

The fascinating story of farming and country life with working watermill, gardens, collections of bygones, farm and nature trails. Excellent for young children. Campers and Caravanners welcome.

DIRECTIONS: off A47, 8 miles west of Peterborough.

OPEN: daily all year.

FHG PUBLICATIONS, ABBEY MILL BUSINESS CENTRE, PAISLEY PA1 1TJ

All-weather entertainment for all the family. Victorian Village, Britain in the Blitz, super family rides, entertainment, gardens and much more.

DIRECTIONS: A394 to Helston.

OPEN: Easter to end October.

FHG PUBLICATIONS, ABBEY MILL BUSINESS CENTRE, PAISLEY PA1 1TJ

Life in Cornwall during the past century. Workmen's tools, domestic items, collection of Cornish and Devonshire pottery.

DIRECTIONS: off A39 18 miles south of Bude.

OPEN: Easter to end September daily except Sundays.

FHG PUBLICATIONS, ABBEY MILL BUSINESS CENTRE, PAISLEY PA1 1TJ

FHG

READERS' OFFER 1995

VALID April to end October 1995

South Tynedale Railway

Alston, Cumbria CA9 3JB Telephone (01434) 381696

Reduction of 40p on adult ticket and 20p on child ticket

NOT TO BE USED IN CONJUNCTION WITH ANY OTHER OFFER

FHG

READERS' OFFER 1995

VALID during 1995 season (museum entry only)

Windermere Steamboat Museum

Rayrigg Road, Windermere, Cumbria LA23 1BN Tel: 015394 45565

ONE FREE ENTRY for every paying adult

NOT TO BE USED IN CONJUNCTION WITH ANY OTHER OFFER

FHG

READERS' OFFER 1995

VALID during 1995

The Donington Collection

Donington Park, Castle Donington, Derbyshire DE74 2RP Tel: 01332 810048

ADMIT two for the price of one

NOT TO BE USED IN CONJUNCTION WITH ANY OTHER OFFER

FHG

READERS' OFFER 1995

VALID Spring Bank Holiday to October 1995

Devonshire Collection of Period Costume

43 High Street, Totnes, Devon TQ9 5NP Tel: (01803) 862827

Admit **TWO** for the price of one

NOT TO BE USED IN CONJUNCTION WITH ANY OTHER OFFER

FHG

READERS' OFFER 1995

VALID during 1995

Kents Cavern Showcaves

91 Ilsham Road, Wellswood, Torquay, Devon TQ1 2JF Tel: 01803 294059

One **FREE** guide book per family when purchasing ticket from Kents Cavern office

NOT TO BE USED IN CONJUNCTION WITH ANY OTHER OFFER

England's highest narrow-gauge railway. Steam and diesel engines carry pasengers through the scenic North Pennines.

DIRECTIONS: station is just off A686 Hexham road north of Alston town centre.

OPEN: service operates April to November (daily July and August).

FHG PUBLICATIONS, ABBEY MILL BUSINESS CENTRE, PAISLEY PA1 1TJ

The finest collection of steamboats in the world. Motor boats and other vintage craft are also displayed afloat, under cover.

DIRECTIONS: A591 from Kendal to Rayrigg Road; A592 from Newby Bridge.

OPEN: Easter to October 10am to 5pm daily.

FHG PUBLICATIONS, ABBEY MILL BUSINESS CENTRE, PAISLEY PA1 1TJ

World's largest collection of single seater racing cars, housed in five halls. Fully licensed restaurant. Ample free parking.

DIRECTIONS: 2 miles east of East Midlands Airport; 3 miles from M1 Junction 23a; approach via Birmingham by M42/A42.

OPEN: Daily except Christmas Day, Boxing Day and New Year's Day. 10am to 5pm daily.

FHG PUBLICATIONS, ABBEY MILL BUSINESS CENTRE, PAISLEY PA1 1TJ

A selection of costumes and accessories (changed each year) on show in one of the oldest and most interesting houses in the heart of Totnes.

DIRECTIONS: part of the Butterwalk which is near main town car park.

OPEN: Spring Bank Holiday to October 1st (closed Saturdays).

FHG PUBLICATIONS, ABBEY MILL BUSINESS CENTRE, PAISLEY PA1 1TJ

Underground world packed with secrets of times gone by. One of the most important archaeological sites in Britain.

DIRECTIONS: From Torquay Harbour follow brown tourist signs – Ilsham Road is off Babbacombe Road.

OPEN: April to Sept 10am-5.15pm (plus evenings in July and Aug). Oct to March: 10am-4.15pm.

FHG PUBLICATIONS, ABBEY MILL BUSINESS CENTRE, PAISLEY PA1 1TJ

FHG

VALID during 1995

READERS' OFFER 1995

Tank Museum

Bovington, Wareham, Dorset BH20 6JG Telephone: (01929) 463953

50p Restaurant Voucher to be used in Gauntlet Restaurant

NOT TO BE USED IN CONJUNCTION WITH ANY OTHER OFFER

FHG

VALID during 1995

READERS' OFFER 1995

BERKELEY CASTLE

Berkeley, Gloucestershire GL13 9BQ Telephone: (01453) 810332

Admit one **FAMILY** at group rates

NOT TO BE USED IN CONJUNCTION WITH ANY OTHER OFFER

FHG

VALID during 1995 Season

READERS' OFFER 1995

Cotswold Farm Park

Guiting Power, Cheltenham, Gloucestershire GL54 5UG Tel: (01451) 850307

Admit one child **FREE** with an adult paying full entrance fee

NOT TO BE USED IN CONJUNCTION WITH ANY OTHER OFFER

FHG

VALID April to October 1995

READERS' OFFER 1995

The Cider Museum Centre

Pomona Place, Hereford HR4 0LW Telephone: (01432) 354207

Admit **TWO ADULTS** at group reduction rate

NOT TO BE USED IN CONJUNCTION WITH ANY OTHER OFFER

FHG

VALID during 1995 Season

READERS' OFFER 1995

FRONTIERLAND

Promenade, Morecambe, Lancashire LA4 4DG Telephone: (01524) 410024

Buy one Day Pass and get another **FREE**

NOT TO BE USED IN CONJUNCTION WITH ANY OTHER OFFER

Over 300 armoured fighting vehicles from 25 countries. Drive-a-tank simulators, video theatres, restaurant.

DIRECTIONS: A352 between Dorchester and Wareham.

OPEN: 10am-5pm daily except at Christmas period.

FHG PUBLICATIONS, ABBEY MILL BUSINESS CENTRE, PAISLEY PA1 1TJ

Magnificent home of the Berkeley family for nearly 850 years.
Full of treasures including paintings, tapestries, porcelain.

DIRECTIONS: off A38 midway between Bristol and Gloucester. From M5 use Exit 13 or 14.

OPEN: April to Sept: open daily except Mondays. Oct: open Sunday afternoons only.

FHG PUBLICATIONS, ABBEY MILL BUSINESS CENTRE, PAISLEY PA1 1TJ

The home of rare breeds conservation, with over 50 breeding flocks and herds of rare farm animals. Adventure playground, pets' corners, picnic area, farm nature trail.

DIRECTIONS: M5 Junction 9, off B4077 Stow-on-the-Wold road. 5 miles from Bourton-on-the-Water.

OPEN: daily 10.30am to 5pm – April to September.

FHG PUBLICATIONS, ABBEY MILL BUSINESS CENTRE, PAISLEY PA1 1TJ

Cider Museum and Distillery telling the fascinating story of traditional cider making through the ages. Programme of temporary exhibitions and activities throughout the year.

DIRECTIONS: off A438 from Hereford to Brecon.

OPEN: April to October daily 10am-5.30pm; November to March Mon-Sat 1-5pm.

FHG PUBLICATIONS, ABBEY MILL BUSINESS CENTRE, PAISLEY PA1 1TJ

Western theme park with over 30 rides and attractions for all the family.

DIRECTIONS: on coast 8 miles south of M6 Junction 34.

OPEN: March to October – Main season – May 28th to September 18th.

FHG PUBLICATIONS, ABBEY MILL BUSINESS CENTRE, PAISLEY PA1 1TJ

FHG

READERS' OFFER 1995

VALID Jan-March and Sept-Oct 1995

SNIBSTON DISCOVERY PARK

Ashby Road, Coalville, Leicestershire LE67 3LN Telephone: (01530) 510851

20% DISCOUNT on adult and concessionary tickets

NOT TO BE USED IN CONJUNCTION WITH ANY OTHER OFFER

FHG

READERS' OFFER 1995

VALID during 1995

NATURELAND SEAL SANCTUARY

North Parade, Skegness, Lincolnshire PE25 1DB Telephone: (01754) 764345

FREE entry for one child when accompanied by paying adult

NOT TO BE USED IN CONJUNCTION WITH ANY OTHER OFFER

FHG

READERS' OFFER 1995

VALID during 1995 except Bank Holidays

SOUTHPORT ZOO AND CONSERVATION TRUST

Princes Park, Southport, Merseyside PR8 1RX Telephone: (01704) 538102

One child **FREE** entry with two full paying adults

NOT TO BE USED IN CONJUNCTION WITH ANY OTHER OFFER

FHG

READERS' OFFER 1995

VALID March to October 1995

HEXHAM HERBS

Chesters Walled Garden, Chollerford, Hexham, Northumberland NE46 4BQ Tel: (01434) 681483

One adult FREE with paid adult entry

NOT TO BE USED IN CONJUNCTION WITH ANY OTHER OFFER

FHG

READERS' OFFER 1995

VALID during 1995

White Post Modern Farm Centre

Farnsfield, Near Newark, Nottinghamshire NG22 8HL Tel: (01623) 882977

TWO child admissions for the price of one

NOT TO BE USED IN CONJUNCTION WITH ANY OTHER OFFER

Five main gallery areas tell the story of the county's rich industrial heritage. Hands-on *Science Alive!*, nature trail and picnic areas.

DIRECTIONS: 12 miles north-west of Leicester.

OPEN: daily except Christmas and Boxing Day.

FHG PUBLICATIONS, ABBEY MILL BUSINESS CENTRE, PAISLEY PA1 1TJ

Rescues and rears abandoned seal pups before returnng them to the wild. Specialised collection includes penguins, reptiles etc.

DIRECTIONS: coastal resort 19 miles north-east of Boston.

OPEN: daily except Christmas Day, Boxing Day and New Year's Day.

FHG PUBLICATIONS, ABBEY MILL BUSINESS CENTRE, PAISLEY PA1 1TJ

Lions, snow leopards, chimpanzees, penguins, reptiles, aquarium and lots more set amidst landscaped gardens.

DIRECTIONS: On the coast 16 miles north of Liverpool; follow brown tourist signs.

OPEN: daily except Christmas Day. Summer 10am to 6pm; Winter 10am to 4pm.

FHG PUBLICATIONS, ABBEY MILL BUSINESS CENTRE, PAISLEY PA1 1TJ

Beautiful walled garden with nearly 900 types of herbs, woodland walk, nursery, shop. Guide dogs only.

DIRECTIONS: 6 miles north of Hexham, next to Chesters Roman Fort.

OPEN: daily March to October/November.

FHG PUBLICATIONS, ABBEY MILL BUSINESS CENTRE, PAISLEY PA1 1TJ

A modern working farm with over 3000 animals including ducklings, deer, bees, rheas, piglets, snails, lambs (all year). New pet centre.

DIRECTIONS: off the A614 at Farnsfield, 12 miles north of Nottingham. From M1 Junction 27 follow 'Robin Hood' signs for 10 miles.

OPEN: daily all year round.

FHG PUBLICATIONS, ABBEY MILL BUSINESS CENTRE, PAISLEY PA1 1TJ

FHG

READERS' OFFER 1995

VALID April to end October 1995

Cogges Manor Farm Museum

Church Lane, Witney, Oxfordshire OX8 6LA Tel: (01993) 772602

FREE pot of tea on production of voucher

NOT TO BE USED IN CONJUNCTION WITH ANY OTHER OFFER

FHG

READERS' OFFER 1995

VALID until 26 November 1995

Didcot Railway Centre

Didcot, Oxfordshire Telephone: (01235) 817200

One child **FREE** when accompanied by full paying adult

NOT TO BE USED IN CONJUNCTION WITH ANY OTHER OFFER

FHG

READERS' OFFER 1995

VALID during 1995

PERRY'S CIDER MILLS

Dowlish Wake, Near Ilminster, Somerset TA19 0NY Telephone: (01460) 52681

10% OFF all shop goods excluding cider and cider brandy (free entry to Cider Mills)

NOT TO BE USED IN CONJUNCTION WITH ANY OTHER OFFER

FHG

READERS' OFFER 1995

VALID during 1995

RODE BIRD GARDENS

Rode, Near Bath, Somerset BA3 6QW Telephone: (01373) 830326

One child **FREE** with each full paying adult

NOT TO BE USED IN CONJUNCTION WITH ANY OTHER OFFER

FHG

READERS' OFFER 1995

VALID during 1995

Planet Earth

Garden Paradise, Avis Road, Newhaven, East Sussex BN9 0DH Tel: (01273) 512123

Admit one **FREE** adult or child with one adult paying full entrance price

NOT TO BE USED IN CONJUNCTION WITH ANY OTHER OFFER

A museum of the Oxfordshire countryside, with Manor House, working farm, riverside walks etc, plus daily demonstration of cooking on the kitchen range.

DIRECTIONS: follow signs from A40, close to Witney town centre.

OPEN: 4th April to end October. Closed Mondays except Bank Holidays.

FHG PUBLICATIONS, ABBEY MILL BUSINESS CENTRE, PAISLEY PA1 1TJ

The golden age of the Great Western Railway – steam trains, original equipment; picnic area and refreshment room. Rides on trains all Sundays June to August, Bank Holidays - enquire for other times.

DIRECTIONS: 10 miles south of Oxford, signposted from M4 (Junction 13) and A34. At Didcot Parkway Rail Station.

OPEN: weekends all year; daily April to September.

FHG PUBLICATIONS, ABBEY MILL BUSINESS CENTRE, PAISLEY PA1 1TJ

Traditional cider and cider brandy on sale all year – sample before you buy. Shop, museum of farm tools, country photographs.

DIRECTIONS: approximately 2 miles from Ilminster off A303, 3 miles from Cricket St Thomas.

OPEN: all year except Sunday afternoons.

FHG PUBLICATIONS, ABBEY MILL BUSINESS CENTRE, PAISLEY PA1 1TJ

Hundreds of brilliant exotic birds in 17 acres of woodlands, lakes and flower gardens. Children's play area. Woodland steam railway (summer, weather permitting).

DIRECTIONS: turn off the A36 10 miles south of Bath (follow brown tourist signs).

OPEN: all year except Christmas Day.

FHG PUBLICATIONS, ABBEY MILL BUSINESS CENTRE, PAISLEY PA1 1TJ

World of Natural History including Plantasia Desert and Tropical Gardens, World of Dinosaurs, and Fossil Museum

DIRECTIONS: signposted 'Garden Paradise' off A26 and A259.

OPEN: all year, except Christmas Day and Boxing Day.

FHG PUBLICATIONS, ABBEY MILL BUSINESS CENTRE, PAISLEY PA1 1TJ

FHG

VALID during 1995 Season

READERS' OFFER 1995

Cadeby Steam & Brass Rubbing Centre

Nuneaton, Warwickshire CV13 0AS Telephone: (01455) 290462

Train ride for two, and two cream teas or similar

NOT TO BE USED IN CONJUNCTION WITH ANY OTHER OFFER

FHG

VALID during 1995

READERS' OFFER 1995

Museum of British Road Transport

St Agnes Lane, Hales Street, Coventry, West Midlands CV1 1PN Tel: 01203 832425

45p OFF, full child & adult admission prices

NOT TO BE USED IN CONJUNCTION WITH ANY OTHER OFFER

FHG

VALID until 31st October 1995

READERS' OFFER 1995

Dyson Perrins Museum of Worcester Porcelain

Severn Street, Worcester WR1 2NE Telephone: (01905) 23221

Admit **TWO** Adults for the price of one museum entry

NOT TO BE USED IN CONJUNCTION WITH ANY OTHER OFFER

FHG

VALID during 1995

READERS' OFFER 1995

FRIARGATE WAX MUSEUM

Lower Friargate, York YO1 1SL Telephone: (01904) 658775

One **FREE** admission when one of equal value is purchased

NOT TO BE USED IN CONJUNCTION WITH ANY OTHER OFFER

FHG

VALID Easter to end Sept 1995 (except Bank Holidays)

READERS' OFFER 1995

Flamingo Land Family Fun Park

Kirby Misperton, Malton, North Yorkshire YO17 0UX Tel: 01653 668287

One **FREE** entry when accompanied by two full paying persons

NOT TO BE USED IN CONJUNCTION WITH ANY OTHER OFFER

Working narrow gauge steam railway, railway museum and over 70 replica brasses to rub

DIRECTIONS: on the A447 six miles north of Hinckley.

OPEN: second Saturday each month.

FHG PUBLICATIONS, ABBEY MILL BUSINESS CENTRE, PAISLEY PA1 1TJ

Largest display of British road transport telling the story of Coventry's motor industry.

DIRECTIONS: in City centre.

OPEN: daily except Christmas Eve and Day plus Boxing Day.

FHG PUBLICATIONS, ABBEY MILL BUSINESS CENTRE, PAISLEY PA1 1TJ

World's largest and most comprehensive collection of Worcester Porcelain, including magnificent Chicago Exhibition Vase (4ft 6 inches tall). Reg. Charity No. 22375

DIRECTIONS: M5 Junction 7 to city centre, then left at 3rd set of traffic lights.

OPEN: Mon-Fri. 9.30am-5pm – Sat & Bank Holidays 10am-5pm.

FHG PUBLICATIONS, ABBEY MILL BUSINESS CENTRE, PAISLEY PA1 1TJ

As winner of the BTA 'Come to Britain Award', expect something special here. Educationally entertaining. Black Cave now in 11th year.

DIRECTIONS: off Clifford Street in central York.

OPEN: daily from mid-January to end November.

FHG PUBLICATIONS, ABBEY MILL BUSINESS CENTRE, PAISLEY PA1 1TJ

Over 100 great rides, slides, shows and attractions including The Bullet, Waikiki Wave, Skyflyer and Corkscrew.

DIRECTIONS: off A169 Malton to Pickering road.

OPEN: daily from Easter to October.

FHG PUBLICATIONS, ABBEY MILL BUSINESS CENTRE, PAISLEY PA1 1TJ

FHG

READERS' OFFER 1995

VALID until 30th June 1995

RHONDDA HERITAGE PARK

Lewis Merthyr, Coed Cae Road, Trehafod, Mid-Glamorgan CF37 7NP Tel: (01443) 682036

Admit one child **FREE** with each full paying adult

NOT TO BE USED IN CONJUNCTION WITH ANY OTHER OFFER

FHG

READERS' OFFER 1995

VALID during 1995

Big Pit Mining Museum

Blaenafon, Gwent NP4 9XP Tel: 01495 790311

Admit one child **FREE** per voucher with a full paying adult

NOT TO BE USED IN CONJUNCTION WITH ANY OTHER OFFER

FHG

READERS' OFFER 1995

VALID during 1995

Sygun Copper Mine

Beddgelert, Gwynedd LL55 4NE Tel: 01766 890595

10% OFF full adult and child admission prices

NOT TO BE USED IN CONJUNCTION WITH ANY OTHER OFFER

FHG

READERS' OFFER 1995

VALID: Phone for details

MUSEUM OF CHILDHOOD

1 Castle Street, Beaumaris, Anglesey LL58 8AP Telephone: (01248) 712498

Admit one child or Senior Citizen **FREE** when accompanied by 2 paying adults

NOT TO BE USED IN CONJUNCTION WITH ANY OTHER OFFER

FHG

READERS' OFFER 1995

VALID April to Oct 1995 on timetabled service trains

Talyllyn Railway

Wharf Station, Tywyn, Gwynedd LL36 9EY Tel: 01654 710472

One child **FREE** with each fare paying adult passenger

NOT TO BE USED IN CONJUNCTION WITH ANY OTHER OFFER

Journey back in time with the new underground tour; 'Black Gold'; audio-visual presentation; artefact exhibitions.

DIRECTIONS: just off A470 between Pontypridd and Porth.

OPEN: April to September: open daily; October to March: Tuesday to Sunday.

FHG PUBLICATIONS, ABBEY MILL BUSINESS CENTRE, PAISLEY PA1 1TJ

Underground tours of original colliery workings guided by experienced miners. On the surface: exhibitions, forge, stables, craft shop and licensed cafeteria.

DIRECTIONS: M4 Junction 26, then A4042/3 to Pontypool and Blaenafon. From M50, A449 to Raglan, then A40 to Abergavenny and A4246 to Blaenafon.

OPEN: daily March to November. Phone for Winter opening times. Last admission 3pm.

FHG PUBLICATIONS, ABBEY MILL BUSINESS CENTRE, PAISLEY PA1 1TJ

Set in the heart of Snowdonia, Prince of Wales Award-winning underground audio-visual tours. Magnificent stalactite and stalagmite formations.

DIRECTIONS: one mile from Beddgelert on A498 towards Capel Curig A5.

OPEN: all year.

FHG PUBLICATIONS, ABBEY MILL BUSINESS CENTRE, PAISLEY PA1 1TJ

Superb collection of over 2000 items illustrating the habits and interests of children and families over the past 150 years. Shop.

DIRECTIONS: 4 miles from Britannia Bridge, opposite Beaumaris Castle.

OPEN: Easter to November 1st.

FHG PUBLICATIONS, ABBEY MILL BUSINESS CENTRE, PAISLEY PA1 1TJ

The world's first preserved railway running from Tywyn to Dolgoch Falls, Abergynolwyn and Nant Gwernol in Snowdonia National Park.

DIRECTIONS: Tywyn is on Mid-Wales coast on A493.

OPEN: from April to October and during Christmas/New Year period.

FHG PUBLICATIONS, ABBEY MILL BUSINESS CENTRE, PAISLEY PA1 1TJ

LONDON

HAMMERSMITH. Golden Strand Hotel, 85 Shepherds Bush Road, Hammersmith, London W6 7LR (0171-603 7384). Small family Hotel. All rooms have washbasin, colour TV and tea/coffee making facilities. Double glazing. Children welcome. Non-smoking accommodation available. Bed and Breakfast £18. Please write or telephone for further details.

LONDON. Stanley House Hotel, 19-23 Belgrave Road, Victoria, London SW1V 1RB (0171-834 5042/7292; Fax: 0171-834 8439; Telex: 24699 KISMET G). Centrally located and convenient for London's sights and West-End Theatreland. Excellent connections to Heathrow and Gatwick Airports. Stanley House Hotel offers very good accommodation for the individual, family, tourist or group in 44 comfortably furnished bedrooms, either single, double, twin or family. Most rooms have private shower or bathroom and toilet and all have colour TV, radio and intercom. Tea/coffee and hot and cold drinks available. There is a lounge with colour TV, dining room serving full English breakfast and also a licensed restaurant and bar. The Hotel is very well run with efficient, friendly and helpful staff. Children welcome.

LONDON. Mr Marios Stavrou, Gower Hotel, 129 Sussex Gardens, Hyde Park W2 2RX (0171-262 2262/3; Fax: 0171-262 2006). The Gower Hotel is a small family-run Hotel, centrally located a short distance from Paddington Station. Excellent for sightseeing and shopping. Close to Hyde Park, Madam Tussauds, Oxford Street, Marble Arch and many more attractions. All rooms have private shower and toilet, radio, TV (video and Satellite channels), direct-dial telephone and tea/coffee facilities. The hotel is fully centrally heated. Singles from £24 to £34, doubles from £36 to £48. All prices are inclusive of traditional English Breakfast and VAT.

LONDON. Kirness House, 29 Belgrave Road, Victoria SW1V 1RB (0171-834 0030). A small friendly guest housee, please try us. Situated close to Victoria Station. All European languages spoken. satisfaction guaranteed. Single £20, Double £30. Stay five nights, pay for four.

Key to Tourist Board Ratings

The Crown Scheme

(England, Scotland & Wales)

Covering hotels, motels, private hotels, guesthouses, inns, bed & breakfast, farmhouses. Every Crown classified place to stay is inspected annually. *The classification:* Listed then 1-5 Crown indicates the range of facilities and services. Higher quality standards are indicated by the terms APPROVED, COMMENDED, HIGHLY COMMENDED and DELUXE.

The Key Scheme

(also operates in Scotland using a Crown symbol)

Covering self-catering in cottages, bungalows, flats, houseboats, houses, chalets, etc. Every Key classified holiday home is inspected annually. *The classification:* 1-5 Key indicates the range of facilities and equipment. Higher quality standards are indicated by the terms APPROVED, COMMENDED, HIGHLY COMMENDED and DELUXE.

The Q Scheme

(England, Scotland & Wales)

Covering holiday, caravan, chalet and camping parks. Every Q rated park is inspected annually for its quality standards. The more ✓ in the Q – up to 5 – the higher the standard of what is provided.

AVON

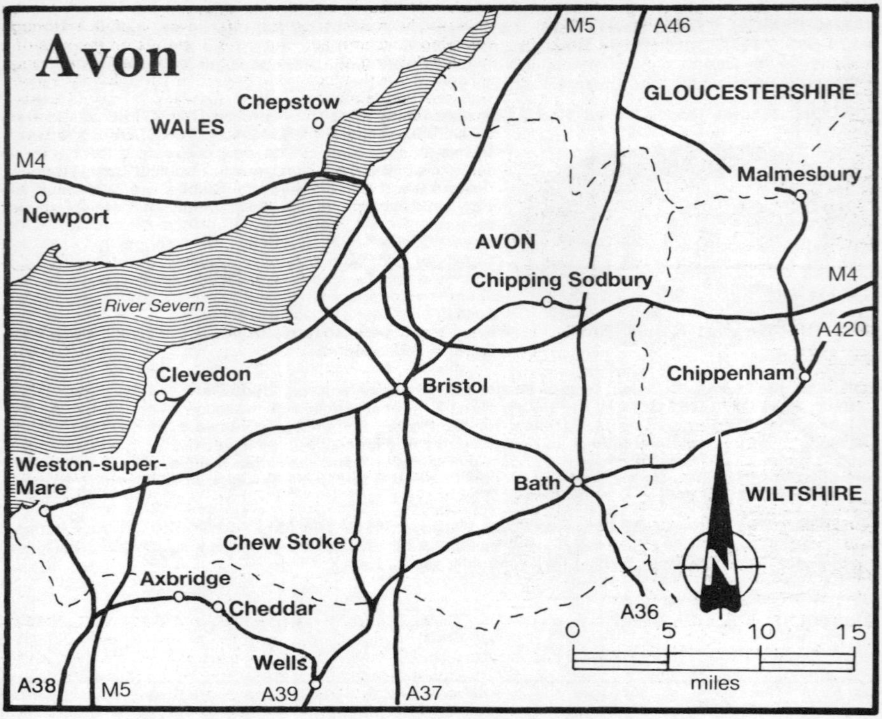

BATH near. Mrs Pam Wilmott, Pool Farm, Wick, Bristol BS15 5RL (0117 937 2284). Working farm, join in. May we welcome you to our 350 year old farmhouse, a listed building on a working dairy farm. We are on the A420, only six miles from Bath, nine miles from Bristol, and a few miles from exit 18 on the M4. This makes us an ideal touring centre for these cities and places of interest such as the Cotswolds, Wells, Badminton, etc. Nearby is a shop with newspapers, local pub with good food, Golf and Country Club with squash, tennis, croquet and open air pool. TV lounge, central heating. Parking. Open all year except Christmas. Terms for Bed and Breakfast on request.

BATH near. Wheelbrook Mill, Laverton, Near Bath BA3 6QY (01373 830263). A warm welcome, log fires on chilly nights, and good food await you in our picturesque Watermill overlooking the Wheel Brook, fields and woodland. We offer centrally heated, oak beamed, en suite double bedrooms, twin bedroom and single room, furnished with antique pine and Laura Ashley linens. TV, tea/coffee are provided in the bedrooms and there is a cosy sitting room with open fire. Laverton is a quiet hamlet 15 minutes' drive south of Bath, one and a half miles from the A36, an ideal base for touring the West Country, being within reach of Wells, Longleat, Stourhead, Salisbury, Bristol, etc.

BATH near. Mrs B.M. Martin, The Old Inn Farmhouse, Farmborough, Near Bath BA3 1BY (01761 470250). The Old Inn Farmhouse is very attractive, built 1684, and was at one time a Coaching Inn, but has been extensively modernised to offer every comfort, though retaining its charm and character. It stands on the side of a hill overlooking the valley on the edge of Farmborough Village. Attractive landscaped garden. It is highly recommended and maintains a high standard of home cooked food, a family atmosphere prevails, with personal attention. All bedrooms (doubles, twins, and family size) have washbasins. Lounge with TV. Ample parking space. Very central for touring Bath, Wells, Cheddar, Wookey Hole, Longleat, Chew Lake, Wye Valley. Open all the year. Bed and full English Breakfast. Fire Certificate held. SAE or telephone for terms.

BRISTOL. Margaret Hasell, The Model Farm, Norton Hawkfield, Pensford, Bristol BS18 4HA (01275 832144). ♛♛ The farmhouse is a Listed building situated two miles off the A37 in a peaceful hamlet nestling under the Dundry Hills. A working arable and beef farm in easy reach of Bristol, Bath, Wells, Cheddar and many interesting places. The accommodation consists of one family room en suite and one double room with washbasin, both with tea/coffee facilities. Guests' lounge with TV and dining room. Open all year except Christmas and New Year. I can assure you of a warm welcome and a peaceful and comfortable stay.

BRISTOL. Mrs Sandra Hasell, Herons Green Farm, Compton Martin, Bristol BS18 6NL (01275 333372). A natural stone-built farmhouse by the side of the Chew Valley Lake. Enjoy freedom and peace walking the fields with beautiful views of surrounding Mendip Hills and Lakes. A warm, friendly atmosphere awaits you. Attractive oak beamed dining room featuring the original water well. Double and family rooms with washbasins, razor points, tea/coffee making facilities. Guests' own shower room. Large breakfast served. Children welcome. No smoking. Bed and Breakfast from £14 to £20 per person per night. Open March to November. Tourist Board Listed.

BRISTOL. Mrs Doreen Keel, Valley Farm, Sandy Lane, Stanton Drew, Bristol BS18 4EL (01275 332723). ♛♛ *Highly Commended.* 1994 Award-Winning Valley Farm is a modern farmhouse offering Bed and Breakfast accommodation. Pleasantly situated on the edge of an ancient village near the River Chew with Druid Stones and many footpaths to walk. It is located near the Chew Valley Lakes, renowned for trout fishing, and in easy reach of Bath, Bristol, Wells and Cheddar. There are three rooms with double beds; each has washbasin and tea/coffee making facilities; there are also two rooms with en suite and another with private bathroom. The house is double glazed and centrally heated. We try to create a friendly and relaxed atmosphere in lovely countryside and we are always pleased to give information about the area. Brochure.

BRISTOL near. Mrs Colin Smart, Leigh Farm, Pensford, Near Bristol BS18 4BA (01761 490281). Working farm. Close to Bath, Bristol, Cheddar, Mendip Hills. Large, comfy, stone-built farmhouse with lawns. Twin, single, family, double rooms; cot and high chair available. Guests' private lounge with night storage heating and open log fires in cold weather. Traditional farmhouse breakfasts. Tea/coffee facilities, hair dryer available. Carp and tench fishing close to the farmhouse. Floodlit car park with plenty of space. Payphone. Close to Blagdon and Chew Valley reservoirs. Fire Certificate. Sorry, no pets. Bed and Breakfast from £18 to £25. Also self catering accommodation available, graded 2/3 Keys: from £95 to £350 weekly.

WESTON-SUPER-MARE. Mrs T.G. Moore, Purn House Farm, Bleadon, Weston-Super-Mare BS24 0QE (Bleadon [01934] 812324). ♛♛ Seventeenth-century creeper-clad house standing on a 400-acre mixed farm at the foot of Purn Hill where there are panoramic views of the Bristol Channel, Glastonbury Tor in the east to Exmoor and the Welsh Mountains in the west. The house contains some period furniture in day rooms. Tastefully decorated bedrooms — three double, one single, four family en suite rooms (one ground floor); modern conveniences; sitting-room, diningroom and games room for use of visitors. Excellent home cooking with traditional menus using home produce when possible. Special diets by arrangement. No pets. Open February to December. A car not essential, though parking provided. Evening Dinner, Bed and Breakfast. Three day Special Breaks available. Fire Certificate held. Miles of sandy beaches a short distance at Uphill, Weston, Berrow and Brean. Fishing, golf, sailing available; also riding and pony trekking locally. En route for the West Mendip Way walk. Milking may be watched through observation window in very modern milking parlour. SAE for brochure, please. AA Listed. Merit Award from local Tourist Board.

BEDFORDSHIRE

BEDFORD. Mrs Sheila Mousley, Lea Cottage, Old Harrowden Road, Bedford MK42 0TB (01234 740182). Members of the Bedfordshire Farm and Country Accommodation Group can offer a selection of Bed and Breakfast and Self Catering accommodation in rural areas. Thirteen properties offering Bed and Breakfast with prices from £14; 16 self catering units with prices from £90 to £245. Further information and a colour brochure on application.

PULLOXHILL. Phil and Judy Tookey, Pond Farm, 7 High Street, Pulloxhill MK45 5HA (01525 712316). Pond Farm is situated opposite the village green in Pulloxhill. Three miles from the A6 and five miles from the M1 Junction 12. We are within easy reach of Woburn Abbey and Safari Park, Whipsnade Zoo, the Shuttleworth Collection of Historic Aircraft at Old Warden and 11 miles from Luton Airport. Flitwick mainline station is only three miles away and 45 minutes by train to London. Pond Farm, built in the 17th century, is mainly arable although we have horses grazing on the meadowland. We also have a resident Great Dane. All bedrooms have tea/coffee facilities, washbasins and colour TV as no guest lounge is available. Price from £14. Evening Meals at local inn. ETB Listed.

SANDY. Mrs M. Codd, Highfield Farm, Sandy SG19 2AQ (01767 682332). *Highly Commended.*

Tranquil welcoming atmosphere on attractive arable farm. Set well back off A1 giving quiet, peaceful seclusion yet within easy reach of the RSPB, the Shuttleworth Collection, the Greensand Ridge Walk, Grafham Water and Woburn Abbey. Cambridge 22 miles, London 50 miles. All rooms have tea/coffee facilities, most have bathrooms en-suite and two are on the ground floor. There is a separate guests' sittingroom with TV. Family room. Dogs welcome by arrangement. No smoking. Guestaccom "Good Room" Award. Most guests return! Prices from £15 per person per night.

BERKSHIRE

ALDWORTH, near Reading. Mrs B.M. Chapman, Woodrows Farm, Aldworth, Near Reading RG8 9RS (Compton [01635] 578 336). Working farm. This attractive farmhouse is set in peaceful Berkshire countryside, near the River Thames and the Ridgeway. Within easy reach of Oxford, Newbury and Henley-on-Thames. Old world pub within half-a-mile serving excellent evening meals. Accommodation comprises one double room, one twin room and one single room; two bathrooms, three toilets. Bed and Breakfast £15 per person per night. Open April to October. Tourist Board registered.

MAIDENHEAD near. Mrs G. Reynolds, Moor Farm, Holyport, Near Maidenhead SL6 2HY (Tel & Fax: 01628 33761). *Highly Commended.* In the pretty village of Holyport, Moor Farm is four miles from Windsor in a lovely country garden setting. The farmhouse is a timber-framed 700 year old listed manor with charming en suite rooms, furnished with antiques. Well placed for touring the Thames Valley and visiting London; also close to Heathrow. Children welcome. Open all year. Bed and Breakfast from £19 to £22. Also self catering cottages available, graded 4 KEYS Highly Commended, sleeping two to four persons, from £200 to £380 per week.

BUCKINGHAMSHIRE

AYLESBURY. Foxhill Farm, Thame Road, Kingsey, Aylesbury HP17 8LZ (01844 291650). A delightful 17th century white-painted farmhouse, listed as being of architectural and historical interest, situated in the Aylesbury Vale with lovely views to the Chiltern Hills. This peaceful and comfortable oak-beamed farmhouse offers accommodation in three double/twin bedded rooms, two with en suite showers; all have colour TV and tea/coffee making facilities and there is a TV lounge/breakfast room. The large garden has lawns, shrubs, trees, ornamental ducks and a heated swimming pool available in the Summer. There is a wide choice of good local pubs and restaurants. Waddesdon Manor, Oxford and Windsor are all easily accessible for day visits as are London and Heathrow Airport.

CAMBRIDGESHIRE

CAMBRIDGE. Mrs Jean Wright, White Horse Cottage, 28 West Street, Comberton, Cambridge CB3 7DS (Cambridge [01223] 262914). A 17th century cottage with all modern conveniences situated in a charming village four miles south-west of Cambridge. Junction 12 off M11 — A603 from Cambridge, or A428 turn off at Hardwick Turning. Accommodation includes one double room, twin and family rooms. Own sitting room with colour TV; tea/coffee making facilities. Full central heating; parking. Excellent touring centre for many interesting places including Cambridge colleges, Wimpole Hall, Anglesey Abbey, Ely Cathedral, Imperial War Museum at Duxford, and many more. Bed and Breakfast from £17 per person. Children welcome.

CAMBRIDGE near. Mrs J.L. Bygraves, Elms Farm, 52 Main Road, Little Gransden SG19 3DL (01767 677459). Situated south west of Cambridge on B1046 from Junction 12 on the M11 or from A1 at St. Neots. Excellent touring centre for Cambridge, Duxford War Museum, Wimpole Hall, Woburn Abbey, Audley End House, Ely Cathedral, etc. Working arable farm with rural views and country walks around picturesque village. Recently renovated farmhouse offering a friendly atmosphere. Accommodation comprises one double, one twin with en suite facilities and one single bedrooms, all with colour TV, tea/coffee making facilities and central heating. Four pubs nearby for evening meals. Bed and Breakfast from £16 per person.

ELY. Mrs Valerie Fuller, Spinney Abbey, Wicken, Ely CB7 5XQ (Ely [01353] 720971). Working farm. Spinney Abbey is a spacious Georgian farmhouse. A Grade II Listed building of historical interest, rebuilt from the former priory in 1775. It stands in a large garden with tennis court adjacent to our dairy farm which borders the National Trust Nature Reserve "Wicken Fen". The accommodation comprises two double en suite rooms and a twin-bedded room with private bathroom, all with TV and tea/coffee tray. Guests' sittingroom. Central heating and electric blankets for colder months. Regret no pets and no smoking upstairs. Bed and Breakfast from £18 per person. Situated just off the A1123 half a mile west of Wicken. Open all year.

ELY. Mrs Margaret Sicard, The Laurels, 104 Victoria Street, Littleport, Ely CB6 1LZ (01353 861972; 0850 199299 mobile). A large, attractive Victorian House in a quiet location offering excellent accommodation and cooking. Set in pretty, old-fashioned garden, 200 yards from riverside pub. Situated on the Norfolk/Suffolk/Cambridge borders, four miles from Ely Cathedral; Wildfowl and Wetlands Trust, Cambridge's ornate colleges and famous Backs 30 minutes, Sandringham one hour. Twin/double en-suite rooms, one suitable for partially disabled person, with easy chairs, tea/coffee facilities, radio, colour TV, door locks and central heating. Drawing room, dining-room leading to sub-tropical garden room. Evening Meal. Cot/high chair, Z-bed. Private parking. Non smoking guests only. Special diets catered for. Bed and Breakfast from £15.

Enjoy FREE visits to Sacrewell Farm and Country Centre, Peterborough – see our READERS' OFFER vouchers.

CHESHIRE

CHESTER. Mrs C. Hibbert, Twomills Farm, Parkgate Road, Woodbank, Chester CH1 6EZ (01244 880232). A warm welcome awaits you at this 18th century farmhouse on a working farm, just six miles from Chester. We have a lovely quiet double room with colour TV and tea/coffee making facilities, also a pleasant bathroom. You can enjoy free range eggs and fresh milk with your breakfast and in the evening there is a choice of many and varied restaurants in the area for dining out. We are within easy reach of the hills and coast of North Wales, also North Shropshire and Cheshire. Rates are very reasonable at £14.50 per person.

CONGLETON. Mrs Sheila Kidd, Yew Tree Farm, North Rode, Congleton CW12 2PF (01260 223569). This working farm has a peaceful village setting with scenic country walks on our doorstep. It is central for the Peak District, Potteries, Alton Towers and the historic houses of Cheshire. Just 20 minutes from the M6. You can be assured of a warm welcome, a cosy atmosphere and good food. One double en-suite room and two twin rooms. Lounge with open log fire. Children are welcome and guests are invited to look around the farm and get to know the animals and wide range of pets. Bed and substantial cooked Breakfast from £15; optional Evening Meal £10. ETB Listed/Commended. Write or phone for brochure.

CONGLETON. Dorothy and Joe Gilman, Pedley House Farm, Pedley Lane, Timbersbrook, Congleton CW12 3QD (01260 273650). A family farm run on traditional lines with dairy cows, beef and sheep. The countryside is very beautiful with good walks nearby. Well situated for easy access to the Peak District and Staffordshire moorland; Alton Towers is 15 miles away. Little Moreton Hall, Gawsworth Hall, Biddulph Grange Gardens, Macclesfield Silk Museum are all within a 10 mile radius and well worth visiting. Accommodation is offered in a family room with double and bunk beds and a double room; bathroom; lounge with TV and tea-making facilities. Full English breakfast served using home and local farm produce whenever possible. Brochure with full details on request. Self catering accommodation also available.

HYDE. Monica Sidebottom, Shire Cottage, Benches Lane, Chisworth, Hyde SK14 6RY (01457 866536). ♛♛ *Commended.* Real home from home accommodation in peaceful location. Magnificent views overlooking Etheroe Country Park. Convenient for Manchester Airport, city centre, Peak District, stately homes and numerous places of interest. Ground floor bedrooms and bathroom. All rooms have vanity units, shaver points, tea-making facilities, TV. Family room has own shower and toilet. Bathroom has shower and bidet. Early breakfast for businessmen and travellers. Open all year. Suitable for disabled visitors. Children and pets welcome. Bed and Breakfast from £18 to £22.

Terms quoted in this publication may be subject to increase if rises in costs necessitate

HYDE, Near Manchester. Mrs Charlotte R. Walsh, Needhams Farm, Uplands Road, Werneth Low, Gee Cross, Near Hyde SK14 3AQ (0161-368 4610).

♛♛♛ *Commended.* **Working farm.** A cosy 16th century farmhouse set in peaceful, picturesque surroundings by Werneth Low Country Park and the Etherow Valley, which lie between Glossop and Manchester. The farm is ideally situated for holidaymakers and businessmen, especially those who enjoy peace and quiet, walking and rambling, golfing and riding, as these activities are all close by. At Needhams Farm everyone, including children and pets, receives a warm welcome. Good wholesome meals available in the evenings. Residential licence and Fire Certificate held. Open all year. Bed and Breakfast from £18 single minimum and £32 double maximum; Evening Meal £7. AA Listed. RAC Acclaimed.

MACCLESFIELD. Mrs I. Kennerley, Sandpit Farm, Messuage Lane, Marton, Macclesfield SK11 9HS (01260 224254).

♛♛ A friendly welcome to our 200 acre arable farm in peaceful surroundings. Well maintained farmhouse with two rooms en-suite, one room with washbasin, all with TV and tea/coffee making facilities. Visitors' bath/shower room. Separate diningroom. TV lounge. Heated throughout. Excellent touring centre for Peak District, Chester and Potteries. Manchester Airport 14 miles. National Trust properties, stately homes and Jodrell Bank radio telescope nearby. Open all year. Non-smokers preferred. Bed and Breakfast from £14; from £18 for en-suite facilities.

MACCLESFIELD. Mrs P.O. Worth, Rough Hey Farm, Leek Road, Gawsworth, Macclesfield SK11 0JQ (01260 252296).

♛♛ Delightfully situated overlooking the Cheshire Plain and on the edge of the Peak National Park, Rough Hey is an historic former hunting lodge dating from before the 16th century. Tastefully modernised yet retaining its old world character. This 300 acre sheep farm consists of wooded valleys and hills with plenty of wildlife and lovely walks. In the locality there are numerous old halls and villages to visit. Double room en-suite, twin room and two single rooms, all with washbasins, TV and tea/coffee making facilities. Large comfortable lounge with TV. A warm and friendly welcome is assured. Terms from £13.50; from £17 for en suite facilities.

NANTWICH. Mrs Jean E. Callwood, Lea Farm, Wrinehill Road, Wybunbury, Nantwich CW5 7NS (01270 841429).

♛♛ *Commended.* **Working farm, join in.** A charming farmhouse set in landscaped gardens, where peacocks roam, on 150 acre dairy farm. Spacious bedrooms with washbasins, colour TV, electric blankets and tea/coffee making facilities. Family, double and twin bedrooms, en suite facilities. Luxury lounge, diningroom overlooking gardens. Pool/snooker; fishing in well stocked pool in beautiful surroundings. Bird watching. Children welcome, also dogs if kept under control. Help feed the birds and animals and see the cows being milked. Near to Stapeley Water Gardens, Bridgemere Garden World and Wild Life Park. Also Nantwich, Crewe, Chester, the Potteries and Alton Towers. Bed and Breakfast from £13.50 per person; Evening Meal from £7.50. Children half price. Weekly terms available.

CHESHIRE

Salt and silk, cheese and canals, trains and telescopes – just some of the intriguing features of this picturesque county. Make time to visit Chester Zoo, Stapeley Water Gardens, Jodrell Bank Science Centre, Port Sunlight Heritage Centre and Tatton Park – all a great day out and easily accessible from the motorway network.

CORNWALL

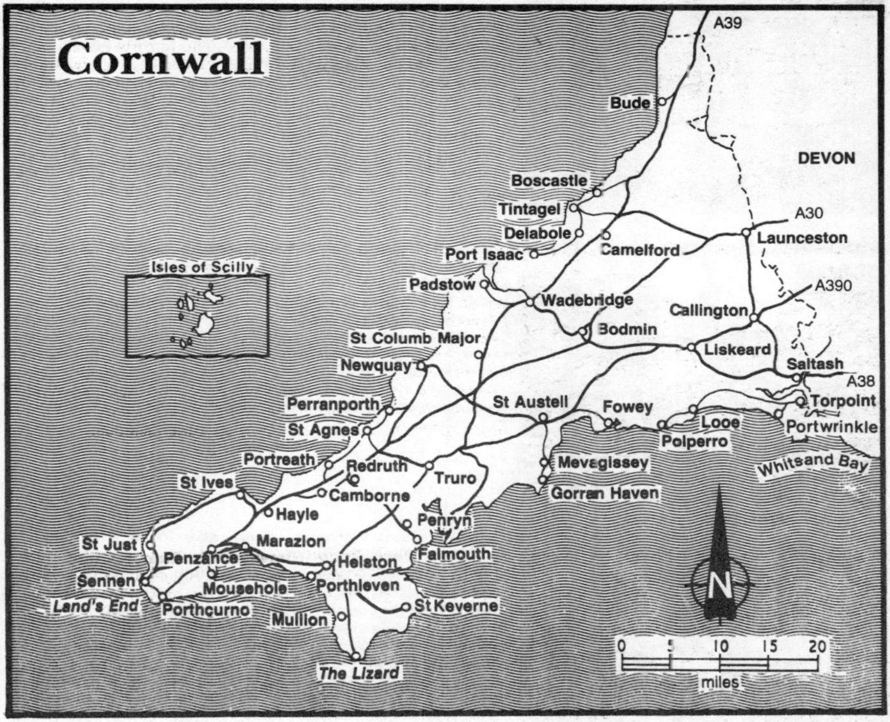

BODMIN. Mrs S. Menhinick, Loskeyle Farm, St. Tudy, Bodmin PL30 3PW (01208 851005). *Approved.* Loskeyle is a working dairy farm in the Duchy of Cornwall where a warm welcome awaits you. Relax and enjoy the peace and tranquillity of farm life here where you can watch the milking, feed the hens, collect eggs or enjoy leisurely walks through open fields. Children especially welcome with reduced rates. Delicious farmhouse cooking using fresh local produce. Pretty bedrooms with tea/coffee facilities and vanity units. Ideal base for north/south coasts. Golf, Camel Trail nearby, also pony trekking over the moors only a stone's throw away. Bed and Breakfast from £13; Evening Meal £7.50.

BODMIN. Mrs Jenny Bass, Trehannick Farm, St. Teath, Bodmin PL30 3JW (Bodmin [01208] 850312). Working farm. First mentioned in the Domesday Book in 1086, Trehannick is a 180-acre family farm situated in the beautiful Allen Valley. Safe sandy beaches, coastal walks, golf, sailing, surfing and fishing are all within easy reach of this peaceful farmhouse. One family room, two double rooms, twin-bedded room with washbasin and one single bedroom. Bathroom; lounge with colour TV (log fires when needed). Good home cooking using own farm produce when available. Car essential. Sorry, no pets. Reductions for children sharing parents' room. Bed and Breakfast, or Bed, Breakfast and Evening Meal. SAE please or telephone for terms and further details.

BODMIN. Mrs Marilyn Hawkey, Tregolls Farm, St. Wenn, Bodmin PL30 5PG (01208 812154). Set in a picturesque rural valley in mid-Cornwall, Tregolls farmhouse is conveniently situated approximately five miles from the main A30 trunk road. The rugged North Cornish coast, the holiday resort of Newquay and the well known harbour village of Padstow are approximately 12 miles away; South Cornish coast is approximately 15 miles, Truro with its cathedral and good shopping centre 20 miles and famous Land's End 50 miles. Tregolls is a family-run farm of 570 acres of cattle and sheep with some arable crops grown. Spacious traditional farmhouse offers four guest bedrooms with tea/coffee facilities. Bathroom/shower and separate toilet. Traditional English meals served in diningroom and lounge has feature fireplace and colour TV. Bed and Breakfast from £11.50 to £13.50. Send for brochure.

BOSCASTLE. Mrs Sarah James, Trehane Farm, Trevalga, Boscastle PL35 0EB (01840 250510). ♛♛ *Commended.* Welcome to Trehane, a dairy farm on the spectacular North Cornwall Heritage coast. Farmhouse set in magnificent position overlooking sea, superb coastal views. We offer a comfortable friendly atmosphere and wholesome nourishing food using fresh farm produce and home baked bread. Enjoy fine walks along the coast or inland on to Bodmin Moor. And you can learn to spin in this very lovely place. We can accommodate six guests. Children and pets welcome. Open all year. Bed and Breakfast from £14.50.

BOSCASTLE. Mrs Cheryl Nicholls, Trerosewill Farm, Paradise, Boscastle PL35 0DL (01840 250545). Working farm. ♛♛♛ *Highly Commended.* AA QQQQ Selected. Bed and Breakfast accommodation in modern farmhouse on working dairy farm, only short walk from the picturesque village of Boscastle. Rooms have spectacular coastal and rural views, all en-suite with tea making facilities. Colour TVs and telephones available if required. Licensed. Centrally heated. Seasonal log fires. Large gardens. Traditional farmhouse fayre. Watch the milking and feed the calves. Superb coastal and countryside walks. Specially negotiated rates for nearby golf and pony trekking. One way walks arranged. Packed lunches available. Spring and Autumn breaks. Regret no pets or smokers. Bed and Breakfast from £15.

TREROSEWILL FARMHOUSE

BUDE. Mrs Rosina Joyner, Penrose, Dizzard, St. Gennys, Bude EX23 0NX (01840 230318). Penrose is a delightful 17th century cottage with beamed ceilings and inglenook fireplaces. Tastefully modernised, yet retaining all its Olde Worlde charm. Set in one and a half acres of lawns and gardens within the National Trust area close to the coastal path, it is ideal for those seeking peace and quiet. Nearby is the beautiful beach of Widemouth Bay. The views from the cottage are extensive. All rooms have washbasins, TV and tea/coffee making facilities; two rooms with double four-poster beds (one with en suite facilities). Good English breakfast; optional Evening Meal. Also available is a mobile home and self-catering cottage annexe. SAE for booking form and brochure, or telephone. Bed and Breakfast from £17 per night.

CORNISH CUISINE!

The traditional Cornish Pasty was originally the tin-miners' portable lunch — shaped like a torpedo to fit in his pocket! The filling is usually mutton mixed with potatoes and swedes, and is enclosed in pastry pinched high along its entire length. Another Cornish speciality is Stargazey Pie, where pilchards are arranged in a dish like the spokes of a wheel, the pastry cover being cut to allow the eyes to gaze out. And to finish off — a clotted cream tea with scones and strawberry jam!

Court Farm

Mrs Mary Trewin, Court Farm, Marhamchurch, Bude, Cornwall.
Telephone: (01288) 361494

Court Farm is set in the centre of the pretty village of Marhamchurch, close to Bude and various beaches. Bedrooms (mainly ensuite) have coffee/tea making facilities and colour TV. Large, comfortable TV lounge and separate dining room. Guests are welcome to use our heated outdoor swimming pool, hard tennis court, children's play area and pool room. We are a 200 acre beef and sheep farm, and guests are welcome to wander round. Bed and Breakfast from £14. Evening meal optional. Reductions for children. Weekly rates. Open all year.

HIDEAWAY FARM HOLIDAYS

On the Cornwall/Devon borders a group of farmers' wives have got together to offer you a unique experience staying in rural countryside. A warm welcome awaits everyone in English Tourist Board inspected accommodation, ideal for countryside/Heritage/coastal walking.

For accommodation brochure apply to:
Hideaway Farm Holidays,
Lower Northcott, Poughill, Bude,
Cornwall EX23 7EL
Tel. (01288) 352350
24 hr answering service

Children welcome
Ensuite accommodation
Home cooking our speciality using home grown and fresh produce
Open all year

Play areas
Log fires
Bed and Breakfast
Short Breaks

FOR THE MUTUAL GUIDANCE OF GUEST AND HOST

Every year literally thousands of holidays, short-breaks and overnight stops are arranged through our guides, the vast majority without any problems at all. In a handful of cases, however, difficulties do arise about bookings, which often could have been prevented from the outset.

It is important to remember that when accommodation has been booked, both parties — guests and hosts — have entered into a form of contract. We hope that the following points will provide helpful guidance.

GUESTS: When enquiring about accommodation, be as precise as possible. Give exact dates, numbers in your party and the ages of any children. State the number and type of rooms wanted and also what catering you require — bed and breakfast, full board, etc. Make sure that the position about evening meals is clear — and about pets, reductions for children or any other special points.

Read our reviews carefully to ensure that the proprietors you are going to contact can supply what you want. Ask for a letter confirming all arrangements, if possible.

If you have to cancel, do so as soon as possible. Proprietors do have the right to retain deposits and under certain circumstances to charge for cancelled holidays if adequate notice is not given and they cannot re-let the accommodation.

HOSTS: Give details about your facilities and about any special conditions. Explain your deposit system clearly and arrangements for cancellations, charges, etc, and whether or not your terms include VAT.

If for any reason you are unable to fulfil an agreed booking without adequate notice, you may be under an obligation to arrange alternative suitable accommodation or to make some form of compensation.

While every effort is made to ensure accuracy, we regret that FHG Publications cannot accept responsibility for errors, omissions or misrepresentation in our entries or any consequences thereof. Prices in particular should be checked because we go to press early. We will follow up complaints but cannot act as arbiters or agents for either party.

BUDE. Mrs Sylvia Lucas, Elm Park, Bridgerule, Holsworthy EX22 7EL (01288 381231). Elm Park is a 205 acre dairy, beef, sheep farm six miles from surfing beaches at Bude and ideal for touring Devon/Cornwall. Children are especially welcomed with pony rides and a tractor and trailer ride around the farm. There are spacious family rooms (two en-suite) and a twin-bedded room, all with tea/coffee making facilities. Ample four-course dinners with freshly produced fare and delicious sweets. Games room with snooker, table skittles, darts, etc, and golf putting. Bed, Breakfast and Evening Meal, reasonable terms. Reductions for children and everyone is made welcome and comfortable. Brochure available.

BUDE. Michael and Pearl Hopper, West Nethercott Farm, Whitstone, Holsworthy (Devon) EX22 6LD (Week-St-Mary [0128884] 394). Working farm, join in. A warm welcome awaits you on this dairy and sheep farm. Watch the cows being milked, help with the animals. Free pony rides, scenic farm walks. Short distance from sandy beaches, surfing and the rugged North Cornwall coast. Ideal base for visiting any part of Devon or Cornwall. We are located in Cornwall though our postal address is Devon. The traditional farmhouse has TVs in bedrooms; diningroom and separate lounge with colour TV. Plenty of traditional home cooking. Access to the house at anytime. Bed and Breakfast from £11, four-course Evening Meal available. Children under 12 years reduced rates. Weekly terms available.

BUDE. Mrs C. Cholwill, Tackbeare Farm, Marhamchurch, Bude EX23 0HH (01288 810264; from March 1995, 01288 381264). A friendly welcome awaits you at our 16th century manor farmhouse on a 240 acre dairy and beef farm. Light spacious rooms are well equipped and comfortable. There are two family bedrooms (one en suite), two double rooms (one en suite), and one single room; all have tea/coffee making facilities: Large lounge with colour TV and log fire. Our speciality is home cooked country fare using our own and local produce. Children welcome; cots and high chairs provided. People with special needs catered for. Bed and Breakfast from £15 per night; Bed, Breakfast and Evening Meal £21 per night. Reductions for weekly bookings and children. Mountain bikes for hire.

See also Colour Display Advertisement **BUDE. The Cliff Hotel, Crooklets Beach, Bude EX23 8NG (01288 353110).** A small, top-class hotel where quality matters. Indoor swimming pool, spa pool, solarium, all weather tennis court, putting green, par-3 chipping hole, and children's play area (swings, see-saw) and new all weather bowling green. Set in five acres of grounds 200 yards from Crooklets Beach, adjoining National Trust cliffs and farm. Bedrooms are all en suite, with colour TV (with video and satellite), radio, drinks facility, and phone. The chef proprietor ensures that food has the highest priority, with choice and quality second to none. Mr Peter Savill, ETB Inspector, said "This hotel is like an oasis in a desert". Weekly half board from £200.

CALLINGTON. Higher Manaton, Callington PL17 8PX (01579 370460). Higher Manaton is a working 90 acre mixed farm situated two and a half miles north west of Callington on the B3257, 13 miles from Plymouth. Located on the Cornwall/Devon border midway between Bodmin Moor and Dartmoor, it is ideal for touring with golf, riding, fishing, swimming in easy reach. The farmhouse is early 18th century, with granite open fireplace, dining room and separate lounge with colour TV. One spacious family room and one twin-bedded room. Non-smoking accommodation available. Open April to October. Bed and Breakfast from £13 to £15 nightly; £90 weekly. Reductions for children.

CAMBORNE. Mrs Christine Peerless, Cargenwen Farm, Blackrock, Praze-an-Beeble, Camborne TR14 9PD (01209 831442). Cargenwen is a comfortable, quiet, and ideally situated base from which to explore the beautiful Cornish countryside and magnificent coastline, set on a south-west-facing hillside with extensive country views towards St. Ives Bay. We offer good traditional home made and varied meals using fresh home and local produce whenever available; vegetarian and special diets catered for. TV lounge. Tea/coffee making facilities and washbasins in all rooms; en-suite facilities available. Easy parking. Fire Certificate. No smoking. Bed and Breakfast from £91 per week; Evening Meal (optional) £8. Sorry, no children under 12 years. Open all year except Christmas and New Year. Cornwall Tourist Board registered.

A REAL COUNTRY HOUSE HOTEL JUST OUTSIDE OF FALMOUTH

THE HOME

PENJERRICK, FALMOUTH

Telephone: Falmouth (STD 01326) 250427 and (Fax) 250143

Situated in lovely unspoilt countryside, yet only 2½ miles from Falmouth. Ideal for lovers of the country, yet within 18 minutes' walk of Maenporth Beach.

An Ashley Courtenay Highly Recommended Hotel

Our house, in its large garden, has lovely views over tree-clad countryside to Maenporth and the bay. Close to the Helford River with its beautiful walks and boating facilities. Ideal base for touring.

Majority of bedrooms completely refurbished with full en-suite facilities, TV, heating and tea/coffee making facilities. Our home is graciously furnished and carpeted to a high standard. All beds are modern divans. Partial central heating. Our elegant dining room has separate tables. Large lounge with colour TV. In addition there is a spacious sun lounge overlooking the garden.

★

TABLE LICENCE GOOD ENCLOSED CAR PARK BUS SERVICE

★

Mr & Mrs P. Tremayne have welcomed guests to their lovely house for the past 30 years

★

Dinner, Room and Breakfast from £130 per week, including 17.5% VAT

Illustrated brochure from Mrs. T. P. Tremayne

We are of a farming family and our visitors' book is blushingly complimentary over the home-cooked food and its presentation. This is our home and as such we welcome you to it and hope you will enjoy it as much as we do.

Also Self-Catering Furnished Farmhouse and Cottage at Constantine, Falmouth

FOWEY. Mrs S.C. Dunn, Menabilly Barton, Par PL24 2TN (01726 812844). Working farm. MENABILLY BARTON is a secluded farmhouse set in wooded valley leading to a quiet cove, accessible by footpath and safe for bathing. Farmhouse with spacious diningroom and large lounge with TV, also peaceful garden available during the day. Good traditional farmhouse cooking. National Trust cliff walks round the coast. Fowey, 10 minutes by road, offers fishing, sailing, quaint shops, etc. Golfing on the coast nearby. North coast about 40 minutes' drive; Land's End two and a half hours. Several National Trust properties in the area. Open March to October with accommodation in three family bedrooms with washbasins and one single bedroom; bathroom with shower, toilet. Facilities for making drinks. Cot, high chair, babysitting. Pets allowed. Bed and full English Breakfast only from £13 per adult; reductions for children.

HELSTON. Mrs Dorothy Jenkin, Treworgie Farm, Manaccan, Helston TR12 6JB (01326 231327). Working farm. Treworgie is a 140 acre dairy farm offering true farmhouse accommodation with a Cornish family. Situated in an area of outstanding natural beauty, two miles from the quaint old village of Manaccan, three miles from the beautiful Helford River with its well known walks including Frenchman's Creek. Within easy reach of many beaches and coastal paths on the Lizard Peninsula. Helston eight miles. Many tourist attractions and places of interest within easy reach by car. Two double/family rooms, bathroom, lounge/diner with colour TV, sun lounge. Full English breakfast. Evening meal by arrangement only. Children welcome, reasonable terms.

HELSTON. Mrs Maureen Dale, Polgarth Farm, Crowntown, Helston TR13 0AA (Helston [01326] 572115). Working farm. Polgarth Farm is central for touring West Cornwall, three miles from the market town of Helston (home of the famous Furry Dance —8th May) on the main Helston-Camborne road (B3303). Market gardening includes early potatoes and cabbage. Maureen Dale, having cooked at The London Dairy Show, Ideal Home Exhibition, on TV, and broadcast on local radio, takes great pleasure in producing sumptuous meals for all her guests and, with her husband, welcomes you to their home. Children welcome. Pets welcome by prior arrangement. Open January to end November. Bed and breakfast £13 to £15. SAE for terms please. RAC Listed.

HELSTON. Mrs P. Roberts, Hendra Farm, Wendron, Helston TR13 0NR (Falmouth [01326] 40470). Hendra Farm, just off the main Helston/Falmouth road, is an ideal centre for touring Cornwall; three miles to Helston, eight to both Redruth and Falmouth. Safe sandy beaches within easy reach — five miles to the sea. Beautiful views from the farmhouse of the 60-acre beef farm. Two double, one single, and one family bedrooms; bathroom and toilets; sittingroom and two diningrooms. Cot, babysitting and reduced rates offered for children. No objection to pets. Car necessary, parking space. Enjoy good cooking with roast beef, pork, lamb, chicken, genuine Cornish pasties, fish and delicious sweets and cream. Open all year except Christmas. Evening Dinner, Bed and Breakfast from £85 per week which includes cooked breakfast, three course evening dinner, tea and homemade cake before bed. Bed and Breakfast only from £11 per night also available.

One FREE adult entry with every paid adult entry when visiting North Cornwall Museum and Gallery – see our READERS' OFFER VOUCHERS for full details.

HELSTON. Mrs Margaret Jenkin, Boderloggan Farm, Trenear, Helston TR13 0ES (01326 572148). Working farm. "Boderloggan" is a 120-acre dairy farm, ideally situated for touring the main towns and beauty spots of South and West Cornwall. Within easy reach of the coast, Newquay, Falmouth, St. Ives, Penzance, Truro; Helston three miles. Also well situated for visiting holiday attractions and National Trust properties and gardens in the area. Two double (family) bedrooms with washbasins and tea/coffee making facilities; bathroom; dining room, lounge with colour TV. Mrs Jenkin will give her guests a value-for-money holiday with plenty of fresh vegetables, clotted cream, with a three-course Evening Meal. English Breakfast. Friendly homely atmosphere, children welcome. FHG Diploma Winner.

HELSTON. Mrs Joan Gilbert, Erisey Barton, Ruan Minor, Helston TR12 7LJ (Mullion [01326] 240296). Working farm. Erisey Barton is a working beef and sheep farm with a historic 17th century farmhouse set in walled gardens. Guests can enjoy many walks on the farm which borders the peaceful Goonhilly Downs. There is a Nature Reserve and Farm Museum, also sandy beaches, golf and fishing nearby. There are local pubs and seafood restaurants which serve excellent meals and snacks. Two double (family) rooms with tea/coffee making facilities. Large beamed lounge with piano and TV. Bed and Full English Breakfast only, served in farmhouse kitchen. Access to rooms at all times. Children welcome, babysitting if required. Mrs Gilbert and family will warmly welcome their guests for a secluded and peaceful holiday. Holder of Basic Food Hygiene Certificate.

LAUNCESTON. Mrs Valerie Griffin, Wheatley Cottage, Wheatley Farm, Maxworthy, Launceston PL15 8LY (Tel & Fax: 01566 781232). ♛♛♛ *Highly Commended.* Escape and unwind at Wheatley where personal attention and friendly atmosphere is a priority, as is our traditional and imaginative farmhouse cuisine. Lovely old farmhouse set in landscaped gardens on working farm in the peace of the Cornish countryside. Delightful pretty bedrooms all with en suite facilities; one with romantic four-poster bed. Beautifully situated just a few miles from spectacular rugged North Coast and sandy coves. Bed and Breakfast from £19 per person; Evening Meal from £10.50.

HELP IMPROVE BRITISH TOURIST STANDARDS

You are choosing holiday accommodation from our very popular FHG Publications. Whether it be a hotel, guest house, farmhouse or self-catering accommodation, we think you will find it hospitable, comfortable and clean, and your host and hostess friendly and helpful. Why not write and tell us about it?

As a recognition of the generally well-run and excellent holiday accommodation reviewed in our publications, we at FHG Publications Ltd. present a diploma to proprietors who receive the highest recommendation from their guests who are also readers of our Guides. If you care to write to us praising the holiday you have booked through FHG Publications Ltd. – whether this be board, self-catering accommodation, a sporting or a caravan holiday, what you say will be evaluated and the proprietors who reach our final list will be contacted.

The winning proprietor will receive an attractive framed diploma to display on his premises as recognition of a high standard of comfort, amenity and hospitality. FHG Publications Ltd. offer this diploma as a contribution towards the improvement of standards in tourist accommodation in Britain. Help your excellent host or hostess to win it!

FHG DIPLOMA

We nominate ....

....

Because

Name ....

Address ....

.... Telephone No. ....

LAUNCESTON. Mrs A. E. Werren, Waterloo Farm, North Petherwin, Launceston PL15 8LL (01566 785386). Family accommodation provided in our comfortable, six-bedroomed farmhouse situated amid peaceful countryside overlooking the beautiful Ottery Valley. The river, ancient county boundary, offers lovely walks and one and a half miles of good, private trout fishing. Shooting and sea fishing trips can be arranged. The village and Otter Sanctuary are ten minutes' walk from farm. Rural town of Launceston (four and a half miles) has 18-hole golf course, Norman Castle and Steam Railway. Excellent farmhouse cooking and a relaxed, friendly atmosphere make Waterloo an ideal touring centre for the moors and coasts of Devon and Cornwall. Bed and Breakfast from £12.50 per night; Evening Meal optional. Reductions for children. SAE please for terms.

LISKEARD. Mrs Elizabeth Rowe, Trewint Farm, Menheniot, Liskeard PL14 3RE (Liskeard [01579] 347155 or 62237). Working farm, join in. Trewint Working Farm is situated one and a half miles off the A38. Set in peaceful, rural surroundings, four miles from old market town of Liskeard, local popular attractions and National Trust. The 200 acre farm has attractive valley walks, cattle, sheep, pigs; pony for children and play area. Ideal for touring Cornwall and South Devon. The south coast is within easy reach with fishing harbours at Looe, Polperro, Mevagissey. Bodmin Moor four miles and St. Mellion Golf Course eight miles. Vegetables and naturally fed meat, all home produced, provide a delicious four course Evening Meal. Full English Breakfast, bedtime drink. Double, twin and family rooms, all with TV, en suite facilities, tea/coffee making facilities and electric blankets. Cot, high chair, babysitting (reductions for children). Lounge with colour TV, large open fire for the cooler evenings. Five minutes' walk from popular village pub. Sorry, no pets. Open all year. SAE for brochure or ring for a chat about your requirements. Cornwall Tourist Board registered. RAC listed. Also self catering accommodation sleeping five plus cot.

LISKEARD. Mrs A.R. Hawke, Cartuther Barton, Liskeard PL14 3PS (01579 343244). Cartuther Barton is a pleasant Cornish manor farmhouse, situated one mile from Liskeard on the A38 Plymouth road. Within easy reach of Looe, Polperro and many other coastal resorts. Also golf course approximately four miles. Ideal for touring. Lounge with TV; dining room with separate tables, and hot and cold water in bedrooms. Ample free parking space. Bed, Breakfast and Evening Dinner. Terms on application.

LISKEARD. Mrs Stephanie Rowe, Tregondale Farm, Menheniot, Liskeard PL14 3RG (Liskeard [01579] 342407). ♛♛ *Highly Commended.* **Working farm, join in.** Feeling like a break? Come and join our family with the peace of the countryside amidst wildlife, flowers and woodland walks — breathtaking in Spring — on a 180 acre mixed farm, situated between A38 and A390 near Looe. See pedigree animals being naturally reared, and pony rides and play area for children. This charming characteristic farmhouse, which dates back to the time of the Domesday Book, provides a high standard of comfort with en suite facilities; lounge, diningroom with log fires and colour TV. Sun porch. Home grown produce tastefully presented, beautifully set in an old walled garden with picnic table. Ideal for exploring Cornwall's holiday attractions, National Trust properties, new sports centre at Liskeard. Bed and Breakfast from £16 to £18. Weekly reductions and reduced rates for children. Babysitting. AA QQQQ. Open all year. Brochure available or phone for your requirements. Self catering cottage also available, graded 4 Keys Highly Commended

LISKEARD. Mrs E.R. Elford, Tresulgan Farm, Near Menheniot, Liskeard PL14 3PU (Tel & Fax: 01503 240268). ♛♛ *Highly Commended.* **Working farm, join in.** Tresulgan is a 115-acre Pedigree Holstein Friesian dairy farm situated off the Plymouth/Liskeard road, set in quiet surroundings. The farmhouse, built in the 1700s, still retains its quiet character and original beams. The attractive bedrooms, which overlook the large enclosed garden, have picturesque views of the wooded Seaton Valley. Nearest beach at Seaton (four miles), and the popular fishing village of Looe (six miles), shark fishing, water sports, etc. Sailing, fishing, golf, riding, Woolly Monkey Sanctuary, Dobwalls Family Adventure Park, National Trust properties and other attractions within a few miles. Friendly accommodation — one double, one treble and one family bedrooms, all with en suite, colour TV and tea/coffee making facilities. Colour TV in guests' lounge. Price includes full English Breakfast every day, three-course Evening Meals. SAE, please, for terms and brochure.

LISKEARD. Mrs Lindsay M. Pendray, Caduscott, East Taphouse, Liskeard PL14 4NG (Liskeard [01579] 320262). Working farm. Down the lane where the wild flowers nod in passing; to relax and unwind in attractive 17th century listed farmhouse peeping over the valley where streams converge to make the 10 mile journey to the sea at Looe. Double room (en-suite toilet/shower), adjoining twin-bedded room. Traditional Bed and Breakfast with Evening Meal served in a large lounge/diningroom where a log fire assures you of a warm welcome, also central heating. Children especially welcome; cot, high chair and open spaces to play in with swing and climbing frame. Bed and Breakfast from £13.50 to £17 per person per night. No Smoking. The Pendray family have farmed Caduscott for over 60 years and will make every effort to ensure that you discover Cornwall.

LOOE. Mrs D. Eastley, Bake Farm, Pelynt, Looe PL13 2QQ (Lanreath [01503] 220244). Working farm. This is an old farmhouse, bearing the Trelawnay Coat of Arms (1610) situated midway between Looe and Fowey. There are three double bedrooms all with washbasins and night storage heaters; bathroom/toilet, shower room/toilet; combined sitting/diningroom. Children welcome at reduced rates, babysitting available. Sorry, no pets. Open from May to October. Plenty of fresh farm food, a lot of home produce including Cornish clotted cream and an abundance of roasts. A car is essential for touring the area, ample parking. There is much to see and do here — horse riding four miles, golf seven. The sea is only five miles away and there is shark fishing at Looe. SAE, please for terms for Evening Meal, Bed and Breakfast. Cleanliness guaranteed.

ENGLISH TOURIST BOARD
HIGHLY COMMENDED

Coombe Farm

WIDEGATES, Nr. LOOE
CORNWALL PL13 1QN
Tel: Widegates (01503) 240223

WINNER AA Guest House of the Year Award West of England 1981

A warm welcome assured by Alexander and Sally Low

A lovely country house surrounded by lawns, meadows, woods and streams with superb views to the sea. Log fires. Delicious home cooking. Candlelit dining. Licensed. All bedrooms are ensuite and have colour TV, radio, tea and coffee-making facilities and direct dial telephone.

In the grounds – many birds, animals and flowers, a lovely heated swimming pool, a croquet lawn and a stone barn for games including snooker and table tennis. Nearby – golf, fishing, tennis, horse riding and glorious walks and beaches.

The perfect centre for visiting all parts of Cornwall and Devon.

Bed and Breakfast from £18.00. Four course dinner from £12.00.

Special Short Break discounts.

AA QQQQ

RAC Highly Acclaimed

LOOE. Mrs Jean Henly, Bucklawren Farm, St. Martin, Looe PL13 1NZ (Tel & Fax: 01503 240738). *Highly Commended.* **Working farm.** Bucklawren is situated deep in the unspoilt countryside yet only one mile from the beach, two and a half miles from Looe and only one mile from the Woolly Monkey Sanctuary. It is mentioned in the Domesday Book, but the manor house is now replaced by a 19th century spacious farmhouse, which has a large garden and beautiful sea views. We offer excellent accommodation in en suite and family rooms, with farmhouse cooking in a friendly relaxed atmosphere. There is ample parking. Open all year. Reduced rates for children. Bed and Breakfast from £16 to £18 per person per night; Evening Meal £9 (optional). Brochure on request. Farm Holiday Bureau member.

Bucklawren Farm

LOOE. Mrs J.M. Gill, Cleese Farm, Nomansland, Looe PL13 1PB (01503 240224). Cleese Farm is a dairy farm, just off the main B3253 Looe Road, in an ideal position for touring Cornwall. Sandy beach at Looe one and a half miles, Monkey Sanctuary, golf course, horse riding, water sports within five minutes' drive. Also relaxing woodland walks on farm. Set in beautiful unspoilt countryside. All rooms have sea and valley views, washbasins and tea/coffee making facilities. We offer a friendly atmosphere, babysitting, ample parking. Pets welcome. Garden furniture available. Bed and Breakfast from £12. Cornwall Tourist Board registered.

MEVAGISSEY. Mrs Dawn Rundle, Lancallan Farm, Mevagissey, St. Austell PL26 6EW (01726 842284). Lancallan is a large 17th century farmhouse on a working 200 acre dairy and beef farm in a beautiful rural setting, one mile from Mevagissey and surrounded by lovely coastal walks and sandy beaches. We are well situated for day trips throughout Cornwall. Enjoy a traditional farmhouse breakfast in a warm and friendly atmosphere. Accommodation comprises one family room, one double room; bathroom; lounge with colour TV and tea-making facilities. Terms available on request, reductions for children. SAE please. Tourist Board registered.

PLEASE SEND A STAMPED ADDRESSED ENVELOPE WITH ENQUIRIES

MEVAGISSEY. Mrs Jane Youlden, Steep House, Portmellon Cove, Mevagissey PL26 2PH (01726 843732). Steep House stands in an acre of ground by the sea, in a natural cove which has a safe, sandy beach 20 yards from the large garden. Comfortable, centrally heated double bedrooms with washbasins and sea or beach views, colour TV and tea/coffee maker; some en-suite. English Breakfast and imaginative home cooked dinners of a very high standard served in wood panelled diningroom overlooking Portmellon Cove. All meals include as much home grown produce as possible and barbecue evening meals are a popular event during the summer months. Covered summertime swimming pool. Guests welcome all year. Modest prices, special weekly and winter break rates. Christmas celebrations. Residential drinks licence. Private parking. Fire Certificate. All enquiries welcomed.

MEVAGISSEY. Mrs Anne Hennah, Treleaven Farm, Mevagissey PL26 6RZ (Mevagissey [01726] 842413). Working farm. Treleaven Farm is situated in quiet, pleasant surroundings overlooking the village and the sea. The 200-acre mixed farm is well placed for visitors to enjoy the many attractions of Mevagissey with its quaint narrow streets and lovely shops. Fishing and boat trips are available and very popular. The house offers a warm and friendly welcome with the emphasis on comfort, cleanliness and good food using local produce A licensed bar and solar heated swimming pool add to your holiday enjoyment, together with a games room and putting green. Tastefully furnished throughout, with central heating, there are five double bedrooms and one family bedroom, all en-suite with tea/coffee making facilities and TV; bathroom, two toilets. Sittingroom and diningroom. Open February to November for Evening Dinner, Bed and Breakfast from £26; Bed and Breakfast from £16. Sorry, no pets. SAE, please, for particulars or telephone.

MEVAGISSEY near. Mrs Sally Wade, Tregidgeo Farm, Grampound, Truro TR2 4SP (Tel & Fax: 01726 882450). Working farm. Tregidgeo is a spacious tastefully furnished farmhouse in a beautifully secluded and peaceful setting overlooking garden and pond. On the edge of the unspoilt Roseland Peninsula and within easy reach of the main St. Austell to Truro Road. It is ideally situated for touring and any part of the county is easily reached on a day's excursion. There are several sandy beaches and the fishing village of Mevagissey nearby. Delicious home cooking. Children welcome at reduced rates, cot and babysitting available. Bedrooms are all en suite and have colour TV, radio alarm, heating and tea-making facilities. Luxury bathroom, lounge and dining room. Bed and Breakfast; Evening Dinner optional.

MEVAGISSEY. Mrs Linda Hennah, Kerryanna Country House, Treleaven Farm, Mevagissey PL26 6RZ (Mevagissey [01726] 843558). *Commended.* **Working farm.** AA QQQ; FHB Member. Kerryanna Country House enjoys a superb position overlooking the quaint fishing village of Mevagissey surrounded by rambling farmland, abundant wildlife and flowers. You are welcome to meet our goats, ponies and assorted chickens. Swim in our beautiful outdoor pool — heated May to September — or try your skills in the games barn or putting green. All rooms are en-suite with colour TV and tea/coffee facilities. Large lounge with open fire and cocktail bar in our plant-filled conservatory. Local fish, vegetables and meat used daily in our lovingly prepared dishes with plenty of choice. Bed and Breakfast or Bed, Breakfast and Dinner. Colour brochure.

See also Colour Display Advertisement **NEWQUAY near. Marian and Derrick Molloy, Tregurrian Hotel, Watergate Bay, Near Newquay TR8 4AB (St. Mawgan [01637] 860280).** Peaceful position between Newquay and Padstow — 100 yards from glorious sandy beach and spectacular Atlantic coastline. Open Easter to November, 27 rooms (most en-suite) have tea makers, radio/listening, heaters and colour TV. Heated pool, sun patio, games room, solarium. Licensed. Central for touring Cornwall; parties and coaches by arrangement. Spring and Autumn Breaks. Dinner, Bed and Breakfast £144 to £230 inclusive. Children welcome at reduced rates. Brochure from resident proprietors **Marian and Derrick Molloy.**

See also Colour Display Advertisement **NEWQUAY near. Dalswinton Country House Hotel, St. Mawgan, Near Newquay TR8 4EZ (St Mawgan [01637] 860385).** ♛♛♛ An old Cornish house of immense character in one and a half acres of secluded grounds, overlooking the beautiful Valley of Lanherne with views to the sea. Ideally situated between Newquay and Padstow, reputed to be the finest coastline in Europe. Excellent beaches and coves within one and a half miles with many picturesque walks. Some of the best coarse fishing in Cornwall, two new golf courses, plus horse riding are all available locally. The Hotel offers superb cooking in a comfortable, friendly atmosphere. Bed and Breakfast from £15.50 per night, weekly from £95; Dinner, Bed and Breakfast from £137. Bargain Breaks available. Colour brochure on request.

NEWQUAY. Porth Enodoc Hotel, 4 Esplanade Road, Pentire, Newquay TR7 1PY (01637 872372).

♛♛♛ Standing in its own grounds overlooking Fistral Beach and Newquay Golf Course this delightful hotel offers a warm friendly welcome. Family owned and managed. Delicious home cooking. There are 15 well appointed bedrooms, most with sea views, all with en suite facilities, colour TV, radio/intercom/child listening, tea/coffee making and central heating. There is a comfortable bar and the lounge and dining room have panoramic views over the Bay. Parking space for all within the hotel grounds. Dinner, Bed and Breakfast from £129 to £185 per week including VAT. Short Breaks available throughout the year. AA QQQQ, RAC Highly Acclaimed.

NEWQUAY. Mrs J.C. Wilson, Manuels Farm, Quintrell Downs, Newquay TR8 4NY (01637 873577).

♛♛ *Highly Commended.* **Working farm.** AA QQQQ Selected. Built in the early 17th century on a site mentioned in Domesday Book "Manuels" is situated two miles inland from Newquay off the A392. In a sheltered wooded valley it offers peace of the countryside with charm of traditional Cornish farmhouse. Emphasis placed on comfort, good farm produced food and a friendly relaxed atmosphere. Pets galore and a play area. Children especially welcome, free babysitting every night. One double, one single and one family bedrooms; cot and high chair available. Open all year except Christmas. Log fires and central heating. Reduced rates for children. Pets accepted but not in the house. Terms from £16 per night per person for Bed and Breakfast; Evening Meal from £9.50. Packed lunches and suppers also available. Farm cottage for self catering also available from £90 to £395 weekly.

See also Colour Display Advertisement **NEWQUAY near. Mr and Mrs Rowlands, Crantock Plains Farm, Near Newquay TR8 5PH (Crantock [01637] 830253).** Charming character farmhouse in peaceful countryside. Comfort, home cooking and personal service combine to make an enjoyable, relaxing holiday. Crantock Plains Farm is situated two and a half miles from Newquay and half a mile off the A3075 Newquay-Redruth road. One and a half miles to the village of Crantock with Post Office, village stores, tea rooms, two pubs and beautiful sandy beach. Riding stables and many sporting activities nearby. Choice of four doubles (one twin en-suite), two family bedrooms; ground floor bedrooms are available; shower room, toilets. Electric blankets for your comfort on chilly nights. Sittingroom and diningroom. Home grown vegetables where available. Table licence. Sorry, no pets. Bed, Breakfast and Evening Meal or Bed and Breakfast. Terms and brochure on request with SAE please. Non-smoking establishment. Tourist Board and HASS registered. Cream Tea Award. Award winners of "Newquay in Bloom" 1990, 1991 and 1992.

PADSTOW. Andrew and Sue Hamilton, Trevone Bay Hotel, Trevone, Near Padstow PL28 8QS (Padstow [01841] 520243). *Commended.* We invite you to relax in our friendly, non-smoking hotel, tastefully refurbished to provide superior accommodation. Set in an attractive, peaceful village and overlooking a beautiful sandy beach and rugged coastline. Family run, offering a warm welcome to all. Excellent home cooking with a choice for all courses. Licensed bar, lounges and spacious dining room. 13 comfortable en suite bedrooms with tea-making facilities. Ideal for walking, touring, bird watching or simply relaxing on the beach. From £25 for Dinner, Bed and Breakfast. Open Easter to October. Please contact us for further details and a colour brochure.

PENZANCE. Mrs Monica Olds, Mulfra Farm, Newmill, Penzance TR20 8XP (Penzance [01736] 63940). Superb accommodation is offered on this 50 acre hill farm high on the Penwith moors. The 17th century stone built farmhouse has far reaching views, is attractively furnished and offers two double en suite bedrooms with tea/coffee trays and TV. The comfortable lounge with ing enook fireplace and Cornish stone oven has a good selection of books and TV. Diningroom with separate tables, sun lounge and good food. Car essential, ample parking. Ideal centre for exploring West Cornwall's beaches and places of historic interest. We even have our own Iron Age village, as well as cows, calves and horses. Warm friendly atmosphere. Beautiful walking country. Penzance three miles, St. Ives nine miles. Bed, Breakfast and Evening Meal from £125 per week. Further details sent with pleasure.

PENZANCE. Mrs A.R. Blewett, Menwidden Farm, Ludgvan, Penzance TR20 8BN (Penzance [01736] 740415). Menwidden Farm is centrally situated in west Cornwall four miles from St. Ives (north coast) and three miles from Marazion (south coast). Within easy reach of Land's End and The Lizard. It is a dairy and market gardening farm of 40 acres. Comfortable bedrooms and good home cooking including roast meats, pasties and Cornish Cream. Four double, two family bedrooms, one with washbasin; bathroom, shower room and toilet; sittingroom, diningroom. Cot, high chair, reduced rates for children. Pets allowed. Open February to November. Car essential — parking. Lots of interesting places nearby including many beaches and coves, St Michael's Mount, Bird Paradise. Fire Certificate held. Tourist Board Listed and Commended, AA listed and winner of Farm Holiday Guide Diploma 1986. Evening Meal, Bed and Breakfast from £120 per week or Bed and Breakfast from £13.50 per night.

PORT ISAAC. Mr and Mrs D. Phelps, Trewetha Farm, Port Isaac PL29 3RU (Port Isaac [01208] 880256). 18th century traditional Cornish Farmhouse with 20 acres of grazing land in "Betjeman country", on the Heritage Coast. Superb sea and countryside views. Poultry, sheep, miniature Shetland ponies kept. Ideal area for water sports, beaches, fishing, bird watching and walking; footpath to beach from the farm. Wadebridge is nine miles and has sports facilities and cycling along old railway track to Padstow. Separate dining room and sittingroom with colour TV. Access to house throughout day. Tea-making facilities. Reductions for children. Bed and Breakfast; Vegetarians welcome. Fire Certificate held. Also available, self catering cottages. Member of the Cornwall Tourist Board.

PORTSCATHO. Hillside House, 8 The Square, Portscatho, Truro TR2 5HW (01872 580523). Small fishing village on the beautiful Roseland Peninsula. Hillside House Bed and Breakfast accommodation is just 100 yards from the sea, ideal for exploring the wonderful National Trust coastline and miles of cliff path walks. Lovely safe sandy beaches, perfect for swimming and sailing. Within easy reach of Trelissick Gardens, Heligan Gardens and the cathedral city of Truro. Comfortable rooms have own TV, washbasin and tea/coffee making facilities. Guests' lounge and dining room. Two inns and a restaurant in the village for evening meals plus other pubs and restaurants with good food close by. Double, single and family rooms. Bed and breakfast from £15, reduced rates for children.

Terms quoted in this publication may be subject to increase if rises in costs necessitate

ROSELAND PENINSULA. Mrs Shirley E. Pascoe, Court Farm, Philleigh, Truro TR2 5NB (01872 580313). Working farm, join in. Situated in the heart of the Roseland Peninsula at Philleigh, with its lovely Norman church and 17th century Roseland Inn, this spacious and attractive old farmhouse, set in over an acre of garden, offers Bed and Breakfast accommodation. There are double, single and family bedrooms with washbasins and tea making facilities; bathroom, separate toilet; large comfortable lounge with colour TV. Enjoy a full English breakfast in the traditional farmhouse kitchen. Children welcome, cot, high chair, baby-sitting available. Sorry, no pets indoors. Car essential — ample parking. The family livestock and arable farm includes 50 acres of woodlands which border the beautiful Fal Estuary providing superb walking, picnic areas and bird-watching opportunities, while the nearest beaches are just over two miles away. Tourist Board registered. Please write or telephone for brochure and terms.

ST. AGNES. Cleaderscroft Hotel, 16 British Road, St. Agnes TR5 0TZ (01872 552349). This small, detached, family-run Victorian hotel stands in the heart of the picturesque village of St. Agnes, convenient for many outstanding country and coastal walks. Set in mature gardens and having a separate children's play area we can offer peace and relaxation after visits to the beach, which is approximately half a mile away. Accommodation is provided in generous sized rooms, mostly en suite with colour TV. Public rooms comprise lounge, bar, dining rooms and games room. Non smoking and smoking areas. Private parking. Bed and Breakfast £19.50 to £22.50 with discounts for children sharing. Evening set menu and picnic lunch available.

ST. AGNES. Mrs Dorothy Gill-Carey, Penkerris, Penwinnick Road, St. Agnes TR5 0PA (St. Agnes [01872] 552262). 👑👑 An enchanting Edwardian residence in garden with large lawn in unspoilt Cornish village. AA, RAC and Les Routiers recommended. Penkerris has fields on one side yet there are pubs, shops, etc only 100 yards away on the other side. Attractive dining room, lounge with colour TV, video, piano and log fires in winter. Bedrooms with washbasins, TV, kettles, shaver points, radios. There is a shower room as well as bathrooms. Delicious meals, traditional roasts, fresh vegetables and home made fruit tarts. Beaches, swimming, surfing, gliding and magnificent cliff walks nearby. From £13.50 per night Bed and Breakfast and from £20 with Dinner. Open all year.

ST. AGNES. Driftwood Spars Hotel, Trevaunance Cove, St. Agnes TR5 0RT (01872 552428 or 553323). 👑👑👑 Sample some proper Cornish hospitality! Have a lie-in with morning tea and breakfast TV — come down to an enormous breakfast, then laze on the beach or explore the numerous inland and coastal footpaths. Come home and over-indulge in good home cooking, then have a natter with the locals in a choice of two "timeless" bars. All rooms have colour TV, telephone, hairdryers and tea/coffee facilities. Sea fishing, surfing, swimming, walking all available locally. Children and pets welcome. Short Breaks include three nights for the price of two 30th September to 30th April excluding Christmas, New Year and Easter. Bed and Breakfast from £29 per person, from £174 per week. Please phone for details of our informal holidays.

See also Colour Display Advertisement **ST. AGNES. Mr S. Manico, Rosemundy House Hotel, St. Agnes TR5 0UF (01872 552101).** Rosemundy House Hotel occupies a most sheltered and secluded position in the village of St. Agnes and within a mile of Trevaunance Cove beach. Built around 1780, Rosemundy has been tastefully extended to provide a charming diningroom and many bedrooms with en-suite facilities. Our amenities include an attractive licensed bar, 45ft outdoor heated swimming pool and a large games room with table tennis, pool, snooker, darts, etc. The informal grounds comprise some four acres of gardens and woodland secluding the property and making Rosemundy ideal for a restful holiday. Badminton, croquet and putting may be enjoyed in the grounds. Our hotel boasts a warm and friendly atmosphere with good English home cooking. Dinner, Bed and Breakfast from £140 to £235 per week, Bed and Breakfast from £115 to £210 weekly (including VAT).

ST. AUSTELL. Mrs Liz Berryman, Polgreen Farm, London Apprentice, St. Austell PL26 7AP (01726 75151). Polgreen is a family run dairy farm nestling in the beautiful Pentewan Valley. One mile from the coast and four miles from the picturesque fishing village of Mevagissey. A perfect location for a relaxing holiday in the glorious Cornish countryside with farm and woodland walks. Centrally situated, Polgreen is ideally placed for touring all of Cornwall's famous beauty spots, gardens and attractions. Nearby activities include golf, sea fishing and horse riding. Bed and Breakfast accommodation includes en-suite rooms, colour TV in bedrooms, tea/coffee facilities, guests' lounge. Children welcome. Terms from £15 per night — £98 per week. Registered Cornwall Tourist Board.

ST. IVES. Miss B. Delbridge, Bella Vista Guest House, St. Ives Road, Carbis Bay, St. Ives TR26 2SF (01736 796063). ♛ First class accommodation, highly recommended, satisfaction guaranteed. Extensive views of sea and coastline. Washbasins in all rooms. Colour TV. Central heating. Own keys to rooms. Free parking on premises. Personal supervision. Fresh farm produce. Radio intercom and baby listening service in all rooms. Fire Certificate held. Bed and Breakfast from £15. Open all year. Non-smokers welcome. Registered with English Tourist Board and West Country Tourist Board. SAE for brochure.

ST. IVES. Mrs N.I. Mann, Trewey Farm, Zennor, St. Ives TR26 3DA (Penzance [01736] 796936). Working farm. On the main St Ives to Land's End road, this attractive granite-built farmhouse stands among gorse and heather-clad hills, half-a-mile from the sea and five miles from St Ives. The mixed farm covers 300 acres, with Guernsey cattle and fine views of the sea; lovely cliff and hill walks. Guests will be warmly welcomed and find a friendly atmosphere. Five double, one single and three family bedrooms (all with washbasins); bathroom, toilets; sittingroom, diningroom. Cot, high chair and babysitting available. Pets allowed. Car essential — parking. Open all year. Electric heating. Bed and Breakfast only. SAE for terms, please,

ST. KEVERNE. Mrs P. Peters, Gallentreath Guest House, Porthallow, St. Keverne, Helston TR12 6PL (01326 280400). Situated in a pretty fishing village; quiet and peaceful. Lovely coastal walks and panoramic sea views. All bedrooms en suite and all have colour TV, coffee and tea-making facilities. Full English breakfast. Table licence. Car essential. Children and pets welcome. Under personal supervision. Bed and full English Breakfast from £17.50; Evening Meal £9 per person (optional). Also available, selection of self catering accommodation; details on request.

ST. MAWES/TRURO. Mrs A. Palmer, Trenestrall Farm, Ruan High Lanes, Truro TR2 5LX (Truro [01872] 501259). Working farm, join in. A tastefully restored 200 year old barn, now a farmhouse offering comfortable accommodation on a 300 acre mixed farm. Situated on beautiful Roseland Peninsula, within easy reach of St. Mawes and Truro. Close to safe beaches and beautiful Fal estuary for sailing, bird watching etc. Accommodation consists of double or twin room with washbasins and tea/coffee facilities, own sittingroom with TV, bathroom and shower room. Amenities include private fishing lake and snooker room, table tennis and pony riding. Pride taken with presentation of food using home produce whenever possible. Children welcome, babysitting service. Pets accepted. Truro Tourist Board registered. Phone or write for details of Bed and Breakfast.

TRENESTRALL FARM

Ruanhighlanes
Truro, Cornwall

CORNWALL – SOMETHING FOR EVERYONE!

Sea, sand, cliffs and quite often the sun, but that's not all you will find in this interesting county. Cornwall has many fascinating places to visit, such as the Charlestown Shipwreck Centre, the Tropical Bird Gardens at Padstow, Cornwall Aeronautical Park near Helston, Botallack Tin Mine, The Cornish Seal Sanctuary, Perranporth and of course, St. Michael's Mount.

See also Colour Display Advertisement

TINTAGEL. C. and R. Savage, Bossiney House Hotel, Tintagel PL34 0AX (Tintagel [01840] 770240; Fax: 01840 770501). ♛♛♛ An ideal base to tour and explore an area packed with interest and beauty. Bossiney House is situated about half a mile from Tintagel on the cliffs overlooking a magnificent stretch of coastline. Nearly all of the 20 bedrooms have sea or country views. Spacious diningroom and cocktail bar; three lounges. Colour TV. Good English cooking with excellent choice of menu. Personal attention. Indoor heated pool, sauna, solarium. Nearby activities include surfing, riding, golf, squash, pony trekking and shark fishing. Reductions for children. Open Easter to end of October.

TROON, near Camborne. Mrs S. Leonard, Sea View Farm Guesthouse, Troon, Near Camborne TR14 9JH (Praze [01209] 831260). Farmhouse on small horticultural holding, one mile from Troon village. Six double, one single and three family bedrooms, all with individual heating, washbasins etc. Large lounge with colour TV; bathroom, two shower rooms, three toilets; diningroom. Good home cooking. Residential licence. Heated swimming pool. Well recommended by previous guests. Cot, high chair, babysitting and reduced rates for children. Pets permitted. Panoramic views from some bedrooms. Within easy reach of north and south coasts, only 15 minutes by car. Open all year round for Bed and Breakfast from £75 weekly; Dinner £8 per night. AA Approved, Cornwall Tourist Board.

TRURO. Mrs Jo Roberts, Carvean Farm, Probus, Truro TR2 4HY (01872 520243). A warm welcome, delicious cooking (vegetarians welcome) and comfy, heated en-suite rooms await you. Flowers, log fires, antiques and friendly informality make Carvean the ideal spot for a relaxing break for non-smokers. Licensed. This secluded stone farmhouse is just 10 minutes from Truro, convenient for the A30 and near the beautiful Roseland Peninsula. A settlement at Carvean is mentioned in the Domesday Book but facilities have been improved since then! Bed and Breakfast from £16; Dinner from £12. Open all year. Brochure on request.

AA RECOMMENDED · RAC appointed · CORNWALL REGISTERED ACCOMMODATION

Trevispian-Vean Farm

Commended

Trevispian-Vean is an attractive 300-year-old farmhouse nestling in the Cornish countryside. It has recently been extended to give increased lounge facilities; most bedrooms have en-suite facilities. Meals are prepared with great care by Bridget who provides a good variety of home cooking. Residential licence. For the "active" – a fishing lake, a games room and participation in the feeding of the animals on this 300-acre mixed farm. With its location four miles from Truro, Trevispian-Vean is an ideal centre for touring the whole of Cornwall. Dinner, Bed & Breakfast £146. Children's prices according to age.

A warm welcome, good food and a friendly atmosphere guaranteed

Mrs B. Dymond, Trevispian-Vean Farm, St. Erme, Truro, Cornwall TR4 9BL. Truro (01872) 79514

ENGLISH TOURIST BOARD COMMENDED

AA SELECTED QQQQ

Lands Vue

You will find a special welcome for all our guests at our peaceful country home. Set in 2 acres of informal gardens, Lands Vue enjoys a secluded position yet is central for exploring all Cornwall and close to Truro and beaches. The lovely diningroom offers superb views over the Cornish countryside, and friendly atmosphere in which to enjoy delicious home made food using fresh local produce. Guests are welcome to bring their own wine. There is a cosy lounge with log fires and TV. Most bedrooms have en suite facilities. Highly recommended by many of our guests who return year after year. Write or phone for brochure. B&B from £16.00, Dinner by arrangement. Open all year except Christmas and New Year.

Mrs M.A. Hutchings, Lands Vue, Three Burrows, Truro TR4 8JA
Telephone: (01872) 560242

TRURO. Mrs S. Mason, Great Trewirgie Farm, Probus, Truro TR2 4HW (01872 520274). A 225 acre working farm situated in the Roseland Peninsula. The 17th century farmhouse is set in beautiful countryside, and within easy reach of all main places of interest such as Truro, St. Michael Penkevil, Veryan with attractive round houses, River Fal and Carrick Roads. Accommodation consists of family room, double rooms and single rooms. Own sittingroom with TV; shower room and separate toilet. Open fireplaces. Warm welcome at all times. Open from April to October. Please telephone, or SAE, for details

TRURO. Mrs Diane Dymond, Great Hewas Farm, Grampound Road, Truro TR2 4EP (01726 882218). Great Hewas is ideally situated in central Cornwall offering extensive views, ideal for relaxing. Good homely atmosphere and personal attention. One double/family room with washbasin, one double room en suite, one twin/large family room en suite; all have TV, tea/coffee facilities; guests' bathroom/WC, separate WC; towels/soap supplied. Lounge, dining room with separate tables. Central heating. Fire Certificate held. Holders of Food and Hygiene Certificate. Choice of traditional breakfast or fresh fruit and yoghurt. Bed and Breakfast £13/£14 nightly, en suite £16/£17 nightly; Evening Dinner (6.30/7.30pm) £6/£7. Small well behaved dogs welcome. Open January to December except Christmas. Car essential. October 1st to June 30th minimum four consecutive nights, two adults' occupancy 10% reduction or one free child sharing with parents.

TRURO. Mrs Margaret Retallack, Treberrick Farm, Tregony, Truro TR2 5SP (01872 530247). Working farm. Treberrick is a 250 acre working farm situated on the edge of the Roseland Peninsula and two miles from unspoilt beaches at Carhays and Portholland and six miles from Mevagissey. Most parts of Cornwall reached by car within one hour. Guests are welcome to walk around the farm. Spacious house, bedrooms have washbasin and tea-making facilities. Diningroom with separate tables, lounge with TV always available. Guests can expect traditional home cooked food using own produce where possible. Member of the Cornish Tourist Board. Maximum number of guests six. Sorry no smoking. Bed and Breakfast from £13.50; Evening Meal available. Near Heligon Manor Gardens — Restoration Project. Please telephone or write for brochure.

WADEBRIDGE. Mrs V.M. Davey, Carns Farm, Trewethern, Amble, Wadebridge PL27 6ER (Bodmin [01208] 880398). Working farm. A fully-modernised 15th century farmhouse with its original oak beams and open fires situated on a dairy farm. Guests are welcome to explore the farm and watch the milking. Only four miles from the safest beaches in North Cornwall, sailing, fishing, surfing and golf. Horse riding available. Lovely walks nearby. Mrs Davey's aim is to give guests a restful holiday and real farmhouse fare, with home-produced eggs, cream, etc. One double, one single and two family bedrooms with washbasins; bathroom, two toilets; shower; own lounge and TV; diningroom. Cot, high chair available, babysitting on request. Please enquire about pets. Car essential — parking. Open Easter to October. SAE, please, for terms for Evening Dinner/Meal, Bed and Breakfast or Bed and Breakfast only. Reductions for children.

WHITSAND BAY. Mrs Sarah Blake, Stone Farm, Whitsand Bay, Millbrook, Torpoint PL10 1JJ (01752 822267). A 350 acre working dairy farm where you can wander around, watch the milking, help feed the calves and pigs; free pony rides for the children. Large garden with traditional tree swing and croquet lawn, games room with pool table. Close to Whitsand Bay and within 350 yards across field to the cliff path leading to miles of sandy beach. Enjoy the rugged coastline and sandy coves along the bay to Looe and Polperro. Plymouth lies only a short drive and ferry crossing away and boasts many theatres and restaurants. National Trust properties nearby. Added attractions include the Dobwalls Theme Park, Monkey Sanctuary and National Shire Horse Centre. Ideal for touring Cornwall and Devon. We have double and family rooms, all en suite, with TV and tea/coffee making facilities. Electric blankets, cot, high chair, babysitting can all be provided. Lounge with log fire and colour TV and video. Sorry no pets. Bed and full English Breakfast, optional four-course Evening Meal. Open all year. SAE for brochure or ring for details. Self Catering accommodation also available.

ZENNOR. Dr E.G. Gynn, Boswednack Manor, Zennor, St. Ives TR26 3DD (01736 794183). Working farm, join in. An organic smallholding with free-range ducks, hens, geese, goats. Our granite farmhouse overlooks both sea and moorland with a quiet cove nearby and fine walks with much natural history and archaeological interest all around. Pub and church at Zennor, art galleries, restaurants, beaches at St. Ives (five miles) and Penzance (six miles). One family, one twin, one double, two double en suite bedrooms; two bathrooms; lounge and diningroom. Open all year. Bed and full English Breakfast from £14 per person, vegetarian Evening Meal. No smoking. No pets. Bird watching, natural history and archaeology courses on selected weeks, and guided natural history walks available on a daily basis. Self catering cottage sleeping four also available from £180 weekly. SAE, please, for further details.

CORNWALL – LAND'S END AND THE ISLES OF SCILLY

Britain's most westerly point, Land's End, is now under private ownership and offers multi-sensory exhibitions, craft workshops and play areas to the many thousands of visitors who are attracted by its unique, breathtaking views.

The 200-odd Isles of Scilly lie 22 miles south-west of Land's End (access by plane, ferry or helicopter). The temperate climate allows visitors to enjoy exotic flowers, palm trees and tropical gardens, and the islands are a bird-watcher's paradise (May and June are the best months).

CUMBRIA — including "The Lakes"

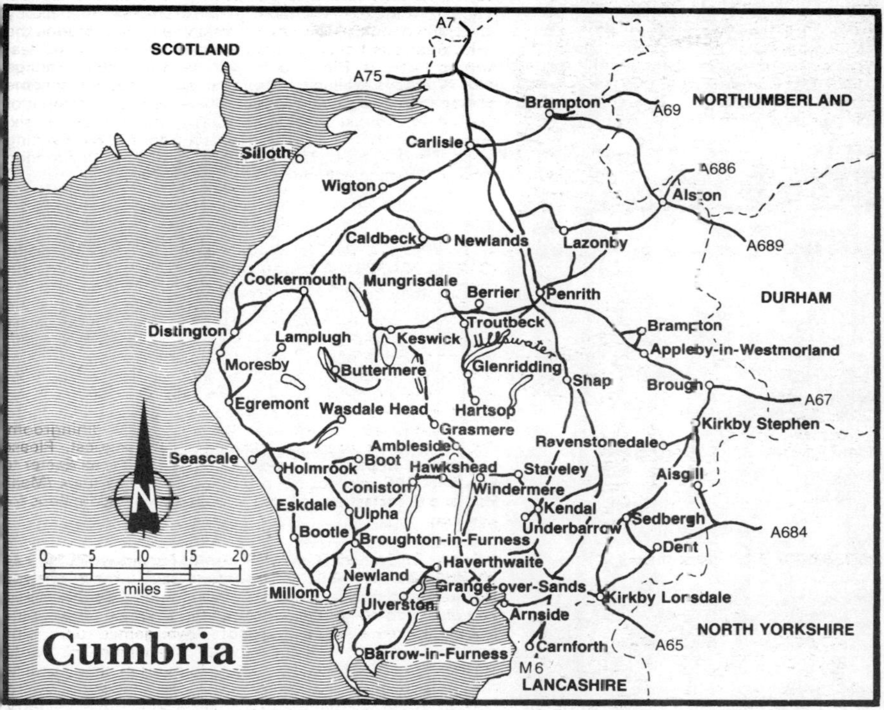

ALSTON. Mrs C. Williams, Bridge End Farm, Alston CA9 3BJ (01434 381261). 👑👑 *Commended.* A warm welcome awaits at our tastefully furnished 18th century farmhouse. Good home cooking with traditional fayre and generous breakfasts. We have a separate dining room where evening meals and breakfasts are served. In the evening relax in our guests' lounge with open fire. We offer one double bedroom with en suite facilities, one family room with washbasin. All rooms are centrally heated. The farmhouse is ideal if you are looking for peace and tranquillity away from the hustle and bustle of everyday life. We are ideally situated for exploring the Lakes, Hadrian's Wall, Weardale and the Pennine Way.

AMBLESIDE. Peter and Anne Hart, Bracken Fell, Outgate, Ambleside LA22 0NH (015394 36289). 👑👑 *Commended.* Bracken Fell is situated in beautiful open countryside between Ambleside and Hawkshead, in the picturesque hamlet of Outgate. Ideally positioned for exploring the Lake District and within easy reach of Coniston, Windermere, Ambleside, Grasmere and Keswick. All major outdoor activities are catered for nearby including wind-surfing, sailing, fishing, pony trekking, etc. All six bedrooms have private facilities, complimentary tea/coffee making and outstanding views. There is central heating throughout, a comfortable lounge and diningroom, together with ample parking and two acres of gardens. Fire Certificate. Open all year. Bed and Breakfast from £18.50. Non-smoking. Self catering accommodation is also available. Write or phone for brochure and tariff.

See also Colour Display Advertisement **AMBLESIDE. Summer Hill Country House, Hawkshead Hill, Hawkshead, Ambleside LA22 0PP (015394 36311).** *Highly Commended.* Set in the heart of the English Lakes yet in a secluded and tranquil setting. Our central position is ideal for whatever type of holiday you require, whether this be walking, climbing, pony trekking, bird watching, country walks, water sports or touring throughout the Lakeland area, being equally suitable for an energetic or a pleasant, relaxing holiday. Although extensively modernised, the house has retained its olde worlde friendly atmosphere which is enhanced throughout by central heating, together with a cosy log fire in the lounge (on cooler evenings). Bedrooms are well appointed with private shower and WC, hairdryer, complimentary tea/coffee facilities, colour TV. Traditional full English breakfast or Continental breakfast in our well appointed dining room. Parking. Pets welcome by arrangement. A strictly non-smoking establishment. Bed and Breakfast from £19 to £22 per person.

AMBLESIDE. Anne and Edward Miller, High Grassings, Sunny Brow, Outgate, Hawkshead, Near Ambleside LA22 0PU (015394 36484). Here is one of the most tranquil settings in the heart of the Lakes. The house nestles against a Woodland Trust coppice and has seven acres of grounds inhabited by deer and red squirrels with views over fields and woods which are the haunt of curlews to majestic mountain ranges. Walk by bridle path to the pub or take a short drive into the quaint village of Hawkshead with its wide variety of pubs and restaurants. Enjoy log fires in the beamed lounge and take a leisurely breakfast in our spacious conservatory. If you would like to escape from life's hustle and crowds rest at High Grassings for a while. All rooms en suite with TV and tea/coffee facilities. Ample parking. Bed and Breakfast from £19.50 per person.

AMBLESIDE. Mrs D.E. Wrathall, The Oaks, Loughrigg, Ambleside LA22 9HQ (015394 37632). Set in the secluded Loughrigg Valley in the heart of the Lake District, this 18th century farmhouse is the property of the National Trust. Accommodation is offered in three family and one double bedrooms all with washbasins; two bathrooms; sittingroom with TV; dining room. Central heating in bedrooms during colder months. Bed and Breakfast. Meals available in tea room until 6.30pm except Thursday and Friday. Good food served in a friendly atmosphere. Reductions for children sharing parents' room. Open February to November. Car essential, parking. SAE for terms.

AMBLESIDE. Mrs Judith King, Holmeshead Farm, Skelwith Fold, Ambleside LA22 0HU (015394 33048). Working farm. A warm, comfortable 17th century farmhouse nestling between Ambleside and Hawkshead, just outside the hamlet of Skelwith Fold. The Drunken Duck Inn is within easy walking distance (one mile). Family, twin and double rooms, all with washbasin, colour TV and tea/coffee making facilities. Cosy lounge/dining room. Central heating, log fire in winter. Full breakfast, traditional and vegetarian. Home-made Evening Meals £6.50 to £10.50. Open all year. An ideal base for all outdoor activities. Walkers' paradise.

AMBLESIDE. Chris and Jane Amos, Brantfell House, Rothay Road, Ambleside LA22 0EE (015394 32239). *Approved.* Ambleside is a picturesque village in the heart of the Lake District and Brantfell House is superbly situated for your stay. A warm, friendly Victorian house where Chris and Jane enjoy the company of their guests and offer every comfort including excellent cuisine; traditional and vegetarian meals are freshly cooked each day. Residential licence. Car parking. Wonderful views of the fells. Single, double, twin, family rooms with en suite facilities are available. Open all year. Bed and Breakfast £15 to £20 per person. Optional Evening Meal £10. Special Breaks, discounts for long stays and groups.

AMBLESIDE near. Mrs Edmondson, Wall End Farm, Great Langdale, Near Ambleside LA22 9JU (015394 37226). Wall End Farm is a working farm located at the head of Great Langdale Valley, ideal for walking and activity holidays and a good stop-over on the Cumbrian Way walk. Accommodation comprises one double, one family bedrooms with tea/coffee making facilities; cot available. Shower room. Bed and Breakfast; packed lunches and vegetarian food available if requested when booking. Sorry, no dogs. £14 per person, reductions for children up to 14 years. Within easy walking distance for bar meals.

See Also Colour Display Advertisement

AMBLESIDE. Linda & Alan Bleasdale, Borwick Lodge, Outgate, Hawkshead, Ambleside LA22 0PU. Telephone: Hawkshead (015394) 36532.

Twice winners of the AWARD for "Accommodation of the Highest Standards". A leafy driveway entices you to the most enchantingly situated house in the Lake District, a very special 17th century country lodge with magnificent panoramic lake and mountain views, quietly secluded in beautiful gardens. Ideally placed in the heart of the Lakes and close to Hawkshead village with its good choice of restaurants and inns. Beautiful ensuite bedrooms with colour televisions and tea/coffee facilities including 'Special Occasions' and 'Romantic Breaks', two king-size four-poster rooms. Prize-winning homemade breads. Tourist Board 'Two Crown Highly Commended'. Linda and Alan welcome you to their 'haven of peace and tranquillity' in this most beautiful corner of England. Ample parking. NON-SMOKING THROUGHOUT. Bed and Breakfast from £18. May we send you our brochure?

AMBLESIDE. Ann and David Vatcher, Wanslea Guest House, Lake Road, Ambleside LA22 0DB (015394 33884). ♛♛♛ Wanslea is a spacious Victorian house within easy walking distance of Ambleside village and the pier and lake shore at Waterhead. With fine views, it is readily accessible and walks begin at the door. Scenic beauty lies all around and the area offers outdoor pursuits of all kinds plus stately homes, literary associations, Roman remains and steam railways. Wanslea offers every comfort including private facilities. TV lounge, bar, garden and superb home and vegetarian cooking. Children welcome. Pets by arrangement. Bed and Breakfast from £18.50; Bed, Breakfast and Evening Meal from £28.50. Autumn, Winter and Spring Breaks at reduced rates. Brochure available. We look forward to welcoming you.

AMBLESIDE. Jim and Joyce Ormesher, Rothay House, Rothay Road, Ambleside LA22 0EE (Ambleside [015394] 32434). Rothay House is an attractive modern detached Guest House, set in pleasant gardens with views of the surrounding fells. All bedrooms, most en-suite, are comfortable and well furnished with colour TV, tea and coffee trays. Our visitors are assured of warm and friendly service in attractive surroundings. The house is within easy walking distance of the village centre. Ambleside has a variety of interesting shops and restaurants and makes an ideal base for walking, touring or enjoying sailing, watersports and angling on Lake Windermere. Car not essential, but ample parking space in the grounds. Open all year. Bed and Breakfast from £17 to £20. Children welcome. Sorry, no pets. Winter Weekend Breaks available.

AMBLESIDE. Mrs S. Briggs, High Wray Farm, High Wray, Near Ambleside LA22 0JE (015394 32280). Working farm. A charming 17th century farmhouse once owned by Beatrix Potter. Friendly accommodation on this working sheep and beef farm in quiet, unspoilt location, ideal centre for touring and walking. Panoramic views and lake shore walks close by. Follow B5286 from Ambleside towards Hawkshead; turn left for Wray, follow road to High Wray; the farm is on the right. A ramblers' paradise with a hearty breakfast to start the day. Families and children welcome. Terms from £13.50. Tourist Board Listed. FHG Diploma Winner.

AMBLESIDE. Mrs E. Culbert, Kingswood, Old Lake Road, Ambleside LA22 0AE (015394 34081). Kingswood is ideally situated near the town centre, yet off the main road. Ample car parking. Well equipped and comfortable bedrooms with washbasins and tea/coffee making facilities. Colour TV. Central heating. Single, double, twin and family rooms. Pets welcome. Open most of the year, with special bargain breaks off season. Non-smoking. Write or phone for rates and details.

AMBLESIDE. Sally and Anthony Marsden, Betty Fold, Hawkshead Hill, Ambleside LA22 0PS (Hawkshead [015394] 36611). ♛♛ *Commended.* Betty Fold is a large country house in its own spacious grounds with magnificent views and set in the heart of the Lake District National Park. The quaint village of Hawkshead is nearby and Coniston and Ambleside are within four miles. The beauty spot Tarn Hows is 20 minutes' walk away. This privately licensed guest house run by the resident owners offers Bed, Breakfast, Evening Meals and Packed Lunches. All bedrooms are en suite. Children are welcome, cots are available and babysitting can be arranged. Parties are particularly welcome. We regret, no pets in the guest house. Open all year. Terms approximately £34 per night for Bed, Breakfast and Evening Dinner. See also advertisement in SELF CATERING section of the guide.

APPLEBY-IN-WESTMORLAND. Mrs Edith Stockdale, Croft House, Bolton, Appleby-in-Westmorland CA16 6AW (017683 61264). Croft House is situated in Bolton, an unspoiled village of sandstone houses and an inn on the banks of the River Eden, three miles north of Appleby off A66. This is an excellent base for exploring Eden Valley, Lakes, Dales and Border Country or as a midway break from Scotland. The historic town of Appleby welcomes visitors to its ancient castles and churches and to the country's oldest Gypsy Fair, which is held annually in June. Local attractions include pony trekking, golf, fishing and swimming. The comfortable farmhouse offers traditional farmhouse breakfast and guest accommodation comprises sittingroom with colour TV; diningroom; one twin and two double bedrooms with washbasims. Separate bathroom and shower. Children welcome at reduced rates, cot, babysitting. Pets welcome by arrangement. Private fishing on River Eden available to our guests. Open all year (except Christmas). Rates from £14.

BRAMPTON. Mrs Margaret Mounsey, High Rigg Farm, Walton, Brampton CA8 2AZ (016977 2117). ♛ *Approved.* **Working farm, join in.** Pleasant welcoming family dairy/sheep farm on the roadside close to Walton village and the Roman Wall, three and a half miles Brampton, 10 miles Carlisle. An attractive 18th century Listed farmhouse with comfortable, spacious rooms. Snooker/pool table available. All bedrooms have washbasin, shaver points, colour TV and tea/coffee making facilities. Double/family room available. There is a lovely large garden to relax in with patio and children's play area. Excellent parking. Delicious home cooking. Bed and Breakfast from £13.30; Evening Meal by arrangement. Reductions for children under 14 years and for stays of two or more days. Panoramic views of the Pennines and Lakes; plenty to do — follow the farm trail to the waterfall, help feed the animals, enjoy fishing, water sports, pony trekking, golf.

CALDBECK. Mrs Dixon, The Height Farm, Caldbeck, Wigton CA7 0LU (016974 78668). ♛ Beautifully situated with 25 mile views over Northern Lakeland, Solway Coast, Eden Valley and Hadrian's Wall. The elegant farmhouse, built in 1836, is both spacious and homely. All rooms have central heating and lovely views. The family, twin and double bedrooms all have washbasins; two bathrooms; lounge with TV; dining room and garden. Non-smoking. Children welcome but sorry, no dogs. Ample parking. Laundry services; hot drinks are always available. The farm has Swaledale ewes with lambs and fell ponies with foals which can be seen on walks through and from the farm, for example to the beautiful historic village of Caldbeck. Bed and Breakfast from £15.

FUN FOR ALL THE FAMILY IN CUMBRIA

Muncaster Mill, near Ravenglass; World of Beatrix Potter, Bowness-on-Windermere; Carlisle Castle; Wordsworth Museum, Dove Cottage, Grasmere; Appleby Castle Conservation Centre; Cumberland Toy and Model Museum, Cockermouth; Wildlife Oasis, near Milnthorpe; Brockhole National Park Centre, near Windermere; Cumberland Pencil Museum, Keswick; Windermere Steamboat Museum.

Swaledale Watch

Ours is a mixed farm of 300 acres situated in beautiful countryside within the Lake District National Park. Easy reach of Scottish Borders, Roman Wall, Eden Valley. Primarily a sheep farm (everyone loves lambing time), with 60 dairy cattle. Visitors are welcome to see farm animals and activities. Many interesting walks nearby or roam the peaceful fells where John Peel hunted. Enjoyed by many Cumbrian Way walkers. Very comfortable accommodation with excellent home cooking. Two rooms en-suite. Central heating. Tea making facilities. **Registered with the English Tourist Board** ♛♛. We are a friendly Cumbrian farming family and make you very welcome. Bed and Breakfast from £15 to £18; Evening Meal £9.00.

Mr & Mrs A. Savage, Swaledale Watch, Whelpo, Caldbeck CA7 8HQ. Telephone: (016974) 78409.

CARLISLE. Mrs Elizabeth Woodmass, Howard House Farm, Gilsland, Carlisle CA6 7AN (016977 47285). ♛♛ *Highly Commended.* **Working farm.** A 250 acre mixed farm with a 19th century stone-built farmhouse situated in a rural area overlooking the Irthing Valley on the Cumbria/Northumbria border. Half a mile from Gilsland village and Roman Wall; Haltwhistle five miles and the M6 at Carlisle, 18 miles. Good base for touring — Roman Wall, Lakes and Scottish Borders. Trout fishing on farm. Guests' lounge with colour TV where you can relax anytime in comfort. Diningroom. One double room en-suite, one twin and one family room with washbasins, bath or shower. All bedrooms have tea/coffee making facilities. Bathroom with shower, toilet. Children welcome at reduced rates. Sorry, no pets. Car essential — parking. Open January to December for Bed and Breakfast from £17 to £19; Evening Meal optional. Weekly terms available. SAE or telephone for further details.

CARLISLE. Mrs Georgina Elwen, New Pallyards, Hethersgill, Carlisle CA6 6HZ (01228 577 308). ♛♛♛ *Commended.* **Working farm, join in.** GOLD AWARD WINNER. Farmhouse filmed for BBC TV. Relax and see beautiful North Cumbria and the Borders. A warm welcome awaits you in our country farmhouse tucked away in the Cumbrian countryside, yet easily accessible from M6 Junction 44. In addition to the surrounding attractions there is plenty to enjoy, including hill walking, peaceful forests and sea trout/salmon fishing or just nestle down and relax with nature. Two double en-suite, two family en-suite rooms and one twin/single bedroom, all with tea/coffee making equipment. Bowls, putting, etc. Bed and Breakfast from £18 per night; Bed, Breakfast and Evening Meal from £26.50. Half Board from £150 to £170 weekly. Menu choice. Self catering offered. Disabled facilities. We are proud to have won a National Salon Culinaire Award for the "Best Breakfast in Britain".

CARLISLE. Jean and Dennis Martin, The Hill Cottage, Blackford, Carlisle CA6 4DU (01228 74739). ♛ *Highly Commended.* One minute from M6/A74 Junction 44, three miles north of city centre, 19th century cottage recently modernised and extended. Spacious, centrally heated rooms (most on ground floor), high standard of furnishings and decor. Enjoying a rural setting in farming country, an ideal base for Solway coasts, Lakes, Scottish Borders, Hadrian's Wall and historic Carlisle (expert historical/tourism advice) or for Scottish stopover. Golf, fishing and bird watching nearby. Accommodation in single, twin, double or family rooms with washbasins, shaver points, tea-making facilities, Yale locks and really comfortable beds. Bathroom/shower, two toilets; visitors' lounge with colour TV; diningroom. Excellent Cumbrian breakfast. Sorry, no pets. Ample parking, though car not essential, convenient for public transport. Special weekly terms, out of season bookings, etc. Evening Dinner available if booked in advance. Non-smokers especially welcome. Cumbria Tourist Board member. SAE for details.

CARLISLE. Mrs Dorothy Nicholson, Gill Farm, Blackford, Carlisle (0122875 326). ♛ In a delightful setting on a beef and sheep farm, this Georgian style farmhouse dated 1740 offers friendly welcome to all guests breaking journey to or from Scotland or having a holiday in our beautiful countryside. Near Hadrian's Wall, Borders and Lake District. Golf, fishing, swimming and large agricultural auction market all nearby. Accommodation is in one double, one family and one twin or single bedrooms, all with washbasins, shaver points and tea/coffee making facilities; two bathrooms, shower; lounge with colour TV; separate diningroom. Open all year. Reductions for children; cot and babysitting available. Central heating. Car essential, good parking. Pets permitted. Telephone for further details.

COCKERMOUTH. Pardshaw Hall, Cockermouth CA13 0SP (Cockermouth [01900] 822607). Old farmhouse in small, quiet village, three-and-a-half miles from Cockermouth with views to the fells. Children most welcome; cot, highchair and babysitting available, also large garden to play in. Pardshaw Hall is ideally situated for touring the Lakes and children delight in the miniature railway at Ravenglass; there are some lovely walks. Good home cooking with fresh produce. Accommodation in one double, one single and one family or twin room, most with washbasins. Log fires. Open all year. Sorry, no pets in house. Car essential, parking. B&B from £14; Evening Meal optional. Reduced rates for children.

COCKERMOUTH. Mrs Alison Hewitson, High Stanger Farm, Cockermouth CA13 9TS (01900 823875). Working farm. Everyone is made to feel welcome here on this 17th century working farm, situated two miles from Cockermouth, the birthplace of Wordsworth. Keswick is 12 miles away and there are lovely views of the Lorton Valley as well as beautiful countryside close to Loweswater, Crummock and Buttermere Lakes. Accommodation is in two family bedrooms; shower room; diningroom; lounge with colour TV. Ideal for children — cot, high chair and babysitting provided. Pets by arrangement. Bed and Breakfast from £15. OS Ref: NY138277.

CONISTON. Mrs M.C. Dutton, Knipe Ground, Coniston LA21 8AE (Coniston [015394] 41221). Working farm. Knipe Ground is a small agricultural holding situated on the hillside, two miles east of Coniston. Tucked away in its old-fashioned garden with commanding views of the Lake and mountains, the 16th century farmhouse provides a quiet, homely atmosphere with log fires which enhance the old oak timbers. Local produce is used in traditional and vegetarian fare. Two double and two single bedrooms. Bed and Breakfast from £14 to £16. Sorry, no dogs in the house. No smoking. SAE for brochure.

ENNERDALE. Mrs E. Loxham, Beckfoot Farm, Ennerdale, Cleator CA23 3AU (Lamplugh [01946] 861235). Our homely comfortable NO SMOKING accommodation stands on the northern shore of Ennerdale Lake, two miles from Ennerdale village. Though not a working farm we are situated in a mainly sheep farming community, in one of Lakeland's wildest and most spectacular valleys. We can offer guests' lounge with colour TV, tea making facilities; two double rooms and one twin room, all with washbasins, lake views, continental quilts and electric underblankets. Central heating. Superb home cooking with quality, variety and quantity being our aim. Bed and Breakfast (with choice of menu) £15 to £17; three-course candle-lit Evening Dinner plus coffee and mints and complimentary glass of wine £10.

FAR SAWREY. Irene and Brian Forbes, West Vale Country Guest House, Far Sawrey, Hawkshead, Ambleside LA22 0LQ (015394 42817). ♛♛♛ *Highly Commended.* Superbly situated on the edge of the village of Far Sawrey with fine views, West Vale offers you personal service and home-cooked food in a warm, friendly atmosphere. We have full central heating, and log fire and TV in one lounge. Most bedrooms have private facilities en-suite, and all rooms have tea and coffee making facilities. Residential licence. Horse riding available locally, also free trout and coarse fishing. AA QQQQ Selected and RAC Highly Acclaimed. Bed and Breakfast from £21.50; Half Board from £31.50 per day. Weekly terms £206.50. Children under 11 years two thirds. For further details please send for brochure to Resident Proprietors — Irene and Brian Forbes.

GRANGE-OVER-SANDS. Mrs Jean Jackson, Templand Farm, Allithwaite, Grange-over-Sands LA11 7QX (Grange-over-Sands [015395] 33129). Working farm, join in. Though built in 1687, Templand offers comfortable and quiet accommodation with all modern conveniences. This 100 acre mixed farm is close to the Grange-over-Sands/Cartmel road and is within easy reach of the Lake District. Under two miles to the sea. Fishing and hill walking, swimming pool, golf and tennis at Grange. Superb 12th century Priory at Cartmel. One double, one single and one family bedrooms; bathroom, toilet; lounge and diningroom. Children welcome — cot, high chair and babysitting available. Car not essential but parking provided. Open 1st March to 31st October. SAE brings prompt reply. Terms for Evening Dinner/Meal, Bed and Breakfast from £17 or Bed and Breakfast from £10. Half price for children. No pets.

GREAT LANGDALE. Mrs J. Rowand, Baysbrown Farm, Great Langdale, Ambleside LA22 9JZ (015394 37300). Working farm, join in. Set at the beginning of the Great Langdale Valley, Baysbrown farm is a 12th century farm with 825 acres of land with beef cows and Herdwick sheep. It is an excellent base to visit Ambleside, Coniston, Keswick, Grasmere, Bowness and Windermere. Accommodation comprises one family, one twin, one single and two double bedrooms, all are beautifully furnished, carpeted and have washbasins and tea/coffee making facilities. Non-smoking accommodation available. Guest lounge with open log fire and colour TV, separate dining room offering English, Continental or vegetarian food. Children welcome, cot and high chair available. Pets weclome. Bed and Breakfast from £15; Evening Meal (optional) £8. Reductions for weekly bookings and children. ETB Listed "Approved". ELD HCA Award.

HAWKSHEAD. Peter and Anne Hart, Bracken Fell, Outgate, Ambleside LA22 0NH (015394 36289).

Commended. Bracken Fell is situated in beautiful open countryside between Ambleside and Hawkshead in the picturesque hamlet of Outgate. Ideally positioned for exploring the Lake District and within easy reach of Coniston, Windermere, Ambleside, Grasmere and Keswick. All major outdoor activities are catered for nearby including wind surfing, sailing, fishing, pony trekking, etc. All six bedrooms have private facilities, complimentary tea/coffee making and outstanding views. There is central heating throughout, a comfortable lounge and dining room together with ample private parking and two acres of gardens. Fire Certificate. Open all year. Bed and Breakfast from £18.50. Non-smoking. Self catering accommodation also available. Write or phone for brochure and tariff.

HAWKSHEAD. Anne and Edward Miller, High Grassings, Sunny Brow, Outgate, Hawkshead, Near Ambleside LA22 0PU (015394 36484).

Here is one of the most tranquil settings in the heart of the Lakes. The house nestles against a Woodland Trust coppice and has seven acres of grounds inhabited by deer and red squirrels with views over fields and woods which are the haunt of curlews to majestic mountain ranges. Walk by bridle path to the pub or take a short drive into the quaint village of Hawkshead with its wide variety of pubs and restaurants. Enjoy log fires in the beamed lounge and take a leisurely breakfast in our spacious conservatory. If you would like to escape from life's hustle and crowds rest at High Grassings for a while. All rooms en suite with TV and tea/coffee facilities. Ample parking. Bed and Breakfast from £19.50 per person.

CUMBRIA – THE LAKES (AND SO MUCH MORE!)

The magnificent Lakeland scenery attracts thousands of visitors each year, but there are many other unspoiled areas of the county well worth a visit. The Eden Valley is a walkers' and anglers' paradise, while the North Pennines (an Area of Outstanding Natural Beauty) is a haven for wildlife. Don't forget the county town of Carlisle, where traces of a rich history dating from pre-Roman times blend with excellent shopping and leisure facilities.

See also Colour Display Advertisement **HAWKSHEAD. Linda and Alan Bleasdale, Borwick Lodge, Outgate, Hawkshead, Ambleside LA22 0PU (015394 36332).** *Highly Commended.* Twice winners of the AWARD for "Accommodation of the Highest Standards". A leafy driveway entices you to the most enchantingly situated house in the Lake District, a rather special 17th century country lodge with magnificent panoramic lake and mountain views, quietly secluded in beautiful gardens. Ideally placed in the heart of the Lakes and close to Hawkshead village with its good choice of restaurants and inns. Beautiful en suite bedrooms with colour TVs and tea/coffee facilities, including "Special Occasions" and "Romantic Breaks" — two king-size four-poster rooms. Prize-winning home-made breads. Linda and Alan welcome you to their "haven of peace and tranquillity" in this most beautiful corner of England. Ample parking. Non-smoking throughout. Bed and Breakfast from £18. May we send our brochure?

HAWKSHEAD. Mrs Diane Rackham, Silverholme, Graythwaite, Hawkshead LA12 8AZ (Newby Bridge [015395] 31332). Situated in an elevated position on the west side of Lake Windermere, this unique small Georgian mansion house set in its own grounds is furnished in traditional style and provides a special atmosphere for relaxation. All rooms are large, comfortable and have spectacular views over the lake. Enjoy a full English Breakfast in our beautiful sunny diningroom overlooking the colourful garden and see the first pleasure cruise passing down the lake. A beautiful lounge is available with log fire. Central heating throughout. We are open all year. Bed and Breakfast from £19.50 per person.

HAWKSHEAD. Mrs Nancy E. Penrice, Violet Bank Farmhouse, Hawkshead, Ambleside LA22 0PL (015394 36222). Violet Bank is a beautifully situated farmhouse of charm and character on a quiet country lane only half-a-mile from Hawkshead village and within walking distance of the famous Tarn Hows beauty spot. The owners keep rare breeds of pigs and poultry and have an interest in country bygones. Ideally situated for touring, walking and fishing. Two double rooms with washbasins. Central heating and open fires. Open all year. Bed and Breakfast from £15 — £16. Tourist Board Listed and Commended. Non-smoking accommodation available. Self catering-cottage also available — *Highly Commended.*

KENDAL. Mrs Sylvia Beaty, Garnett House Farm, Burneside, Kendal LA9 5SF (01539 724542). Working farm. This is an AA/RAC Acclaimed 15th century farmhouse on large dairy/sheep farm situated half a mile from A591 Kendal/Windermere road. Accommodation comprises double, twin and family bedrooms, (most en suite), all with washbasins, colour TV, clock/radio and tea making facilities. Lovely oak panelling, beams, door and spice cupboard. Full English breakfast and five-course dinners served at separate tables; all prepared in the farmhouse kitchen including homemade soups, lamb and beef from the farm and delicious sweets. Children welcome at reduced rates if sharing with two adults. Good private parking. Near village and public transport. Special offer during January, February and March — three nights Bed and Breakfast £39, en suite £45.

KENDAL. Mrs Catherine E. Packham, Docker Hall, Docker, Kendal LA8 0DB (01539 824216). Docker Hall is a dairy/sheep farm three miles north east of Kendal, three and a half miles from M6 Junction 37, situated in very peaceful and relaxing countryside. Excellent touring base for the Lakes, Dales, Borders, coast and for local walks. Guests are assured of a warm welcome in a homely atmosphere with five course breakfast. Accommodation consists of one double, one twin-bedded/family room, both with washbasins, shaver points, bath towels and tea/coffee facilities; bathroom suite with shower plus extra toilet room; dining/sittingroom with colour TV. Full central heating. Children welcome, cot, high chair and babysitting available. Open March to November for Bed and Breakfast. Parking. Tourist Board registered. SAE for terms or telephone.

PLEASE ENCLOSE A STAMPED ADDRESSED ENVELOPE WITH ENQUIRIES

KENDAL. Mrs Anne Knowles, Myers Farm, Docker, Grayrigg, Kendal LA8 0DF (01539 824610). A mixed farm of 204 acres with sheep and dairy cows. Children are welcome to see the working of the farm. The house is over 250 years old with oak beams and a beautiful partition in the lounge/dining room where a log fire burns. One family, one double and one single bedrooms. Bathroom, shower and toilet. Lovely area for walking locally and further afield. Many scenic views to enjoy. Guests are made to feel at home with a friendly atmosphere. Two and a half miles from Junction 37 on M6 motorway. Within easy reach of the Lakes, Dales and the seaside. Good halfway stop between England and Scotland. Central heating. Reduced rates for children under 10 years with cot, high chair and babysitting available. Open from March to November for Bed and Breakfast; Dinner served every other night. Car essential, parking. SAE please.

KENDAL. Mrs D.M. Swindlehurst, Tranthwaite Hall, Underbarrow, Near Kendal LA8 8HG (015395 68285). Working farm. Commended and AA Selected for excellent standards of comfort and quality. Tranthwaite Hall is said to date back to 1186. A charming olde world farmhouse with beautiful oak beams, doors and rare black iron fire range. This working dairy/sheep farm has an idyllic setting half a mile up an unspoilt country lane where deer can be seen, with herons fishing in the stream and lots of wild flowers. This is a very peaceful and quiet retreat yet only minutes from all Lakes and local attractions. Attractive bedrooms, all with tea/coffee makers, en suite facilities and full central heating. Lounge with colour TV. Full English breakfast is served with milk and eggs from our farm and home made jam and marmalade. We like guests to enjoy our home and garden as much as we do. Walking, pony trekking, golf and many good country pubs and inns nearby. Bed and Breakfast £16 to £18.50.

KENDAL. Mrs Jean Bindloss, Grayrigg Hall, Grayrigg, Near Kendal LA8 9BU (Kendal [01539] 824689). Working farm. Comfortable, peaceful, 18th century farmhouse set in a beautiful country location, ideal for touring the Lakes and famous Yorkshire Dales. We run a beef and sheep farm only four and a half miles from Kendal and with easy access to M6 motorway Junction 38. Guests are assured of the finest accommodation and a friendly welcome. One spacious family room and one double bedroom; tasteful lounge/diningroom with colour TV; bathroom. Children most welcome; cot, babysitting if required. Open March to November. Tourist Board registered and inspected. Bed and Breakfast from £14 per person, with Evening Meal on request. Good home-made meals using local produce from £5 to £7. Further information gladly supplied.

KENDAL. Mrs A.E. Bell, Hill Fold Farm, Burneside, Kendal LA8 9AU (01539 722574). Working farm. Situated three miles north of Kendal close to rolling hills of Potter Fell, with many quiet walks and within easy reach of lakes and sea. Genuine working farm of over 1000 acres; beef and sheep. Three double rooms with washbasins, heaters, TV, shaving points and tea/coffee making facilities. Sittingroom; diningroom; bathroom, toilet. Cot and babysitting; reduced rates for children under 12 years. Wholesome meals served. Car essential, parking. Open January to December (including Christmas and New Year). Sorry, no pets. Terms on request.

CUMBRIA – THE GREAT OUTDOORS

Lakes, rivers, mountains and moors (and a mild climate) make Cumbria a paradise for the outdoor enthusiast — with something to suit every age group and every level of ability. Practically every kind of watersport can be enjoyed — if you haven't tried water ski-ing, canoeing, windsurfing or yachting, then now's your chance! Climbing, abseiling, walking, cycling, mountain biking, pony trekking, fishing, orienteering . . . the list is endless!

KENDAL. Mavis and Trevor Carey, Lyndhurst Guest House, 8 South Road, Kendal LA9 5QH (01539 727281). Lyndhurst is situated in a quiet road at the southern end of town overlooking the River Kent. A bustling market town, the shopping centre is nearby whilst the whole Lakeland area and Yorkshire Dales are within easy reach by car or one of many coach tours operating during the holiday season. With their intimate knowledge of the Lakes, Mavis and Trevor will be pleased to help you plan your day's driving or walking. All bedrooms have washbasins, tea/coffee facilities; two public bathrooms. Bed and Breakfast from £14 to £15.50; Evening Dinner available. Open all year round. Full Fire Certificate; central heating.

KENDAL. Mrs Margaret Hodgson, Patton Hall, Kendal LA8 9DT (01539 721590). Guests welcome in friendly home on working farm overlooking Kendal (three miles). Private fishing River Mint one and a half miles A6 (Kendal/Shap road). Comfortable clean rooms with good home cooking. Available two double and one twin rooms, all with washbasins, razor plugs, tea/coffee facilities; guests' bathroom and separate toilet. Lounge with colour TV; dining room with view over Kendal and Lakeland Fells. Guests are free to wander on farmland. Delighted guests have stayed on the farm since 1972, many returning. Within easy reach of Lakes and Dales. Kendal offers a host of interesting things to do. Bed and Breakfast from £14; Evening Meal from £5.50. Children and dogs welcome.

KENDAL near. Mrs Julia H. Thom, Riverbank House, Garnett Bridge, Near Kendal LA8 9AZ (01539 823254). *Commended.* Lovely family-built Victorian house situated in a peaceful hamlet at the foot of the beautiful and totally unspoilt valley of Longsleddale, four miles north of Kendal, half a mile from A6. Guests are free to wander through 20 acres of pastureland bordered by the River Sprint which provides good late season fishing. Comfortable bedrooms with shower. No smoking upstairs. Sittingroom with open fire, TV and background central heating. Ideally situated for walking or touring the Lakes, Eden Valley and Yorkshire Dales. Bed and excellent Breakfast from £14.

KENDAL near. S.J. Lennon, 'The Birks', Underbarrow, Kendal LA8 8HJ (015395 68360). A secluded and peaceful 17th century Lakeland farmhouse set in two acres of garden and surrounded by the beautiful scenery of the uncommercialised Lyth Valley. A family-run guesthouse with a warm welcome. The oak beams and inglenook fireplace complement the many old-world features. Underbarrow is a small village within the National Park. It nestles in an enchanting location yet is only six miles from Lake Windermere, and is convenient for access to all parts of the Lake District. The area is ideal for walking and cycling and has many varied routes. Non-smoking. Double, twin and family rooms, en suite available. Bed abd Breakfast from £15. Self catering accommodation available from £95 weekly. Please phone for brochure.

KENDAL. Rod and Maggie Bowker, Sundial House, 51 Milnthorpe Road, Kendal LA9 5QG (01539 724468). *Approved.* Sundial House is on the A6, quarter of a mile from Kendal town centre, directly opposite the college. Known as "The Gateway to the Lakes" Kendal is a charming and historic market town and is the perfect base to visit the Lake District. Whatever your pastime, walking, golfing, fishing or sightseeing, Kendal has it all. We offer you a homely and warm welcome with Dinner on request at Sundial House. The cosy bedrooms all have tea/coffee making facilities and colour TV. There is a reading lounge and ample parking. Follow the Kendal signs from Junction 36, we are 10 minutes from the M6. Bed and Breakfast from £15.

KESWICK. I. and M. Atkinson, "Dancing Beck", Underskiddaw, Keswick CA12 4PY (017687 73800). Large Lakeland country house two and a half miles from Keswick just off A591 Carlisle road, signposted Millbeck. Situated in its own elevated, spacious grounds with summerhouse. Magnificent views of Derwent Valley and surrounding mountains. Walks onto Skiddaw Mountain are possible from the grounds of "Dancing Beck". All rooms are centrally heated. Bedrooms have washbasins and tea/coffee facilities. Children welcome. Car essential. Bed and Breakfast from £18. Weekly terms available. Open Spring to November. A pleasant welcome assured. A self catering cottage also available.

KESWICK. Mrs Jean McNichol, Glendene, 8 Southey Street, Keswick CA12 4EF (017687 73548). A long established guesthouse with a reputation for comfort and warm hospitality, ideal for family holidays. Situated close to town centre and amenities. Double, twin and family rooms are available; all are tastefully decorated and have comfortable beds, washbasin, shaver point, colour TV, hospitality tray and electric blankets. Generous portions of high quality home cooking served in the pleasant non-smoking dining room. There is also a relaxing residents' lounge. Central heating throughout. All guests have their own keys for access to house at all times. Private parking. Bed and Breakfast from £13; Dinner, Bed and Breakfast from £19. Brochure on request.

KESWICK. Mrs F.J.M. Dawson, Goodwin House, 29 Southey Street, Keswick CA12 4EE (017687 74634). Goodwin House is a detached imposing three storey residence with central hall and staircase of solid pine with verandah on first landing. It affords easy access to parks and town shopping centre and is an ideal base for walks and drives to fells and lakes. All rooms have central heating, washbasin, tea making facilities and colour TV. There are en suite rooms and guests have own front door keys. Guests can enjoy delicious home cooking; packed lunches on request; Evening Meal optional. Bed and Breakfast from £12, Evening Meal from £8. Weekly Bed and Breakfast terms by arrangement. Reduced rates for children. Sorry no dogs. Open all year. ETB and Cumbria Tourist Board registered.

KESWICK. Mr and Mrs G. Turnbull, Rickerby Grange, Portinscale, Keswick CA12 5RH (017687 72344). ♛♛♛ *Commended.* Quiet location in the pretty village of Portinscale, three-quarters of a mile west of Keswick. Ideal base for explorers of the Lakes, by foot or car. Family-run 14 bedroom hotel (most en-suite), all with tea/coffee making facilities, direct-dial telephones, colour TV and central heating. Three ground floor bedrooms, and four-poster available. The lounge and cosy bar offer a relaxing atmosphere before a delicious five course meal in the elegant diningroom. Private car park. Bed and Breakfast from £22; Dinner, Bed and Breakfast from £33 per person. RAC Acclaimed, AA QQQ. Non-smoking available. Write or phone for brochure.

KESWICK. Mrs D. Mattinson, Bassenthwaite Hall Farm, Keswick CA12 4QP (017687 76279). Working farm. A sheep and cattle farm in Bassenthwaite Village, with beautiful views of the Skiddaw Range on the front and the river rippling past at the rear. Flower garden and lawn. Ample parking. Open April to November, the four bedrooms all have washbasins; one room en suite. Bath/shower room, two toilets. Living/diningroom with colour TV. Coal/log fires when needed. Home cooking and hospitality. Children and pets welcome. Golf, riding and fishing nearby. Bed and Breakfast from £14; Bed, Breakfast and Evening Meal from £21. Cumbrian Tourist Board and AA Listed.

Terms quoted in this publication may be subject to increase if rises in costs necessitate

KESWICK near. Mrs Rosalind Hunter, Croft House, Applethwaite, Near Keswick CA12 4PN (Keswick [017687] 73693). ♛♛ Beautifully situated house, enjoying magnificent views of Lakeland mountains, in a lovely quiet village at the foot of Skiddaw, one-and-a-half miles from Keswick. An excellent base for touring all parts of the Lake District, walking, pony trekking and all Lakeland pursuits. A warm welcome is assured and good home cooking a speciality. The comfortable accommodation in our non-smoking house comprises three double, two single and two family rooms en-suite, all with washbasins and showers. Lounge, diningroom. Children welcome. Well-behaved pets accepted. Ample private parking. SAE, please, or telephone for terms for Bed and Full English Breakfast, or Dinner, Bed and Breakfast. Open all year.

KESWICK near. Muriel Bond, Thornthwaite Hall, Thornthwaite, Near Keswick CA12 5SA (Tel & Fax: 017687 78424). ♛♛♛ *Approved.* Thornthwaite Hall is a traditional 17th century farmhouse, modernised and converted into a very comfortable guesthouse. All rooms are en-suite with TV, tea/coffee making facilities. Catering includes good home cooking, residential licence. The Hall lies in an acre of grounds complete with a lovely garden. Thornthwaite is a lovely quiet hamlet three miles west of Keswick. There are numerous walks from Thornthwaite, with a different feel to other parts of the Lake District. Climbing in pine forest locations on the numerous paths and forest trails, spectacular views rewarding those who climb to the tops of Barf, Lords Seat, Seat How. Dogs and children most welcome. Open all year, except Christmas. Bed and Breakfast from £19 to £24. Send for brochure, please.

KESWICK. Mrs E.M. Richardson, Fold Head Farm, Watendlath, Borrowdale, Keswick CA12 5UW (017687 77255). Working farm. Fold Head Farmhouse is a white Lakeland farmhouse situated on the banks of Watendlath Tarn in this picturesque hamlet. It is a 3000 acre sheep farm and an ideal centre for touring, climbing, fell walking and fishing. Fly-fishing for rainbow trout at Watendlath Tarn; permits available. Guests are accommodated in two double bedrooms and one twin bedroom, with washbasins; bathroom, two toilets; sittingroom; diningroom. Full central heating; separate TV lounge. Pets are allowed free. Open from February to December. Car essential; parking. Sir Hugh Walpole used this farmhouse in his book "Judith Paris" as the home of Judith Paris. Evening Dinner, Bed and Breakfast or Bed and Breakfast. Terms on request.

KIRKBY STEPHEN. Mrs Sylvia Capstick, Duckintree House, Kaber, Kirkby Stephen CA17 4ER (017683 71073). Duckintree is a working family farm set in the quiet Eden Valley countryside just off the A685 Kirkby Stephen to Brough road. Easy access to the Lakes and Yorkshire Dales or ideal for breaking your journey from the South of England/Midlands to Scotland. Car essential, ample parking. The rooms comprise family, double and twin (cot available) with tea/coffee making facilities. Lounge/diningroom with colour TV. All rooms overlook a large garden and countryside. Bed and Breakfast from £14. Reductions for children under 12 years. Pets welcome by arrangement. Evening Meal can be provided. Open from March to October. Write or phone for details.

LAKESIDE/NEWBY BRIDGE. Brian and Sylvia Slingsby, Landing Cottage, Lakeside, Newby Bridge, Ulverston LA12 8AS (015395 31719). ♛♛ Traditional Lakeland stone cottage built about 1870, situated at the southern tip of Lake Windermere, about 100 yards from the Lake Steamer and Lakeside/Haverthwaite Steam Railway terminals. Conveniently located as a touring base to all the Lakes, places of interest and the Morecambe Bay coast. The cottage has en suite, standard double and family bedrooms with pretty, colour co-ordinated decor, tea/coffee making facilities. Just starting our 11th year, we shall be extending a warm welcome to all our new and returning guests. Good home cooking, packed lunches available on request. Complimentary pot of tea/coffee on arrival. Car parking. Open all year. Bed and Breakfast £16 to £18.50. Brochure on request.

PLEASE SEND A STAMPED ADDRESSED ENVELOPE WITH ENQUIRIES

LANGDALE VALLEY. Mrs Audrey Whittle, Meadow Bank, Elterwater, Ambleside LA22 9HW (015394 37278). A warm welcome awaits you at Meadow Bank, Elterwater, peacefully situated in the beautiful Langdale Valley in its own mature garden. We offer high class accommodation in three double rooms and one twin, all with washbasins; one double en suite; central heating, tea making facilities, shaver points and new firm beds; two bathrooms with showers; comfortable lounge and dining room. Private parking. Bed and English Breakfast from £15. Sorry, no dogs or children. Ideal for walking or touring. Non-smokers. Also available, a self catering apartment for two persons.

LOWESWATER. Mrs A. Hayton, Brook Farm, Thackthwaite, Loweswater, Cockermouth CA13 0RP (Lorton [01900] 85606). ♛ *Commended.* **Working farm.** This 300-acre stockrearing hill farm is a good centre for walking and touring; Loweswater and Crummock Water two miles; boating, fishing and pony trekking nearby. Guests are assured of a quiet and comfortable holiday, with bedrooms having washbasins, razor points and tea making facilities. Two double rooms, bathroom, shower and toilet; sittingroom. Homely atmosphere and good food. Children welcome at reduced rates. Sorry, no pets. Car essential — parking. Open from May to October for Evening Meal, Bed and Breakfast from £23; Bed and Breakfast from £16. Weekly terms Evening Meal, Bed and Breakfast from £154.

MILNTHORPE. Mrs Lynn Green, "Springlea", Heversham, Milnthorpe LA7 7EE (015395 64026). Situated in South Lakeland, Springlea faces rolling farmland framed by woods and stone walls with the Kent estuary glinting between the trees. It is ideally positioned for the Lakes, Yorkshire Dales and the Morecambe Bay resorts. Historic houses, nature reserves and many other centres of attraction are within easy reach. Local pubs and restaurants serve good food at reasonable prices. There are twin and double en-suite rooms with central heating, TV and tea/coffee making facilities. A lounge, sunroom and terrace are available as is safe off-road parking. Bed and Breakfast or Bed, Breakfast with Evening Meal. Open all year. Terms from £15 per person per night. AA QQQ Recommended.

MOSEDALE. Colin and Lesley Smith, Mosedale House, Mosedale, Mungrisdale, Penrith CA11 0XQ (017687 79371). ♛♛♛ *Commended.* Traditional 1862 built, Lakeland farmhouse. Listed building. A smallholding with sheep, ducks and hens, it enjoys a magnificent position, nestling at the foot of Carrock Fell, overlooking open fields, the River Caldew and Bowscale Fell. Off the beaten track, yet only three and a half miles to the A66 Keswick to Penrith road. Vegetarians welcome. Home baked bread, farm produce — our own free-range eggs. Packed lunches. Non-smoking establishment. Central heating. Open all year. Most bedrooms have en-suite facilities. Visitors' diningroom and lounge. Excellent facilities for disabled guests — ground floor twin-bedded room with en-suite bathroom; no steps throughout. Also self catering cottage in adjacent barn. SAE, please, for brochure.

NEAR SAWREY. Ms. Gillian Fletcher, High Green Gate Guest House, Near Sawrey, Ambleside LA22 0LF (Hawkshead [015394] 36296). ♛♛ The Guest House is a converted 17th-century farmhouse in the quiet hamlet where Beatrix Potter lived and wrote. Her house, owned by the National Trust, is close by and open to the public. The area abounds with pleasant easy walks and is a good centre for the Southern Lakes. Open from March to October. Good food and service under the personal attention of the owner. Spacious diningroom, lounge and separate TV lounge. All bedrooms have hot and cold water and individual heating in addition to central heating. Rooms with private facilities available. Reduced rates for children sharing with parents. Cot and highchair are available and babysitting can be arranged. Dogs welcome. A car is desirable and there is parking for seven cars. AA listed, RAC acclaimed. Bed and Breakfast from £17 per night; Bed, Breakfast and Evening Meal from £26 per night (£163 weekly).

NEAR SAWREY. Little Ees Wyke, Near Sawrey, Ambleside LA22 0JZ (015394 36335). Little Ees Wyke is set in half an acre of mature gardens and is on the edge of this picturesque village where Beatrix Potter lived and wrote many of her well known books. We have outstanding views of Esthwaite Water, Grizedale Forest, Coniston Old Man and round to the Langdale Pikes. Although we are only a small establishment our rooms are large and equipped to a high standard, all having private bathrooms, tea making facilities and a TV. Guests have use of a lounge with open fire. We offer a warm welcome with good food and views to match.

NEWBY BRIDGE near. Mr and Mrs F. Cervetti, Lightwood Farmhouse, Cartmel Fell, Grange-over-Sands LA11 6NP (Newby Bridge [015395] 31454). 👑👑

Commended. This 17th century farmhouse with original oak beams is in a two acre garden with streams. Situated two miles from southern end of Lake Windermere, just off the A592, near Bowland Bridge. An ideal place for families with young children. Three rooms have washbasins and tea making facilities, six rooms are en suite. Guests' own sitting-room with colour TV and log fire. Offering personal, friendly attention at all times. Bed and Breakfast from £18.50 with reduced rates for stays of seven or more nights, and for children under 12 years.

NEWLANDS. Mrs M.A. Relph, Littletown Farm, Newlands, Keswick CA12 5TU (017687 78353).

Working farm. Littletown has all the facilities of a small hotel and most bedrooms are en-suite. Situated in a peaceful part of the beautiful Newlands Valley, with surrounding hills providing excellent walking and climbing. Market towns of Keswick and Cockermouth, Lakes, Derwentwater and Bassenthwaite all within easy distance. Farmhouse, though fully modernised, still retains a traditional character with comfortable lounge, diningroom, and cosy licensed bar. All bedrooms have tea-making facilities, heating and wash-basins. Traditional four-course dinner (roast beef, lamb etc) served six nights a week; full English Breakfast every morning. Littletown Farm is featured in Beatrix Potter's "Mrs Tiggy Winkle". Ample parking. Dinner, Bed and Breakfast from £32 to £36 per person; Bed and Breakfast from £20 to £25 per person. SAE please.

PATTERDALE. Mrs A.M. Knight, Fellside, Hartsop, Patterdale, Penrith CA11 0NZ (017687 82532).

Fellside is a 17th century Cumbrian farmhouse, built in local stone, situated in a beautiful Lake District valley, close to high mountains, surrounded by magnificent scenery and with a panoramic view overlooking Brotherswater. Perfect for fell-walkers, and artists are also welcome. There is boating on Ullswater (boats for hire) two and a half miles away — fishing in lakes and tarns; pony trekking in Patterdale two miles away. Accommodation comprises one double-bedded room, one twin-bedded room and one-single bedded room; two bathrooms; lounge with TV, piano, guide books and maps. Central heating and log fire when cold. Tea/coffee making facilities. Children welcome. Dogs accepted. Bed and Breakfast from £15.50, reductions for stays of three nights or more. ETB Listed and Approved.

PENRITH. Tim and Jane Metcalfe, Home Farm, Edenhall, Penrith CA11 8SS (01768 881203).

Working farm. A warm welcome awaits you at Home Farm, situated on the outskirts of the peaceful village of Edenhall three miles east of Penrith. This a a working farm and is ideally situated for seeing the Eden Valley, North Pennines, Hadrian's Wall and is conveniently located for the Lake District or en route to/from Scotland. Full English Breakfast, evening meals obtainable locally. Accommodation comprises double, family or twin rooms. Reduced rates for children. Bed and Breakfast from £14 per person.

PENRITH. Mrs Brenda Preston, Pallet Hill Farm, Penrith CA11 0BY (Greystoke [017684] 83247). Pallet Hill Farm is pleasantly situated two miles from Penrith on the Penrith-Greystoke-Keswick road (B5288). It is four miles from Ullswater and has easy access to the Lake District, Scottish Borders and Yorkshire Dales. There are various sports facilities in the area — golf club, swimming pool, pony trekking; places to visit such as Lowther Leisure Park and the Miniature Railway at Ravenglass. Good farmhouse food and hospitality with personal attention. Double, single, family rooms; diningroom and sittingroom. Children welcome — cot, high chair available. Sorry, no pets. Car essential, parking. Open Easter to November. Bed and Breakfast from £9 (reduced rates for children and weekly stays). Excellent bar meals available locally.

Welcome to the White House

A small licensed Guest House for Non-Smokers ETB ♛♛ Commended

The 18th century converted Farmhouse is set in an interesting rural area close to Ullswater, Haweswater and the Eden Valley. Our comfortable home with attractive gardens is centrally heated and double glazed throughout. Bedrooms consist of two double/twin ensuite. Two singles and one family room. There are two bathrooms. Children most welcome at reduced prices. B&B from £17, Evening Meal £11.50. Car essential – ample parking. For further details please contact **Anne and Chris Broadbent at the White House, Clifton, Near Penrith CA10 2EL. Tel: (01768) 65115.**

PENRITH. J.A. Wilson, Gill Head Farm, Troutbeck, Penrith CA11 0ST (017687 79652). Gill Head is a working hill farm set against the backdrop of Blencathra and the Northern Fells in the Lake District. Stay in the comfortable 17th century farmhouse with oak beams and log fire and enjoy traditional home cooked meals. There are twin and double-bedded en suite rooms, all with tea/coffee making facilities, central heating and colour TV. There is also a kitchen for guests' use. We are open all year including Christmas and New Year. Special rates for July and August. Please contact us for further information.

PENRITH. Mrs M.R. Taylor, Tymparon Hall, Newbiggin, Stainton, Penrith CA11 0HS (Greystoke [017684] 83236). ♛♛ *Commended.* **Working farm.**

Relax in this charming character Manor House standing in half-acre of garden on 160 acre mixed farm, combining comfort, home cooking and personal service for an enjoyable holiday. Within easy reach are pony trekking, fell walking, swimming and golf. Situated in peaceful rural area close to Lake Ullswater. Accommodation for guests in two double en suite and one double standard bedrooms, all with tea/coffee making facilities; two bathrooms, two toilets; sittingroom with colour television; separate dining room with individual tables. Open 1st April to 1st November. Car essential. Evening Dinner, Bed and Breakfast terms on request. RAC Acclaimed, AA QQQ. Farm Holiday Bureau member.

SHAP. Mr and Mrs D.L. and M. Brunskill, Brookfield, Shap, Penrith CA10 3PZ (01931 716 397).

Situated one mile from M6 motorway (turn off at Shap interchange No.39), first accommodation off motorway. Excellent position for touring Lakeland, or overnight accommodation for travelling north or south. Central heating throughout, renowned for good food, comfort and personal attention. All bedrooms are well appointed and have colour TV and tea/coffee making facilities. Diningroom where delicious home cooking is a speciality. Well stocked bar. Residents' lounge. Sorry, no pets. Open from February to December. Terms sent on request. Car essential, ample parking. Tourist Board registered. AA listed. Fire Certificate granted.

TROUTBECK. Mrs E.S. Nicholson, Lane Head Farm, Troutbeck, Penrith CA11 0SY (017687 79220). Charming 17th century farmhouse set in beautiful gardens overlooking undisturbed views of Lakeland Fells. Midway between Keswick and Penrith. The house has been tastefully decorated throughout with many rooms featuring beams. Some rooms with en suite and colour TV, and all have washbasins. Residents' licence. Open all year. Traditional Christmas Break. Bed and Breakfast from £17 per person. We will be happy to supply further details on receipt of SAE. AA recommended.

ULLSWATER. Mrs S. Hunter, Grove Foot Farm, Watermillock, Penrith CA11 0NA (017684 86416). Working farm. Grove Foot is a 90 acre dairy farm just off the A66 and two miles from Lake Ullswater. The house, built around 1650, has oak beams and open fires and sleeps six guests. Close by are historic houses and gardens, fishing, swimming pools, golf and pony trekking. Open March to October. Children welcome. Sorry, no pets. Bed and Breakfast from £13.50.

ULLSWATER (3 miles). Mrs Julia Thompson, Gill House, Stainton, Penrith CA11 0ES (01768 890785). Lovely house in own grounds situated in pretty village. Good bar meals just five minutes' walk. Central heating, TV lounge, twin and double bedrooms with washbasins and tea/coffee making facilities. One room en suite. All home comforts with personal attention. Ideal base for touring Lakes or stop-off for Scotland. Open March to October. Two miles from M6 (Exit 40); on A66 Keswick road or Ullswater A592. Bed and Breakfast from £15 per person. Reductions for children.

WINDERMERE. Mrs R. Phelps, Winbrook House, 30 Ellerthwaite Road, Windermere LA23 2AH (015394 44932). *Commended.* A friendly welcome awaits you at Winbrook House which is convenient for village and lake. Ideal touring centre. We offer personal service, together with excellent English cooking, under the personal supervision of the proprietors. All rooms are decorated to a high standard; residents' lounge with colour TV; full central heating. All bedrooms have private shower/baths, colour TV, tea/coffee making facilities and most have private toilets. Access to rooms at all times. Private parking. Full Fire Certificate. RAC Acclaimed. Open all year. Bed and Breakfast from £15 to £20.

See also Colour Display Advertisement **WINDERMERE. Glencree Private Hotel, Lake Road, Windermere LA23 5EQ (015394 45822).** Be sure to enjoy your stay in this most beautiful corner of England by choosing "Glencree" which offers lovely spacious en suite rooms with colour TV and pretty woodland outlook and comfortable beds (some kingsize) and a delicious and generous English breakfast cooked to perfection. Close to rail and bus stations. A short walk to Lake and many varied restaurants. Minibus tours can be arranged. Very convenient location. A warm welcome awaits you in our lovely small hotel. Tourist Board registered, AA Recommended, RAC "Highly Acclaimed".

See also Colour Display Advertisement **WINDERMERE. Irene and George Eastwood, Sandown, Lake Road, Windermere LA23 2JF (015394 45275).** Superb Bed and Breakfast accommodation. All rooms en suite with colour TV and tea/coffee making facilities. Situated two minutes from Lake Windermere, shops and cafes. Many lovely walks. Open all year. Special out of season rates, also two-day Saturday/Sunday Breaks. From £18 to £27 per person per night. Well-behaved dogs welcome. Each room has own safe private car parking. SAE or telephone for further details.

See also Colour Display Advertisement **WINDERMERE. Hawksmoor Guest House, Lake Road, Windermere LA23 2EQ (015394 42110).** *Highly Commended.* Situated mid-way between Bowness and Windermere within easy walking distance of both villages and backed by woodland. All rooms have bath/shower and toilet en-suite, tea/coffee making facilities and colour TV. Fourteenth year in same ownership, Hawksmoor enjoys a reputation for good home cooking, personal service by the proprietors and has a superb private car park. Some ground floor rooms are available. Please telephone for room availability or brochure. November — mid-May, excluding Bank Holidays; Dinner, Bed and Breakfast from £70 — £85 for 2/3 nights. Discounts for Sunday. AA Selected, RAC Highly Commended.

WINDERMERE. Broadoaks Country House, Bridge Lane, Troutbeck, Windermere LA23 1LA (015394 45566). This luxury country house is set in the heart of Troutbeck Valley and a warm and friendly welcome is offered to old and new guests. Family-owned, personal attention is assured at all times. Situated approximately two miles from Windermere or Ambleside and set in seven acres of beautiful gardens and woodland, surrounded by superb scenery. Delicious food, fine wines and pleasant views of Troutbeck Fells complement our picturesque dining room. Bedrooms are all individually designed with colour TV, hairdryers, tea/coffee making facilities, four poster and Victorian beds with Victorian spa, jacuzzi and power shower bathroom en suite. Perfect base for your walking holiday; added attractions include all water sports, fishing, pony trekking, clay pigeon shooting, archery, mountain bikes, hot air ballooning, golf, free use of local leisure centre — full activity list available. Terms from £28 — £45 per person Open all year. Licensed. RAC Highly Acclaimed.

WINDERMERE. Mr M. Brown, Haisthorpe Guest House, Holly Road, Windermere LA23 2AF (015394 43445). ♛♛ *Commended.* Haisthorpe is a comfortable family house situated in a quiet part of Windermere yet close to the village centre and local amenities. It is within 10 minutes' walk of the station and coach park (free collection by arrangement). Ideal location for touring the Lakes. All rooms have colour TV with Satellite channel, tea/coffee facilities; most are en suite. No smoking in bedrooms. Children welcome, reduced rates for under 14 year olds. Pets by prior arrangement. Special breaks October to June. Private parking for three cars. Credit cards accepted. Bed and Breakfast from £13; Evening Meal £6.50. AA QQQ, RAC Acclaimed.

See also Colour Display Advertisement **WINDERMERE. The Beaumont Hotel, Holly Road, Windermere LA23 2AF (015394 47075).** ♛♛ *Highly Commended.* AA QQQQ Selected, RAC Highly Acclaimed. Elegant Victorian House Hotel displays all the grace and charm of its time skilfully combined with all the comforts of today. Ideally situated for Windermere and Bowness and the perfect location for touring the Lakes. All 12 luxury bedrooms are en suite, each has TV, tea-making facilities and hairdryer; four-poster rooms are available for that special occasion and a "Romantic Presentation" of wine, chocolates, fruit and flowers may be ordered. Private parking. Standards are high, breakfasts are hearty, and the hospitality is warm and sincere. Bed and Breakfast from £20. Full details on request.

Westlake

Proprietors:
Steve and Elaine Loveland

LAKE ROAD, WINDERMERE,
CUMBRIA LA23 2EQ
TELEPHONE: 015394 43020

RAC HIGHLY ACCLAIMED — English Tourist Board COMMENDED — AA

A warm welcome awaits you from your hosts Steve & Elaine at their small private hotel. Situated midway between Windermere and the Lake, we are ideally positioned as a base for exploring the many attractions and places of interest the Lake District has to offer. Providing comfortable and well decorated bedrooms, including our Four Poster room. Rooms are en-suite (bath or shower), with colour TV, tea/coffee facilities. Residents' lounge. Licensed. Private parking. All making your stay in the Lakes a memorable one. Bed and Breakfast from £18-£24.

WINDERMERE. Mrs Sandra Garside, Boston House, 4 The Terrace, Windermere LA23 1AJ (Tel & Fax: 015394 43654). *Commended.* A delightful Victorian Gothic building dating from 1849. Situated in peaceful cul-de-sac on the edge of the village with panoramic views of the lake and surrounding fells, yet close to village centre, train and coach stations (collection by arrangement). Six spacious double/twin/family rooms with tea trays, hairdryers, radio alarms and colour TV; five are en suite, two have four-poster and another has an oak half-tester bed — very romantic! Choose hearty breakfasts from an extensive menu; superb home-cooked dinners are also available. Restaurant/residential licence. NO SMOKING PLEASE. Private parking. Bed and Breakfast from £16 to £22 per person. Brochure on request. RAC Highly Acclaimed.

WINDERMERE. John and Liz Christopherson, Villa Lodge, Cross Street, Windermere LA23 1AE (Tel & Fax: 015394 43318). Friendliness and cleanliness guaranteed. Extremely comfortable accommodation in peaceful area overlooking Windermere village, yet only two minutes from station. All seven bedrooms are tastefully decorated, mostly en-suite (some four-posters) with colour TV, tea/coffee making facilities and full central heating, most with magnificent views of Lake and mountains. Access to rooms at all times. Superb English breakfast served in our delightful dining room. Vegetarian and special diets catered for. Dogs welcome by prior arrangement. Open all year. Special offers November to March. Safe, private parking for six cars. An excellent base for exploring the whole of the Lake District. Bed and Breakfast from £16. Ring John and Liz Christopherson.

WINDERMERE. Mr and Mrs J.N. Fowles, Rockside Guest House, Ambleside Road, Windermere LA23 1AQ (015394 45343). Rockside is a family run Guest House, 100 yards from Windermere village, bus stop and railway station. If any help is needed to plan a day's outing the proprietors, Neville and Mavis Fowles, will book trips, loan maps, suggest car routes and plan walks. Single, twin, double and family rooms are all centrally heated and have colour TV, clock radio and telephone; most rooms en-suite with tea/coffee making facilities. A car park at the rear holds 12 cars. Open all year — as every season has its own magic and beauty. RAC Acclaimed. Bed and Breakfast from £14.50 to £22.50 per person. Visa, Mastercard and Access accepted.

WHEN MAKING ENQUIRIES PLEASE MENTION
FARM HOLIDAY GUIDES

DERBYSHIRE

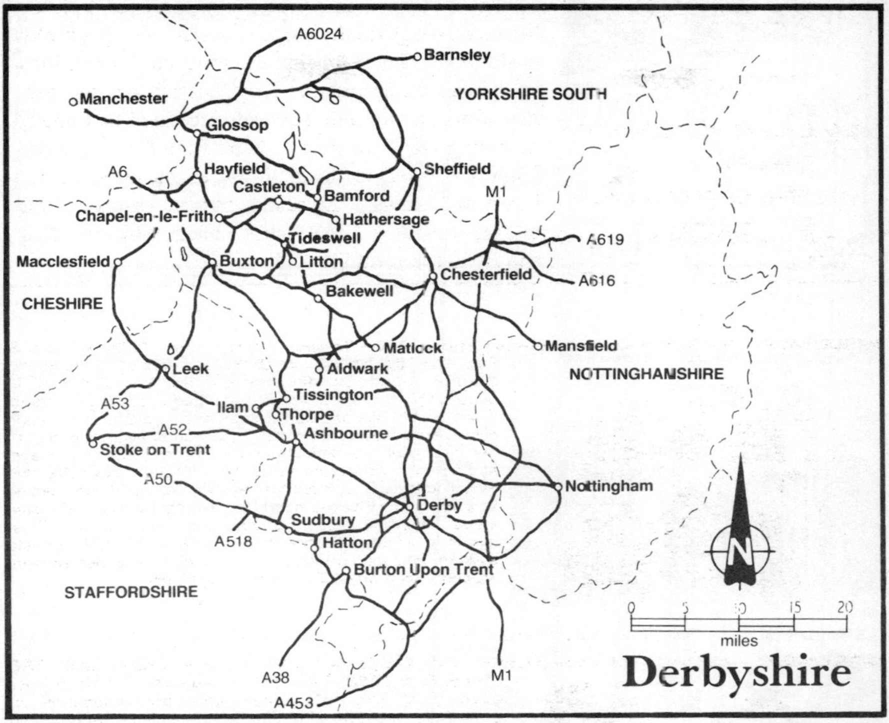

ALDWARK. Mrs D. Forsey, Tithe Farm, Aldwark, Grange Mill, Matlock DE4 4HX (01629 540263).

Commended. Overlooking open countryside, Tithe Farm is a Grade II Listed building, eight miles from Ashbourne, Matlock and Bakewell. Peacefully situated, it is an ideal centre for exploring the Dales and visiting Derbyshire's historic houses. Splendid walking country with much to interest the naturalist. Both the twin-bedded and the family rooms have private bathrooms colour TV and tea/coffee making facilities. Noted for extensive breakfast menu with homemade bread and preserves. Open April to October. Regret no dogs. Bed and Breakfast £18 with reduced rates for children, also for visits of three nights or longer. Brochure on request.

AMBERGATE. Mrs Carol Oulton, Lawn Farm, Whitewells Lane (off Holly Lane), Ambergate DE56 2DN (01773 852352). Working farm, join in. Enjoy comfortable Bed and Breakfast accommodation on a working beef and sheep farm, one mile off the A6 at Ambergate. Ambergate has many woodland walks and a picturesque canal which leads to nearby Cromford, home of the Arkwright Mill. Matlock Bath is 10 miles away and offers many attractions including cable cars. Within easy travelling distance of Alton Towers, American Adventure, Haddon Hall, Chatsworth House and Gardens, The Peak District National Park and The National Tramway Museum at Crich. Accommodation comprises one family room and one double room en-suite, both with washbasins, tea/coffee equipment, hair dryers and clock radio alarms. Sittingroom/diningroom with colour TV. Terms from £12.50 per night. Children welcome at reduced rates. Pets welcome by arrangement.

Biggin Mill Farm

Penny & Mark Bazeley,
Biggin Mill Farm, Biggin-by-Hulland,
Nr. Ashbourne, Derbyshire, DE6 3FN.

(Telephone Bookings Only Please).

01335 370414

In the heart of the beautiful Derbyshire Dales, yet within easy reach of local interest, our 18th Century stone farmhouse stands in 3 acres of wooded grounds with lawns, ducks and stream in a rural 'hideaway' location. Here you are assured of peace, tranquillity, the highest standards & attention to detail. Our two exquisite double guest rooms have every comfort with en-suite or private 'spa' bath facilities. We have an extensive breakfast menu & optional dinner menu comprising 4 delicious courses. Your cosy lounge has a log burner & we are fully licensed. 3 day special rates. Open all year including Christmas. No smoking.

Prices per person - Double B&B £35.00 D,B&B £47.50
Single B&B £47.50 D,B&B £65.00

AAQQQQ Selected ETB 2 Crown Highly Commended
Johansens Recommended

ASHBOURNE. Mrs Julia Brookfield, Green Gables, Thorpe, Near Ashbourne DE6 2AW (Thorpe Cloud [0133-529] 386). ♛ This old farmhouse has been renovated to offer comfortable accommodation for its guests. Two double rooms and one twin-bedded room. Two en-suite, one with own bathroom. Diningroom with oak beams; lounge with colour TV (log fire in winter). Full central heating. Tea and coffee making facilities. Children and pets welcome. Ample parking space. Open March 1st to November 30th. Bed and Breakfast £17; Singles £19.

ASHBOURNE near. Mrs Heathcote, Yerley Farm, Oakeover, Near Ashbourne DE6 2BR (01335 350244). Working farm. Working farm set in 180 acres of beautiful countryside situated two miles north of Ashbourne. Ideal for walking in the Dales and visiting historic houses. Five miles from Alton Towers and within easy reach of the American Adventure Park. Lounge tastefully decorated. Cosy diningroom with good wholesome cooking. One twin, two double rooms with washbasins. Central heating, log fires, colour TV. Bed and Breakfast from £13.50; Evening Meal by arrangement. Reductions for children. Non-smoking.

ASHBOURNE near. Mrs H. Leason, Overdale, Lode Lane, Alstonefield, Near Ashbourne DE6 2FZ (0133-527 206). Overdale is a beautiful, spacious house situated in one and a half acres of landscaped gardens, including shaded walks, orchard and lily pond. Alstonefield is a quiet, extremely pretty village adjacent to Dovedale, the spa towns of Buxton and Matlock, Chatsworth House and Haddon Hall. The guest house has full central heating, two family and five double bedrooms, all equipped with washbasins; three toilets, bathroom. A charming sittingroom and pleasant diningroom complete this perfect holiday home in its exclusive setting. Bed and Breakfast including evening drink from £15. Open all year.

ASHBOURNE near. Mr and Mrs P.J. Watson, Weaver Farm, Waterhouses, Near Ashbourne ST10 3HE (Oakamoor [01538] 702271). Working farm. Situated off A52 on the Weaver Hills close to Ashbourne, Dovedale and Alton Towers. Stone farmhouse with central heating and open fires offering family, twin and double bedrooms with washbasins. Cot. Bathroom with shower and WC. Guest diningroom and lounge with TV. Children welcome. Home produced fresh farmhouse cooking is served. The 320 acre farm with dairy cows, calves, sheep and lambs provides many activities which guests are welcome to watch and they can also enjoy extensive walks and views. Car essential; ample parking. No pets. SAE or ring for terms. A warm welcome awaits you.

ASHFORD. Mrs Ann Lindsay, Gritstone House, Greaves Lane, Ashford in the Water, Bakewell DE45 1QH (Bakewell [01629] 813563). *Highly Commended.* Be assured of a warm welcome at this charming Georgian house located in Peak National Park on B6465 leading to Monsal Dale and set in picturesque village on the Wye, one and a half miles north-west of Bakewell off A6. Lounge with TV; one twin-bedded room en suite, two double bedrooms with washbasins, all with TV, tea/coffee facilities. Luxury bathroom with bath, shower, etc; two toilets. Full central heating. A perfect location for visiting the Stately Homes and Dales of Derbyshire. Bed and Breakfast from £17 to £22; reduced for weekly stays. Sorry, no pets.

BAKEWELL. Mrs Sheila Gilbert, Castle Cliffe Private Hotel, Monsal Head, Bakewell DE45 1NL (Great Longstone [01629] 640258). *Commended.* Monsal Head is a popular beauty spot in the heart of the Derbyshire Dales. There are superb views from all the bedrooms in Castle Cliffe Hotel, some overlooking Monsal Dale and the famous viaduct. It is an ideal centre for visiting the dales, caverns and historic houses. Some of the hotel's three double, two family and four twin rooms have en-suite shower/WC, all have tea making facilities. Centrally heated plus open fires in the lounge and bar. Food is home cooked with the emphasis on British dishes from old traditional recipes. Children welcome. Sorry, no pets. Christmas and New Year and Special Mini Breaks available. Licensed. Bed and Breakfast from £21 to £27.50. AA Listed QQQ.

BAMFORD. Ye Derwent Hotel, Main Road, Bamford S30 2AY (01433 651395). Ye Derwent Hotel is situated in the beautiful Peak District National Park and in the heart of Jane Eyre country. All rooms have colour TV, tea/coffee making facilities and fine views of the Derbyshire hills. The proprietors pride themselves on the quality of the home cooking on offer, and there is a selection of fine traditional ales. The hotel is comfortable, with central heating throughout. Close to the spectacular Ladybower Reservoirs, Chatsworth House, Haddon Hall and the Castleton Caverns. Children and pets welcome. Short Breaks available. Further details and tariff on request.

BASLOW. Mrs S. Mills, Bubnell Cliff Farm, Wheatlands Lane, Baslow, Bakewell DE45 1RH (01246 582454). Working farm. A 300 acre working farm situated half a mile from the village of Baslow in the beautiful Derbyshire Peak District. Guests can enjoy, from their bedroom window, breathtaking views of Chatsworth Park and surrounding area. Chatsworth House, the majestic home of the Duke of Devonshire, medieval Haddon Hall and the traditional market town of Bakewell (famous for its puddings), are all close by. Accommodation comprises one double and one family room, guests' lounge/dining room with TV and log fires in the winter. NON-SMOKERS ONLY. Bed and Breakfast from £14 per person. Reductions for children. Varied breakfast menu.

BUXTON. Mr Rys Edge, "Lakenham", 11 Burlington Road, Buxton SK17 9AL (Buxton [01298] 79209). *Commended.* Kathryn and Rys invite you to LAKENHAM, their beautifully appointed Victorian Guest House in residential area, set on a broad tree-lined avenue overlooking the Pavilion Gardens. The bedrooms are spacious and furnished with your comfort in mind. All have en-suite bathrooms, hospitality trays, colour TVs and Satellite; many rooms have refrigerators. Decorated throughout in a Victorian manner, our elegantly furnished lounge and diningroom overlook our own peaceful and private gardens. Close to all amenities, Lakenham is the perfect base for exploring the Peak District. Children welcome. Private parking. We hope to give a personal service in a friendly, relaxed atmosphere and provide plenty of good home cooked food. Bed and Breakfast from £20. AA QQQ. For colour brochure contact **Rys Edge.**

DERBYSHIRE

The major portion of the Peak District, England's first National Park, lies within the county, high wind-swept heather moors and gritstone outcrops providing a vivid contrast to the softer rural landscapes of the south. Derbyshire's rich industrial heritage can be traced at Arkwright's Mill, Cromford; National Tramway Museum, Crich; Peak District Mining Museum, Matlock Bath; Royal Crown Derby Works, Derby, plus a host of other fascinating exhibitions and museums.

MOUNT PLEASANT FARM

Mrs E. B. Faulkner, Mount Pleasant Farm, Elkstones, Longnor, nr. Buxton, Derbyshire SK17 0LU.
Telephone: 01538 300 380.

Commended. FHG Diploma

This BTA and ETB "Commended" farmhouse is set on a two acre smallholding surrounded by lovely countryside, peaceful and relaxing with beautiful open views. It makes a comfortable centre for touring the Peak District; a car is essential to get the most out of your holiday. Plenty of parking space. One spacious double bedroom with en-suite bathroom and one twin bedroom with adjacent private bathroom. Both bedrooms have bath and shower, easy chairs, colour TV, and beverage making facilities. Guest lounge, dining room, table tennis room. Traditional English breakfast using local bacon, free range eggs, locally baked bread, and with home made preserves. Full central heating. Children over 6 years welcome. We prefer people not to smoke in the house. Pets by arrangement only. Open March to November inclusive for bed and breakfast. Terms on receipt of SAE please, or telephone for personal attention and full details.

Fernydale Farm

Fernydale Farm
Earl Sterndale, Buxton
Telephone: (01298) 83236/83605
Proprietor: Mrs Joan Nadin
Reg: East Midlands Tourist Board

Our luxury farmhouse is part of our 200 acre dairy/sheep farm and is ideally situated in a quiet rural setting within the Peak District National Park amidst superb scenery. We are a short distance from Buxton, famous for its water, and within twenty minutes of Ashbourne and the market town of Bakewell. The accommodation, which is open from January to November offers our guests dining room, luxury lounge and conservatory for relaxed comfort.
There are two double bedrooms furnished to a very high standard of comfort with shower, toilet, tea/coffee making facilities and colour television. There is full central heating and access to rooms during the day. B&B from £18.

Barms Farm

HIGHLY COMMENDED

Superb accommodation within warm and spacious luxury farmhouse, delightfully situated overlooking 18 hole golf course and within one mile of Buxton. Guests return to our dairy farm where attention to detail is second to none and individual requirements are personally catered for. The three pretty bedrooms are ensuite with tea/coffee facilities and colour TVs. Traditional features and high quality fixtures and fittings are complemented by beautiful decor throughout. Relax within our cosy oak-beamed lounge after sampling our excellent home cooking. Illuminated parking and use of payphone. No pets or smoking guests. Open all year. Bed and Breakfast from £19 per person. Evening meal £12.50 per person. Contact Mrs Lorraine Naden for brochure. (FHB Member, Tourist Board Inspected and Registered.)

Barms Farm, Fairfield, Buxton, Derbyshire SK17 7HW. Telephone: (01298) 77723. Fax: (01298) 78692.

BUXTON. Mrs S. Harrison, Thornsett, Chelmorton, Buxton SE17 9SL (01298 85779). Enjoy the seclusion and tranquillity of your own stone built cottage, adjoining our 17th century oak beamed farmhouse. Ideal for couples or families. Here you can relax in your own lounge; pretty double bedroom (plus bunks, also cot if required); separate bathroom with shower. Enjoy breakfast in front of a log fire in our dining room exclusive to you. Chelmorton is a peaceful farming village a short drive from Bakewell and Buxton. Local inn serves good food and has friendly atmosphere (200 yards). Terms from £18 for Bed and Breakfast.

BUXTON. Mrs Lynne P. Fearns, Heath Farm, Smalldale, Buxton SK17 8EB (01298 24431). Farm in Peak District with walking, caving, parks, gardens, caverns, pony trekking, historic houses, hang gliding, riding stables and rock climbing all within reasonable driving distance. Four and a half miles from Buxton (A6), two miles from Peak Forest (A623). One double and one family bedroom; bathroom, two toilets; sittingroom and diningroom. Cot and babysitting available. Pets welcome. Open all year except Christmas, mid-week bookings accepted. Car essential, parking. Bed and Breakfast from £13.50 per night; reductions for children and weekly stays. Registered with East Midland Tourist Board.

CASTLETON. Mrs B. Johnson, Myrtle Cottage, Market Place, Castleton, Near Sheffield S30 2WQ (Hope Valley [01433] 620787). Myrtle Cottage is pleasantly situated near the village green in the picturesque village of Castleton, famous for its castle and caverns. It is an ideal base for walking, caving, hang gliding or touring the Peak District and Derbyshire Dales. Buxton, Bakewell, Chatsworth House and the plague village of Eyam are within 20 minutes' drive. Registered with the English Tourist Board. The guest accommodation comprises family, twin and double bedrooms all with private shower/toilet and tea/coffee making facilities; sittingroom with TV and diningroom. Central heating. Fire Certificate. Parking. Regret no pets. Open all year (except Christmas) for Bed and Breakfast only from £17.50 per person.

See also Colour Display Advertisement **CHELMORTON. Christine Holland, Shallow Grange, Chelmorton, Near Buxton SK17 9SG (01298 23578; Fax: 01298 78242).** *Highly Commended.* Shallow Grange is situated in the heart of the Peak District set amidst beautiful open views. This working dairy farm has numerous unspoilt breathtaking walks, whilst Chatsworth, Haddon Hall, Bakewell and Buxton are all within a short drive. This 18th century farmhouse has recently been fully modernised without detracting from its original character; oak beams, inglenook fireplace, etc. are all complemented with antique furniture. All bedrooms are en-suite with tea/coffee making facilities and colour TVs. The house is fully centrally heated, double glazed and carpeted throughout. Fully licensed. Also holiday cottage, sleeps 4. Deluxe caravan site. Terms and brochure on request.

DERBY. Mrs Catherine Dicken, Bonehill Farm, Etwall Road, Mickleover DE3 5DN (01332 513553). This 120 acre mixed farm with Georgian farmhouse is set in peaceful rural surroundings, yet offers all the convenience of being only three miles west of Derby, on the A516 between Mickleover and Etwall. Within 10 miles there is a choice of historic houses to visit; Calke Abbey, Kedleston Hall, Sudbury Hall. Peak District 20 miles, Alton Towers 25 miles. Accommodation in three bedrooms (one twin, one double, one family), all with tea/coffee making facilities. Cot and high chair provided. Open all year. Bed and Breakfast from £15. Tennis, croquet available. A warm and friendly welcome awaits you.

DOVEDALE. Mrs Joan Wain, Air Cottage Farm, Ilam, Ashbourne DE6 2BD (01335 350475). Working farm, join in. Holidaymakers to the Peak District will enjoy staying at Air Cottage Farm situated at the edge of Dovedale with picturesque views of Thorpe Cloud and Dovedale Valley. The famous Stepping Stones are just 10 minutes away and it is an ideal base for touring the Peak District National Park, stately homes and many other places of local historic interest. Unlimited walks in the Manifold Valley and the Tissington Nature Trail and scenic routes for motorists. Within easy reach of Alton Towers and Carsington Reservoir for water sports. Activities available include swimming, squash and horse riding, all within easy reach. Two double bedrooms and one single (sleeping two); bathroom, two toilets; sittingroom; diningroom. Cot and high chair provided for children. Open March to November. A car is essential — parking. Terms and further details on request.

PLEASE ENCLOSE A STAMPED ADDRESSED ENVELOPE WITH ENQUIRIES

GLOSSOP. Margaret Child, Rock Farm, Glossop SK13 9JZ (01457 861086). For an easy-going restful break amid beautiful scenery and with warm friendly service, come to Rock Farm, hidden away in the hills above Glossop, with nearby pony trekking and good walks, and plenty of local pubs offering excellent food. An ideal base for seeing the Peak District and yet only 40 minutes from Stockport, Manchester and the Airport. Carefully restored and tastefully furnished with full central heating, we offer one double and one twin-bedded room, both with south-facing views, beams, tea/coffee making facilities and TV; guest bathroom with shower; separate lounge overlooking Kinder Scout. Ample parking. £15 per person per night for Bed and full English Breakfast. Member of Glossop and District Association for Tourism.

HARTINGTON. Mrs Jane Gibbs, Wolfscote Grange Farm, Hartington, Near Buxton SK17 0AX (01298 84342). Find an ideal "country hideaway" on our secluded hill farm, set high above Wolfscote Dale overlooking Berrisford Dale, with Dovedale downstream. Just a couple of miles along a stone-walled road from the pretty village of Hartington. Feel at home in our ancient 15th century farmhouse with all its character of original oak beams, spiral stairs, old mullion windows. The spacious guest lounge has a cosy log fire and grandfather clock ticking steadily in the corner. Separate dining room. Three bedrooms (one double, one twin/family, one single), have antique furnishings, tea/coffee facilities, washbasins and central heating; some en suite facilities. Breakfast, then explore the beautiful surrounding hills and hidden dales below. Bed and Breakfast from £16.

HATHERSAGE. Mrs Jill Salisbury, Lane End Farm, Abney, Hathersage, Via Sheffield S30 1AA (01433 650371). Working farm, join in. Relax in our award-winning Derbyshire farmhouse. We are a working hill farm in the Peak District National Park. Lane End, having panoramic views, is situated in the small hamlet of Abney midway between Hathersage and Tideswell. The area is ideal for most outdoor pursuits and for visiting all local places of interest. We offer a high standard of accommodation — one double en-suite room, one double room and one twin room, all with washbasins and tea/coffee making facilities. Car recommended. Farm trail. Own horse welcome. Self catering cottage also available. Bed and Breakfast from £15.50. Reductions for children. Open all year. East Midlands Tourist Board member, Listed and Highly Commended.

HATHERSAGE. Mrs Caroline B. Colley, Sladen, Jaggers Lane, Hathersage, The Peak District S30 1AZ (Hope Valley [01433] 650706). Sladen is a substantial Victorian residence surrounded by a large and attractive garden. The house has panoramic views over the Derbyshire hills and is situated on a quiet lane only two minutes' walk from the centre of the picturesque village of Hathersage in the beautiful Peak National Park. The house has one family and two double rooms, all with tea/coffee making facilities, and there are two separate bathrooms for guests. There is ample private parking and Sladen is within only a few minutes' walk from train and bus services. Hathersage is an excellent centre from which to visit the Peak District's attractive villages and stately homes. For the more energetic the surrounding area offers a wide range of activities including rambling, rock climbing, fishing, golf, tennis, swimming, pony trekking, para and hang gliding, to name only a few of the opportunities available to visitors. A warm welcome for all, including children and pets. Bed and Breakfast from £16 per night.

MAPPLETON. Mrs E.J. Harrison, Little Park Farm, Mappleton, Ashbourne DE6 2BR (0133-529 341). ♛ *Commended.* **Working farm.** This 125 acre dairy farm is set in the peaceful Dove Valley, ideally situated for the Derbyshire Dales, National Trust properties and Alton Towers. Nearby cycle hire. Five minutes' ride from Ashbourne and in walking distance of the village local, where bar meals are served. Plenty of wildlife and beautiful walks, ideal place for unwinding. The oak beamed listed farmhouse, over 300 years old, is tastefully furnished; lounge with colour TV, diningroom with separate tables and tea making facilities; two double and one twin bedded rooms with washbasins; bathroom and toilet. Sorry no pets. Open March to end of October. Bed and Breakfast from £13.

MATLOCK. Mrs D. Wootton, Old School Farm, Uppertown Lane, Uppertown, Ashover, Near Chesterfield S45 0JF (Chesterfield [01246] 590813). ♛ **Working farm, join in.** This working farm in a small hamlet on the edge of the Peak District enjoys unspoilt views. Ashover is three miles away and mentioned in the Domesday Book; Chatsworth House, Haddon Hall, Hardwick Hall, Matlock Bath and Bakewell all within seven miles. Accommodation comprises two family rooms with en suite facilities, one double, one single rooms. Guests have their own bathroom; washbasins in three of the large rooms. Plenty of hot water; fitted carpets; large livingroom/diningroom with colour TV. Non-smoking accommodation available. Car essential. NO PETS. Disabled guests welcome. Children welcome. Open from April to October. Bed and Breakfast from £16 or Bed, Breakfast and Evening Meal (reductions for children). Take the B5057 Darley Dale Road off the A632 Chesterfield to Matlock main road. Take second left. Keep on this road for approximately one mile. Old School Farm is on left opposite the stone water trough. AA and RAC listed.

MATLOCK BATH. Daphne and Peter West, Sunnybank Guest House, 37 Clifton Road, Matlock Bath DE4 3PW (01629 584621). ♛♛♛ *Commended.* Sunnybank is a spacious, comfortable Victorian residence with lovely views in peaceful surroundings, convenient for touring and walking in the Derbyshire Peaks and Dales. Five well-appointed and attractively furnished bedrooms with tea/coffee making facilities; some with colour TV. Three en suite, the other two with washbasins. Separate shower and two toilets. Cosy dining room with two large tables which guests share — promotes conversation and friendly atmosphere. Comfortable lounge with colour TV. Central heating throughout. Home cooking and personal service. Residential licence. Non-smokers only, please. Bed and Breakfast from £18. Bargain Breaks available. Guestaccom Good Room Award. Open all year except Christmas. Brochure on request. Access and Visa accepted.

MATLOCK near. Ray and Pauline Sanders, Sycamore Guest House, Town Head, Bonsall, Near Matlock DE4 2AA (Wirksworth [01629] 823903). ♛♛ A lovely 18th century family guest house in the village of Bonsall, nestling high on Masson Hill on the edge of the Peak District National Park. Easy access to Matlock Bath (for cable cars), Chatsworth House, Haddon Hall, Dovedale, Alton Towers and Carsington Water. Five very comfortable en suite rooms equipped with tea/coffee makers, colour TV, hair dryers and alarm clocks. Full central heating. Residential licence. Own off street car park. Bed and Breakfast from £20; Evening Meal from £10.50. Open all year with special breaks from November to March. AA Listed. Ring or write for brochure.

TISSINGTON. Mrs Herridge, Bent Farm, Tissington, Ashbourne DE6 1RD (01335 390214). Busy working farm situated approximately three-quarters of a mile from the picturesque village of Tissington, famous for its annual Well Dressings. Ideal for a walking holiday or touring the Peak District and within easy reach of Chatsworth House, Dovedale and Alton Towers. Cycle hire available in the village. Comfortable homely accommodation is offered in double, twin and family rooms, all with washbasins and tea/coffee making facilities. Some rooms en suite. Comfortable lounge with open fire and colour TV. No children under five years or pets allowed. Bed and Breakfast available.

DEVON

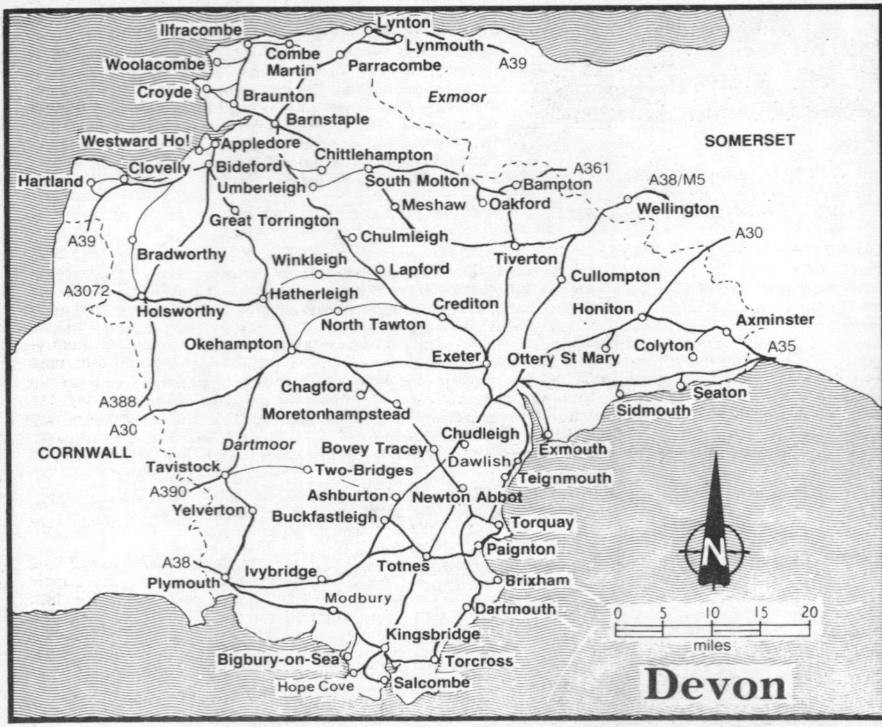

ASHBURTON. Mrs D.M. Dent, Adams Hele Farm, Ashburton TQ13 7NW (Ashburton [01364] 652525). ♛♛ Working farm. This 16th century farmhouse nestles on the south facing hill overlooking the Dart Valley and the Moors. The farm consists of 90 acres stocked with cattle, sheep and ponies on pleasant grassland. It is an ideal base for exploring the unspoilt scenery of Dartmoor. The accommodation consists of two double bedrooms each with shower and toilet, one twin and one family room both with washbasins; two bathrooms, three toilets; sittingroom; two diningrooms. Children are welcome: cot, high chair, babysitting, special mealtimes and reduced rates. Pets by arrangement. Open March to October. Car essential, parking. The South Devon beaches are only 15 miles; Plymouth and Exeter within half an hour's drive. Excellent fishing, beautiful walks, moorland pony rides and many golf courses within easy reach. A warm welcome to all guests.

ASHBURTON. Chris and Annie Moore, Gages Mill, Buckfastleigh Road, Ashburton TQ13 7JW (01364 652391). Relax in the warm and friendly atmosphere of our lovely 14th century former wool mill, set in an acre of gardens on the edge of Dartmoor National Park. Eight delightful en suite bedrooms, one on the ground floor, all with tea-making facilities, central heating, hair dryers, radio and alarm clocks. We have a large comfortable lounge with corner bar and granite archways leading to the dining room, and a cosy sittingroom with colour TV. Home cooking of a very high standard. Licensed. Ample car parking. Being one mile from the centre of Ashburton, this is an ideal base for touring South Devon or visiting Exeter, Plymouth, Dartmouth, the many National Trust properties and other places of interest. Children over five years welcome. Sorry no pets. Bed, Breakfast and Evening Meal or Bed and Breakfast only. AA Selected, RAC Acclaimed.

ASHBURTON (Dartmoor). Mrs Anne Torr, Middle Leat, Holne, Near Ashburton TQ13 7SJ (01364 631413). Middle Leat, set in three acres, offers very comfortable accommodation with wonderful views, in the picturesque village of Holne, three and a half miles west of Ashburton in the Dartmoor National Park. We have one large ground floor bedroom with private bathroom and full facilities; this has a double bed, bunk beds and a single bed and is available as a double or family room. Full English Breakfast. Good home cooking, home grown produce. Optional Evening Meal. Vegetarians welcome. Large garden, free-range rare breed chickens and ducks cows and calves, horse and pets. Visitors are welcome to join in, feeding chicks and ducklings, collecting eggs, etc. A warm welcome and relaxed friendly atmosphere assured in very peaceful surroundings. Sorry, no smoking in the house. Bed and Breakfast from £16. SAE for details or phone for brochure.

AXMINSTER. M. Keenes, "White Hall", Kilmington, Axminster EX13 7SB (Axminster [01297] 32067). Your visit to White Hall will be a treasured memory, your room will have washbasin and colour TV. White Hall is a small, comfortable Georgian House situated off the main road. Standing in four acres, the house enjoys fabulous views from all rooms over the beautiful Devonshire countryside. Kilmington is the ideal centre for exploring this most beautiful part of Devon; Dorset, Somerset and the sea only six miles away. Dartmoor, Exmoor, Lyme Regis and Beer are easily reached. Sailing, golf, riding, historic houses and Wildlife Parks are all within a few miles. We have our own Spring Water and guests would naturally expect to have home made marmalade, jam and free range eggs with their breakfast. You must not be surprised if, coming here once you find yourself, like so many others, returning year after year. Bed and Breakfast from £14. Evening Meals available in the 16th century Inn. SAE, please.

AXMINSTER. Christopher and Sandra Holmes, Higher Bruckland Farm, Musbury, Axminster EX13 6SU (01297 552371). Working farm. Chris and Sandie welcome guests to the friendly atmosphere of their 16th century farmhouse situated on the Devon/Dorset border, close to the beach at Lyme Regis, Seaton and the market town of Axminster. Guests are free to walk the 250 acres, with 40 acres of woodland and abundant wildlife, set in an area of outstanding natural beauty. We offer our guests traditional home cooking in the oak-beamed diningroom with comfortable lounge area with colour TV. One family, one double and one twin-bedded rooms, all with washbasins. Children welcome, babysitting available. Open all year. Terms on request.

BAMPTON. Mrs Lindy Head, Harton Farm, Oakford, Tiverton EX16 9HH (Dakford [0139-85] 209). Working farm, join in. Lovely 17th century farmhouse with original fireplaces and witches' window on 53-acre mixed farm with own friendly cows, pigs, chickens, sheep, goats, home spun wool, etc. Secluded, but accessible, it is an ideal touring centre for Exmoor, the Exe Valley and Devon. Comfortable accommodation in three double bedrooms with washbasins and tea-making facilities; luxury bathroom with a view; dining room serving real country cooking with farm-produced additive-free meat and organic vegetables; home baking a speciality; guests' lounge with colour TV. Garden. Children over four welcome. Pets accepted. Car essential — parking. Open for Evening Meal, Bed and Breakfast from £18; Bed and Breakfast from £13. Reductions for children. Farm walks. Fishing, shooting, riding can be arranged. Vegetarian meals available on request.

FHG DIPLOMA WINNERS 1994

Each year we award a small number of diplomas to holiday proprietors whose services have been specially commended by our readers and the following advertisers were our FHG Diploma winners for 1994.

ENGLAND

Mrs Judith Goddard, Cherry Tree Villa, 7 Newbridge Hill, Bath Avon
Mrs S. Briggs, High Wray Farm, High Wray, Ambleside, Cumbria
Mr & Mrs F. Cervetti, Lightwood Farmhouse, Bowland Bridge, Cumbria
Mrs Jenny Fox, Highstead Farm, Bucks Cross, Near Bideford, Devon
Mrs B. Williams, Abbots Court, Church End, Twyning, Gloucestershire
Mr & Mrs Hayward, Castlemere Hotel, 13 Shaftesbury Avenue, Blackpool
Mrs Wainwright, Homestead House, 5 Ashley Road, Medbourne, Leics
Mrs Sheila Potts, Aydon, 1 Osborne Avenue, Hexham, Northumberland
Mr & Mrs B. Joyner, Anro, 90 Kings Road, Harrogate, N. Yorks

SCOTLAND

Mr & Mrs I. Weir, Appin Holiday Homes, Appin, Argyl

WALES

Mrs J.E. Thom, The Grange, Penrose, Raglan, Gwent

BARNSTAPLE. Mrs Hazel Kingdon, Waytown Farm, Shirwell, Barnstaple EX31 4JN (01271 850396). *Commended.* Waytown is a family run beef and sheep farm situated three miles from the town of Barnstaple. Our attractive 17th century farmhouse is set in pleasant countryside within easy reach of Exmoor and the sandy beaches of Woolacombe, Croyde and Saunton. An ideal touring centre with riding, fishing and a Leisure Centre nearby. Good home cooked farmhouse food. Accommodation consists of two double/family en-suite rooms, one twin-bedded room, all with colour TV, heating and tea/coffee making facilities; bathroom; lounge with colour TV; dining-room. All children welcome, babysitting, cot, high chair. Ample parking. Bed and Breakfast, Dinner optional. Reductions for weekly stays. Brochure and terms on request. Welcome Host Award.

BARNSTAPLE. Mrs Marilyn Purchase, Bridwick Farm, Kentisbury, Barnstaple EX31 4NN (01598 763416). *Commended.* A warm friendly welcome awaits at this working livestock farm beautifully set in quiet Exmoor Valley, where everything possible is done to ensure the enjoyment of your stay. Situated in A39 half a mile from Blackmoor Gate crossroads towards Barnstaple and midway between Woolacombe and Lynton. Spacious guest rooms equipped with colour TV, washbasins, drinks making facilities; en suite or private bathrooms. Comfortable guest lounge. Ideal location for moors, beaches, fishing or exploring market towns. Pony rides, children encouraged where possible to meet our pet sheep and cows. Excellent restaurant only half a mile away. Bed and Breakfast from £16 per night, £105 per week. Reductions for children and stays of over three days.

BARNSTAPLE. Mrs Pat Burge, Haxton Down Farm, Bratton Fleming, Barnstaple EX32 7JL (01598 710275). Dear all, having a wonderful time. It's so peaceful here, quiet and welcoming with room to relax and so much to do nearby. We've been to the beach and Exmoor, visited a wildlife park and National Trust house and tomorrow we're going sheep racing. We start the day with a huge breakfast and come back each evening to a delicious four-course dinner. Bedrooms are clean and comfortable with lots of extras and babysitting and washing machines on hand. Wildlife outside, animals and trailer rides for the children. Super views, great value for money. Come and see for yourself. Tourist Board Listed Commended. Bed and Breakfast from £13.50; Evening Meal from £7.50.

BARNSTAPLE. Mrs J. Ley, West Barton, Alverdiscott, Near Barnstaple EX31 3PT (01271 858230). Working farm. West Barton is a mixed family-run farm of 210 acres with a pedigree Friesian herd of cattle and also sheep. An ideal touring base with Dartington Glass, RHS Rosemoor Gardens at Torrington, Clovelly, Hartland Point and many other beauty spots readily accessible; many golf courses close by. Pleasantly situated beside the B3232 Barnstaple to Torrington road with Bideford only five miles away. Sandy beach only six miles. Children welcome. Regret no pets. One twin bedded room with washbasin, one family room and one single room. Lounge with colour TV. Evening drinks. Bed and Breakfast from £12. Evening Meal optional from £6. Reduced rates for children under 12.

BARNSTAPLE. Mrs L.P.A. Joslin, Stone Farm, Brayford, Barnstaple EX32 7PJ (01271 830473).

Charming 16th century Devon Longhouse on 180 acre working sheep farm and seven acres woodland. Peacefully situated in unspoilt countryside, six miles from the market town of Barnstaple, six miles from Exmoor and 12 miles from North Devon coast with sandy beaches. Spacious, warm and comfortable accommodation in en suite family/double/twin bedrooms with all facilities and colour TV. Oak beams, inglenooks and games room with pool table and darts. Plentiful fresh food of the highest quality offered in four-course Dinner and choice of breakfast menu. Vegetarian and special diets catered for. Bed and Breakfast from £16; Dinner £9. Reductions for children and weekly booking. Brochure with colour photo.

BEAFORD. Mrs R. Hookway, "East Villavin Farm", Roborough, Near Winkleigh, North Devon EX19 8TF (018053 272). Working farm. Guests are made welcome at our small, friendly, relaxed farmhouse in the quiet countryside. This mixed farm has cows, sheep, tame lambs, chickens, cats, free donkey rides. Entrance situated on a good road, B3217. Golf course and fishing nearby. Excellent touring centre for Dartmoor, Exmoor and within easy reach of the beautiful North Devon beaches. Farmhouse tastefully decorated; diningroom; lounge, colour TV; bedrooms have washbasins and tea-making facilities. We serve good food. Sweets served with cream made on the farm. A warm welcome awaits you. Bed and Breakfast. Evening Meal optional.

BIDEFORD. Mrs C. Colwill, Welsford Farm, Hartland EX39 6EQ (01237 441296). Working farm, join in.

Relax, enjoy the peaceful countryside yet be within easy reach of towns, interesting places and picturesque beaches with miles of scenic cliff walks. This 360-acre dairy farm is situated two miles from Hartland Village; four miles from cobble-stoned Clovelly and the rugged Hartland coastline. Comfortably furnished farmhouse with colour TV lounge and washbasins in bedrooms. Children welcome at reduced rates. Wander around the farm and "pets' corner". Babysitting always available. Good country food using home grown produce. Car essential. Bed, Breakfast and four-course Evening Meal from £112 weekly. Warm welcome. Regret no pets. Open April to October.

BIDEFORD near. Mr and Mrs J. Ridd, Bakers Farm, Torrington EX38 7ES (01805 623260). This is a

farm of just over 100 acres with attached 16th century farmhouse. A warm welcome awaits all visitors, who are free to come and go as they please. The food and accommodation are both highly recommended by previous guests, and visitors are assured of delicious meals prepared from fresh produce only, including meat, vegetables, milk, eggs, cream and cheese. Accommodation consists of one family and two double rooms; two toilets, one shower room, one bathroom. Comfortable lounge with colour TV which visitors may use at any time. Full Fire Certificate. Local amenities in Torrington include indoor swimming pool, golf, tennis and fishing (coarse fishing available within the farm), as well as the famous Dartington Glass Factory. We are within easy reach of the coast, Exmoor, Dartmoor and many other places of interest, including Tarka Trail for cycling or walking, and are just under a mile from Torrington. Guests are welcome to walk around the farm and see our various animals. Reasonable rates for Evening Meal, Bed and Breakfast (from £17) or Bed and Breakfast only. Reductions for children. Please send SAE for full particulars.

BIDEFORD near. Mrs Yvonne Heard, West Titchberry Farm, Hartland, Near Bideford EX39 6AU (01237 441 287). Working farm, join in.

Spacious, completely renovated 17th century farmhouse, carpeted and well appointed throughout. One family room with washbasin, one double room with washbasin and one twin room; bathroom and two toilets. Downstairs lounge with colour TV; toilet; diningroom where excellent home cooking is served using fresh farm produce. A games room and sheltered walled garden are available for guests' use. The coastal footpath winds its way around this 150 acre mixed farm situated between Hartland Lighthouse and the National Trust beauty spot of Shipload Bay (sand at low tide). Hartland three miles, Clovelly six miles, Bideford and Westward Ho! 15 miles, Bude 18 miles. Children welcome at reduced rates; cot, high chair and babysitting available. Open all year except Christmas. Sorry no pets. Tourist Board registered. SAE for terms for Evening Dinner/Meal, Bed and Breakfast. Also self catering cottage available.

BOVEY TRACEY. Mrs Linda Harvey, Frost Farmhouse, Frost Farm, Bovey Tracey TQ13 9PP (01626 833266). ♛ *Commended.* A pretty pink-washed thatched farmhouse with pictures, pottery and pretty bed linen. Large, comfy double rooms en-suite (one ground floor), double/twin with private bathroom. Pine furnished, tea/coffee making facilities, colour TV in bedrooms. Feast on traditional home cooked foods. Hearty breakfast, traditional three-course evening meal. Quiet location. One and a half miles to Bovey Tracey, the town that is the gateway to Dartmoor. Bed and Breakfast from £18, Evening Meal from £9.50. For further details please ring.

RADDICOMBE LODGE

Set in peaceful surroundings overlooking the sea and country, midway between the picturesque harbour towns of Brixham and Dartmouth. Raddicombe Lodge has a charm and character all of its own, with pitched ceilings and lattice windows. Scrumptious traditional English Breakfast. Attractive bedrooms with TV and tea making facilities. Ensuite rooms available. Bed and Breakfast only. Ample parking. AA and RAC listed. Les Routiers Recommended. Prices from £15.50.

Graham and Yvonne Glass, Raddicombe Lodge, 102 Kingswear Road, Brixham TQ5 0EX. Telephone: (01803) 882125.

BRIXHAM. Ian and Carol Hayhurst, "Richmond House", Higher Manor Road, Brixham TQ5 8HA (01803 882391). ♛♛ *Commended.* Detached Victorian house, decorated in the "Laura Ashley" style, with pretty diningroom and elegant lounge, including colour TV. Quiet location (turn first left after "Golden Lion" on New Road), central for shops and historic harbour. Licensed restaurant 100 yards. Excellent base for touring South Hams and Dartmoor. 40 minutes from M5. Ideal sea-fishing, boating, painting, walking and golf. Our eight spacious bedrooms are heated, have vanity units, hot drinks facilities and pleasant views. All types of room available plus en-suites, family-size and ground floor. South-facing gardens and car park. Bed and varied four-course breakfast from £16.00 per person per night. VISA, ACCESS. Midweek bookings. Colour brochure available.

COLYTON. Mrs Ruth Gould, Bonehayne Farm, Colyton EX13 6SG (01404 87396). Working farm. Bonehayne Farm, situated in beautiful Coly Valley, set amidst 250 acres dairy farmland on banks of the River Coly, where daffodils are a feature in springtime, and Mallard duck and Kingfishers are a common sight. Trout fishing freely available. Woodlands to explore. Visitors welcome to participate in some farm activities and make friends with the animals. One family, one double bedrooms, with washbasins; bathroom, toilet. Spacious, homely lounge with inglenook fireplace, TV. A good English breakfast with our traditional Devonshire farmhouse menu, vegetarian or special diets on request. Play area for children and extended large lawn overlooking surrounding countryside. Reduced rates, cot, high chair, babysitting for children. Small pets accepted. Parking. Farway Country Park, two riding schools, Honiton Golf Course, weekly cattle market, coastal area, all within four and a half miles. Open April to October. Bed and Breakfast; Evening Meal. Terms on request.

DEVON – ENDLESS CHOICES!

People never tire of visiting Devon. There's so much to do, like visiting Alscott Farm Museum, Berry Head Country Park, Bickleigh Mill Farm, Farway Countryside Park, Haytor Granite Railway, Kent's Cavern, Dartmoor National Park, Exmoor National Park and of course Plymouth and its Hoe.

COLYTON. Mrs Norma Rich, Sunnyacre, Northleigh, Colyton EX13 0QE (01404 87422). Working farm, join in. Have a relaxing holiday in Bed and Breakfast and Evening Meal accommodation set in an area of outstanding natural beauty with plenty of things to do and see. Accommodation is in a bungalow on a working dairy farm. Join in with farm activities, feeding all the animals, watch cows being milked. Enjoy excellent and varied meals, all home cooked using fresh produce. Full English Breakfast, early morning tea, evening drinks. Three bedrooms with washbasins, separate WC, TV in lounge, games room. Children welcome, cot, high chair and babysitting available. Reasonable rates.

CREALY BARTON. Mrs M. Prouse, Crealy Barton, Clyst St. Mary, Exeter EX5 1DR (01395 232567). ♛♛♛ A delightful farmhouse offering three en-suite bedrooms — family, double and twin; colour TV; tea/coffee trays. Spacious lounge and diningroom overlooking peaceful garden, patio and barbecue area. Access at all times. Ideally situated two miles from the M5 Junction 30 making Devon's moors and coast within easy reach. Walk to Crealy Country Park (on the farm, free admission for guests) with its attractive shop, restaurant, animals, adventure playground. Good restaurants and pubs nearby. Feed the ducks on the lake. Short or long stay, a warm welcome awaits throughout the year. Bed and Breakfast from £18.

CREDITON. Mr and Mrs R. Barrie-Smith, Great Leigh Farm, Crediton EX17 3QQ (01647 24297). Working farm, join in. Great Leigh Farm is delightfully set in the mid-Devon hills in a quiet position between Cheriton Bishop and Crediton, two miles off the A30. Ideally situated for a quiet holiday or for touring Devon and Cornwall. Guests are free to wander over the 80 acre sheep farm and may join in farm activities. Outstandingly comfortable accommodation with full central heating. One family room, one double room and two single rooms. Two rooms with bathroom en-suite. Children welcome. Good home cooking. Open all year. Car essential. Babysitting available. Bed, Breakfast and Evening Dinner £20; Bed and Breakfast £14. Children half price.

CREDITON. Derek and Rosemary Webber, Hensley Farm, Worlington, Crediton EX17 4TG (Tiverton [01884] 860346). Working farm, join in. A friendly farming family offers accommodation in their thatched farmhouse near a picturesque country village overlooking one of the prettiest valleys in Devon. A 180 acre dairy and sheep farm which extends to the river where there are superb walks. Local riding school nearby. Ideal centre for Exmoor, Dartmoor and North Coast beaches. Within easy reach of Tiverton Link road (A361). Large lawns. Large bedrooms with washbasins, colour TV. Diningroom; lounge. Play room, table tennis, darts and games, etc. Wide range of toys for children and babysitting available. Delicious food using local and home grown produce. Bed and Breakfast £13; Evening Meal very reasonable. Send or telephone for details. Tourist Board inspected.

CROYDE. Mrs Jean M. Barnes, Denham Farm, North Buckland, Braunton EX33 1HY (Tel and Fax: 01271 890297). ♛♛♛ *Commended.* **Working farm, join in.** This is a 160 acre beef farm where guests are allowed to roam around and join in with the farming activities. We provide everything for a relaxing holiday. Peace and quiet, countryside, good food, friendly atmosphere and super, comfortable accommodation. All the food is personally prepared by Mrs Barnes to ensure a high standard, desserts are a speciality. The rooms are of an equally high standard, all are en-suite and have own colour TV, radio alarm and tea/coffee making facilities; TV lounge; bar lounge; large diningroom; reading room; laundry facilities. Games room outside. A short drive to long sandy beaches, rolling surf, cliff walks and rugged moorland. Nearby you will find golf, riding, sailing, windsurfing and miles of country walks. This 17th century farmhouse has been tastefully decorated to offer you the best. AA QQQ and RAC Acclaimed. Telephone now and book your break. Open all year. Bed and Breakfast from £20; Evening Dinner optional. Sorry, no pets.

CULLOMPTON. Mrs Sylvia Baker, Wishay Farm, Trinity, Cullompton EX15 1PE (01884 33223).

♛♛ **Working farm.** Wishay Farm is a 200 acre working farm with a recently modernised Grade II Listed farmhouse with some interesting features. It is situated in a quiet and peaceful area with scenic views, yet is central for touring the many attractions Devon has to offer. Comfortable and spacious accommodation in family room with en suite bathroom, double room with washbasin and private bathroom, both with colour TV and tea/coffee making facilities. Central heating, log fire when cold. Children welcome with ample toys and games provided. Cot and high chair available. Bed and Breakfast from £14 to £16; Evening Meal by arrangement. Reduced rates for children.

CULLOMPTON. Mrs Margaret Chumbley, Fig Tree Farm, Butterleigh, Cullompton EX15 1PQ (01884 855463).

Set in a magnificent position with spectacular views overlooking the Burn Valley, an idyllic rural retreat, you are assured of a peaceful relaxing holiday at Fig Tree. There are many lovely walks in the area, with both coarse and trout fishing nearby. The coast, Exmoor, Dartmoor and many National Trust properties are all within easy reach; Cullompton (M5) four miles. Full menu, delicious four-course Evening Meals using the best of local produce, with home grown fruit and vegetables. Special diets catered for with pleasure. Comfortable guests' lounge with colour TV, video, tea/coffee making facilities. Guest accommodation includes double bedroom with verandah; all rooms have washbasins and shaver points. Children welcome at reduced rates. Bed and Breakfast from £14; Bed, Breakfast and Evening Meal £125 per week.

DARTMOUTH. Mr Nigel Peter Jestico, The Captain's House, 18 Clarence Street, Dartmouth TQ6 9NW (Dartmouth [01803] 832133). ♛♛ *Highly Commended.* The Captain's House is a small Georgian listed house built about 1730 and is only a few minutes' level walk from the shops and 50 yards or so from the River Dart promenade. Attractions include historic Dartmouth itself, nearby beaches, sailing, fishing and coastal walks. The house is centrally heated and all bedrooms have private facilities, colour TV, radio and alarm clock, tea and coffee making equipment, and hairdryer, etc. Access to your room at all times. Open January to December. AA QQQQ, RAC. Bed and Breakfast from £17.

Key to Tourist Board Ratings

The Crown Scheme

(England, Scotland & Wales)

Covering hotels, motels, private hotels, guesthouses, inns, bed & breakfast, farmhouses. Every Crown classified place to stay is inspected annually. *The classification:* Listed then 1-5 Crown indicates the range of facilities and services. Higher quality standards are indicated by the terms APPROVED, COMMENDED, HIGHLY COMMENDED and DELUXE.

The Key Scheme

(also operates in Scotland using a Crown symbol)

Covering self-catering in cottages, bungalows, flats, houseboats, houses, chalets, etc. Every Key classified holiday home is inspected annually. *The classification:* 1-5 Key indicates the range of facilities and equipment. Higher quality standards are indicated by the terms APPROVED, COMMENDED, HIGHLY COMMENDED and DELUXE.

The Q Scheme

(England, Scotland & Wales)

Covering holiday, caravan, chalet and camping parks. Every Q rated park is inspected annually for its quality standards. The more ✓ in the Q – up to 5 – the higher the standard of what is provided.

See also Colour Display Advertisement **DAWLISH. Mr and Mrs T.C. Crump, MHCI, Radfords Country Hotel, Dawlish EX7 0QN (Dawlish [01626] 863322).** Come and relax at Radfords in one of our lounges, comfortable bar, our lovely garden or alternatively enjoy an action-packed holiday — many activities and sports available here and in the locality. We have family bedrooms or two family suites available, all with private bathroom; accommodation for about 30 families. The children will love their special heated indoor swimming pool, the outdoor playground, the freedom of our large gardens and the assorted ponies and dogs there are to talk to. In the evening they can look forward to a swimming gala, live entertainment, a party and their own cartoon show, etc. Playroom now available. The adults can look forward to superb food lovingly cooked and served and the various entertainments we arrange for them from skittles tournaments to a feature film. We also have a fully equipped launderette and an evening babysitter to help make your holiday as relaxing as possible. Mothers can bring babies and small children here with every confidence. Member West Country Tourist Board. Featured on TV by Judith Chalmers. Farm Holiday Guide Diploma winner. Please telephone or send for illustrated brochure.

EXETER. Mrs Jackie Bolt, Wood Barton, Farringdon, Exeter EX5 2HY (01395 233407). Wood Barton is a Grade II Listed farmhouse in quiet position facing south with good views. Three spacious en suite rooms with central heating and hospitality tray. Bedtime drinks served in the TV lounge with woodburner. Electric blankets available. Traditional farmhouse breakfast is served, cooked on the Aga. There is a good restaurant/pub half a mile away. Situated three miles from M5 Junction 30 and Cathedral city of Exeter, half a mile from children's adventure park and carp fishing; three miles from Bird Reserve at Aylesbeare Common, and six miles from sandy beaches and coastal path at Exmouth. Guests have access to rooms all day. Open all year. Plenty of parking space. Bed and Breakfast from £15.

EXETER near (Doddiscombsleigh). Mrs B. Lacey, Whitemoor Farm, Doddiscombsleigh, Near Exeter EX6 7PU (01647 52423). Working farm. ♛ Listed 16th century thatched farmhouse set in the seclusion of 284 acres of farmland within easy reach of Exeter, coast, Dartmoor, birdwatching and forest walks. The cobb house has exposed oak beams and doors. Accommodation in one twin, one double and two single bedrooms, all with washbasins, razor points and tea/coffee making facilities; bathroom. Non-smoking accommodation available. Home produce. Bed and Breakfast from £16; Evening Meals on request by prior arrangement. Reductions for children. Pets welcome. Outdoor swimming pool available.

EXETER. Mrs Mary Brown, Cottles Farm, Woodbury, Exeter EX5 1ED (Woodbury [01395] 232547). ♛ Working farm. A charming thatched farmhouse with comfortable accommodation. Our dairy farm is situated in 200 acres of peaceful countryside with wonderful views as far as Dartmoor. Four miles to Exmouth and the nearest sandy beach, and seven from Exeter. Dartmoor and Exmoor are within easy driving distance. One double, one twin bedrooms with washbasins and one family room en-suite, all with tea/coffee facilities. Large lounge/diner with TV. Children welcome; cot and high chair provided. Access to rooms anytime. Bed and Breakfast from £15 per night. Non-smoking accommodation available. Open all year. Reductions for children aged 11 and under.

COTTLES FARM

EXETER. Mr Chris Morris, Clock Tower Hotel, 16 New North Road, Exeter EX4 4HF (01392 424545; Fax: 01392 218445). ♛♛ The greatest care and comfort offered by caring resident proprietors of this Grade II Listed historically interesting city centre hotel with its award winning patio/garden and the modern facilities expected of larger hotels at a fraction of their cost. En suite rooms with baths and Satellite TV. Licensed bar. All major credit cards accepted. Bed and Breakfast rates start from £12.50 per person per night. Send for colour brochure with details of free holiday insurance

EXETER. Mrs Sally Glanvill, Rydon Farm, Woodbury, Exeter EX5 1LB (Woodbury [01395] 232341).

Working farm. Come, relax and enjoy yourself in our lovely 16th century Devon longhouse. We offer a warm and friendly family welcome at this peaceful dairy farm. Three miles from M5 Junction 30 on B3179. Ideally situated for exploring the coast, moors and the historic city of Exeter. Only 10 minutes' drive from the coast. Inglenook fireplace and oak beams. All bedrooms have central heating, private or en suite bathrooms, hair dryers and tea/coffee making facilities. One room with romantic four-poster. A traditional farmhouse breakfast is served with our own free range eggs and there are several excellent pubs and restaurants close by. Pets by arrangement. Farm Holiday Bureau member. As featured in the "Daily Mail". Open all year. Colour brochure available. Bed and Breakfast from £16 to £22.

EXMOOR. Mrs Jane Jeyes, Winsley, Brayford, Barnstaple EX32 7QW (01598 710388). "Far from the maddening crowd" — Winsley farmhouse is set on a hillside overlooking a wooded valley. This recently built house, set in beautiful scenic countryside just within the Exmoor National Park, incorporates many traditional features and offers comfortable centrally heated accommodation including lounge with colour TV; separate dining room; en suite double bedroom and twin bedroom with washbasin. An excellent place to relax and enjoy the countryside, especially for those who like walking as the Tarka Trail runs past the door. A short walk will show breathtaking views to Hartland and Clovelly, to Dartmoor and to Dunkery Beacon. The location is central for visiting many areas of interest — Barnstaple, the main centre for North Devon, is 10 miles, Lynton 15 miles, South Molton nine miles. Bed and Breakfast from £18; Bed, Breakfast and Evening Meal from £27. Weekend breaks or weekly terms available.

EXMOUTH. Mrs J. Hallett, Gulliford Farm, Lympstone, Near Exmouth EX8 5AQ (Topsham [01392] 873067). You are assured of a warm welcome to our 16th century farmhouse with its spacious rooms and beautiful garden with sun terrace, lawns, tennis court and swimming pool. This working farm stands in the beautiful Exe Valley only a short distance from the many beaches. One family suite, two double or family rooms, one single room, most with washbasin and tea-making facilities. Lounge with colour TV and inglenook fireplace, diningroom with separate tables. Ample parking. There is access to rooms at all times. A full English breakfast is served and there are many delightful inns and restaurants to provide your evening meal. Terms for Bed and Breakfast are from £18 per person per night. **We also have two delightful self catering cottages. From £100 to £300 plus VAT.**

PLEASE SEND A STAMPED ADDRESSED ENVELOPE WITH ENQUIRIES

HOLSWORTHY. Mrs Linda Cole, The Barton, Pancrasweek, Holsworthy EX22 7JT (01288 381315).

Standing in a peaceful position just off the A3072, half a mile from Devon/Cornwall Border. Six miles from Cornish Coast with beautiful beaches and famous Clovelly. The 200 acre working dairy farm has a 16th century farmhouse with three bedrooms for visitors, two double and one twin rooms with en suite or private facilities. Games room, lounge with TV and separate dining room. Traditional farmhouse cooking with home grown produce. Tea making facilities in rooms. Children's play area in garden. Bed and Breakfast from £13; Evening Meals available. Open Easter to September. Brochure on request.

HONITON. Mrs Elizabeth Tucker, Lower Luxton Farm, Upottery, Honiton EX14 9PB (01823 601269). Working farm.

Get away from the toil of everyday life and come to Lower Luxton Farm where a warm welcome awaits you in an area of outstanding natural beauty. Set overlooking peaceful Otter Valley facing south, this olde worlde farmhouse, fully modernised but retaining its charm, is on 140 acres of farmland keeping usual animals and pets to make it a real farm. Carp fishing on site included in terms. Peaceful walks. Ideal base for touring. Several places of interest in area. Coast 14 miles; village inn one mile. Good home cooking assured using fresh farm produce (four-course breakfasts and dinners) — including sweets topped with Devon cream; bedtime beverages with biscuits included. Family, double or twin rooms available with washbasins and razor points. Tea making facilities. Children welcome at reduced rates. Snooker table and darts available for guests. Mid-week bookings and reductions early and late in season. Pets welcome. Terms from £105 for six Evening Dinners and weekly Bed and Breakfast, £13 Bed and Breakfast nightly. SAE for brochure and terms. Open all year.

ILFRACOMBE. Mrs E.A. Barleycorn, Epchris Hotel, Torrs Park, Ilfracombe EX34 8AZ (01271 862751).

A comfortable small hotel with lovely grounds and views in a peaceful setting in Ilfracombe. Perfect for families in high season and for those looking for peaceful walks and touring, all year. Yards from the footpath to the Torrs Walks over National Trust coastline, yet only a short walk to the famous Tunnels Beaches, town centre and seafront. We have a heated swimming pool and paddling pool, putting green, games chalet and a cheerful bar and comfy residents' lounge. All rooms have tea/coffee making facilities, TV and are en suite except one room which has private facilities. Bed and Breakfast from £15 to £18. Brochure available, please telephone.

ILFRACOMBE. Michael and Lynda Hunt, Sunnymeade Country House Hotel, Dean Cross, West Down, Ilfracombe EX34 8NT (01271 863668).

Approved. AA QQQ. A charming country house hotel in its own large gardens set in the rolling Devon countryside. Every effort is made to ensure that guests feel welcome and relaxed from the moment they arrive, a feeling which is enhanced by the standard of food and accommodation. Most of the 10 pretty bedrooms are en suite and all have tea-making facilities, colour TV, phones and radios; some of the rooms are on the ground floor. Fresh local ingredients are used in the traditional English cooking which has a regional flavour. On the menu there is always a vegetarian choice and any special diets can be accommodated. Sunnymeade is close to Woolacombe, Exmoor and Ilfracombe. Access and Visa accepted. Bed and Breakfast from £16.50 daily; Dinner, Bed and Breakfast from £149 weekly. Open all year.

IVYBRIDGE. Mr and Mrs D. Johns, Hillhead Farm, Ugborough, Ivybridge PL21 0HQ (01752 892674). Working farm, join in. Comfortable accommodation and good home-produced food. Busy farm with plenty to see. Beautiful views of the rolling Devonshire countryside. Within walking distance of Dartmoor. Choice of beaches within 10 miles. Nearby towns of interest include Plymouth (15 miles approximately), Totnes, Kingsbridge and Salcombe. Pony trekking and golf available in the area. Bed and Breakfast — £14 per night; Bed, Breakfast and Evening Meal £21 per night. Reduced rates for over two nights and for children — cot, baby equipment available. One double bedroom with TV, one double with washbasin, one twin with washbasin and one bunk bedded room; tea/coffee making facilities in all rooms. Guests' private sittingroom with woodburning stove and TV; also private bathroom and separate toilet. Log fire in diningroom. Full central heating throughout. Non-smoking rooms available. Open all year. From A38 at Wrangaton Cross, turn left to Ermington A3121, turn right at first crossroads (Venn Cross signposted Ugborough), across next crossroads, continue for three-quarters of a mile to Hillhead Cross, turn left — farm 75 yards on left. ETB Listed.

IVYBRIDGE. Pat Stephens, Venn Farm, Ugborough, Ivybridge PL21 0PE (01364 73240). *Commended.* Venn Farm is situated in a peaceful position in the South Hams. We are a busy working farm and have always encouraged our guests to help on the farm — this is especially popular with children. We are near Dartmoor and many sandy beaches. Carve your own roast is a favourite here and many come back for more! Gardens are expansive, we are bordered by streams and a wild garden has been added recently. Two family rooms en-suite and a two-bedroomed garden cottage also en suite available. Send for brochure for more details.

IVYBRIDGE. Mrs Paula Salter, Strashleigh Farm, Ivybridge PL21 9JP (01752 892226). Working farm. Enjoy a relaxing holiday in a friendly atmosphere. Strashleigh is a working farm set between Dartmoor and Bigbury Bay. Easily accessible, it is a perfect base for touring, city entertainment, horse riding, golf and many other attractions. The farm has an interesting history. The house has comfortable, spacious rooms and wide views of the rolling countryside. If you are interested we will be pleased to show you the animals. Children welcome. Two double and one twin rooms, all with washbasins and tea making facilities. Non-smoking accommodation available. Cot available. Lounge with colour TV. ETB Listed, Commended; Member of FHB. Self catering accommodation (3 Keys Approved) also available. Brochure.

IVYBRIDGE near. Mrs Susan Winzer, "The Bungalow", Marridge Farm, Ugborough, Near Ivybridge PL21 0HR (01548 821560). Working farm. Marridge Farm is a traditional family run dairy farm with its own drive, completely off the main road, and situated in the heart of the peaceful South Hams countryside. Near Dartmoor and local unspoilt sandy beaches. A new bungalow, built in the old orchard setting with beautiful garden and meadow views. One double with washbasin and one en-suite family room. Good home cooked food, cream and fresh home grown vegetables. Children welcome — cot, high chair and babysitting available. Bed and Breakfast from £14 daily; optional Evening Meal extra. Open all year. A379 turnoff from the main A38 Exeter to Plymouth road.

See also Colour Display Advertisement **KINGSBRIDGE near. Mr and Mrs C.M. Davies, Maelcombe House, East Prawle, Near Kingsbridge TQ7 2DA (01548 511300). Working farm.** This small coastal working farm nestles beneath wooded cliffs overlooking Lannacombe Bay. The beach is one minute from the comfortable farmhouse which is nearly the most southerly in Devon. Guests have a choice of family, double or single rooms. Food is excellent — much being produced on the farm, and freshly caught seafood is a speciality. There is a lot to do — fishing, bathing, spectacular walking, exploring, climbing, boating, tennis or just relaxing in the gardens. Prices from £104.50 per week for Bed and Breakfast or £149.50 for Bed, Breakfast and Evening Meal, with special reductions for children. Also two self-catering flats to sleep six, and limited camping facilities are provided. Telephone or write for colour brochure.

KINGSBRIDGE. Nikki and Philip Higgin, Karrageen, Bolberry, Malborough, Kingsbridge TQ7 3EN (01548 561230; Fax: 01548 560192). Karrageen is an elegant country family house with superb views over Bigbury Bay and surrounded by National Trust coastline walks. The setting is very peaceful and relaxing yet only three and a half miles from Salcombe with its excellent boating and sailing facilities and one mile from the beaches at the old fishing village of Hope Cove. Very comfortable accommodation in one three-bedded and one double rooms with washbasin and one single room, all with tea/coffee making facilities and a colour TV. Comfortable lounge with colour TV, two bathrooms, spacious diningroom, conservatory, patios and gardens. Delicious breakfasts. Evening Meal by arrangement. Non-smoking. Regret no pets. Open Easter to October. Brochure with terms available.

KINGSBRIDGE. Mrs B. Kelly, Blackwell Park, Loddiswell, Kingsbridge TQ7 4EA (01548 821230). ♛♛ Blackwell Park is a 17th century farmhouse situated five miles from Kingsbridge and two miles from Loddiswell. Many beaches within easy reach, also Dartmoor, Plymouth, Torbay and Dartmouth. Seven bedrooms for guests, all with washbasins and tea-making facilities, some en suite. Separate tables in diningroom; lounge with colour TV. Large games room with darts, snooker, skittles etc. Garden with plenty of grass for games adjoining 54 acres of woodland/ nature reserve. Large car parking area. Ample food with choice of menu. Help yourself to tea and coffee at any time. Fire Certificate. Children and pets especially welcome. Baby-sitting. Open all year round for Bed, Breakfast and Evening Meal. Reduced rates out of season.

KINGSBRIDGE. Anne Rossiter, Burton Farm, Galmpton, Kingsbridge TQ7 3EY (Kingsbridge [01548] 561210). ♛♛ *Highly Commended.* **Working farm, join in.** Working farm in South Huish Valley, one mile from the fishing village of Hope Cove, three miles from famous sailing haunt of Salcombe. Walking, beaches, sailing, windsurfing, bathing, diving, fishing, horse-riding — facilities for all in this area. We have a dairy herd and three flocks of pedigree sheep. Guests are welcome to take part in farm activities when appropriate. Traditional farmhouse cooking and home produce. Four-course Dinner, Bed and Breakfast. Access to rooms at all times. Tea/coffee making and washbasins in rooms, all of which have private facilities, some en-suite. Games room. No smoking. Open all year, except Christmas. Warm welcome assured. Small functions catered for. Self-catering also available. Dogs by arrangement. Details and terms on request.

KINGSBRIDGE. Yvonne Helps, Hillside, Ashford, Kingsbridge TQ7 4NB (Kingsbridge [01548] 550752). Character house set in acre of orchard garden surrounded by lovely countryside, in a quiet hamlet just off the A379 Plymouth to Kingsbridge road. Superb beaches and sandy coves nearby. Dartmoor 20 minutes' drive. Very comfortable accommodation with washbasins, shaver points, tea/coffee making facilities in all bedrooms. Two bathrooms. Colour TV in lounge. Diningroom with separate tables. Car parking. Visitors find a friendly, relaxed atmosphere with own keys. Full central heating. Bed and full English Breakfast from £14; Evening Meal optional. Open all year. Booking any day of the week. Write or phone for brochure.

KINGSBRIDGE near. Mrs L.M. Smith, Yeo Farm, Topsham Bridge, Woodleigh, Near Kingsbridge TQ7 4DR (Kingsbridge [01548] 550586). Working farm. ETB registered. Beautiful farmhouse tastefully renovated to high standard of comfort, nestling in Avon Valley, bounded by river with one mile of salmon and sea trout single bank fishing lying within property boundary. Behind and to the north of the house are woods rich in bird and animal life. Ideal situation for bird watching and walking; beaches and Dartmoor within 15 minutes. Accommodation comprises two double, one family bedrooms; two bathrooms, three toilets. Sittingroom, large colour TV, diningroom. Central heating and log fires. Children welcome at reduced rates, babysitting available. Pets accepted at small charge. Car essential — parking. Bed and Breakfast; Dinner optional. Prices on request.

KINGSBRIDGE near. Mrs M. Newsham, Marsh Mills, Aveton Gifford, Near Kingsbridge TQ7 4JW (Kingsbridge [01548] 550549). Former Mill House, overlooking the River Avon, with gardens, mill leat and duck pond. Small farm with friendly animals. Peaceful and secluded, just off A379. Kingsbridge four miles, Plymouth 17 miles, Bigbury and Bantham, beautiful beaches nearby, or enjoy a walk along our unspoilt river estuary. Salcombe seven miles, Dartmoor eight miles. A warm welcome awaits our guests, who have access to the house at any time. Bedrooms have washbasins, tea/coffee making and room heaters. Guest bathroom, WC; lounge/dining room with colour TV. Car essential, ample parking. Bed and Breakfast from £13 per person. SAE for brochure, or telephone.

LYNTON. Don and Jenny Bowman, Gable Lodge Hotel, Lee Road, Lynton EX35 6BS (Tel & Fax: 01598 752367). 👑👑👑 You can be sure of a warm welcome at this elegant Victorian hotel situated in a level part of Lynton. Nestling at the foot of Hollerday Hill with views over Countisbury Hill, the East Lyn Valley and Exmoor National Park. Comfortable and pretty bedrooms, both standard and en suite. Family, double and twin rooms, all with TV, beverage facilities and central heating. The cosy lounge is warmed by an open fire in winter. Car parking at rear. Bed and Breakfast from £16; Evening Meals are available if required. Special offers for out of season Short Breaks.

LYNTON. Waterloo House Hotel, Lydiate Lane, Lynton EX35 6AJ (01598 753391). The Waterloo House Hotel is a delightful Georgian building combining the spirit of the early 19th century — in which it has its origins — with all the comforts of the present day. Historically one of the oldest, original lodging houses in all of Lynton, its renovations and exquisite decor have created a unique, gracious and warmly welcoming hotel. Quietly situated in the heart of "olde" Lynton, Waterloo House is host to those who wish to enjoy the variety of pursuits which the area can offer. Discover the tranquil beauty at Watersmeet or marvel at the famous Valley of the Rocks. Whether walking, touring, fishing, stalking, bird watching or simply enjoying the opportunity for total relaxation, a welcome awaits you.

LYNTON. Mr Alan Wayman, The Turret, 33 Lee Road, Lynton EX35 6BS (01598 753284). 👑👑 A delightful family run Victorian guest house situated in the centre of this picturesque village ideal for exploring Exmoor and its magnificent coastline. All of our rooms have colour TV and beverage making facilities. Most are en suite. Superb home cooking, vegetarians catered for. Children and pets welcome. Licensed. Open all year. Bed and Breakfast from £15 to £20; Evening Meal £11. Reduction for Short Breaks and weekly bookings. Telephone for a free brochure.

INGLESIDE HOTEL

Lynton, North Devon EX35 6HW Tel: 01598 752223

Ingleside, a family run AA/RAC hotel in premier position. High standards of accommodation, food and wine assured. All rooms ensuite, colour TV, tea/coffee makers. Safe car park in hotel grounds. Lynton is the perfect centre to enjoy the magnificent beauty of Exmoor's coast, cliffs, rivers and countryside, whether walking, strolling or motoring. Brochure with sample menus and information sheet of local and surrounding area gladly sent.

Mr & Mrs C. S. Horn. B&B from £22 p.d. (£140 p.w.) Dinner £12.

LYNTON. Ben and Jane Bennett, Victoria Lodge, Lee Road, Lynton EX35 6BS (Lynton [01598] 753203). *Highly Commended.* Elegant Victorian, family-run, non-smoking hotel, RAC Highly Acclaimed and AA Premier Selected for its comfort, hospitality and outstanding cuisine. All bedrooms are en suite and beautifully decorated, with colour TV and beverage making facilities; some are de-luxe four-poster rooms. Dine by candlelight in our elegant dining room and enjoy our four-course dinner which combines an imaginative blend of English and Continental cuisine, complemented by fine wines. Victoria Lodge is ideally situated for exploring Exmoor and its spectacular coastline. Full central heating and private car park. Open all year. Bed and Breakfast £18 to £30, Dinner £14. Special tariff for weekly bookings and Short Breaks. Children welcome. Please send or telephone for free brochure.

LYNTON. Mr and Mrs B. Peacock, Seawood Hotel, North Walk, Lynton EX35 6HJ (Lynton [01598] 752272). *Commended.* Seawood Hotel is set in its own grounds overlooking the sea with breathtaking views of Lynmouth Bay and Exmoor. The Peacock family make guests very welcome in their charming old-world house. Five-course dinners with imaginative home cooking, for which great praise is received. Both lounges, diningroom and all bedrooms enjoy sea views. The latter all have en-suite bathroom and/or shower/WC, colour TV and tea/coffee making facilities. Four-posters are also available. Full central heating. Residential licence. Pets welcome. Terms from £230 weekly, daily rates available. Colour brochure on request. Open March to November. RAC one star. Special award for Hospitality, Service and Comfort. AA one star.

MODBURY. Mrs A. Rogers, Weeke Farm, Modbury, Near Ivybridge PL21 0TT (01548 830219). This family-run dairy and beef farm set in a picturesque valley one mile from Modbury offers comfortable farmhouse accommodation with central heating. Guests breakfast in the conservatory overlooking peaceful scenic views. Lounge with colour TV for guests' use. One double bedroom and one family bedroom with tea/coffee making facilities. Children welcome, cot available. Garden and parking. We are ideally situated for touring Dartmoor and the South Hams, close to beaches, National Shire Horse Centre; fishing and riding nearby. Bed and Breakfast from £12. Reductions for stays over three nights. Evening Meal if required. Plenty of good local eating places can be recommended. ETB Listed.

MORETONHAMPSTEAD. Mrs T.M. Merchant, Great Sloncombe Farm, Moretonhampstead TQ13 8QF (01647 440595). *Highly Commended.* **Working farm.** Share the magic of Dartmoor all year round while staying in our lovely 13th century farmhouse full of interesting historical features. A working dairy farm set amongst peaceful meadows and woodland abundant in wild flowers and animals, including badgers, foxes, deer and buzzards. A welcoming and informal place to relax and explore the moors and Devon countryside. Comfortable double and twin rooms with en suite facilities, TV, central heating and coffee/tea making facilities. Delicious Devonshire suppers and breakfasts with new baked bread. Open all year. No smoking. Farm Holiday Bureau member.

MORTEHOE. Roger and Dena Sells, Lundy House Hotel, Mortehoe, Woolacombe EX34 7DZ (Woolacombe [01271] 870372). ♛♛♛ *Commended.* Small friendly Hotel spectacularly situated on the cliff side with gardens adjoining the coastal path, access to secluded beach and magnificent sea views over Woolacombe Bay to Lundy Island. Traditional home from home cooking with vegetarian and special diets catered for, extensive selection of fine wines and comfortable well stocked licensed bar. Full gas centrally heated en-suite bedrooms. Satellite TV lounge and separate colour TV and video lounge for non-smokers. Ample car parking. National Trust land surrounding the hotel makes an excellent base for local award-winning beaches, walking, rambling, visiting local beauty spots or exploring Exmoor. Open February to October. Les Routiers Commended. Please write or telephone now for colour brochure, tariff and full details of Spring, Summer and Autumn Bargain Breaks. Discounts for children (six to 13 years) and Senior Citizens. Pets welcomed free of charge.

NEWTON ABBOT. Ms. Valerie Dean, Oakwood Farm, Luton Cross, Ideford, Newton Abbot TQ13 0BQ (01626 853226). Working farm, join in. Modern bungalow set on the level in the rolling Devon countryside, one mile from A380 and A30 two miles. We can offer you a choice of cosy single, double or family rooms, all with washbasins. We have downstairs rooms for those less mobile and colour TV if required. Non-smoking accommodation available. Close by there is golf, fishing, watersports at Teignmouth, Dawlish and Dartmoor. Qualified instructor can provide horse riding instruction and hacking on site. A full English breakfast is cooked on a wood fuelled range and eggs are from our own hens; vegetarians welcome. Children and pets welcome. Bed and Breakfast from £11 to £13.50.

NEWTON ABBOT. Mrs Mary Lloyd-Williams, Hooks Cottage, Bickington, Near Newton Abbot TQ12 6JS (01626 821312). The house is situated in 12 acres of woods and fields in a very quiet and picturesque setting. Lovely walks and an abundance of wildlife on the doorstep; relax by the swimming pool or enjoy the river that runs through the grounds. Torbay beaches only 20 minutes' drive away and Dartmoor much closer. Central for the many attractions the area has to offer. Family suite for guests comprising double bedded room, twin room and connecting bathroom; dining room; lounge, colour TV; tea making facilities. Excellent meals with fresh produce a speciality; cream tea on Saturday arrival. Children very welcome. Bed and Breakfast; Evening Meal available. SAE for brochure.

NEWTON ABBOT. Mrs G.A. Stone, Milton Farm, East Ogwell, Newton Abbot TQ12 6AT (Newton Abbot [01626] 54988). Homely accommodation in farm bungalow in pleasant village with good view of Dartmoor, two miles west of Newton Abbot. Village lies equal distance from Torbay and Dartmoor National Park, both about eight miles. Three golf courses nearby. Dairy farm with cows and calves. Five minutes' walk from bus; railway two miles. Parking. One double room with H & C, one twin bedded room. Bathroom with shower, separate WC. Lounge/diningroom. Sorry, no pets. Mostly fresh produce served. Terms on request. Evening Meal optional. Reduced rates for children. Closed November to April. Details with SAE. Mid-week bookings if required.

NEWTON ABBOT. Mrs M.R. Chitty, Bittons Guest House, Ipplepen, Newton Abbot TQ12 5TW (Ipplepen [01803] 812489). Delightfully situated Guest House offering every comfort, good food and personal attention. Ideal touring centre within easy reach of both sea and moorland. We offer all that you would expect to ensure a pleasant and happy holiday base: golf course one mile. Guest accommodation in three double, one family bedrooms, all with washbasins. Bathroom, two toilets. Guests' lounge and separate diningroom Central heating in all rooms. Children welcome, cot, high chair available, also reduced rates. Car essential — parking. Open all year for Bed and Breakfast from £15. Please write or telephone for further details.

NORTH TAWTON. Mrs Pam Jordan, Higher Nichols Nymett, North Tawton EX20 2BP (01837 82181). A warm welcome and friendly atmosphere await you in our 15th century thatched hall house with its wealth of beams and old world charm. Situated between Okehampton and Crediton, close to Dartmoor, ideal for touring Devon countryside and coast. Enjoy the moors with their lovely walks, good coarse and fly fishing or local sporting facilities just 10 minutes away. We have three bedrooms, one double and one twin together with a further double downstairs, all en suite and with tea making facilities and colour TV. Ample private parking. Bed and Breakfast from £16.50; optional Evening Meal available. Traditional cooking using garden produce.

OTTERY ST. MARY. Mrs E.A. Forth, Fluxton Farm Hotel, Ottery St. Mary EX11 1RJ (01404 812818). ♛♛♛ CAT LOVERS' PARADISE! Lovely 16th century farmhouse in beautiful Otter Valley, with two acre gardens including stream, trout pond and garden railway. Only four miles from beach at Sidmouth. Beamed candlelit diningroom; two lounges with colour TV, one non-smoking. Log fires, central heating; Teasmaids in all rooms, all double rooms en-suite. Large garden room, lily pond. Good home cooking our speciality, using all local fresh produce superbly cooked. Children welcome. Pets welcome free of charge. Parking. Licensed. Open at Christmas. AA listed. Terms from £200 per person per week for Dinner, Bed and Breakfast.

OTTERY ST. MARY near. Mrs J. Burrow, Claypitts Farm, East Hill, Ottery St. Mary EX11 1QD (01404 814599). ♛♛ Have a relaxing holiday on our mixed farm situated in the beautiful Otter Valley, one mile off the B3176 at Tipton St. John. Enjoy walks through woods and wonderful views, also many tourist attractions nearby. Sidmouth with its pebble and sand beaches only four and a half miles away. Excellent accommodation is offered in double room en-suite, also double and twin rooms with washbasins; guests' own bathroom and toilets. Tea/coffee facilities in all rooms. Beamed ceilings and central heating throughout. Massive lounge with log burner, colour TV; large diningroom serving good farmhouse cooking. Spacious garden to relax in, children's play area, many small animals and birds. Regret no pets or children under three years. Bed and Breakfast from £16 to £18; Evening Meal from £9 (optional).

PAIGNTON. St. Marguerite Guest House, The Riviera, Paignton TQ4 5EX (01803 556428). Why not relax with Cath and Maurice on the "English Riviera". Paignton is not just a summer resort, there are lots of things to do and see throughout the year including steam railway, firework displays, special events, carnivals and shows to suit all tastes. Our guest house is situated in a level residential part of Paignton and is within a few minutes' walk of the town centre, harbour, beach, Goodrington Sands and leisure centre. We have TV and tea making facilities in all rooms, provide good clean accommodation and home cooked food is served in pleasant surroundings. Come as a guest and leave as a friend.

PLYMOUTH. Mrs Margaret MacBean, Gabber Farm, Down Thomas, Plymouth PL9 0AW (Plymouth [01752] 862269). *Commended.* **Working farm, join in.** Come and join us on this 120 acre working farm in an area of outstanding natural beauty with lovely walks on the farm and coastline. It is ideally situated for touring and near the historic city of Plymouth. Good food and a warm welcome are assured with Bed and Breakfast or Bed, Breakfast and Evening Meal available. One double and one family room en suite, two twins and family room with washbasins. All have tea/coffee making facilities and clock radios. Iron, ironing board, hair dryer available. Open March to November. TV lounge, dining room. Fire Certificate. Bed and Breakfast from £15. Special rates for Senior Citizens and children. Brochure available on request.

PLYMOUTH near. Slade Barn and Netton Farm Holiday Cottages, Noss Mayo, Near Plymouth PL8 1HA (01752 872235). Coastal South Devon beside the beautiful Yealm estuary. Sandy Cherrington assures you of a warm welcome to Slade Barn. Only three bedrooms — one twin, one double and one with shower en suite. All rooms have central heating, TV/radio and hairdryers. Tea/coffee on request. Full English breakfast naturally! Lovely indoor pool, games room, tennis court and private gardens. Easy access to fabulous National Trust cliff walks; nearby sandy beaches, golf, fishing, riding. Ideal base for day trips to Cornwall or the Moors. Plenty of parking. Non smoking. Open all year. Bed and Breakfast from £15, Evening Meal £7.50. Tourist Board Listed "Commended". SPECIAL INTEREST: professional Reflexology/Aromatherapy Massage by appointment.

SALCOMBE. Mrs Madge Bullock, Pine Cottage, Froude Road, South Sands, Salcombe TQ8 8LH (Salcombe [0154-884] 2170). A comfortable detached cottage in wooded surroundings with beautiful sea views from all bedrooms; lounge, diningroom and sun terrace. Car preferable, but not essential — parking space provided. Log fires out of season — bedrooms with heaters. Safe, sandy beach within 100 yards for swimming, sailing, windsurfing, diving and fishing. Ideal countryside for walkers and visitors appreciative of wild life, with magnificent views of the estuary and English Channel. Other beaches and coves nearby. Children over three years welcome at reduced rates if sharing parents' room. Substantial cooked breakfast, pot of tea with biscuits early morning and afternoon from £15 inclusive — no extra charge. Bed and Breakfast only. Open from January to December. Reductions for Senior Citizens November to March. SAE, please.

SALCOMBE. Mrs M.E. Lonsdale, Fern Lodge, Hope Cove, Kingsbridge TQ7 3HF (Kingsbridge [01548] 561326). "Fern Lodge" is a detached guest house with colourful garden, flanked by palm trees. It is delightfully situated in Hope Cove, an uncommercialised fishing village with safe, sandy beaches, surrounded by National Trust land, offering beautiful cliff and country walks. The scenery is truly magnificent and totally unspoilt. Dartmoor is nearby, Totnes 19 miles, Dartmouth 21, Torbay 25 and Plymouth 23 miles. The eight bedrooms, most en-suite, have either a sea or landscape view (sea approximately 250 yards). Full central heating. Two lounges, one with colour TV. Diningroom. Beverage making facilities. Car parking. Children and pets welcome.

DEVON – LAND OF DOONE AND DRAKE

Exmoor is the setting of R.D. Blackmore's "Lorna Doone", and visitors today can still soak in the romantic atmosphere of Doone Valley where the outlaws lived, and Oare Church, near Lynmouth, the scene of Lorna's wedding. Devon's most famous son is undoubtedly Sir Francis Drake, born at Crowndale, near Tavistock. It was to Plymouth he returned after sailing round the world in 1580 and on Plymouth Hoe he reputedly finished his game of bowls before tackling the Spanish Armada in 1588.

SIDMOUTH. Mrs Kerstin Farmer, Higher Coombe Farm, Tipton St. John, Sidmouth EX10 0AX (Ottery St. Mary [01404] 813385). ♛ *Commended.* **Working farm.** Comfortable farmhouse accommodation, peacefully situated in the beautiful Otter Valley only four miles from Sidmouth seafront and the surrounding National Trust and Devon Heritage Coast. Half a mile off B3176, it is within easy reach of many beaches, ideal for touring all of East Devon, but also Exeter, Dartmoor and Exmoor. Enjoy the good, mainly home produced, farmhouse food, full English Breakfast and friendly relaxed atmosphere. Family, double and single bedrooms, all with washbasins, tea-making facilities and electric blankets, some with TVs. Guests' bathroom, toilet; diningroom and lounge with colour TV. Children very welcome with cot, high chair and babysitting available. Terms from £105 weekly for Bed and Breakfast (from £18 nightly), and from £165 weekly for Bed, Breakfast and Evening Meal.

SIDMOUTH. Mrs Betty F. Sage, Pinn Barton, Peak Hill, Sidmouth EX10 0NN (Sidmouth [01395] 514004). ♛♛ *Commended.* **Working farm.** Pinn Barton is a farm of 330 acres situated on the coast, two miles from Sidmouth, where there is a good choice of eating places. There are many safe bathing beaches nearby and lovely walks along the cliffs and around the farm. Pony trekking nearby. It is very peaceful, being just off the coast road, between Sidmouth and the village of Otterton. Pinn Barton has been highly recommended and you will be given a friendly welcome in comfortable surroundings, and a good farmhouse breakfast. All bedrooms have en-suite facilities and all have colour TV, central heating, tea/coffee making facilities, razor plugs and electric blankets for chilly nights. There is a diningroom and separate sittingroom for guests (with colour TV and a fire). Children are very welcome. Bed and Breakfast including bedtime drink from £18. Reductions for children sharing parents' room. Own keys provided. Open all year.

SIDMOUTH. Mrs B.I. Tucker, Goosemoor Farm, Newton Poppleford, Sidmouth EX10 0BL (01395 568279). Goosemoor Farmhouse is an old Devon Long House with bread oven in diningroom. The 25-acre mixed farm is on the Exeter/Lyme Regis bus route about four miles from the sea and has streams running through its meadows. Coarse fishing available. There are many delightful walks in country lanes or over Woodberry and Alsbeare Commons. Guests may wander freely on the farmland. There are four double and one family rooms, all with washbasins; two bathrooms, three toilets; sitting room; dining room. Children over eight years welcome. Sorry, no pets. Open all year with log fires. Central heating throughout. Car not essential but there is parking. Bed and Breakfast from £10; Bed, Breakfast and Evening Meal from £15 daily, £105 weekly. Cream teas also available.

SIDMOUTH. Mrs Elizabeth Tancock, Lower Pinn Farm, Peak Hill, Sidmouth EX10 0NN (Sidmouth [01395] 513733). Working farm. Lower Pinn is in an area of outstanding natural beauty, two miles west of the unspoilt coastal resort of Sidmouth and one mile to the east of the pretty village of Otterton. Comfortable spacious rooms, two double/twin en-suite, one double with washbasin. All rooms have colour TV, hot drink facilities, electric blankets and central heating. Bathroom has bath and shower, separate toilet. Guests have their own keys and may return at all times throughout the day. Ample parking. Substantial breakfast served in dining room. Local inns and restaurants nearby provide excellent evening meals. Children and pets welcome. Open most of the year. Full details on request.

SOUTH MOLTON near. Mrs Cheryl Woollacott, Capitol Farm, Bishop's Nympton, Near South Molton EX36 4PH (01769 550435). Welcome to our warm and cosy atmosphere here at Capitol Farm. We are pleasantly situated, within easy reach of Exmoor, the coast and many other attractions. Accommodation provided in two bedrooms — one double and one twin-bedded; bathroom; separate lounge. We serve breakfasts of your choice and three-course dinners (optional). Since we limit the number of guests our visitors are assured of personal attention. Couples can relax and be spoilt or a family with children are most welcome; pony rides available, house cow to milk and eggs to find! Whether a short break or a longer stay we aim to make your holiday a happy one. Further details and terms on request.

SOUTH MOLTON near. Messrs H.J. Milton, Partridge Arms Farm, Yeo Mill, West Anstey, Near South Molton EX36 3NU (Anstey Mills [013984] 217). *Commended.* **Working farm, join in.** "Partridge Arms" Farm was, until 1909, a country inn, off the A361, four miles west of Dulverton on the Devon/Somerset border. Ideal for touring Exmoor National Park or the North Devon and West Somerset coastal resorts. Riding, trekking and fishing available. Guests enjoy the atmosphere of a one-time country inn now a guest house and family farm of over 200 acres. Pony on the farm for children's amusement. Open all year. Original four-poster bedroom, single, double and twin-bedded rooms, some of which have en-suite facilities; two sittingrooms and three diningrooms. Traditional farmhouse fare. Children welcome with reduced rates according to age; cot. Full Fire Certificate. Residential licence. Pets by arrangement. Car essential, ample parking. Farm Holiday Guide Diploma Winner. Les Routiers. Evening Dinner, Bed and Breakfast from £175 weekly; Bed and Breakfast from £122.50 weekly.

PLEASE ENCLOSE A STAMPED ADDRESSED ENVELOPE WITH ENQUIRIES

STOKE-IN-TEIGNHEAD (near Torquay). Mrs Rozamund Wilkinson, Deane Thatch Accommodation, Stoke-in-Teignhead, Near Torquay TQ12 4QU (Tel & Fax: 01626 873724). *Commended.* Bed and Breakfast is offered in Deane Thatch, a charming thatched Devonshire cob cottage, and thatched cob Linhay. Situated in a secluded rural spot enjoying uninterrupted views of farmland with an atmosphere of total tranquillity. Only half a mile from the coast and the village of Stoke-in-Teignhead. All rooms have private bathroom/shower or bidet, colour TV and tea/coffee making facilities. An added bonus is that Deane Thatch has its own supply of pure spring water, and the breakfast eggs come from our own hens. Barbecue available. The cottage is set in its own lovely one acre garden. Children welcome, reduced rates and babysitting available. Reductions also offered for stays of two or more nights. Open all year. Bed and Breakfast from £15. Please write to us for further information. Brittany Ferries recommended.

TAVISTOCK. Mrs B. Anning, Wringworthy Farm, Mary Tavy, Tavistock PL19 9LT (01822 810434). Working farm. This farm is set in a valley with the entrance on the A386. It is mentioned in the Domesday Book and the main part is Elizabethan. It has been modernised for comfort yet retains its old charms such as beams and flagstones. Log fires and a friendly greeting ensure guests of a warm welcome at Wringworthy. The guests have a lounge to themselves with TV; two double bedrooms and one family size with TV and tea/coffee making facilities; two bathrooms; diningroom. Children over two years are welcome and there is a cot and reduced rates. Sorry, no pets. Open from April to October. Car is essential and there is parking. Bed and Breakfast only, from £15. It is near the sea and there is fishing in Tamar and Tavy. Also near the moors; riding, walking and golfing. Tourist Board Listed/Approved. SAE please for further details.

TEIGN VALLEY. S. and G. Harrison-Crawford, Silver Birches, Teign Valley, Trusham, Newton Abbot TQ13 0NJ (Chudleigh [01626] 852172). A warm welcome awaits you at Silver Birches, a comfortable bungalow at the edge of Dartmoor. A secluded, relaxing spot with two acre garden running down to river. Only two miles from A38 on B3193. Exeter 14 miles, sea 12 miles. Car advisable. Ample parking. Excellent pubs and restaurants nearby. Good centre for fishing, bird watching, forest walks, golf, riding; 70 yards salmon/trout fishing free to residents. Centrally heated guest accommodation with separate entrance. Two double bedded rooms, one twin bedded room, all with own bath/shower, toilet. Guest lounge with colour TV. Diningroom, sun lounge overlooking river. Sorry, no children under eight. Terms including tea on arrival, full English Breakfast from £20 nightly, £140 weekly. Evening Meal optional. Open all year. ETB registered.

TIVERTON. Mrs Sylvia Hann, Great Bradley Farm, Withleigh, Tiverton EX16 8JL (01884 256946). *Highly Commended.* Lovely 16th century farmhouse, still retaining its original oak screens and cruck beams. 20 minutes from the M5 into glorious countryside, peace and quiet. We offer comfortable bedrooms (one twin, one double, each with private bathroom), the warmth of central heating and tea/coffee trays. The attractive lounge, with a fire on chilly evenings, overlooks the garden and fields beyond. We invite you to linger over a delicious breakfast, walk in the country, explore your surroundings, come back for dinner; or visit the pub nearby. Regret no young children or pets. No smoking in the house please. Bed and Breakfast from £17.50 to £19.50; Dinner £10. Weekly terms and brochure available.

TIVERTON near. Mrs F. A. Luxton, Thorne Farm, Stoodleigh, Near Tiverton EX16 9QG (Rackenford [0188-488] 232). Working farm, join in. Thorne Farm is quietly situated in Devon's rolling hills, overlooking wooded valleys with marvellous views. There is a suckler herd and sheep, and visitors are welcome to take an interest in the various jobs on the farm and walk on the 120 acres of farmland. Within easy reach of the Exmoor National Park and many local beauty spots. Food is a speciality, with fresh vegetables, milk, cream, meat and home-made bread. Two double (one with washbasin), one family bedrooms; bathroom, two toilets; sittingroom. Central heating. Reduced rates, cot and occasional babysitting. Sorry, no pets. Open April to October. Car essential; ample parking. Evening Meal, Bed and Breakfast from £120 (weekly); Bed and Breakfast from £14. Reduced rates for children under fourteen years. SAE, please.

TIVERTON. Mrs Barbara Pugsley, Hornhill Farm, Tiverton EX16 4PL (01884 253352). *Highly Commended.* Explore Devon from Hornhill where a friendly relaxed atmosphere awaits you. Old country house with superb views over Exe Valley. Double and twin bedrooms with private bathroom, heating, colour TV and tea/coffee making facilities; Victorian four-poster bed available. Ground floor room with en-suite shower. Excellent breakfasts. Comfortable drawing room for guests' use. Ample parking. No smoking please. 10 minutes from M5. Open March to October. Bed and Breakfast from £17.50; Evening Meal by arrangement. FHB Member. AA QQQQQ Premier Selected.

TIVERTON. Mrs Anne Boldry, Newhouse Farm, Oakford, Tiverton EX16 9JE (013985 347; from May 1995 01398 351347). *Commended.* Home-baked bread, delicious puddings, home-made pies, pates and preserves . . . the best of country cooking! Newhouse is a 17th century farmhouse tucked down our own stone lane in a peaceful valley. We have prettily and comfortably furnished twin and double rooms, all with private bathrooms and tea trays. We specialise in relaxed, friendly holidays with many guests returning. Newhouse Farm is a perfect base for touring and exploring Exmoor and Devon. We have been awarded QQQQ for Quality by the AA. Sorry, but we do not take children under 10 years or pets. Bed and Breakfast from £16 to £18; Dinner £10. Weekly Bed, Breakfast and Dinner £165 to £175.

TORBAY. Pamela & John Hill, Bowden Close Hotel, Teignmouth Road, Maidencombe TQ1 4TJ (01803 328029; Fax: 01803 327215). Delightful elevated family-run Victorian country house hotel midway between Torquay and Teignmouth with panoramic sea and coastal views. Friendly informal atmosphere with emphasis on comfort, courtesy and good food. Ideal for walking, touring or just relaxing. Close to Torbay attractions without the hustle and bustle. 15 en suite bedrooms with colour TV and tea making facilities. Central heating. Ample private parking. Peaceful garden. Open all year. Just 600 yards from sheltered beach. Bed, Breakfast and Evening Meal from £168 weekly, £26 daily; Bed and Breakfast only from £19 daily. Special children's rates. Well behaved pets welcome. Credit cards accepted. Please write or phone for further details.

TORQUAY. Mrs J. Grops, "Furzeacre", Teignmouth Road, Maidencombe, Torquay TA1 4SZ (01803 326436). Comfortable family home enjoying glorious sea and country views from all rooms. Situated midway between Torquay and Teignmouth and half a mile from Maidencombe beach, coastal footpath and country tavern for excellent meals and bar snacks. Accommodation comprises one double room with en suite shower and one twin-bedded room, both with clock radio, colour TV and tea/coffee making facilities. Central heating. Own key and choice of breakfast menu. Lovely gardens with ample parking. Bed and Breakfast only from £15 to £17 per person. Reductions for short breaks and weekly bookings.

See also Colour Display Advertisement **TORQUAY. Lindum Hotel, Abbey Road, Torquay TQ2 5NP (01803 292795).** A friendly, family-run licensed Hotel conveniently situated for beach, shops, theatre and harbour. Within 600 yards of Abbey Sands, Gardens and main shopping area. An established reputation for good food, first class service in a relaxed and friendly atmosphere. Children welcome. Bed and Breakfast from £15. AA and RAC Listed.

ONE FREE GUIDEBOOK per family when purchasing tickets to KENT'S CAVERN SHOWCAVES, Torquay, Devon. See our READERS' OFFER VOUCHERS for details.

TORQUAY. Mr and Mrs D.E. Anning, Craig Court Hotel, 10 Ash Hill Road, Torquay TQ1 3HZ (Torquay [01803] 294400). RAC Acclaimed. AA QQQ. Resident proprietors Joyce and David Anning supervise this Grade II listed building beautifully situated facing south in one of the most convenient positions in Torquay, although away from the main road, within easy walking distance of beaches, amusements and shops. Pleasant TV lounge and separate bar overlook a secluded garden in which there is a model railway. Diningroom has separate tables and there is a choice of menu at all meals. The hotel has six double bedrooms (three en-suite), two family rooms (both en-suite) and two single rooms, all with hand basins; three bathrooms and toilets. Children are welcome. Parking on the premises. Bed and Breakfast from £16.50 per person, Dinner, Bed and Breakfast from £154 per week. Reduced rates for children sharing parents' room. SAE for colour brochure.

See also Colour Display Advertisement **TORQUAY. Mike and Verna James, Hotel Fiesta, 50 St. Marychurch Road, Torquay TQ1 3JE (01803 292388/211497).** An elegant neo-Georgian Listed building standing in its own spacious grounds with large sunny garden. Ample free parking is available. All rooms have central heating, washbasins and tea/coffee making facilities. Comfortable colour TV lounge, attractive dining room serving excellent home cooked meals. Games room, pool table, children's play area; ironing facilities available. Fire Certificate. Children welcome. Early breakfast and packed lunches available on request. Amenitites near to the hotel include an 18 hole golf course, bowls, tennis putting, swimming pools, horse riding and water sports. Torquay town centre within easy reach with its fine beaches, shops and entertainments. Brochure and terms available.

TOTNES near. Mrs Sheree Palmer, Hatchlands Farm, Bluepost, Avonwick, Near Totnes TQ9 7LR (01364 72224). Working farm. A warm welcome awaits you at Hatchlands, a luxury farmhouse set in panoramic countryside with wonderful views in such a peaceful setting. Two guest bedrooms, each with double bed and bunks, both en suite with colour TV, radio, tea/coffee making facilities, clean towels and shaver points; two bathrooms; main lounge has woodburning fire in centre of the room, colour TV, video; the sun lounge has snooker table, golf practice machine, bar and fabulous views over the garden and fields. There are many excellent places to eat out, most welcome children. A hearty four-course English Breakfast is provided with optional dinner. On the farm there are opportunities for fishing, walking, bird watching, helping on the farm and clay pigeon shooting. Terms on request. Reductions for children and weekly and Winter bookings. Ring for brochure.

TOTNES. Jeannie and Peter Allnutt, The Old Forge at Totnes, Seymour Place, Totnes TQ9 5AY (01803 862174). *Highly Commended.* A charming 600 year old stone building, recently converted from blacksmith and wheelwright workshops and coach houses. Meet Peter Allnutt working in his traditional forge, complete with blacksmith's prison cell. We have our own bit of "rural England" close to the town centre. Very close to the River Dart steamer quay, shops and station (also steam train rides). Ideally situated for touring most of Devon — including Dartmoor and Torbay coasts. A day trip from Exeter, Plymouth and Cornwall. May to September — Elizabethan costume worn Tuesdays. Double, twin and family rooms, most en-suite/ground floor. Ground floor rooms suitable for disabled guests. All rooms have colour TV, beverage trays (fresh milk), colour co-ordinated Continental bedding, central heating. Licensed lounge and patio. No smoking indoors. Parking, walled gardens. Excellent choice of breakfast menu including vegetarian and special diets. Children welcome but sorry, no pets. Bed and Breakfast £20 per person; en suite facilities £25 per person. AA Selected (QQQQ) Award Cottage suite for two or four, suitable for disabled visitors.

1991/1992 WINNER SOUTH HAMS
FOR ALL SEASONS AWARD

TOTNES. Mrs Jan Finch, Island Farm, Moreleigh, Totnes TQ9 7SH (01548 821441). Working farm, join in. This working sheep/arable farm is ideally situated in the South Hams, enjoying a panoramic view extending to Torquay. Seven miles between Totnes/Kingsbridge/Dartmouth. Within easy reach of coast with windsurfing beaches and Dartmoor with many walks. There is a trout farm nearby and many old pubs. Open all year. A car is essential. Visitors may use lounge with TV. Children are welcome and a cot and high chair are provided. One double-bedded room, two twin-bedded rooms. Guests' own bathroom and toilet. Bed and Breakfast from £13. Children and Senior Citizens welcome at reduced rates.

TOTNES. Mrs Geraldine Nicholls, Berry Farm, Berry Pomeroy, Totnes TQ9 6LG (01803 863231). Mixed family working farm surrounded by lovely old cider orchards in village one and a half miles from historic Totnes with narrow streets, ancient buildings, castle and river trips, and a short distance to the beauty spots of Dartmoor. Clean, comfortable and good food guaranteed; warm, relaxed welcome. As featured in the *Daily Telegraph* Magazine. Spacious, well appointed bedrooms. Bathroom, shower, separate WC. Lounge with TV. Open all year. Bed and Breakfast from £13.50; Evening Meal from £8 by arrangement. Reductions for children. Good local eating places. No smoking in the house. ETB Listed "Commended".

TOTNES. Mrs Anne Barons, Charford Farm, Avonwick, Totnes TQ9 7LT (South Brent [013647] 3263). 🌸🌸 Working farm, join in. A warm and friendly welcome awaits you at this lovely old farmhouse on a 340-acre dairy and arable farm where visitors are free to roam. Centrally situated for coast, Dartmoor, Plymouth and Torbay; within easy reach of many tourist attractions. Family, double and twin-bedded rooms available with en suite facilities. Tea-making facilities. Diningroom and lounge with colour TV. Home from home comfort in a relaxed, informal atmosphere. Children are very welcome at reduced rates. Cot, high chair and babysitting available, also children's ponies. Open Easter to October for Bed and Breakfast from £14.00; Evening Meal £8.50. Weekly reductions available. Please telephone or write for terms and brochure.

WOOLACOMBE. Dave and Chris Ellis, Crossways Hotel, The Seafront, Woolacombe EX34 7DJ (Woolacombe [01271] 870395). 🌸🌸🌸 Cosy, family-run, licensed hotel, situated in one of the finest sea front positions in Woolacombe, overlooking the pretty Combesgate beach and Lundy Island and being surrounded by National Trust land. Bathing and surfing from hotel and ideally situated for golf, horse riding and beautiful walks. Menu choice for breakfast and evening dinner, and children's menu. Varied bar snacks available at lunchtime. All bedrooms individually refurbished to a high standard, many en suite and with fabulous sea views. Colour TV and tea/coffee making facilities in all rooms. Children half or Free. Pets welcome. Free on-site parking. AA/RAC one star, RAC Merit for Hospitality and Service. Why not find out why many of our guests return year after year?

RUSTIC DEVON

Inland from the coastal resorts lies the heart of Devon and the 365 square miles of Dartmoor National Park. Take time to explore the spectacular tors, hills and lakes, and watch out for the famous wild ponies. Picturesque rural villages reflect the unhurried pace of Devon life and there are traces everywhere of the Moor's rich heritage, dating back to the Bronze Age. In the north is Exmoor, one of Britain's smallest National Parks, ideal for rambling, pony trekking and bird watching.

DORSET

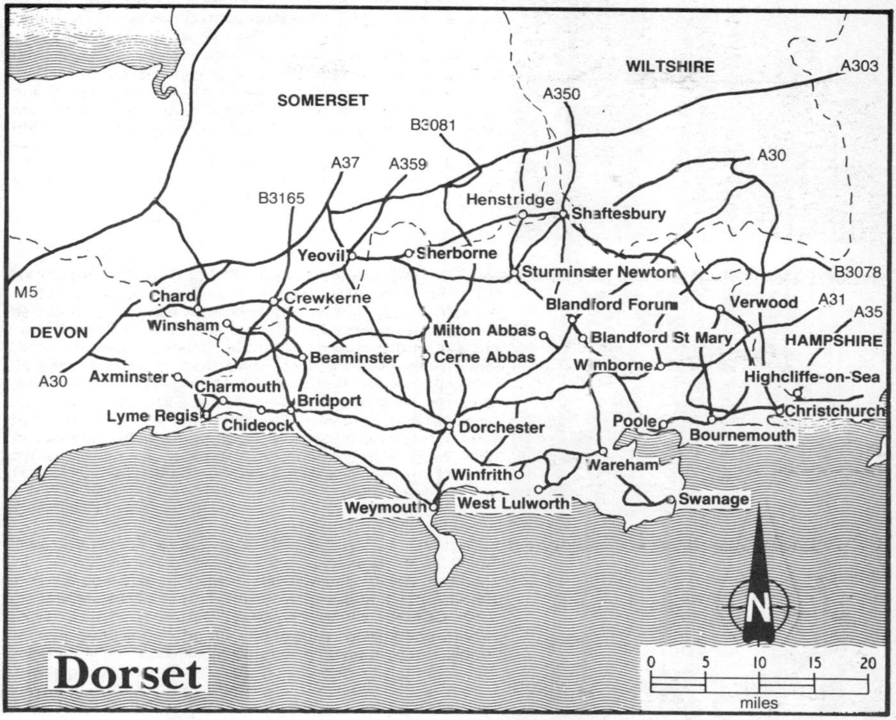

BEAMINSTER. Mrs A. Hasell, Kitwhistle Farm, Beaminster Down, Beaminster DT8 3SG (01308 862458). Kitwhistle Farm is a working dairy farm situated on the peaceful Beaminster Down. As you have your breakfast you can watch the cows amble out to their pasture. We are two miles from the small town of Beaminster with its many eating houses. The town is featured in many of Thomas Hardy's tales. Forde Abbey, Parnham House and Mapperton Gardens attract many visitors. Crewkerne and Bridport are six miles away, West Bay seven miles, Lyme Regis 14 miles and Crinkley Bottom (Cricket St Thomas) eight miles. Bed and Breakfast from £15 per adult with full English breakfast. You are assured of a warm welcome and personal attention at all times. Directions: from Beaminster Square take North Street to top of hill, turn right (signposted Maiden Newton), Kitwhistle Farm half a mile on right.

See also Colour Display Advertisement **BEAMINSTER. Mrs Jackie Spooncer, Lewesdon Farm, Stoke Abbot, Beaminster DT8 3JZ (Broadwindsor [01308] 868270).** Lewesdon Farm is situated in an area of outstanding natural beauty, five and a half miles from Bridport, close to the Heritage Coast. Free from noise and traffic, off a private road. Warm comfortable double room with en-suite shower. Tea-coffee making facilities and TV. Superb location for walking or just relaxing. NON-SMOKERS PLEASE. See also entry in Self Catering section.

FUN FOR ALL THE FAMILY IN DORSET

Brewers Quay, Weymouth; Deep Sea Adventure, Weymouth; Dinosaur Museum, Dorchester; Dinosaurland, Lyme Regis; Maiden Castle, Dorchester; Natural World, Poole Aquarium; Sea Life Centre, Weymouth; Upton Country Park, Poole; Waterfront Museum, Poole.

BLANDFORD FORUM. Mrs C.M. Old, Manor House Farm, Ibberton, Blandford Forum DT11 0EN (01258 817349). Working farm, dairy and sheep. Situated nine miles west of Blandford Forum. Small 16th century manor house, now a farmhouse, surrounded by large colourful garden in a quiet unspoilt village which at one time was given to Katherine Howard by Henry VIII. The oak beams and nail studded doors confirm its centuries-old past. Two double bedrooms (one with en suite facilities) and one twin-bedded room, both with tea-making facilities. Bathroom and toilet; lounge with TV, dining room with separate tables. Children welcome, cot and high chair provided. Bed and Breakfast from £12 to £15. Open all year. No evening meal. Good food at Crown Inn nearby. Self catering accommodation also available.

BLANDFORD FORUM. Mr and Mrs D.N. Cross, Gold Hill Organic Farm, Childe Okeford, Blandford DT11 8HB (01258 860293). Working farm, join in. 60 acres grass and horticulture in beautiful North Dorset countryside. Explore Hardy's country, National Trust houses and the Purbeck coast. Family and twin rooms, both with washbasins, razor points, TV and tea/coffee making facilities; two separate bathrooms; comfortable sittingroom with log fire. Non-smokers only. Breeding Shires, DIY livery, safe good hacking, own ponies welcome for long or short stays; coarse fishing; organic horticulture, harvesting help welcomed. Farmhouse offers Bed and Breakfast for long or short stays in friendly family atmosphere, no Evening Meal (sorry), but good inns within walking distance. Terms from £16 per night. Ample parking. Self catering annexe available, sleeps two/three.

BOURNEMOUTH. Mrs Annie Habgood, Northover Hotel, 10 Earle Road, Alum Chine, Bournemouth BH4 8JQ (Bournemouth [01202] 767349). OLD-FASHIONED COURTESY AWAITS YOU AT THE NORTHOVER HOTEL situated facing Alum Chine, 400 yards from sea and sandy beaches and only 20 minutes' walk from Bournemouth Pier. Near bus routes for town centre where there is superb shopping and all types of entertainment. The New Forest, Purbeck Hills and lovely Dorset and Hampshire countryside within easy reach. Choice of double, single or family rooms with double or twin beds, tea/coffee making facilities FREE; most rooms with en-suite facilities. Attractive lounge, colour TV; spacious diningroom serving varied and excellent food. Residential licence. Central heating. Under personal supervision of proprietor, the hotel is open all year including Christmas. Bed and Breakfast from £16; Dinner, Bed and Breakfast from £23. **STAY FOR 7 PAY FOR 6 DAYS.** Mid-week bookings accepted. Special rates for Senior Citizens early and late season. PRICES FOR 1995 SEASON REDUCED BY 10%. Children and pets welcome. Ample parking. Off season bargain breaks. Our aim is to make you want to return. AA/RAC listed. AWARDED FHG DIPLOMA 1988/89 — ONLY FIVE AWARDED TO HOTELS IN ENGLAND!

BRIDPORT. Mrs L.M. Hutchings, Dunster Farm, Broadoak, Bridport DT6 5NR (Bridport [01308] 424626). Working farm, join in. 17th century thatched farmhouse amidst beautiful, peaceful surroundings in the Marshwood Vale. Ideal touring centre for Lyme Regis, Charmouth and West Bay. Swimming, fishing, horse riding etc, five miles. The farm consists of dairy cows, calves, beef cattle, sheep and chickens. Guests are welcome to join in farm activities. One double and one family room both with tea/coffee making facilities; bathroom, toilet; sittingroom with TV, diningroom. Washbasins in all rooms. Open wood fire. Cot, high chair, babysitting. Car essential. Sorry, no pets. Open Easter to October. Dinner, Bed and Breakfast or Bed and Breakfast only. Food mostly home produced including own meat and fresh garden vegetables. SAE, please for terms. Prompt reply. Reductions for children.

PLEASE ENCLOSE A STAMPED ADDRESSED ENVELOPE WITH ENQUIRIES

FARM GUEST HOUSE

This farm/guest house, built in Victorian times, set in ten acres of pastures and woods, bordered by streams, lies in beautiful peaceful surroundings, only five miles from Charmouth's unspoilt beach with its store of fossils. The

house has a comfortable, relaxed and informal atmosphere and really good food is a speciality, including home made bread, jams, farm butter etc. The gardens provide fresh fruit and vegetables. Heated outdoor swimming pool. Car essential. Ample parking space provided. Six double and family rooms, most en-suite. Colour TV in all bedrooms. Comfortable lounge. Cots and high chairs provided. Children can play safely in fields and large indoor games room. Central heating, log fires. Evening Dinner, Bed and Breakfast. Tea/coffee making facilities in all rooms. Reductions for children. Pets welcomed. Riding nearby. Open all year. Special "off season" rates.

TERRY & TRICIA SHAKESHAFT, MARSHWOOD MANOR
Bridport, Dorset DT6 5NS
Tel: Broadwindsor (01308) 868442

TOURIST BOARD ♛♛♛ COMMENDED

AA LISTED

FOR THE MUTUAL GUIDANCE OF GUEST AND HOST

Every year literally thousands of holidays, short-breaks and overnight stops are arranged through our guides, the vast majority without any problems at all. In a handful of cases, however, difficulties do arise about bookings, which often could have been prevented from the outset.

It is important to remember that when accommodation has been booked, both parties — guests and hosts — have entered into a form of contract. We hope that the following points will provide helpful guidance.

GUESTS: When enquiring about accommodation, be as precise as possible. Give exact dates, numbers in your party and the ages of any children. State the number and type of rooms wanted and also what catering you require — bed and breakfast, full board, etc. Make sure that the position about evening meals is clear — and about pets, reductions for children or any other special points.

Read our reviews carefully to ensure that the proprietors you are going to contact can supply what you want. Ask for a letter confirming all arrangements, if possible.

If you have to cancel, do so as soon as possible. Proprietors do have the right to retain deposits and under certain circumstances to charge for cancelled holidays if adequate notice is not given and they cannot re-let the accommodation.

HOSTS: Give details about your facilities and about any special conditions. Explain your deposit system clearly and arrangements for cancellations, charges, etc, and whether or not your terms include VAT

If for any reason you are unable to fulfil an agreed booking without adequate notice, you may be under an obligation to arrange alternative suitable accommodation or to make some form of compensation.

While every effort is made to ensure accuracy, we regret that FHG Publications cannot accept responsibility for errors, omissions or misrepresentation in our entries or any consequences thereof. Prices in particular should be checked because we go to press early. We will follow up complaints but cannot act as arbiters or agents for either party.

BRIDPORT. Ann and Dan Walker MHCIMA, Britmead House, West Bay Road, Bridport DT6 4EG (01308 422941). ♛♛♛ *Commended.* AA QQQQ Selected. RAC Acclaimed. Guestaccom Good Room Award 1995. Delightful freshly cooked food, personal service and putting guests' comfort first means visitors return time after time. Situated between Bridport, West Bay harbour with its beaches/golf course/walks, Chesil Beach and the Dorset Coastal Path. Fully en suite rooms (one ground floor), all with colour TV, tea making facilities, hair dryers and mini bar. South facing lounge and dining room overlooking the garden. Optional table d'hôte dinner menu, incorporating local fish and produce. Licensed. Full central heating. Private parking. Dogs by arrangement. Children welcome. Reservations starting any day for any length of stay. Break rates all year. Weekly Bed and Breakfast from £105 to £140; Dinner, Bed and Breakfast from £189 to £220.50.

BRIDPORT near. Mrs Sue Norman, Frogmore Farm, Chideock, Bridport DT6 6HT (01308 456159). Working farm, join in. Set in the rolling hills of West Dorset, enjoying splendid sea views, our delightful 17th century farmhouse offers comfortable, friendly and relaxing accommodation. An ideal base from which to ramble the many coastal and country footpaths of the area (nearest beach Seatown one and a half miles) or tour by car the interesting places of Dorset and Devon. Some bedrooms with en-suite shower room. Cosy TV lounge, with wood fire, guests' diningroom and tea making facilities. Children and well behaved dogs welcome. Open all year, car essential. Bed and Breakfast (Evening Meal optional). Brochure and terms free on request.

CERNE ABBAS. Mrs V.I. Willis, "Lampert's Cottage", Sydling St. Nicholas, Cerne Abbas DT2 9NU (Cerne Abbas [01300] 341659). Bed and Breakfast in unique 16th century thatched cottage in unspoilt village. The cottage has fields around and is bounded, front and back, by chalk streams. Accommodation consists of three prettily furnished, double bedrooms with dormer windows, set under the eaves, and breakfast is served in the diningroom which has an enormous inglenook fireplace and original beams. The village, situated in countryside made famous by Thomas Hardy in his novels, is an excellent touring centre and beaches are 30 minutes' drive. West Dorset is ideal walking country with footpaths over chalk hills and through hidden valleys and is perfect for those wishing peace and quiet. Open all year. Terms on request.

CHARMOUTH. Mrs S.M. Johnson, Cardsmill Farm, Whitchurch Canonicorum, Bridport DT6 6RP (01297 489375). Working farm, join in. ♛♛ A Grade II Listed comfortable quiet farmhouse in picturesque Marshwood Vale, three miles from Charmouth. Ideal for beaches, fossil hunting, touring, walking and golf at Lyme Regis. See the animals, pets and crops on this 450 acre family farm. Walk to the village through the fields. Double and family rooms available with washbasins, shaver points, tea/coffee trays, cot, hairdryer, bathroom for guests' use only. Full central heating and double glazed windows throughout. Lounge with log fires, beams and colour TV; dining room with separate tables. Access at all times. English and varied breakfasts. Children and pets welcome. Babysitting. Ample parking. Large garden, picnic table and barbecue. Bed and Breakfast from £13.50 per person per night. Senior Citizens' and children's reductions. Open February to end November. Please phone or write for brochure. Also self catering farmhouse, sleeps up to 12, short or long stays, available all year.

HOLIDAY ACCOMMODATION Classification Schemes in England, Scotland and Wales

The National Tourist Boards for England, Scotland and Wales have agreed a common 'Crown Classification' scheme for **serviced (Board)** accommodation. All establishments are inspected regularly and are given a classification indicating their level of facilities and services.

There are six grades ranging from 'Listed' to 'Five Crowns ♛♛♛♛♛'. The higher the classification, the more facilities and services offered. Crown classification is a measure of *facilities* not *quality*. A common quality grading scheme grades the quality of establishments as 'Approved', 'Commended', 'Highly Commended' or 'Deluxe' according to the accommodation, welcome and service they provide.

For **Self-Catering**, holiday homes in England are awarded 'Keys' after inspection and can also be 'Approved', 'Commended', 'Highly Commended' or 'Deluxe' according to the facilities available. In Scotland the Crown scheme includes self-catering accommodation and Wales also has a voluntary inspection scheme for self-catering grading from '1 (Standard)' to '5 (Excellent)'.

Caravan and Camping Parks can participate in the British Holiday Parks grading scheme from 'Approved (✓)' to 'Excellent (✓ ✓ ✓ ✓ ✓)'. In addition, each National Tourist Board has an annual award for high-quality caravan accommodation: in England – Rose Awards; in Scotland – Thistle Commendations; in Wales – Dragon Awards.

When advertisers supply us with the information, FHG Publications show Crowns and other awards or gradings, including AA, RAC, Egon Ronay etc. We also award a small number of Farm Holiday Guide Diplomas every year, based on readers' recommendations.

CORFE CASTLE near. Mrs Gillian Hole, Bradle Farmhouse, Bradle, Corfe Castle, Wareham BH20 5NU (Corfe Castle [01929] 480712). *Commended.* **Working farm.** The farmhouse, built in 1862, is situated in the Purbeck Hills and lies in a valley between the villages of Kimmeridge and Church Knowle. The coast is two miles away with safe bathing and windsurfing on a selection of beaches, whilst the surrounding hills and cliffs offer spectacular views and walks. There is local pony trekking and evening entertainment in Bournemouth, Swanage and Wareham. A warm friendly atmosphere with good farmhouse cooking is assured on this 500-acre farm. Family/double and a twin room (one en suite); two bathrooms. All rooms have washbasins and tea-making facilities. Lounge with colour TV, separate diningroom. Open all year for Bed and Breakfast from £16, reductions for children. Evening Meals by arrangement with the local inn, with special weekly rate/children welcome. Apply for brochure.

DORCHESTER. Michael and Jane Deller, Churchview Guest House, Winterbourne Abbas, Near Dorchester DT2 9LS (01305 889296). This 300 year old AA QQQ Guesthouse is set in a small village five miles west of Dorchester and is noted for its warm, friendly hospitality and delicious home cooked food. Churchview makes an ideal touring base for Thomas Hardy country, set in a designated area of outstanding natural beauty. All rooms have full central heating and tea-making facilities, with some en-suite. We have two comfortable lounges, one reserved for non-smokers, a well stocked bar and attractive oak-beamed diningroom. Children and pets welcome. Parking. Bed and Breakfast from £18; four course Evening Meal, Bed and Breakfast from £28. Reductions for children.

DORCHESTER. Mrs Chris Walford, Rectory House, Fore Street, Evershot, Dorchester DT2 0JW (0193-583 273). *Highly Commended.* Lovely 18th century rectory in picturesque Hardy village of Evershot. Six delightfully appointed bedrooms all with en-suite bathrooms, colour TV and hospitality tray. Superb home cooking of traditional and some exotic dishes. Delicious breakfasts including freshly baked bread from the Evershot Bakery and locally made sausages. The village also has its own store and popular pubs. Melbury Estate adjoins the village where beautiful walks and scenery are plentiful. Facilities for fishing, riding and sailing nearby. Ideally located for visiting Bath, Exeter, Bournemouth, Lyme Regis and the coast. Weekly terms from £250.

Terms quoted in this publication may be subject to increase if rises in costs necessitate

DORCHESTER. Mrs Roffey, Coneygar, Turners Puddle, Dorchester DT2 7JA (01929 471375).

Beautiful small country house in six acres of land, lovely garden and setting. Seven miles from coast and beautifully situated in Thomas Hardy country. The accommodation is very comfortable and comprises two double twin-bedded rooms, with private bathrooms, tea making facilities and central heating; TV in one room. Children welcome; regret, no pets. Terms from £17.50 per person per night. All guests are made to feel at home.

DORCHESTER. Maiden Castle Farm, Dorchester DT2 9PR (Tel & Fax: 01305 262356).

Large Victorian farmhouse on a working family farm one mile from Dorchester on the A354 to Weymouth (seven miles), in the heart of Hardy Country; approximately two hours from London. The farmhouse enjoys magnificent views of Maiden Castle and the surrounding countryside. The accommodation comprises en suite bedrooms with central heating, TV and tea-making facilities; large comfortable lounge; log fire on chilly days and telephone for guests' use combine to offer comfort, peace and quiet — ideal for the perfect holiday. Children welcome, babysitting by arrangement. Pets welcome by arrangement. Open all year.

See also Colour Display Advertisement **LULWORTH COVE. Cromwell House Hotel, Lulworth Cove BH20 5RJ (01929 400253; Fax: 01929 400566).** Catriona and Alistair Miller welcome guests to their comfotable family-run Hotel, set in secluded gardens with spectacular sea views. Direct access to Dorset Coast Path. Heated swimming pool May to October. Accommodation in 14 double bedrooms, all en suite with tea/coffee facilities, radio, TV and telephone. Cottage annexe also available, 300 yards. Please write, or telephone/Fax, for further details.

LULWORTH COVE. Mr and Mrs J. Else, The Old Barn, West Lulworth, Wareham BH20 5RL (01929 400305).

The Old Barn is situated in a superb position with a glorious view of the rolling Dorset hills, yet only a few hundred yards from the famous beauty spot of Lulworth Cove. Choice of Bed and Breakfast and/or "Please Yourself" rooms (equipped for self-catering). Central heating. Fire Certificate. Large garden. Parking. Shops and sea nearby and wide choice of restaurants offering local specialities. Entertainment at Bournemouth (22 miles) and Weymouth (15 miles). Southern Tourist Board listed. Details on request with SAE, please.

LYME REGIS. Mr and Mrs C.S. Ansell, Providence House, Lyme Road, Uplyme, Lyme Regis DT7 3TH (01297 445704).

Set in the lovely village of Uplyme, one mile from Lyme Regis, our small Regency guest house has been beautifully renovated — we even have a Minstrels' Gallery! — and welcomes you as do we, Clem and Jean Ansell. The meals are special, the beds very comfortable and as some guests recently said "It's like being at home without the washing up". We have a small cat but your dog is welcome. There are always fresh flower arrangements around and part of our garden is upstairs where you are very welcome to sit and enjoy the sun. This is wonderful walking country. Cricket is played regularly in the village, and there are also tennis courts. All rooms are freshly decorated and are either en suite or have private facilities. Bed and Breafast from £15.50; four-course Dinner and coffee £7.50.

FHG PUBLICATIONS LIMITED publish a large range of well-known accommodation guides. We will be happy to send you details or you can use the order form at the back of this book.

LYME REGIS. Mrs S.G. Taylor, Buckland Farm, Raymonds Hill, Near Axminster EX13 5SZ (01297 33222). Smallholding of five acres, three miles from Lyme Regis and Charmouth. Children, Senior Citizens all welcome. Bed and Breakfast. Accommodation on ground floor. We are situated back off the A35 in quiet and unspoilt surroundings, ideal for guests to relax or stroll. Two family bedrooms, one double en suite and one twin-bedded room, all with TV, washbasins and tea/coffee making facilities. Lounge with colour TV and log fire if needed. Diningroom with separate tables. Bathroom, shower in bath, WC, plus separate WC. Plenty of good food with free range eggs. Cot and high chair available. Guests welcome to stay in if wet. Full English Breakfast served. Payphone. Pets welcome. Bed and Breakfast from £12. Friendly pub within two minutes' walk for evening meals. No smoking in bedrooms. Send SAE for further details.

LYME REGIS. Jenny and Ivan Harding, Coverdale Guest House, Woodmead Road, Lyme Regis DT7 3AB (01297 442882). ♛♛ AA Recommended QQ. Friendly, well established Guesthouse situated in a quiet residential area of Lyme Regis, a few minutes' walk from the sea and town centre. Fine views over Woodland Trust's land to rear and sea to front. Double, twin, family and single rooms (en suite available). Tea/coffee facilities all rooms. Comfortable TV lounge. Attractive dining room with separate tables. Good home cooking using own garden produce. Access to house all day. Private parking. No smoking please. Ideal base for exploring countryside and unspoilt scenic coastline on foot or by car. Walkers welcome — South Coast path/Liberty Trail close by. Bed and Breakfast from £12; Dinner optional. Weekly reductions. Write or phone for brochure.

POWERSTOCK. Mrs D.P. Read, The Old Station, Powerstock, Bridport DT6 3ST (01308 485301). Peacefully situated deep in the glorious Dorset countryside, one mile south east of Powerstock, in two and a half acres of garden, this former railway station enjoys beautiful views. Conveniently situated for drives into neighbouring counties; many rural walks; can be reached by public transport. Two double bedrooms, one single, all with washbasins and tea-making facilities; bathroom, second toilet; central heating. Daytime access. Off road parking; tennis, unheated swimming pool, fun golf. Hearty English breakfast prettily served (vegetarian breakfast by previous arrangement). Evening meals available locally. Open March through October, from £13. No pets. Badger watching possible most evenings from house. SAE, please, for details.

SHAFTESBURY. Mrs G. Gosney, Kington Manor Farm, Church Hill, Kington Magna, Near Gillingham SP8 5EG (01747 838371). Working farm. Attractive farmhouse situated in a quiet, pretty village, with splendid views over the picturesque Blackmore Vale. The village lies one mile off A30 between the historic towns of Shaftesbury and Sherborne; Stourhead National Trust house and gardens and stately home of Longleat and Safari Park nearby. Bath 45 minutes' drive. Spacious and comfortable accommodation comprising one double/family room with adjoining private shower room with WC, one twin-bedded room with/without private bathroom. Tea/coffee making facilities. Visitors' dining room and lounge with TV. Bed and hearty breakfast £15 per person per night. Reductions for children. Excellent pub food nearby or evening meals on request.

SHERBORNE. Mrs Pauline Tizzard, Venn Farm, Milborne Port, Sherborne DT9 5RA (01963 250598). The perfect stop when travelling, easy to find on main A30, three miles east of historic castles and abbey town of Sherborne, 30 minutes' drive to coast. Our 200 acre working dairy farm is situated in beautiful wooded parkland within walking distance of local village inn. Attractively furnished accommodation includes one twin, one double and one family rooms, all with washbasin, colour TV and tea/coffee making facilities; bathroom equipped with shower and separate WC; guests' lounge with log fire. Full central heating. Children welcome, cot available. Bed and Breakfast from £13. Reductions for children. Open all year. AA QQ Listed.

SHERBORNE. Mrs J. Mayo, Almshouse Farm, Hermitage, Sherborne DT9 6HA (01963 210296).

Working farm, join in. This charming old farmhouse was a monastery during the 16th century, restored in 1849 and is now a listed building. A family-run working dairy farm surrounded by 140 acres overlooking the Blackmoor Vale, just one mile off A352. Accommodation is in three comfortable rooms with tea/coffee making facilities. Diningroom with inglenook fireplace, lounge with colour TV, for guests' use at all times. Also garden and lawn. Plenty of reading material and local information provided for this ideal touring area. Bed and Breakfast from £15. Excellent evening meals in all local inns nearby. Situated six miles from Sherborne with its beautiful Abbey and Castle. SAE for further details.

SHIPTON GORGE. Mrs Margaret Tewson, Icen Farm, Shipton Gorge, Near Bridport DT6 4PW (01308 897376).

A small sheep farm situated in beautiful unspoilt countryside with breathtaking views in all directions. Ideal for walkers or anyone who wants to relax in peaceful surroundings. Just four miles to Bridport and the busy little harbour of West Bay and 12 miles to the famous county town of Dorchester, this makes a perfect base for a country lovers' holiday. Walk across our fields to the local inn where really good food at sensible prices is always available. One double room with en-suite facilities, tea/coffee making equipment and colour TV. SAE, or telephone for details. Bed and Breakfast only from £12 to £14.

STURMINSTER NEWTON. Mrs Sheila Martin, Moorcourt Farm, Moorside, Marnhull, Sturminster Newton DT10 1HH (Marnhull [01258] 820271).

Working farm. Marnhull is situated four miles from Sturminster Newton, five from Shaftesbury. Central for touring; Longleat, New Forest, coast within 28 miles. We are a modern dairy farm of 120 acres lying in the Blackmore Vale in the midst of Hardy country. Visitors will enjoy wandering around meeting Sunny the little white donkey and his friend Buster the big horse, watching the milking and farm activities or just lazing in our large gardens. The accommodation comprises one bedroom with twin beds and two with double beds; all are adjacent, colour co-ordinated and have washbasins, tea/coffee making facilities and biscuits, colour TV. Flowers, plants; keys to bedrooms. There is a shower room and toilet next to these bedrooms, and a further toilet and bathroom downstairs. There is a sittingroom with woodburner fire and a dining room. Enormous breakfast menu. Children over 10 years welcome, but sorry no pets. A car is essential to explore our lovely Dorset countryside and coastline. There is ample parking. There are two public houses in the village, which both do excellent evening meals. There is a friendly atmosphere created here "Down on the Farm" and Sheila does her best to make your holiday a happy and enjoyable one. Bed and Breakfast from £13. SAE for brochure.

SWANAGE. Mrs Justine Pike, Downshay Farm, Haycrafts Lane, Harmans Cross, Swanage BH19 3EB (01929 480316).

A working dairy farm on beautiful Isle of Purbeck, half a mile from A351 and midway between Corfe Castle and Swanage. Sandy beaches, coastal path, steam railway nearby. One family room with TV and one double room, both with washbasins. Shower room and bathroom; sittingroom with TV; diningroom. Tea/coffee facilities. Ample car parking and large garden. Children welcome, cot provided on request and babysitting available. Open March to end October for Bed and Breakfast from £15 to £17.

SWANAGE. Mrs Rosemary Dean, Quarr Farm, Valley Road, Swanage BH19 3DY (01929 480865). Quarr is a working family farm steeped in history dating back to the Domesday Book. Animals kept naturally — cows, calves, horses, poultry. Bring your children to feed ducks, chickens, peacocks and watch steam trains passing through our meadows. Accommodation in family room with en suite bathroom, own sitting room with colour TV, real log fire, tea making facilities. Old Dairy, low beamed ceilings, small windows, double room with en suite shower, sittingroom with colour TV, kitchen. Choice of Bed and Breakfast or self catering. Cot and Z-bed available. Easy reach high class restaurants, pubs; sea three miles. Studland, sandy beach just five miles away. Ideal for walking, cycling, coastal path, RSPB Reserves, golf courses, riding. Please write, or telephone, for further details and terms.

SWANAGE. Judy and Graham Rudd, Skelmorlie House, 50 Queens Road, Swanage BH19 2EU (01929 424643). ♛♛ *Commended.* Small detached guesthouse with superb sea views, situated in a quiet part of town. Four comfortable bedrooms, each with colour TV and tea/coffee facilities. One family room en suite and one double room en suite and two single rooms sharing a bathroom. Evening meals are optional and feature a choice of delicious home cooked food, including vegetarian. There is a separate lounge with reference and guide books on the area. Off street parking is available. We are open April to September inclusive. Children of five years and over are welcome. Sorry, no pets. Our Bed and Breakfast tariff starts at £15 and Half Board at £23. Please write or telephone for brochure.

WAREHAM. Mrs Harvey, Bucknowle House, Bucknowle, Wareham BH20 5PQ (01929 480352). Bucknowle is a large Victorian house standing in its own grounds between Corfe Castle and Church Knowle with stunning views of the surrounding Purbeck Hills. The spacious bedrooms are recently redecorated and furnished in comfortable period style; all have en suite facilities. Breakfast served in the magnificent dining room with delicious home produced sausages, eggs and marmalade. Ideally situated for exploring the wonderful Dorset coastline — we are only three miles from the sea. Sandy beaches, golf, sailing, fishing, bird watching and riding are all nearby. Please write or telephone for terms and further details.

WAREHAM/KIMMERIDGE. Mrs Annette Hole, Kimmeridge Farm House, Kimmeridge, Near Wareham BH20 5PE (01929 480990). Beautiful 16th century farmhouse on a mixed farm situated in the heart of the Purbeck countryside showing views of the rolling hills and the sea, offering many long coastal walks. Other sandy beaches such as Studland Bay and Swanage are easily reached by a short car journey. Good entertainment and shopping can be found at nearby Bournemouth or Poole. Spacious and comfortable accommodation; one double suite with private bathroom, one twin and one double with shared bathroom facilities. All rooms have TV and tea-making equipment; two bathrooms. Comfortable sittingroom with colour TV and central heating. Bed and Breakfast from £16 to £18 per person.

WEST LULWORTH. Mr and Mrs T.H. Williams, Shirley Hotel, West Lulworth, Wareham BH20 5RL (01929 400358). ♛♛♛ *Commended.* Comfortable, friendly hotel of 18 bedrooms, all en-suite, with colour TV, radio, tea-making facilities and direct-dial telephones. Situated in the middle of the village of West Lulworth, a conservation area, it is half a mile from the famous Lulworth Cove with its wonderful cliff scenery and walks. Local beaches are shingly but sandy ones are within 17 miles at Weymouth, Swanage and Studland. Bournemouth is 20 miles away. Light, airy diningroom with bar; varied menu with several choices prepared by hosts and served by friendly staff. The lounge has a pool table, card table and reading area. There is a coin-op laundry, an indoor heated swimming pool and spa with patio and a giant chess set. Car park within the grounds. Children and pets welcome. Please call for a colour brochure giving full details of this family run, licensed hotel. Member of the Southern Tourist Board, RAC/AA one star, Les Routiers. Open February to November. Terms: Half Board £230 to £252 per person per week; Bed and Breakfast £25.50 to £28 daily. Bargain Breaks out of season.

FREE and REDUCED RATE Holiday Visits!
See our Readers' Offer Vouchers for details.

WINTERBORNE ZELSTON. Mrs Irene Kerley, Brook Farm, Winterborne Zelston, Blandford DT11 9EU (01929 459267). A warm welcome awaits you at Brook Farm, a friendly working farm situated in a pretty, peaceful hamlet overlooking the River Winterborne, between Wimborne and Dorchester. Central for coast and exploring the beautiful Dorset countryside, New Forest, etc. Two spacious family rooms, washbasins, TV, easy chairs, beverage facilities and central heating. One room has en suite shower. No parking problems. Payphone available. Access to rooms all times. Hearty breakfasts are served with own free range eggs and home-made marmalade! Excellent inns nearby with extensive menus. Open all year except Christmas. From £15 per person per night, reductions for children sharing and longer stays.

DURHAM

CHESTER-LE-STREET. Mrs H. Johnson, Low Urpeth Farm, Ouston, Chester-le-Street DH2 1BD (0191 410 2901; Fax: 0191 410 0081). Come and relax in our traditional farmhouse. Our rooms (two twin-bedded rooms en suite, one double room with washbasin) are spacious and comfortably furnished with TV and beverage facilities. Easy access to Beamish Museum, Durham, Metro Centre and Northumberland. Directions — leave A1M at Chester-le-Street, A693, at second roundabout turn right/ Ouston, continue down hill, over roundabout, turn left into farm at "Trees Please" sign. OS Map Ref: NZ 257 556. Bed and Breakfast from £16 to £20. NTB Listed, Highly Commended.

CONSETT. Liz Lawson, Bee Cottage Farm, Castleside, Consett DH8 9HW (01207 508224). Working farm, join in. ♛♛ *Highly Commended.* A working farm set in peaceful picturesque surroundings with access to quiet, pleasant and interesting walks with unspoilt views. Ideally situated for visits to Beamish Museum, the Metro Centre, Durham Cathedral, Hadrian's Wall, the scenic and historic Northumbrian coastline and Border country, and within easy travelling distance of the new Slaley Hall Golf Complex and numerous other interesting places to visit. Accommodation comprises two family, two twin, one single and two double bedrooms; also two external ground floor bedrooms. Non-smoking accommodation available. Lounge with open fire and colour TV. Fire Certificate. Evening meals available. Self catering bungalows also available. Tea room open Easter to September 11am to 6pm. Bed and Breakfast from £18; Self Catering from £265 per week. Brochure available for full details.

DURHAM/NORTH YORKSHIRE BORDERS. Mr and Mrs D. Needham, The Ashes, Low Dinsdale, Neasham, Darlington DL2 1PL (01325 720149). Peacefully situated country house overlooking the River Tees. We offer a happy family atmosphere with home cooking. There is an oak beamed room with large log fire. Situated five miles from Darlington within easy reach of Durham City, Herriot Country, the Dales, North Yorkshire Moors and a large number of historic houses and gardens. Just two miles from a golf course, stabling (if required), local hunts — Bedale, Zetland and Hurworth. Lovely walks and ideal for bird watching. One twin and two double rooms, one en-suite. Bed and Breakfast from £18 to £20; Evening Meal available if required. Children and pets welcome.

MIDDLETON-IN-TEESDALE. Mrs S.E. Parmley, Snaisgill Farm, Middleton-in-Teesdale, Barnard Castle DL12 0RP (01833 40343). Working farm, join in. Our smallholding is situated in beautiful scenic and peaceful countryside, one mile from Middleton-in-Teesdale. Ideal base for walking or touring the Dales, visits to Beamish, Durham City, Bowes Museum and local places of interest. Spacious and comfortable accommodation in two double bedrooms with washbasins. Bathroom with shower, two toilets. Large comfortable guests' lounge with colour TV. Tea/coffee served on request. Bed and Breakfast from £13.50 to £14.50. Tourist Board listed.

STANLEY. Mrs P. Gibson, Bushblades Farm, Harperley, Stanley DH9 9UA (01207 232722). Ideal base for visiting Beamish Museum (two miles), Durham City (20 minutes), Metro Centre (15 minutes), Hadrian's Wall and Northumberland coast (under an hour). Excellent eating places close by. Comfortable Georgian farmhouse set in large garden. Ground floor twin en suite room plus two double first-floor bedrooms. All rooms have tea/coffee making, colour TV and easy chairs. Ample parking. Children over 12 years welcome. Sorry, no pets. Bed and Breakfast from £16 per person per night. Tourist Board Listed.

ESSEX

BRAINTREE. Mrs Delia Douse, Spicers Farm, Rotten End, Wethersfield, Braintree CM7 4AL (01371 851021). *Commended.* **Working farm.** Previous FHG Diploma Winner. Attractive farmhouse with large garden in quiet rural area designated of special landscape value. Excellent for walking or touring and convenient for Stansted, M11, Harwich, Cambridge and Constable country. Plenty of parking. Comfortable centrally heated bedrooms, en suite shower rooms or private bathrooms, colour TV, tea/coffee making facilities, clock radio and lovely views. Separate lounge for guests which overlooks the garden. Children are welcome at special rates. Non-smoking accommodation can be arranged. Bed and Breakfast from £15 to £18. Reduced weekly terms available.

COLCHESTER. Mrs Jill Tod, Seven Arches Farm, Chitts Hill, Lexden, Colchester CO3 5SX (01206 574896). Working farm. Georgian farmhouse set in large garden close to the ancient town of Colchester. The farm extends to 100 acres and supports both arable crops and cattle. Private fishing rights on the River Colne, which runs past the farmhouse. This is a good location for visits to North Essex, Dedham and the Stour Valley which have been immortalised in the works of John Constable, the landscape painter. Children welcome. Pets welcome. Open all year. Bed and Breakfast from £20; Evening Meal from £5. Twin room £36; family room en-suite. Static caravan on caravan site also available.

ESSEX – CHOICES!

Essex offers the choice between rural farmland, a marshy coastline, and industrial towns. Worth a visit are Abberton Reservoir, Blackwater Estuary, the country park at Danbury, Hatfield Forest and the Naze.

SAFFRON WALDEN. Mrs L. Vernon, Thistley Hall, Widdington, Saffron Walden CB11 3ST (01799 540388). ETB registered. A friendly welcome awaits you at this 17th century farmhouse where personal attention and guests' comfort are a feature including choice of breakfast menu. Approached by a tree-lined drive Thistley Hall stands in 30 acres of pasture and gardens, adjacent to Wildlife Park and Butterfly House. One mile from unspoilt village with Tythe Barn and 15th century inn where good food is available. Within easy reach of local tourist attractions. Local amenities include horse riding, swimming, walking, golf and fishing. Two miles from B1383 with easy access to M11 London-Cambridge. Accommodation comprises one double and one twin-bedded rooms with washbasins and adjacent to bathroom and separate toilet. Shower room on ground floor. All rooms have razor points, tea making facilities and central heating. Guests' spacious lounge/dining room available, very comfortable, with colour TV; inglenook fireplace. Bed and Breakfast only £15 per person. Ring or write for further details.

WIX. Mrs H.P. Mitchell, New Farm House, Spinnells Lane, Wix, Manningtree CO11 2UJ (Clacton [01255] 870365; Fax: 01255 870837). 👑👑👑 *Commended.* **Working farm.** A comfortable, centrally heated modern farmhouse ideally situated for touring the famous Constable countryside, local seaside resorts, historic Colchester and other towns. Convenient for Harwich (Parkeston Quay) Car Ferry to Holland, Denmark, Germany and Sweden. Seven bedrooms with en-suite facilities, TV etc; all other bedrooms have washbasins, tea/coffee making facilities and colour TV. Guests' lounge with colour TV, second quiet lounge with kitchenette available for making snacks. Children welcome at reduced prices, cot, high chair and babysitting provided. Large play area with swings, etc. Good farmhouse cooking; licensed. Open all year. AA QQQ and RAC Acclaimed. Bed, Breakfast and Evening Meal. SAE for brochure.

HELP IMPROVE BRITISH TOURIST STANDARDS

You are choosing holiday accommodation from our very popular FHG Publications. Whether it be a hotel, guest house, farmhouse or self-catering accommodation, we think you will find it hospitable, comfortable and clean, and your host and hostess friendly and helpful. Why not write and tell us about it?

As a recognition of the generally well-run and excellent holiday accommodation reviewed in our publications, we at FHG Publications Ltd. present a diploma to proprietors who receive the highest recommendation from their guests who are also readers of our Guides. If you care to write to us praising the holiday you have booked through FHG Publications Ltd. – whether this be board, self-catering accommodation, a sporting or a caravan holiday, what you say will be evaluated and the proprietors who reach our final list will be contacted.

The winning proprietor will receive an attractive framed diploma to display on his premises as recognition of a high standard of comfort, amenity and hospitality. FHG Publications Ltd. offer this diploma as a contribution towards the improvement of standards in tourist accommodation in Britain. Help your excellent host or hostess to win it!

FHG DIPLOMA

We nominate ....

....

Because

Name ....

Address ....

.... Telephone No. ....

GLOUCESTERSHIRE

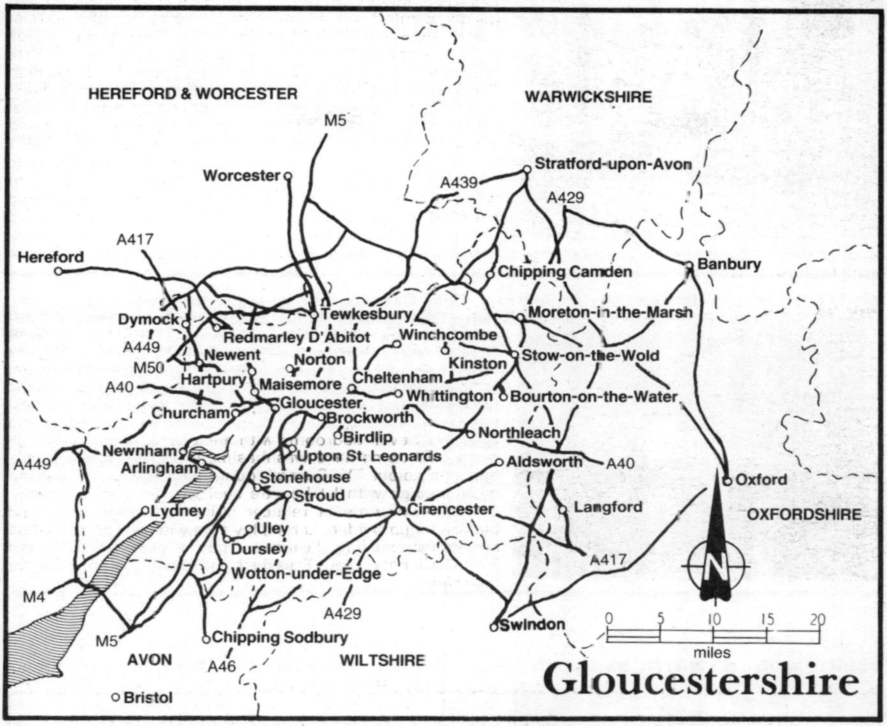

ARLINGHAM. Mrs D. Turrell, Horseshoe View, Overton Lane, Arlingham, Gloucester GL2 7JJ (Gloucester [01452] 740293). Guests are given a friendly welcome, all year round, in this comfortable private house enjoying beautiful views of River Severn and Forest of Dean. Within easy reach of A38 and M5, and excellent base for touring the Cotswolds, Bath, Slimbridge Wildfowl Trust, Berkeley Castle and many other places of interest. Dry ski slope, Gloucester Leisure Centre and Three Choirs Festival attract many visitors. Accommodation in two double bedrooms (one en suite), one twin-bedded and one single room, with usual amenities; non-smoking accommodation available. Children over five years welcome. Sorry, no pets. Car essential — ample parking. Bed and Breakfast. Reductions for children and Senior Citizens. SAE, please, for terms. HETB registered.

BIRDLIP. Mrs P.M. Carter, Beechmount, Birdlip GL4 8JH (Gloucester [01452] 862262).

Commended. Good central base for touring Cotswolds, conveniently situated for many interesting places and picturesque views with lovely walks. "Beechmount" is in centre of Birdlip Village, convenient for garage, post office/village store. Choice of menu for breakfast. Front door key is provided so that guests may come and go freely. All bedrooms with colour TVs, tea/coffee making facilities, washbasins, some with en suite facilities; bathroom, separate shower, shaver points, toilet. Children welcome at reduced rates, cot, high chair provided. Pets allowed by arrangement. Evening Meal by prior arrangement. Home produce when available. Competitive rates. Family-run guest house, highly recommended. Terms on application.

PLEASE ENCLOSE A STAMPED ADDRESSED ENVELOPE WITH ENQUIRIES

BOURTON-ON-THE-WATER. Mrs K. Bolton, Clapton Manor, Clapton-on-the-Hill, Bourton-on-the-Water GL54 2LG (01451 810202). Clapton Manor is a 17th century Cotswold stone house located at the top of the village with spectacular views across the Windrush Valley. The layout of the house lends itself to either complete privacy or more integration with the family as preferred. The interior with its beams and huge inglenook fireplaces is both informal and comfortable. Children of all ages welcome. TV in guests' own sittingroom. Coffee/tea making facilities provided. Non-smoking accommodation available. Sorry, no pets. Bed and Breakfast from £18 to £25 per person per night.

BOURTON-ON-THE-WATER. Mrs Della Trott, Cosy Cottage, The Avenue, Bourton-on-the-Water, Near Cheltenham GL54 2BB (01451 821748). Quietly situated in the heart of the Cotswolds, four minutes' walk from the centre of Bourton-on-the-Water and surrounded by many beautiful and historic places of interest. Cosy Cottage, a Grade II Listed building, offers clean, comfortable accommodation and a friendly atmosphere. One twin and two double bedrooms with TV, washbasins, shaver points and tea/coffee making facilities. Bathroom with shower, two toilets. Central heating. Dining room with separate tables. Genuine good home cooking. Evening Meal by arrangement. Terms from £16.

BOURTON-ON-THE-WATER. Mr and Mrs Farley, Rooftrees, Rissington Road, Bourton-on-the-Water GL54 2EB (01451 821943). Warmth, comfort and hospitality are offered in the relaxed atmosphere of this detached Cotswold stone guest house, situated on the edge of the famous village of Bourton-on-the-Water which is eight minutes' level walking distance from the centre of the village. Bourton is central to all the main Cotswold attractions. Rooftrees offers four bedrooms, all en suite, two on the ground floor. Two of the rooms have four-poster beds, TV and tea-making facilities. A payphone is available. Optional traditional English home cooked dinners provided using fresh local produce. An enjoyable stay is assured here while visiting the Cotswolds. No smoking. Double rooms from £36 to £40; four-poster rooms from £39.

BREDON'S NORTON. Michael and Pippa Cluer, Lampitt House, Lampitt Lane, Bredon's Norton, Tewkesbury GL20 7HB (01684 72295). *Commended.* Lampitt House is situated in a large informal garden on the edge of a quiet village at the foot of Bredon Hill. Splendid views across to the Malverns. Ideal for visiting the Cotswolds, Stratford, Worcester, Cheltenham, Gloucester and the Forest of Dean. All rooms are furnished to a high standard and have private bathrooms, central heating, colour TV and tea/coffee making facilities. Ground floor room available. Children are welcome. Ample parking. No smoking. Open all year. Hill and riverside walks. Arrangements can be made for windsurfing and riding. Double room £35, single £25. Bed and Breakfast.

See also Colour Display Advertisement **CHELTENHAM. Mr and Mrs A.E. Hughes, Ham Hill Farm, Whittington, Cheltenham GL54 4EZ (Cheltenham [01242] 584415).** *Commended.* All visitors will be made welcome and everything will be done to make their stay enjoyable at this new farmhouse on a 160-acre farm. Leisure activities nearby include riding, golf, walking on the Cotswold Way. All bedrooms with washbasins, TV and Teasmaid, three rooms with full en-suite facilities. Central heating. Open all year. Bed and Breakfast from £16.50; £17.50 en suite; £20 singles. No smoking. Children over seven years welcome.

BURROWS COURT HOTEL

NIBLEY GREEN, NORTH NIBLEY,
DURSLEY GL11 6AZ
Tel: Dursley (01453) 546230

This 18th century mill is idyllically set in an acre of garden surrounded by open country with beautiful views of the Cotswolds. Decorated and furnished in the country style, the house has eight bedrooms, all with private shower room or bathroom, colour TV, beverage facilities and radio. A choice of dishes is offered at dinner with a range of wines. Other facilities include two lounges, one with residents' bar, central heating. Log fires in winter, outside swimming pool and croquet lawn. Children over 5 years. AA Listed, RAC Highly Acclaimed. Dinner, Bed and Breakfast from £154 weekly, two days from £56.

DURSLEY. Mrs E. Williams, Claremont House, 66 Kingshill Road, Dursley GL11 4EG (01453 542018). Claremont, a large Victorian house with fine views of the Cotswold Escarpment overlooking the Cam Valley, offers most comfortable accommodation and a warm welcome to all visitors. It is ideally situated for touring the Severn Vale and many Cotswold beauty spots; convenient for visits to Berkeley Castle, Slimbridge Wildfowl Trust, Cirencester, Wye Valley, Cheltenham and Severn Bridge. Fresh farm produce always available. Double, family and twin bedded rooms available, all with either hot and cold or en-suite facilities. Tea/coffee making facilities. Ample parking. Bed and Breakfast; Evening Meals by arrangement.

DURSLEY near. Mrs H.A. Shipton, The Elms, Coaley, Near Dursley GL11 5EA (01453 890222). The Elms is within a short distance of the famous Slimbridge Wildfowl and Wetlands Trust, Berkeley Castle, Woodchester Mansion, Owlpen Manor and many more places of interest in the area. We have three double bedrooms, TV lounge and separate dining room and offer a homely and friendly atmosphere. There are plenty of places nearby to eat. Tariff is £20 per person per night.

DURSLEY near. Susan Strain, Cotswold House, 57 The Street, Uley, Dursley GL11 5SL (01453 860305). Bed and Breakfast is offered in this charming Georgian style house with private parking set in the centre of the pretty village of Uley. We have good access to the Cotswold Way, many local walks and excellent local pubs offering good food. The location is ideal for visits to Tetbury, Berkeley, Badminton, Gatcombe and Slimbridge with easy access to both Cheltenham and Bath. Some bedrooms have en-suite facilities, all have TV, tea/coffee making and double or twin beds. Clothes drying facilities are available. We are open throughout the year and aim to make your visit to our village a relaxing and carefree occasion. Please phone or write for further details.

FREE and REDUCED RATE Holiday Visits!
See our Readers' Offer Vouchers for details.

DURSLEY near. Gerald and Norma Kent, Hill House, Crawley Hill, Uley, Near Dursley GL11 5BH (01453 860267). Cotswold stone house situated on top of a hill with beautiful views of the surrounding countryside, near the very pretty village of Uley. Ideal spot for exploring the various walks in the area including the Cotswold Way and there are many places of interest within reasonable driving distance of Uley. Bed and Breakfast offered though Evening Meals are normally available on request. Choice of bedrooms with or without en-suite facilities, all with washbasins, central heating, shaver points, tea/coffee making facilities. Guests' lounge with colour TV. Your hosts' aim is to make your stay in the Cotswolds an enjoyable and memorable one, with comfort and hospitality of prime importance. Please phone or write for brochure.

Hill House

FALFIELD. Mr and Mrs B.C. Burrell, Green Farm Guest House, Falfield GL12 8DL (01454 260319). Delightful 16th century stone farmhouse, beautifully converted into a country guest house with style and traditional charm. Open all year. Excellent food always available from simple snacks to a full à la carte menu. Bath, Cheltenham, Cardiff, Forest of Dean, Cheddar are all approximately 35 minutes away. Easy access M4 and M5 Junction 14. The ideal touring centre. Tourist Board registered. Bed and Breakfast from £15; en suite available. A warm welcome assured at Green Farm.

FOREST OF DEAN. Mrs Joan Thorpe, Brook House Guest House, Bridge Street, Blakeney GL15 4DY (01594 517101). *Commended.* Enjoy a relaxing break in the Forest of Dean and Wye Valley. This area is ideal for walking, canoeing, golf, fishing or simply enjoying the scenery. Brook House is an attractive 17th century building. We offer a warm welcome, personal service and comfortable accommodation. All rooms have central heating, colour TV and tea/coffee making facilities. En suite room and a four-poster room are available. Enjoy home cooked evening meals; supper licence. Blakeney is midway between Gloucester and Chepstow on A48. Car parking. Bed and Breakfast from £15. Two nights Dinner, Bed and Breakfast from £46. Send for colour brochure.

GLOUCESTER. Mrs S. Carter, Severn Bank, Minsterworth GL2 8JH (01452 750357). Severn Bank is a fine country house standing in its own six-acre grounds on the bank of the River Severn, four miles west of Gloucester. Ideally situated for touring Cotswolds, Forest of Dean and Wye Valley, and at the recommended viewpoint for the Severn Bore tidal wave. Severn Bank has a friendly atmosphere and comfortable accommodation in spacious rooms with superb view over river and countryside. Full central heating, en-suite rooms, tea/coffee making facilities and colour TV in non-smoking bedrooms. Ample parking, with several excellent restaurants and pubs nearby. Terms: Bed and Full English Breakfast from £17 to £19.50, with rates reduced for children.

GLOUCESTERSHIRE – THE IDYLLIC COTSWOLDS COUNTY!

A combination of the Cotswolds and The Vale of Severn, Gloucestershire is a popular tourist destination. Visit Chipping Campden, Cirencester, The Cotswolds Farm Park, The Forest of Dean, Keynes Park and Tewkesbury and you will not be disappointed. If you are around at the right time, the Severn Bore can also be quite a spectacle.

GLOUCESTER near. S.J. Barnfield, "Kilmorie Guest House", Gloucester Road, Corse, Staunton, Near Gloucester GL19 3RQ (01452 840224). Built in 1848 by the Chartists, Kilmorie is Grade 2 listed in a conservation area, and is a smallholding keeping farm livestock and fruit in a lovely part of Gloucestershire. Good home cooking with own produce and eggs when available. Large garden. Children are welcome to "help" with the animals if they wish, and a child's pony is also kept. There are many places of both historic and natural interest to visit, and river trips can be enjoyed from Tewkesbury and Upton-on-Severn. Kilmorie is situated close to the borders of Herefordshire and Worcestershire and the Forest of Dean, the Cotswolds, Malvern Hills, the Wye Valley and four castles are all within easy reach. Four double, one twin, one single and one family bedrooms, all with washbasins and some with private facilities; two bathrooms and two additional toilets, shower. Lounge with colour TV; diningroom. Central heating. Fire Certificate. Children over five years welcome. Pets accepted; kennels available if required. Ample parking. Three course Dinner, Bed and Breakfast from £19; Bed and Breakfast from £12.50. Reduced rates for children. Open all year.

LECHLADE near. Mrs Elizabeth Reay, Apple Tree House, Buscot, Near Faringdon, Oxfordshire SN7 8DA (01367 252592). ♛♛ 17th century Listed house situated in small interesting National Trust village, two miles Lechlade, four miles Faringdon on A417. River Thames five minutes' walk through village to Buscot lock and weirs. Ideal touring centre for Cotswolds, Upper Thames, Oxford, etc. Good fishing, walking and cycling area. Access at all times to the three guest bedrooms all of which have washbasins, razor points, tea/coffee facilities and central heating when necessary. En-suite room available. Residents' TV lounge with log fire in winter. Bed and Breakfast from £16 per person per night; choice of many restaurants, etc within five mile radius of Buscot. I look forward to welcoming you to Apple Tree House.

MINCHINHAMPTON (near Stroud). Mrs Margaret Helm, Hunters Lodge, Dr Brown's Road, Minchinhampton Common, Near Stroud GL6 9BT (01453 883588; Fax: 01453 731449). Hunters Lodge is a beautiful stone-built Cotswold country house set in a large secluded garden adjoining 600 acres of National Trust commonland at Minchinhampton. Accommodation available — one family room and two double rooms, all with washbasins, tea/coffee making facilities, full central heating, colour TV, en suite and private bathrooms. All rooms furnished and decorated to a high standard. Private lounge with TV and a delightful conservatory. Car essential, ample parking space. Ideal centre for touring the Cotswolds, Bath, Cheltenham, Cirencester with many delightful pubs and hotels around for meals. You are sure of a warm welcome, comfort and help in planning excursions to local places of interest. Bed and Breakfast from £16 per person. Non-smokers preferred. SAE, please, for further details or telephone.

MORETON-IN-MARSH near. Mrs P.A. Allen, Lines Farm, Chastleton Road, Little Compton, Near Moreton-in-Marsh GL56 0SL (Barton on the Heath [0160874] 343). ♛♛ Beautiful Cotswold stone house with lovely views situated on the edge of pretty village midway between Moreton-in-Marsh and Chipping Norton. Ideal for touring Cotswolds, Stratford-upon-Avon, Oxford, etc. Centrally heated rooms with guests' TV lounge; diningroom; one en-suite family bedroom; one double and one twin, both with washbasins; all with tea/coffee making facilities. Pets and children welcome. Prices from £15 to £16 per person per night. Dinner by arrangement. Discounts for three or more nights. Horses and cattle kept.

PAINSWICK. Michele Burdett, Damsels Farm, Painswick GL6 6UD (01452 812148). ♛♛ **Working farm, join in.** Welcome to Damsels Farm, where Henry VIII is reputed to have hunted with Anne Boleyn. Children may help feed the ducks, geese, chickens, calves and orphan lambs. The house is set in a quiet Cotswold Valley on the Cotswold Way. We are within easy reach of Cheltenham, Cirencester, Bath, Slimbridge and The Malverns. Open March to October. Pets and children welcome. Bed and Breakfast from £19.50; Evening Meal from £10.50 to £16.50.

SAUL. Mrs Wendy Watts, Saul Farm, Saul GL2 7JB (01452 740384). ♛♛ Take a break and relax in the comfort and homely atmosphere of our 17th century house overlooking a lake. Guests are welcome to lend a hand around the farm, which is situated between the River Severn and the Berkeley Canal. Many interesting places to visit nearby. TV lounge with open fire, spacious bedrooms with en suite and home cooking are waiting for you and your family; children and pets welcome. Two miles from M5 Junction 13. Bed and Breakfast from £15. Open all year.

STOW-ON-THE-WOLD. Mrs E. Graham, Banks Fee House, Longborough, Moreton-in-Marsh GL56 0QF (01451 830292; Fax: 01451 830605). ♛♛ Banks Fee is an 18th century Manor House set in parkland with extensive views across the Evenlode Valley. All rooms have en suite bath/shower rooms and tea/coffee making facilities; some have open fires and TV. Banks Fee is two miles north of Stow-on-the-Wold off the A424, 18 miles from Cheltenham, Cirencester and Stratford-upon-Avon, 28 miles from Oxford and situated in the heart of beautiful walking/cycling countryside. Many beautiful gardens and places of interest are close by. Children welcome. Bed and Breakfast from £18.50 per night. Opera season in July.

STOW-ON-THE-WOLD. Mrs V. Keyte, The Limes, Evesham Road, Stow-on-the-Wold GL54 1EN (01451 830034). ♛♛ Over the last 20 years this RAC and AA listed guesthouse has established a reputation for its homely and friendly atmosphere. It is just four minutes' walk from the town centre; central for visiting Stratford-upon-Avon, Burford, Bourton-on-the Water, Cirencester, Cheltenham, etc. The Limes overlooks fields and has an attractive large garden with ornamental pool and waterfall. Single, double, twin and family rooms with washbasins. Two rooms en-suite, one four poster and two twin bedrooms; two public showers, four toilets. All rooms have tea/coffee making facilities and colour TV. Central heating. TV lounge. Diningroom. Children welcome, cot. Pets welcome. Car park. Fire Certificate held. Bed and full English Breakfast from £15.50 to £18.50 per person. Reductions for children. Vegetarians catered for. Open all year except Christmas. Les Routiers Recommended.

BANKS FARM

The Cotswold stone farmhouse is situated in an elevated position in the centre of the village of Oddington, 3 miles from Stow-on-the-Wold. All rooms enjoy lovely views over fields to the XI Century Church. It is centrally situated for all the Cotswold villages, while Blenheim Palace, Warwick Castle, Oxford, Stratford-upon-Avon, Cheltenham, Cirencester and Gloucester are within easy reach. Accommodation comprises a double and twin-bedded room, both with washbasins, tea/coffee making facilities and electric blankets. The dining/sitting room with colour TV is available for guests' use in the evening. Guests, and children over 10 years, are welcomed to our home March to October. No smoking in public areas. Car essential – ample parking. Sorry, no pets. Bed and good English breakfast, bedtime drink and biscuits from £16.50; weekly from £109. Pubs, good food, within walking distance. E.T.B. Listed and Commended.

Mrs F. J. Adams, Banks Farm, Upper Oddington, Moreton-in-Marsh GL56 0XG. Telephone: Cotswold 01451 830475.

STOW-ON-THE-WOLD. Robert and Dawn Smith, Corsham Field Farmhouse, Bledington Road, Stow-on-the-Wold GL54 1JH (01451 831750). Homely farmhouse with traditional features and breathtaking views, one mile from Stow-on-the-Wold. Ideally situated for exploring all the picturesque Cotswold villages such as Broadway, Bourton-on-the-Water, Upper and Lower Slaughter, Chipping Campden, Snowshill, etc. Also central point for places of interest such as Blenheim Palace, Cotswold Wildlife Park, Stratford and many stately homes and castles in the area. Twin, double and family rooms, some with en suite facilities, all with washbasins, TV and tea/coffee making facilities. Pets and children welcome. Good pub food five minutes' walk away. AA Listed. Bed and Full English Breakfast from £12 to £17.50 per person.

STOW-ON-THE-WOLD. Mrs S. Davis, Fairview Farmhouse, Bledington Road, Stow-on-the-Wold, Cheltenham GL54 1AN (Cotswold [01451] 830279). You are assured of a warm welcome at Fairview Farmhouse, situated one mile from Stow-on-the-Wold on a quiet B road with outstanding panoramic views of the surrounding Cotswold Hills. Ideal base for touring the pretty villages of Bourton-on-the-Water, The Slaughters, Broadway, Chipping Campden, also famous Stratford etc. The cosy bedrooms are furnished to a high standard and all are en-suite with colour TV and tea/coffee making equipment. Lounge and additional lounge area with books, maps, etc. Central heating. Ample parking. Open all year. Evening Meals by arrangement.

STROUD near. Miss E.M. MacSwiney, New Inn House, The Camp, Near Stroud GL6 7HL (01285 821336). New Inn House, built in 1694 as a posting-inn, is a Grade II listed building. It stands in half an acre of grounds in a small Cotswold hamlet 820 feet above sea level amidst unspoilt countryside. Excellent touring centre for Cotswolds and Wye Valley, Bath, Stratford-upon-Avon. Gloucester 10 miles, Cheltenham nine miles and Cirencester 10 miles. Nearby are the Cotswold Way and Prinknash Abbey; three golf courses within easy reach and riding stables in the village. The Severn Wild Fowl Trust approximately 15 miles. Both bedrooms (one twin-bedded and one single with extra folding bed) have washbasins, tea-making facilities. Central heating. Full English breakfast, separate tables. Large garden. TV. Guests have own sittingroom. Access at all times. Dogs by prior arrangement. Children over 10 welcome. Car essential. Bed and Breakfast from £14. Weekly terms available. SAE, please. English Tourist Board Approved, Listed.

Barnhill Farmhouse

Bredons Norton, Nr Tewkesbury
Gloucestershire GL20 7HB
Telephone 01684 72704
Commended. ***AA QQQ***

Peacefully situated on the slopes of Bredon Hill, an area of outstanding natural beauty. Two large comfortable bedrooms, one en suite, one with private bathroom, both with colour TV and tea/coffee making facilities. A spacious guest lounge with inglenook wood fire and generous farmhouse cooking makes our Grade II Listed home an ideal centre for touring or business. Barnhill is set in large gardens and has ample tarmac parking. Pets welcome by arrangement, we also have stables and paddocks. Regrettably no children. We are a non-smoking household. Bed and Breakfast from £32 double; Dinner from £8 per person. Mrs Jane Archer.

TEWKESBURY. Mrs Bernadette Williams, Abbots Court, Church End, Twyning, Tewkesbury GL20 6DA (Tel and Fax: 01684 292515). Working farm. A large, quiet farmhouse set in 350 acres, built on the site of monastery between the Malverns and Cotswolds, half a mile M5-M50 junction. Large bedrooms, six en-suite, fully carpeted, with washbasins, tea making facilities and colour TV. Centrally heated. Open all year. Large lounge with open fire and colour TV. Spacious diningroom. Licensed bar. Good home cooked food in large quantities, home produced where possible. Children's own TV room, games room and playroom. Tennis lawn. Play area and lawn. Cot, high chair and babysitting available. Laundry facilities. Ideally situated for touring with numerous places to visit. Swimming, tennis, sauna, golf within three miles. Coarse fishing available on the farm. Bed and Breakfast from £16.50. Reduced rates for children and Senior Citizens.

HAMPSHIRE

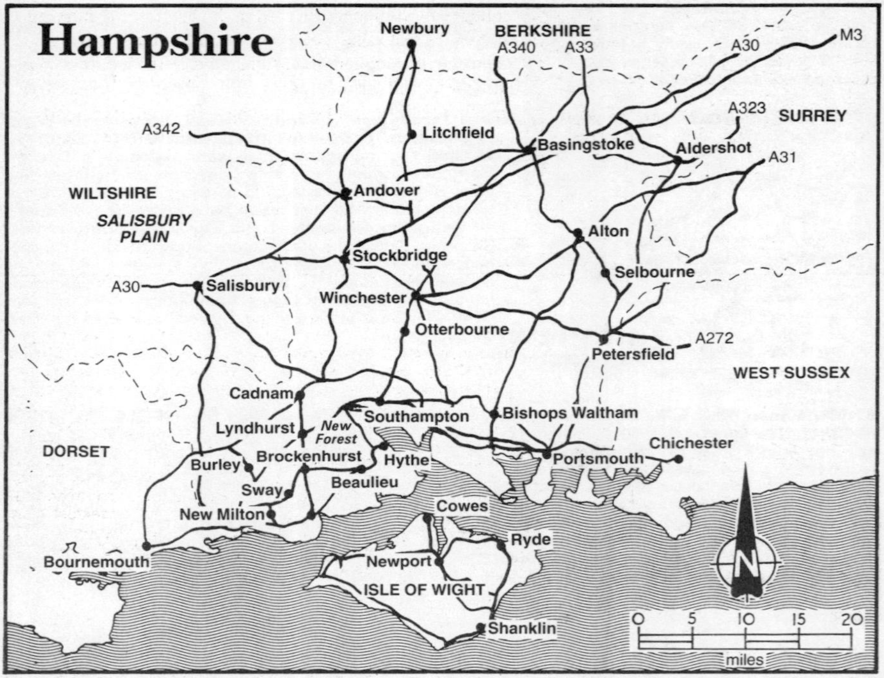

BARTON-ON-SEA. Mrs J. Copeland, Laurel Lodge, 48 Western Avenue, Barton-on-Sea BH25 7PZ (01425 618309). A superb area in all seasons for that special break. Scenic clifftop walks, beaches, golf, sailing, riding and the delights of the nearby historic New Forest. Laurel Lodge offers every possible comfort in a cosy atmosphere, friendly personal service, great home-cooked food. Bed and four-course Breakfast from £16 (single occupancy from £19); optional four-course Dinner from £9. Popular Half Board short breaks. The centrally heated en suite double, twin and family rooms all have remote control colour TV, tea/coffee facilities and more; ground floor bedroom available. An ideal touring base, and we are open all year.

BURLEY. Mrs Gina Russell, "Charlwood", Longmead Road, Burley BH24 4BY (01425 403242). Charlwood is situated on the edge of Burley, a picturesque little village in the midst of the New Forest. An ideal walking and touring base with Bournemouth and Southampton only 16 miles and the Isle of Wight ferry 12 miles. Riding and golf are nearby. The bedrooms, one double, one twin, have washbasins, colour TV and tea/coffee facilities. Central heating throughout. The friendly family home stands in its own attractive grounds on a no-through Forest road offering visitors a peaceful "away from it all" break. A full traditional English breakfast is served. Pets welcome. No smoking. Open January to November. Bed and Breakfast from £16.

LYMINGTON. Mrs R. Sque, Harts Lane Nurseries, 242 Everton Road, Everton, Lymington SO41 0HE (01590 645902). Bungalow (non-smoking) set in three acres; large garden with wildlife pond and an abundance of bird life. Quiet location, convenient for A337, three miles west of Lymington. Friendly comfortable accommodation comprising three double bedrooms, two en suite, all with tea/coffee making facilities and colour TV. The sea and forest are five minutes away by car. Horse riding, golf, fishing and a real ale pub serving homemade meals are all nearby. Children and pets welcome. Bed and Breakfast from £15 to £17 per person per night.

THE NURSE'S COTTAGE

This popular licensed guest house, once home of the District Nurse, provides every possible comfort in a cosy cottage environment. Situated in the heart of the thriving New Forest village of Sway, this is an ideal touring centre, with excellent road/rail access to the area's many attractions. All ensuite rooms, with colour TV, tea/coffee making facilities and much more – from £22.50 nightly per person. Early booking advised for good value half-board Short break packages including FREE New Forest Encounters.

Colour brochure and tariff on request.

ETB 👑👑 Commended
AA QQQQQ Premier Selected

VISA MasterCard AMERICAN EXPRESS

Station Road, Sway, Lymington SO41 6BA
Telephone/Fax: (01590) 683402

LYMINGTON. Mrs B. Tee, Gorse Meadow, Sway Road, Lymington SO41 8LR (Tel & Fax: 01590 673354). The house, in thirteen and a half acres, has charming gardens; horses graze the paddocks. Lymington is one and a half miles away with two excellent marinas, the forest is one mile away and beaches five miles. Seven golf courses, riding stables, tennis courts and many charming country pubs are all nearby. Self contained flat: Bed and Breakfast or self catering from £220 per week low season (monthly terms by arrangement). Family room: room and full breakfast from £50. Doubles: room and full breakfast from £40 to £46 (ensuite); all with central heating, washbasins, TV, tea/coffee makers, etc. Excellent home cooked dinners at £12. Accommodation and food prices reduced for children. Heated swimming pool.

HELP IMPROVE BRITISH TOURIST STANDARDS

You are choosing holiday accommodation from our very popular FHG Publications. Whether it be a hotel, guest house, farmhouse or self-catering accommodation, we think you will find it hospitable, comfortable and clean, and your host and hostess friendly and helpful. Why not write and tell us about it?

As a recognition of the generally well-run and excellent holiday accommodation reviewed in our publications, we at FHG Publications Ltd. present a diploma to proprietors who receive the highest recommendation from their guests who are also readers of our Guides. If you care to write to us praising the holiday you have booked through FHG Publications Ltd. – whether this be board, self-catering accommodation, a sporting or a caravan holiday, what you say will be evaluated and the proprietors who reach our final list will be contacted.

The winning proprietor will receive an attractive framed diploma to display on his premises as recognition of a high standard of comfort, amenity and hospitality. FHG Publications Ltd. offer this diploma as a contribution towards the improvement of standards in tourist accommodation in Britain. Help your excellent host or hostess to win it!

FHG DIPLOMA

We nominate ....

....

Because

Name ....

Address ....

.... Telephone No. ....

In the Heart of The New Forest

Surrounded by some of England's most beautiful countryside, this smart family-run hotel offers en-suite, colour TV and tea/coffee facilities as well as large car park to the rear. Comfortable licensed bar with satellite TV, and residents' lounge. Walking, riding, golf, animal sanctuaries and many other activities and attractions are close by. *Ring for a brochure.*

The Penny Farthing Hotel
Romsey Road, Lyndhurst,
Hampshire SO43 7AA.
Tel: 01703 284422 Fax: 01703 284488

AA RAC

English Tourist Board COMMENDED

The Penny Farthing

NEW FOREST. Mrs Sandra Hocking, Southernwood, Plaitford Common, Sailisbury Road, Near Romsey (01794 323255 or 322577). Modern country family home, surrounded by farmland, on the edge of the New Forest. Two double, one family and one twin bedrooms; lounge. Terms from £11. Full English breakfast. Cots and high chairs available for babies. Four miles from M27 off A36. Salisbury, Southampton 11 miles, Stonehenge 17 miles, Portsmouth half an hour, Winchester 14 miles, Romsey five miles and within easy reach of Continental ferries. Large garden. Ample parking. TV. Tea/coffee always available. Horse riding, golf, fishing, swimming, walking in New Forest 10 minutes. Local inns for good food. Terms from £12. Open all year. Tourist Board registered.

NEW FOREST (near Beaulieu). Mrs M. Stone, Heathlands, Lepe Road, Langley SO45 1YT (01703 892517). New Forest bungalow, near Beaulieu, offers large breakfast in comfortable bedrooms for non-smoking couples. Washbasins, central heating, tea-making facilities and colour TV; shower room, WC. Two miles from Lepe Beach, an unspoilt natural beach and country park opposite Isle of Wight. Three miles Beaulieu, three miles Exbury Azalea Gardens (Rothschild's collection). Half an hour's drive to Isle of Wight ferries at Lymington; half an hour Southampton, one hour Bournemouth. Central for touring the Forest which is especially beautiful in Autumn and Spring with the new-born foals. Non-smokers only. Bed and Breakfast from £14 per person per night. Car parking. For full details send SAE, please.

NEW MILTON. Mr and Mrs Michael and Judith Pearce, St. Ursula, 30 Hobart Road, New Milton BH25 6EG (01425 613515). Large, detached family home between New Forest and sea offering every comfort in a friendly relaxed atmosphere. Quiet, but central for town, station and leisure centre (with pool). Sea one mile, four miles to New Forest with ponies and beautiful walks. Ideal touring base for Bournemouth, Salisbury, etc. Twin, family, double and singles, most en suite, with washbasins and tea making facilities. Excellent beds. Beautiful ground floor twin en suite bedroom suitable for wheelchair/disabled guests. Children and pets welcome. Two bathrooms, one shower, four toilets. Lounge with colour TV, two dining rooms. Pretty "cottage" garden with barbecue. Smoke detectors installed. Full central heating. Open all year. Bed and Breakfast from £15 to £18. AA QQQ Recommended.

HAMPSHIRE – VARIED ATTRACTIONS!

Coastal resorts like Southsea, river valleys like that of the Itchen, The New Forest and the nautical centres of Southampton and Portsmouth combine to give Hampshire its reputation as a holiday destination. Also of interest in this large county are places like Bucklers Hard, a preserved 18th century ship building village; Broadlands, home of the late Lord Mountbatten; New Forest Butterfly Farm, Longdown; and Paulton's Park, a family leisure park with lots to do and see.

Built about 1800, overlooking Otterbourne Common, near the entrance to Cranbury Park Estate; standing in 3/4 acre of mature woodland garden. Within easy reach of Winchester, New Forest and Southampton. Ferries to Isle of Wight from Portsmouth are 30 minutes' drive away. Our accommodation is of the highest standard, each twin bedded room having its own bathroom, air conditioning, tea/coffee facilities, colour TV; independent access, including a ground floor en suite. Open all year. Enclosed parking. Regret no animals and no smoking. We pride ourselves on having a homely and welcoming atmosphere. Terms from £19 per person. For reservations please contact:

Vera and Peter Walford, Lilac Cottage, Otterbourne Hill, Otterbourne, Hampshire SO21 2HJ. Tel: (01703) 267070.

PORTSMOUTH. Graham and Sandra Tubb, "Hamilton House", 95 Victoria Road North, Southsea, Portsmouth PO5 1PS (Tel & Fax: 01705 823502). *Commended.* Delightful AA Recommended/RAC Acclaimed family-run guesthouse. Centrally located five minutes by car from Continental and Isle of Wight ferry terminals, M27, stations, city centres, sea front tourist attractions and museums. Bright, modern rooms, all centrally heated with colour TV and tea-making facilities; some en suites available. Ideal touring base for Southern England. Full English, vegetarian and Continental breakfasts served from 6am (for early travellers). Nightly/weekly stays welcome all year.

RINGWOOD. New Forest. Mrs M.E. Burt, Fraser House, Salisbury Road, Blashford, Ringwood BH24 3PB (Ringwood [01425] 473958). Fraser House is situated one mile from the market town of Ringwood, overlooking the Avon Valley. This comfortable family house is on the edge of the New Forest, famous for its ponies, deer and pleasant walks. It is ten miles from Bournemouth and the south coast, and is convenient for visiting Southampton, Stonehenge and the Cathedral city of Salisbury. All rooms have central heating, hot and cold water, shaver points, comfortable beds, colour TV, tea/coffee making facilities. Some en-suite rooms available at extra charge. Fishing and water sports available nearby. Non-smokers preferred. Ample parking space. Open all year. Bed and Breakfast from £16 — £19 per night.

ROMSEY (New Forest). Mrs J. Hayter, "Woodlands", Bunny Lane, Sherfield English, Romsey SO51 6FT (01794 884840). ♛♛♛ Woodlands is situated on the edge of the New Forest near the Hampshire/ Wiltshire border with the historic city of Salisbury and the ancient town of Romsey only a matter of minutes away in opposite directions. Southampton is also an easy journey away, Isle of Wight ferry at Beaulieu close by. Located in a quiet country lane with bedrooms overlooking dairy fields. All rooms have washbasins and tea making facilities; en suite facilities available. Comfortable lounge with colour TV. Children welcome. Our aim is to provide a personal, friendly service, home cooked food and a comfortable stay in pleasant surroundings — home from home. Bed and Breakfast from £13.50; Evening Meal available. Reductions for Senior Citizens.

SOUTHAMPTON. Mrs Christine Archdeacon, Dale Farm Guest House, Manor Road, Applemore Hill, Dibden, Southampton SO45 5TJ (01703 849632). ♛ This attractive 18th century farmhouse nestles in a large wooded garden on the edge of Marchwood enclosure in the New Forest. All six bedrooms are tastefully furnished with vanity basins, shaver points, courtesy trays and comfortable beds; some rooms are en suite and have TV. The house is quietly located next door to a riding stables and farmland yet only 250 yards from the A326. We welcome families and can offer large family bedrooms, cots and high chairs and a large safe garden to play in with swings and slide. We are open all year except Christmas. Bed and Breakfast from £16 to £18, weekly from £100. Reduced rates are also available for stays over four nights. AA QQ Listed.

SWAY. Joan Dowson, Redwing Farm, Pitmore Lane, Sway SO41 6BW (01590 683319). Small farm specialising in pedigree show cattle. Ideally situated in the New Forest between Brockenhurst and Lymington, the 200 year old cob cottage has been picturesquely extended, the beamed bedrooms having en suite and tea/coffee making facilities, and overlooking fields and gardens. There is also a small guest lounge with colour TV. Ample parking. Redwing is beautifully situated and an excellent base for walking and touring, offering the warmest of welcomes. Bed and Breakfast £18 per person per night. ETB Listed.

HEREFORD & WORCESTER

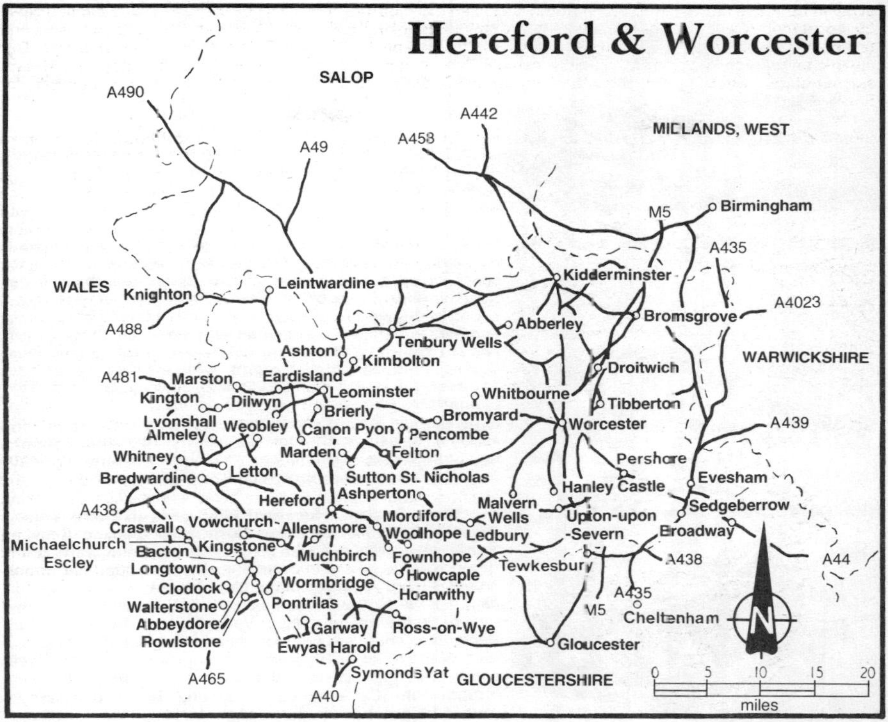

ALMELEY. Mrs J.A. Kingdon, Rose Cottage, Woonton, Almeley HR3 6QW (01544 340436).

Enjoy country hospitality at its best at Rose Cottage — a romantic 16th century house set in two acres of old world gardens and grounds. Located in a peaceful lane with fine views towards the Black Mountains, the perfect base to relax and unwind. Furnished with antiques, interesting collection of old china, samplers and bygones. Beautiful bedrooms, one with four-poster and en suite facilities. Oak beamed guests' parlour with good books, colour TV and log fires in winter. Generous breakfasts, vegetarian choice available; free range eggs and home-made preserves. Nearby activities include riding, golf, walking, gliding and micro-lighting. Come and meet our pet sheep!

BREDENBURY. Mrs G. Evans, Red Hill Farm, Bredenbury, Bromyard HR7 4SY (01885 483255 or 01885 483535). 17th century farmhouse situated in the beautiful peaceful countryside, within easy driving distance of Worcester, Hereford, Malvern, Ledbury and Ludlow. Guest accommodation includes one family room, two double bedrooms, one twin-bedded room all with washbasins and TV; bathroom and shower; lounge with colour TV; central heating throughout. Good food at local pub (one mile) at reasonable prices (small hot evening meals available on premises also — optional). Home from home. Children and pets welcome. Bed and Breakfast from £14 to £15 per person. English Tourist Board Listed (Commended applied for). Situated on A44. From Worcester take A44 to Bromyard, proceed towards Leominster for two miles on right hand side, then right turn — signposted. You will receive a very warm welcome on arrival.

WHEN MAKING ENQUIRIES PLEASE MENTION THIS *FHG* PUBLICATION

BROADWAY. Mrs Helen Perry, Mount Pleasant Farm, Childswickham, Broadway WR12 7HZ (Broadway [01386] 853424). ♛♛ *Highly Commended.* **Working farm.** Large Victorian farmhouse set in 350 acres of mixed farm with cattle and horses. Excellent views. Open all year round, guests are offered a warm welcome and a good, traditional farmhouse Breakfast. An ideal centre for touring the Cotswolds — three miles from Broadway, 15 miles from Stratford-on-Avon, within easy reach Warwick, Oxford, Cheltenham, Burford and many other attractions. All the bedrooms are en suite with TV, tea/coffee making facilities and central heating. Bed and Breakfast from £20 per person. Superior self catering accommodation also available in converted barns sleeping two to six persons. Graded 🔑🔑🔑🔑 by Tourist Board.

BROMSGROVE. Mrs C. Gibbs, Lower Bentley Farm, Lower Bentley, Bromsgrove B60 4JB (01527 821286). An attractive Victorian farmhouse with modern comforts on a dairy and beef farm is an ideal base for a holiday, Short Break or business stay. Overlooking peaceful countryside, we are situated a few minutes away from M5 and M42 in "Archer" country between Redditch, Bromsgrove and Droitwich. The accommodation comprises spacious double, twin and family rooms with en suite or private bathroom, colour TV and tea/coffee making facilities. The comfortable lounge and separate dining room overlook the large garden. Young children are welcome. We are ideally situated for visits to Stratford-upon-Avon, Warwick, Worcester, Stourbridge, Birmingham, the Black Country, the NEC and International Convention Centre.

HEREFORD. Mrs Catherine B. Smith, Tremorithic, Bacton, Hereford HR2 0AU (Golden Valley [01981] 240291). Working farm. Have a peaceful away-from-it-all holiday in a 17th century farmhouse offering good home cooking and comfortable accommodation. The house enjoys panoramic views of the Black Mountains and provides easy access to the Brecon Beacons, Wales and the many beauty spots of the Wye Valley. Open from April to December. There are two double and one single bedrooms; bathroom, toilet; sittingroom, diningroom. Children welcome; cot, high chair and babysitting provided. Pets by arrangement. Car essential — parking. Bed and Breakfast from £14 per person per night. Evening Meal available. Reduced rates for children by arrangement. Send SAE for brochure.

HEREFORD. Mrs R.T. Andrews, Webton Court, Kingstone, Hereford HR2 9NF (01981 250220). ♛♛ **Working farm.** Georgian Black and White Farmhouse situated in open country in the heart of beautiful Wye Valley amidst green fields. This is ideal touring country at any time of the year for Symonds Yat, Forest of Dean, Chepstow and the Severn Bridge or, to the west, the rugged grandeur of the Welsh Mountains. Malvern and Stratford-upon-Avon also offer peace and tranquillity. Two family, two double, two twin-bedded rooms and two en-suite rooms, all with wash-basins; two bathrooms, five toilets; sittingroom; dining-room. Children are welcome, cot, high chair and babysitting. Pets welcome. Open all year with electric heating. Plain home cooking using fresh garden and farm produce. Roasts of all meats are enjoyed. Early morning tea. Children under 10 and Senior Citizens are welcome at 10 per cent reductions. Riding can be enjoyed and riding lessons are available. Full Board, Evening Dinner, Bed and Breakfast or Bed and Breakfast only. Fire Certificate granted. Bed and Breakfast from £14 but reductions for two nights or more (except en-suite). En-suite from £20. We can also cater for large parties of up to 20 persons.

FREE and REDUCED RATE Holiday Visits!

See our Readers' Offer Vouchers for details.

HEREFORD. Ashgrove House, Wellington Marsh, Hereford HR4 8DU (01432 830608). Mike and Sandra Fletcher welcome you to luxurious accommodation with high standard furnishings and lovely gardens. Situated in a quiet rural location, overlooking cider apple orchards, three miles north of the historic Cathedral City of Hereford. Lovely walks nearby, golf and fishing 10 minutes by car. Double, twin-bedded or single rooms, all en suite with TV and tea-making facilities. Good pub food within easy walking distance. Bed and full English Breakfast £16 to £18 per person.

HEREFORD. Mr David Jones, Sink Green Farm, Rotherwas, Hereford HR2 6LE (01432 870223). Working farm, join in. Warm and friendly atmosphere awaits your arrival at this 16th century farmhouse, on the banks of the River Wye. Three miles south of the cathedral city of Hereford, with Ross-on-Wye, Leominster, Ledbury, Malvern and the Black Mountains within easy reach. All rooms en-suite, tea/coffee making facilities and colour TV. One room with four-poster, family room by arrangement. Guests' own lounge. Pets by arrangement. Bed and Breakfast from £18 per person. Heart of England Tourist Board. AA QQQ.

KINGTON. Mrs E.E. Protheroe, Bucks Head House, School Farm, Hergest, Kington HR5 3EW (Kington [01544] 231063). Working farm. Newly modernised farmhouse on 290-acre mixed farm which has been worked by the Protheroe family since 1940 and carries cattle, sheep and crops. Wye Valley, Black Mountains, Elan Valley, Ludlow, Hereford Cathedral, Black and White villages all within easy reach. Pony riding available at extra charge. Two double, two single, two family bedrooms, with washbasins; two bathrooms, two showers, four toilets; two sitting rooms; tea/coffee making facilities in all rooms; diningroom. Snooker room with full size table. Cot, high chair and reduced rates for children; babysitting by arrangement. Pets free of charge, by arrangement only. Car essential, parking. Central heating. Peaceful walks around the farm and its sheep walk "Hergest Ridge". Evening Dinner/Meal, Bed and Breakfast or Bed and Breakfast only. Two six-berth mobile homes also available. ETB registered.

KINNERSLEY. Pearl and Jon Taylor, Upper Newton Farmhouse, Kinnersley HR3 6QB (Tel & Fax: 01544 327727). 17th century farmhouse, totally redecorated during last four years. Lovely fabrics, crafts and paint techniques abound coupled with traditional fare, tasty farmhouse quantities served with fresh produce — vegetarians welcomed! Ideally situated for touring — the Black and White village trail, equidistant to Hay-on-Wye, Leominster and Hereford. Local activities range from the academic to the dangerous and in-between. Stencil craft courses available. Four-poster beds, private bathrooms, twin and family room. Drinks trays, extra blankets, fluffy towels and toiletry baskets in all rooms. Guests' own bathroom/dining/drawing rooms. We enjoy taking guests around the farm and try always to make your stay special. Open all year. Self catering cottage also available. No smoking.

HEREFORD & WORCESTERSHIRE – THE HEART OF ENGLAND!

A beautiful county which includes The Vale of Evesham and the rugged – if petite – Malvern Hills. It has been designated an "Area of Outstanding Beauty". Places of interest include The Avoncroft Museum of Buildings, Brockhampton, Ross-on-Wye, The Teme Valley and The Hereford & Worcester County Museum.

LEDBURY. Mrs Jane West, Church Farm, Coddington, Ledbury HR8 1JJ (01531 640271). Working farm. A Black and White 16th century listed farmhouse on a working farm, close to the Malvern Hills. Ideal for touring. Warm hospitality assured. There is accommodation in three double bedrooms, one with washbasin. Bathroom, toilet; sittingroom; diningroom. Children are welcome (reduced rates under 10 years). Plenty of good English fare, everything home made wherever possible. Log fires, TV, pets allowed. Open all year. Bed and Breakfast from £18; bedtime drink included. Car essential — parking. Situated midway between Ross-on-Wye, Hereford, Gloucester and Worcester. Tourist Board Listed. SAE, please, for further details. Excellent self catering cottage also available.

LEDBURY near. Mrs Elizabeth Godsall, Moor Court Farm, Stretton Grandison, Near Ledbury HR8 2TR (01531 670408). ♛♛♛ *Commended.* Relax and enjoy our attractive 15th century timber-framed farmhouse with its adjoining oast-houses, whose picturesque location will ensure a peaceful stay. We are a traditional hop and livestock farm situated in the beautiful countryside of Herefordshire being central to the local market towns, with easy access to the Malverns, Wye Valley and Welsh Borders. Guests will enjoy spacious bedrooms, all with en suite facilities, their own oak-beamed lounge, dining room and the peaceful setting of the garden or walks through surrounding woods and farmland with their rural views. Fishing is available in our own pool and there are stables on the farm. Bed and Breakfast £16; Evening Meal £12.50. Residential licence.

LONGTOWN. Mrs I. Pritchard, Olchon Cottage Farm, Longtown, Hereford HR2 0NS (0187-387 233). ♛ *Approved.* **Working farm.** An ideal location for a peaceful holiday in lovely walking country close to Offa's Dyke Path and Welsh Border. A smallholding of 32 acres, mostly sheep and cattle. The farmhouse is noted for its good, wholesome, home-produced food, and many guests return to enjoy the homely, relaxing atmosphere. Magnificent views and many places of interest to visit. Accommodation comprises two family bedrooms with washbasins, electric blankets, radios, colour TV, hairdryers and tea/coffee facilities; guest bathroom, toilet; sitting room and dining room with separate tables. Towels and soap provided. Reductions for children under 10; cot, high chair and babysitting offered. Pets accommodated. Open all year round except Christmas. Bed, Breakfast and Evening Meal, or Bed and Breakfast from £14.50. Car essential, parking provided. Terms on application with stamp for brochure, please.

MALVERN. Mrs F.W. Coates, Mill House, 16 Clarence Road, Great Malvern WR14 3EH (Malvern [01684] 562345). Originally a Georgian Water Mill at the foot of the beautiful Malvern Hills. Situated in tranquil grounds with croquet lawn and hill views. A few minutes' walk from the town centre or Great Malvern station. Malvern is an ideal centre for touring the Cotswolds, the Severn and Wye Valleys and Welsh Marches. Comfortable accommodation with full central heating, washbasins and tea/coffee making facilities in all bedrooms; (one double room with shower en-suite). Payphone. Parking within grounds. Bed and Breakfast from £16. No smoking. Also Mill Cottage for self-catering. SAE, please.

If you've found
FARM HOLIDAY GUIDES
of service please tell your friends

MALVERN. Jean and John Mobbs, Rock House, 144 West Malvern Road, Malvern WR14 4NJ (01684 574536). ♛ *Approved.* Attractive, family-run early Victorian guest house situated high on hills in peaceful atmosphere with superb views of over 40 miles. Ideal for rambling on hills or open country. 1[illegible] comfortable bedrooms, most overlooking our splendid view; hot and cold showers/ bathrooms, TV lounge, separate quiet room. Licensed to enhance excellent home cooked dinners. Groups welcome. Parking on premises. Bed and Breakfast from £16.50. Stamp only, please, for brochure. Also pretty self catering cottage available.

MALVERN WELLS. Mrs J.L. Morris, Brickbarns Farm, Hanley Road, Malvern Wells WR14 4HY (Malvern [016845] 61775). Working farm. Brickbarns, a 200-acre mixed farm, is situated two miles from Great Malvern at the foot of the Malvern Hills, 300 yards from the bus service and one-and-a half miles from the train. The house, which is 300 years old, commands excellent views of the Malvern Hills and guests are accommodated in one double, one single and one family bedrooms with wash-basins; two bathrooms, shower room, two toilets; sitting-room and diningroom. Children welcome and cot and babysitting offered. Central heating. Car essential, parking. Open Easter to October for Bed and Breakfast from £14 nightly per person. Reductions for children and Senior Citizens. Birmingham 40 miles, Hereford 20, Gloucester 17, Stratford 35 and the Wye Valley is just 30 miles.

APPLE TREE COTTAGE – Near HEREFORD

15th-century Cruck-construction cottage (full central heating) set in beautiful Hereford countryside – quiet, peaceful and friendly. Ideal for walkers and birdwatchers. Within easy reach of Cotswolds, North and South Wales, Black Mountains and many historic sites. One twin-bedded room with en-suite facilities, one double (single) and one twin-bedded room with shared bathroom; hot drinks tray; extra WC; lounge with TV. No smoking in bedrooms. BED AND BREAKFAST £18 (en-suite) and £15, reductions for 2 & 7 nights. Evening Meal and Packed Lunch by arrangement. We are open throughout the Winter. Car essential. Situated in the small hamlet of Mansel Lacy, seven miles N.W. of HEREFORD CITY, off the A480.

Enquiries to MONICA BARKER,
Apple Tree Cottage, Mansel Lacy,
Near Hereford HR4 7HH.
Tel: (0198 122) 688 – 24 hrs.

ROSS-ON-WYE. Mrs M.E. Drzymalska, Thatch Close, Llangrove, Ross-on-Wye HR9 6EL (Llangarron [01989] 770300). ♛♛ *Commended.* **Working farm, join in.** Secluded Georgian farmhouse set in large colourful gardens in 13 acres of pasture situated in the beautiful Wye Valley between Ross and Monmouth. Thatch Close offers a comfortable, homely atmosphere where guests are welcome to help feed the sheep, cows, calves, or just relax and enjoy this traditionally run farm. Places of scenic beauty and historic attractions nearby include Forest of Dean, Black Mountains, Cathedral Cities, old castles and buildings. Guests have their own lounge and diningroom with colour TV. Twin bedroom and one double room, both with bathrooms en-suite, one double room with private bathroom; all bathrooms have showers. Central heating. Non-smokers please. Breakfast and optional Evening Meal are prepared using mainly home grown produce. Vegetarian and diabetic meals arranged. Bed and Breakfast from £14 to £18 with reductions for longer stays. Reduced rates for children. SAE for further details.

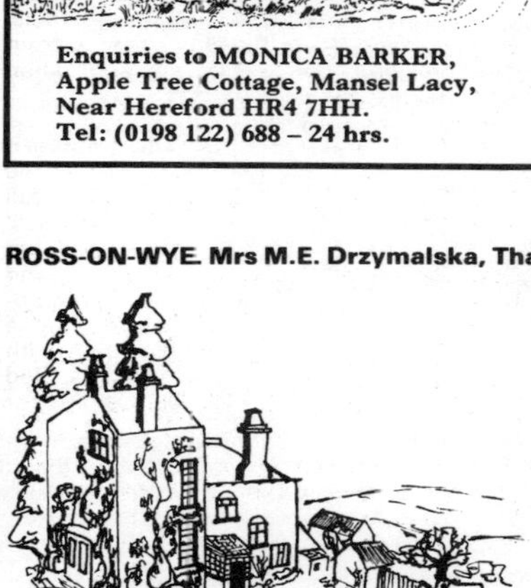

Terms quoted in this publication may be subject to increase if rises in costs necessitate

ROSS-ON-WYE. Mrs Susan Dick, Merrivale Place, The Avenue, Ross-on-Wye HR9 5AW (01989 564929). ♛ *Commended.* Merrivale Place is a lovely big Victorian house set in half an acre of gardens in a splendid tree-lined avenue. Peaceful surroundings overlooking trees and hills, yet close to the old market place centre of Ross, and near the River Wye. Guest accommodation in three spacious, comfortable bedrooms (double, twin and family) with wash-basins and shaver points. Three bathrooms, three toilets. TV lounge and separate diningroom. Full central heating. Good home cooking with garden produce. A very warm welcome extended to all guests. Sorry, no pets. Ample parking space inside grounds. Open April to October. Bed and Breakfast from £16 (Dinners available). Weekly terms. Come and see the lovely Wye Valley, Malverns, Brecon Beacons and the Golden Valley.

ROSS-ON-WYE. The Skakes Guest House, Glewstone, Ross-on-Wye HR9 6AZ (01989 770456). An 18th century former farmhouse, surrounded by gardens and the unspoilt, rolling Herefordshire countryside. All bedrooms have washbasins, colour TV, beverage trays, clock radios and some are fully en suite. Cosy lounges with log fire, and bar to relax in after a hard day's exploring. Evening meal available. Situated between Ross-on-Wye, Monmouth and Hereford and perfect for the Wye Valley, Forest of Dean and the Welsh Borders. A wealth of local attractions and characterful market towns will ensure that you are never at a loose end. We welcome children 10 years and over. Dogs by arrangement. Bed and Breakfast from £15. AA/ETB registered. For brochure and special Spring & Winter rates please ring.

ROSS-ON-WYE. Mrs Julie Kimpton, Brook House, Lea, Ross-on-Wye HR9 7JZ (Tel & Fax: 01989 750710). ♛♛ A fine Grade II Listed Queen Anne house in the centre of Lea, four miles from Ross on the Gloucester Road. We like to welcome all guests personally in an informal, friendly atmosphere with emphasis on comfort and good food. All rooms are comfortably furnished in country style, are centrally heated, and have colour TV and tea and coffee making facilities. Some are en suite. Breakfast isn't just a question of bacon and eggs! There is a wide choice and homemade muffins and cinnamon bread are a speciality. If you opt for "English" Breakfast we guarantee excellent local bacon, sausage and free range eggs. Evening meals are just as good and most types of diet can be catered for by arrangement. Bed and Breakfast from £15; Evening Dinner £10.75. Special weekly terms available. Non-smokers preferred.

ROSS-ON-WYE. Jean and James Jones, The Arches Hotel, Walford Road, Ross-on-Wye HR9 5PT (Ross-on-Wye [01989] 563348). ♛♛♛ Small family-run hotel, set in half an acre of lawned garden, ideally situated only 10 minutes' walk from town centre. All rooms are furnished and decorated to a high standard and have views of the garden. Tea/coffee making facilities and colour TV are available in bedrooms; some en suite rooms, also one ground floor en suite bedroom available. Full central heating. There is a delightful Victorian-style conservatory to relax in and the garden to enjoy in the summer months. Licensed. Ample parking in grounds. A warm and friendly atmosphere with personal service. Generous weekly reductions. Bed and Breakfast £15, en suite rooms £21. Dinner by arrangement. AA Listed, RAC Acclaimed, Les Routiers Award. Please telephone or send SAE for colour brochure.

TENBURY WELLS. Mrs Margaret Jane Yarnold, Court Farm, Hanley Childe, Tenbury Wells WR15 8QY (01885 410265). Working farm, join in. Court Farm is a charming 15th century renovated farmhouse with adjoining listed buildings, on a 200 acre mixed farm located in a quiet village with beautiful church nearby. From April to October, accommodation available in one double room with en suite facilities, one twin-bedded room with adjoining bathroom; visitors' lounge and dining room. Large garden. Home cooking and a comfortable, friendly atmosphere assured. Children welcome. Cot and high chair available. Special diets can be catered for. Regret no pets. Extensive, delightful views within short walking distance across Teme Valley. Market town of Tenbury Wells six miles. Close by are the historic towns of Ludlow, Worcester, Bewdley and Bromyard. Further afield is Stratford, the Cotswolds and Welsh Borders. Several gardens and National Trust properties locally. ETB Listed. Car essential. Local shop/post office in village. Terms from £15. SAE for further details please.

WEOBLEY. Tony and Una Williams, "The Gables Guest House", Broad Street, Weobley, Hereford HR4 8SA (Weobley [01544] 318228). ♛♛ Beautiful old 14th century Tudor house situated in the centre of one of England's prettiest villages. Open from January to November, "The Gables" is renowned for its hearty English Breakfasts. Several small cafes, restaurants and hotels in the village. An area of great natural beauty with the Malvern Hills and the Welsh Mountains easily accessible, it is also an antique and art lovers' paradise. "The Gables", set in one acre of lovely gardens, offers a choice of double, single and family bedrooms, all with washbasins, shaver points, tea/coffee making facilities; three rooms en-suite. All rooms are beautifully and comfortably furnished. Guests' lounge with colour TV. Three garden rooms. Two rooms available in Coach House, with shower/toilet. Pets accepted. Car not essential, but there is ample parking. Several golf courses nearby. Teas, coffees, snacks served all day. Registered with Heart of England and Promotion of Herefordshire Tourist Boards. Bed and Breakfast from £15.

WORCESTER near. Miss Jo Morris, Knowle Farm, Suckley, Near Worcester WR6 5DJ (01886 884347). Part-timbered 17th century farmhouse with 25 acres grassland, used mainly for horses. Adjacent to a small, quiet country inn, the house is in an elevated position with unrivalled views of the Malvern Hills and offers accommodation all year round. Large colourful garden. The quaint market towns of Bromyard, Ledbury and Hereford are nearby, and Knowle Farm is in the heart of a fruit-growing area where visitors enjoy the magnificent spring blossoms. Superb walking country. One double and two single bedrooms (one with washbasin); bathroom, toilet. Sittingroom with woodburner fire, diningroom. Central heating keeps the house comfortable throughout the year. Car essential — parking. Traditional hearty English Breakfast. Fresh farm eggs. Bed and Breakfast from £12.50 (bedtime drink). This is a non-smoking establishment.

WORCESTER near. Sylvia and Brian Wynn, The Old Smithy, Pirton, Worcester WR8 9EJ (Worcester [01905] 820482). A 17th century half-timbered country house set in peaceful countryside with many interesting walks. Centrally situated, within easy reach of Stratford-upon-Avon, Cotswolds, Malvern and Bredon Hills, Worcester Cathedral and Royal Worcester Porcelain. Four and a half miles from the motorway M5 Junction 7. Relaxed homely atmosphere. Lounge with inglenock log fire and colour TV. Two/three double bedrooms (one twin-bedded), bathroom and toilet. Private facilities and non-smoking accommodation also available. Central heating. Gardens and paddock. Ample parking. Bed and farmhouse Breakfast from £14.50 to £20; Evening Meal optional extra. Sorry, no pets or children under 10 years. Heart of England Tourist Board "Listed" — Highly Commended. Craft Workshop — Harris Tweed, woollens, etc.

PUBLISHER'S NOTE

While every effort is made to ensure accuracy, we regret that FHG Publications cannot accept responsibility for errors, omissions or misrepresentation in our entries or any consequences thereof. Prices in particular should be checked because we go to press early. We will follow up complaints but cannot act as arbiters or agents for either party.

KENT

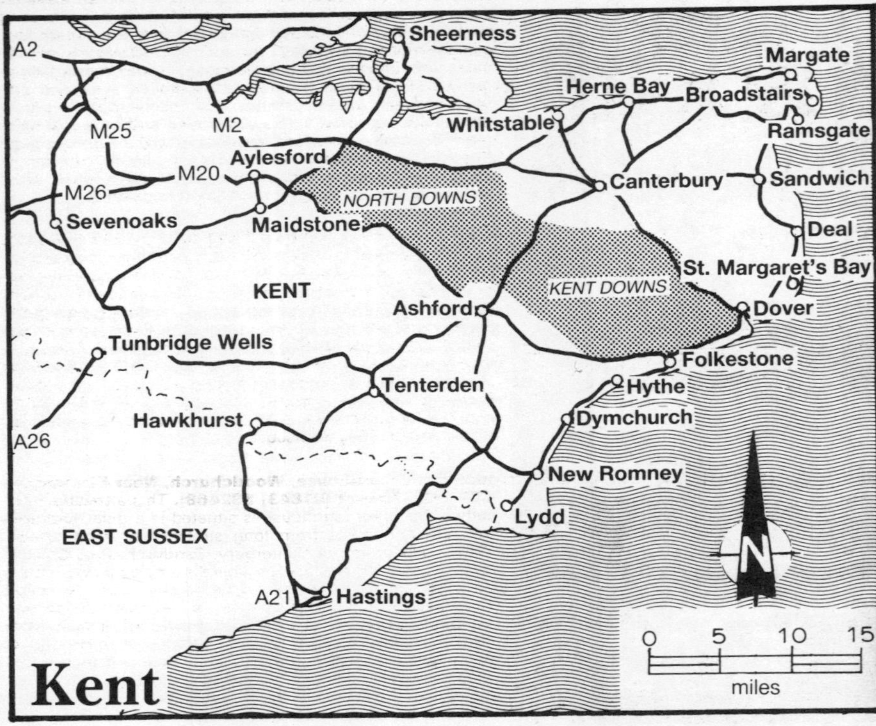

ALDINGTON. Ros and John Martin, Hogben Farm, Church Lane, Aldington, Ashford TN25 7EH (01233 720219). This farmhouse, dating from the sixteenth century, lies in a very quiet location, down its own drive, set among extensive gardens and lawns and bordered by 16 acres of meadows. It is an ideal centre for visits to Canterbury, Rye, Tenterden etc, and handy for the ferries and the Channel Tunnel. Accommodation comprises one double room and two twin rooms (no extra charge for single occupancy). A sitting room with inglenook fireplace and colour TV is available for guests. Not only tea and coffee in your room but also good home cooking for your Evening Meal (available by arrangement). Open all year. Bed and Breakfast from £15. Tourist Board Listed.

ASHFORD. Mrs I. Wreathall, Court Lodge, Appledore, Ashford TN26 2DD (01233 758403). *Highly Commended.* Arable farm. Court Lodge is an imposing Victorian farmhouse standing in four acres of mature garden and farmland grazed by sheep, with panoramic views over Romney Marsh. Just a short walk through the garden leads to the picturesque village of Appledore which is situated between Rye and Tenterden. Ideal base to visit Canterbury (28 miles), Chilham, Leeds Castle, Sissinghurst and the Marsh Churches. Near Channel Tunnel. Accommodation comprises one twin and one double rooms, both with private bathrooms. Bed and Breakfast only from £18.50 (minimum two nights). Supper Trays by arrangement, £7. Ample parking. Regret, no children.

ASHFORD. Mrs E. Ashby, Bevenden House, Spicers Hill, Great Chart, Ashford TN26 1JP (01233 820226). A warm welcome awaits you in this superior 17th century country residence set in 10 acres with an elevated position and beautiful views. Ideally situated for touring south-east England. On A28 Ashford to Tenterden road: four miles Ashford, eight miles Tenterden, 18 miles Maidstone, 48 miles from London. Full central heating. Diningroom; sitting-room with TV; one twin-bedded room en suite and one double room with en suite shower and washbasin, plus a further double room with guests' own bathroom. All with tea/coffee making facilities. Heated outdoor swimming pool. Bed and Breakfast from £17.50; Evening Meals by arrangement. Light supper available. Children over eight years welcome. Non-smoking. Tourist Board registered.

ASHFORD near. Elvey Farm Country Hotel, Pluckley, Near Ashford TN27 0SU (01233 840442). Completely secluded, this working farm offers luxury accommodation in converted oak beamed farm buildings. Five one or two bedroomed ground floor Stables adjoin the old Kent Barn which has two large family rooms. Oast House has a family room and two twin-bedded rooms. Each bedroom has colour TV, central heating and en-suite facilities. Pluckley is ideally situated for visiting the coast, Channel Ports and local attractions, with all outdoor activities being available nearby. Excellent farmhouse meals offered for a minimum of 10 people with home made produce to make your stay a holiday to remember. Fully licensed.

BIRCHINGTON near. Mrs Liz Goodwin, Woodchurch Farmhouse, Woodchurch, Near Birchington CT7 0HE (Thanet [01843] 832468). This attractive Elizabethan/Georgian farmhouse is situated in a quiet rural area yet only two miles from long stretches of sandy beach. Within easy reach of Canterbury, Sandwich, Rye, Chilham and the cross-Channel ferries. There is ample parking, a car is essential. Very comfortable bedrooms with tea/coffee making facilities. Sittingroom with TV. Bathroom and shower for guests' use only. Separate beamed diningroom. A warm welcome and a comfortable stay assured at Woodchurch. Bed and Breakfast from £14.50. Please write or telephone for further details.

CANTERBURY. Mrs Joan Hill, Renville Oast, Bridge, Canterbury CT4 5AD (01227 830215). Renville Oast is situated amongst apple orchards in beautiful Kentish countryside, only two miles from the Cathedral City of Canterbury, 10 miles from the coast and two hours' drive from London. Many interesting castles and historic houses within easy reach. Nature reserves, golf courses and Howletts Zoo nearby. A day trip to France is a possibility. All rooms are comfortable and attractively furnished, with tea making facilities. One family room en-suite, a twin-bedded room and double room with washbasins; separate bathroom; lounge/TV room. Bed and Breakfast from £19 per person includes good farmhouse breakfast. Excellent pub food nearby.

CANTERBURY. Mrs Lewana Castle, Great Field Farm, Misling Lane, Stelling Minnis, Canterbury CT4 6DE (01227 709223). In own pastures with friendly ponies, on a quiet country lane, adjacent B2068, comfortable farmhouse with Aga and full central heating. One double bedroom with own stairs, lounge, colour TV, kitchen and bathroom (also available for self catering); double bedroom, en-suite bathroom; twin-bedded room sharing separate bathroom. Guests welcome in elegant lounge with colour TV, dining room and farmhouse kitchen. Babysitting, refreshments and laundry available. Local restaurants. Bed and farmhouse Breakfast from £15.50 to £20. Reductions for children. Pets by arrangement. Non-smoking establishment. SAE or telephone. ETB Listed.

CANTERBURY. The Woodpeckers Country Hotel, Womenswold, Near Canterbury CT4 6HB (01227 831319). Charming Victorian Hotel situated six miles from Canterbury and nine miles from the coast. Woodpeckers boasts an attractive heated swimming pool, water slide, diving board and is set in two and a half acres of lawns and flower beds. Play area for children with sandpit and swing. 11 comfortable rooms, all en suite and with tea/coffee making facilities. TV lounge and quiet lounge; four-poster, brass bedstead, bridal bedrooms with colour TV, showers and WC. Central heating. Highly recommended English and Continental cuisine. Wealth of historic places to visit nearby. Packed lunches. Licensed. Bargain two/three-day breaks available October to April. RAC.

CANTERBURY. Mr and Mrs R. Linch, Upper Ansdore, Duckpit Lane, Petham, Canterbury CT4 5QB (Petham [01227] 700672). Beautiful secluded Listed Tudor farmhouse with various livestock, situated in an elevated position with far-reaching views of the wooded countryside of the North Downs. The property overlooks a Kent Trust Nature Reserve, it is five miles south of the cathedral city of Canterbury and only 30 minutes' drive to the ports of Dover and Folkestone. The accommodation comprises three double and one twin bedded rooms and family room. All have shower, WC en-suite and tea making facilities. Dining/sitting room, heavily beamed and with large inglenook. Car essential. Bed and Full English Breakfast from £18 per person. South East Tourist Board Listed. AA QQQ.

English Tourist Board

Listed

CANTERBURY. Mrs A. Hunt, Bower Farmhouse, Stelling Minnis, Near Canterbury CT4 6BB (01227 709430). Anne & Nick Hunt welcome you to Bower Farm House, a traditional 17th-century Kentish farmhouse situated in the midst of Stelling Minnis, a medieval common of 125 acres of unspoilt trees, shrubs and open grassland; seven miles south of the cathedral city of Canterbury and nine miles from the coast; the countryside abounds in beauty spots and nature reserves. The house is heavily beamed and maintains its original charm. The accommodation comprises a double room and a twin-bedded room, both with private facilities. Full traditional English breakfast is served with home-made bread, marmalade and fresh free-range eggs. Children welcome; pets by prior arrangement. Open all year (except Christmas). Car essential. Excellent pub food five minutes away. Bed and Breakfast from £17.50 per person. Tourist Board Listed.

DEAL. Mr and Mrs P.S.F. Jailler, "Blencathra Country Hotel", Kingsdown Hill, Kingsdown, Deal CT14 8EA (01304 373725). Blencathra is a small private hotel situated in the picturesque unspoilt village of Kingsdown. With panoramic views over the Channel and countryside, it is an ideal centre for a touring, walking or golfing holiday (close to four golf courses). Kingsdown is only five miles from the ferries at Dover and early breakfasts are available. Blencathra is a family run hotel offering eight bedrooms, personal service and attention from the proprietors. The hotel is in a private road and a peaceful stay is guaranteed. Open all year. Evening snacks available by prior arrangement. AA and RAC Listed. Bed and Breakfast from £17 per person.

ELMSTED. Mrs Jennifer Denny, High Lodge, Elmsted, Near Wye, Ashford TN25 5JL (0123 3750 234). Bed and Breakfast from £17, children two-thirds of adult price, toddlers free; Evening Meal by prior arrangement £8 per head. The cottage with the view. We extend a warm personal welcome to our 250-year-old Kent cottage, modernised and comfortable, with large garden and wholly exceptional all-round views over unspoiled Downland sheep/cereal farming countryside. Nine miles from Canterbury in seven o'clock direction, and nine miles from Ashford in two o'clock direction, in easy reach of the ports and most places of interest in East Kent. Ideal for walkers and connoisseurs of unspoilt countryside. One high ceilinged double bedroom with big views and own bathroom plus two single/double bedrooms and separate bathroom. Self catering accommodation also available. Details on application.

FOR THE MUTUAL GUIDANCE OF GUEST AND HOST

Every year literally thousands of holidays, short-breaks and overnight stops are arranged through our guides, the vast majority without any problems at all. In a handful of cases, however, difficulties do arise about bookings, which often could have been prevented from the outset.

It is important to remember that when accommodation has been booked, both parties — guests and hosts — have entered into a form of contract. We hope that the following points will provide helpful guidance.

GUESTS: When enquiring about accommodation, be as precise as possible. Give exact dates, numbers in your party and the ages of any children. State the number and type of rooms wanted and also what catering you require — bed and breakfast, full board, etc. Make sure that the position about evening meals is clear — and about pets, reductions for children or any other special points.

Read our reviews carefully to ensure that the proprietors you are going to contact can supply what you want. Ask for a letter confirming all arrangements, if possible.

If you have to cancel, do so as soon as possible. Proprietors do have the right to retain deposits and under certain circumstances to charge for cancelled holidays if adequate notice is not given and they cannot re-let the accommodation.

HOSTS: Give details about your facilities and about any special conditions. Explain your deposit system clearly and arrangements for cancellations, charges, etc, and whether or not your terms include VAT

If for any reason you are unable to fulfil an agreed booking without adequate notice, you may be under an obligation to arrange alternative suitable accommodation or to make some form of compensation.

While every effort is made to ensure accuracy, we regret that FHG Publications cannot accept responsibility for errors, omissions or misrepresentation in our entries or any consequences thereof. Prices in particular should be checked because we go to press early. We will follow up complaints but cannot act as arbiters or agents for either party.

FAVERSHAM. N.J. and C.I. Scutt, Leaveland Court, Leaveland, Faversham ME13 0NP (01233 740596). Guests are warmly welcomed to our enchanting timbered 15th century farmhouse which nestles between Leaveland Church and woodlands in rural tranquillity. Offering high standards of accommodation whilst retaining their original character, all bedrooms are en suite with colour TV and hot drinks trays. Traditional breakfasts, cooked on the Aga, are available with a choice of alternatives. There is a large attractive garden with heated outdoor swimming pool for guests' use and ample car parking. Ideally situated for visiting Kent's historic cities, castles, houses and gardens with Canterbury only 20 minutes by car and also easy access to Channel ports, 30 minutes. Good walking country, being close to both the Pilgrim's Way and the coast.

HEADCORN. Mrs Jane Harman, Vine Farm, Waterman Quarter, Headcorn TN27 9JJ (01622 890203; Fax: 01622 891819). Working farm. Vine Farm is situated amongst sheep meadows in a peaceful position along its own private track, surrounded by colourful gardens and ponds (Jane Harman is a keen gardener). The Listed farmhouse is 16th century, comfortable yet retaining its original charm and attractively furnished. There is a guests' sittingroom and two double and one twin bedrooms with en suite or private bathrooms, tea/coffee facilities and files full of information on Kent's historic sites and gardens. Excellent base for touring since Headcorn is centrally situated in Kent. Bed and Breakfast from £19.50. Dinner by arrangement. Open all year except Christmas. Visa/Mastercard accepted.

South East England Tourist Board MEMBER

MAIDSTONE. The White Lodge, Linton, Maidstone ME17 4AG (01622 743129). Guests return again and again to this elegant house beautifully situated in parkland overlooking the Weald of Kent. 15 minutes from Leeds Castle, four miles from Central Maidstone and within easy reach of Sissinghurst Castle and many other interesting places. Well established with a friendly relaxed atmosphere, guests are encouraged to enjoy the two and a half acre garden with two ponds. Ample parking. Quiet location. Terms £19 per person per night with full English breakfast. En suite double/family room with sitting room and kitchen available. Directions: south on A229, onto B2163, first right Loddington Lane, near to the bottom of hill, on right. Tourist Board registered.

ROLVENDEN. Mrs B.J. Hilder, Little Halden Farm, Rolvenden, Cranbrook TN17 4JL (01580 241254). Working farm. The farmhouse on a working hop and livestock farm is situated in an area of outstanding natural beauty. The picturesque town of Tenterden with its steam railway and leisure centre is only two miles away. Visit the old Cinque Port town of Rye, Canterbury Cathedral, Dover Castle and many other places of interest in the area. There are two double rooms and one twin, each furnished to a high standard and having washbasins, colour TV and tea/coffee making facilities. Separate shower and bathroom for guests' use. All rooms are centrally heated. Bed and Breakfast from £15 per person. Non-smoking.

KENT – THE GARDEN OF ENGLAND!

The pleasant landscape of Kent, including The North Downs and The Weald, is the host of many engaging places to visit. These include Chiddingstone – the half-timbered village, the sophisticated spa town of Tunbridge Wells and Swanton Mill. There are also day trips to the continent and for railway enthusiasts, The Sittingbourne & Kensley Light Railway, The Kent & East-Sussex Railway and the 'World's Smallest Public Railway' from Hythe to Dungeness.

SEVENOAKS. Mrs Amanda Webb, Pond Cottage, Eggpie Lane, Weald, Sevenoaks TN14 6NP (Sevenoaks [01732] 463773). Beautiful Grade II listed 16th century farmhouse with inglenook fireplace and oak beams. Set in three and a half acres of grounds with tennis court and a large, safely fenced pond with fish, kingfishers and wild duck. This is beautiful countryside and yet only 30 minutes by train to London; one hour to the coast at Dover, Eastbourne and Brighton. Sir Winston Churchill's Chartwell, Penshurst, Knole and some excellent and historic pubs nearby. Accommodation in one family room/double room (own bathroom, toilet and shower). Mrs Webb provides lovely cooked Breakfasts plus fruit juice, cereal and home made bread. Colour TV in sittingroom. Children welcome at reduced rates; babysitting. Pets by prior arrangement. Open all year. Registered with English Tourist Board. Please telephone for reservation or more information.

SUTTON VALENCE. Mrs Stephanie Clout, Sparks Oast Farm, Forsham Lane, Sutton Valence, Maidstone ME17 3EW (01622 842213). Sparks Oast is a characteristic converted Kentish Oasthouse, on a small sheep farm in quiet country lane overlooking the Weald of Kent. Ideally situated for visiting the many attractive castles, famous gardens such as Sissinghurst, Scotney Castle, etc and other places of interest in the Garden of England, or just rambling amid orchards and hop gardens. There is a wealth of excellent pubs offering good food. A warm welcome by the family including the animals, waterfowl, barn owls, etc. Bed and Breakfast from £16 per person. One double room with sofa bed, one twin and one en suite. TV. Guests' bathroom and beverage facilities. ALSO SELF CATERING SUITE.

TENTERDEN. Mrs M.R. O'Connor, The Old Post House, Stone-in-Oxney, Tenterden TN30 7JN (01233 758258). Experience the peace and tranquillity of rural England at its best. This guest house overlooks the historic expanse of Romney Marsh and nestles against the hill of the Isle-in-Oxney in the heart of Kentish farmland. Only about ten minutes' drive to the delightful market towns of Rye and Tenterden, where excellent meals can be enjoyed. All rooms are equipped with central heating, washbasins, razor points, tea/coffee making facilities. One room with en suite facilities. Bathroom and shower room. Open all year round. Children over eight years welcome. Pets must be left in car. Bed and traditional English Breakfast from £18 to £20 per person; delicious food can also be had in the village. Car essential, ample parking.

WEST HYTHE. Mrs Emma Catt, Harveyland Farm, West Hythe CT21 4NR (01303 873738). Peaceful, friendly farmhouse set in 25 acres of countryside and situated three and a half miles from the Cinque Port of Hythe. Ideal for visiting France, Canterbury, Rye and the beautiful Weald of Kent. Rooms have TV and own bathroom. Amenities are on one level and rooms open onto a patio with lovely views. Mrs Emma Catt provides a delicious English breakfast; in winter tea is served in front of log fires. Supper is served on request and special diets catered for. Ideal area for fishing, walking, cycling Bed and Breakfast £15. All welcome.

Please mention this guide when you write or phone to enquire about accommodation.

If you are writing, a stamped, addressed envelope is always appreciated.

LANCASHIRE

BACUP. Ann Isherwood, Pasture Bottom Farm, Bacup OL13 9UZ (01706 873790). We offer farmhouse accommodation in a quiet rural area on a true working beef farm with delicious home cooked meals in a relaxed away-from-it-all atmosphere. Two twin-bedded rooms are available with washbasins, colour TV and tea/coffee making facilities. Evening meals by prior arrangement. Magnificent country views, centrally located for the Pennines and Yorkshire Moors, Lancashire hill country and within easy reach of Manchester by M66 making it ideal for business people. Bed and Breakfast from £13 per night; Evening Meal from £6. A Farm Holiday Bureau Member.

BLACKPOOL near. Mrs Maureen Smith, Todderstaffe Hall Farm, Singleton, Near Blackpool FY6 8LF (01253 882537). ♛♛ *Commended.* Todderstaffe Hall Farm is a 260 acre arable farm which is situated in the heart of the Fylde countryside just four miles from Blackpool and within easy reach of Lake District and Trough of Bowland. As well as the obvious attractions of Blackpool, nearby activities include swimming, golf, horse riding and fishing. We aim to keep a friendly old-world atmosphere in our oak beamed farmhouse, recently renovated to provide all modern comforts. En suite family room, centrally heated, with tea/coffee making facilities and colour TV. Children welcome. Reduced terms May and June. Ring **Mrs Smith** for details.

CLITHEROE. Mrs Frances Oliver, Wytha Farm, Rimington, Clitheroe BB7 4EQ (01200 445295). Working farm. Farmhouse accommodation on stockrearing farm in Ribble Valley with extensive views. Within walking distance of Pendle Hill. Ideal touring centre for Lake District, Yorkshire Dales, Bronte Country, interesting and historic Clitheroe. Children welcome. Babysitting service. Beautiful picnic area. Packed lunches available. Farm produce when possible, and home cooking. Accommodation comprises family and double rooms; TV lounge; central heating. Ample car parking. Pets by prior arrangement (£1 per day). Bed and Breakfast from £13.50; Evening Meal £8. Reduced rates for children under 11 years. Open all year.

GARSTANG near. Mrs D.J. Hodge, Lower House Farm, Bilsborrow Lane, Bilsborrow, Near Garstang PR3 0RQ (Brock [01995] 640581). Working farm. A warm Christian welcome awaits you when you decide to stay on this working dairy farm deep in the Lancashire countryside. Peaceful surroundings, yet only 10 miles from Preston and 15 miles from Lancaster. An ideal base for the seaside, the Lake District and the Universities of Lancaster and Central Lancashire. One double bedded room and one twin bedded room with en-suite facilities. Non-smoking accommodation available. Own dining/sittingroom with TV. Hospitality trays in bedrooms. Terms from £13.50 per person per night. Sorry no pets. SAE for details.

LANCASTER. Roy and Helen Domville, Three Gables, Chapel Lane, Galgate, Lancaster LA2 0NP (01524 752222). A large detached bungalow, three miles south of Lancaster and 400 yards from Lancaster University. Access from M6 Junction 33 and A6 in Galgate village. Two double bedrooms with colour TV and tea/coffee facilities. One bedroom has private bathroom, the other has washbasin and use of the main bathroom with shower. Open all year with full central heating. Cot and high chair are available. Spacious parking. Sorry, no pets. A good location for visiting Blackpool, Morecambe, the Lake District and Yorkshire Dales. You will be sure of a friendly welcome and a homely atmosphere. Non-smokers only please. Bed and Breakfast only £15 single, £25 double.

Buy one day pass and get another free on visits to FRONTIERLAND, Morecambe, Lancashire, when you use our READERS' OFFER VOUCHER.

PRESTON. Mrs. Heather Smith, Swarbrick Hall Farm, Singleton Road, Weeton, Near Kirkham PR4 3JJ (01253 836465). ♛♛ **Working farm.** Georgian farmhouse on 200-acre working farm, situated in rural area. Swarbrick Hall is within easy reach of the hustle and bustle of Blackpool, and also the quieter resort of Lytham St. Annes. The location is also ideal for access to the Lake District, Trough of Bowland and the Yorkshire Dales. Comfortable spacious accommodation is offered, comprising one double/family room with ensuite bathroom. Central heating, colour TV, tea/coffee making facilities, separate lounge and dining room. Children welcome, cot, high chair, reduced rates for children under 14 years. Pets by arrangement. Open all year. Also available is one self-contained cottage, sleeps four/five. Open May to October. Car essential. Bed and Breakfast from £15 per night.

SOUTHPORT. Mrs Wendy E. Core, Sandy Brook Farm, 52 Wyke Cop Road, Scarisbrick, Southport PR8 5LR (Scarisbrick [01704] 880337). ♛♛ Bill and Wendy Core offer a homely, friendly atmosphere at Sandy Brook, a small working farm situated three and a half miles from the seaside resort of Southport and five miles from the historic town of Ormskirk. Motorways are easily accessible, and the Lake District, Trough of Bowland, Blackpool and North Wales are within easy reach. Six en suite bedrooms with colour TV and tea/coffee making facilities. Central heating throughout. Sittingroom with colour TV; diningroom. High chair, cots and babysitting available. Open all year round. Member of North West Tourist Board. Bed and Breakfast from £15; reductions for children. Weekly terms on request.

LEICESTERSHIRE

OLD DALBY. Mr and Mrs Anderson, Home Farm, Church Lane, Old Dalby, Near Melton Mowbray LE14 3LB (Melton Mowbray [01664] 822622). Comfortable 18th/19th century listed farmhouse and attractive gardens on edge of conservation village in lovely Vale of Belvoir. Peaceful overnight stop, yet only two miles from A46, A606, A6006. Half hour from A1, M1, M42, M69; and from Nottingham, Leicester, Loughborough, Oakham, Grantham, Belvoir Castle, etc. Seven miles north west Melton Mowbray. Single and twin en suite rooms. Generous country breakfasts. Excellent meals at acclaimed Crown Inn just a five minute walk across village green. Open all year. Advance bookings only. Bed and Breakfast from £18 to £27 per person per night. Non-smoking accommodation available. ETB registered, AA listed. Elizabeth Gundrey recommended. Guestaccom inspected and approved. Visa/Master/Euro cards accepted.

LINCOLNSHIRE

BENNIWORTH. Mrs Olivant, Skirbeck Farm, Panton Road, Benniworth LN3 6JN (01507 313682. Fax: 01507 313692). Enjoy a stay on a working farm, whilst visiting the beautiful Lincolnshire Wolds. This peaceful location is surrounded by good walking country including the Viking Way. It is 16 miles east of the Cathedral city of Lincoln and only a few miles from the interesting market towns of Louth, Horncastle and Market Rasen. The east coast and South Yorkshire (via the Humber Bridge) all within easy touring distance. The farm has trout and coarse fishing, also an off-road driving course: tuition available. The farmhouse is comfortably furnished, has central heating and log fires. All bedrooms have colour TV and Teasmaid, with bathrooms adjacent. Sun lounge overlooking secluded garden. Children welcome. Non-smokers only please. Self catering cottages also available.

GRANTHAM. Mrs Freda Mival, Woodlands, West Willoughby, Near Ancaster, Grantham NG32 3SH (01400 230340). This quiet farmhouse accommodation is set on a 12 acre smallholding on the A153 coast road, with Grantham and Sleaford seven miles, Lincoln 20 miles. Within easy reach of Robin Hood country, and Belton House is four miles away. A car is essential and there is ample parking. We are open Easter to October. There is a twin-bedded room and a family room, tea/coffee making facilities available; bathroom and toilet. Evening Meal provided by arrangement using mainly home produced food. Children are welcome and there is a cot, high chair and babysitting. Tourist Board registered. AA listed. Bed and Breakfast from £16 single, £28 double. Reductions for children.

HOLBEACH. Maureen Biggadike, Cackle Hill House, Cackle Hill Lane, Holbeach PE12 8BS (01406 426721). We welcome you to our farm situated in rural position just off the A17. Comfortable accommodation comprises one twin-bedded room en suite, one double and one twin-bedded rooms with washbasins and sharing guest bathroom. Traditional farmhouse fare. Farm walks. Large patio and gardens. Close to the shores of the Wash with its marshes, trails and nature reserves, Spalding, Boston, Norfolk and Cambridgeshire. Open all year. Bed and Breakfast from £16; Evening Meal from £10.

HORNCASTLE. Mrs J. Bankes Price, Greenfield Farm, Minting, Near Horncastle LN9 5RX (01507 578457). Judy and Hugh welcome you to their comfortable farmhouse set in a tranquil location, surrounded by open countryside and spacious gardens with a large pond. It is centrally placed for the main Lincolnshire attractions and borders the Chambers Wood Forest Nature Reserve. Guests have their own sittingroom with colour TV and woodburning stove; pretty en suite shower rooms, heated towel rails; radios, tea/coffee making facilities, central heating. One double and one twin with en suite facilities, one double with private bathroom. Excellent pub with traditional country cooking within one mile. Non-smoking household. AA QQQQ Selected. Farm Holiday Bureau member. Bed and Breakfast from £18.

LANGTON-BY-WRAGBY. Miss Jessie Skellern, Lea Holme, Langton-by-Wragby LN3 5PZ (01673 858339). Ground floor accommodation in comfortable, chalet-type house set in own half-acre peaceful garden. All amenities. Central for touring Wolds, coast, fens, historic Lincoln etc. So much to discover in this county with wonderful skies and room to breathe. Attractive market towns, Louth, Horncastle (famed for antiques), Boston, Spilsby, Alford, Woodhall Spa (noted for golf). Accommodation offered in two double bedrooms (can be let as single), with washbasins; bathroom, toilet adjoining; lounge with colour TV always available to guests, separate dining room. Drinks provided. Children welcome at reduced rates. Pets welcome (no charge). Car almost essential, parking. Basically Room and Breakfast, but Evening Meals can be had by arrangement. Bed and Breakfast from £15 per person; limited Evening Meals £7. Numerous eating places nearby. Open all year.

LINCOLN near. Mrs Brenda Williams, Gallow Dale Farm, Sturton by Stow, Lincoln LN1 2AH (01427 788387). AA QQQQ Selected. Situated eight miles north-west of Lincoln on the A1500 road between the villages of Sturton by Stow and Marton (one mile west of Sturton by Stow village centre). Tastefully refurbished, centrally heated, Grade II Listed Georgian farmhouse set in 33 acres of grass paddocks. TV lounge with beamed ceiling and separate dining room for guests. Tea/coffee making facilities in all bedrooms. Full English farmhouse breakfast provided. Lunch and evening meals available at three local public houses. Sorry, no smoking. Terms from £14 to £15 (adult) Bed and Breakfast.

LUDFORD. Tom and Mary Thornalley, Hainton Walk Farm, Ludford, Lincoln LN3 6AP (01507 313242). Our Georgian house is situated in an area of outstanding natural beauty on the edge of the Wolds. Within easy reach of Lincoln City, a market town and antique centre of the North. Trout fishing, car racing, horse racing, the coast all nearby, and there are many popular walks. Accommodation comprises large TV lounge with log fires if required; large diningroom with separate tables. One family/twin room, one double bedroom with washbasin; one single. Large bathroom with shower. Wireless alarm, tea/coffee making facilities available. Central heating and electric fires. Three quarters of an acre garden with lawns. Ample parking. Bed and Breakfast from £13 to £14; Evening Meals by request. Tourist Board Listed "Commended".

MAXEY. Mrs Fitton, Abbey House, West End Road, Maxey PE6 9EJ (Market Deeping [01778] 344642). 👑👑 Comfortably furnished guest house in one acre of mature gardens. Dating in part from 1190, it belonged to Thorney Abbey and Peterborough Minster before serving as a vicarage and possesses several features of historical interest. All bedrooms are well appointed, offering refreshment facilities and colour TV. The locality abounds in attractive stone built villages, stately homes and castles. Stamford (five miles), Crowland Abbey, Rutland Water, Peakirk Wildfowl Trust and Peterborough Cathedral are close at hand, whilst Ely and Cambridge are reached within one hour. Private carp lake. SAE, please, or telephone for details.

NORFOLK

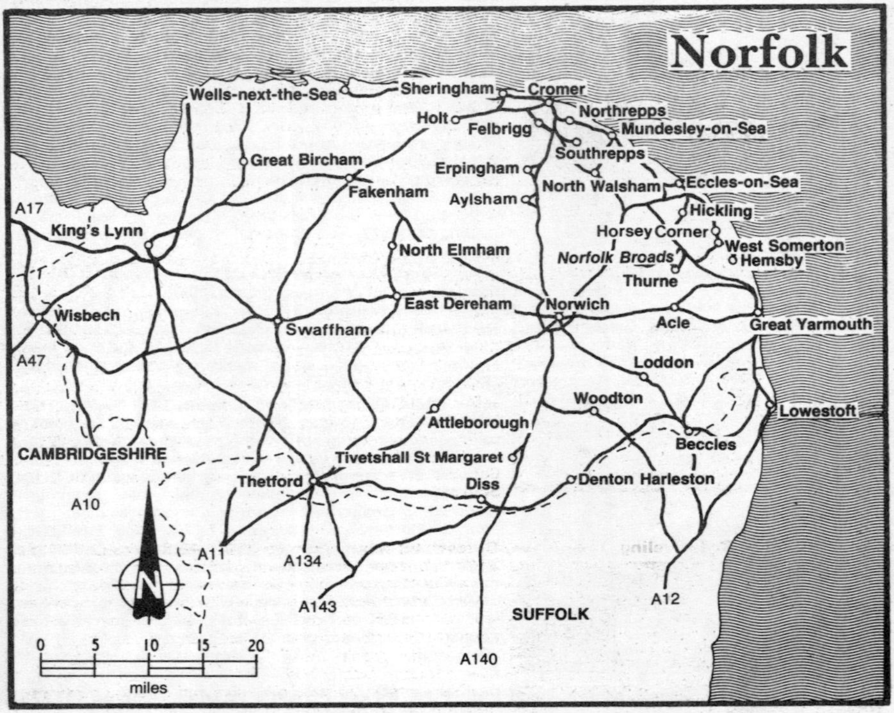

AYLSHAM. The Old Pump House, Holman Road, Aylsham, Norwich NR11 6BY (01263 733789).

This comfortable 1750's family house, facing the thatched pump a minute from Aylsham's church and historic marketplace, has five bedrooms, three en suite, all with colour TV and tea/coffee making facilities. English Breakfast (with free range eggs and local produce) or Continental Breakfast is served in the pine-shuttered Red Sitting Room overlooking the garden. Aylsham is central for Norwich, the coast, the Broads, National Trust houses, steam railways and unspoilt countryside. Well behaved children are very welcome. Bed and Breakfast from £17 to £20. Dinner by prior arrangement. Half Board Awaybreaks are available from October to June. Non-smoking.

BECCLES near. Mrs R. M. Clarke, Shrublands Farm, Burgh St. Peter, Near Beccles, Suffolk NR34 0BB (01502 677241). *Commended.* This attractive homely farmhouse which is pleasantly situated in the Waveney Valley on the Suffolk border is surrounded by one acre of garden and lawns. The River Waveney flows through the 550 acres of mixed working farmland; opportunities for bird-watching. Ideal base for touring Norfolk and Suffolk; Beccles, Lowestoft, Great Yarmouth and Norwich are all within easy reach. The house has two double rooms and one family room, with washbasins; two toilets, shower room, bathroom; sittingroom, diningroom, separate lounge with colour TV and tea/coffee making facilities. All bedrooms have satellite colour TV. Games room for snooker and darts. Tennis court available; swimming pool and food at River Centre nearby. Children over five welcome at reduced rates. Car essential, parking. Open all year. Bed and Breakfast from £16 to £17. No pets. SAE, please.

BUNGAY. Mrs Bobbie Watchorn, Earsham Park Farm, Harleston Road, Earsham, Bungay, Suffolk NR35 2AQ (01986 892180). ♛♛ *Highly Commended.* Stay with every comfort in our outstanding Victorian farmhouse with beautiful views, set in the middle of a 600 acre farm. The rooms are warm and elegantly furnished, all having beverage facilities, colour TVs, radios and en suite bathrooms; four-poster bed available. Enjoy our large gardens and collection of unusual farm animals. Lots of lovely home produced food. Evening Meal available by arrangement. Many local attractions including the Otter Trust. Easy access Norwich and the coast. This is a real "home from home". Open all year. FHB Member. Bed and Breakfast from £35 double/twin. Sorry no pets or smoking.

COLTISHALL. The Hedges Guest House, Tunstead Road, Coltishall NR12 7AL (01603 738361; Fax: 01603 738983). ♛♛ The Hedges Guest House, in picturesque Coltishall, is situated seven miles from Norwich and two miles from Wroxham, in a delighful rural part of the Norfolk Broads, England's newest National Park, close to the River Bure and village amenities. Each room has colour TV and tea/coffee making facilities, most are en-suite. Comfortable lounge with log fire; residential licence. Diningroom serving full English breakfast. An acre and a half of garden for you to enjoy. Facilities are available nearby for fishing, sailing, wind surfing, birdwatching and country walks, as well as the many places of interest which Norfolk has to offer. Bed and Breakfast from £20 en suite per person. AA QQQQ Selected.

CROMER. Mr J. R. Graveling, The Grove, Overstrand Road, Cromer NR27 0DJ (Cromer [01263] 512412). ♛♛ The Grove is an 18th-century holiday home magnificently set in its own three-acre grounds of fields, gardens and trees. There are walks through the fields and woods to cliffs, golf courses and beach. The small fishing town of Cromer is within walking distance, with its pier, lifeboat, fine church, museum, shops and eating places. We have a lounge, games room, large garden and we grow our own vegetables. We also have five self catering cottages in the grounds. Ideal holiday for young or old. Six double, two single, three family bedrooms with washbasins; four rooms have showers; six with en-suite bathrooms; four toilets. Diningroom. Cot, high chair, reduced rates for children. Sorry, no pets. Open April to October for Evening Meal, Bed and Breakfast from £157 per week; Bed and Breakfast from £105 per week.

DISS. Mrs Susan Chubbock, Rookery Farm, Aslacton, Norwich NR15 2ER (01379 677250). Working farm. You are assured of a warm welcome at Rookery Farmhouse, our 16th century home, which has a wealth of oak beams and an inglenook fireplace. Our 120 acre mixed farm has a variety of animals of all ages including rare breeds and is ideal for a family holiday or just a short break in peaceful countryside. Many interesting places to visit close by: Banham Zoo only seven miles. Situated 14 miles south of Norwich, only three and a half miles from A140. There is a spacious family/double room with vanity unit, colour TV and tea/coffee making facilities. Separate toilet. Diningroom. Disabled facilities. Children welcome at reduced rates, cot and high chair available. Bring your dog/horse by arrangement. Reductions on stays of four nights or more. Tourist Board Listed and Approved. Bed and Breakfast from £15.

NORFOLK – THE BROADS!

Formed by the flooding of medieval peat diggings, the Broads have a unique quality which attracts thousands of visitors each year. Slow moving waterways are bounded by reed and sedge, and despite the pressures of the modern world are home to rare birds, butterflies and plants. Motor boats and sailing boats can be hired in most towns and villages and there are lots of lively riverbank pubs to round off a day afloat.

DISS near. "The Strenneth", Airfield Road, Fersfield, Diss IP22 2BP (01379 688182; Fax: 01379 688260). ♛♛ *Commended.* This family run 17th century farmhouse standing in a lovely lawned garden close to the market town of Diss has been renovated to a very high standard while retaining the period features of the building: oak beams, open fires, window seats. All bedrooms are decorated and furnished with taste and style and now have en suite facilities and colour TVs, most of them are on the ground floor. One of the Executive rooms has a magnificent four poster bed and a "Pharaoh" bath; there is an especially attractive residents' lounge which has been furnished with period furniture to harmonise with the heavily beamed ceiling and walls. The food is of very high standard indeed, special diets can be catered for and local produce is used extensively by the chef/owner. Diss is a charming little town and is central to most of East Anglia's tourist attractions. Open all year. No smoking in part of dining room, some bedrooms and one lounge. Vegetarian and other diets, but not Vegan, by arrangement. Licensed. Tea/coffee making in all rooms. Pets welcome. Bed and Breakfast from £22; Dinner £18. Ladies and gents HAIRDRESSING SALON now open.

EAST DEREHAM. Old Hall Farm, Scarning, Dereham NR19 2LG (01362 691754). A large 16th century Grade II Listed timber frame farmhouse with one acre garden and lawns, plus private fishing available to guests. Set amongst open countryside, two miles from Dereham town centre, one mile off A47 bypass. Norfolk offers sandy beaches, golf, sailing, riding, swimming and the Norfolk Broads. Also stately homes, museums, bird sanctuary and wildlife parks. Accommodation comprises one double room with en suite facilities, one double and one twin with separate bath/WC. Central heating, TV and tea/coffee facilities in all rooms. Guest lounge with TV and log fire. Open all year for weekly or short stays. Bed and Breakfast from £15 to £17.50 per person per day. Car essential, ample parking. Sorry no pets and no children under eight years.

FAKENHAM. Mrs Maureen Walpole, "Hardlands", East Raynham, Fakenham NR21 7EQ (Fakenham [01328] 862567). A friendly welcome and relaxing atmosphere await you at "Hardlands". Peaceful countryside surrounds the house and its pleasant one-acre gardens. Furnished to high standards the comfortable five-bedroomed house is four miles from Fakenham on A1065, ideally situated for visiting Royal Sandringham, historic King's Lynn, North Norfolk coast, bird sanctuaries, Pensthorpe Waterfowl Trust, National Trust properties, Norwich and the Broads. Double and twin-bedded rooms with tea/coffee making facilities. Guests' TV lounge/dining room. Log fires and central heating. Bed and full English Breakfast from £15. Seasonal Short Breaks and weekly terms on request. ETB Listed "Highly Commended".

HAPPISBURGH. Mrs Jill Morris and Miss Diana Wrightson, Cliff House Guest House, Restaurant and Teashop, Beach Road, Happisburgh, Norwich NR12 0PP (Walcott [01692] 650775). Commanding views of sea and lighthouse, Cliff House is situated in an attractive, unspoilt and friendly village, six miles east of North Walsham. Happisburgh's wide sandy beach — safe for bathing — is rated as one of the cleanest Norfolk beaches so it is a favourite family resort. Visitors can enjoy the Broads, craft centres, windmills, stately homes and interesting small market towns. Accommodation comprises one twin/family room, one double and one single room — all with washbasins and tea/coffee making facilities; two bathrooms and a residents' lounge with TV. We offer a warm welcome, excellent home cooking, fresh vegetables and home-made bread. Diets catered for. Bed and Breakfast from £14.50; other meals available. Special prices for childen and Senior Citizens. Budget Breaks.

HEMSBY. Mrs Margaret Lake, Old Station House, North Road, Hemsby, Near Great Yarmouth NR29 4EZ (01493 732022). This large country house, set in the village of Hemsby, is only half a mile from golden beaches and is ideally situated for touring the Norfolk Broads and National Trust properties. The lovely accommodation comprises guest lounge with colour TV; separate dining room; three double bedrooms and one family room, all with vanitory units and washbasins. Separate toilet and bathroom. Free tea-making facilities. Full central heating. No smoking. Bed and Breakfast from £14. Open all year except Christmas. Telephone or send SAE for further details.

WHEN MAKING ENQUIRIES PLEASE MENTION THIS *FHG* PUBLICATION

HOLT. Mrs Lynda-Lee Mack, Hempstead Hall, Holt NR25 6TN (01263 712224). ♛♛ Enjoy a relaxing holiday and a friendly atmosphere in our 19th century flint farmhouse attractively set on a 300 acre arable farm with ducks, donkeys and large gardens. Close to the North Norfolk Coast and its many attractions, Hempstead Hall is ideally situated for walking, sailing and bird watching. There is a five mile circular walk through our conservation award winning farm to Holt Country Park. Large en suite family room, double with private bathroom. Colour TV, tea/coffee facilities. Large lounge with log burning stove. Non smoking. Sorry, no pets indoors. Bed and Breakfast from £16 per person. Children's reductions. Member of Farm Holiday Bureau.

HUNSTANTON. Arthur and Jenny Chapman, "Coralyn", 12 Glebe Avenue, Hunstanton PE36 6BS (01485 534672). A warm welcome awaits you at "Coralyn", a small, friendly, family-run guest house, close to town centre, beach and all amenities. We can guarantee personal attention as "Coralyn" is our home. Bedrooms are provided with TV, tea/coffee making facilities; full central heating throughout. Guests are supplied with their own keys for unlimited access. We have a comfortable sittingroom/breakfast room for guests at all times. Delicious home cooked food for breakfast and optional three-course evening dinner. There is a lockable store in the garden for cycles. Hunstanton offers plenty to do for all the family — Winner of Clean Beach and Seawater Award. Ideal base for exploring beautiful Norfolk countryside, Royal Sandringham six miles. Bed and Breakfast from £15 per night. Reductions for weekly stays; Senior Citizens low season rates. Tourist Board registered, Holder of Food Hygiene Certificate.

KING'S LYNN, Central Norfolk. Mrs G. Davidson, Holmdene Farm, Beeston, King's Lynn PE32 2NJ (Fakenham [01328] 701284). Working farm, join in. Holmdene Farm is a mixed farm with rare breeds situated in central Norfolk within easy reach of the coast and Broads. Sporting activities are available locally, and the village pub is nearby. The 17th century farmhouse is comfortable and welcoming with log fires and beams. Two double rooms, one en-suite, both with beverage trays. Pets welcome. Bed and Breakfast from £13 per person; Evening Meal from £9. Weekly terms available and child reductions. There is also a self catering flint cottage for eight and a mobile home for six available. Both fully equipped. From £70 per week. Tourist Board registered.

HELP IMPROVE BRITISH TOURIST STANDARDS

You are choosing holiday accommodation from our very popular FHG Publications. Whether it be a hotel, guest house, farmhouse or self-catering accommodation, we think you will find it hospitable, comfortable and clean, and your host and hostess friendly and helpful. Why not write and tell us about it?

As a recognition of the generally well-run and excellent holiday accommodation reviewed in our publications, we at FHG Publications Ltd. present a diploma to proprietors who receive the highest recommendation from their guests who are also readers of our Guides. If you care to write to us praising the holiday you have booked through FHG Publications Ltd. – whether this be board, self-catering accommodation, a sporting or a caravan holiday, what you say will be evaluated and the proprietors who reach our final list will be contacted.

The winning proprietor will receive an attractive framed diploma to display on his premises as recognition of a high standard of comfort, amenity and hospitality. FHG Publications Ltd. offer this diploma as a contribution towards the improvement of standards in tourist accommodation in Britain. Help your excellent host or hostess to win it!

FHG DIPLOMA

We nominate ....

....

Because

Name ....

Address ....

.... Telephone No. ....

LONG STRATTON, near Norwich. Mrs Joanna Douglas, Greenacres Farm, Woodgreen, Long Stratton, Norwich NR15 2RR (01508 30261). A 17th century farmhouse, warm friendly atmosphere — wealth of character, exposed beams and inglenook fireplace. In idyllic situation on 30 acre common. Long Stratton one and a half miles, with shops, public houses, restaurants, sports centre; facilities nearby for golf, fishing, horse riding, swimming. Beautiful historic city of Norwich is 12 miles, central location provides easy access to Norfolk Broads, coast and the Suffolk/Constable country. Car essential. Accommodation comprises one double room with en-suite bathroom, one twin room with en-suite shower/WC and washbasin. Both have tea/coffee facilities. Sittingroom with colour TV. Games/snooker room. All weather tennis court. Children welcome, reduced rates, cot, high chair, climbing frame available. Large garden. Bed and Breakfast from £18; Evening Meal from £8. Reductions for seven nights or more. ETB Listed and Approved. Self catering accommodation also available.

NEATISHEAD (Norfolk Broads). Alan and Sue Wrigley, Regency Guest House, The Street, Neatishead, Near Norwich NR12 8AD (Horning [01692] 630233). ♛♛ *Commended.* An 18th century guest house in picturesque, unspoilt village in heart of Broadlands. Personal service top priority. Long established name for very substantial English Breakfasts. 20 minutes from interesting old city of Norwich and six miles from coast. Ideal location for touring East Anglia, boating activities, sailing, hiring, cruising, sightseeing. Easy access to wild life and bird watching grounds. Guesthouse, holder of "Good Care" Award for high quality services, has five tasteful Laura Ashley style decorated rooms (including two king-size doubles with en-suite bathrooms). All rooms have colour TV and tea/coffee making facilities. Two main bathrooms. Separate tables in beamed-ceiling breakfast room. Guests' sittingroom. Bed and Breakfast from £18. Cot, babysitting, reduced rates for children and all stays of more than one night. Pets welcome. Parking. Open all year. Fire Certificate held. AA listed. Also self catering cottage, sleeps six, available next to Guest House.

NORTH WALSHAM. Mr Lindsay Spalding, Beechwood Hotel, 20 Cromer Road, North Walsham NR28 0HD (01692 403231). ♛♛♛ *Commended.* The Beechwood is a Georgian hotel with a warm and friendly atmosphere, situated in the attractive market town of North Walsham. Set in an acre of mature gardens and yet only three minutes' walk from the town square, the hotel has ten well appointed en-suite bedrooms. There is a small intimate Bar, an attractive Dining Room and a cosy Residents' Lounge in which to relax. The hotel makes an ideal touring base for North Norfolk, the Broads and Norwich. Johansens Recommended. Fully Licensed. Please write or telephone for a brochure. We look forward to welcoming you. See Outside Back Cover for our display advertisement.

NORWICH. Mrs M.A. Hemmant, Poplar Farm, Sisland, Loddon, Norwich NR14 6EF (Loddon [01508] 520706). Working farm. This 400-acre mixed farm is situated one mile off the A146, approximately nine miles south east of Norwich. An ideal spot for the Broads and the delightful and varied Norfolk coast. Close to Beccles, Bungay, Diss and Wymondham. We have a Charolais X herd of cows, with calves born March-June. The River Chet runs through the farm. Accommodation comprises double, twin and family rooms; bathroom; TV sittingroom/diningroom. Central heating. Tennis court. Children welcome. A peaceful, rural setting. Car essential. Open all year for Bed and Breakfast. Terms from £15 per person per night.

NORWICH. Mrs V.M. Dewing, Old Hall Farm, South Walsham, Norwich NR13 6DT (01603 270271). Thatched Norfolk farmhouse in peaceful surroundings, an ideal centre for the coast, the Broads and the city of Norwich. Accommodation offered in two double, one single and one twin-bedded rooms, all with TV, radio and tea/coffee making facilities; one private bathroom and one shared bathroom. Bed and Breakfast only. Good pub serving food in the village. Terms from £27 per room (double), £13.50 per person; en suite from £37 (double).

SLOLEY (Norfolk Broads). Mrs Ann Jones, Sloley Farm, High Street, Sloley, Norwich NR12 8HJ (01692 536281; Fax: 01692 535162). ♛ *Commended.*

Sloley Farm is a working mixed farm set in peaceful countryside approximately four miles from the Broadland village of Wroxham, ideally situated for seaside resorts and Norwich, where one can visit the Cathedral, Castle Museum and theatre. Accommodation comprises one double, one family and one twin bedrooms, all with washbasins, TV and tea/coffee making facilities; separate bathroom and WC; diningroom, lounge with log fire in winter and TV. Children welcome, cot available. Open all year (closed Christmas). Sorry, no pets and no smoking. Bed and Breakfast from £15; Evening Meal by arrangement £8.

THETFORD. Mrs Cynthia Huggins, Malting Farm, Blo Norton Road, South Lopham, Diss IP22 2HT (01379 687201). ♛♛ **Working farm.**

Malting Farm is situated on the Norfolk/Suffolk border amid open countryside. It is a working dairy farm where it is possible to see the cows being milked and there are farmyard pets. The farmhouse is Elizabethan timber-framed (inside) with inglenook fireplaces. Central heating. Some four-poster beds. Easy reach of Norfolk Broads, Norwich, Cambridge, Bressingham Steam Museum and Gardens. Cynthia is a keen craftswoman in quilting, embroidery, spinning and weaving. Bed and Breakfast from £17.

THURSFORD. Mrs Ann Green, Old Coach House, Thursford, Near Fakenham NR21 0BD (Thursford [01328] 878273). Working farm.

This peaceful Norfolk farmhouse, converted from 17th century coach house, affords modern comforts but retains its charm. Entered from the main King's Lynn to Cromer road (A148), by a straight drive curving into a sheltered sunny courtyard. Norfolk offers miles of sandy beaches, golf, sailing, fishing and riding also stately homes, museums, bird sanctuary and wildlife park to visit. Main bedroom has four-poster bed, washbasin, shaver point and kettle; second bedroom with twin beds and washbasin; third bedroom with twin beds and en-suite bathroom and WC; guests' bathroom and WC. All bedrooms have tea/coffee making facilities. Farmhouse kitchen/diningroom. Sittingroom with sun lounge and access to garden. Good country cooking and personal attention. Children welcome and pets by arrangement. Bed and Breakfast from £15 per night (from £100 per week); optional Evening Meal £6/£8 (six nights per week). Reduced rates for children. Open all year. Also self-catering accommodation sleeping five available. From £100 per week, linen and electricity included.

WELLS-NEXT-THE-SEA. Sylvia and Andrew Strong, The Cobblers Guest House, Standard Road, Wells-next-the-Sea NR23 1JU (01328 710155/711092). The Cobblers is a friendly eight bedroomed licensed guest house (four double, one twin, one family and two single rooms); centrally heated and double glazed with full Fire Certificate. There is a large diningroom and two guest lounges (one overlooking the attractive, secluded garden). Three en suite bedrooms; others have washbasins; all have TV and tea/coffee facilities. Ample car parking. Personal keys provided for free access at all times. Bed and Breakfast from £14.50; Dinner £8.95. En-suite and single room supplement. Come and discover the glorious North Norfolk Coast.

WOODTON. Mrs J. Read, George's House, Woodton, Near Bungay, Suffolk NR35 2LZ (01508 482214). This is a charming late 17th century cottage with a six acre free range egg unit and a blacksmith on site. It is situated in the centre of the village, just off the main Norwich to Bungay road. Wonderful holiday area, ideal for touring Norfolk and Suffolk. Historic Norwich, with its castle, cathedral, theatre and good shops is only nine-and-a-half miles and everyone should find something there to suit them. Sea 18 miles. Guest accommodation comprises three double bedrooms, with washbasins. There is a bathroom and toilet. Diningroom and TV lounge. A car is essential to make the most of your holiday and there is ample parking. The house is open to guests for Bed and Breakfast; Evening Meal by arrangement. SAE, please, for terms.

WYMONDHAM. Mrs J. Durrant, Rose Farm, School Lane, Suton, Wymondham NR18 9JN (01953 603512). Rose Farm is situated two-and-a-half miles from Attleborough and the charming market town of Wymondham, with its historic twin-towered abbey church. On our smallholding of three acres we keep ducks, chickens and geese, and offer free-range eggs. We also have donkeys which young children are welcome to ride. All bedrooms are ground floor and have colour TV and beverage making facilities. Central heating throughout. 18-hole golf course in vicinity. Bed and Breakfast from £18; Evening Meal from £9. Reductions for children under 10 years. English Tourist Board Listed.

NORTHAMPTONSHIRE

KETTERING. Mrs A. Clarke, Dairy Farm, Cranford St. Andrew, Kettering NN14 4AQ (01536 330273). ♛♛♛ *Commended.* Dairy Farm is a 17th century thatched Jacobean manor house, prettily set on a 350 acre mixed farm. It is a home of great character, thoughtfully furnished and complemented by straightforward home cooking using garden produce. Accommodation offered in one twin-bedded room and one double bedded room, both en-suite; one family room also available. The large garden with its medieval stone dovecote, and the local walks, are further aids to relaxation. With a car the permutation for sightseeing trips to other villages, historic houses, market towns and even the cities of Peterborough and Cambridge are almost endless. Nearest road A14 (A604). Bed and Breakfast from £18; Double from £36; Evening Meal from £10 (by arrangement). Children under 10 years half price.

NORTHAMPTONSHIRE – WHAT TO DO AND SEE!

Rolling farmland and woods contrasted against industrial towns such as Corby and Kettering, this is what makes up Northamptonshire. The canal centre at Stoke Bruerne, the coloured stone church at Stanford-on-Avon and the country parks at Barnwell and Irchester all make for interesting visits.

NORTHUMBERLAND

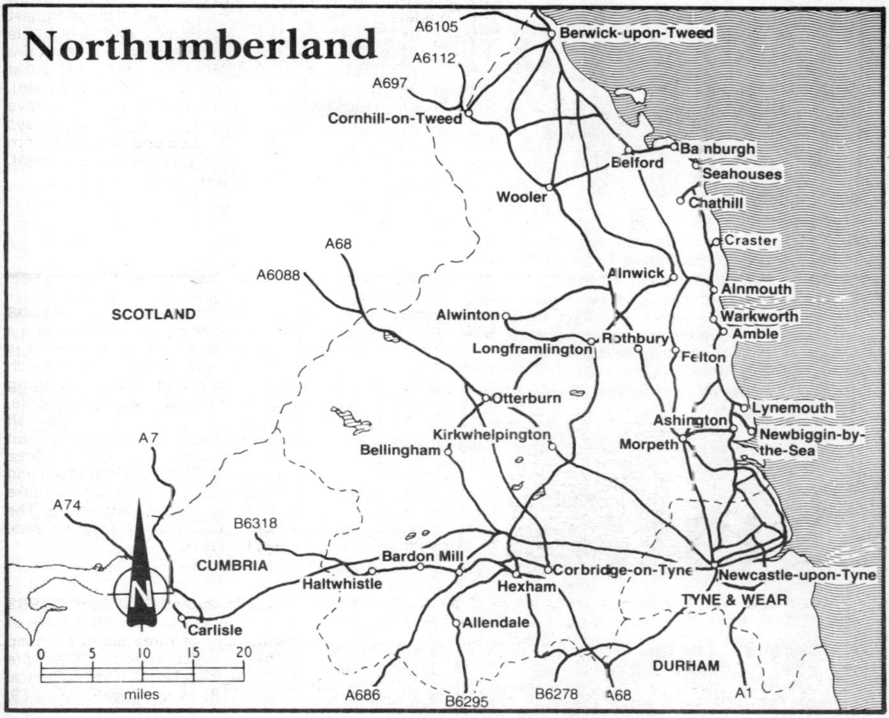

ALLENDALE. John and Isabel Wentzel, Crowberry Hall, Allendale, Hexham NE47 9SR (01434 683392). *Approved.* Allendale is ideally situated for visiting the Roman Wall, Scottish Borders and Lake District as well as the majestic North Pennines. Crowberry Hall lies one and a half miles off the B6295 between Allendale and Nenthead, along the minor road signposted Acton. Crowberry Hall offers comfortable accommodation in twin-bedded and family rooms with washbasins and private bath or shower. Children over five and dogs welcome. No smoking in house, please. Self-guided walks, pony trekking and golf can be enjoyed locally with swimming, windsurfing and other activities nearby. Open March to November. Traditional English cooking plus vegetarian menu available. Bed and Breakfast from £13.50 to £15. Evening Meal if pre-booked.

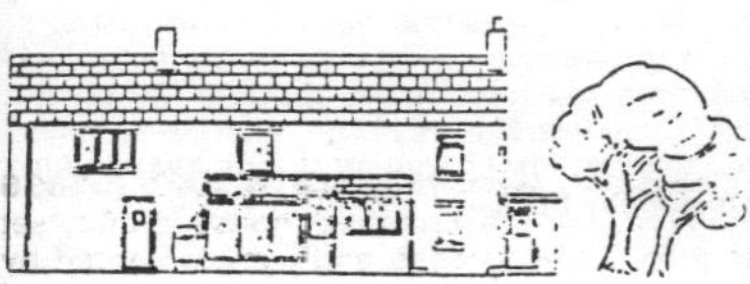

ALNMOUTH. Mrs A. Stanton, Mount Pleasant Farm, Alnmouth, Alnwick NE66 3BY (01665 830215). Mount Pleasant is situated on top of a hill on the outskirts of the seaside village of Alnmouth, with spectacular views of the surrounding countryside. We offer fresh air, sea breezes, green fields, beautiful beaches, country roads and peace and quiet. There are two golf courses and a river meanders around the farm with all its bird life. There are also historic castles, Holy Island, the Farnes and the Cheviots to explore. Farmhouse has large rooms, with washbasins, TV, tea-making and en suite facilities. Guest bathroom with shower. Ample parking. Prices from £16. Self catering accommodation can be booked in two caravans. Full details on request.

ALNMOUTH. Janice and Norman Edwards, Westlea, 29 Riverside Road, Alnmouth NE66 2SD (Alnmouth [01665] 830730). *Commended.* We invite you to relax in the warm friendly atmosphere of Westlea situated at the side of the Aln Estuary. We have an established reputation for providing a high standard of care and hospitality. Guests start the day with a hearty breakfast of numerous choices and in the evening a varied and appetising four-course traditional meal is prepared using local produce. All bedrooms are bright and comfortable with colour TVs, hot drink facilities, central heating, electric blankets. Two bedrooms on the ground floor. En suite available. Large visitors' lounge and diningroom overlooking the estuary. Ideal for exploring castles, Farne Islands, Holy Island, Hadrian's Wall. Fishing, golf, pony trekking, etc within easy reach. Bed and Breakfast from £19; Bed, Breakfast and Evening Meal from £29. English Tourist Board and Northumberland Tourist Board registered. Alnwick District Council Hospitality Award 1989. Alnwick District Council Most Popular Hotel/Guesthouse Award 1991/1992.

ALNWICK. Mrs S. Patton, "Cenac", 50 Swansfield Park Road, Alnwick NE66 1AR (01665 603304). *Commended.* Cenac ia a quietly situated, comfortable, private house offering excellent Bed and Breakfast accommodation only 10 to 15 minutes' stroll from the town centre. We have two lovely guestrooms, one double and one twin, both en suite with TV and tea/coffee making facilities. For the benefit of our guests we have a no smoking policy. Sorry, we cannot take dogs. Bed and Breakfast from £17.50 per person per night. Please telephone for further details.

ALNWICK. Mrs B. Gaines, Crosshills, 40 Blakelaw Road, Alnwick NE66 1BA (01665 602518). *Highly Commended.* Come and join us at Crosshills for your stay in historic Northumberland. A friendly family-run house situated in a quiet area near golf course and only a short walk into town. We have two double rooms and one twin room, all en suite and having colour TV and tea/coffee making facilities. Twin room has balcony with a beautiful view of coast and countryside. Sorry, no dogs. Bed and Breakfast from £19 per person; Evening Meal optional. Parking available.

ALNWICK. Mrs L. Edridge, "Norfolk", 41 Blakelaw Road, Alnwick NE66 1BA (01665 602892). *Highly Commended.* A private detached house, quietly situated, offering high standards of comfort. Two spacious bedrooms — one double room, one twin room, both en suite. Tea/coffee tray. Guests' sittingroom with TV, separate diningroom. Central heating throughout. Good home cooking using own garden produce. Traditional evening meals. Full English breakfast. Alnwick is a historic market town ideal for open countryside with quiet roads leading to unspoilt Northumbrian coastline, only three miles away. Historic houses and castles are plentiful. Bed, Breakfast and four-course Evening Meal £25 inclusive. No smoking throughout.

ALNWICK near. Mrs Celia Curry, Howick Scar Farm, Craster, Alnwick NE66 3SU (01665 576665). Comfortable farmhouse accommodation on working mixed farm situated on the Heritage Coast between the villages of Craster and Howick. Ideal base for walking, birdwatching or exploring the coast, moors and historic castles. The Farne Islands famous for their colonies of seals and seabirds, and Lindisfarne (Holy Island) are within easy driving distance. Accommodation is in two double rooms. Guests have their own TV lounge/dining room with coal fire and full central heating. Bed and Breakfast from £14. Reductions for three nights or more. Closed April. Tourist Board Listed. Also member of Farm Holiday Bureau.

AMBLE near. Mrs L.A. Marshall, Togston Hall Farm House, North Togston, Near Amble NE65 0HR (01665 712699). Tranquil farmhouse atmosphere and personal service. En suite bedrooms plus adjacent cottage for four or more. Varied breakfast menu and traditional home cooked food served in the evenings. Bed and Breakfast from £17 per person per night; Dinner, Bed and Breakfast from £27 per person per night.

BERWICK-UPON-TWEED. Mrs J. Gray, Middle Ord Manor House Farm, Berwick-upon-Tweed TD15 2XQ (01289 306323). *De Luxe.* **Working farm.** NTB Nominated Best Bed and Breakfast 1993. An attractive Georgian residence, built 1783, with a Victorian extension, on mixed cattle, sheep, arable farm, set in unspoilt position surrounded by woodland and walled gardens. Period lounge and dining room overlook the garden. Colour TV. Tea/coffee making facilities. En suite rooms or rooms with washbasin only; four-poster if desired. Central heating. Car essential, parking. Three miles from coast. Bed and Breakfast from £16.50 to £22. Many places of interest to visit and sporting activities are within easy reach. Also available, Middle Ord Farmhouse, for self catering holidays all year round — an 18th century farmhouse, completely detached to accommodate nine people plus cot for small baby if required. Three double and one twin-bedded room; bathroom; sittingroom; dining room; kitchen. Fully equipped except linen. Pets accepted. Other self catering accommodation also available. Weekly terms £90 to £310. ETB Listed and inspected.

CORBRIDGE. Mr and Mrs F.J. Matthews, The Hayes, Newcastle Road, Corbridge NE45 5PL (Corbridge [01434] 632010). Spacious, attractive stone-built guesthouse. Set in seven acres of grounds. Single, double, twin, family bedrooms; lounge and dining rooms. Open 11 months of the year. Bed and Breakfast from £16. Children's reductions. Stair lift for disabled visitors. Also self catering properties — three cottages, flat and caravan. Awarded two Farm Holiday Diplomas. Car parking. For brochure/booking SAE/phone. ETB registered.

CORNHILL-ON-TWEED. Mrs V. Watson, Flodden Edge Farm, Mindrum, Cornhill-on-Tweed TD12 4QG (016686 287). Large country house set in own grounds in quiet rural area, one-and-a-half miles from A697 Newcastle to Edinburgh road. Central for hills and coast. Within half an hour's drive of Lindisfarne and Bamburgh Castle, also Border Abbeys. Edinburgh one and a quarter hours' drive. Four miles from Scottish border and one and a half miles from Flodden Field. Ideal for children. Dogs welcome. Homely atmosphere and no restrictions. Bedrooms have washbasins, tea/coffee facilities and TV. Bathroom with shower. Residents' lounge with TV. Separate diningroom. Ideal for fishing, walking and exploring the National Park. Gliding and horse riding nearby, also miniature steam railway. Open all year. Reduced rates for children and for Senior Citizens early and late season.

HALTWHISTLE. Mrs Mary Dawson, Park Burnfoot Farm, Featherstone Park, Haltwhistle NE49 0JP (01434 320378). Working farm. When visiting the Roman Wall area for an overnight stop or a longer visit, you can be sure of a friendly welcome at this 18th century farmhouse on a 200-acre working farm. Park Burnfoot, with the waterfalls to the front of the house and the River South Tyne at the back, makes an ideal setting. Woodland walk 100 yards away. Two miles from Haltwhistle, one mile from Featherstone Castle and about four miles from the best parts of the Roman Wall, the farm is an ideal touring centre; Ullswater and the Scottish Borders within easy motoring distance. One double and one family bedrooms, with washbasins, soap and towels, colour TV and tea makers; bathroom with shower, separate toilet; large, warm visitors' lounge. Terms for accommodation and good English Breakfast from £13.50 to £14.50, late drink included. Evening Meal available. Self-catering cottage also available from £99 per week. Inspected and Listed by the English Tourist Board.

Terms quoted in this publication may be subject to increase if rises in costs necessitate

HEXHAM. Mrs Ruby Keenleyside, Struthers Farm, Catton, Allendale, Hexham NE47 9LP (01434 683580). ♛♛ *Commended.* Struthers Farm offers a warm welcome in the heart of England, with many splendid local walks from the farm itself. Panoramic views. Double/twin rooms, en suite, central heating. Good farmhouse cooking. Ample safe parking. Come and share our home and enjoy beautiful countryside. Children welcome, pets by prior arrangement. Open all year. Bed and Breakfast from £16.50; Evening Meal £8.50. Farm Holiday Bureau Member.

HEXHAM. Mrs Ailsa A. Dixon, Anick Grange Farm, Hexham NE46 4LP (01434 603807). ♛♛ *Commended.* This is a mixed farm of 363 acres in the Tyne Valley, and the south-facing farmhouse which dates back to the 1600's is warm, welcoming and comfortable. One mile from the market town of Hexham and two miles from Corbridge, a lovely old village to browse around, we are 20 minutes' drive from Hadrian's Wall and the same from the beautiful North Pennines. The Northumbrian coastline is only one and a half hours away — perhaps you could take in one or two National Trust properties en route. One twin-bedded en suite room, one family and one single rooms, all have washbasins and tea/coffee and biscuits. TV lounge. Terms from £15 to £17 per person. Brochure available.

HEXHAM. Mrs Doreen Cole, Hillcrest House, Barrasford, Hexham NE48 4BY (01434 681426). ♛♛♛ *Highly Commended.* Hillcrest House has been specifically extended to provide a high standard of accommodation, with a homely, comfortable atmosphere. One family, one double, one twin, one single rooms, all with ensuite shower rooms, colour TV, tea/coffee facilities. Evening meal optional; packed lunches on request. Comfortable lounge, separate tables in diningroom. Residential licence. Accommodation suitable for disabled visitors. Situated seven miles from historic Hexham in beautiful North Tyne Valley. Ideal for touring Hadrian's Wall and within easy distance of Kielder, the Borders, Newcastle and Gateshead Metro Centre. Car essential. Bed and Breakfast £17 single, £29 double.

LOWICK. Janet and John Dunn, The Old Manse Guest House, 5 Cheviot View, Lowick, Berwick-upon-Tweed TD15 2TY (Berwick-upon-Tweed [01289] 388264). ♛♛ *Highly Commended.* The Old Manse Guest House, situated in the quiet farming village of Lowick, is a Georgian Grade II Listed former church manse of considerable character. The adjoining church (circa 1821), which is still used every Sunday, was the first Scottish church to be built in England. The house, which overlooks the village common, offers comfortable accommodation which comprises double and twin-bedded rooms with en-suite bathrooms. Bed and Breakfast from £16.50 per person; Evening Meal, which is four-course with choice of menu, is £11.

ROTHBURY. Mrs Helen Farr, Lorbottle West Steads, Thropton, Morpeth NE65 7JT (01665 574672). Situated in the quite beautiful Whittingham Vale, five miles from Rothbury on a 320 acre farm. Stone-built spacious farmhouse with panoramic views of Thrunton Craggs, Simonside and Cheviot Hills, a perfect base for exploring Northumberland's natural beauty and heritage. Many facilities within four miles — e.g. golf, pony trekking, mountain bikes, fishing and woodland walks. The farmhouse offers spacious TV lounge/diningroom with open fires in colder weather. Bedrooms have tea/coffee making and TV facilities. Guests' bathroom and use of garden. Bed and Breakfast from £13.50. Evening Meal negotiable. ETB Listed. Self catering cottage, sleeps five, also available. Further details on request.

PLEASE ENCLOSE A STAMPED ADDRESSED ENVELOPE WITH ENQUIRIES

ROTHBURY. Mrs Alison Giles, Thropton Demesne Farmhouse, Thropton, Morpeth NE65 7LT (Tel & Fax: 01669 20196). ♛♛ *Highly Commended.* Comfortable farmhouse with a friendly atmosphere lying in the beautiful Coquet Valley overlooking the river and the Simonside Hills. Privately situated on the edge of a quiet village, two miles from Rothbury where there is golf, riding, tennis, fishing and swimming. Superb walking country within easy reach of the coast and Cheviots. The farmhouse has full central heating. There is one double/family room, one double and one twin-bedded room, each with private bathroom. Comfortable guest lounge and separate diningroom. Cot etc available and also babysitting if required. Colour TV in every bedroom. Non-smoking throughout. Bed and Breakfast from £17.50. Reductions for children. Packed lunches available. Open all year.

SLALEY, near Hexham. Mrs Elizabeth Courage, Rye Hill Farm, Slaley, Near Hexham NE47 0AH (Hexham [01434] 673259). ♛♛♛ *Commended.* Rye Hill Farm is a 300 year old Northumbrian stone farmhouse, set in its own 30 acres of rural Tynedale. Guests have the unique opportunity to see life on a small working farm, while the self-contained accommodation in the converted farm buildings offers all the comforts of good farm hospitality. We provide full English Breakfast and optional three course Evening Meal. Table licence held. All bedrooms are centrally heated with colour TV and tea/coffee making facilities and have bathrooms en-suite. Northumberland Moors, Kielder Forest, Kielder Water nearby. Visit the historic city of Durham, or the market town of Hexham which is only five miles away. Bed and Breakfast from £18; Evening Meal £10.

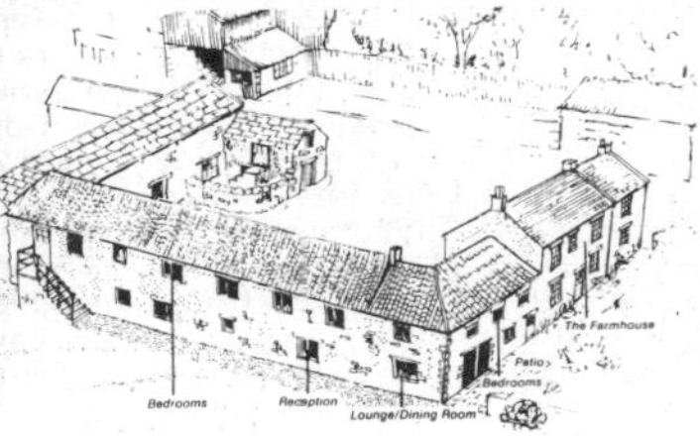

NOTTINGHAMSHIRE

BURTON JOYCE. Mrs V. Baker, Willow House, 12 Willow Wong, Burton Joyce NG14 5FD (0115 931 2070). A Victorian house in a quiet village location within walking distance of beautiful stretch of River Trent, excellent for angling, sailing, etc and yet only five miles from Nottingham city. Short drive to Sherwood Forest, Dukeries, D.H. Lawrence/Byron birthplaces and historic Southwell Minster. Good local eating places and many surrounding picturesque villages. Very comfortable accommodation. Luxury bathroom facilities. Tea making facilities and TV in room. Central heating. Children welcome, cot available. Babysitting/Evening Meal by arrangement. Bed and Breakfast from £16 per person, with reduced rates for children.

HOLBECK (Sherwood Forest). Mrs J. Brown, "Browns", The Old Orchard Cottage, Holbeck, Worksop S80 3NF (01909 720659). Listed, Highly Commended; Winner of EMTB Bed and Breakfast of the Year 1991. The Old Orchard Cottage is a 1730 Grade II Listed stone cottage with character and charm, situated in a one acre garden with ample parking. Holbeck is a quiet hamlet close to Sherwood Forest, half a mile off A60 Nottingham to Worksop road, six miles M1, eight miles A1. Enjoy your stay in a separate, comfortable Lodge sleeping two, three or four people, en suite, colour TV, tea/coffee facilities, central heating: £17.50 per person per night. Breakfast with a wide choice of menu is served in the elegant dining room of the tastefully restored cottage. "Room Service" for home made afternoon tea.

MANSFIELD. Mrs L. Palmer, Boon Hills Farm, Nether Langwith, Mansfield NG20 9JQ (Mansfield [01623] 743862). Working farm. Farmhouse accommodation in stone-built farmhouse standing in 155 acres of mixed farmland, 300 yards back from A632 on edge of the village. Comfortably furnished with fitted carpets throughout, the house has electric heating, open fire. Large sitting/diningroom with colour TV. One family room, one double room and another room with twin beds. Children welcome and there are many pets for them on the farm. Babysitting arranged. Pets accepted. Situated on edge of Sherwood Forest, six miles from Visitors' Centre; eight miles M1; 10 miles A1. Places of interest include Hardwick Hall, Thoresby Hall, Chatsworth House, Newstead Abbey. Pleasant half-mile walk to picturesque village inn serving evening meals. Car essential, ample parking. Tourist Board registered. Bed and Breakfast only from £14 per night. Non-smokers only. Reductions for children. Open March to October inclusive.

NOTTINGHAM. Mrs M. Watchorn, The Dairies, 22 The Green, Barkestone-le-Vale, Nottingham NG13 0HH (01949 842495). Farmhouse in the middle of small village with quiet country lanes for walking. On Leicestershire, Nottinghamshire and Lincolnshire border, it is an ideal location for exploring the East Midlands, convenient for Robin Hood country, also associations with Byron and D.H. Lawrence and the Dukeries. Central for several market towns — Melton Mowbray, Newark-on-Trent, Nottingham. Eight miles from A1 (Grantham), two miles Belvoir Castle. Central heating. One double room en-suite from £15 per person Bed and Breakfast, one twin and single from £14 per person Bed and Breakfast. Family room available. Reductions for children sharing. Evening meal by arrangement. TV, tea/coffee facilities in all rooms. Bathroom plus separate shower, three toilets.

REDMILE (Vale of Belvoir). Redmile House Hotel, Main Street, Redmile NG13 0GA (01949 43086 or 843086). Redmile House Hotel and Restaurant is a Grade II Listed (c. 1740) former Georgian farmhouse, set in one and a half acres. Notable for old world charm with period furniture and open fires, yet with TV and tea making facilities in all bedrooms, most of which have full en suite facilities. Totally relaxed atmosphere. Bed and Breakfast from £19 to £23. Evening meal available by arrangement as we only use fresh local produce. Close to Belvoir Castle and Nottinghamshire/Lincolnshire/Leicestershire borders. Telephone for brochure.

STANTON-ON-THE-WOLDS. Mrs V. Moffat, Laurel Farm, Browns Lane, Stanton-on-the-Wolds, Nottingham NG12 5BL (0115 937 3488). Laurel Farm is an old house standing in four acres of garden and paddocks. There are pet sheep, horses, dogs, cats, chickens and ducks. The garden may be used by guests. All rooms have shower and washbasin, two rooms have full private facilities, all have colour TV and real coffee; very large family room with cot and high chair also available. Babysitting free by prior arrangement. 24 hours notice for evening meals. Pets welcome. Bed and Breakfast from £14 to £17. Many reasonably priced eating places locally. Laurel Farm is on a quiet lane with easy access to main roads, many old towns and castles, Sherwood Forest. Smoking is not allowed. Fully registered.

OXFORDSHIRE

BANBURY near. Mrs E.J. Lee, The Mill Barn, Lower Tadmarton, Near Banbury OX15 5SU (01295 780349). ♛♛ Tadmarton is a small village, three miles south-west of Banbury. The Mill, no longer working, was originally water powered and the stream lies adjacent to the house. The Mill Barn has been tastefully converted, retaining many traditional features such as beams and exposed stone walls, yet it still has all the amenities a modern house offers. Two spacious en-suite bedrooms, one downstairs, are available to guests in this comfortable family home. Base yourself here and visit Stratford, historic Oxford, Woodstock and the beautiful Cotswolds, knowing you are never further than an hour's drive away. Open all year for Bed and Breakfast from £17.50, reductions for children. Weekly terms available.

BLETCHINGDON. Mrs P.M. Hedges, Stonehouse Farm, Bletchingdon, Oxford OX5 3EA (01869 350585). Working farm. 17th century Cotswold farmhouse set in 560 acres. For those who want to get off the beaten track! Situated between A34 Oxford to Bicester and A4260 Oxford to Banbury. 10 minutes from Blenheim Palace and 15 minutes from Oxford; one hour to Heathrow Airport off Junction 9 or 10 M40. Accommodation comprises one double, one twin, one family and one single bedrooms, all with washbasins, TV, tea/coffee facilities. Non-smoking accommodation available. Lovely walks in beautiful countryside. Children welcome. Bed and Breakfast from £15 to £20 per person per night. Tourist Board Listed.

Stonehouse Farm
Bletchington

BRAILES. Mrs M. Cripps, Agdon Farm, Brailes, Banbury OX15 5JJ (01608 685226). Working farm.

A warm welcome awaits all our guests. Our comfortable Cotswold stone farmhouse is set in 500 acres of mixed farming, in an unspoilt part of the countryside. Two miles from B4035, five miles from A422. Within walking distance of Compton Wynyates, in close driving range of the Cotswolds, Warwick, 10 miles Stratford-upon-Avon and Banbury Cross. Many local village pubs. Accommodation with TV room, separate diningroom, guests' bathroom, pleasant bedrooms with tea/coffee facilities. Central heating. Evening Meals available.

BURFORD. Mrs S. Fryer, Rookery Farm, Brize Norton OX18 3UL (01993 842957). Enjoy a welcome stay in our Listed farmhouse. We have one twin, one double and one family room, all with washbasins, remote-control colour TV and tea/coffee making facilities. We provide a generous traditional breakfast. There is a lovely period-style bathroom. Rookery Farm is a smallholding pleasantly situated in this Oxfordshire village with lovely views of surrounding countryside. We have a variety of pets including dogs, cats, horses and sheep. We are pleasantly located on the edge of the Cotswolds being 15 miles west of Oxford and four miles from Burford, making it an ideal base for visiting Oxford, Stratford and the Cotswolds. Tourist Board Highly Commended, AA Listed QQ. Car parking. Heated outdoor swimming pool. Bed and Breakfast; Evening Meals available in nearby pub. Rates from £20 single room, £35 double room.

DEDDINGTON. Mrs Audrey Fuller, Earls Farm, Deddington, Oxford OX15 0TH (Deddington [01869] 38243). ♛♛ Working farm. Delightfully situated on edge of village 200 yards from main Banbury to Oxford road, this farm covers 230 acres of cropping fields. Open all year, it has two double, one family bedrooms, all with washbasins; two bathrooms, two toilets; sittingroom, diningroom. Central heating. Children very welcome and facilities for them include cot, high chair, babysitting and reduced rates; also swing and slide. Fishing available on River Swere. Trout fishing on local lake by arrangement. Golf five miles away, tennis two. Banbury six miles. This is an ideal touring base. Pets accepted. Car essential, parking. Bed and Breakfast from £15 to £17 per person per night.

FARINGDON. Mr D. Barnard, Bowling Green Farm, Stanford Road, Faringdon, Oxfordshire SN7 8EZ (01367 240229; Fax: 01367 242568). ♛♛ Attractive 18th century farmhouse offering 20th century comfort. Situated in the Vale of White Horse, just one mile south of Faringdon on the A417. Easy access to M4 Exit 13 for Heathrow Airport. An ideal place to stay for a day or longer. A working farm of cattle, horse breeding, poultry and ducks. Large twin-bedded/family room on ground floor, en suite. All bedrooms have colour TV, tea/coffee making facilities and full central heating throughout. Perfect area for riding, golf, fishing and walking the Ridgeway. Interesting places to visit include Oxford, Bath, Windsor, Burford, Henley, Blenheim Palace and the Cotswolds. Open all year. Registered with the Heart of England Tourist Board. Member of the Farm Holiday Bureau.

FARINGDON. Mrs Pat Hoddinott, Ashen Copse Farm, Coleshill, Faringdon SN6 7PU (01367 240175). ♛♛ Working farm. Perfect spot to tour or relax. Our 580 acre National Trust farm is set in peaceful countryside on borders of Oxfordshire, Wiltshire and Gloucestershire. The large stone and brick farmhouse has two family bedrooms for guests; one has en suite facilities. Cot available. Large garden, farm animals, lovely views. So much to do and see — tourist information available. Facilities locally for fishing, riding, golfing, swimming, boating and walking. Good choice of places to eat out. Open all year. Bed and Breakfast from £17 to £20, reductions for children sharing. A non-smoking household.

FREELAND. Mrs B.B. Taphouse, "Wrestler's Mead", 35 Wroslyn Road, Freeland, Oxford OX7 2HJ (01993 882003). A warm welcome awaits you at the home of the Taphouses. We are conveniently located for Blenheim Palace (10 minutes), Oxford (20 minutes) and the Cotswolds (25 minutes). Accommodation comprises one double and one single room both with washbasins and at ground level. Our first floor family room has its own en-suite shower room with washbasin and toilet. The double and the family room each have a colour TV. Cot, high chair and babysitting service available. Pets by arrangement. No hidden extras. Bed and Breakfast from £15.

HENLEY-ON-THAMES. Mrs Liz Roach, The Old Bakery, Skirmett, Near Henley-on-Thames RG9 6TD (01491 638309). This welcoming family house is situated on the site of an old bakery, seven miles from Henley-on-Thames and Marlow; half an hour from Heathrow and Oxford; one hour from London. It is in the Hambleden Valley in the beautiful Chilterns with many excellent pubs selling good food. Riding school nearby; beautiful walking country. Two double rooms with TV, one twin-bedded and two single rooms; two bathrooms. Open all year. Parking for five cars (car essential). Children and pets welcome. Bed and Breakfast from £18 to £21 single, £35 to £38 double. Registered with English and Chiltern Tourist Boards.

OXFORD. Mr and Mrs L.S. Price, Arden Lodge, 34 Sunderland Avenue (off Banbury Road), Oxford (01865 52076). Modern detached house in select area of North Oxford off Banbury Road. Within easy reach of Oxford centre, riverside inns, country walks, river, meadows, etc. Excellent position for touring; Cotswolds, Blenheim Palace, Stratford and visits to London. Colour TV, tea/coffee making equipment and private facilities in all rooms. Parking available. Bed and Breakfast from £19 per person.

OXFORD. Ann Warwick, The Close Guest House, Witney Road, Long Hanborough, Oxford OX8 8HF (01993 882485). ♛♛ *Commended.* We offer comfortable accommodation in house set in own grounds of one and a half acres. Two family rooms, one double room. All are en suite and have colour TV and tea/coffee making facilities. Lounge. Full central heating. Use of garden and car parking for eight cars. Close to Woodstock, Oxford and the Cotswolds. Babysitting. Open all year except Christmas. AA Listed. Bed and Breakfast from £15.

OXFORD. Mrs E. Neville, Ascot Guest House, 283 Iffley Road, Oxford OX4 4AQ (Oxford [01865] 240259/727669). This pleasant Victorian guest house, situated one mile from the city centre, offers six most charming and comfortable rooms with modern furnishings, TV and tea/coffee making facilities. En-suite available. Cots also provided upon request. One four-poster bed. Mrs Neville makes all her guests very welcome and will help plan tours. A good base for visiting the city of "Dreaming Spires". A short drive takes you to Blenheim Palace, the Cotswolds, Stratford-upon-Avon and within a day's drive is Windsor Castle. A vegetarian Breakfast is provided if required. Terms from approximately £15 per person. Thames and Chiltern Tourist Board Registered.

STANTON HARCOURT. Mrs Margaret Clifton, Staddle Stones, Linch Hill, Stanton Harcourt OX8 1BB (01865 882256). A chalet bungalow situated in a peaceful location on the outskirts of the village with four acres of atttractive surroundings, including a carp pond; visitors are allowed to fish. A full breakfast is offered to satisfy the keenest of appetites. Disabled persons, children and dogs are welcome. In easy reach of the Cotswolds and Oxford. One double or family room en suite, two twin bedrooms with private bathrooms; also a comfortable TV lounge with tea/coffee available. Bed and Breakfast from £13.

TETSWORTH. Julia Tanner, Little Acre, Tetsworth, Near Thame OX9 7AT (01844 281423). A charming secluded country house retreat, offering every comfort, set in 18 acres of private grounds, nestling under the Chilterns escarpment. Single, twin and double rooms, all with central heating, colour TV, tea/coffee making facilities; some with en suite facilities. One ground floor room suitable for disabled guests. Full English or Continental breakfast. A perfect place to relax and enjoy the local countryside in a quiet location but only three minutes from Junction 6 on the M40. Children and well behaved family dog welcome. Lovely walking area (Oxfordshire Way and Ridgeway Path). Riding, fishing and excellent golf course nearby. Little Acre offers a warm welcome and REAL VALUE FOR MONEY from just £13 per night. Reductions for weekly bookings and children. Highly recommended by previous guests. Plenty of good restaurants nearby. Open all year.

WOODSTOCK near. Mrs B. Jones, Gorselands Farmhouse Auberge, Near Long Hanborough, Near Woodstock OX8 6PU (01993 881895; Fax: 01993 882799). ♛♛ Situated in an idyllic location in the Oxfordshire countryside, Gorselands has its own grounds of one acre. This Cotswold stone farmhouse has exposed beams, flagstone floors, billiards room (full size table), guest lounge, dining conservatory and tennis court. En-suite rooms, family room, double/twin rooms available. Near to Oxford, Blenheim Palace, East End Roman Villa, Cotswold villages. Children welcome. Bed and Breakfast from £14 per person; Evening Meal from £9.95. Licensed. RAC Listed. Elizabeth Gundrey Recommended.

SHROPSHIRE

BUCKNELL. Mrs Christine E. Price, The Hall, Bucknell SY7 0AA (015474 249). *Commended.*

You are assured of a warm welcome at The Hall, which is a Georgian farmhouse with spacious accommodation. The house and gardens are set in a secluded part of a small South Shropshire village, an ideal area for touring the Welsh Borderland. Offa's Dyke is on the doorstep and the historic towns of Shrewsbury, Hereford, Ludlow and Ironbridge are within easy reach as are the Church Stretton Hills and Wenlock Edge. Three bedrooms — one twin en-suite, two doubles with washbasins. All have tea-making facilities and TV. Guest lounge. Ample parking. Bed and Breakfast from £16; Dinner £8. Heart of England Tourist Board Approved. SAE, please, for details.

DINNEY FARM

The Dinney is a small working farm deep in Shropshire's rolling countryside with views across the Severn Valley and nearby lake. There are safe play areas and farm walks from the door, and fishing nearby. The Severn Valley Railway runs through the owners' land. Historic Bridgnorth is five minutes away, with Ironbridge Gorge Museum and the hills of the Long Mynd and Wenlock Edge around seven miles. All bedrooms are centrally heated with en-suite bathrooms. Tea/coffee making facilities are available. You are assured of a warm welcome at Dinney Farm. Dogs welcome. Brochure available.

Mr & Mrs Roberts, Dinney Farm, Chelmarsh, Bridgnorth WV16 6AU. Telephone: 01746 861070

CHURCH STRETTON. Mrs Barbara Norris, Court Farm, Gretton, Church Stretton SY6 7HU (01694 771219). *Highly Commended.* **Working farm.**

Stone Tudor farmhouse in a very quiet and peaceful area of outstanding natural beauty, ideally situated for visiting Ironbridge, Bridgnorth, Ludlow and Shrewsbury. This is excellent walking country and, round about, there is much to interest the visitor — or simply enjoy relaxing at Court Farm. Riding and trout fishing can be arranged. Three double rooms, one en-suite and two with private bathrooms, all with tea/coffee making facilities. Colour TV; central heating. High quality cuisine served, and the house is open from February to the beginning of November. Car preferable, ample parking. Sorry, no pets. Non-smoking household. Bed and Breakfast from £19; Evening Meal from £11. Further details may be obtained from Mrs Norris. Tourist Board registered. RAC Acclaimed. RAC comment: "A place worth seeking".

CHURCH STRETTON. Mrs Mary Jones, Acton Scott Farm, Acton Scott, Church Stretton SY6 6QN (01694 781260). *Commended.* **Working farm.**

Lovely 17th century farmhouse in peaceful village amidst the beautiful hills of South Shropshire, an area of outstanding natural beauty. The house is full of character; the rooms, which are all heated, are comfortable and spacious. Bedrooms have washbasins and tea/coffee making facilities; en suite available. Colour TV lounge. Children welcome, pets accepted by arrangement. We are a working farm, centrally situated for visiting Ironbridge, Shrewsbury and Ludlow, each easily reached within half an hour. Visitors' touring and walking information available. Bed and full English Breakfast from £13 per person. Farm Holiday Bureau member. Open all year excluding December and January.

CHURCH STRETTON. Mrs Isobel Burgoyne, Churchmoor Farm, Marshbrook, Church Stretton SY6 6PU (01694 781365). Situated at the foothills of the Long Mynd, the farmhouse has panoramic views of all the hills of South Shropshire. Ideal for rambling and wildlife. Convenient to the A49 and for local places of interest. Homely atmosphere with personal attention. Two double rooms with own bathroom, tea/coffee facilities. Central heating. Bed and Breakfast from £14.

CHURCH STRETTON. Mrs Josie Griffiths, Gilberries Farm Cottage, Wall-under-Heywood, Church Stretton SY6 7HZ (01694 771400). ♛ *Commended.* Country cottage adjoining family farm within easy reach of many places of interest. Ideal walking country. One double, one twin bedrooms, both with washbasins, tea making facilities and radios. Also one bathroom and separate toilet. Guests' lounge with colour TV and separate diningroom are available to guests at all times. Log fires, central heating. Spacious parking. A friendly homely atmosphere. Bed and Breakfast from £16 per person. Excellent evening meals available within five minutes' drive.

CHURCH STRETTON. Mrs Joanna Brereton, Woolston Farm, Church Stretton SY6 6QD (01694 781201). ♛ Woolston Farm lies within the tiny hamlet of Woolston above the village of Wistanstow, with lovely views of Wenlock Edge. Convenient for the A49 for sightseeing, Ludlow and Ironbridge within easy reach. Offa's Dyke and Long Mynd offer excellent walking facilities. Woolston farmhouse is Victorian, brick built, with lovely garden and peaceful atmosphere. Children very welcome — cot, high chair and babysitting available. All bedrooms have tea-making facilities and washbasins. Lounge with colour TV. Bed and Breakfast from £14.50; Evening Meal optional. Reductions for children under 12 years

SHROPSHIRE – HISTORIC BORDER COUNTY!

The lonely Shropshire Hills – an "Area of Outstanding Natural Beauty" – are much favoured by walkers. Those seeking more traditional tourist activities would do well to visit the Acton Scott Working Museum, Ironbridge, Offa's Dyke, the black and white Tudor town of Shrewsbury or the market town of Bridgnorth.

CLUN. Mrs I. Evans, Springhill Farm, Clun, Craven Arms SY7 8PE (01588 640337). A working farm of 250 acres with sheep, cattle and mixed crops. Situated on Offa's Dyke footpath with panoramic views of the Clun Valley. Close by are many places of historic interest — Clun Castle, Ludlow Castle, Ironbridge. Accommodation comprises one double, one twin, one family rooms. Central heating in all rooms. Sitting room with TV; coffee and tea served. Good home cooking; evening meals available. Children welcome at reduced rates; pony to ride; babysitting can be arranged. Car parking, car essential. SAE, please, for terms.

CLUN. Mrs M. Jones, Llanhedric, Clun, Craven Arms SY7 8NG (Clun [01588] 640203). Working farm. A mixed farm just two miles off the A488 road, overlooking the picturesque Clun Valley, near the Welsh border and Offa's Dyke. Ideal for walking or exploring the many places of historic interest including Ludlow and Shrewsbury. Attractive old stone house with lawns and garden, spacious accommodation, friendly atmosphere and good food. One double and one family bedroom, both with washbasins and tea/coffee making facilities; bathroom, toilet; lounge; separate diningroom. Sorry no dogs. Open Easter to October. Bed and Breakfast from £14; Bed, Breakfast and Evening Meal from £21.50. Reductions for children. HETB member.

CLUN. Mrs Miriam Ellison, New House Farm, Clun, Craven Arms SY7 8NJ (Bishops Castle [01588] 638314). ♛♛ *Commended.* Isolated peaceful 18th century farmhouse set high in the Clun Hills near Welsh border. Hill farm in the Environmentally Sensitive Area of South Shropshire. Additional sheep hill farm which includes an Iron Age Hill Fort. Three major walking routes within striking distance: Offa's Dyke, Shropshire Way and Kerry Ridgeway. Scenic views from large comfortable bedrooms, furnished to high standard with TV and tea and coffee making facilities. Twin room en-suite, family room with adjacent bathroom, and double room with shower room nearby. Home cooking; packed lunches; evening meal. Comprehensive selection of books. Our aim is to offer clean, comfortable accommodation with a friendly atmosphere in quiet peaceful surroundings. Bed and Breakfast from £16.50. Evening Meal from £9.

CLUN. Bob and Margaret Wall, The Old Farmhouse, Woodside, Clun SY7 0JB (Clun [01588] 640695). ♛ Featured in Elizabeth Gundrey's "Staying off the Beaten Track". A warm welcome is extended to all guests, seeking peace and quiet in idyllic surroundings, at this 300-year-old farmhouse situated about one mile from Clun, on the sheltered side of Soudley Hill. Offa's Dyke is only three miles away and the surrounding countryside, for many miles, affords delight to ramblers — combined with the historic interest of the many castles and towns of the Border Country making this an ideal holiday location for people of all ages. Accommodation comprises one double and one (twin) family bedrooms, with washbasins; bathroom, toilet; sitting-room; diningroom. Non-smoking accommodation available. Central heating. Car not essential, but an advantage to make the most of touring this picturesque and historic part of England. Parking. Cot, high chair, babysitting, reduced rates for children. Pets welcome. Open March to October for Bed and Breakfast from £14. Evening Meal by arrangement from £8.50. SAE for brochure, please.

CRAVEN ARMS. Mrs P.M. Reynolds, Newcastle Hall, Newcastle on Clun, Craven Arms SY7 8QL (01588 640350). A Georgian farmhouse with lovely views, occupying a pleasant position on the edge of the tranquil, picturesque village of Newcastle in the Clun Valley. The 300 acre family farm, breeding cattle and sheep, offers delightful picnic areas beside the River Clun with glorious walks and fishing; close to many places of interest including Powis and Stokesay Castles; four miles from Welsh Border and half a mile from Offa's Dyke. Four bedrooms, three with washbasin; bathroom and toilet; sitting and dining rooms. Cot and babysitting available. Pets permitted. Wholesome farmhouse fare; packed lunches, vegans catered for. Bed and Breakfast from £18; Evening Meal available. SAE for terms. ETB registered, English Wanderer Approved.

CRAVEN ARMS. Mrs S.J. Williams, Hurst Mill Farm, Clunton, Craven Arms SY7 0JA (01588 640224). ♛♛ **Working farm.** "Hurst Mill Farm" is situated in the prettiest part of the Clun Valley, renowned as a completely unspoilt part of England. One mile from the small town of Clun, which has a Saxon church and a Norman castle. Legend says one is wiser after crossing Clun Bridge. Within easy reach are Ludlow, Newtown, Elan Valley, Ironbridge and Long-Mynd Hills. Through the fields runs the River Clun where one can bathe. Woods and hills provide wonderful walks, which can be organised. Fishing and pony trekking locally. The farm has cattle, sheep, two quiet riding ponies. Three double, one single bedrooms, all with washbasins and tea/coffee making facilities; guests' lounge, diningroom. Parking. Children and pets welcome; cot and babysitting. Good food, pretty garden. Dinner, Bed and Breakfast from £23; Bed and Breakfast from £15. Lunches. Open all year. AA listed. Mrs Williams is the Winner of "Shropshire's Great Farm Breakfast Challenge". Also two holiday cottages available.

CRAVEN ARMS near. Mrs Caroline Morgan, Strefford Hall, Craven Arms SY7 8DE (01588 672383). ♛♛ *Commended.* An elegant Victorian farmhouse situated in the peaceful hamlet of Strefford with outstanding views of the Wenlock Edge and Long Mynd Hills. A 360 acre working farm with sheep, cattle and arable. Rooms are spacious and comprise two double en suite and one twin room with private bathroom, all comfortably furnished, having tea/coffee making facilities and TVs. Separate dining room and lounge for guests. Ample parking. Vegetarians catered for. Bed and Breakfast from £18; weekly terms available. Non-smoking household. Closed Christmas. Farm Holiday Bureau member.

IRONBRIDGE/TELFORD. Mrs Julia Thomas, Stoke Manor, Stoke-on-Tern, Market Drayton TF9 2DU (01630 685222; Fax: 01630 685666). ♛♛ *Highly Commended.* A warm welcome awaits you at Stoke Manor, which has a large garden and is situated on a working farm. Three charming bedrooms, each with bathroom, colour TV and tea/coffee making facilities. Unusual features include a particularly welcoming cellar bar, an 18th century bread oven, collections of vintage tractors, cast iron seats, artefacts from an archaeological dig on the farm's castle site and farm trails. Central to Ironbridge, Wedgwood Pottery and Cosford Aerospace Museum, Shrewsbury Chester and North Wales. An abundance of good eating places nearby. Residents' bar. Terms from £20 to £25 per person. AA Listed QQQQ.

LUDLOW. Clare and David Currant, Corndene, Coreley, Ludlow SY8 3AW (Ludlow [01584] 890324). ♛♛ This spacious 18th century country home stands in two acres of attractive grounds in the beautiful South Shropshire hills, 20 minutes' drive from Ludlow. Convenient for exploring Shropshire, Herefordshire and the Welsh Border. Ground floor rooms (twin and family) with en-suite modern bathrooms; single room with private bathroom; guests' own diningroom and sittingroom with TV and open fire. Central heating throughout. Ideally suited for disabled visitors. Good home cooking; packed lunches, special diets by arrangement Children welcome, cot, highchair. Own transport essential. Regret, no dogs. Bed, Breakfast and Evening Meal from £27 per day or from £170 per week. Bed and Breakfast from £18.50 per day. Reduced rates for children under 12 years. Brochure on request. No smoking please.

LYDBURY NORTH. Mr and Mrs R. Evans, "Brunslow", Lydbury North SY7 8AD (Lydbury North [0158-88] 244). Working farm, join in. "Brunslow" is a beautiful Georgian style farmhouse, centrally heated throughout, ideal for walking and those who enjoy the peace and quiet of unspoiled countryside. The house is set in large gardens with lovely views in all directions and the farm mainly produces milk; pigs, poultry and calves are reared and "feeding time" is very popular with younger guests. One double, one single and two family rooms, all having washbasins. Bathroom, toilets; separate sittingroom and diningroom; colour TV, high chair and babysitting available. Open all year, except Christmas, for Bed and Breakfast. Evening Dinner if required. SAE, please, for terms. Packed lunches available. Car essential, parking.

PONTESBURY. "Pinehurst", Shrewsbury Road, Pontesbury SY5 0QD (01743 790737). John and Kath Farmer welcome you to their home in the heart of Mary Webb country, with the South Shropshire hills, the Stiperstones and the Welsh Border near. On the bus route between Shrewsbury and Bishop's Castle. Accommodation comprises one single room, one double and one double with en suite shower, etc and TV. Tea/coffee trays in all rooms. Large lounge with open fire. Parking. Sorry, no smoking and no pets. Bed and Breakfast from £12.50 to £16. Children welcome at a reduced rate. At least 10 local establishments serve evening meals.

SHREWSBURY. Mrs Janet Jones, Grove Farm, Preston Brockhurst, Shrewsbury SY4 5QA (01939 220223). ♛ *Commended.* AA QQQ. This lovely 17th century farmhouse with a beautiful view offers warmth and comfort to all visitors. It is set in a little village on the A49, seven miles north of Shrewsbury. The house has a large lounge/dining room with log fires and colour TV; three pretty bedrooms (large double/family with shower, washbasin, colour TV, twin and single with washbasins) with easy chairs, tea/coffee facilities, hair dryers, etc. Guests' bathroom. Centrally heated throughout. You will be welcomed with tea and home-made cakes, and there is always a variety of delicious food offered for breakfast. Sorry, no smoking. No pets. Bed and Breakfast from £16.50. We look forward to welcoming you into our home.

SHREWSBURY. Mrs Mary Edwards, Cardeston Park Farm, Ford, Shrewsbury SY5 9NH (01743 884265). ♛ *Commended.* Spacious farmhouse set in quiet countryside with easy access to mid and north Wales, about eight miles west of Shrewsbury, 13 miles from Welshpool. Take A458 Welshpool Road from Shrewsbury, the farm is well signposted. One double and one twin room, both en suite, and one single room with washbasin; all rooms have colour TV and hot drinks facilities. Open all year. From £15 per person.

STIPERSTONES near. Mrs Rachel Lawton, Hill Cottage, The Bog, Stiperstones, Shrewsbury SY5 0NL (01743 791918). Delightfully situated on the South Shropshire hills, adjacent to the Stiperstones National Nature Reserve, with the Long Mynd three miles away. Excellent base for walking and centrally situated for visiting Shrewsbury, Powis Castle, Ludlow, Church Stretton and Ironbridge. Accommodation comprises one double with en suite facilities, one twin with separate bathroom and one small single room; tea/coffee making facilities, central heating, log burning stoves, TV. Non-smoking. No pets. Bed and Breakfast from £15; three course Evening Dinner with complimentary glass of wine and coffee £11. Excellent home cooking, home-made bread and preserves. Come and enjoy a peaceful, very comfortable relaxed stay, surrounded by beautiful unspoilt countryside and magnificent views. ETB Listed. Brochure available.

WEM. Mrs Elizabeth A. Jones, Lowe Hall Farm, Wem SY4 5UE (01939 232236). ♛♛ Working farm. Historically famous 16th century listed farmhouse, once country residence of Judge Jeffreys (1648-1689). Situated one mile north of Wem and convenient to Shrewsbury, Ironbridge, Chester and Llangollen. Two golf courses within seven miles and only one mile to Welsh Border. Ideal touring centre. Ample parking space. Inside is a splendid Jacobean staircase and Charles II fireplace. Fully centrally heated. En-suite bedrooms comprising family, double and twin rooms, all with colour TV and tea/coffee making facilities. Hair dryer and ironing board available on request. All guests have separate tables for breakfast with a choice of menu. Lowe Hall is one of only a few farmhouses classified two crowns by the English Tourist Board — a guarantee of the highest standard of food, decor and accommodation. Recommended on BBC 1 "Good Morning". Bed and Breakfast from £16. Reduced rates for children and weekly bookings. SAE or telephone for further details.

WHITCHURCH. Miss J. Gregory, Ash Hall, Ash Magna, Whitchurch SY13 4DL (01948 663151). Working farm. An early 18th century house set in large garden with ample room for children to play, on a medium-sized farm with pedigree Friesians. Situated in the small North Shropshire village of Ash, approximately one and a half miles from A41. Within easy reach of Chester and Shrewsbury (about 20 miles); Crewe 15 miles. Interesting features of this house are two oak-panelled reception rooms and an oak staircase; one of the two guest bedrooms is also panelled. One bedroom has en-suite facilities. Bathroom, toilet; sittingroom; diningroom. Children welcome, cot, high chair and reduced rates available. Open all year for Evening Meal, Bed and Breakfast or Bed and Breakfast. Tourist Board Listed.

FOR THE MUTUAL GUIDANCE OF GUEST AND HOST

Every year literally thousands of holidays, short-breaks and overnight stops are arranged through our guides, the vast majority without any problems at all. In a handful of cases, however, difficulties do arise about bookings, which often could have been prevented from the outset.

It is important to remember that when accommodation has been booked, both parties — guests and hosts — have entered into a form of contract. We hope that the following points will provide helpful guidance.

GUESTS: When enquiring about accommodation, be as precise as possible. Give exact dates, numbers in your party and the ages of any children. State the number and type of rooms wanted and also what catering you require — bed and breakfast, full board, etc. Make sure that the position about evening meals is clear — and about pets, reductions for children or any other special points.

Read our reviews carefully to ensure that the proprietors you are going to contact can supply what you want. Ask for a letter confirming all arrangements, if possible.

If you have to cancel, do so as soon as possible. Proprietors do have the right to retain deposits and under certain circumstances to charge for cancelled holidays if adequate notice is not given and they cannot re-let the accommodation.

HOSTS: Give details about your facilities and about any special conditions. Explain your deposit system clearly and arrangements for cancellations, charges, etc, and whether or not your terms include VAT

If for any reason you are unable to fulfil an agreed booking without adequate notice, you may be under an obligation to arrange alternative suitable accommodation or to make some form of compensation.

While every effort is made to ensure accuracy, we regret that FHG Publications cannot accept responsibility for errors, omissions or misrepresentation in our entries or any consequences thereof. Prices in particular should be checked because we go to press early. We will follow up complaints but cannot act as arbiters or agents for either party.

SOMERSET

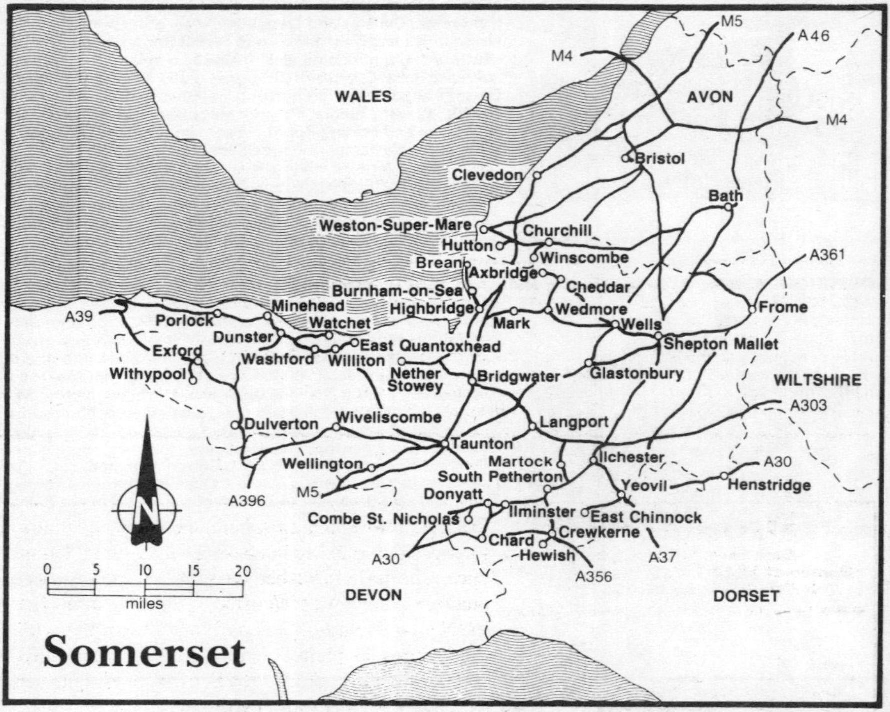

BURNHAM-ON-SEA near. Mrs F. Young, Lower Wick Farm, Wick Lane, Lympsham BS24 0HG (01278 751333). A warm welcome awaits you at our delightful old farmhouse, pleasantly situated in peaceful countryside within easy reach of Somerset attractions such as Cheddar Gorge, Wells and Glastonbury. All bedrooms have toilet, shower and washbasin en-suite and views over surrounding countryside. In addition to the diningroom, the large inglenook guests' lounge with colour TV offers quiet relaxation. Lovely garden and spacious lawns for just sitting or sunbathing. Regret unable to accommodate young children. Restricted smoking. Bed and Breakfast £16 daily. Weekly reductions. Brochure available.

CHARD. Mrs Sue Eames, Wambrook Farm, Wambrook, Chard TA20 3DF (01460 62371). Our farm is in a pretty rural village two miles from Chard in the Blackdown Hills. It has an attractive farmhouse and buildings which are listed. On our 350 acre farm we have beef cattle, breeding sheep, corn and koi carp in several ponds, with an abundance of wild life all around. We are half an hour from the Devon/Dorset coast. One double en-suite, one double with washbasin and one twin. Bed and Breakfast from £14. Children welcome, reduced rates, cot and babysitting available.

CHARD. Mrs J. Wright, Yew Tree Cottage, Hornsbury Hill, Chard TA20 3DB (01460 64735).

Attractive cottage, tastefully modernised, situated in lovely countryside with an acre garden. One mile from Chard on A358 between Chard and Ilminster, 15 miles from the coast, it makes an ideal base for touring Devon, Dorset and Somerset. Nearby are many historic houses, beautiful gardens, Wildlife Park, and golf and squash facilities. Comfortable, friendly accommodation consisting of twin/single and double rooms, all with washbasins and central heating. Ground floor apartments and en suite rooms; tea-making on request. Lounge/dining room with colour TV. Parking. Pets by arrangement. Good home cooking. No smoking. English Tourist Board registered. Bed and Breakfast from £14 to £19 per person per night; Evening Meal £9 by arrangement. SAE please for further details.

CHEWTON. Mrs B. Clothier, Franklyns Farm, Chewton Mendip, Near Bath BA3 4NB (01761 241372). Working farm. ♛♛ Situated just off the main A39 road on the B3114, amid the peaceful setting of the Mendip Hills. It is a 400 acre mixed farm with cows and corn. Plenty of interesting places to visit — Bath being only 12 miles away, Cheddar and the Chew Valley Lake eight miles, the city of Wells five miles and the West coast only 20 miles. First class comfortable farmhouse Bed and Breakfast accommodation offered in two twin-bedded and one double-bedded rooms, all with washbasins. Excellent eating out places close at hand. Lounge/dining room; bathroom. TVs and tea/coffee making facilities in all bedrooms. Pets permitted if kept under control. Bed and Breakfast from £18 single, £32 double.

Broadview

East Street, Crewkerne, Somerset TA18 7AG (Dorset Border)
Tel: Mrs G. Swann (01460) 73424

♛♛♛ De Luxe ETB & QQQQQ Premier Selected AA
BOTH TOP QUALITY AWARDS

Friendly informal atmosphere and extremely comfortable and relaxing in an unusual Colonial ambience. Carefully furnished en-suite rooms with easy chairs, colour TV, tea/coffee, central heating. Set in 'National Garden Scheme' feature gardens with many unusual plants. Award-winning traditional English home cooking. B&B £23 per person per day; Dinner £12. Stay awhile and explore varied and contrasting places; National Trust gardens, houses, moors, quaint old villages, Dorset coast and Hardy country. List of 50 places provided.
A NO SMOKING HOUSE. Open all year.

CREWKERNE. Mrs Sally Gregory, Dryclose, Newbery Lane, Misterton, Crewkerne TA18 8NE (01460 73161). ♛ *Commended.* Dryclose is a 16th century former farmhouse set in two acres of garden with swimming pool in a quiet area of the village of Misterton. Close by are historic buildings, beautiful gardens and, within half an hour, the Devon and Dorset coast. Explore Thomas Hardy's countryside, with wonderful walks. We offer Bed and Breakfast with optional Evening Meals. Three bedrooms — one twin en suite with TV, one twin and one single. Two separate guest sittingrooms with TV. All bedrooms have hot drinks facilities. Non-smokers please. Bed and Breakfast from £15.50. Reductions for weekly bookings. Write or phone for further details.

FHG PUBLICATIONS LIMITED publish a large range of well-known accommodation guides. We will be happy to send you details or you can use the order form at the back of this book.

DULVERTON. Mrs A.M. Spencer, Dassels, Dulverton TA22 9RZ (013984 203). Superb Georgian-style country guest house magnificently situated on the edge of Exmoor, three miles west of Dulverton on the outskirts of East Anstey. Set in nine and a half acres of tranquil grounds with panoramic views. A spacious house, large dining room, separate lounge, TV and log fires. 10 bedrooms, all en suite and with colour TV and tea/coffee making facilities. A high standard of comfort is maintained and Dassels is noted for its excellent home cooked food, farm produce, delicious sweets served with clotted cream, fresh baked rolls. A beautiful area near the Exmoor National Park where horse riding, walking, fishing and nature study are available. Many beauty spots within easy reach, also places of archaeological and historic interest, with easy access to North Devon and West Somerset coastal resorts. Residential licence. Ample parking. Fire Certificate. Stabling. Open all year. Children welcome. Dinner, Bed and Breakfast from £28.

DULVERTON. Mrs Brenda Coates, Chapple Farm, Bury, Dulverton TA4 2DP (01398 331364). Chapple Farm is situated on the slopes of Haddon Hill overlooking a wooded valley rich in wildlife. The farm is an Exmoor working beef and sheep hill farm of 220 acres; chickens, ducks, pheasant and sometimes partridge roam the farmyard. The farmhouse is 16th century and retains its oak beams and original character. It comprises three bedrooms, each with washbasin and tea/coffee making facilities; bathroom with separate toilet; dining room, comfortable lounge with TV and pleasant views across the valley. We serve traditional farmhouse breakfasts and evening meals using farm and dairy produce when available and fresh vegetables from the garden. Children and dogs welcome.

DUNSTER. Mr & Mrs W.A. Greenfield, Burnells Farm, Knowle Lane, Dunster TA24 6UU (Dunster (01643) 821841). Working farm. Comfortable and friendly farmhouse accommodation, one mile from Dunster, two miles from sea, with glorious views of Exmoor. Ideal walking or touring centre for the National Park. Accommodation comprises one double, one family and one single bedroom, all with washbasins; one public bathroom and one shower room, toilet upstairs and down; lounge with TV and diningroom. Guests are requested to refrain from smoking indoors. Ample parking. Packed lunches on request. Open all year. Bed and Breakfast £15.50. Evening Meal, Bed and Breakfast £21.50. Weekly £139.

EXMOOR **Ann & Philip Durbin, Cutthorne Farm, Luckwell Bridge, Wheddon Cross, TA24 7EW Tel: (0164 383) 255 ETB**

Set in the heart of Exmoor, one of the last truly unspoilt areas of the country. Cutthorne, a working farm with lots of animals and poultry, is beautifully secluded and dates from the 14th century. It is an ideal base for exploring the coast and countryside – good touring, walking and riding. Fly-fishing is also available in our well-stocked trout pond. The house is spacious and comfortable with log fires and central heating. The three bedrooms have en-suite bathrooms and the master bedroom has a four-poster bed. Candlelit dinners with good home cooking and an excellent choice of breakfasts. Bed and Breakfast from £19.50. Dogs welcome. No smoking.

PUBLISHER'S NOTE

While every effort is made to ensure accuracy, we regret that FHG Publications cannot accept responsibility for errors, omissions or misrepresentation in our entries or any consequences thereof. Prices in particular should be checked because we go to press early. We will follow up complaints but cannot act as arbiters or agents for either party.

EXMOOR. Jean and Ian Hamilton, Fern Cottage, Allerford, Near Porlock TA24 8HN (Porlock [01643] 862215). ♛♛ *Commended.* The forgotten part of the West. Never crowded, this is the place to find peace and solitude within the 260 square miles of the National Park's dramatic, beautiful scenery. The soft, warm climate nurtures the wonderful wooded coombes and furze-mantled hills. Forest paths are adorned with wild flowers; here wild red deer browse whilst buzzards soar the rising thermals. The heron's loping flight follows the river, falcons and ravens enjoy the sea cliff vistas. The villages of this, Exmoor's most spectacular vale, reflect a bygone way of life. Our large 17th century cottage has all the expected comforts of a country home, log fires, central heating. Noted for fine classic cooking and comprehensive wine list. Parking. Open all year. Bed and Breakfast £25; Dinner, Bed and Breakfast £36.25; weekly £228. Exmoor Short Breaks: three nights Dinner, Bed and Breakfast £103. Non-smoking. Credit cards accepted.

GLASTONBURY. Mrs Mary Dodds, Twelve Hides, Quarry Lane, Butleigh, Glastonbury BA6 8TE (01458 50380). Six acre smallholding with small pedigree Wensleydale flock (own handspinning). Four miles from Glastonbury, within easy reach of Wells, Bath, Cheddar Gorge, Wookey Caves, Camelot, Wetlands, etc, yet peaceful and away from it all. Exceptional view across Vale of Avalon to Glastonbury Tor, Wells Cathedral and Mendip Hills. Own tennis court (coaching available) overlooking picturesque Butleigh village. Good pub food within walking distance. Accommodation: one double-bedded room, two twin-bedded rooms (one with washbasin); tea/coffee facilities. Guest bathroom with bath, WC and washbasin. Separate guest shower room with WC/washbasin. Bed and traditional English Breakfast from £15.

GLASTONBURY. Mrs D.P. Atkinson, Court Lodge, Butleigh, Glastonbury BA6 8SA (01458 50575). A warm welcome awaits at attractive, modernised 1850 Lodge with homely atmosphere. Set in picturesque garden on the edge of Butleigh, three miles from historic Glastonbury. Only a five minute walk to pub in village which serves lovely meals. Accommodation in one double, one twin and one single bedrooms; constant hot water, central heating. Bathroom adjacent to bedrooms. TV lounge. Tea/coffee served. Bed and Breakfast from £12.50; Evening Meal by arrangement. Children welcome at reduced rates.

GURNEY SLADE. Mrs Jacqueline Hawkins, Cockhill Farm, Marchants Hill, Gurney Slade, Near Bath BA3 4TY (01749 840125). Farmhouse accommodation on a working farm keeping a small beef suckler herd in the heart of the Mendips. A friendly atmosphere is assured in this Victorian farmhouse. Excellent home cooking from local produce. Bed and Breakfast, optional Evening Meal. Spacious rooms with period furnishings, TV, tea/coffee making facilities. Ideally situated for the Cathedral City of Wells, Glastonbury, Cheddar, Georgian Bath and historic Bristol. Royal Bath and West Showground 10 minutes. Magnificent Chew Valley Lake for bird watching, fly fishing and picnicking 20 minutes. Good local pubs and peaceful country walks. Children welcome, baby facilities available. One twin, one double bedroom and one single bedroom. Open all year. Bed and Breakfast from £13.50.

HIGHBRIDGE near. Mrs B.M. Puddy, "Laurel Farm", Mark Causeway, Near Highbridge TA9 4PZ (01278 641216). ♛♛ Laurel Farm is over 200 years old with 120 acres and 70 milking cows, Friesian and Holstein. We are about two miles from Mark Church and village on the Wells to Burnham-on-Sea B3139 road, two miles from M5 Junction 22. Ideal touring centre or halfway house. There is a large sittingroom with a colour TV, log fires September to May. Central heating, electric blankets. Washbasins in all bedrooms. Nicely decorated with fitted carpets throughout. Separate tables in diningroom. Doubles, singles and family rooms; shower, two baths, three toilets. Car essential/or bike. Undercover garages. Open all year. Bed and Breakfast from £12.50.

LYMPSHAM. Mrs C.M. Ball, Lower Farm House, South Road, Lympsham BS24 0DY (01934 750206). Our traditional Somerset farmhouse is on the edge of the picturesque village of Lympsham between the Mendip Hills and the sea, yet is only three miles from the M5 Junction 22. Relax in our peaceful garden and meet the goats or wander close by to see a variety of farm animals. Our bedrooms have washbasins, TV and tea making facilities. The ground floor bedrooms are suitable for less able guests. We especially welcome children and have a range of outdoor play equipment. Pets by arrangement. Good parking. Bed and full English Breakfast from £14 daily, £90 per week. Reductions for children.

MARTOCK. Mr and Mrs S.R. Peach, Falconers Farm, Milton, Ash, Martock TA12 6AL (01935 823363). Working farm. A Georgian farmhouse set in 320 acres of mixed farmland on a Duchy of Cornwall farm belonging to the Prince of Wales Estates. Visitors welcome to tour farm and watch. Nearest town Yeovil seven miles. A family farm ideal for walking on the Somerset Levels or Polden Hills, horse riding and coarse fishing or convenient for shopping in Taunton. Local attractions include Montacute House and Cricket St. Thomas Wildlife Park. The coast is three-quarters of an hour's drive. Accommodation in three guest rooms (one family), own bathroom. All children welcome, cot, high chair and babysitting available. Car essential. Bed and Breakfast from £13 to £18 per person per night. Telephone or write for further details.

MARTOCK. Mrs Turton, "Wychwood", 7 Bearley Road, Martock TA12 6PG (01935 825601). *Highly Commended.* Quality, comfortable accommodation. Excellent home cooking. In quiet position just off A303. Central touring location. Close to Montacute House, Tintinhull Gardens, Fleet Air Arm Museum, and much more. Walk the "Leyland Trail" through Camelot Country and the Legend of King Arthur. Yeovil 10 minutes, Sherborne 15 minutes; Glastonbury, Wells, Taunton, M5 Junction 25 approximately 30 minutes. TV, radio and tea/coffee making facilities in all bedrooms. Double and single rooms en suite, twin with private bathroom. Comfortable residents' lounge, separate dining room. Garden. Bed and full English Breakfast from £16; Dinner £12. Brochure. Open all year. Credit cards accepted.

MARTOCK. Mrs Jacqui Dodd-Noble, Parrett House, Martock TA12 6AE (Tel & Fax: 01935 826539). Parrett House is an old rambling listed hamstone house with a wonderful one and a half acre walled garden on the River Parrett. Situated on an old historic mill site between Martock and South Petherton, it is just two miles off A303. The garden is full of wildlife and you can wander and relax, or play croquet. Golf and riding are nearby, and coarse fishing on the Parrett. We are close to many National Trust properties, gardens, some wonderful old Somerset pubs and many fine churches. All bedrooms have colour TV, tea/coffee facilities and washbasins. One has an en suite shower. Accommodation is spacious with a real country house atmosphere. Bed and Breakfast from £16 per person; Evening Meal by arrangement.

MINEHEAD near. Mrs Rosemary Tucker, West Luccombe Farm, Porlock, Near Minehead TA24 8HT (01643 862478). Working farm. West Luccombe is a working farm of 340 acres carrying beef cattle, sheep, arable. An ideal location for tourists needing bed and breakfast, with Porlock one mile, Minehead five miles and Horner quarter of a mile. West Luccombe was originally a Manor House on the National Trust Estate and stands amidst lovely gardens, with a river running close to the grounds 100 yards away and surrounded by beautiful countryside of great interest to walkers. Accommodation comprises two double and one family bedrooms, all with washbasins (hot and cold water) and tea/coffee making facilities; bathroom, two toilets; sittingroom with colour TV; dining room. Pets by arrangement. Children welcome at reduced rates. Open Easter to October. A car is essential and ample parking space is provided. Bed and Breakfast from £14 nightly; weekly rates quoted on request.

Take a child free to RODE BIRD GARDENS, near BATH, Somerset – use our READERS' OFFER VOUCHER.

MINEHEAD. Mr and Mrs G. Collop, Alcombe Cote Guest House, 19 Manor Road, Alcombe, Minehead TA24 6EH (Minehead [01643] 703309). *Approved.* Alcombe Cote is a charming 19th century residence situated at the entrance to Alcombe Coombe and within a short distance of Exmoor. Ideal base for exploring the coast and countryside by foot, car or coach. Castles, manor houses, churches, ancient monuments and historic villages abound, also many famous beauty spots and the West Somerset Steam Railway in Minehead. Two double, one single, one family, two twin bedrooms all with washbasins; two bathrooms, two toilets, diningroom. Central heating plus log fire in lounge. Children over five years welcome — reduced rates. Sorry, no pets. Open March to November. Parking. ETB and WCTB registered. Evening Meal, Bed and Breakfast from £17.50 daily, £115.50 weekly; Bed and Breakfast from £13.50 daily.

MINEHEAD near. Mrs Penny Webber, Hindon Farm, Near Minehead TA24 8SH (Minehead [01643] 705244). Working farm, join in. Our guests say "This is a real farm!" Superbly situated on our own in valley between Minehead (three miles) and Selworthy (one mile). 500 acres and direct access to moor — terrific walks, views and horse riding. Great atmosphere, farm and wildlife; many animals including donkey, horses, cows, spotted pigs, lots of sheep, goats, etc.; poultry roam freely. Help with feeding, lambing, haymaking, etc., or relax on large lawn with stream and picnic table, volleyball/badminton net. Games barn. Big breakfasts in lovely 17th/18th century farmhouse. All pretty bedrooms have washbasins and drinks trays. Guests' bathroom and toilet. Sitting room with TV and video. Dogs and horses welcome. ETB Listed and Commended. Farm Holiday Bureau member. Write or phone for brochure.

SHEPTON MALLET. Mrs M. White, Barrow Farm, North Wootton, Shepton Mallet (01749 890245). Working farm. This farm accommodation is AA QQQ Listed and registered with the English Tourist Board. Barrow is a dairy farm of 146 acres. The house is 15th century and of much character, situated quietly between Wells, Glastonbury and Shepton Mallet. It makes an excellent touring centre for visiting Somerset's beauty spots and historic places, for example, Cheddar, Bath, Wookey Hole and Longleat. Guest accommodation consists of two double rooms, one family room, one single and one twin bedded room, each with washbasin, TV and tea/coffee making facilities. Bathroom, two toilets; two lounges, one with colour TV; diningroom with separate tables. Guests can enjoy farmhouse fare in generous variety, home baking a speciality. Bed and Breakfast from £14 to £15; Evening Meal from £8. Weekly rates from £140. Car essential; ample parking. Children welcome; cot and babysitting available. Open all year except Christmas. Sorry no pets.

SHERBORNE near. Mrs Sue Stretton, Beech Farm, Sigwells, Charlton Horethorne, Near Sherborne, Dorset DT9 4LN (01963 220524). A warm welcome awaits you on our 150 acre dairy farm carrying beef and horses in an area with wonderful views and excellent for walking, cycling and horse riding (guests' horses welcome). Located on the Somerset/Dorset border, six miles from Wincanton, four miles from Sherborne and just two miles off the A303. A comfortable, centrally heated farmhouse with a family room en suite and a twin room with private bathroom, both with colour TV and tea/coffee facilities. Laundry facilities and packed lunches available. Bed and Breakfast from £14 to £15 per person. Evening meals at village inn or by prior arrangement. Open all year.

TAUNTON. Mrs Chris Jordan, Waterpitts Farm, Broomfield, Quantock Hills, Bridgwater TA5 1AT (01823 451679). Working farm, join in. Quiet, friendly, secluded smallholding set in the beautiful Quantock Hills. Situated six miles from both Taunton and Bridgwater. Good pubs nearby. Ideally placed for all outdoor pursuits including walking, golfing, fishing, riding and mountain biking. Facilities for cleaning and storing of bikes; stables for guests' horses. Large safe parking area for cars. Animals on smallholding include free-range chickens, ducks, sheep, cats and dogs. No smoking in house. Accommodation comprises one family room and one double room. Central heating. Bed and Breakfast from £14. Children under 10 years half price.

Hall Farm Guest House

Stogumber, Taunton TA4 3TQ Tel: (01984) 56321

Hall Farm is situated on a working farm in the centre of Stogumber Village, surrounded by the Quantocks and Exmoor. Within easy reach of the sea, Minehead, Blue Anchor, Watchet and St. Audries Bay. Accommodation for 12 to 14 guests. The bedrooms are comfortable and have ensuite facilities. The catering is under the personal supervision of the proprietress, whose concern it is to make your holiday a happy one. Dogs are welcome if kept well under control. Good parking. Breakfast at 9am with Evening Dinner at 6.30pm. Traditional Sunday lunches at 1pm. **Proprietress: Christine M. Hayes.**

TAUNTON. Mrs Lucy Parker, North Down Farm, Wiveliscombe, Taunton TA4 2BL (01984 23730).

Set on the edge of Exmoor, approximately 20 minutes from the M5 Junctions 25, 26, 27. Very quiet situation, with no passing traffic. Outstanding views over the Vale of Taunton and Quantock Hills. Guests are free to watch the milking and other activities on this family-run dairy farm. Accommodation is a family suite of rooms sleeping three/four with en suite toilet, and a double room. Full central heating, tea/coffee facilities provided. Bed and Breakfast from £15 per person per night, discounts for weekly bookings. Evening Meal available from £9.50. Vegetarian and special menus catered for. Open all year round except Christmas.

TAUNTON. Mrs M.A. Woollaston, Greenway Farm, Wiveliscombe, Taunton TA4 2UA (01984 623359; Fax: 01984 624051). ♛ The farm is British Tourist Board graded and classified. This is a working dairy farm boasting a beautiful Regency farmhouse with all guest facilities, comfortable lounge, excellent views, gardens, good home prepared food. Children welcome. Comfort with peace and quiet without being isolated; for action take part in a country pursuit, enjoy excellent walks, riding, game or coarse fishing, clay pigeon shooting; all can be arranged. The coast is also close by. Open March to October. Bed and Breakfast £15; Evening Meal £7. Special diets catered for. Farm Holiday Bureau Member. O.S. Map Ref: ST080270.

WATCHET. Mrs Sheena White, Glasses Farm, Roadwater, Watchet TA23 0QH (01984 640552). Working farm. Thatched 16th century farmhouse situated in a beautiful rural setting on the edge of the Brendon Hills, within the Exmoor National Park. Ideal for touring and walking around the picturesque countryside. Also available riding, hunting (stabling if needed). The farm consists of 220 acres, arable and dairy. Three bedrooms, all with washbasins, tea/coffee making facilities and central heating. Bathroom and shower room. Ample parking, car essential. Open all year round except Christmas. Terms available on request.

WATCHET. Mrs H. North, Swansea Farm, Brendon Hill, Watchet TA23 0LH (013987 202). Historic 17th century spacious farmhouse on Brendon Hills. Working farm of 300 acres carrying sheep and beef. Stabling available; riding school nearby. Pets and children welcome; cot, high chair and babysitting available. Excellent area for walking, Wimbleball Lake nearby for fishing and sailing. Ideal base for exploring Exmoor, excellent pubs nearby for meals. Four miles from Brompton Regis with its post office/stores and pub. Situated in hamlet of Withiel Florey which boasts charming Norman Church. Bed and Breakfast £15, reductions for children. Two bedrooms — one twin en suite, one family; two bathrooms, two toilets. Central heating. A warm welcome awaits.

WEDMORE. Mrs Sarah Willcox, Townsend Farm, Sand, Near Wedmore BS28 4XH (01934 712342).

♛♛ Townsend Farm is delightfully situated in peaceful countryside with extensive views of the Mendip Hills. Set on the outskirts of the picturesque Georgian village of Wedmore with easy access to many places of natural and historic interest, such as the famous Cheddar Gorge, Wells Cathedral, Glastonbury Tor and Abbey ruins and only six miles from the M5 motorway, Junction 22 (one night stops welcome). We offer Bed and Breakfast with optional Evening Meal. All bedrooms have tea/coffee making facilities and some have portable TVs. Guests can be assured of a warm and pleasant atmosphere. Bed and Breakfast from £15 per person, en-suite from £18; Evening Meal from £10. Phone for availability. Farm Holiday Bureau member.

WELLS. Mrs Janet Gould, Milton Manor Farm, Old Bristol Road, Upper Milton, Wells BA5 3AH (Wells [01749] 673394). ♛ Working farm.

Manor Farm is a Grade 2 star listed Elizabethan Manor House superbly situated on southern slopes of Mendip Hills one mile north from Wells. It is a beef farm of 130 acres. Three large rooms for visitors with hot and cold water, central heating and tea/coffee facilities. Full English Breakfast with choice of menu served at separate tables in panelled diningroom. Colour TV. Large peaceful garden with lovely view towards the sea. Ideal for walking on the Mendip Hills and exploring local places of historic interest. Access to house at all times. Fire Certificate held. AA listed QQQ. No smoking. Open January to December for Bed and Breakfast from £14 per person. Reductions for children and week-long stays. Brochure on request.

WELLS near. Mrs Pamela Keen, Crapnell Farm, Dinder, Near Wells (01749 342683).

A 300 acre mixed farm of arable, dairy and pigs, situated on the Mendip Hills in beautiful surroundings. Listed 16th century house with much character within easy reach of Wells, Cheddar, Wookey Hole, Glastonbury, Bath and many more interesting places. Only a mile from lovely Mendip Golf Club, four miles from Bath and West Showground at Shepton Mallet. All rooms are large and comfortably furnished with washbasins, some with showers, tea/coffee facilities. TV lounge available. Children welcome. March to October. Parking. Bed and Breakfast; Dinner available.

WELLS near. Mrs H.J. Millard, Double-Gate Farm, Godney, Near Wells BA5 1RZ (Glastonbury [01458] 832217). Working farm. Located in the heart of beautiful Somerset, Double-Gate nestles on the banks of the River Sheppey, on a mixed farm. This charming Georgian farmhouse (now listed) is tastefully renovated to include comfortable guest lounge with colour TV; spacious bedrooms with washbasins; luxury bath and shower room. Non-smoking accommodation available. Children most welcome. Morning teas and evening beverages available; Evening Meals available at village inn close by. Food Hygiene Certificate held. No restrictions on access. Ideal for touring: six miles from the magnificent city of Wells, three miles from Glastonbury — legendary home of King Arthur — and central for most attractions; Bath, Cheddar Gorge, Wookey Hole Caves, Weston-super-Mare. Car essential, free parking. Sorry, no pets except guide dogs. Country Rover Farm Holidays. T.H.A Approved accommodation. Brittany Ferries. Full Fire Certificate. Bed and Breakfast from £14. Reduced terms children/weekly stays.

See also Colour Display Advertisement WESTON-SUPER-MARE. Margaret and David Holt, Moorlands, Hutton, Near Weston-Super-Mare BS24 9QH (Bleadon [01934] 812283). *Approved.* Enjoy fine food and warm hospitality at this impressive late Georgian house set in landscaped gardens below the slopes of the Western Mendips. A wonderful touring centre, perfectly placed for visits to beaches, sites of special interest and historic buildings. Families with children particularly welcome, reduced terms and pony rides in our paddock. Good wholesome meals with the emphasis on our own home-grown produce. Full central heating, open fire in comfortable lounge. Licensed. Open January to early November.

WHEDDON CROSS. Mr L.J. Maxwell, Little Brendon Hill, Wheddon Cross TA24 7DG (01643 841556). *Highly Commended.* Enjoy a stay with us and experience the true peace of the countryside in our beautifully appointed farmhouse in a quiet location where we keep sheep, horses and chickens; ducks and other fowl roam freely. We are in the centre of the Exmoor National Park, an outstanding area of unspoilt natural beauty and tranquillity. Log fires, cosy candle-lit dinners, good food — the essential ingredients of a splendid holiday. Short stay or long you will be most welcome. Bed and Breakfast from £16; Evening Meal £10.

STAFFORDSHIRE

LEEK. Mrs Laura Melland, Newhouse Farm, Bottomhouse, Near Leek ST13 7PA (01538 304350). Situated four miles from Leek off the A523 Ashbourne Road. This is a small, family-run farm set in the Staffordshire Moorlands, convenient for Alton Towers, Carsington Water Reservoir, Peak District National Park, Dovedale, Manifold Valley, Hartington, Potteries, Chatsworth House and cycleways. Full English breakfast, packed lunch on request. One twin room en suite and one family room, both with colour TV, tea making facilities, central heating. Pets by arrangement. Children welcome, cot available. Ample parking. Bed and Breakfast from £13.50 to £15. Reductions for children under 12 years. Guests are assured of a warm friendly welcome.

LEEK near. Mrs E. Lowe, Fairboroughs Farm, Rudyard, Near Leek ST13 8PR (Rushton Spencer [01260] 226341). ♛ **Working farm.** Established 1979. This is a working beef/sheep farm of 150 acres. The house is 17th century with oak beams and log fires when necessary. All the large rooms have panoramic views and central heating. The bedrooms (one family, one double) have washbasins and shaver points, with tea/coffee facilities provided. Separate lounge with colour TV, dining room for visitors' use. Situated in Staffordshire Moorlands within easy reach of Peak Park, Alton Towers, Potteries and Cheshire. Fishing at Rudyard and Tittesworth Reservoirs; Biddulph Grange Gardens nearby. Children welcome at reduced rates. We endeavour to make your stay comfortable and happy. Phone for availability. Bed and Breakfast from £15 single, £30 double. CC/CL.

LEEK near. Stan and Elizabeth Winterton, Brook House Farm, Cheddleton, Leek ST13 7DF (Churnet Side [01538] 360296). ♛♛♛ *Commended.* **Working farm, join in.** Brook House is a 180-acre dairy farm situated in a picturesque valley with scenic views and pleasant walks, half a mile from the A520 and near to Cheddleton Village with its Brindley Mill Railway Museums, Cauldon Canal and beautiful Churnet Valley. Convenient for the Peak District, the Pottery Museum, Alton Towers, Coombes Valley RSPB Reserve and much more of interest. Two family rooms in a tasteful farm building conversion with patio doors; two rooms in the farmhouse; all with en-suite facilities, central heating, colour TV and tea/coffee makers. Dine in our attractive conservatory with magnificent country views. A warm welcome and good food a speciality. Reduced rates for children. Bed and Breakfast from £15.50; optional Evening Meal from £8. Farm Holiday Bureau member.

OAKMOOR. Muriel and John Egerton Orme, Bank House, Farley Lane, Oakmoor ST10 3BD (01538 702810). ♛♛ *Highly Commended.* This exceptional private country home overlooks the picturesque Churnet Valley and provides de luxe en suite accommodation with fine cuisine and relaxed and friendly "house party" style. Licensed. All rooms are handsomely furnished and offer baskets of fruit and home made biscuits, tea/coffee making facilities, radio, TV. Bank House is conveniently situated for Alton Towers, Bakewell, Ashbourne, The Potteries, the Peak District and Staffordshire moorlands. Bed and Breakfast from £23 to £35 per person; Dinner from £12 to £18. Open all year. AA QQQQQ Premier Selected.

STAFFORD. Mrs Judy Palmer, Oulton House Farm, Norbury, Stafford ST20 0PG (Woodseaves [01785] 284264). ♛♛ *Highly Commended.* **Working farm.** Oulton House Farm is a 300 acre dairy farm situated on the Staffordshire/Shropshire border. Our large Victorian farmhouse offers warm, comfortable and well appointed bedrooms, all en-suite and with TVs and tea trays. Within easy driving distance there are many interesting places to visit, ranging from the historic county towns of Stafford and Shrewsbury, the famous Ironbridge Gorge Museum, Wedgwood, the Potteries and many stately homes to the modern splendours of Alton Towers and the National Sports Centre. For dinner we have many excellent local pubs and restaurants to choose from. Bed and Breakfast from £18.50.

STAFFORDSHIRE'S

Farm & Country Holidays

BED & BREAKFAST

BANK END FARM MOTEL, Longsden, Stoke-on-Trent, Staffs. (Mrs B. Robinson) 01538 383 638. Tastefully converted accommodation in 15th century stone barn. All ensuite. Licensed bar. Award-winning restaurant. Indoor pool. Superb views. **From £22 pp. (★★ AA Recommended).**

BONEHILL FARM, Mickleover, Derby. (Mrs C. Dicken) 01332 513 553. Georgian farmhouse in quiet rural setting, on A516 3 miles west of Derby. Convenient for many Derbyshire attractions. Children welcome. Tea/coffee in room. Large garden. **1D 1T 1F. From £15. ETB Listed.**

BROADFIELDS FARM, Pessall Lane, Edingale, Tamworth, Staffs B79 9JW. (Mrs K. Cliffe) 01827 383 225. Traditional beamed farmhouse situated in peaceful countryside. Five minutes M42 and A38. Tastefully furnished rooms. H&C, tea making, own bathroom and lounge, colour TV. **From £15.**

LITTLE BROOKHOUSE FARM, Cheddleton, Leek, Staffs. (Mrs N. Sherratt) 01538 360 350. A warm welcome, good food and high level of comfort ensures guests of a memorable stay in this delightfully peaceful rural location. All ensuite rooms. **From £16.50 pp.**

MAIDENSLEY FARM, Foston, Derbyshire. (Mrs A. Weston) 01283 585 724. Beautiful old farmhouse, very relaxed and comfortable. Central for Derby, Ashbourne, Alton Towers, Burton and potteries. Residents' lounge with TV and open fire. Full breakfast. **2D 1T. From £14.50.**

MARSH FARM, Abbots Bromley, Rugeley, Staffs. (Mrs M. Hollins) 01283 840 323. You will be made welcome at this spacious farmhouse; tastefully furnished bedrooms and good home cooking. Close to Lichfield, Alton Towers and Cannock Chase. **1F 1T. From £15 each. (ETB ♛).**

MOORS FARM & COUNTRY RESTAURANT, Codshall, Wolverhampton, W. Midlands. (Mrs D. Moreton) Tel & Fax 01902 842 330. Picture an Oak Beamed Farmhouse in a quiet valley with superb cuisine and comfortable bedrooms with wonderful views, tea/coffee, TV etc. **3 ensuite; 2D 2T 2F. From £19. (ETB ♛♛♛ Commended).**

NORTON FARM, Stone, Staffs. (Mrs M. Brown) 01785 760 224. A beautiful Georgian farmhouse on working dairy and stock farm overlooking a golf course. Ideally situated for the potteries (Wedgwood 4 miles), Alton Towers and stately homes of the area. **2D 1T. From £15.**

OFFLEY GROVE FARM, Adbaston, Staffs. (Mrs M. Hiscoe-James) 01785 280 205. You'll consider this a good find! Quality accommodation. Excellent breakfasts. Attractive house and traditional farm buildings. Ideal for Stoke-on-Trent, Ironbridge etc. Children welcome. Many guests return. **1D 2T. From £15. (♛ Highly Commended).** AA & RAC Listed.

PARK FARM, Weston Road, Stafford. (Mrs J. Williams) 01785 40257. Period farmhouse situated by County Showground, with lovely views. Private bathroom, TV and tea trays in rooms. Fire Certificate held. **1F 1T. From £15. (♛♛ Highly Commended).**

RIBDEN FARM, Nr Oakamoor, Staffs. (Mrs C. Shaw) 01538 702 830. Stone farmhouse in Staffordshire Moorlands. Ensuite bedrooms with TV, clock-radios, toiletries. TV lounge, Car Park. Alton Towers 5 minutes. Close to potteries and Peak District. **1F 2D 1F Suite. From £15 pp. (♛♛ Highly Commended).**

SLINDON HOUSE FARM, Slindon, Eccleshall, Staffs. (Mrs H. Bonsall) 01782 791 237. Comfortable accommodation situated on the A519 in tiny village of Slindon. Ideal for M6 Junctions 14 & 15. **1T Ensuite 1D. From £15 pp. (ETB ♛♛).**

STRAMSHALL FARM, Stramshall, Uttoxeter, Staffs. (Mrs L. Bailey) 01889 562 363.. Late Victorian Farmhouse complete with neglected Aspidistra and mega bedrooms. Experience a great British Breakfast served with a helping of hospitality. **2F (max. 6 persons). (Listed/Commended).**

SUMMERHILL FARM, Grindon, Staffs. (Mrs P. Simpson) 01538 304 264. Working farm tastefully, comfortably furnished. Period furniture. Panoramic views overlooking the Dove, Manifold Valley and Staffordshire Peaks. **1D 1T Ensuite 1T Private Bathroom. From £16. (Listed/Commended. AA Recommended QQQ).**

SEE ALSO FULL PAGE SELF CATERING ADVERTISEMENT UNDER STAFFORDSHIRE.

Phone or send a 9 × 4" SAE to any member of our group for their own individual or the group brochure.

STOKE-ON-TRENT. Mrs Anne Hodgson, The Hollies, Clay Lake, Endon, Stoke-on-Trent ST9 9DD (Stoke-on-Trent [01782] 503252). ♛♛ Beautiful Victorian house in a quiet country setting off the B5051 convenient for the M6, Alton Towers, Staffordshire Moorlands and the Potteries. Five spacious comfortable bedrooms (including three en-suite) all with central heating, washbasins, tea/coffee facilities and TV. Children welcome sharing family room. Dogs by prior arrangement. Secluded garden with ample parking. Choice of breakfast with own preserves. No smoking, please. Bed and Breakfast from £16 with reductions for children. Guests are assured of a warm friendly welcome.

STOKE-ON-TRENT. Mrs Barbara White, Micklea Farm, Micklea Lane, Longsdon, Near Leek, Stoke-on-Trent ST9 9QA (Leek [01538] 385006; Fax: 01538 382882). Quietly situated off A53 yet ideally located for touring the area, this delightful old stone house, boasting a warm friendly atmosphere and comfortable accommodation, is the perfect base for a family holiday. Open all year; guest lounge with TV; large garden; ample parking. Children welcome. Visitors will enjoy pleasant canal and country park walks, fishing, golf, gliding and hang gliding. Alton Towers and the beautiful Peak District and Potteries are near at hand. Tourist Board Listed "Approved". Bed, Breakfast and Evening Meal £25. Further details on request.

UTTOXETER. Stramshall Farm, Stramshall, Uttoxeter ST14 5AG (01889 562363). Visiting Alton Towers, the Potteries, the Derbyshire Peak District and a multitude of other attractions, then come and experience a friendly home from home atmosphere at Stramshall Farm with its late-Victorian farmhouse (complete with neglected aspidistra), mega-sized bedrooms and attractive gardens. The two family bedrooms have washbasins, shaver points, towels, TV and tea/coffee making facilities. All this completed by a great English breakfast. From £13 per person per night; maximum six people.

SUFFOLK

BEYTON. Mrs Kay Dewsbury, "Manorhouse", The Green, Beyton, Near Bury St. Edmunds IP30 9AF (01359 270960). ♛♛ *Highly Commended.* Lovely 16th century timber framed former farmhouse overlooking a delightful village green, with its resident geese, in the conservation village of Beyton. Good local hostelries, the nearest inn is just a walk across the green. The historic town of Bury St. Edmunds is nearby with its cathedral and lovely abbey gardens. Lavenham, Long Melford, Cambridge or the coast are all within 30 minutes' drive. Both en suite rooms are attractively decorated to a high standard, are non smoking and have colour TV, tea making facilities, radio and hair dryers. AA QQQQ Selected. Bed and Breakfast from £18 to £19 per person per night. Self catering accommodation for two people also available.

BRAMFIELD, Near Halesworth. Mrs Patricia Kemsley, Broad Oak Farm, Bramfield, Halesworth IP19 9AB (01986 784232). ♛♛ *Commended.* A 400 acre dairy and arable farm about quarter of a mile from the road, one and a half miles from Bramfield Village. Spacious 16th century farmhouse has been carefully modernised and offers three double rooms (one en suite shower and one en suite bathroom); separate bathroom; sittingroom with colour TV and dining room where good home cooking is served (optional Evening Meal). Non-smoking accommodation available. We are surrounded by attractive gardens and within easy reach of the sea; Southwold is seven miles. Pets and children welcome. Golf, fishing and cycle hire available close by. Bed and Breakfast from £13 to £16.

BUNGAY/BECCLES. Mrs Sarah Cook, Butterley House, Leet Hill Farm, Yarmouth Road, Kirby Cane, Bungay NR35 2HJ (01508 518301). Working farm. A warm welcome awaits at this dairy/arable farm set in the heart of the Waveney Valley, with excellent rural views, situated between the historic towns of Beccles and Bungay, 15 miles from Norwich, 20 minutes' drive from Norfolk/ Suffolk coasts, and nearby the famous Otter Trust. Accommodation comprises one double/family room with en-suite facilities, one double room with washbasin and one twin room; bathroom, two toilets. Guests have their own sittingroom with TV, separate diningroom. Full English Breakfast. Evening Meal by arrangement. Farm produce used whenever possible. Car essential. No pets please. Reductions for children. Terms on request. Tourist Board registered.

BURY ST. EDMUNDS. Mrs N.B. Less, Broad Acre, 10 Parklands Green, Fornham St. Genevieve, Bury St. Edmunds IP28 6UH (Bury St. Edmunds [01284] 769340). A large attractive house in a quiet location offering excellent accommodation and cooking, and set in delightful partly wooded grounds of one-and-a-half acres. The village of Fornham St. Genevieve is two miles north of the historic market town of Bury St. Edmunds. Cambridge, Newmarket, Thetford and medieval wool towns such as Lavenham are within easy reach. The house has double, twin and single bedrooms with hot and cold water. Shower-room, bathroom and diningroom/lounge with TV are for guests' exclusive use. Children are welcome and there is a reduced rate up to the age of 10. Open year-round for Bed and Breakfast; Evening Meals available. Write or 'phone for bookings or full details.

BURY ST. EDMUNDS. Mrs Sarah Rush, Rymer Farm, Barnham, Thetford IP24 2PP (01842 890233; Fax: 01842 890653). ♛♛ *Commended.* 17th century farmhouse situated eight miles north of the historic town of Bury St. Edmunds. A wonderful welcome awaits guests with tea in the garden room or by the log fire in the elegant sittingroom. Fruit from the garden and full English breakfast offered. Double and single en suite rooms and a twin-bedded room with private bathroom. All centrally heated. Farm walks with wild life everywhere! Open all year except Christmas. Bed and Breakfast from £16 nightly.

COLCHESTER. Mrs C.A. Somerville, Rosebank, Lower Street, Stratford St. Mary, Colchester, Essex CO7 6JS (Colchester [01206] 322259). Attractive 14th-century part Manor House, with river frontage and fishing rights, in peaceful village in the Dedham Vale, which is renowned for its period architecture and old inns. Our boathouse is reputed to have featured in Constable's paintings. Guests are accommodated in two double and two twin bedrooms, all with washbasins, some en suite including a family room; two bathrooms and three toilets. Diningroom. Central heating; woodburner on chilly nights. Rooms are comfortable and attractive with television and tea/coffee making facilities. Delightful chalet set in the grounds, double-bedded with bathroom en-suite. English Breakfast of your choice — good cooking. Tourist Board registered. Terms from £16.50 for Bed and Breakfast. Winter Breaks with Evening Meal available. Open all year except Christmas week.

SUFFOLK – CONSTABLE COUNTRY!

To be precise Dedham Vale is Constable Country and it is only one of Suffolk's attractions. The others include the country parks at Brandon and Clare Castle, Debenham, Lavenham, Newmarket, The Museum of East Anglian Life and the river port of Woodbridge.

EYE. Shelia Webster, Elm Lodge Farm, Chippenhall Green, Fressingfield, Eye IP21 5SL (01379 586249). ♛♛ *Commended.* This 112 acre working farm with early Victorian farmhouse overlooks a large common (SSSI) where animals graze in summer — the perfect spot for an after-dinner stroll. Spacious bedrooms with washbasins, separate dining and sitting rooms, log fires and excellent food ensure that a comfortable, relaxing holiday is enjoyed by all those we warmly welcome to this attractive and peaceful corner of Suffolk. Open March to November. Children 10 years and over and pets welcome. Bed and Breakfast from £15 to £19; Dinner by arrangement. Non-smokers preferred. FHB Member.

FRAMLINGHAM. Brian and Phyllis Collett, Shimmens Pightle, Dennington Road, Framlingham, Woodbridge IP13 9JT (01728 724036). Shimmens Pightle is situated in an acre of landscaped garden, surrounded by farmland, within a mile of the centre of Framlingham, with its famous castle and church. Ideally situated for the Heritage Coast, Snape Maltings, local vineyards, riding, etc. Cycles can be hired locally. Many good local eating places. Double and twin-bedded rooms, with washbasins, on ground floor. Comfortable lounge with TV overlooking garden; central heating and log fires in winter. Morning tea and evening drinks offered. Sorry, no pets or smoking indoors. Bed and traditional English Breakfast, using local cured bacon and home made preserves. Vegetarians also happily catered for. ETB Listed "Commended". Open all year. SAE please. Self catering flats also available in Southwold.

FRAMLINGHAM. Mrs Ann Proctor, Grove Farm, Laxfield, Framlingham, Woodbridge IP13 8EY (01986 798235). This is a Georgian farmhouse standing in a 30 acre mixed farm with pigs and sheep, ponies and pedigree breeding dogs. Beautiful view of village and only 12 miles from the coast. Within easy reach of Norwich, Norfolk Broads, historic houses and quaint unspoilt villages. The accommodation is in two double and two family bedrooms (with washbasins); diningroom; lounge with colour television; bathroom, three toilets; full central heating. Children welcome, cot, high chair and babysitting. Sorry, no pets. Open March to November. The emphasis is on a friendly atmosphere with good home cooking — meat, vegetables, honey, etc., mainly produced on farm. Car essential, ample parking. Bed and Breakfast or Bed, Breakfast and Evening Meal; children under 12 years reduced rates. Please phone or send SAE for terms.

FRAMLINGHAM. Mrs C. Jones, Bantry, Chapel Road, Saxtead, Woodbridge IP13 9RB (01728 685578). ♛♛♛ Bantry is set in half an acre of gardens overlooking open countryside in the picturesque village of Saxtead, which is close to the historic castle town of Framlingham. Best known for its working windmill beside the village green, Saxtead is a good central base from which to discover East Anglia. Accommodation is offered in self-contained apartments (one ground floor), each comprising its own private diningroom/TV lounge and bathroom for secluded comfort. Good home cooking from home grown produce. Terms: Bed and Breakfast from £18 per night. Non Smoking.

FRAMLINGHAM near. Gordon and Teresa Craggs, Red House Farm, Maypole Green, Dennington, Woodbridge IP13 8AQ (01728 638628). A warm, friendly welcome to this attractive 17th century farmhouse set in four acres of wooded grounds on small side road half a mile from Dennington village and A1120. Red House offers a peaceful interlude: two twin-bedded rooms, one single; private bathrooms. Full English breakfast, home made bread, local produce. Oak beamed sittingroom, TV, separate diningroom. Tea/coffee making facilities. Packed lunches by arrangement. Historic Framlingham three miles, easy reach Heritage coast (Southwold, Dunwich, Aldeburgh, Orford). No smoking in bedrooms. Children over 10 years welcome. Plenty of good eating places nearby. Open February to December (not Christmas). From £18.50 per person.

FRAMLINGHAM. Mrs Jennie Mann, Fiddlers Hall, Cransford, Near Framlingham, Woodbridge IP13 9PQ (01728 663729). Working farm, join in. Signposted on B1119, Fiddlers Hall is a 14th century, moated, oak-beamed farmhouse set in a beautiful and secluded position. It is two miles from Framlingham Castle, 20 minutes' drive from Aldeburgh, Snape Maltings, Woodbridge and Southwold. A Grade II Listed building, it has lots of history and character. The bedrooms are spacious; one has en-suite shower room, the other has a private bathroom. Use of lounge and colour TV. Plenty of parking space. Lots of farm animals kept. Traditional farmhouse cooking. Bed and Breakfast terms from £18. Tourist Board registered.

FRAMLINGHAM. Mrs J.R. Graham, Woodlands Farm, Brundish, Near Woodbridge IP13 8BP (01379 384444). ♛♛ *Highly Commended.* Woodlands Farm has a cottage-type farmhouse set in quiet Suffolk countryside. Near historic town of Framlingham with its castle and within easy reach of coast, wildlife parks, Otter Trust, Easton Farm Park and Snape Maltings for music lovers. Open all year. Twin room wih private shower, washbasin and WC; two double bedrooms with bathroom en-suite. Diningroom and sittingroom with inglenook fireplaces for guests' use. Good home cooked food assured. Full central heating. Car essential, good parking. Sorry, no pets. Bed and Breakfast from £15; Evening Meal £12 (six nights). SAE or telephone. FHB Member.

HADLEIGH. Mrs P. Redman, Mount Pleasant Farm, Offton, Ipswich IP8 4RP (Tel & Fax: 01473 658896). ♛♛♛ *Approved.* **Working farm, join in.** Secluded 16th century farmhouse situated on a working farm with many different animals. Genuinely secluded, yet sea only 30 minutes away, Water Park only five minutes. Sports centres with varied activities 15 minutes. Many local beauty spots to visit and enjoy. En-suite facilities available. Evening Meals a speciality, by arrangement. Bed and Breakfast — single rates from £18, double £27.50. Evening Meal £8.

HALESWORTH. Mrs Eileen Webb, "Saskiavill", Chediston, Halesworth IP19 0AR (Halesworth [01986] 873067). ♛♛♛ "Saskiavill" is set back from the road and stands in one-and-a-half acres of garden. The spacious bungalow offers holidaymakers an ideal touring base for the fine City of Norwich, the coast and nearby Minsmere Bird Sanctuary. The village has many thatched cottages and an old church and is only two miles from the market town of Halesworth. Convenient for golf courses, nature reserves, museums, National Trust houses, gardens, etc. One double, one family, one twin adapted for disabled guests, all en-suite; two bathrooms, two toilets; TV lounge, sittingroom, diningroom. Children welcome at reduced rates, babysitting available. Sorry, no pets. Car essential — parking. Open all year for Evening Dinner/Meal, Bed and Breakfast or Bed and Breakfast. Varied menus with good home cooking including home made pastries, bread and preserves. Telephone or SAE for terms. Reductions for Senior Citizens out of season. EATB member.

HITCHAM. Mrs Philippa McLardy, Hill Farmhouse, Bury Road, Hitcham IP7 7PT (Bildeston [01449] 740651). Hill Farmhouse has lovely views and is set in its own grounds of three acres. It is an ideal touring centre, close to Lavenham, Constable and Gainsborough country. The coast, Cambridge, Norwich, Ipswich and Colchester are within an hour's drive. Restaurant and three pubs serving food all within two miles. Accommodation is in the main farmhouse and adjoining oak timbered Tudor cottage. Twin and double suites all have private or en-suite bathrooms, colour TVs, tea/coffee making facilities. Pets by arrangement. Special diets catered for. Bed and Breakfast £16.50 (one to four nights), £14.50 (five or more nights). Reductions for children. Dinner (choice of menu) available at £10.

IPSWICH. Mrs Rosemary Bryce, College Farm, Hintlesham, Ipswich IP8 3NT (Tel & Fax: 01473 652253). *Highly Commended.* A 15th century beamed farmhouse once owned by Cardinal Wolsey in quiet rural setting on a 600 acre arable/beef farm, six miles west of Ipswich. Double room en suite, single and double/family room sharing guests' bathroom. Comfortably furnished with tea/coffee trays and central heating in all bedrooms. Guests' lounge with colour TV and inglenook fireplace. Close to "Constable Country" and Lavenham. Marked footpaths around the farm, golf and horse riding nearby. Children over five years welcome. Sorry, no dogs. No smoking in bedrooms or dining room. Good food available locally. Open mid-January to mid-December. Bed and Breakfast from £16.

SAXMUNDHAM. Philip and Janet Maricic, Rose Farm, Mill Street, Middleton, Saxmundham IP17 3NG (01728 648456). Delightful 17th century farmhouse set in seven acres on the edge of rural village. Conveniently situated for Suffolk and Norfolk Heritage Coasts. The two large (double/twin) bedrooms in the main house are beautifully furnished with their own private en suite or enormous bathroom. Reached via the garden is the self contained "Dairy" double bedroom with en suite shower room; this, situated on the ground floor, makes easy ONE LEVEL access to the farmhouse where breakfast is served in the dining room. TV, tea/coffee making facilities in rooms. Open all year.

SAXMUNDHAM. Mrs Margaret Gray, Park Farm, Sibton, Saxmundham IP17 2LZ (01728 668324). *Commended.* Park Farm is a working farm of 250 acres in gentle Suffolk countryside, where a friendly welcome awaits all guests. We can offer one double and two twin bedrooms, each with washbasin. Guests have their own dining and sitting rooms, with colour TV. A three-course dinner is optional, cooked from our own or local produce. All tastes and special diets are gladly catered for. Early morning/bedtime drinks on request. We are within easy reach of the sea, Minsmere Bird Reserve and Snape Maltings. We can arrange cycle hire or you can wander over our fields at your leisure. Bed and Breakfast from £14 to £17; Evening Meal £10.50. Farm Holiday Bureau member.

TRIMLEY ST. MARTIN (Near Felixstowe). Mrs Claire Whight, Little Street Farm, 240 High Road, Trimley St. Martin, Ipswich IP10 0RG (01394 278874). Lovingly restored detached farmhouse. We promise a warm welcome and informal atmosphere. All rooms have central heating, and the comfortable bedrooms include vanity units, shaver sockets, TV and tea/coffee making facilities. Separate guest toilet and bathroom (bath and shower). Fresh home-made farmhouse-range cooking; full varied English breakfast and evening meal, if required. Set in picturesque Suffolk, many local walks, easy access to Constable country and local places of interest (Dedham, Woodbridge, Lavenham, etc). 30 minutes' drive from Colchester and Harwich. Bed and Breakfast from £30 double; Evening Meal from £10. Sorry no pets and no smoking. Special diets catered for. Directions: A12 from London, A14 to Felixstowe, turn off at Trimley villages roundabout, left at next roundabout, 400 yards on your left on Trimley High Road.

SURREY

LINGFIELD. Mrs Vivienne Bundy, Oaklands, Felcourt Road, Lingfield RH7 6NF (01342 834705).

Oaklands is a spacious country house of considerable charm dating from the 17th century. It is set in its own grounds of one acre and is about one mile from the small town of Lingfield and three miles from East Grinstead, both with rail connections to London. It is convenient to Gatwick Airport and is ideal as a "stop-over" or as a base to visit many places of interest in south east England. Dover and the Channel Ports are two hours' drive away whilst the major towns of London and Brighton are about one hour distant. One family room en-suite, one double and one single bedrooms, one with washbasin; three bathrooms, two toilets; sittingroom; diningroom. Cot, high chair, babysitting and reduced rates for children. Gas central heating. Open all year. Parking. Bed and Breakfast from £16. Evening Meal by arrangement.

LINGFIELD. Mrs Vanessa Manwill, Stantons Hall Farm, Eastbourne Road, Blindley Heath, Lingfield RG7 6LG (01342 832401).

Stantons Hall Farm is an 18th century farmhouse set amidst 18 acres of farmland and adjacent to Blindley Heath Common. Family, double and single rooms, most with toilet, shower and washbasins en-suite. Separate bathroom. All rooms have colour TV, tea/coffee facilities and are centrally heated. There are plenty of parking spaces. We are conveniently situated within easy reach of M25 (London Orbital), Gatwick Airport (car parking facilities for travellers) and Lingfield Park Racecourse. Enjoy a traditional English Breakfast in our large farmhouse kitchen. Bed and Breakfast from £16 per person, reductions for children sharing. Cot and high chair available. Well behaved dogs welcome by prior arrangement.

Key to Tourist Board Ratings

The Crown Scheme

(England, Scotland & Wales)

English Tourist Board COMMENDED

Covering hotels, motels, private hotels, guesthouses, inns, bed & breakfast, farmhouses. Every Crown classified place to stay is inspected annually. *The classification:* Listed then 1-5 Crown indicates the range of facilities and services. Higher quality standards are indicated by the terms APPROVED, COMMENDED, HIGHLY COMMENDED and DELUXE.

The Key Scheme

(also operates in Scotland using a Crown symbol)

English Tourist Board COMMENDED

Covering self-catering in cottages, bungalows, flats, houseboats, houses, chalets, etc. Every Key classified holiday home is inspected annually. *The classification:* 1-5 Key indicates the range of facilities and equipment. Higher quality standards are indicated by the terms APPROVED, COMMENDED, HIGHLY COMMENDED and DELUXE.

The Q Scheme

(England, Scotland & Wales)

Covering holiday, caravan, chalet and camping parks. Every Q rated park is inspected annually for its quality standards. The more ✓ in the Q – up to 5 – the higher the standard of what is provided.

SUSSEX

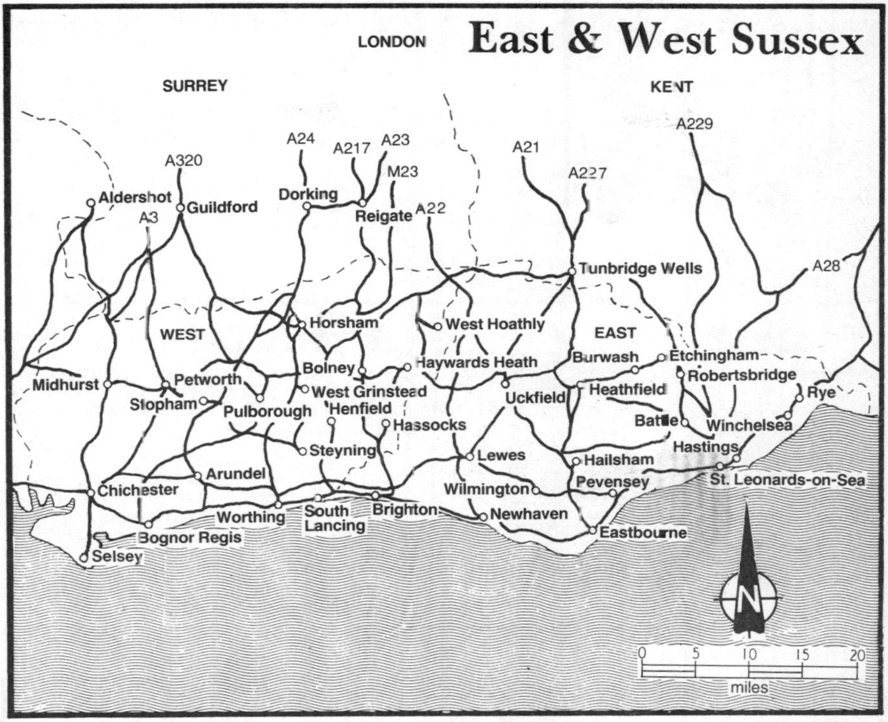

EAST SUSSEX

BATTLE. Mrs Howard, Platnix Farm Oasthouse, Harts Green, Sedlescombe, Battle TN33 0RT (01424 870214). A delightful oasthouse, with heavily beamed interior and full central heating, situated in beautiful countryside on a working sheep farm between Battle and Rye. Accommodation is in three comfortable bedrooms, two en suite, and one round twin-bedded room, all with TV and tea/coffee making facilities. Within easy reach of Bodiam and Sissinghurst Castles. You can be sure of a warm and friendly welcome. Bed and Breakfast from £20 per person per night. There are a number of excellent local pubs where delicious meals can be obtained.

EAST SUSSEX – 1066 AND ALL THAT!

The story of the famous battle can be traced from Pevensey, where William the Conqueror first landed; to Hastings, where the Norman and Saxon armies met and King Harold was slain; to Battle, where the victorious William founded an abbey. Visit too the Cinque Port of Rye (now a hilltop town), Michelham Priory and the magnificent moated Bodiam Castle.

BRIGHTON. Amblecliff Hotel, 35 Upper Rock Gardens, Brighton BN2 1QF (01273 681161). 👑👑👑

This stylish hotel was recommended by the Sunday Times and on TV. Excellently located close to the sea front with the Pier, The Lanes, Royal Pavilion, Conference Centre and Marina only a short stroll away. Individually designed rooms with king-size, four-poster and non-smoking rooms available. All double, twin and family rooms are en suite. A choice of full English breakfast in the diningroom or Continental breakfast in bed. Unrestricted access. We believe you deserve an excellent service and value for money. AA QQQQ, RAC Highly Acclaimed. Bed and Breakfast from £17.50, supplements for one night stays and en-suite facilities.

Sea Breeze

PROBABLY BRIGHTON'S FRIENDLIEST GUEST HOUSE
"ARRIVE AS A GUEST, LEAVE AS A FRIEND"

Sea Breeze is your home from home. **All** rooms are fully en-suite. Hospitality tray, Radio alarm, Colour TV with video & satellite channels. Rooms individually designed (have we your colour?). Perhaps the Four-Poster suite.

Brighton has much to offer ie: Entertainments, Shops. Pier, Lanes, Marina, Brighton Centre & The Sea.

Sea Breeze's standards are very high. Friendship and a good time at Sea Breeze guaranteed.

Own keys. Credit Cards & cash accepted. Pets by request. Prices from £17.

12a Upper Rock Gardens, Brighton, E. Sussex BN2 1QE
Tel: 01273 602608 Fax: 01273 607166

AVALON GUEST HOUSE

7 Upper Rock Gardens, BRIGHTON BN2 1QE
Telephone (01273) 692344

Bob Sharp extends a warm welcome to his small, friendly Guest House in the centre of Brighton, close to seafront, Conference Centre, Marina and tourist attractions. Fully centrally heated. All rooms have colour TV and tea/coffee making facilities. Some rooms en suite. Good English Breakfast. All from £15.00. Special rates for weekly stays. Credit cards accepted. Members of the Brighton Guest House and Hotel Association. Registered with Brighton Tourist Board. Satellite TV. In-house films.

BRIGHTON. Kempton House Hotel, 33/34 Marine Parade, Brighton BN2 1TR (01273 570248).

👑👑👑 *Commended.* AA/RAC Highly Acclaimed. We are a private seafront hotel offering a relaxed and friendly holiday or short break. Rooms available with magnificent views overlooking beach and pier, all with full en-suite shower and toilet, central heating, tea/coffee facilities, direct-dial telephones, colour TV, Satellite TV, radio, hair dryer. Full English Breakfast served or Continental Breakfast in bed. Four-poster bed available overlooking sea. Residents' bar and sea-facing patio garden for your use. Ideally situated for business or pleasure. Children and pets always welcome. Please telephone for details. From only £22 per person per night Bed and Breakfast. Weekly rate — seven nights for the price of six. Open all year.

BURWASH. Mrs E. Sirrell, Woodlands Farm, Burwash, Etchingham TN19 7LA (Burwash [01435] 882794). Working farm, join in. Woodlands Farm stands one third of a mile off the road surrounded by fields and woods. This peaceful and beautifully modernised 16th century farmhouse offers comfortable and friendly accommodation. Sitting/dining room; two bathrooms, one en suite, double or twin bedded rooms (one has four poster bed) together with excellent farm fresh food. This is a farm of 55 acres with mixed animals, and is situated within easy reach of 20 or more places of interest to visit and half an hour from the coast. Open Easter to October. Central heating. Literature provided to help guests. Children welcome. Dogs allowed if sleeping in owner's car. Parking. Evening Meal optional. Bed and Breakfast from £15.50. ETB registered. AA listed. Telephone or SAE, please.

DITCHLING. Mrs R. Norfolk, The Old Rectory, Westmeston, Ditchling BN6 8RL (01273 843711; Fax: 01273 844918). Sample traditional English country family life in this comfortable and intriguing Victorian Gothic rectory. Enjoy its 10 acres beside the South Downs. Large, light rooms full of character, magnificent views, log fires in the winter. Be near to Brighton without its excesses, also convenient for Lewes, Newhaven, Hickstead, Glyndebourne; Gatwick is 30 minutes away. Cyclists/walkers face the challenge of Ditchling Beacon and the South Downs Way, golfers may tackle the East Sussex National and other local courses. Charleston Farmhouse and a clutch of other historic houses and gardens are within easy reach. Double/twin rooms £21.25 per person, single £31, including memorable breakfasts.

HASTINGS. Mr and Mrs S. York, Westwood, Stonestile Lane, Hastings TN35 4PG (01424 751038). Working farm. Small farm with pet sheep, chickens, etc. Quiet rural location off country lane half a mile from B2093 approximately two miles from seafront and town centre. Central position for visiting places of interest to suit all ages. Elevated situation with outstanding views over Brede Valley. All bedrooms have washbasins, tea making facilities and TV; some en suite and two bedrooms on ground floor. Full English breakfast. Off-road parking. Bed and Breakfast from £15 to £20 per person for two persons sharing. Reduced rates for weekly booking. Also available six-berth self catering caravan — details on request.

HASTINGS. Mrs B.M. Beck, Lower Lidham Hill Farm, Guestling, Near Hastings TN35 4LX (Hastings [01424] 814225). Working farm. Lovely, fully beamed 18th century farmhouse situated on working farm. Prize winning beef herd, sheep and arable. Two double rooms with colour TV and tea/coffee making facilities. Ideal for touring with Battle seven miles, Hastings five miles and Rye six miles away. No smoking. Open all year for Bed and Breakfast £17 per person per night; £16 per person for two nights or more. Car essential, parking.

HERSTMONCEUX. Mr and Mrs R.E. Gentry, The Stud Farm, Bodle Street Green, Near Hailsham BN27 4RJ (Tel & Fax: 01323 833201). ♛♛ *Commended.* **Working farm.** The Stud Farm keeps mainly cattle and sheep. It is peacefully situated between A271 and B2096 amidst beautiful undulating countryside. Ideal for walking and touring lovely East Sussex, being within easy reach of Eastbourne (12 miles), Bexhill (10 miles) and Hastings (15 miles). There are many places of historic interest in the vicinity and the coast is only eight miles away at Pevensey. Upstairs there is a family unit (only let to one set of guests — either two, three or four persons — at a time), consisting of one twin-bedded room and one double-bedded room, both with handbasins and shaver points and their own bathroom with toilet. There is also downstairs one twin-bedded room with shower, handbasin, tea/coffee making facilities and toilet en-suite. Guests have their own sittingroom with TV and diningroom and sunroom. Sorry, no pets. Open all year. Central heating in winter. Car essential — parking available. Bed and Breakfast from £17; Evening Meals from £8.50 by arrangement. SAE, please. AA Commended QQ.

Don't miss the FREE entrance offer at PLANET EARTH, Newhaven, East Sussex. See our READERS' OFFER VOUCHERS for details.

RYE. Pat and Jeff Sullivin, Cliff Farm, Iden Lock, Rye (01797 280331 long ring please). Working farm. Our farmhouse is peacefully set in a quiet elevated position with extensive views over Romney Marsh. The ancient seaport town of Rye with its narrow cobbled street is two miles away. We are an ideal touring base although the town and immediate district have much to offer — golden beaches, quaint villages, castles, gardens etc. Comfortable guest bedrooms with washbasins and tea/coffee making facilities; two toilets; own shower; diningroom and sitting-room. Home produce. Open March to October for Bed and Breakfast from £13.50 to £14.50. Reduced weekly rates. AA and RAC Recommended.

RYE near. Mrs Sheena Austen, Birds Farm House, Bixley Lane, Beckley, Near Rye TN31 6RY (01797 260443). All you require for a peaceful stay in secluded countryside. Situated six miles from the ancient Cinque Port of Rye on the edge of the Romney Marsh. Close to many areas of historical interest including Bodiam, Scotney and Sissinghurst Castles. Birds Farm House offers you a warm welcome and comfortable bedrooms with your own bathroom. Excellent English breakfast served. Beverages available. Open all year. Bed and Breakfast £17. Please call for further details.

RYE near. David and Eliane Griffin, Kimblee, Main Street, Peasmarsh, Near Rye TN31 6UL (01797 230514 or 0831 841004 mobile). ♛♛ *Commended.* Friendly country house. View from all aspects. Rye five minutes' drive, beaches 15 minutes. Ample off road parking. Ideal base for visiting Kent and Sussex. Two large rooms with shower, toilet, washbasin en suite. Smaller room with adjacent private bathroom. Single room possible. All rooms have colour TV, radio alarm, tea/coffee facilities, hair dryers. Locally renowned pub/restaurant 250 metres. Generous English breakfast, vegetarian on request. Reduction for substantial Continental breakfast. French spoken. On A268 three miles from Rye direction London. £15 to £18 per person. Reductions for three nights or more. Brochure on request.

WEST SUSSEX

BOGNOR REGIS. Mr and Mrs G.E. Soothill, Black Mill House Hotel, Princess Avenue, Bognor Regis PO21 2QU (Bognor Regis [01243] 821945). ♛♛♛ A family-run hotel in Aldwick, the quieter west side of Bognor Regis, only 300 yards from the sea and Marine Gardens. The hotel faces south and has all the characteristics of a large private house, surrounded by enclosed gardens. The hotel is centrally heated throughout. 27 bedrooms (21 with private bathroom/shower and toilet) including 11 twin or double, six family and ten single. All with telephone, colour TV and tea/coffee making facilities. There is an attractive Cocktail Bar and Restaurant, fully licensed. Lift. Two lounges, one non-smoking; large games room with table tennis, darts, small snooker table. Bed and Breakfast; Dinner, Bed and Breakfast or Full Board on request. Picnic lunches and afternoon teas available; special diets catered for. Children sharing with two adults accommodated free. "Listening Service", washing and drying facilities. Out of season Mini-Breaks, two days from £60 Dinner, Bed and Breakfast. Also Spring and Summer Short Breaks. Open all year including Christmas. Dogs welcome. Own car park. Illustrated brochure. An excellent centre for touring in the south. MinOtels. AA/RAC. Ashley Courtenay recommended. Member South East England Tourist Board.

BOGNOR REGIS. Mrs M. Hashfield, Taplow Cottage, 81 Nyewood Lane, Bognor Regis PO21 2UE (01243 821398). The Cottage lies in a residential part, west of the town centre, 600 yards from the sea and shops. Proximity to many beaches and contrasting towns and countryside make for an ideal touring centre. Chichester, Goodwood Racecourse, Arundel Castle, Brighton, Portsmouth and Southsea are but a few of the places of interest within easy reach. Accommodation comprises one double, one twin-bedded and one family bedroom, all with vanity units, tea/coffee making facilities and colour TV. Lounge, diningroom. The cottage is well appointed and the area is served by public transport. Parking space available. Bed and Breakfast from £14. Dogs by prior arrangement. SAE, please. Arun Tourist Board registered.

DIAL POST. Mrs E.C. Sawyer, Swallows Farm, Dial Post, Horsham RH13 8NN (Partridge Green [01403] 710385). ♛♛ Working farm. Swallows Farm is a 200-acre mixed farm, family run since 1928, and is situated in mid-West Sussex. Horses are a highlight of the farm and are available for riding the South Downs Way or hacking out, or whatever you require. The farmhouse is Grade II Listed, and is situated half a mile from the busy A24 which goes from London to the coast, 40 minutes from Gatwick Airport. Many places of historic interest such as Arundel Castle, Petworth House, the South Downs, and many well-known gardens are all within 20 miles. Hacking locally or downland rides, prices on application. All rooms have washbasins, tea/coffee making facilities and colour TV. Guests' lounge with colour TV. Open February to November. Bed and Breakfast from £15; Evening Meal, optional, from £7.25. SAE for brochure, or phone please.

HENFIELD. Mrs J. Forbes, Little Oreham Farm, off Horne Lane, Near Woodsmill, Henfield BN5 9SB (Henfield [01273] 492931). Delightful old Sussex farmhouse situated in rural position down lane, adjacent to footpaths and nature reserve. One mile from Henfield village, eight miles from Brighton, convenient for Gatwick and Hickstead. Excellent base for visiting many gardens and places of interest in the area. The farmhouse is a listed building of great character; oak-beamed sittingroom with inglenook fireplace (log fires), and a pretty diningroom. Three comfortable attractive bedrooms with en-suite shower/bath; WC; colour TV; tea-making facilities. Central heating throughout. Lovely garden with views of the Downs. Situated off Horne Lane, one minute from Woodsmill Countryside Centre. Winner of Kellog's award: "Best Bed and Breakfast" in the South East. You will enjoy a friendly welcome and pleasant holiday. Sorry, no children under 10. Bed and Breakfast from £17.50 per person. Evening Meals by arrangement. No smoking. Open all year. ETB registered.

HENFIELD. Mrs M. Wilkin, Great Wapses Farm, Henfield BN5 9BJ (Henfield [01273] 492544). Working farm. The Tudor/Georgian farmhouse is set in rural surroundings, ten miles north of Brighton, off the B2116 Albourne/Henfield road. Hickstead is nearby. There are horses etc. The three comfortable rooms (one with four-poster bed) all have their own bathroom, shower en-suite, TV and tea/coffee making facilities. Children and well behaved dogs are welcome. Hard tennis court. Open all year round for Bed and Breakfast from £17 per person. Snacks usually available by arrangement. There is also an attractive self-contained comfortable cottage, sleeps two/three. Let on weekly basis £110 including electricity, TV etc. Tourist Board registered.

WEST SUSSEX – COASTAL RESORTS AND DOWNS!

Although dominated perhaps by Chichester and Bognor Regis, West Sussex does have much to offer. Places like Arundel, Marden-Stoughton Forest, Midhurst, and its historic inn, the open-air museum at Singleton and the National Butterfly Museum at Bramber are worth a visit.

The Old Cottage

Opening May 1995. Idyllic, peaceful, 16th century, stone-built farm cottage, newly restored and extended to architect's design and surrounded by Sussex downland. Lovely views. Perfect for South Downs explorers, gardening and wildlife enthusiasts; access to Portsmouth continental ferries, beautiful and historic Chichester, racing at Goodwood, polo and golf at Cowdray Park and south coast watersports and yachting. Three centrally heated double bedrooms (two with twin beds), washbasins, TV/radio, tea/coffee-making facilities. Conservatory, huge garden, wildlife pond, chickens and small orchard. Optional, light evening meals. Home produce. Vegetarians catered for. No children or smokers. Bed and breakfast £19.00.

Sue & Mike Hook, The Old Cottage, Didling, Near Midhurst, West Sussex GU29 0LQ Tel: 01730 813680

PETWORTH. Mr and Mrs Nick Moss, River Park Farm, Lodsworth, Petworth GU28 9DS (Lodsworth [01798] 861362). Working farm. Situated at the end of a mile long private drive the farm is a perfect spot for nature lovers and walkers. In our 17th century farmhouse we offer full English Breakfast and optional light evening meals using home made produce. The farm comprises 340 acres of corn and grassland which guests are encouraged to walk. Behind the house is a four and a half acre lake attracting an abundance of wildlife. Coarse fishing is available. Most bedrooms have washbasins, all have electric blankets and tea/coffee making facilities. Our Channel Island house cow provides milk and cream for us. Bed and Breakfast from £14.50 to £16.

WEST HOATHLY. Mrs R. Blackman, Duckyls Farm, Selfield Road, West Hoathly RH19 4QY (01342 810429; Fax: 01342 811047). Enjoy the relaxed atmosphere and good food at Duckyls Farmhouse, built in the 16th century and situated in an area of outstanding beauty. The house has an historic background and features in Peter Brandon's book "The Sussex Landscape" as typical of the area. All rooms are spacious and well appointed with beautiful views. Dining room, sitting room with colour satellite TV. Delightful bedrooms — en suite bathroom available, TV, tea/coffee making facilities. Spectacular local hill and forest walks. Excellent base for touring Sussex, four miles from Junction 10 of M23. Close to South of England Showground, Wakehurst Place, Bluebell Railway, Haywards Heath, Gatwick; 30 minutes' drive to Brighton. Bed and Breakfast £35 double, £20 single. Evening Meal £12.50. Minimum stay — two nights. Car parking. Dogs welcome.

PUBLISHER'S NOTE

While every effort is made to ensure accuracy, we regret that FHG Publications cannot accept responsibility for errors, omissions or misrepresentation in our entries or any consequences thereof. Prices in particular should be checked because we go to press early. We will follow up complaints but cannot act as arbiters or agents for either party.

WARWICKSHIRE

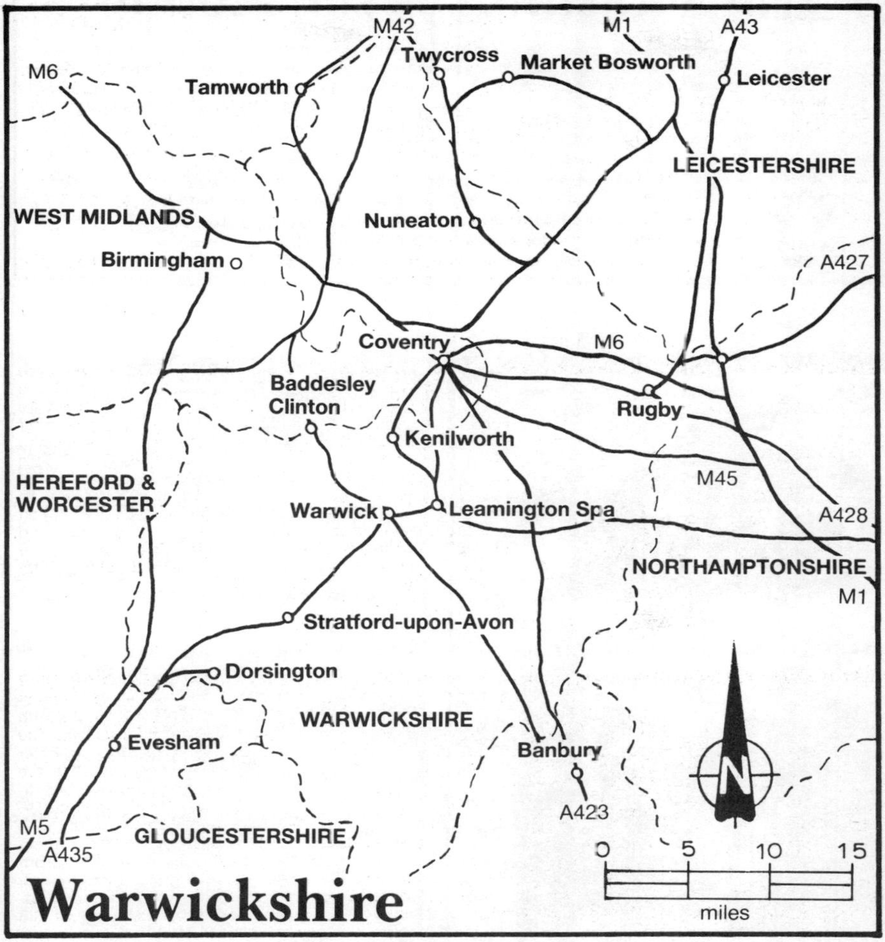

COVENTRY. Mrs Barbara Chamberlain, Mill Farmhouse Country Residence, Mill Lane, Fillongley, Near Coventry CV7 8EE (01676 541898).

Experience the peace and tranquillity of our beautiful country home offering exceptional standards of comfort in idyllic surroundings. All rooms are centrally heated and immaculately furnished. Ample private car parking. No smoking. Tariff: Luxury Double en suite room with colour TV, etc £40; Luxury Twin en suite room with colour TV, etc £45; Luxury Single en suite room with colour TV, etc £30. Non en suite single room £17. Near Corley Services on M6; 15 minutes NEC/Coventry, 30 minutes Birmingham and Stratford. Near Forest of Arden and The Belfry.

CADEBY STEAM & BRASS RUBBING CENTRE, Nuneaton, Warwickshire, offers a train ride for two and two cream teas or similar on production of our READERS' OFFER VOUCHER.

Warwickshire Farm Holidays

Warwickshire farming families welcome guests into their homes to enjoy the comforts of a traditional English farmhouse and discover the peace of the English countryside. Each home listed has it own unique character and differs in size, style, and price, but all offer a high standard of accommodation, good food, a warm welcome and excellent value for money to holidaymakers and business travellers. All owners are members of the Farm Holiday Bureau, all properties are inspected and classified by the English Tourist Board, some also participate in the ETB grading scheme. Warwickshire, in the heart of England, provides the perfect setting for the perfect holiday. Mile upon mile of rolling countryside, picturesque villages and meandering waterways. There are castles, stately homes, theatres, country gardens and some of the prettiest villages to be found.

FARM HOLIDAY BUREAU

Places to visit within easy reach include Stratford-upon-Avon, Warwick, Royal Leamington Spa, The Cotswolds, Oxford, Coventry, National Exhibition Centre and National Agricultural Centre.

For further details about Bed & Breakfast or Self-catering cottages, please write or telephone for a free brochure to: Warwickshire Farm Holidays (FHG), Crandon House, Avon Dassett, Leamington Spa CV33 0AA. Telephone: (01295) 770652.

COVENTRY near. Mrs Sandra Evans, Camp Farm, Hob Lane, Balsall Common, Near Coventry CV7 7GX (01676 533804). Camp Farm is a farmhouse 150 to 200 years old. It is modernised but still retains its old world character. Nestling in the heart of England in Shakespeare country, within easy reach of Stratford-upon-Avon, Warwick, Kenilworth, Coventry with its famous Cathedral, and the National Exhibition Centre, Camp Farm offers a warm, homely atmosphere and good English food, service and comfortable beds. The house is carpeted throughout. Dining-room and sun lounge with colour TV. Bedrooms — five double, three family rooms and five single, all with wash-basins. Part of the house is suitable for disabled guests. Children welcome. Cot and high chair, babysitting on request. Fire Certificate granted 1974. All terms quoted by letter or telephone.

FRANKTON. Mrs Mary Pritchard, Frankton Grounds Farm, Frankton, Near Rugby CV23 9PD (01926 632391). Frankton Grounds is made up of a listed house and buildings, beautifully situated on a mixed farm of horses, sheep, pedigree and commercial cattle. A warm welcome for the visitor who enjoys peace and quiet, yet with the benefit of very easy access to Warwick, Leamington Spa and Stratford. Full central heating, log fires. Excellent food. Evening Meals made of fresh home produce a speciality. One double room with TV and bathroom, one twin-bedded room; tea-making facilities in both rooms. Bed and Breakfast from £15. HETB Listed. Further details on request.

HASELEY. Mrs Cathy Dodd, Shrewley Pools Farm, Haseley CV35 7HB (01926 484315). Why not sample the delights of staying in a beautiful 17th century traditional farmhouse? Set in an acre of landscaped garden with four-acre pool, Shrewley Pools has many interesting features including timbered barn, huge fireplaces and beamed ceilings. Two bedrooms, one en suite, with tea/coffee tray. Close to Warwick, Stratford-upon-Avon, the NEC and NAC. Open all year (closed Christmas). Children and pets welcome. Non-smoking. Bed and Breakfast from £18 to £25; Evening Meal from £6. Tourist Board Listed "Commended".

WHEN MAKING ENQUIRIES PLEASE MENTION
FARM HOLIDAY GUIDES

KINETON. Mrs C. Howard, Willowbrook Farm House, Lighthorne Road, Kineton, Warwick CV35 0JL (01926 640475; Fax: 01926 641747). ♛♛ Very comfortable and interesting house and small farm in rolling countryside, half a mile from Kineton Village, handy for Warwick, Stratford, the Cotswolds, the NEC and NAC. En-suite facilities available; all rooms with washbasins, tea trays, colour TV, and beautiful views. Guests' own large sitting room and dining room with antiques and interesting collections. The house is surrounded by gardens and paddocks with terrace and pond. Old breeds of free-ranging poultry supply your breakfast eggs. There is central heating, and winter log fires. Plenty of local eating places. B&B from £15.00. Friendly, attentive service assured. No smoking in the house. We are 3 miles from Junction 12, M40.

LEAMINGTON SPA. Mrs R. Gibbs, Hill Farm, Lewis Road, Radford Semele, Leamington Spa CV31 1UX (01926 337571). ♛ **Working farm.** Guests are welcome all year to this friendly, comfortable farmhouse on 350 acre mixed farm, ideally situated for Warwick, Stratford-upon-Avon, Leamington, Coventry, Royal Showground, Birmingham and N.E.C. and the Cotswolds. Children welcome; reductions for under 12's. Cot and high chair. Large garden. Babysitting. Excellent farmhouse fare using home produce. Central heating. Log fires in chilly weather. Four double bedrooms and two twin rooms, some with en-suite facilities. Guests' sittingroom, colour TV and diningroom. Car preferable; ample parking. Supper drinks available. Spacious five van site available. AA Recommended. Farm Holiday Bureau member. FHG Diploma. Bed and Breakfast from approximately £16 to £20.

LEAMINGTON SPA. Miss Deborah Lea, Crandon House, Avon Dassett, Leamington Spa CV33 0AA (01295 770652). ♛♛ *Highly Commended.* **Working farm.** Guests receive a specially warm welcome at our comfortable farmhouse offering an exceptionally high standard of accommodation. Set in 20 acres, with beautiful views over unspoilt countryside, the small working farm with rare breeds of cattle, sheep and poultry provides produce used in our excellent meals. Three attractive bedrooms with private facilities, tea/coffee making equipment and colour TV. Guests' dining room and sitting rooms, one with colour TV. Full central heating and log fire in chilly weather. Electric blankets available. Car essential. Ample parking. Children over eight years welcome. Pets by arrangement. Peaceful and quiet yet offers easy access for touring the Heart of England, Warwick, Stratford-upon-Avon, the Cotswolds. Open all year. Bed and Breakfast from £17.50; Dinner, Bed and Breakfast from £29. Evening Meal by prior arrangement. Farm Holiday Bureau member. Write or ring for further details.

LEAMINGTON SPA Near. R. Hancock, Snowford Hall, Snowford Hall Farm, Hunningham, Near Royal Leamington Spa CV33 9ES (01926 632297). ♛♛ *Commended.* Snowford Hall is set on a 250 acre mixed working farm. The 18th century house stands on elevated ground overlooking the peaceful surrounding countryside. Rooms are centrally heated, have coffee/tea making facilities and most are fully en-suite. A comfortable lounge with colour TV awaits the visitor, and a full English breakfast is served. There are excellent pubs and restaurants nearby for lunches and evening meals. Warwick, Stoneleigh Park, Exhibition Centre, Sky Blue Centre, Stratford-upon-Avon and the Motor Museum are within easy reach. Bed and Breakfast from £17 per person per night. Open all year except Christmas and New Year.

LIGHTHORNE (near Warwick). Mrs J. Stanton, Redlands Farm, Banbury Road, Lighthorne, Near Warwick CV35 0AH (01926 651241). ♛♛ A beautifully restored 15th century farmhouse built of local stone, the "Old Farm House" is set in two acres of garden with its own swimming pool, well away from the main road yet within easy travelling distance of Stratford and Warwick, and handy for the Cotswolds. Guest accommodation is one double (with bathroom), one single and one family bedrooms; bathroom; beamed lounge with TV; diningroom. Rooms are centrally heated and the farmhouse also has open fires. Bed and Breakfast from £15 to £17.50. No extra charge for evening drinks. Children welcome — facilities available. No pets. A car is recommended to make the most of your stay. AA QQQ.

BTA's "Stay on a Farm"

Nolands Farm

Nolands Farm and Country Restaurant is an 18th century working farm situated on 300 acres of arable farmland in a tranquil valley.

The guest accommodation is mostly on the ground floor, located in annexed converted stables which have been tastefully restored, preserving the old timbers and beams, enhancing their atmosphere and charm.

For the romantic at heart, we can offer beautiful four poster bedrooms.

All rooms have en suite bathrooms, central heating, TV and hostess trays. There is a stocked lake for fishing, a large garden, woods and walks, clay pigeon shooting, bicylces for hire and riding at nearby stables. To complement your stay – dine in our licensed restaurant with only the finest, freshest cuisine.

Prices from £15.00 per person.

We can assure the country lover a happy, relaxing stay.

Situated eight miles from Stratford-upon-Avon; just off the A422 to Banbury.

AA QQQQ Selected

NOLANDS FARM · OXHILL · WARWICKSHIRE · CV35 0RJ
Telephone: (01926) 640309 · Fax: (01926) 641662

RAC ACCLAIMED

LONG COMPTON. Mrs J.R. Haines, Ascott House Farm, Ascott, Whichford, Near Long Compton, Shipston-on-Stour CV36 5PP (01608 684655). 🌷🌷 **Working farm.** Cotswold stone farmhouse with peaceful surroundings in designated area of natural beauty on edge of the Cotswolds. 500 acre arable/sheep farm, lovely views, attractive garden, outdoor swimming pool, snooker room and interesting walks. Ascott House Farm is ideal for relaxing, as well as being very well situated for exploring Cotswolds, Oxford, Stratford-upon-Avon and Warwick. One mile north of Long Compton on A3400. M40 Banbury 10 miles. One double room en-suite, one family room en-suite and one twin room with vanity unit; all rooms have TV, tea/coffee making facilities, central heating; TV lounge; traditional diningroom. Riding two miles, golf three miles with reduced green fees for guests. Children welcome, dogs by arrangement. Bed and Breakfast from £15 per person. Closed Christmas. Farm Holiday Bureau Member.

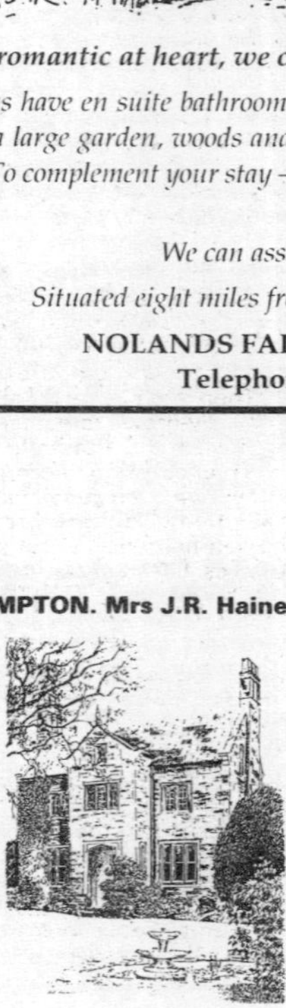

SHIPSTON-ON-STOUR. Mrs Fox, Kirby Farm, Whatcote, Shipston-on-Stour (01295 680525). Kirby Farm is situated in beautiful countryside within easy reach of Cotswolds, Stratford-upon-Avon, Banbury, Warwick Castle and many other places of interest. Our spacious, stone built farmhouse is set in 450 arable acres and a long driveway gives it an "off the beaten track" feel. Visitors will receive a warm welcome. Bedrooms have tea/coffee making facilities and en suite accommodation is available. Evening meals are available at two local pubs; both reached within five minutes by car. Breakfast is served in separate dining room and guests have access to their own drawing room with TV and log fire on cold evenings. Please telephone for further details.

STRATFORD-UPON-AVON. Prim and John Finnemore, Walcote Farm, Walcote, Haselor, Alcester B49 6LY (01789 488264). En suite comfortable accommodation in one double and one twin room, both with lovely views, in our easy to find, attractive, listed oak-beamed farmhouse, in a tranquil picturesque hamlet near Stratford-upon-Avon. Bed and Breakfast from £17. Full central heating with log fires in winter. No smoking in the house. Open all year. For local history we have a large collection of old photographs and documents including the Earl of Warwick's accounts for 1782 to 1786. It makes fascinating reading of detailed expenditure at Warwick Castle. Children welcome but sorry, no pets. Bed and Breakfast £17 per person.

STRATFORD-UPON-AVON. Mrs Marion J. Walters, Church Farm, Dorsington, Stratford-upon-Avon CV37 8AX (01789 720471; Fax: 01789 720830; Mobile: 0831 504194). *Commended.* **Working farm.** A warm and friendly welcome awaits you all year at our 127-acre mixed farm with woodlands and stream which you may explore. Our Georgian Farmhouse is situated on the edge of an extremely pretty village. Stratford-upon-Avon, Warwick, NEC, Royal Showground, Cotswolds, Evesham and Worcester all within easy driving distance. Family, twin and double bedrooms, all with tea/coffee facilities; some en-suite with TVs in converted stable block. Cot and high chair available. Central heating. Gliding, fishing, boating and horse riding nearby. Full Fire Certificate held. AA listed. Bed and Breakfast from £13.50. Write or phone for further details.

STRATFORD-UPON-AVON. Mrs J.M. Everett, Newbold Nurseries, Newbold-on-Stour, Stratford-upon-Avon CV37 8DP (Stratford-upon-Avon [01789] 450285). Working farm. You can be sure of personal attention and a friendly welcome here. The modern farmhouse has country views on all sides, but is easy to find, standing just off the A3400. There are 20 acres of arable crops and half an acre of hydroponically-grown tomatoes. Stratford is seven miles, Warwick Castle, the Cotswold area and Blenheim Palace within very easy reach. Accommodation comprises family and double rooms, en suite available. TVs and tea/coffee facilities in all rooms. Dogs accepted. Bed and Breakfast from £14.50, children half-price. Local pub serves excellent meals at budget prices. ETB registered.

STRATFORD-UPON-AVON. Mrs R.M. Meadows, Monk's Barn Farm, Shipston Road, Stratford-upon-Avon CV37 8NA (01789 293714). Working farm. One and a half miles south of Stratford-upon-Avon on the A3400 (formerly A34) is Monk's Barn, a 75 acre mixed farm welcoming visitors all year. Monk's Barn dates back to the 16th century and succeeds in combining real traditional character with first class amenities and the utmost comfort. Two double rooms, one twin-bedded room and one family room en suite, and one single bedroom. Beautiful riverside walk to village. Bed and Breakfast from £14. Tea/coffee facilities and colour TV in rooms. Reductions for children. Pets welcome on application. Non-smokers preferred. AA QQ. Details on request.

STRATFORD-UPON-AVON. Mrs J. Wakeham, Whitfield Farm, Ettington, Stratford-upon-Avon CV37 7PN (Stratford-upon-Avon [01789] 740260). Working farm. Situated down its own private drive, off the A429, this 220-acre mixed farm (wheat, cows, sheep, geese, horses, hens) is ideal for a quiet and relaxing holiday. Convenient for visiting the Cotswolds, Warwick, Coventry, Stratford, Worcester, near M40. Fully modernised centrally heated house with separate lounge and colour TV; one double with washbasin, one double and one twin en-suite, all with tea/coffee making facilities. Car essential, parking. Open all year (except Christmas) for Bed and Breakfast from £13.50 per night. Home produced food served. Full English Breakfast. AA registered. SAE, please.

Moonraker House

You'll feel at home at the Moonraker!©

English Tourist Board
COMMENDED

* ALL rooms are elegantly decorated and designed with your comfort in mind
* CAR PARK (open and garage)
* Ideal centre for exploring the Cotswolds, Shakespeare's Countryside, Warwick Castle and Shakespeare Theatres
* ALL rooms have ensuite bathrooms, tea and coffee making facilities, colour TV, clock radios and fitted hairdryers
* There are also extra special rooms with FOUR POSTER BEDS, lounge area and garden patio (non-smoking)
* Enjoy an excellent English Breakfast prepared with care by the resident proprietors, **Mauveen and Mike Spencer.**

AA QQQ
Michelin

40 Alcester Road, Stratford-upon-Avon CV37 9DB
Tel: (01789) 267115/299346 Fax: (01789) 295504

MinOtels
Les Routiers

HUNTER'S MOON GUEST HOUSE

All rooms are ensuite and are comfortably furnished with colour television, tea and coffee making facilities, and fitted hairdryers. Single, twin, double and family rooms are available. Hunter's Moon is close to Anne Hathaway's cottage, and is an ideal base for visiting the Cotswold villages, Warwick Castle and all other Shakespearean properties. Car parking is for guests' use and there is also a garden patio and ornamental fountain to relax by. An excellent English breakfast is served by resident hosts – Stratfordians Rosemary and David Austin. Visa, Access and American Express accepted. Recommended by Arthur Frommer. Telephone for further details and reservations.

AA *QQQ* Recommended

150 Alcester Road, Stratford-upon-Avon,
Warwickshire CV37 9DR. Telephone: 01789 292888

RECOMMENDED SHORT BREAK HOLIDAYS IN BRITAIN

Introduced by John Carter, TV Holiday Expert and Journalist

Specifically designed to cater for the most rapidly growing sector of the holiday market in the UK. Illustrated details of hotels offering special 'Bargain Breaks' throughout the year.

Available from newsagents and bookshops for £3.60 or direct from the publishers for £4.20 including postage, UK only.

FHG PUBLICATIONS LTD
Abbey Mill Business Centre, Seedhill,
Paisley, Renfrewshire PA1 1TJ

STRATFORD-UPON-AVON. Mrs A. Millington, Larkstoke Cottage, Ilmington, Shipston-on-Stour CV36 4JH (01608 682220). Luxury en-suite accommodation and a warm welcome await you in this lovely Cotswold-stone country house with its stone-tiled roof, beamed ceilings and elegant furniture. Standing in beautiful half acre garden in an area of outstanding natural beauty at the foot of Larkstoke Hill, it is the perfect base for visiting Stratford-upon-Avon, Warwick Castle, the Cotswold villages or simply relaxing in the peace and tranquillity of the glorious surroundings. Family, double or twin rooms are spacious, bright and tastefully decorated, each with remote control colour TV and tea/coffee making facilities. Bed and Breakfast from £16.50 to £18.50 per person. Book early to avoid disappointment.

STRATFORD-UPON-AVON. Mrs M. Turney, Cadle Pool Farm, The Ridgway, Stratford-upon-Avon CV37 9RE (Stratford-upon-Avon [01789] 292494). Working farm. Situated in picturesque grounds, this charming oak-panelled and beamed family house is part of a 450-acre mixed farm. It is conveniently situated two miles from Stratford-upon-Avon town, between Anne Hathaway's Cottage and Mary Arden's House, also only eight minutes from The Royal Shakespeare Theatre. Ideal touring centre for Warwick, Kenilworth, Oxford, the Cotswolds and Malvern Hills. Accommodation comprises one family, one double, one twin-bedded and one single rooms, one with en suite bathroom, all with central heating and tea/coffee making facilities. There is an antique oak diningroom, and lounge with colour TV. The gardens and ornamental pool are particularly attractive, with peacocks and ducks roaming freely. Children welcome at reduced rates; cot, high chair, babysitting. Sorry, no pets. Non-smoking accommodation available. Bed and Breakfast from £17 to £22.50 per person. Open all year.

The Barn – built in 1840 and a Listed Building

Oxstalls Farm Stud

For Farmhouse Bed & Breakfast

English Tourist Board
COMMENDED

Warwick Road, Stratford on Avon, Warwickshire CV37 4NR
Telephone: (01789) 205277

- Five minutes from The Royal Shakespeare Theatre.
- One mile from town centre Shakespeare properties
- Thoroughbred Stud Farm, overlooking beautiful Welcombe Hills
- Adjacent to 18 hole Golf Course
- All rooms are pleasantly furnished, many with ensuite facilities and TV, Tea & Coffee making etc.
- Convenient for touring the Cotswolds
- Twenty minutes from the N.E.C. Birmingham
- Additional ensuite rooms in the Cow Shed & Stables Complex
- Easy access from Junction 15, M40

Prices: From £15 per person to £25 per person.
Also the Old Cowshed has now been renovated into delightful ensuite bedrooms and Self Catering accommodation is available.

Main House

Oxstalls Farm is situated on the A439, Stratford Road to Warwick. 1 mile from Stratford on Avon

STRATFORD-UPON-AVON near. Mrs Joan James, Whitchurch Farm, Wimpstone, Near Stratford-upon-Avon CV37 8NS (Alderminster [01789] 450275). ♛♛ **Working farm.** This large Georgian farmhouse is set in parklike surroundings, four-and-a-half miles from Stratford-upon-Avon, on the edge of the Cotswolds and ideal for a touring holiday. It is open to guests all year with central heating. The accommodation is in one family room en-suite and two double rooms en-suite with tea/coffee making facilities; bathroom, toilet, shower room; sittingroom, dining room. Children are welcome; there is a cot and babysitting is offered. Sorry, no pets. A car is essential and there is parking space. Good farmhouse English Breakfast served. Evening Meal. Reduced rates for children. Bed and Breakfast from £15 to £17 per person nightly; optional Evening Meal £9.

STRATFORD-UPON-AVON near. Mrs Janet Haimes, Yew Tree Farm, Wootton Wawen, Solihull, West Midlands B95 6BY (01564 792701). ♛♛ *Commended.* Georgian farmhouse situated on A3400 in village of Wootton Wawen, one mile south of Henley-in-Arden, six miles north of Stratford-upon-Avon. Within easy reach of Warwick Castle, Royal Showground, NEC and the Cotswolds. 700 acre dairy/arable farm with lake and woodland walks. Two large double bedrooms, central heating, en-suite, tea/coffee making facilities. Cot available, high chair and child's bed. Comfortable visitors' lounge with colour TV. Excellent pubs and restaurants nearby. Open all year. Bed and Breakfast from £35 double, £22.50 single.

Terms quoted in this publication may be subject to increase if rises in costs necessitate

WARWICK. Mrs Louise Smith, Oaktree Farm, Buttermilk Lane, Yarningale Common, Claverdon CV35 8HW (01926 842413). ♛♛ Based in 34 acres of traditional meadow and woodland, Oaktree Farm offers country accommodation of the highest standard. Bedrooms are attractive, comfortable and cosy, all with en suite bathrooms, colour TV and tea/coffee making facilities. In winter months our log fires give that special warmth. The farm is also home to a small herd of rare breed cattle and is ideal for nature lovers. We serve excellent home cooked food, with vegetarian food being our speciality. We are ideally situated for Warwick (six miles), Stratford-upon-Avon (eight miles), NEC and NAC. Bed and Breakfast from £20 per night. AA QQQ.

WARWICK. Mr and Mrs D. Clapp, The Croft, Haseley Knob, Warwick CV35 7NL (01926 484447). ♛♛ *Commended.* Join David and Pat on their four acre smallholding and share the friendly family atmosphere, the picturesque rural surroundings, home cooking and very comfortable accommodation. Bedrooms, most en-suite, have colour TV, tea/coffee making equipment. Ground floor en-suite bedrooms available. Dinners by arrangement. Bed and full English Breakfast from £19. Centrally located for touring Warwick (Castle), Stratford (Shakespeare), Coventry (Cathedral) and Birmingham. Also ideal for the businessman visiting the National Exhibition Centre or Birmingham Airport, both about 15 minutes. No smoking inside. Ample parking. Mobile home available, also caravan parking. Large gardens. Open all year. AA and RAC Acclaimed. French spoken.

FOR THE MUTUAL GUIDANCE OF GUEST AND HOST

Every year literally thousands of holidays, short-breaks and overnight stops are arranged through our guides, the vast majority without any problems at all. In a handful of cases, however, difficulties do arise about bookings, which often could have been prevented from the outset.

It is important to remember that when accommodation has been booked, both parties — guests and hosts — have entered into a form of contract. We hope that the following points will provide helpful guidance.

GUESTS: When enquiring about accommodation, be as precise as possible. Give exact dates, numbers in your party and the ages of any children. State the number and type of rooms wanted and also what catering you require — bed and breakfast, full board, etc. Make sure that the position about evening meals is clear — and about pets, reductions for children or any other special points.

Read our reviews carefully to ensure that the proprietors you are going to contact can supply what you want. Ask for a letter confirming all arrangements, if possible.

If you have to cancel, do so as soon as possible. Proprietors do have the right to retain deposits and under certain circumstances to charge for cancelled holidays if adequate notice is not given and they cannot re-let the accommodation.

HOSTS: Give details about your facilities and about any special conditions. Explain your deposit system clearly and arrangements for cancellations, charges, etc, and whether or not your terms include VAT.

If for any reason you are unable to fulfil an agreed booking without adequate notice, you may be under an obligation to arrange alternative suitable accommodation or to make some form of compensation.

While every effort is made to ensure accuracy, we regret that FHG Publications cannot accept responsibility for errors, omissions or misrepresentation in our entries or any consequences thereof. Prices in particular should be checked because we go to press early. We will follow up complaints but cannot act as arbiters or agents for either party.

WILTSHIRE

BIDDESTONE. Mrs R.E. Sexton, Elm Farmhouse, The Green, Biddestone, Chippenham SN14 7DG (01249 713354). A peaceful 17th century Grade II Listed farmhouse now run as a Bed and Breakfast establishment located in the heart of North Wiltshire. Situated opposite the pond and close to the village pub, Elm Farmhouse is traditionally decorated and retains many striking features such as original fireplaces and mullioned windows. Accommodation is offered in two double bedrooms (one with private bathroom), both with colour TV, tea/coffee making facilities and good views. Biddestone is only four miles from the M4 and is between the famous villages of Lacock and Castle Combe. Just nine miles from Bath and close to many National Trust properties and beautiful countryside. Bed and Breakfast from £17.50 per person. Children and pets welcome.

CHIPPENHAM. Mrs K.M. Addison, The Old Rectory, Lacock, Chippenham SN15 2JZ (01249 730 335). Working farm. Situated in the National Trust village of Lacock and standing in its own grounds with tennis and croquet, The Old Rectory offers easy access to a variety of interesting things for the visitor to see and do. Lacock Abbey, the home of Fox Talbot, is one of the few abbeys Henry VIII did not destroy, and a visit to the Fox Talbot Photographic Museum is well worthwhile. The village is centrally placed for touring such places as Bath, Avebury, Stonehenge, Salisbury and many other towns and villages. Pleasant drives and walks through the West Country. Elegant accommodation is offered with private bathroom to all bedrooms. Ample free parking space. Bed and Breakfast from £17.50 per person per night.

CHIPPENHAM near. Suzanne Candy, Olivemead Farm, Dauntsey, Near Chippenham SN15 4JQ (01666 510205). *Commended.* Relax and enjoy the warm informal hospitality at our charming 18th century farmhouse on a working dairy farm in the Dauntsey Vale. Twin, double and family rooms with washbasins, colour TVs and tea/coffee making facilities. Generous breakfasts. Oak beamed dining room/lounge for guests' exclusive use. Large garden, children's play area, cot, high chair, baby listening. Excellent food available locally. Convenient for Bath, Cotswolds, Salisbury, M4, South West and Wales. Bed and Breakfast from £14 to £17 per person per night. Reductions for children and long stay guests.

CORSHAM. Mrs Carol Pope, Hatt Farm, Old Jockey, Box, Corsham SN14 9DJ (01225 742989). *Commended.* We warmly invite you to enjoy the peace and comfort of our family home. Hatt Farm was built in the 18th century overlooking magnificent views of the rolling Wiltshire countryside, approximately five miles from Bath. Ideal for visiting many National Trust properties, picturesque villages, ancient historical sites and the Cotswolds. One twin, one double/family room, both with private facilities. Tea/coffee facilities, central heating. TV lounge; log fire in Winter. Children welcome. Open January to November. Bed and Breakfast from £16.

CORSHAM. Gill Stafford, Pickwick Lodge Farm, Corsham SN13 0PS (01249 712207). Pickwick Lodge Farm is half a mile off the A4 between Chippenham and the Georgian city of Bath, only eight miles away. Ideally situated for visiting the many sites of historical interest such as Wiltshire White Horses, Avebury and Stonehenge and for touring the many National Trust properties, quaint villages and stately homes. Enjoy walking or riding (stabling can be provided) or visit one of the many country pubs for lunch or supper. Accommodation comprises two large double/family rooms and one large twin with washbasins, colour TV and tea/coffee making facilities; three guests' bathrooms. Babysitting is available by arrangement. Ample car parking. Bed and full English Breakfast from £17. Tourist Board Listed, Commended, Farm Holiday Bureau member.

DEVIZES. Mr and Mrs C. Fletcher, Lower Foxhangers Farm, Rowde, Devizes SN10 1SS (01380 828254). *Commended.* **Working farm.** Tranquillity awaits you on our 18th century canalside working farm. Situated alongside the Kennet and Avon Canal, at the base of the staircase of 29 locks; assist boats through the locks; scenic walks to pubs. Fish and boat to your heart's desire. Ideal for cycling. Bed and Breakfast in family/double and twin rooms with washbasins, twin room en suite; two bathrooms, three toilets; lounge with TV for visitors' use. Children and pets welcome. Cot, high chair available. Open Easter to end of October. Bed and Breakfast from £15. FHB Member. Also available, self catering units and small campsite with electricity and toilets/shower. Brochure on request.

MALMESBURY. Mrs R. Eavis, Manor Farm, Corston, Malmesbury SN16 0HF (01666 822148; 0374 675783 mobile). *Commended.* Within easy reach of Lacock, historic Bath, Tetbury, Badminton and the beautiful Cotswolds, Manor Farm is the ideal location for touring. Two miles from Junction 17 of the M4, the farm nestles in the small village of Corston. The accommodation is comfortable, comprising single, twin, double and family rooms, all with washbasins, colour TV and tea/coffee making facilities. Three rooms have en suite bathrooms. Sittingroom with colour TV, and guests also have use of lovely gardens. Children welcome. Sufficient parking. Bed and Breakfast from £16 to £22. Good pub food available within walking distance. Full Fire Certificate. Les Routiers and AA QQQ. Farm Holiday Bureau member.

MALMESBURY. Mrs D. Freeth, Vancelettes Farm, Tetbury Road, Sherston, Malmesbury SN16 0LU (Malmesbury [01666] 840253). **Working farm.** 90-acre mixed farm, situated at side of quiet country road, one-third-of-a-mile from the Cotswold type village, one-and-a-half miles from Westonbirt Arboretum. Convenient for Tetbury, Cheltenham, Cirencester, Bath, Slimbridge, Castle Combe. Ideal touring centre. Varied menu, home-produced vegetables. Two double, one twin bedrooms, with washbasins; bathroom, toilet; sittingroom and separate diningroom. Pets permitted. Car essential — parking. Full central heating. Open all year round, except Christmas. Mid-week bookings. Evening Dinner, Bed and Breakfast from £22; Bed and Breakfast from £15. SAE please.

MALMESBURY. John and Edna Edwards, Stonehill Farm, Charlton, Malmesbury SN16 9DY (01666 823310). Working farm. Stonehill Farm is a 15th century farmhouse situated three and a half miles from Malmesbury, England's oldest borough, eight miles from M4. This working dairy farm is ideally situated for days out at Bath, the Cotswolds, Berkeley Castle, Salisbury and Stonehenge. Horse riding is available nearby and there are Water Parks six miles away with fishing, boating and windsurfing. A warm welcome is assured at this traditional farmhouse where full English breakfast is served. Three bedrooms, one with en-suite facilities. Ample parking. Children and dogs welcome. Terms from £14. ETB and AA Listed.

WILTSHIRE – "WHITE" HORSE COUNTY!

Many "White" horses adorn the Wiltshire chalk downs and the prehistoric theme continues with Stonehenge and Avebury. Also of interest are the landscape gardens at Studley, Chiselbury Camp, the Kennet and Avon canal with lock "staircase", Salisbury Plain, and the abandoned city Old Sarum.

MARLBOROUGH. Mrs C. Orssich, Mayfield, West Grafton, Marlborough SN8 3BY (01672 810339).

Listed, Highly Commended, AA Premier Selected. This beautiful Listed thatched house with parts dating back to the 15th century is very peacefully situated yet ideal for visiting Stonehenge to Avebury, Bath to Oxford and Salisbury to Marlborough. The whole house is decorated with taste and style incorporating an inglenook fireplace, a conservatory and an Aga in the farmhouse kitchen which is the centre of life in this happy family home. There are lovely gardens with tennis court and heated swimming pool. Two double and one twin bedrooms, all en suite. Bed and Breakfast from £19 per person.

MERE. Mr and Mrs C. Ross, Chetcombe House Hotel, Chetcombe Road, Mere BA12 6AZ (Mere [01747] 860219). ♛♛♛ *Commended.* AA QQQQ Selected. This Country House Hotel, set in one acre of lovely gardens, is situated just off the A303 on the eastern approach road to the picturesque little town of Mere. Ideal as a stopover en route to the West Country or as a centre to explore the delights of Wiltshire. Close to Stourhead and Longleat, with Stonehenge, Salisbury, Wilton and Shaftesbury all within 20 mile radius. All bedrooms have private bath/shower rooms, colour TV and tea/coffee making facilities. The hotel has a residential licence and is open all year. Bed and Breakfast from £25 to £33 per person per night. Write or phone for brochure. Off Season two or three day breaks available.

SALISBURY. Mrs Suzi Lanham, Newton Farmhouse, Southampton Road, Whiteparish, Salisbury SP5 2QL (Whiteparish [01794] 884416). ♛♛ *Approved.* Bordering the New Forest and no longer a working farm, the property was originally part of the Trafalgar Estate gifted to Lord Nelson. All rooms (one with four-poster bed) are fully en suite and have colour TV and tea/coffee making facilities. The dining room has original flagstone floors, oak beams and huge open fireplace. The garden covers two acres and includes a swimming pool. Ideal location for Stonehenge, Salisbury, Wilton House, Broadlands, Beaulieu, Paultons Park, Winchester, Southampton and Bournemouth area, plus golfing, walking, cycling and horse riding nearby. Central heating. Children welcome. No pets. Evening Meals by arrangement. AA QQQ Recommended.

SWINDON. Mrs Mary Richards, Little Cotmarsh Farm, Broad Town, Wootton Bassett, Swindon SH4 7RA (01793 731322). Listed 17th century farmhouse situated in the quiet hamlet of Cotmarsh. Comfortable, attractive bedrooms with washbasins, one with toilet and shower en suite. All have tea/coffee making facilities and electric heating. Colour TV on request. Beams throughout, flagstone dining room with inglenook fireplace and wood-burning stove. Lounge for guests' use. Close to Avebury, Marlborough, Oxford and the Cotswolds. Bath 26 miles. M4 Junction 16, four miles. Good local pub food within two to three miles. No smoking. Children welcome, reductions available. Bed and Breakfast from £15. Directions: from Wootton Bassett take Broad Hinton Road. After approximately two miles, turn left for Cotmarsh, follow road bearing left. We are second farm on the right.

PUBLISHER'S NOTE

While every effort is made to ensure accuracy, we regret that FHG Publications cannot accept responsibility for errors, omissions or misrepresentation in our entries or any consequences thereof. Prices in particular should be checked because we go to press early. We will follow up complaints but cannot act as arbiters or agents for either party.

TROWBRIDGE near. Jill Awdry, Spicers Piece Farm, Steeple Ashton, Trowbridge BA14 6HG (01380 870266). ♛ *Commended.* Follow a treasure trail and find a warm welcome to our spacious Georgian farmhouse with its fantastic views and family run arable and stock farm. Take A350 from Melksham, follow the Keevil Airfield signs and find us within easy reach of many tourist attractions. Two doubles and a twin-bedded room with washbasins. Tea/coffee making facilities and central heating. Guests' lounge and bathroom. Children and pets welcome. Open February to November inclusive. Bed and Breakfast from £15 to £17.

WARMINSTER. Mrs Jean Crossman, Stalls Farm, Longleat, Warminster BA12 7NE (01985 844323). Working farm. Stalls Farm is a 350 acre dairy farm on Wiltshire/Somerset border, situated at Longleat on road from Longleat House to Safari Park. Pleasant garden with terrace, lawns and pond, games room. Lovely walks. Ideally situated for visiting Longleat Stourhead, Bath, Cheddar, Wells, Salisbury, Stonehenge, Avebury, Castle Combe, Rode Bird Gardens, Claverton Manor, Westbury White Horse etc. A car is essential. All bedrooms with comfortable divans, fitted carpets, washbasins and colour TV. Children welcome, cot and high chair. Access to house at all times. Open all year for Bed and Breakfast. SAE or telephone for terms. Full central heating. AA QQQ. Tourist Board registered.

WARMINSTER. Mrs M. Hoskins, Spinney Farmhouse, Chapmanslade, Westbury BA13 4AQ (01373 832412). ♛♛♛ **Working farm.** Off A36, three miles west of Warminster; 16 miles from historic city of Bath. Close to Longleat, Cheddar and Stourhead. Reasonable driving distance to Bristol, Stonehenge, Glastonbury and the cathedral cities of Wells and Salisbury. Golf, pony trekking and fishing available locally and an 18 hole golf course within walking distance. Washbasins, tea/coffee-making facilities and shaver points in all rooms. Family room available. Guests' lounge with colour TV. Central heating. Children and pets welcome. Ample parking. Open all year. Bed and Breakfast from £15 per night, £90 per week. Reduction after two nights. Evening Meal £9. Farm fresh food in a warm, friendly, family atmosphere.

YORKSHIRE

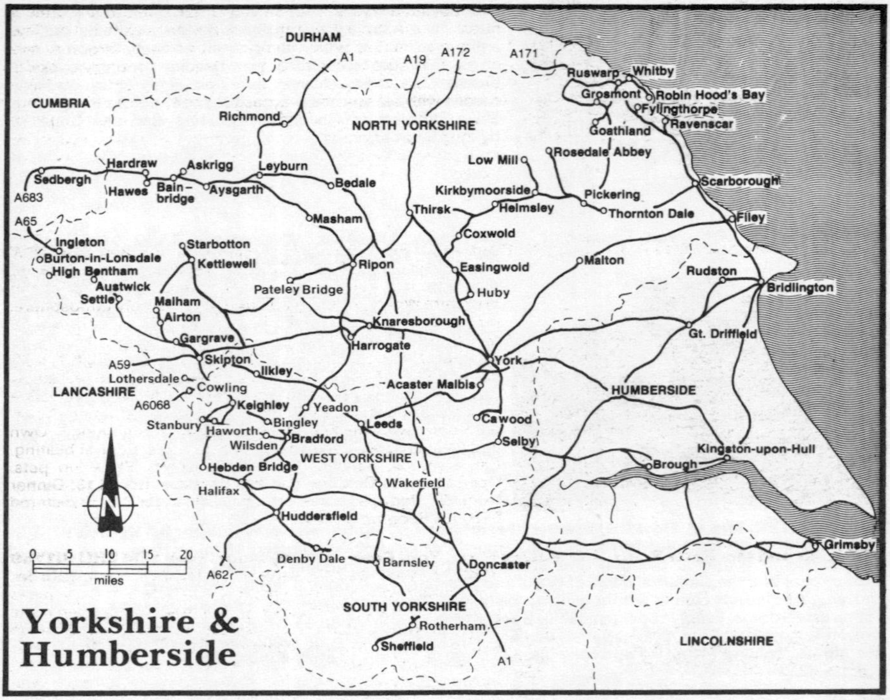

EAST YORKSHIRE (Humberside)

BRIDLINGTON. Mrs J.M. Thompson, The Grange, Bempton Lane, Flamborough, Bridlington YO15 1AS (Bridlington [01262] 850207). Working farm. This attractive 150-year-old house is situated on 475 acres of stock and arable land, half-a-mile from Flamborough Village on the B1229, 100 yards off the road with tarmac drive and ample parking space. It has a large garden with tennis court. Within easy reach of sandy beaches at Bridlington or Filey, also Yorkshire moors and Wolds. Golf at Flamborough, Puffin and Gannet colonies and RSPB Reserve at Bempton. Guests welcome all year except Christmas and New Year, and can look around the farm. One double, one single and one family bedrooms, all with tea-making facilities; two bathrooms and toilets; sittingroom and diningroom. Children welcome at reduced rates. Cot, high chair, babysitting available (free of charge). Pets permitted. Car advisable — ample parking. Terms on request for Bed and Breakfast only. Evening Meals in Flamborough or Bridlington four miles away. Tourist Board Listed.

GREAT DRIFFIELD. Mrs Tiffy Hopper, Kelleythorpe, Great Driffield YO25 9DW (01377 252297). Working farm. Imagine peacocks strutting, ducks swimming and trout rising. Enjoy a cup of tea on the sun terrace overlooking a crystal clear shallow river. The friendly atmosphere of our lovely Georgian farmhouse with its mellow antique furniture, pretty chintzes and new bathrooms, one en-suite, is sure to captivate you. Delicious country cooking. Children are very welcome, they enjoy playing in our large garden with swings and playcastle. Ideally placed for touring. Bed and Breakfast from £14; optional Evening Meal from £10 by prior arrangement. 10% discount for seven nights or more. Reductions for children under 12 years. Tourist Board Listed.

POCKLINGTON near. Mrs A. Pearson, Meltonby Hall Farm, Meltonby, Near Pocklington YO4 2PW (Pocklington [01759] 303214). Working farm, join in. Meltonby Hall Farm is in a small village at the foot of the Yorkshire Wolds, offering a relaxed and homely atmosphere. It provides a good base for historic York 13 miles, coast 30 miles, as well as the beautiful North Yorkshire Moors with their forest drives, also for Stately Homes. Pocklington, with its magnificent water lilies, is two and a half miles away. Gliding club nearby. Double and twin rooms with tea/coffee making facilities, cot and high chair if required; guests' own bathroom with electric shower, dining room/lounge. Own and local produce used and free range eggs. Central heating. Car essential, parking. Children welcome. Sorry no pets. Open Easter to October. Bed and Breakfast from £13; Dinner from £8. Reduced rates for children under 12. Registered ETB; AA Recommended.

YORK. Mr and Mrs Peter Scott, The Mohair Farm, York Road, Barmby Moor, York YO4 5HU (01759 380308; Fax: 01759 388119). Working farm, join in. The Mohair Farm is on the main A1079 between the villages of Wilberfoss and Barmby Moor. Situated on the main route between York and the Humber Bridge, an ideal centre to explore York and district, coast within easy reach. The farm is a highly productive small-holding with a variety of animals, including rare Angora Goats; the house is set well back from the main road and surrounded by conifers. One double, one twin-bedded, one family bedrooms, all with washbasins, tea-making facilities and TVs. Spa bath. Reduced rates, babysitting for children. Pets welcome. Full central heating. Car essential, parking. Guests welcome to participate in farm activities which may be of interest to people who wish to derive an income from a small acreage. Bed and Breakfast from £12.50 per person. Tourist Board registered.

NORTH YORKSHIRE

AMPLEFORTH. Annabel Lupton, Carr House Farm, Shallowdale, Ampleforth, Near Helmsley YO6 4ED (01347 868526 and 0850 310188). ♛♛ Working farm. Carr House — 16th century farmhouse in peaceful, beautiful 'Herriot' countryside, half an hour from York. Recommended by Sunday Observer — "a fresh-air fiend's dream — good food, good walking and a warm welcome". Tour the Moors, Dales, National Parks, York coast, nearby famous Abbeys, Castles and Stately Homes. Carr House provides a comfortable, relaxing homely base. Romantics will love the four-poster double bedrooms, both en-suite. Central heating, log fires. Enjoy a full Yorkshire farmhouse Breakfast with home-made preserves, free-range eggs, own produce used whenever possible. Bed and Breakfast from £15, Evening Meal £8 — weekly rates available. Sorry, no pets or children under seven. No smoking indoors. Open all year; closed Christmas. SAE, please, for brochure. Farm Holiday Bureau Member.

ARKENGARTHDALE. Ian and Angela Whitworth, The White House, Arkle Town, Arkengarthdale, Near Richmond DL11 6RB (01748 884203). ♛♛ *Commended.* The White House is a 200 year old former farmhouse situated within the Yorkshire Dales National Park, in Herriot country. A family run guest house offering comfort, relaxation, good food and personal attention amidst beautiful scenery. The accommodation consists of two en suite double rooms and one twin-bedded room, all with hospitality trays and panoramic views of the Dale. The visitors' lounge overlooks the surrounding hills and there is a good selection of maps and guides. Off road parking. Sorry, no children under 10, no smoking and no dogs. Open January to November. Bed and Breakfast from £18 per person; Dinner £10. Special rates for two nights or more. Please ask for our brochure.

ASKRIGG. Mrs B. Percival, Milton House, Askrigg, Leyburn DL8 3HJ (Wensleydale [01969] 650217). ♛♛ Askrigg is situated in the heart of Wensleydale and is within easy reach of many interesting places — Aysgarth Falls, Hardraw Falls, Bolton Castle. This is an ideal area for walking. Milton House is a spacious house with all modern amenities. There are two double bedrooms and one family room, two with private facilities. All have washbasins, colour TV and tea making facilities. Bathroom with shower, two toilets; visitors' lounge with TV; diningroom with separate tables. Children are welcome (at reduced rates). Central heating. It is open all year and Askrigg is one of the loveliest villages in the Dales. You are sure of good home cooking, a friendly welcome and a homely atmosphere. Private parking. Evening Meal, Bed and Breakfast or Bed and Breakfast only. Terms on application with SAE, please, or by phone.

BEDALE. David and Thea Smith, Waterside, Glenaire, Crakehall, Bedale DL8 1HS (01677 422908). A warm and friendly welcome awaits you at Waterside where you can relax and enjoy the mature one acre gardens running down to the trout stream. As a holiday centre it is ideal for exploring by car or on foot the glories of the Yorkshire Dales and Moors . . . "The Gateway to Herriot Country" . . . Bed and Breakfast with private facilities £20 per person; reductions for longer stays. Evening Meal (optional) £11. Full details on request. Central heating, TV, tea and coffee facilities, radio in all rooms.

BEDALE. Mrs Sheila Dean, Hyperion House, 88 South End, Bedale DL8 2DS (Bedale [01677] 422334). A lovely quiet house in the charming market town of Bedale with every comfort and facility. COMPLETELY NON-SMOKING. Good, firm, comfortable beds, ideal for back sufferers: one double, one twin, one room with kingsize bed, one single. Excellent varied well-cooked breakfast of your choice. Special diets catered for. Information and advice plus video on all the places of interest in this beautiful area of North Yorkshire. Good north/south stopover — one mile from A1. Excellent bar meals, restaurants, etc either in Bedale or surrounding villages. Private parking. All guests welcomed with complimentary home baked scones and tea. Highly recommended by returning visitors. Open all year (Christmas and New Year excepted). Bed and Breakfast from £14 to £16.50.

BEDALE. Mrs M. Keighley, Southfield, 96 South End, Bedale DL8 2DS (01677 423510). Only five minutes from A1, ideal for breaking a journey to/from Scotland. Good base for touring; attractions in the area include Fountains Abbey, Harewood House, Bolton Castle and Lightwater Valley. Golf and swimming. Marjorie will supply supper and babysitting free. One single, one double, twin and family bedrooms, all with washbasins. Open all year. Bed and Breakfast from £14.

BEDALE. John and Freda Coppin, Richmond House, 6 Beech Close, Scruton, Northallerton DL7 0TU (01609 748369). A warm welcome awaits you at our detached house in a lovely rural village between Bedale and Northallerton. Only three miles from A1. Ideal stopover for north/south travellers. One double room with colour TV, tea/coffee making facilities, central heating, air conditioning and double glazing. Bathroom with shower, shaver point. Home cooked full English breakfast is served in our dining room/lounge overlooking the pleasant garden. Private parking. Central location for touring Yorkshire Dales and Moors. York, Durham and coast all within one hour's drive. Bed and Breakfast from £13. Open April to October. Sorry, no pets or children. Tourist Board registered.

BEDALE. Mrs Patricia Knox, Mill Close Farm, Patrick Brompton, Bedale DL8 1JY (01677 450257).

Commended. Mill Close is a working farm surrounded by beautiful rolling countryside at the foothills of the Yorkshire Dales and Herriot country. Rooms are spacious and furnished to a very high standard. One double or family room, one twin-bedded room, both with tea/coffee making facilities. Guests' own sittingroom with colour TV; diningroom; private bathrooms. Relaxing, peaceful atmosphere with large garden, open fires and central heating. Children welcome, cot available. Pets housed by arrangement. Enjoy wholesome farmhouse cooking using local produce, freshly prepared. Open Easter to October. Bed and Breakfast from £15 to £17. Evening Meal from £10.

BENTHAM. Mrs Betty Clapham, Lane House Farm, Bentham, Near Lancaster LA2 7DJ (Bentham [015242] 61479). *Commended.* **Working farm.**

Lane House Farm is a family run farm on the Yorkshire/Lancashire border. The 17th century beamed farmhouse overlooks the market town of High Bentham (one mile away) and has beautiful views of the Yorkshire Dales. Ideal base for walking or touring. On the edge of the Trough of Bowland and within easy reach of Yorkshire Dales, Lake District or coastal beauty spots. Bedrooms have washbasins, shaver points and tea-making facilities; en suite available. Guests' lounge has colour TV. Separate diningroom. Farm Holiday Bureau member. Bed and Breakfast from £15; Evening Meal from £8.50. Phone or SAE for details.

BENTHAM. Mrs Shirley Metcalfe, Fowgill Park Farm, High Bentham, Near Lancaster LA2 7AH (015242 61630). *Commended.* **Working farm.**

Fowgill is a 200 acre stock rearing farm, situated in an elevated position and having magnificent views of the Dales and Fells. Only 20 minutes from M6 Junction 34. A good centre for touring the Dales, Lakes, coast and Forest of Bowland. Visit Ingleton with its waterfalls and caves only three miles away. Golf, fishing and horse riding nearby. Bedrooms have washbasins, shaver points and tea-making facilities, two bedrooms en-suite. Comfortable beamed visitors' lounge to relax in with colour TV. Separate diningroom. Bed and Breakfast from £12; Evening Meal optional £7.50. Reductions for children. Bedtime drink included in price. Brochure available.

BISHOP THORNTON. Mrs Joyce Kellett, Hatton House Farm, Colber Lane, Bishop Thornton, Near Harrogate HG3 3JA (01423 770315). *Highly Commended.* Farmhouse accommodation at its best on a dairy mixed farm in Nidderdale, close to Harrogate. Quiet and peaceful area. Emphasis on home cooking, beautifully presented. Two double, one twin and one single bedrooms with washbasins and tea making facilities; shared bathroom. Separate tables in dining room; large lounge to relax in. Outdoor smokers welcome. Regret no dogs. Children from 10 years welcome. Parking available. Open all year. Bed and Breakfast; Evening Dinner available on request. Farm Holiday Guide Diploma Award for accommodation of the highest standard.

BRAWBY. Mrs Fairweather, Brawby Grange, Brawby, Malton YO17 0PZ (01653 668245). Working farm. Brawby Grange is a working farm situated in peaceful surroundings, central for the City of York, Yorkshire Moors and the coast. Eight miles from Castle Howard, Pickering and Malton, three miles from Flamingoland. Accommodation offered in two double and one twin-bedded rooms, all with washbasins; bathroom with shower; guests' own sittingroom with colour TV. Full central heating. Bed and Breakfast from £13 per night.

CARLTON-IN-COVERDALE. Mrs Gillian M. Smith, "Abbots Thorn", Carlton-in-Coverdale, Leyburn DL8 4AY (Wensleydale [01969] 40620).

Our 19th successful season! "Abbots Thorn" is an old farmhouse of character which has been modernised to offer every comfort to guests, with double glazing, central heating and coal fires during cool weather. Still surrounded by a working farm, it lies amidst quiet unspoilt countryside in the Yorkshire Dales National Park with Wensleydale, Wharfedale and Swaledale nearby. Good walking and several interesting historic places in the area. One twin-bedded and one family room with en-suite facilities, one double/single with vanity unit and shaver point. All rooms face south and have lovely views across the Dale and are all equipped with electric blankets, tea making facilities and towels. There is also a separate bathroom with bath, shower and toilet. The comfortable lounge with inglenook fireplace and colour TV adjoins the guests' diningroom. Full English Breakfast and optional four course Evening Dinner plus coffee and mints — good home cooking and free range eggs. Car essential. Now a "no smoking" establishment, we are open from approximately Palm Sunday to October. Bed and Breakfast from £14.50 (en suite £17.50); Evening Meal from £9.50. Tourist Board registered.

CARLTON-IN-COVERDALE. Mrs Anne Dinsdale, Town Foot Farm, Carlton-in-Coverdale, Leyburn DL8 4BA (Wensleydale [01969] 640651). Working farm. Run by Dales people. Situated in Coverdale, one of the lesser known Yorkshire Dales. Accommodation comprises two double and one twin bedrooms, all with own shower/toilet/H&C and heated towel rails. Towels provided; poly-cotton sheets used. Spacious "guests' only" lounge, with TV. Guests' kitchen is available for making sandwiches and ingredients provided for a selection of hot drinks. Breakfast is served in our oak-beamed dining room. Free range eggs used. Open May to October inclusive for Bed and Breakfast from £16 to £18. Private parking. Sorry, no pets or children under 12 years. SAE for further details please.

DANBY. Mrs B. Tindall, Rowan Tree Farm, Danby, Whitby YO21 2LE (Guisborough [01287] 660396). Working farm, join in. Rowan Tree Farm is situated in the heart of the North Yorkshire Moors and has panoramic moorland views. Ideal walking area and quiet location just outside the village of Danby. Accommodation comprises one single room, one twin-bedded room and one family room all with full oil-fired central heating. Residents' lounge with colour TV. Children welcome — cot provided if required. Babysitting available. Pets accepted. Good home cooking. Bed and Breakfast from £13; Evening Meals provided on request £6.50 each. Ample car parking space. Tourist Board Listed.

DENT. Mrs Marlene Williamson, Ivy Dene, Gawthrop, Dent, Sedbergh LA10 5TA (015396 25353). Ivy Dene is situated in the Yorkshire Dales within easy reach of the glorious Lake District and ten miles from the M6. Ideal centre for walking and only three-quarters of a mile from the picturesque village of Dent with its cobbled streets. Accommodation comprises two double and one family bedrooms, with washbasins; bathroom; cosy sittingroom with coal fire and TV/diningroom. All home cooking and baking is served. Sorry, no pets. Children welcome at reduced rates. Car essential — parking. Open March to November for Evening Dinner/Meal, Bed and Breakfast or Bed and Breakfast. Terms on request. Also holiday cottage to let.

EASINGWOLD. Mrs Christine Kirman, The Old Vicarage, Market Place, Easingwold, York YO6 3AL (01347 821015). 👑👑 *Commended.* This 18th century house sits in a corner of the square of this quiet Georgian market town just off the A19 halfway between York and Thirsk. It provides an excellent touring centre for York, the Dales and the Moors. The centrally heated "no smoking" accommodation comprises two twin, two double and one single bedrooms, all enjoying en suite facilities, colour TV, radio alarm and beverage tray. A large sitting room is available solely for guests and the private grounds include a croquet lawn and walled rose garden. Tea and Yorkshire biscuits await you on arrival. Bed and Breakfast from £19.50.

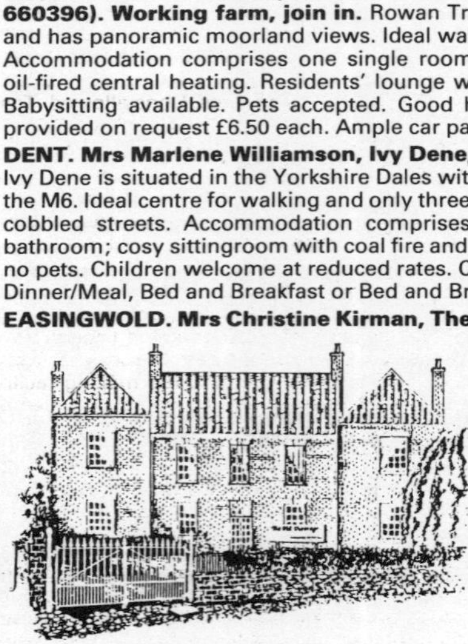

WHEN MAKING ENQUIRIES PLEASE MENTION
FARM HOLIDAY GUIDES

EASINGWOLD. Mrs Rachel Ritchie, The Old Rectory, Thormanby, Easingwold, York YO6 3NN (01845 501417). A warm welcome awaits you at this interesting Georgian rectory built in 1737 and furnished with many antiques including a four-poster bed. Three comfortable and very spacious bedrooms with tea/coffee making faciltiies, two en suite; charming lounge with colour TV and open fire. Separate diningroom. Large mature garden. An excellent base for touring the Moors, Dales and York. This is the centre of "James Herriot" country with many historic houses and abbeys to visit in the area. Thormanby is a small village between Easingwold and Thirsk. York is 17 miles. Many delightful inns and restaurants serving good food locally. Bed and Breakfast from £14 to £17 — reductions for children under 12 years and reduced weekly rates. Ample parking. Open all year. SAE for brochure or telephone.

GLAISDALE. Mrs H. Kelly, The Grange, Glaisdale, Whitby YO21 2QW (01947 897241). Beautiful stone manor house with magnificent hilltop view. It lies amidst our sheep/arable farm bordering the Esk River which boasts the best salmon fishing in the country. Home grown produce used in our generous meals. Excellent position for walks, steam railway and Whitby. Bathroom en-suite or shared between two rooms. Fishing by arrangement. Open all year except December. Children and pets by arrangement. Bed and Breakfast from £15; Evening Meal from £7. Eden Farm, Eden Camp, Flamingoland, etc all within easy reach. ETB Listed.

GOATHLAND. Mrs V.A. MacCaig, Prudom House, Goathland, Whitby YO22 5AN (01947 86368). Situated nine miles from the coast, Goathland offers some of the finest walking countryside and is an ideal touring centre. An added attraction is the North Yorkshire Moors Historic Railway Trust running through the village. Delightful scenery. Prudom House is situated in attractive well-maintained gardens in the centre of the village. Careful restoration of the farmhouse has provided guests with modern amenities whilst retaining its character. Open beams a feature and cosy log fires. Razor points and washbasins. Comfortable accommodation and good food. Children are welcome; cot, high chair, babysitting and reduced rates. Dogs allowed. Tea room with crafts on display. Bed and Breakfast from £17.50 per person. Open all year except Christmas and New Year. Please phone or send SAE for brochure.

GOATHLAND. Mrs Christine Chippindale, Barnet House Guest House, Goathland, Whitby YO22 5NG (Whitby [01947] 896201). Situated in large garden just outside the delightful village of Goathland, an ideal centre for walking and touring the North Yorkshire Moors, Dales and coast. Warm, comfortable accommodation, friendly atmosphere, excellent food. Lounge with colour TV; three double, three twin-bedded, one family room all with washbasins, razor points, heating, tea/coffee making facilities and magnificent views over surrounding moorland. Bathroom, shower room, three toilets. Reductions for children 11 years and under (minimum six years) sharing parents' room. Sorry no pets. Parking. Open from March to November for Bed and Breakfast from £17.50; Evening Meal, Bed and Breakfast from £25. Brochure on request.

GROSMONT. Mrs S. Counsell, Eskdale, Grosmont, Whitby YO22 5PT (Whitby [01947] 895385). Eskdale is a Georgian detached house set in large attractive gardens. The house overlooks the Esk Valley with views to the North Yorkshire Moors. Good walking area and convenient for coast and steam railway. Two double rooms and two single. Families can also be catered for. Separate lounge for guests' use. Ample parking is available. Children welcome with babysitting offered. Pets also welcome. Bed and Breakfast from £15 to £15.50 Full English Breakfast. SAE, please, or telephone. Tourist Board Listed.

HARROGATE. Mrs Margaret Watson, High Winsley Farm, Burnt-Yates, Ripley, Near Harrogate HG3 3EP (01423 770376). A warm welcome is assured on this 120 acre stock rearing farm situated in peaceful scenic countryside just seven miles from and central to Harrogate, Ripon and Pateley Bridge areas. Brimham Rocks and Ripley Castle just three miles away. Accommodation is in two double and one twin-bedded rooms, all comfortable and spacious with washbasins and tea/coffee facilities. Guests' bathroom/shower. TV lounge with open fire. Bed and Breakfast from £13.50; Evening Meal optional, or eat at one of the nearby country inns. ETB Listed. Ideal base for touring the Yorkshire Dales.

HARROGATE. Mrs E. Payne, North Pasture Farm, Brimham Rocks, Summerbridge, Harrogate HG3 4DW (01423 711470). ♛♛♛ Working farm. North Pasture Farm offers farmhouse Bed, Breakfast and Evening Dinner. Guests receive a warm welcome, and best of hospitality assured; home cooking, well presented and served. The farm is a 135 acre dairy farm next to Brimham Rocks, four miles from Fountains Abbey and nine miles from Harrogate. The house is of historic interest with datestone 1657 and the front part dates back to the early 1400s. John Wesley preached in the room which is now the diningroom. There are three en-suite bedrooms. Central heating. Sorry no pets or children. Bed and Breakfast from £17.50; optional Evening Dinner from £9. SAE please.

HARROGATE near. Mrs Brenda Walmsley, Clough House Farm, Summerbridge, Near Harrogate (01423 780823). 17th century farmhouse with attached buildings converted into seven beautiful bed and breakfast rooms, all with private facilities. Lovely TV lounge and dining room with scenic views. Harrogate is just nine miles away and there the new Victoria Garden shopping centre has recently opened; Fountains Abbey and Brimham Rocks are close by. Horse riding and lessons available, tennis, fishing and bowls in the village. We also have one large holiday cottage or six small cottages; these are self catering or meals are available. We offer Short Breaks and gladly cater for walking parties. Please write or telephone for further information and brochure.

HARROGATE. Mrs A. Wood, Field House, Clint, Near Harrogate HG3 3DS (01423 770638). Field House is situated five miles from Harrogate and a mile above the attractive village of Hampsthwaite, commanding beautiful views over the Nidd Valley. Ideal for exploring the Dales and Moors with ancient abbeys, castles and country houses. The market towns of Skipton, Ripon and Knaresborough and the historic city of York are all within easy reach. Accommodation is in one twin and one double room with private bathroom. Private sittingroom with TV, etc. Open all year. Car essential — private parking. Bed and Breakfast from £12.50 with Evening Meals readily available. A warm welcome guaranteed in a peaceful friendly atmosphere. Telephone or SAE, please, for further details.

HARROGATE. Anne and Bob Joyner, Anro Guest House, 90 King's Road, Harrogate HG1 5JX (Harrogate [01423] 503087). ♛♛ *Commended.* AA QQQ, RAC listed. "Excellent!", "Exceptional value!", "Good food!", "Quiet!", "Never had it so good!" — just a few testimonials visitors have written in our book on leaving. Situated in a tree-lined avenue in a central position close to all amenities. Conference and Exhibition Centre two minutes' walk. Valley Gardens, town and local swimming baths close by. Our house is centrally heated, with tea/coffee making facilities and colour TV in all rooms, hot and cold throughout. Some rooms en suite. Home cooking. Bed and Breakfast from £18.50; four-course Dinner, plus tea or coffee on request, £10.25. Ideal centre for touring Dales/Herriot country. Yorkshire and Humberside and English Tourist Board members, well recommended. FHG Diploma Winners.

FHG DIPLOMA WINNERS 1994

Each year we award a small number of diplomas to holiday proprietors whose services have been specially commended by our readers and the following advertisers were our FHG Diploma winners for 1994.

ENGLAND

Mrs Judith Goddard, Cherry Tree Villa, 7 Newbridge Hill, Bath, Avon
Mrs S. Briggs, High Wray Farm, High Wray, Ambleside, Cumbria
Mr & Mrs F. Cervetti, Lightwood Farmhouse, Bowland Bridge, Cumbria
Mrs Jenny Fox, Highstead Farm, Bucks Cross, Near Bideford, Devon
Mrs B. Williams, Abbots Court, Church End, Twyning, Gloucestershire
Mr & Mrs Hayward, Castlemere Hotel, 13 Shaftesbury Avenue, Blackpool
Mrs Wainwright, Homestead House, 5 Ashley Road, Medbourne, Leics
Mrs Sheila Potts, Aydon, 1 Osborne Avenue, Hexham, Northumberland
Mr & Mrs B. Joyner, Anro, 90 Kings Road, Harrogate, N. Yorks

SCOTLAND

Mr & Mrs I. Weir, Appin Holiday Homes, Appin, Argyll

WALES

Mrs J.E. Thom, The Grange, Penrose, Raglan, Gwent

HARROGATE. Mrs Christine Ryder, Scaife Hall Farm, Blubberhouses, Otley, West Yorkshire LS21 2PL (01943 880354). ♛♛ *Highly Commended.* Farm Holiday Bureau member. Scaife Hall is a working farm set in picturesque countryside on the edge of the Yorkshire Dales. Ideal location for visiting the Dales, Harrogate, Fountains Abbey, York, Skipton and Emmerdale country. Sheep and beef cattle are kept and guests are free to roam and even take part in some seasonal activities such as lambing, etc. One twin-bedded and two double rooms, each tastefully decorated and having en suite facilities, central heating and beverage tray. Guests' private sittingroom with colour TV and log fires on chilly nights. Open all year. Local inns provide excellent evening meals. Bed and Breakfast from £18.

HELMSLEY. Mrs Elizabeth Easton, Lockton House Farm, Bilsdale, Helmsley YO6 5NE (01439 798303). Working farm, join in. 16th century farmhouse on mixed family run farm of 400 acres with sheep, cattle and ponies. Ideally situated for touring North Yorkshire moors and the many other attractions of this area. There are peaceful panoramic views from the farm. Guest accommodation is in two double and one family rooms all with washbasins; lounge with colour TV. Good home cooking in abundance. One dog per family welcome. Open March to October. Bed and Breakfast from £13.50; Bed, Breakfast and Evening Meal (optional) from £21. Reduced rates for children. Tourist Board registered.

HELMSLEY. Mrs Sally Robinson, Valley View Farm, Old Byland, Helmsley, York YO6 5LG (01439 798221). ♛♛ *Highly Commended.* **Working farm.** Stylish, well appointed farmhouse accommodation twixt Moors and Dales in the North Yorks Moors National Park with outstanding views across beautiful countryside. Relax in rural peace and tranquillity. Excellent walking country. Warm, spacious en suite rooms, each with tea/coffee making facilities, colour TV and central heating. Residents' lounge furnished traditionally with open fires and your comfort always in mind. Dining room where substantial breakfasts and old fashioned leisurely farmhouse dinners are served. Licensed. Vegetarian meals on request. Open all year. Bed and Breakfast from £22; Dinner, Bed and Breakfast from £35. Special offers available. Please phone for brochure.

HELMSLEY. Mrs Margaret Wainwright, Sproxton Hall, Sproxton, Helmsley YO6 5QE (01439 770225; Fax: 01439 771373). ♛♛ *Highly Commended.* **Working farm.** Enjoy the peaceful atmosphere, magnificent views and comfort of Sproxton Hall, a 17th century Grade II listed farmhouse on a 300 acre family farm. A haven of peace and tranquillity, lovingly and tastefully furbished with antiques and co-ordinating fabrics to give the warm and cosy elegance of a country home. Set amidst idyllic countryside, one and a half miles from Helmsley. Excellent base for touring North Yorkshire Moors, Dales, Coast, National Trust properties and York. One double bedded room with private bathroom, one twin and one double bedded rooms with luxury shower room. Colour TV, central heating, drinks facilities, washbasins and razor points in all rooms. Laundry facilities. No children under 10 years. A "Non-Smoking" household. Special low season breaks. Five self catering award-winning cottages also available. See our separate entry in the Self Catering Section of this guide. Please send stamp for brochure.

PLEASE SEND A STAMPED ADDRESSED ENVELOPE WITH ENQUIRIES

HELMSLEY. Mrs J. Milburn, Barn Close Farm, Rievaulx, Helmsley YO6 5LH (01439 798321). Working farm. Farming family offer homely accommodation on mixed farm in beautiful surroundings near Rievaulx Abbey. Ideal for touring, pony trekking, walking. Home-made bread, own home produced meat, poultry, free range eggs — in fact Mrs Milburn's excellent cooking was praised in the "Daily Telegraph". Modern home — two double bedrooms with washbasins, one family room (one room en-suite); all with tea/coffee making facilities. TV lounge; diningroom. Children welcome, babysitting. Sorry, no pets. Open all year round. Open log fires. Storage heaters in bedrooms. Car essential — parking. Bed and Breakfast from £14-£18. Evening Meals available. Reduced rates for children under 10 sharing parents' room.

INGLETON. Mrs Nancy Lund, Gatehouse Farm, Far Westhouse, Ingleton, Carnforth LA6 3NR (015242 41458/41307). Bryan and Nancy invite you to their farm which they run with their son who lives at Lund Holme (next door). You are welcome to wander round and look at the cows, calves and sheep or stroll in the quiet country lanes and enjoy the wild flowers. Gatehouse, situated in the Yorkshire Dales National Park, is in an elevated position with beautiful views over open countryside; it was built in 1740 and retains the original oak beams. Double or twin rooms (families welcome), all with private facilities and tea/coffee trays; guests' diningroom and lounge with colour TV. M6 turnoff 34, 15 miles, one and a half miles west of Ingleton, just off A65. Bed and Breakfast from £15; Evening Meal from £8.

INGLETON. Carol Brennand, Nutstile Farm, Ingleton, Via Carnforth LA6 3DT (015242 41752). The warm and comfortable farmhouse at Nutstile makes a perfect base for a holiday exploring this scenic area. Nutstile is a typical Dales farm consisting of a dairy herd and sheep. Guests are invited to watch milking and other farm activities. Situated two miles from Ingleton off A65 Settle Road, the local attractions include a waterfall walk, show caves, walking in the Three Peaks area; also convenient for Lakes, Trough of Bowland and Settle to Carlisle railway. Children welcome. Bed and Breakfast. Two double bedrooms, £14 per person. Please telephone for brochure.

See also Colour Display Advertisement **INGLETON. Mrs Mollie Bell, "Langber Country Guest House", Ingleton (Via Carnforth) LA6 3DT (Ingleton [015242] 41587).** Ingleton, "Beauty Spot of the North", in the National Parks area. Renowned for waterfalls, glens, underground caves, magnificent scenery and Ingleboro' mountain — 2,373 ft. An excellent centre for touring Dales, Lakes and coast. Golf, fishing, tennis, swimming and bowls in vicinity. Pony-trekking a few miles distant. Guests are warmly welcomed to "Langber", a detached country house, having beautiful views with 57 acres of gardens, terrace and fields. Sheep and lambs kept. There are three family, three double/twin and one single bedrooms — all with washbasins and razor points; some en-suite. Bathroom, shower and three toilets. Sunny, comfortable lounge and separate diningroom. Central heating. Fire precautions. Babysitting offered. Open all year except Christmas. Fire Certificate granted. AA and RAC Listed. Tourist Board registered. SAE for terms for Evening Dinner, Bed and Breakfast or Bed and Breakfast only. Reductions for children under 13 sharing parents' room.

NORTH YORKSHIRE – RICH IN TOURIST ATTRACTIONS!

Dales, moors, castles, abbeys, cathedrals – you name it and you're almost sure to find it in North Yorkshire. Leading attractions include Castle Howard, the moorlands walks at Goathland, the Waterfalls at Falling Foss, Skipton, Richmond, Wensleydale, Bridestones Moor, Ripon Cathedral, Whitby, Settle and, of course, York itself.

INGLETON (via Carnforth). J.A. and M. Charlton, Stacksteads Farm, Ingleton, Via Carnforth, Lancashire LA6 3HS (015242 41336). Stacksteads Farm, a smallholding situated in the beautiful Yorkshire Dales, dates back to the 1600s. We are approximately one mile from the village centre and half a mile from the main A65 Settle to Kendal road with panoramic views of Ingleborough. Our location is 10 miles from Settle, five miles from Kirkby Lonsdale and 17 miles from Hawes. We are surrounded by some of the most beautiful limestone countryside in England, ideal for walking, with prime historical and geological features in the nearby surrounding area. We offer Bed and Breakfast, together with Evening Meal if required. We have two double en-suite rooms and one twin-bedded room with its own separate bathroom. Residents' diningroom and lounge with TV. All are centrally heated. Open all year round. Bed and Breakfast £14 per person per night; Evening Meal £8. AA QQ.

KEIGHLEY. Joe and Joyce Sawley, The Hawthorns, Ickornshaw, Cowling, Keighley BD22 0DH (01535 633299 or 0831 720796 mobile). "HILTON"! But have you stayed at the "HAWTHORNS", set in its own grounds just off the beaten track in the lovely hamlet of Ickornshaw. Ample parking, heated outdoor swimming pool (weather permitting). Ideally situated for Skipton, Yorkshire Dales, Haworth and the Bronte country. Marvellous centre for touring or walking. Colour TV and tea/coffee facilities in all bedrooms; en suite rooms. Recommended for home cooking and a "BIG" farmhouse breakfast. Guests are assured of a warm, friendly "at home" atmosphere. Situated three miles from Crosshills just off the A6068 road at Cowling. Bed and Breakfast from £14.50; Evening Meal £7.50. SAE for further details. Tourist Board Listed.

KETTLEWELL-WITH-STARBOTTON. Tim and Marie Louise Rathmell, Hilltop Country Guest House, Starbotton, Near Skipton BD23 5HY (01756 760321). *Highly Commended.* RAC Highly Acclaimed. AA Selected. Superbly situated 17th century Country Guest House in 10 acres of beckside grounds overlooking unspoilt Dales village in the heart of the National Park. Beautifully appointed and immaculate bedrooms all have bath or shower and WC en-suite, also colour TV and tea-making facilities. There is a sittingroom with log fires, a wide selection of books and a bar which is well-stocked and often lively. Fine food is served by candlelight in the oak beamed diningroom. And by day, Hilltop is perfectly situated for circular fell and riverside walks and for touring some of England's loveliest countryside. "This delightful house . . . offers the warmth and hospitality of a house party . . .". BTA Commendation. Please telephone for brochure.

KIRKBYMOORSIDE. Mrs M.P. Featherstone, Keysbeck Farm, Farndale, Kirkbymoorside YO6 6UZ (Kirkbymoorside [01751] 433221). Working farm, join in. Friendly accommodation on a 200 acre farm. There are one double, one single or twin bedrooms; diningroom with open log fire where good home cooking is served. Car essential, parking. Children and pets welcome; babysitting available. Open all year round. Evening Meal, Bed and Breakfast £15; Bed and Breakfast £10. Reduced rates for children and weekly terms. Tourist Board registered.

MALTON. Mrs C.P.H. Murray, Manor Farm, Little Barugh, Malton YO17 0UY (0165386 262). Georgian farmhouse with extensive garden and tennis court. Modernised, with central heating, Aga and double glazing. Both double and single rooms with bath are available. Guests' sittingroom with open fire and colour TV. Little Barugh is equidistant, eight miles, from Malton, Pickering and Kirkbymoorside and close to Castle Howard, Flamingoland, Eden Camp, North Yorkshire Moors and the historic railway; Scarborough 22 miles and York 27 miles. Well behaved children and dogs welcome. Open all year except Christmas. Bed and Breakfast from £17 per person per night; Evening Meal on request.

MASHAM. Mrs R. Greensit, Haregill Lodge, Ellingstring, Masham, Ripon HG4 4PW (01677 460272). ♛♛ *Commended.* This attractive 18th century stone farmhouse is set on a family working mixed farm. One bedroom en suite. Large games room. Secluded garden with children's play area, in peaceful surroundings overlooking the Hambleton Hills. Good base to explore the Dales and Herriot country. On A6108 between Masham (two miles) and Leyburn, turn left to High Ellington and Ellingstring is the only farm between villages. Good home cooking with supper tray for all guests. Tea making facilities, log fire, central heating, Satellite TV. Evening meal can be provided. Fishing and trekking nearby. A warm welcome awaits you. Open all year (closed Christmas and New Year). Bed and Breakfast from £15 to £18; Evening Meal from £9.

MASHAM. Mrs Wendy Rodney, Leighton Hall Farm, Healey, Masham, Ripon HG4 4LS (01765 689360). Situated four miles out of Masham, amongst the beautiful Dales, Leighton Hall Farm was once owned by the monks and was built in the 1500's. We have lovely views and a large garden, five minutes' walk from the peaceful fishing reservoir at Leighton. Nearby there is also a trekking centre. Situated between Wensleydale and Nidderdale, we have many public footpaths with walks all round. One en suite room, one twin and one family rooms, all with tea-making facilities; lounge with open fire and a view down the valley. Bed and Breakfast from £13 to £15. Children and pets welcome. Tourist Board Listed/Approved.

MASHAM. Michael and Judy Wilkes, Pinewood Manor, Breary Banks, Healey, Masham HG4 4LW (01765 689082). ♛ *Commended.* Sample the warmth and hospitality awaiting you at our country house set amidst pine trees with beautiful views of Colsterdale. An ideal central base for exploring the Yorkshire Dales. Sporting facilities and places of interest nearby; Leighton Reservoir one mile. Bedrooms have vanity units, TVs, tea/coffee making facilities, towels, robes and electric blankets. Four-poster beds available. Ideal for families. Indoor heated swimming pool and jacuzzi. Lounge with log fire, separate diningroom. First class food, varied and plentiful. Evening Meal optional. Open all year. Bed and Breakfast £18; Evening Meal £13. Brochure available.

NORTH YORKSHIRE MOORS NATIONAL PARK. Mrs Marion N. Cockrem, Dale End Farm, Green End, Goathland, Whitby YO22 5LJ (Whitby [01947] 895371). Working farm. 140 acre working farm, 500 year old stone-built farmhouse in North Yorkshire Moors National Park. Generous portions of home cooked food. Rare breeds of animals kept including wild boar, llama and Vietnamese pot-bellied pigs. Children and pets welcomed. Guests' lounge with TV and log fire. Homely olde worlde interior, oak beams and panelling. Many repeat bookings. Sensible prices. SAE for brochure.

NORTHALLERTON. Mary and John Pearson, Lovesome Hill Farm, Lovesome Hill, Northallerton DL6 2PB (01609 772311). Come and enjoy the experience of staying in our 19th century farmhouse amidst a friendly atmosphere. Tastefully converted granary adjoins house with spacious, well furnished en suite rooms which include TV and beverage facilities. Beamed ceilings are still retained in the two upstairs bedrooms. Our newly converted downstairs includes a bedroom and dining room, both of which overlook the garden and patio. Locally produced food is used when available. Situated in open countryside overlooking Hambleton Hills, four miles north of Northallerton, this is a perfect base for exploring the Dales, Moors, York and Durham. You'll "love" it.

The information in the entries in this guide is presented by the publishers in good faith and after the signed acceptance by advertisers that they will uphold the high standards associated with FHG PUBLICATIONS LIMITED. The publishers do not accept responsibility for any inaccuracies or omissions or any results thereof. Before making final holiday arrangements readers should confirm the prices and facilities directly with advertisers.

OTLEY. Mrs C. Beaumont, Paddock Hill, Norwood, Otley LS21 2QU (01943 465977). ♛ Converted farmhouse on B6451 south of Bland Hill. Open fires, lovely views, in the heart of the countryside. Within easy reach of Herriot, Bronte and Emmerdale country and with attractive market towns around — Skipton, Knaresborough, Otley and Ripon. Harrogate nearby with cinemas, theatre and good eating. Walking, bird watching and fishing on the nearby reservoir. Residents' lounge with TV Comfortable bedrooms. Non-smoking accommodation available. Children welcome. Pets by arrangement. Bed and Breakfast from £13.50 to £16.50.

PICKERING. Mrs Livesey, Sands Farm Country Hotel, Wilton, Pickering YO18 7JY (01751 474405). Enjoy a relaxing holiday in a friendly atmosphere where food, rooms and service are of the highest standard. Laura Ashley style bedrooms, with flowers, colour TV and tea-making facilities, all en-suite; some with four-poster beds. Full English Breakfasts; tea-trays in front of a log fire. Evening Meals on request. Many sporting facilities and places of interest nearby — we are happy to suggest many places to visit. NO SMOKING. No dogs. No children under 10 years. Private parking. Terms **from** £17.50 per person per night. Special Low Season breaks Special low fat diets on request. Self-catering Cottages also available set in 15 acres.

PICKERING. Stan and Hilary Langton, Vivers Mill, Mill Lane, Pickering YO18 8DJ (Pickering [01751] 473640). Vivers Mill is an ancient watermill situated in peaceful surroundings, quarter mile south of Pickering Market Place on Pickering Beck. The Mill is a listed building constructed of stone, brick and pantiles, part of which possibly dates back to the 13th century. The property with its characteristic beamed ceilings is being renovated, whilst most of the machinery, including the water wheel and millstones, is being retained. Pickering is an excellent centre from which to explore the North Yorkshire Moors National Park, Ryedale and the spectacular Heritage Coast. It is the terminal station for the preserved North Yorkshire Moors Railway and is only 26 miles from historic York. Visitors are assured of a friendly welcome with nourishing, traditional breakfast. Large lounge and six comfortable en suite bedrooms. Tea/coffee making facilities. Bed and Breakfast £22 per day; £135 per week. Reductions for family room. Pets welcome.

PICKERING. Mrs J. Allanson, Rains Farm, Allerston, Pickering YO18 7PQ (Scarborough [01723] 859333). ♛♛ Rains Farm is a comfortable modernised farmhouse, situated in the peaceful Vale of Pickering. The ideal base, offering easy access to the coast and moors as well as York. Traditional farmhouse meals served, using fresh local produce whenever possible. Good food and a warm welcome is assured. The centrally heated accommodation comprises double and twin rooms, including ground floor twin. All rooms are en suite and have tea/coffee making facilities and shaver points. Beamed dining room, lounge with colour TV. Car essential, ample parking. No smoking indoors. Bed and Breakfast from £16; Evening Meal optional. Write or phone for further details.

PICKERING. Mrs Ella Bowes, Banavie, Roxby Road, Thornton-le-Dale, Pickering YO18 7SX (Pickering [01751] 474616). ♛ A warm welcome awaits all guests at Banavie, a large stone-built semi-detached house situated in a very nice part of Thornton-le-Dale which, with the stream flowing through the centre, is one of the prettiest villages in Yorkshire. Nearby are two restaurants and three pubs which provide meals. Ideal centre for touring coast, moors, forest, Scarborough, Castle Howard, Flamingo Park and Eden Camp. One family and two double bedrooms, all with washbasins, shaver points, colour TV and tea making facilities. Bathroom, toilet. Dining room and lounge with colour TV. Central heating. Own door keys. A real Yorkshire breakfast is served by Mrs Bowes. Visitors' book reads "Excellent", "Real Yorkshire Hospitality", "Wonderful holiday; will come again". Large car park. Children made very welcome; cot, high chair, babysitting provided. Dogs welcome. Open all year. Bed and Breakfast from £12 to £13 (including tea and biscuits at bedtime). SAE, please, for early reply.

RAVENSCAR. Mrs Joan Greenfield, Smuggler's Rock Country Guest House, Ravenscar YO13 0ER (Scarborough [01723] 870044). ♛♛ Smuggler's Rock is a stone built Georgian Farmhouse between Whitby and Scarborough, with panoramic views over surrounding North Yorkshire National Park and sea. The farmhouse has a homely and relaxed atmosphere. Home cooking is served in our old world diningroom, and there is an open fire and colour TV in our beautiful open-beamed lounge. All bedrooms have private facilities, bedroom TV available. We have a Residential Licence and our own car park. This is an ideal country holiday area, with many picturesque seaside villages on the Heritage Coast, and beautiful Dales just a few miles inland. AA QQQ. Reasonable prices; please send for brochure. Also a self catering cottage available.

RICHMOND. Mr and Mrs Chilton, Mount Pleasant Farm, Whashton, Richmond DL11 7JP (01748 822784). ♛♛ *Approved.* We are situated three miles from the market town of Richmond. A working farm in lovely countryside offering five well furnished comfortable rooms in a converted stable, each with its own bathroom and front door (one equipped for disabled visitors, one family suite). A real Yorkshire Breakfast starts the day. Home cooking. Sitting and diningroom in the farmhouse for dinner. We have a residential licence. We take time to talk to you, show you the farm and give a real Yorkshire welcome. Bed and Breakfast from £17. Children and pets welcome.

RICHMOND. Colin and Helen Lowes, Wilson House, Barningham, Richmond DL11 7EB (01833 21218). ♛ *Commended.* Situated on the North Yorkshire/Co. Durham border, one mile from the A66, this working family farm is ideally situated for a family holiday. The historic towns of Richmond and Barnard Castle are less than 10 miles away and the Lake District, Durham City, York, Beamish Museum and the Metro Centre are within one hour's drive. There is ample walking amidst beautiful scenery plus farm walks and children's play area. Pony trekking at Barnard Castle. The newly renovated accommodation comprises two family apartments with two or three bedrooms, en-suite facilities, colour TV and a kitchenette. Non-smoking accommodation available. Bed and Breakfast or Bed, Breakfast and Evening Meal. Babysitting available. Write or phone for brochure.

RICHMOND. Mrs Hutchinson, Broaches Farm, Dalton, Richmond DL11 7HW (01833 621369). Broaches Farm is in an idyllic setting off the beaten track in 15 acres of meadowland between the historic towns of Richmond and Barnard Castle. An ideal base for touring the Yorkshire Dales and "Herriot Country" and only one hour away from the Lake District. Tennis court on site, and horse riding, golf, fishing and swimming all within six miles. Tea/coffee making facilities and colour TV in family room with private bathroom; central heating throughout. Relax in our sunny conservatory or enjoy the warmth of the log fires in guests' lounge on chillier evenings. There are beautiful views from all windows. Directions: from Scotch Corner (A1/A66) take the A66 for approximately seven miles. Turn left at A66 Motel. After half a mile turn left and continue for one mile. Broaches Farm is on left down a short lane.

RICHMOND. Mrs Dorothy Wardle, Greenbank Farm, Ravensworth, Richmond DL11 7HB (Darlington [01325] 718334). This 170 acre farm, both arable and carrying livestock, is four miles west of Scotch Corner on the A66, midway between the historic towns of Richmond and Barnard Castle, and within easy reach of Teesdale, Swaledale and Wensleydale, only an hour from the Lake District. The farm is one mile outside the village of Ravensworth with plenty of good eating places within easy reach. Guests' own lounge; diningroom; one double/family bedroom, one double en-suite room, one twin-bedded room and a single room. All have washbasins, tea/coffee facilities, heating and electric blankets. Children welcome. Sorry, no pets. Car essential. Bed and Breakfast from £11.50 includes light supper/bedtime drink. Evening Meal on request. Reductions for children and Senior Citizens. Open all year. Luxury mobile home also available.

RIPON near. Peter and Irene Foster, Lime Tree Farm, Hutts Lane, Grewelthorpe, Near Ripon HG4 3DA (01765 658450). ♛♛♛ Working farm, join in. Secluded Dales farm near Ripon where horses are bred; ideal for touring and visiting Yorkshire's many attractions. The farmhouse is almost 200 years old with exposed beams, oak panelling and open fires, clipped rugs, grandfather clocks, etc., plus central heating throughout. All bedrooms are en suite and have colour TV and tea/coffee making facilities. The dining room has separate tables and guests have their own lounge with access to books and games. Full English breakfast, good traditional home cooking with four course Evening Meal. Open all year. Bed and Breakfast from £15 (reductions for weekly stays); Evening Dinner £10. Brochure on request.

ROSEDALE. Mrs B. Brayshaw, Low Bell End Farm, Rosedale, Pickering YO18 8RE (Lastingham [01751] 417451). Working farm. The farm is situated in the North Yorkshire Moors National Park about 15 miles from the nearest seaside resort of Whitby. Scarborough and Bridlington are within easy reach, also York, Pickering and Helmsley, all places of historic interest. The farm, a 173 acre beef and sheep farm, is one mile from the village of Rosedale Abbey and there are many lovely walks to be taken in the area. A car is essential with ample parking space. Sorry, no pets. One double, one bunk-bedded, one family rooms; bathroom and toilet; combined sitting/diningroom with colour TV. Children welcome at reduced rates. Cot, high chair, babysitting available. Central heating and open fires. Open all year. Evening Dinner, Bed and Breakfast or Bed and Breakfast. Terms on request. Tourist Board registered.

ROSEDALE ABBEY. Mrs L. Dale, Sycamores Farm, Rosedale Abbey, Pickering YO18 8RE (01751 417448). Working farm. Welcome to Sycamores Farm, a family-run dairy farm situated in one of the loveliest parts of the North Yorkshire Moors National Park, an ideal location for holidaymakers to walk, fish, ride, golf or visit places of interest including York, Pickering and Helmsley. Comfortable accommodation in two double bedrooms, one twin, all with washbasins, colour TV and tea/coffee making facilities; bathroom, shower, toilet. Enjoy the panoramic views from the guest lounge (colour TV), and the superb cooking of Mrs Dale who specialises in evening meals. Pets accepted. Car essential, parking. Bed and Breakfast from £13.50; Evening Meal £6.50. Open all year.

ROSEDALE ABBEY. Mrs Alison Dale, Five Acre View, Rosedale, Near Pickering YO18 8RE (Lastingham [01751] 417213). Working farm. This 150-acre dairy farm is within easy driving distance from Scarborough, Whitby, York and various leisure parks. Nearer to home there is a wide range of walks set in the North Yorkshire Moors National Park. A small golf course within walking distance is a challenge for any enthusiast. Three-quarters-of-a-mile of trout fishing is also nearby. The "Olde Worlde" farmhouse has all modern-day comforts and offers one family and two double rooms, all with washbasins, tea/coffee making facilities and colour TV. The open-beamed lounge, complete with log fire, has colour TV and satellite. Bed and Breakfast from £13.50; Evening Meal from £6.50. Reductions for children. Pets welcome.

SCARBOROUGH. Mrs M. Edmondson, Plane Tree Cottage Farm, Staintondale, Scarborough (01723 870796). This small mixed farm is situated off the beaten track, with open views of beautiful countryside and the sea. We have rare breed sheep, spotted pigs, hens, two ginger cats and special sheep dog "Bess". This very old beamed cottage, small but homely, has one twin and one double rooms with washbasins and tea makers. Meals of very high standard served with own fresh eggs and garden produce as available. Staintondale is about half way between Scarborough and Whitby and near the North York Moors. Pretty woodland walks nearby. Car essential. Also six-berth caravan available. SAE please for details, or telephone.

Terms quoted in this publication may be subject to increase if rises in costs necessitate

SCARBOROUGH. Mrs Andrea Wood, Wrea Head House, Wrea Head Farm, Barmoor Lane, Scalby, Scarborough YO13 0PB (01723 375844; Fax: 01723 500274). *Highly Commended.* A lovely country house where you are always assured of a warm welcome. A beautiful location with outstanding sea and country views on the edge of the North York Moors National Park, only three miles from Scarborough. All bedrooms en suite with colour TV and tea/coffee trays. Ample parking, telephone, lawns and garden furniture. No smoking in the house please. Sorry, no pets. Bed and Breakfast from £19.50 to £25. Self catering luxury cottages also available (ETB *Highly Commended*). HEATED SWIMMING POOL, JACUZZI AND SAUNA.

SCARBOROUGH. Mrs D.M. Medd, Hilford House, Crossgates, Scarborough YO12 4JU (Scarborough [01723] 862262). Detached country guest house, quietly situated in own grounds adjoining Scarborough — Seamer road just off A64. Near Scarborough, but handy for touring all coast and countryside of North Yorkshire. Three double, one single and one family bedrooms all with washbasins and central heating. Bathroom, two toilets; diningroom with separate tables and guests' lounge with colour TV. Cot, high chair and babysitting available. Full Fire Certificate held. Open all year round. Personal supervision ensures complete satisfaction of guests. Non-smoking accommodation available. Own home grown fruit and vegetables served in season, also fresh Scarborough cod and local meats. Private car parking. Bed and Breakfast from £15 to £18. Reductions for children sharing. Member of English Tourist Board.

SCARBOROUGH near. Mrs K. Simpson, Hazel Hall Farm, Snainton, Near Scarborough YO13 9PN (Scarborough [01723] 859413). Working farm. Stonebuilt in 1700, Hazel Hall is situated on the hillside with panoramic views of the Vale of Pickering. Forest drives north to purple moors, sea to the east and ancient York to the west. Although a working farm with its accompanying tractors, there is an orchard and garden to encourage relaxation. Hazel Hall has been discreetly modernised for comfort, without spoiling its old world charm. Fire Certificate held. Each family room has its own shower and WC. Mrs Simpson personally prepares the farmhouse cooking and helps her guests to plan their daily itinerary. Evening Meal, Bed and Breakfast from £120 per week.

SKIPTON. The Proprietor, Tudor House, Bell Busk, Skipton BD23 4DT (Airton [01729] 830301). A converted country railway station on the Leeds-Settle-Carlisle line. The building is centrally heated throughout and the comfortable accommodation comprises three double, one twin, one family and one single rooms, some with en-suite facilities, and all with tea/coffee makers. Lounge with colour TV and games room. Trains regularly pass the diningroom which was once the station platform. Fire Certificate. Residential licence. Ample parking. Extensive gardens overlooking Malhamdale and bordering on the Yorkshire Dales National Park. Within easy reach of Harrogate, York and Bronte Country. Bed and Breakfast from £15 to £17 per person; Evening Meal an optional extra. Picnic lunches. Brochure and tariff on request. Tourist Board registered, AA Recommended.

THIRSK. Mrs Barbara Ramshay, Garth House, Dalton, Near Thirsk YO7 3HY (01845 577310). Working farm, join in. Garth House is situated in Herriot country amidst beautiful scenery. Near to York, Harrogate and many historic buildings this area with its many attractions is ideal for touring. Guest accommodation is in one family room, one double room and one twin room, all with washbasins and tea/coffee making facilities; TV in lounge; central heating. Large gardens and lawns, children's pets and toys. Access to badminton court and other sporting facilities. Bed and Breakfast from £11 to £13. Easy access — from A1 turn off onto A168 and follow signposts for Dalton. Tourist Board Listed. Brochure on request.

THIRSK. Miss Emma Swiers, Fir Tree Farmhouse, Thormanby, Easingwold, York YO6 3NN (01845 501201 or 501220). Large attractive farmhouse in the Vale of York, five miles south of Thirsk on the A19. Two double rooms, one family room, one room with private facilities; all have washbasins and tea making facilities. Private sittingroom for guests with open fire and colour TV. Children and pets welcome. Ideally located for visiting the Hambleton Hills, Castle Howard, Fountains Abbey, the North Yorkshire Moors and Dales. Also only 15 miles from York. Very convenient for people travelling from the south of England up to Scotland. You are sure of good home cooking and a friendly welcome. Packed lunches are available upon request. Bed and Breakfast from £14; Bed, Breakfast and Dinner from £22.

THIRSK. Mrs Helen G. Proudley, Doxford House, 73 Front Street, Sowerby, Thirsk YO7 1JP (Thirsk [01845] 523238). A warm welcome awaits guests at this handsome Georgian house which overlooks the greens in Sowerby, a delightful village one mile south of Thirsk (James Herriot's Darrowby). Centrally situated for touring the North York Moors and the Dales National Park; within easy reach of York, Harrogate and the East Coast; places of interest include Coxwold, Shandy Hall, Newburgh Priory with beautiful lake and gardens. Ideal walking and riding countryside. Golf at Thirsk. Accommodation has full central heating, all bedrooms have private bath and/or shower, WC, and tea/coffee making facilities; one ground floor bedroom suitable for the disabled. Residents' lounge with colour TV, diningroom. Large garden with a paddock and friendly animals. Children and pets welcome. Cot, high chair, babysitting available. Open all year. Bed and Breakfast from £15 to £16; Evening Meal £7.50. Single occupancy £20 in high season. Reductions for children and weekly bookings.

THIRSK. Mrs Tess Williamson, Thornborough House Farm, South Kilvington, Thirsk YO7 2NP (Tel & Fax: 01845 522103). *Commended.* **Working farm.** This is "James Herriot's" town! Situated one and a half miles north of Thirsk, a warm welcome awaits you in this 200 year old farmhouse set in lovely countryside. Ideal location for a walking or touring holiday. The bedrooms are warm and comfortable: one family room, one double room en suite and one twin room with washbasin and private bathroom. Guests' own sitting and dining rooms with colour TV and open fire. Non-smoking accommodation available. Children most welcome. Babysitting available. Pets accepted. Good home cooking is a speciality; special diets catered for. Guests can choose to have Bed and Breakfast or Bed, Breakfast and Evening Meal. The North Yorks Moors, Pennine Dales, York, the East Coast, Scarborough, Whitby, Ripon, Fountains Abbey, Harrogate are all very near. Golf courses, fishing, horse riding available locally. Bed and Breakfast from £12.

WENSLEYDALE. Mr and Mrs A.K. Butterworth, "Greystone", Preston-under-Scar, Near Leyburn DL8 4AQ (Wensleydale [01969] 22042). "Greystone" is a small, comfortable guest house in a peaceful little village (just off the Wensley to Castle Bolton road). Ideal for walks or drives in an area ("Herriot Country") rich in flowers, birds and history. Richmond, Swaledale, Reeth and Hawes are within a half hour's drive. Beautiful, panoramic views are enjoyed from both bedrooms (one double, one twin), with washbasins, tea/making facilities; the twin-bedded room has shower; double room has TV. Cot available. Lounge; diningroom. Dogs accepted. Evening Meal with interesting and varied menu (including vegetarian) £7.50. Bed and Breakfast from £13.50. Weekly terms available. No smoking please.

Simonstone Hall

Hawes, Wensleydale,
North Yorkshire, DL8 3LY
Tel: (01969) 667255
Fax: (01969) 667741

Elegant 250 year old Country House Hotel in ideal walking country enjoying unsurpassed views across James Herriot Country. Comfortably furnished with antiques giving the aura and grace of a bygone age, but with all the luxuries of the twentieth century. Freshly prepared local produce cooked to order including vegetarian & healthy choice menus, extensive and interesting wine list. All rooms ensuite with colour TV and teamakers. Special walking weekends. Christmas and New Year house parties. Dogs always welcome. Self catering apartments also available. B&B from £44 but check for our special offers.

Personally managed by the resident owners, Mr and Mrs B. Jeffryes.

WHITBY. Mrs Jean Lister, Browside Farm, Glaisdale, Whitby YO21 2PZ (Whitby [01947] 897228). Working farm. This 70 acre dairy and mixed farm is 10 miles from the historic coastal town of Whitby. Surrounded by the beautiful North Yorkshire Moors, it is an ideal area for walking. Hutton-le-Hole, Egton Bridge and the North Yorkshire Moors Railway at Grosmont are all within easy reach. A warm friendly atmosphere is assured, with home grown produce from a large garden, our own meat and free range eggs. Accommodation comprises one double, one family bedroom and one single bedroom, all with washbasins; bathroom and toilet; diningroom; sittingroom with TV. No pets please. Car essential — parking. Evening Meal, Bed and Breakfast or Bed and Breakfast only. SAE, please, for terms.

See also Colour Display Advertisement **WHITBY near. Mrs Pat Beale, Ryedale House, Coach Road, Sleights, Near Whitby YO22 5EQ (01947 810534).** Welcoming non-smoking Yorkshire house of charm and character at the foot of the moors, National Park and "Heartbeat" country, 3½ miles Whitby. Rich in history, magnificent scenery, picturesque harbours, cliffs, beaches, scenic railways, superb walking. 3 double/twin beautifully appointed bedrooms (some private facilities). Guests' lounge and diningroom (separate tables) with breathtaking views over Eskdale. Enjoy our large sun terrace and gardens, relax, we're ready to pamper you! Noted for delicious Yorkshire fare; extensive breakfast and snack menus, picnics (traditional and vegetarian). Recommended local inns and restaurants. Parking, near public transport. Regret no pets. B&B £15.50–£18.00 per person, minimum 2 nights. Weekly reductions, special breaks winter-spring and October. Member Yorkshire & Humberside Tourist Board.

WHITBY near. The Postgate, Egton Bridge, Whitby YO21 1UX (01947 895241). Situated amidst wonderful unspoiled countryside and within easy reach of the magnificent coastline of North East England, this friendly inn offers the perfect touring base for those who want a really relaxing holiday. Comfortable bedrooms have tea making facilities and are available at most reasonable rates for bed and breakfast. Appetising bar lunches and other refreshments are available throughout the day, and in the evenings dinner is served in the attractive dining room. In the convivial atmosphere of the bar a friendly game of darts or dominoes may be enjoyed, as well as a glass of well-kept real ale. CAMRA Pub of the Season. Featured in "Heartbeat".

WHITBY near. Mrs Avril Mortimer, Hollins Farm, Glaisdale, Whitby YO21 2PZ (01947 87516). Hollins Farm is a smallholding ten miles from the historic coastal town of Whitby, surrounded by beautiful countryside and moorland with lovely walks. Places of interest include Moors Steam Railway, Pickering market town and castle, many scenic villages such as Hutton-le-Hole with its extensive museum, the quaint fishing port of Robin Hood's Bay and a host of others. Choice of pony trekking centres and fishing in the vicinity. The 16th century character farmhouse provides comfortable accommodation comprising one large family or double room (sleeps four/five), another large family room (sleeps three plus cot), both with washbasins and TV; also twin-bedded room. Tea/coffee making facilities. Storage heaters. Bathroom; sitting/diningroom with colour TV, conservatory. In winter there are peat and log fires to enjoy. Cot, high chair and babysitting available. Reduced rates for children who will enjoy the farmyard pets. Access to rooms at all times. Bed and Breakfast. Home produced meats and vegetables. Open all year. Phone or send SAE for terms. Camping facilities available.

YORK. Mrs Jackie Cundall, Wellgarth House, Wetherby Road, Rufforth, York YO2 3QB (01904 738592 or 738595). ♛♛ AA Listed. FHG Diploma. Wellgarth House is an individual and most attractive detached house, situated in the delightful village of Rufforth, B1224 five minutes' drive from the historic city of York. Ideal touring base for the North Yorkshire Moors, the Yorkshire Dales and East Coast resorts. All rooms are en-suite with colour TV and tea/coffee making facilities. Residents' lounge and dining room. Private car park. Also shooting, fishing and gliding holidays arranged. Phone or write for brochure. Bed and Breakfast from £15. Reductions November to March.

YORK. City Centre Guest House, 52-54 Walmgate, York YO1 2TJ (01904 624048; Fax: 01904 612494). The only central accommodation with "Guest House" prices. Quietly located in one of York's historic streets within the city walls and surrounded by York's historic attractions. All rooms offer the usual facilities including TVs and tea/coffee making; some rooms en suite. We pride ourselves on our delicious and generous full English breakfast; evening meals are offered in our attached BISTRO — freshly prepared by our French chef Francois (price — under a tenner). We also have our own car park. Bed and Breakfast from £12.50 to £14.50; en suite £2.50 supplement. Evening Meal an experience for under £10.

YORK. Mrs Joan Liversidge, Cuckoo Nest Farm, Wilberfoss, York YO4 5NL (01759 380365). Working farm. Pleasant Victorian oak beamed farmhouse on working farm. Separate sitting room and dining room; two double bedrooms and one twin-bedded room, all with washbasins and hostess trays; separate toilet, shower and bathroom. York six miles, coast 30 miles, Moors and Dales within easy reach. Good country pubs nearby. Warm welcome and good breakfast await guests here.

YORK. Joan and Bill Wharton, Linden Lodge, 6 Nunthorpe Avenue, Scarcroft Road, York YO2 1PF (01904 620107). ♛♛ *Commended.* Under the personal supervision of the owners, this small, friendly hotel is situated in a quiet cul-de-sac; easy access from A64. Only 10 minutes' walk to the city centre, railway station, racecourse and many places of historic interest. Double, twin, family and single rooms all with washbasin, razor points and tea/coffee making, mainly with en suite facilities. Large lounge with TV. Licensed. Fire Certificate. Member of York Hotel and Guest House Association. Low off-season rates. Highly recommended. Bed and good English Breakfast from £16. AA/RAC Inspected.

YORK. Mrs Susan Viscovich, The Manor Country Guest House, Acaster Malbis, York YO2 1YL (Tel & Fax: 01904 706723). ♛♛♛ Atmospheric Manor in rural tranquillity with our own private lake set in five and a half acres of beautiful mature grounds. Close to Racecourse and only 10 minutes' car journey from the city or take the leisurely river bus (Easter to October). Conveniently situated for trips to Dales, Moors, Wolds and splendid coastline. Find us via A64 exiting for Copmanthorpe-York, Thirsk, Harrogate or Bishopthorpe (Sim Bath Lane). Ten centrally heated en suite bedrooms with direct-dial telephones, hairdryer, TV, courtesy tray; dining room with open coal fire. Licensed. Bed and Breakfast from £19 to £26 per person per night. Optional Evening Meal. For details SAE or telephone. Also see our advertisement on the Inside Back Cover of this guide.

One FREE admission when one of equal value is purchased with our READERS' OFFER VOUCHER, to Friargate Wax Museum, Lower Friargate, York. See our READERS' OFFER VOUCHER SECTION.

YORK. Mr Bill Frost, Old Farmhouse Country Hotel, Raskelf, York YO6 3LF (01347 821971; Fax: 01347 822392). ♛♛♛ *Highly Commended.* Old Farmhouse, the small, award-winning comfortable hotel, is ideally situated for exploring the Moors, Dales and York, being some 15 miles north of the City. Huge Yorkshire breakfasts, home baked bread, splendid dinners, with a famous English cheese board, fine wines, malt whiskies, open fires and a warm welcome from the resident chef/proprietors ensure a memorable Short Break or longer holiday. All rooms en suite with central heating, colour TV, phone and hospitality tray. Car parking. Short Breaks at reduced rates available in the winter. Why not ring us for a brochure and sample menu? AA QQQQ Selected; Logis Cuisine Finalist 1993.

YORK. Gordon and Trudi Smith, Rosedale Guest House, Wetherby Road, Rufforth, York YO2 3QB (01904 738297). ♛ *Commended.* Rufforth is a delightful village situated three and a half miles west from the historic city of York, ideally situated for touring Yorkshire Moors and Dales. Rosedale offers you the comfort of a family guest house; all our rooms are furnished to a high standard, some with en-suite facilities, and for the comfort of our guests we provide tea/coffee making facilities and TV in all bedrooms. Guest lounge. Full central heating. Private parking. Children welcome, reduced rates available. Low season rates. Open all year. Bed and full English Breakfast from £16. Registered with Yorkshire and Humberside Tourist Board.

YORK. Mr and Mrs G. Steel, Alder Carr House, York Road, Barmby Moor, York YO4 5HU (01759 380566; Mobile: 0585 277740). ♛♛ *Highly Commended.* A spacious country house situated between the villages of Wilberfoss and Barmbymoor, set in 10 acres of grounds and enjoying lovely views of the Yorkshire Wolds. Close to the historic city of York, Castle Howard, the Moors, etc., also the unspoilt and uncrowded delights of the Wolds, and the free museums of Hull. A gliding club and the National Collection of Water Lilies are only three miles away. All bedrooms are en suite or with private bathroom. They are spacious and tastefully furnished; centrally heated and with TV and tea/coffee making facilities. An excellent range of local restaurants and village pubs offer evening meals. Open all year. Bed and full farmhouse Breakfast from £15 per person. Registered with the Yorkshire and Humberside Tourist Board.

YORK. Mont-Clare Guest House, 32 Claremont Terrace, Gillygate, York YO3 7EJ (01904 627054; Fax: 01904 651011). ♛♛♛ Take advantage and enjoy the convenience of City Centre accommodation in a quiet location close to the magnificent York Minster. A warm and friendly welcome awaits you at the Mont-Clare. All rooms are en suite, tastefully decorated and have colour TV (Satellite), radio alarm, direct-dial telephone, hairdryer, tea/coffee tray, shoe cleaning, etc. All of York's attractions are within walking distance and we are ideally situated for the Yorkshire Dales, Moors and numerous stately homes. Fire and Hygiene Certificates. Cleanliness, good food, pleasant surroundings and friendliness are our priorities. Private car park. Open all year. Reduced rates for weekly stays. Bed and Breakfast from £16 per person per night.

YORK. Mrs P. Stockhill, Marina House, Naburn, York YO1 4RW (York [01904] 627365). ♛♛ Marina House is situated in the unspoilt village of Naburn, overlooking the River Ouse and Naburn Marina, especially appreciated by those who enjoy quiet country surroundings yet only a few minutes' drive from the city. Superior accommodation is offered to guests in tastefully decorated and furnished rooms. Some bedrooms en-suite with TV. Tea/coffee making available. The proprietor offers her personal service at all times to ensure visitors a very pleasant stay. Bed and Breakfast from £14.50 per person. Large private car park. Brochure available on request. RAC listed.

PLEASE SEND A STAMPED ADDRESSED ENVELOPE WITH ENQUIRIES

YORK. Pauleda House Hotel, 123 Clifton, York YO3 6BL (01904 634745; Fax: 01904 621327).

♛♛♛ Enjoy superb accommodation centrally situated only minutes away from all the historic attractions. A warm and friendly welcome awaits you at Pauleda, a small family-run hotel offering excellent value for money. All rooms are en suite and tastefully equipped, some with four-poster, colour TV with satellite, tea/coffee tray, etc Car park. Reduced rates for weekly bookings. Free bottle of house wine per couple with your first evening meal. Bed and Breakfast from £16 to £25; Dinner, Bed and Breakfast from £27 to £36.

YORK. Keith Jackman, Dairy Guesthouse, 3 Scarcroft Road, York YO2 1ND (01904 639367). The Dairy Guest House is a tastefully renovated Victorian town house offering thoughtfully planned and individually styled rooms. Situated only 200 yards south of the Medieval City Walls, it is within easy walking distance of the city centre. Decoration and furnishings are in the style of "Habitat — Sandersons — Laura Ashley", tastefully enhanced by plants and natural pine. All bedrooms have colour TV, hot drinks facilities, washbasin and information folders. Some have en-suite bath/shower room, one of which is at ground floor level. The house is centrally heated and has a lovely enclosed courtyard. Breakfast choice ranges from traditional English to wholefood/vegetarian. Highly Recommended. Bed and Breakfast from £15. A non-smoking environment.

DAIRY GUESTHOUSE
Traditional and Wholefood

YORK. Mrs Cynthia Fell, The Hall Country Guest House, Slingsby, York YO6 7AL (01653 628375).

♛♛♛ *Commended.* The Hall is a Regency house of character set in five acres of delightful grounds, with croquet lawn and stream, situated in a 'real' English village with a ruined castle. A genuine Yorkshire welcome awaits every guest, many of whom return year after year. Excellent varied cuisine with fresh produce. Ideally situated for visiting York, the North Yorkshire Moors, coast and stately homes such as Castle Howard (three miles). We also have bicycles for hire. Double, twin and family rooms, all en suite. A car is essential. Ample parking. Brochure available. Open Easter to October. Table licence. Bed and Breakfast from approximately £16.50; Dinner, Bed and Breakfast from £25 (£125 weekly).

YORK. Mrs C. Firby, Church Farm, Scackleton, York YO6 4NB (01653 628403). A spacious, comfortable stone farmhouse on our sheep and arable farm in a quiet hamlet in the Howardian Hills area of outstanding natural beauty. 14 miles from York, six miles from Castle Howard. Exposed pine beams, log fire in lounge, central heating throughout. Lovely garden. Wonderful views from all bedrooms over fields and woods to moors beyond. Two guest bathrooms, one en suite family suite. Tea/coffee making facilities in all bedrooms. Good home cooking using local produce where possible. Ideal base for walking in quiet lanes or visiting attractive villages and market towns, York, the Moors and coast. Open March to October.

YORK. Mrs K.R. Daniel, Ivy House Farm, Kexby, York YO4 5LQ (01904 489368). Working farm. Bed and Breakfast on a mixed dairy farm six miles from the ancient city of York on the A1079. Central for the east coast, Herriot country and dales. We offer a friendly service with comfortable accommodation consisting of double or family rooms, all with colour TV and tea/coffee making facilities. We provide a full farmhouse English Breakfast served in separate diningroom; colour TV lounge. Ample car parking with play area for children, who are most welcome. Bed and Breakfast from £14 per person. We are within easy reach of local restaurants and public houses serving excellent evening meals. AA and RAC listed.

YORK. Mrs Jackie Cundall, Orillia House, 89 The Village, Stockton on Forest, York YO3 9UP (01904 400600 or 01904 738595). A warm welcome awaits you at Orillia House, conveniently situated in the centre of the village three miles north east of York, one mile from A64. The house dates back to the 17th century and has been restored to offer a high standard of comfort with modern facilities yet retaining its original charm and character. All rooms have private facilities, colour TV and tea/coffee making facilities. Our local pub provides excellent evening meals. We also have our own private car park. Registered with the English Tourist Board. Bed and Breakfast from £16. Telephone for our brochure.

YORK. Mrs D.S. Tindall, Newton Guest House, Neville Street, Haxby Road, York YO3 7NP (01904 635627). John and Diana offer all their guests a friendly and warm welcome to their Victorian Town House, 10 minutes' walk from City centre, York Minster, the City Walls, museums and many other places of interest. All the guest bedrooms have colour TV, tea/coffee making facilities and private showers, some have full en-suite facilities. Breakfast menu to choose from. Keys for access at all times. Fire Certificate. Private car parking. York is an ideal base for touring the beautiful Dales and Moors and the Yorkshire coast is only a 40 mile drive away. Non-smokers please. Write or telephone for prices and further details.

YORKSHIRE DALES (Horton-in-Ribblesdale). Mr and Mrs Colin and Joan Horsfall, Studfold House, Horton-in-Ribblesdale, Near Settle BD24 0ER (01729 860200). This Georgian house, standing in one acre of beautiful gardens, has panoramic views and is near the Three Peaks in the Dales National Park. The house is an ideal centre for visiting the Dales, Lake District and Bronte country. There are oak beams in most rooms and a log fire in the lounge, with colour TV. Rooms with central heating, hot and cold water, colour TV and tea/coffee making facilities. Open all year except Christmas. Vegetarians, children and pets also welcome. Reduced rates for children sharing rooms. Mountain bikes for hire. Pub half a mile away. Bed and Breakfast £14; four course Evening Meal £7. Also available, self-catering unit. SAE for brochure.

WEST YORKSHIRE

NORMANTON. Mrs V. Sharpe, Station Lodge Guest House, 21/27 Lower Station Road, Normanton WF6 2BE (01924 223741). Attractive guest house and tea shop recently converted and refurbished to a high standard in Normanton town centre. 10 bedrooms, excellent en suite accommodation. TV and tea/coffee facilities in each room. Satellite TV. Licensed. Fire Certificate. Good parking. Very good rates from as little as £15 per person per night. Open all year. Dogs by arrangement. Children welcome. Ideally situated near M62/M1 network.

WEST YORKSHIRE – LITERARY CONNECTIONS!

Head for the village of Haworth and sample some of the Bronte atmosphere. The Parsonage is now a museum and well worth a visit. Make sure you also experience the adjacent moors. Also of interest in this county – Harlow Car Gardens, Shibden Hall and the French-style gardens at Bramham Park.

WAKEFIELD. Mrs M. Gill, White Cross Farm, Ash Lane, Emley, Near Huddersfield HD8 9QU (01924 848339). Why not spend a few days on a mixed working farm in a homely 18th century Listed farmhouse? Set in rolling countryside only five minutes from M1 Junction 38/39. Family room and double/single room, one en suite, with central heating, colour TV and tea/coffee making facilities. Good pub meals available within one mile walking distance. Near Yorkshire Mining Museum, Yorkshire Sculpture Park and Holmfirth. Terms from £15 to £17. ETB Listed/Approved.

ISLE OF WIGHT

NEWPORT. Judith Shanks, Youngwoods Farm, Whitehouse Road, Porchfield, Newport PO30 4LJ (01983 522170). Enjoy a friendly welcome at our grassland farm set in open countryside. The 18th century stone farmhouse retains its original character and two guest rooms are spacious and have magnificent views of the West Wight (washbasins in both rooms, central heating throughout). Also single room available. All rooms have tea/coffee making facilities. Close to Newtown Nature Reserve with red squirrels and good bird watching hides. Cowes sailing centre four miles, Carisbrooke Castle three miles, beaches all around from 15 minutes' drive. Children from eight years and non smokers welcome. Stabling available. Open all year. Terms from £14 to £16 per person per night.

RYDE. Mrs M.J. Long, The Brambles, Gatehouse Lane, Upton Cross, Ryde PO33 4BS (01983 565556). Private farmhouse accommodation, one mile from Ryde, in a lovely scenic area. Two double rooms and one family room, all with hot and cold water; two bathrooms with showers; lounge with colour TV; separate dining room. Children welcome; babysitting can be arranged. Very homely atmosphere, with good home cooking and a warm welcome to all our visitors. Open all year, with log fires and electric blankets in winter. Bed and Breakfast from £12 per night; optional Evening Meal. Children under 12 half price if sharing parents' room.

SHANKLIN. Denise and Martin Nickless, Keats Cottage Hotel and Tea Rooms, 76 High Street, Shanklin Old Village PO37 6NJ (01983 866351). Keats Cottage is situated next to the old village in the High Street of Shanklin. A small family-run licensed hotel, centrally heated. TV lounge with log fire. Tea making facilities and washbasins in all rooms; en suite rooms available. Children welcome. Open all year. A five minute walk through tree-lined Chine Avenue to the sandy beach. Bed and Breakfast from £13.50; Bed, Breakfast and Evening Meal from £18.50. 1992 PRICES HELD. Mini Breaks welcome. "One night or more — that's what we're here for." Credit cards accepted. Holiday insurance available. Tourist Board Listed.

CHANNEL ISLANDS

ST. SAVIOUR. The Redwood, St. Saviour, Jersey (01534 26370). An old 17th century Jersey farmhouse has been converted into this comfortable hotel, serving good food in an olde worlde restaurant with a beamed granite cocktail bar. The Redwood has a swimming pool and sun terrace, and guests have use of a large car park. All bedrooms have en suite facilities, telephone, baby listening, TV and tea/coffee making facilities and there are several large family rooms.

COUNTRY INNS

CAMBRIDGESHIRE, CAMBRIDGE. Crown and Punchbowl Inn, Horningsea, Cambridge CB5 9TG (01223 860643; Fax: 01223 441814). This charming, recently restored 17th century inn, situated in the centre of the unspoilt riverside village of Horningsea which lies four miles north-east of Cambridge, is an ideal stop-over, not only for visitors to the city but also those touring East Anglia. The bedrooms all offer the highest standards of comfort with private bathrooms, tea/coffee making facilities and telephones. Colour TVs are also available. The inn is gaining an enviable reputation for its food. A speciality of the house is a five-course dinner included in the daily and weekend rates. Further details and brochure on request.

NORTHUMBERLAND, ALNMOUTH/LESBURY. The Coach Inn, Lesbury, Alnmouth NE66 3PP (01665 830865). Quaint olde worlde village inn set amongst the outstanding natural beauty of Northumberland, close to coast (one mile) and historic county market town of Alnwick (three miles). Ideal for golfing, walking, bird watching or sightseeing holidays. The Coach Inn offer a warm friendly atmosphere, with oak beamed bar and dining room and cosy open fire in the colder months. All rooms are centrally heated, have tea/coffee facilities and colour TV. There is also ample secure parking. We are open all year and serve a full range of bar/restaurant meals with traditional ales a speciality of the house.

SOMERSET, CHARD. Squirrel Inn, Laymore, Winsham, Chard TA20 4NT (0146-030 298). Limited but singularly comfortable accommodation is on hand at this nice little country pub and all guest rooms have the welcome facilities of en suite shower and toilet, colour TV, central heating and tea trays. Bar food is offered seven days a week and a range of home-made specials supplement a good and varied regular menu. Children are greeted with a smile here, and a family room is available together with a safe, well-equipped play area in the inn's extensive gardens. Real ale is served with friendly courtesy and farmhouse cider provides a challenge to the daring.

SOMERSET, TAUNTON. The Hatch Inn, Hatch Beauchamp, Taunton TA3 6SG (01823 480245). A friendly, family-owned and operated village inn, offering bed and breakfast; families catered for. All bedrooms have colour TV and tea/coffee making facilities, and there is a pleasant dining room and comfortable, well-stocked bar serving real ales. Home-cooked meals, including vegetarian dishes, are a speciality. The inn also has a very nice garden, a skittle alley, a spacious function room and large car park. It is situated in a quiet village only a few minutes' drive from the M5 (Junction 25) and the county town of Taunton, amidst spectacular Somerset countryside. It makes a very good base for visiting the many attractions in South and West Somerset.

WARWICKSHIRE, STRATFORD-UPON-AVON. Roy and Valerie Blower, White Horse Inn, Banbury Road, Ettington, Near Stratford-upon-Avon CV37 7SS (01789 740641). We extend a warm welcome to our traditional oak-beamed pub where guests are assured of personal service. We offer Bed and Breakfast at reasonable prices and have a restaurant where good food is always available, also real ale on sale. All our bedrooms are en suite, tastefully furnished and have radiators, TV, tea/coffee facilities. Set in the heart of Shakespeare country, the White Horse Inn is ideal for Stratford-upon-Avon and the Cotswolds, and close to NEC Birmingham, Royal Show Ground at Stoneleigh and also Warwick Castle.

SELF-CATERING HOLIDAYS

AVON

BATH near. Myrtle Cottage, Goose Green, Near Bristol. *Highly Commended.* **Sleeps 6 plus infant.** 250-year-old country cottage modernised and equipped to a high standard, situated in pleasant rural area midway between Bristol and Bath. Ideal centre for visiting the Cotswolds, Slimbridge, Longleat, Weston-super-Mare, Cheddar and Wells. Bath with its Georgian architecture and Roman remains is only 15 minutes' drive, as is Bristol, with Brunel's Suspension Bridge and S.S. Great Britain. Leisure centre nearby for swimming, badminton and squash. Sleeps six in one double bedroom, two twin-bedded rooms. Fully fitted kitchen/diner with automatic washing machine/dryer, microwave, freezer etc; dishwasher available. Lounge with colour TV and telephone. Bathroom. Garden. Garage. Car essential. Night storage heating inclusive in tariff. Linen an optional extra. Children welcome, but sorry, no pets. Terms from £195 to £315 per week. Open all year. SAE to **Mrs S. Thompson, Myrtle House, Goose Green, Syston Hill, Warmley, Near Bristol BS15 5LU (0117 956 4961).**

BRISTOL near. Mrs C.B. Perry, Cleve Hill Farm, Ubley, Near Bristol BS18 6PG (Mendip [01761] 462410). Working farm. This is a dairy farm, set close under the Mendip Hills. Visitors are welcome to explore and watch farm activities. Chew Valley and Blagdon Lakes close, giving trout fishing, birdwatching and walking in beautiful countryside. Bath, Cheddar, Longleat, Wells, Weston, Wookey very near. Two units forming part of main farmhouse. **Belters End,** maisonette with double bedroom, single bed on landing, bathroom upstairs. Downstairs kitchen/diner with double bed settee suite. **Cider House,** single level suitable for wheelchairs. Double bedroom, small twin-bedded room. Lounge with bed settee suite. Large kitchen/diner and bathroom. Units fully equipped except linen. Children welcome. Cot, high chair available. Weekly terms from £70 to £200. Pets by arrangement. SAE for terms. Open all year.

Leigh Farm ETB

Pensford, nr. Bristol BS18 3HA
Tel: Mendip (01761) 490281

Leigh Farm is situated between Bath and Bristol, close to Cheddar Gorge, Wells, Blagdon Lake and the Mendip Hills. Large 3 bedroomed Cottage with heavily beamed lounge, sleeping 6 plus baby. "Lakeside", fully beamed 2 bedroomed, 2 bathroomed Barn Conversion – both overlooking fishing pools. The terraced bungalows built in natural stone, with beams, are either one or two bedroomed, with shower room, W.C. and basin. TV is included in all self-catering units and linen may be hired. Large lawns with picnic sets, barbecue. Pony, donkey, rabbits and goat for the children to pet. Coarse fishing pools with carp and tench close to the farmhouse, heavily stocked. A wildlife haven is being created around the pools with many species of duck, butterflies, dragonflies etc. Ample floodlit car parking. Payphone. Long weekends, split week bookings at short notice. Plenty of good recommended pubs nearby. Unable to accept pets. Open all year. Highchair, cot available. Enquiries – please telephone or SAE – Mrs Josephine Smart.

BUCKINGHAMSHIRE

See also Colour Display Advertisement **WOOBURN GREEN. Thames Valley Holiday Homes. Properties sleep 1/6.** Two holiday homes situated in a picturesque village a short distance from the famous Cliveden Estate, and within easy reach of London (25 miles) and Windsor (10 miles). OVERLEIGH sleeps two to six people and UNDERLEIGH sleeps one to four people. Both properties are fully equipped with central heating, colour TV, telephone, pretty gardens/orchard and plenty of parking. Registered with Tourist Board. For further details send for free colour brochure to **Mrs Griffin, Myosotis, Widmoor, Wooburn Green HP10 0JG (01628 521594; Fax: 01628 850471).**

CAMBRIDGESHIRE

ELY. Quaint Cottage, 10 Nutholt Lane, Ely. Period terrace cottage close to city centre with stunning views to Ely Cathedral which is floodlit at night. Three minutes' walk to shops, cathedral and leisure centre with swimming pool, British Rail Station near marina on River Great Ouse. Accommodation in one double (downstairs), one twin and one double bedrooms, sitting/dining room with colour TV and sofa bed. Kitchen with cooker, fridge/freezer, washing machine and microwave. Gas central heating £1 coin meters. Linen and welcome pack provided. No smoking, no pets, suitable for disabled visitors. Weekly terms from £130 depending on numbers. Minimum stay two nights, £60 for two persons. Contact: **Margaret and Peter Sicard, The Laurels, 104 Victoria Street, Littleport, Ely CB6 1LZ (01353 861972; 0850 199299 mobile).**

IMPINGTON. 7 Villa Road, Impington, Cambridge. Villa style cottage with central heating, open all year. Pets and children welcome. Large fenced garden and garage. Sleeps six in one double, one twin and one bedroom with bunk beds. Kitchen, dining room, lounge with colour TV. Ground floor bathroom, also upstairs loo and outside loo. Washing machine, microwave, payphone. Local shops, pubs and takeaway. Regular bus service. Cambridge three miles, Ely and Fens 16 miles. From £150 to £250 weekly. Contact **Mrs Pat Buck, "Lilac Cottage", 8 Schole Road, Willingham CB4 5JD (01954 260032).**

CHESHIRE

MACCLESFIELD. Mrs D. Gilman, The Old Byre, Pye Ash Farm, Leek Road, Bosley, Macclesfield SK11 0PN (01260 273650). 🔑🔑🔑 The Old Byre at Pye Ash Farm is a sympathetic conversion of an unused shippon into accommodation, particularly well designed to suit two families wishing to spend their holidays together in the countryside; smaller groups may book one half if all rooms not required — one half sleeps six the other four. Fully equipped including electric cookers, fridges, microwave ovens; the rear porch has washing machine, dryer and central heating boiler. All accommodation is on the ground floor, so is suitable for the less able visitor. Many interesting places to visit and plenty to do; Alton Towers is 15 miles away. Brochure giving full details and terms available on request. Bed and Breakfast accommodation also available.

CORNWALL

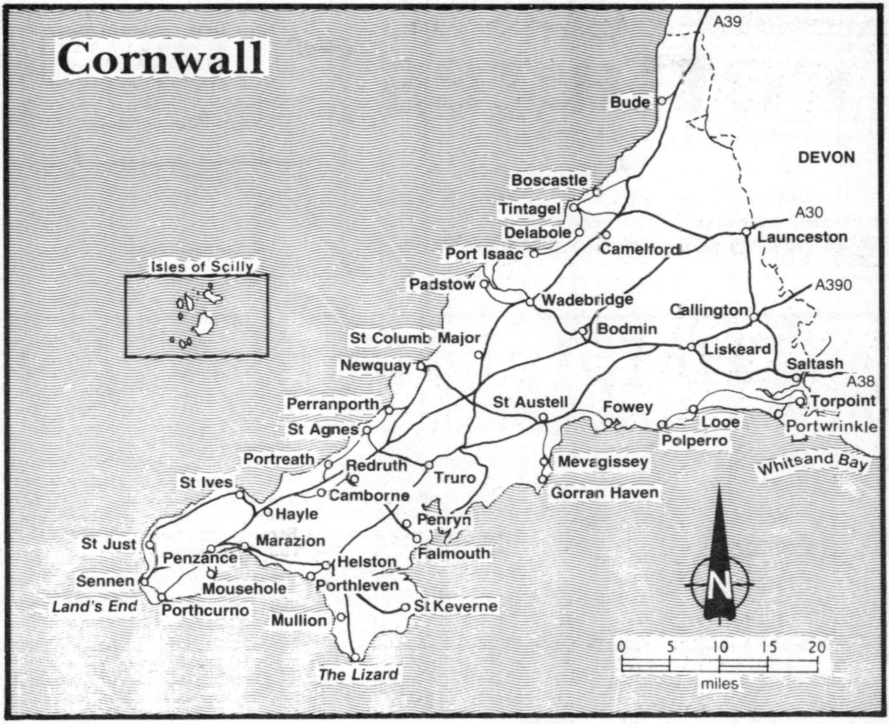

BLISLAND. Mrs M.G. Pestell, "Hockadays", Tregenna, Blisland PL30 4QJ (01208 850146). Two one-bedroom cottages near Blisland converted from a 17th century barn — suitable for couples. Well positioned for remarkable coastal scenery, good beaches and beautiful Bodmin Moor. These charming cottages are very secluded and situated in a peaceful farming hamlet along a private lane, well away from traffic. One cottage is "upside down" with the bedroom downstairs. Rental £90 to £220 per week. Also four listed cottages at St. Tudy carefully refurbished, sleeping up to five. Garden and private parking. Rental £90 to £295 per week. Linen, colour TV, cots and high chairs are included with all cottages. Regretfully no pets. Brochure: **Mrs M.G. Pestell, "Hockadays", Tregenna, Blisland PL30 4QJ (01208 850146).**

BODINNICK-BY-FOWEY. Penmariam Quay Cottage, Yeate Farm, Bodinnick-by-Fowey. Sleeps 6. The cottage, carefully converted from a 14th century barn, is situated in an enviable position, overlooking Mixtow Pill and the Fowey Estuary. With its own quay, slip and mooring, it is ideally placed for sailing, boating and fishing. Nearby footpath leads across our fields to the Old Ferry Inn at Bodinnick, and many other walks are available in surrounding countryside which is mainly National Trust land. Cottage stands in own grounds, 120 yards above the river. Open plan living and dining area contains a feature fireplace of Cornish stone; fuel supplied in winter; colour TV; three double bedrooms; shower room with toilet. Electric cooker. Night storage heater. Well behaved pets welcome. Ample parking. Available all year. Please send SAE (22cm by 11cm) for brochure. **Mrs Angela M. Oliver, Yeate Farm, Bodinnick-by-Fowey PL23 1LZ (01726 870256).**

PLEASE SEND A STAMPED ADDRESSED ENVELOPE WITH ENQUIRIES

BODMIN. Mr T. Chadwick, Skisdon, St. Kew, Bodmin PL30 3HB (01208 441372). Charming flats in lovely old country manor house, Grade II Listed. Beautiful spacious gardens, lawns, streams and woodlands in sheltered peaceful valley only four miles from spectacular North Coast. Outstanding local coastline and countryside; many unspoiled stretches maintained by the National Trust. Bathing, surfing, sailing, sailboarding, golf, hill walking, fishing, pony trekking, cycleways, tennis, squash and modern sports centre all within six miles — Camel Estuary, Polzeath, Daymer, Rock, Port Isaac and Bodmin Moor. Spacious self contained flats sleep from one to seven (for large parties interior communicating doors can be opened). Fully equipped kitchens, colour TVs, night storage heaters, communal laundry facilities. Very attractive village pub serving excellent food only 200 yards away, shops one mile, market town (Wadebridge) five miles. Prices from £100 to £300. Brochure available on request.

BOSCASTLE. Mrs Ann Harding, Ringford Farm, St. Juliot, Boscastle PL35 0BX (01840 250306). Converted barn ideal for two families. Accommodation consists of one double bedroom, one large family room (one double and two single beds); bathroom/toilet; lounge/kitchenette with sofa bed. Electric slot meter, spring water. The Barn is situated on a small working farm two miles from Boscastle with magnificent sea views and set in open countryside. Nearby are the sandy beaches of Crackington Haven, Widemouth Bay, Port Isaac plus King Arthur's Castle at Tintagel. Guests can help around the farm under supervision if they wish. Pets welcome under control. Terms from £70 to £310. The farmhouse also caters for Bed and Breakfast guests from £12.50 per night.

BOSCASTLE. Tresquare, Boscastle. *Approved* / *Commended.* **Working farm. Sleeps 2/8.** Superior accommodation, quietly situated, comfortably furnished, carpeted and fully equipped. Delightful dormer bungalow in own grounds with beautiful valley views, within walking distance of Boscastle. Sleeps eight in three bedrooms (two double, one with en-suite shower; one family room); lounge; sunlounge; fitted kitchen/diner, bathroom, two toilets. Open fire. Also two-bedroomed country bungalow for two/five. Sea views, garden, fitted kitchen. Both properties with private parking, colour TV, electric and storage heating, cot, electric cooker, fridge, washing machine, kettle, iron. Linen hire. Picturesque harbour, National Trust cliff path, Valency Valley, shops. Tintagel Castle, several sandy surfing beaches nearby. Walking, fishing, riding, golf amidst beautiful scenery. Ideal touring centre. Children welcome. Pets on application. Low season from £80 weekly, high season from £175 weekly. SAE please stating dates, numbers in party etc., to **Mrs J.M. Congdon, Tremorle Farm, Boscastle PL35 0BU (01840 250233).**

BUDE. Sharland House, Marhamchurch, Bude. Sleeps 10. From A39 take unclassified turning to Marhamchurch. Pleasantly situated, Sharland House overlooks its own lawned garden adjacent to the square of this attractive village and, in a favoured position, is surrounded by white-painted cottages with thatched or slated roofs. The spacious house dates from Victorian and even earlier times with an interesting interior created by thick walls, low beamed ceilings and window seats. Comfortable accommodation for up to 10 persons is provided by two sittingrooms, diningroom and well-equipped kitchen, five bedrooms and a playroom for young children. Ideally placed for exploring with easy access to many good beaches and cliff walks along the beautiful Cornish Coast. Pets welcome. One and a half miles from Bude. Children welcome. Terms from £210 to £440. SAE for further details to **Mrs P. Gilhespy, 2 Church Cottages, Marhamchurch, Bude EX23 0EN (01288 361570).**

BUDE near. Mrs J. Palmer, Rhude Farm, Launcells, Bude (0128-882 391). Situated five miles from Bude on the B3254, the self catering accommodation comprises lounge, kitchen, bathroom and two bedrooms sleeping up to four people. All electricity and linen provided. Pets welcome. Use of washing machine and tumble dryer at extra charge. Bude is on the North Cornwall coast, easily accessible from the main motorway and along the Atlantic Highway (A39). There are many lovely walks in the area including stretches of the Coastal Path. Other local amenities include golf, fishing and riding, and both Bude and nearby Holsworthy have leisure centres. SAE or telephone for further details.

CAMBORNE. Stable Cottage, Pendarves, Camborne. Situated next to the big house in a quiet corner away from the farmyard is Stable Cottage, attractively converted, yet retaining some of the original character. The property sleeps six and a cot/high chair can be provided. The entrance hall leads into a lounge with a wood-burning stove and colour TV; a second lounge with an open fireplace and a large kitchen/diner with microwave, electric cooker, automatic washing machine, tumble dryer and fridge/freezer. Upstairs there is one double bedded room with fitted wardrobe, a twin-bedded room, a third bedroom with double bed; bathroom with bath, electric shower over, washbasin and toilet. The views, particularly from the bedrooms, are delightful and there is a lawn with garden chairs in front of the property and lots of space for parking. All bed linen included. Electricity by £1 coin meter and logs can be purchased from the owner. Sorry, no pets. Terms from £200 to £365. Contact: **Mr and Mrs G.N.F. Broughton, Orchard House, Wall, Gwinear, Hayle TR27 5HA (01736 850201).**

CAMBORNE. Home Farm, Pendarves, Camborne. The owners started rebuilding work on what was a derelict cottage in the farmyard just over five years ago. It is really now their own home, but with plans to refurbish the big house, most of their time is spent there, and Home Farm is fortunately available for summer visitors. The house has gas central heating/water and sleeps six persons with a cot/high chair available if required. Lounge with open fire, colour TV and superb views of the nearby woods; separate dining room with woodburning stove; kitchen with electric cooker, fridge/freezer, and utility room with an automatic washing machine and tumble dryer. Twin bedded room and two double bedded rooms. Bathroom has bath, washbasin, toilet and separate shower cubicle. All gas and bed linen included in the rental of £225 to £405 per week. Sorry, no pets. Contact: **Mr and Mrs G.N.F. Broughton, Orchard House, Wall, Gwinear, Hayle TR27 5HA (01736 850201).**

CAMBORNE. Little Pendarves, Camborne. Sleeps 6 + cot. This very spacious detached cottage lies just on the edge of the estate and has been completely gutted and rebuilt recently. It is a really superb property with a large south-facing garden, plenty of parking space and oil-fired central heating. The property sleeps six and a cot/high chair can be provided. What was the old dairy is now a utility room with automatic washing machine, tumble dryer, shower cubicle, washbasin and toilet. Large beautifully fitted kitchen with fridge, electric cooker, microwave and coin-operated telephone. Lounge has huge granite fireplace with woodburning stove and colour TV and there is a separate dining room. One double-bedded room, one twin-bedded room with a built-in wardrobe, a bedroom with full-size bunk beds, and a bathroom with electric shower, bath, washbasin and toilet. Electricity by £1 coin meter; logs can be purchased from the owner. Bed linen included. Sorry, no pets. Terms from £225 to £405. Contact: **Mr and Mrs G.N.F. Broughton, Orchard House, Wall, Gwinear, Hayle TR27 5HA (01736 850201).**

CAMELFORD. 12 & 14 Tregoodwell, Camelford. Cottages sleep 4/5. Two semi-detached cottages about 200 years old, though completely modernised and comfortably furnished. Both have lounge and diningroom, all electric kitchens and bathroom. No. 14 has three bedrooms, No. 12 has two bedrooms. Each cottage accommodates four/five with night storage heaters, electric fire and colour TV. Shopping half a mile, seaside five miles. Two miles from Crowdy Dam and Bodmin Moor. Car essential, ample parking space. Fully equipped except linen. Available all year. Children welcome. Terms from £100 to £180 per week including storage heating. Please phone for details to **Mrs M.K. Dixon (0181-346 2549).**

CRACKINGTON HAVEN. Mr and Mrs O.H.F. Tippett, Trelay, St. Gennys, Bude EX23 0NJ (01840 230378). ♀♀♀♀ *Approved.* **Sleep 2/8.** Lovely stone cottages converted from traditional barns and period farmhouse (accommodate two, four, six or eight). Idyllic setting on small working sheep farm at the head of deep wooded valley. Area of outstanding natural beauty. Five minutes to sandy beach at Crackington and coast path along spectacular National Trust cliffs. Ideal area for surfing, walking, birdwatching etc. All cottages furnished in character — much pine and oak, comfortable suites and beds. Log fires, dishwashers, linen, fenced gardens, patios, laundry room and payphone. Pets welcome. Low season from £80 per week, also short breaks. Main season £152 to £550 per week. Colour brochure sent on request.

CUSGARNE. Joyce Clench, Saffron Meadow, Cusgarne, Truro TR4 8RW (01872 863171). Sleeps 2 or 2 plus 1 or 2 children. The Studio, sited within the grounds of Saffron Meadow, is a cosy single storey detached dwelling with own enclosed garden and safe parking. Secluded and surrounded by wooded pastureland. Well appointed main bedroom with vanitory unit. Small children's bedroom. Fully tiled shower, WC and LB suite. Well equipped kitchen/diner, compact TV room. Hot water galore and gas inclusive. Metered heaters, blanket, toaster, fridge, etc., plus use of washing machine. Post shop and inn a short walk. Central to Truro, Falmouth, Perranporth with beaches and golf courses. From £100 to £250.

FALMOUTH. Trebarvah Woon Cottage, Constantine, Falmouth. Trebarvah Woon is a modernised cottage ideally situated for touring the many beauty spots of South Cornwall, being two miles from Gweek, the little creek of the Helford River. Set by the roadside with its own garden, the cottage offers privacy without isolation. Formerly a smallholding, there are meadows for children's play or a breath of fresh air before retiring. Two double bedrooms upstairs; one twin-bedded room downstairs. Modern kitchen and livingroom with a modern toilet/bathroom. TV. Electric cooker, refrigerator, fires. "Off Peak" electric central heating available as an extra. Nicely furnished. Beds have spring interior mattresses. Cot available. Fully equipped with linen, etc., except for towels and iron. Kiddies welcome and also the family dog. Premises thoroughly cleaned and checked by owners between each let. Sea about four and a half miles away. Tourist Board registered. Many guests return year after year. Terms from £150. SAE, please to **Mr T.P. Tremayne, "The Home", Penjerrick, Falmouth TR11 5EE (01326 250427; Fax: 01326 250143).**

FALMOUTH. Nantrissack, Constantine, Falmouth. NANTRISSACK is an impressive farmhouse standing in a delightful garden. It is ideally situated for touring this lovely southern coast of Cornwall. Being two miles from Gweek — the little creek of the Helford River — it is also ideal for visiting Falmouth and the Lizard Peninsula. The farm and small woodland with a freshwater stream is available for those who wish to walk. The furnishings are nice, and beds are new divans. Bathroom; hot and cold water in all bedrooms. Partial central heating. New 30ft Sun Lounge. Colour TV. Fully equipped with all linen except towels; iron provided. Kiddies welcome also well-behaved dog. Premises thoroughly cleaned and checked by owners between each let. Sea about four-and-a-half miles. Illustrated brochure available. SAE please. Terms from £180 including VAT per week. **Mr T.P. Tremayne, "The Home", Penjerrick, Falmouth TR11 5EE (01326 250427; Fax: 01326 250143).**

FALMOUTH. Dolvean Apartments, 48 Melvill Road, Falmouth. Flats sleep 2/4/6. Six completely self-contained, well equipped all electric flats situated 250 yards from safe, sandy bathing beach and sea front, and within a short distance of Falmouth town railway station and buses to town centre. Each flat has a full size cooker and fridge, colour TV, lounge/diner with a double bed settee, one or two double or twin bedrooms, and a bath or shower room and toilet. Bed linen supplied. Pets permitted. Cot available. Electric coin meter. Four flats each sleep up to six, one takes two to four and one takes two. Open all year. Weekly terms from £85 for the smallest in January up to £320 for the largest in July and August. Tourist Board registered. Stamp, please, for details to **Mr and Mrs John Myers, Hillside, St. Mellion, Saltash PL12 6RX (01579 50334).**

GORRAN HAVEN, Near Mevagissey. Ken and Sally Pike, Tregillan, Trewollock Lane, Gorran Haven PL26 6NT (01726 842452 — 24 hours). Beautiful rural area, 600 yards from safe, clean, sandy beach. Ideal for children. Harbour with boat launching facilities, temporary boat moorings arranged. Swimming, fishing. Children and pets very welcome. Ground floor flat sleeping two/seven in bedroom with double bed, double bedroom with twin beds or fullsize bunk beds, plus folding bed available; double bed settee in lounge. Kitchen, shower, toilet. First floor flat sleeping two/six in double en suite bedroom, bunk bedroom, double bed settee in lounge. Kitchen, dining area, shower, toilet. Each flat has colour TV, radio, fridge/freezer, full size electric cooker, microwave, electric heaters (night storage heating out of season). Use of washing machine/tumble dryer. Private parking, secluded garden, sea views. Registered with Cornwall Tourist Board. Cleanliness assured. Pets welcome. Open all year. Weekly terms from £120 to £330.

HELFORD ESTUARY. Mrs S. Trewhella, Mudgeon Vean Farm, St. Martin, Helston TR12 6DB (01326 231341). Leave the hustle and bustle of town life. Come and enjoy the peace and tranquillity of the Helford Estuary. Three homely cottages sleep four/six, equipped to a high standard. Open all year for cosy winter breaks. Open fires/heating. Set amidst a small 18th century working farm with magnificent views across an extensive valley area, surrounded by fields and woodland — a walk through the woods takes you to the Helford River. A superb location in an area of outstanding natural beauty with the rugged coastline of the Lizard Peninsula and beaches only a short drive away. Children and pets welcome. From £120 to £320 per week.

HELFORD RIVER near. Mrs Pamela M.B. Royall, Glebe Hall, Mawgan, Near Helston TR12 6AD (01326 221257). Properties sleep 2/6. Glebe Hall is situated in a quiet sheltered valley on the edge of Mawgan close to the beautiful Helford River. The four cottages are an interesting conversion of the old rectory coach-house and offer well-equipped, all-electric accommodation with two/three bedrooms, kitchen/diner, sittingroom with colour TV and modern bathroom. All linen and towels are provided; cots and high chairs are available; children are most welcome. Two acres of garden include a splendid heated swimming pool, barbecue, swingball, trampoline and games room, with laundry facilities etc. We also have a charming creekside cottage in Helford Village similarly fitted to a high standard. Weekly terms from £125 to £450. Bookings normally Fridays or Wednesdays, or long weekends early or late season. Registered with the Cornwall Tourist Board.

HELFORD RIVER near. Mrs Anne Matthews, Boskensoe Farm, Mawnan Smith, Falmouth TR11 5JP (Falmouth [01326] 250257). Working farm, join in. Sleeps 8. Picturesque farmhouse set in three acres of garden and orchard on 400-acre farm, providing accommodation for eight persons. Five minutes' walk to village of Mawnan Smith, with good selection of shops. The lovely river is approximately one mile away and is famous for its beautiful coastal walks and scenery. Several quiet beaches close by for picnicking, bathing; also excellent sailing and fishing facilities. Other properties also available. Cornwall Tourist Board registered. Terms from £125 to £375. Apply for brochure.

HELSTON. Mrs Una Harvey, "Menifters", Gillan, Manaccan, Helston TR12 6ER (01326 280711). Properties sleep 2/4. MENIFTERS is delightfully set on a hillside one mile inland, with an unobstructed all-round view of the sea and countryside. This area is particularly beautiful with landscapes ranging from rugged coastline, gently rolling fields to the lovely tranquil Helford River. One mile distant is a small fishing village, and there are miles of coastal footpaths between the secluded coves. The converted HAYLOFT is part of the original granite farm buildings, sleeping two/four, and AMY COTTAGE sleeps two. Both properties are tastefully furnished and equipped to make your holiday comfortable and relaxing. Ample parking for cars and boats. Write for brochure, enclosing stamp.

HELSTON. Mrs A.G. Farquhar, Porthpradnack, Mullion, Helston TR12 7EX (Mullion [01326] 240226). At Mullion Cove on the Lizard Peninsula is Porthpradnack, a well built house with two flats, each accommodating four/six persons. A 10 minute walk from house to Mullion Cove. Both flats have fully equipped kitchens with all modern appliances. Colour TV, cots, high chairs (no extra charge). Each flat has separate front door. Pets permitted by arrangement. Car essential, large car park. Panoramic rural views from all rooms. One acre gardens at tenants' disposal. Weekly terms from £100 to £260. Tourist Board registered. Other holiday accommodation also available, please enquire.

PUBLISHER'S NOTE

While every effort is made to ensure accuracy, we regret that FHG Publications cannot accept responsibility for errors, omissions or misrepresentation in our entries or any consequences thereof. Prices in particular should be checked because we go to press early. We will follow up complaints but cannot act as arbiters or agents for either party.

HELSTON. Fuchsia Cottage, Tregarne, Manaccan, Helston. Secluded country bungalow (owner's home) in large, mature garden, one mile from fishing cove of Porthallow. Lovely area for walking, touring, boating and fishing. Shop, pub and beach one mile. Ideal for a relaxing holiday. The well carpeted, fully equipped accommodation comprises three double bedrooms, two with double beds, one with bunks/twin beds, all with Continental quilts; large dining room/kitchen with electric cooker, twin tub washing machine, fridge/freezer, electric water heater and toaster. The large lounge has an inglenook with stone fireplace, TV and radio. Ideal for children, cots available on request. Electricity by meter. Car essential, access by private lane; ample parking. Pets by arrangement. Available April to October. Special rates for Senior Citizens except June, July and August. For dates telephone after 4pm. **Mrs P.M. Jones, "Avisford", Chase Road, Brocton, Stafford ST17 0TL (Stafford [01785] 662470).**

See also Colour Display Advertisement **HELSTON. Mr and Mrs H. Donald, Halwyn, Manaccan, Helston TR12 6ER (St Keverne [01326] 280359 or 565694). Properties sleep 2/12.** Situated in an area of outstanding natural beauty, "Halwyn" is an ancient Cornish farmstead with the original old farmhouse and former farm buildings converted to a choice of holiday homes for two to 12. There are two acres of delightful gardens including an indoor heated swimming pool with sauna and solarium, small lake with boat, badminton court, children's play area and a putting green. A perfect away-from-it-all holiday retreat. Open all year with special low rates out of season. Stamp for colour brochure.

HELSTON. Chapel Cottage, Tregarne, Manaccan, Helston. Sleeps 7. Tregarne is a hamlet one mile from the sea, near the beautiful Helford River, offering safe bathing, boating, fishing and walking. A traditional Cornish cottage with modern single-storey extension. Accommodation for seven (plus cot and folding bed). Large enclosed garden, garage and parking. Children and pets welcome. Comfortable lounge with colour TV, modern kitchen/diner with electric cooker, microwave, automatic washing machine and fridge-freezer. Bathroom/shower and family bedroom on ground floor. Two bedrooms and toilet with washbasin on first floor. Fully equipped except for linen. Three free heatstores October to May. Terms £85 to £330. SAE for brochure to **Mrs H. Dagger, Swanpool House, 65 Long Lane, Aughton, Near Ormskirk, Lancashire L39 5AS (01695 423140).**

HELSTON near. Troon Cottage, Breage, Near Helston. Sleeps 2/5. Take an early or late break in this charming old cottage, attractively furnished to a high standard, situated in a quiet country lane near the sea. Modern kitchen, microwave, tumble dryer, colour TV, oil-fired central heating, beds made up ready. Secluded garden, patio, garage. Children welcome, cot provided. Breage is an ideal centre for exploring the numerous beaches and National Trust coastal walks in the area and within easy motoring distance of Land's End, The Lizard, Helford, Falmouth, Penzance, St. Ives and many other well known beauty spots. Sorry, no pets. Telephone or write to **Mrs A.M. Graham, Long View, Maple Avenue, Bexhill-on-Sea, East Sussex TN39 4ST (01424 843182).**

LAUNCESTON. Mrs Jackie Chapman, Bamham Farm Cottages, Higher Bamhan (FHG), Launceston PL15 9LD (01566 772141; Fax: 01566 775266). Up to 🗝🗝🗝🗝 *Highly Commended.* Enjoy your holiday in one of our eight individually designed cottages and relax in our magnificent indoor swimming pool complex, heated to a comfortable 82° all year and includes a paddling pool, sauna and solarium. The cottages are situated in beautiful countryside, yet only three-quarters of a mile from the ancient market town of Launceston with its impressive Norman castle. All the cottages are superbly fitted and fully equipped, some with microwaves, dishwashers and open fires, and all have Satellite TV. Our other facilities on site include outdoor and indoor children's play areas, games room, laundry room and private fishing. The cottages are open all year and a colour brochure is available on request.

ENJOY A HOLIDAY ON OUR TRADITIONAL WORKING FARM

A warm welcome awaits you at our 17th century farmhouse, centrally situated for touring Devon and Cornwall. Wander across fields to the river or carp lake (good free fishing available) – 20lb salmon caught here on the Tamar in 1993.

Well furnished accommodation including fully fitted kitchen with automatic washing machine, standard electric cooker, microwave and toaster. Sitting room with colour TV, video, storage heaters etc. Three bedrooms (sleeps 2/6) plus cot; tastefully decorated with matching duvets and curtains.

Children very welcome. Games room in nearby barn with snooker, darts, etc – try a tune on our old piano.

TERMS £90-£300 PER WEEK. BED AND BREAKFAST ALSO AVAILABLE FROM £91 PER PERSON PER WEEK: £13.50 PER NIGHT

Mrs K. W. Broad, Lower Dutson Farm, Launceston, Cornwall PL15 9SP. Telephone: 01566 776456

LAUNCESTON near. Mrs A.E. Moore, Hollyvag, Lewannick, Near Launceston PL15 7QH (01566 782309). Working farm, join in. Sleeps 5. Part of 17th century farmhouse, self contained and full of old world charm with own lawns, front and back. Set in secluded position in wooded countryside with views of the moors. Central for North and South coasts. Family farm with ducks on the pond, horses, sheep and poultry. Sleeps up to five, fully furnished with all modern conveniences, folding bed and cot available. Colour TV, fridge, electric cooker, solid fuel heater if needed. Babysitting available free. Linen not provided. Within five miles of market town; golf, fishing and riding nearby. Terms from £100 to £160. Brochure on request.

LAUNCESTON. Mrs H.H. Rowe, Godcott, North Petherwin, Launceston PL15 8NX (01566 785223). Working farm. Sleeps 6. Solid stone farm cottage situated on parish road. The dairy farm is set in beautiful Cornish countryside, with fishing, surfing, golf, squash, tennis and leisure centres at both Launceston and Bude, also in Holsworthy and surrounding districts. Near Devon Border so guests can enjoy the facilities of both Devon and Cornwall. Six people accommodated in one double, one twin and one room with bunk beds and cot. Bathroom and toilet; also immersion heater; mains water and electricity (meter £1). Car essential — parking. Pets welcome. Open January to December; terms from £110 weekly. SAE, please.

LAUNCESTON. Mrs E.M. Budge, Meadow Croft, East Kitcham Farm, St. Giles, Launceston PL15 9SL (01566 784329). Working farm, join in. Enjoy a country holiday in a luxury six-berth caravan, all amenities, equipped and maintained to a high standard, includes two bedrooms, one double, one twin (not bunks). Lounge with colour TV, kitchen with full-size cooker and fridge, shower room with shower, basin and toilet. Linen supplied. The caravan is sited in its own garden (with parking) and has lovely views of the surrounding countryside. Central for coast and Dartmoor; Leisure Centre, golf, bowls, etc. at Launceston (five miles); also fishing, sailing, walks and birdwatching, etc at Roadford Lake nearby. Visitors are encouraged to enjoy farming activities. Own lake for TROUT FISHING on farm. Pets welcome by arrangement. SAE for terms.

LISKEARD. Mrs E. Coles, Cutkive Wood Chalets, St. Ive, Liskeard PL14 3ND (01579 62216). Properties sleep 4 adults; 2 children. Six only detached, self catering cedarwood chalets in 41 acres of private woodland. Personally supervised; the owners take great pride in the cleanliness and condition of these two and three bedroomed chalets which are fully equipped, including bed linen, colour TV, full size cooker, fridge and microwave oven. Terms from £80 to £270 per week. Picturesque resorts of Looe and Polperro a short drive away; Plymouth 30 minutes; St. Mellion Championship Golf Course five miles. On-site shop, milk and papers daily. Pets corner with goats, rabbits, ducks, hens, geese. Children welcome to help feed the animals and milk the goats. Three-hole golf course, tuition available, games room, adventure playground. Dogs welcome.

THE COTTAGES AT *Trefanny Hill* Nr. LOOE

Gorgeous Old World Country Cottages

Sleep 2, 4 and 6, with beams, lovely furnishings and fabulous views. Open all year. Everything from nightstore heating and log fires in winter to heated summer pool. Dishwasher, washing machine/tumble dryer, colour T.V. and video. Meals service, full and generous linen and much, much more. An abundance of country walks from your garden gate and coastal walks only 4 miles away.

Q. Slaughter, St. Mary Manor, Duloe, Liskeard, Cornwall
Telephone: 01503 220622

HILLTOWN

Hilltown

Two superb self-catering cottages for four/five in outstanding area close to moors. Fishing, pony rides/drives, log fires and lots more.
🔑🔑🔑🔑 Commended.

Our visitors wrote: "Hilltown made our holiday . . . Home from home . . . Peace and tranquillity . . . Absolutely brill . . . Almost paradise". Come and try for yourself!

Mrs J. H. White, Hilltown Stud Farm, St. Neot, Liskeard PL14 6PT
Telephone: (01579) 20565

See also Colour Display Advertisement **LOOE.** Holiday Bungalow or Hillside Villa, both semi-detached properties with patio overlooking sea; lovely panoramic views, picturesque, secluded sun trap valley. Walk straight onto sandy beach where windsurfing, parascending, boat trips and all water sports can be enjoyed also tennis, entertainments, indoor pool, golf and restaurant. Launderette. Teletext remote control colour TV with Sky channels, microwave, etc.; shower and bath, duvets and bed linen supplied. Superior accommodation for four/six persons therefore no pets in accommodation or on beach. Highly recommended. Further details and terms from **Mrs J.E. Colloff, 188 Lancaster Drive, Hornchurch, Essex RM12 5SL (01708 444866; Fax: 01708 709483).**

LOOE. The Cottages, Trefanny Hill, Near Looe. Sleep 2,4 and 6. Gorgeous old world country cottages with beams, lovely furnishings and fabulous views. Open all year. Everything from nightstore heating and log fires in winter to heated summer pool. Dishwasher, washing machine/tumble dryer, colour TV and video. Meals service, full and generous linen supplied and much, much more. An abundance of country walks from your garden gate and coastal walks only four miles away. Further details contact: **Mrs O. Slaughter, St. Mary Manor, Duloe, Liskeard (01503 220622).**

LOOE. Alan Pendray, Higher Tregarrick Mill Farm, Tremaine Cross, Pelynt, Looe PL13 2LT (01503 220915). Holiday Cottages in Cornwall. LERRYN COTTAGE can be let as a whole sleeping eight or completely divided sleeping two or six, each having own private entrance door and garden. THE OLD FORGE, originally the Blacksmith's forge, can be rented as a whole sleeping nine or separately sleeping five or four. Quaint TRUDAWEN, first in a row of traditional cottages overlooking Lerryn Creek sleeps five. THE FAIR HOUSE is a Grade II Listed building sleeping five. All properties are fully equipped and all except Lerryn Cottage are suitable for pets. All situated in South East Cornwall which has much to offer everyone ranging from family theme parks to deep sea fishing, not forgetting the many beaches. Boat hire can be arranged for your use during your stay in some of the properties. The cities of Truro and Plymouth are both around an hour away. Please send for our brochure giving full details on all properties and areas plus places to visit.

LOOE. Robert and Jean Henly, Bucklawren Farm, St. Martins, Looe PL13 1NZ (01503 240738; Fax: 01503 240481). *Commended.* Bucklawren is situated deep in unspoilt countryside yet only one mile from the beach and three miles from Looe. Delightful cottages recently converted from farm buildings and furnished to a high standard. Large garden with sea views. Ideal position for beach, coastal paths, Woolly Monkey Sanctuary, National Trust properties, fishing trips, golf and water sports. Evening Meal available in the farmhouse. Terms from £100 to £395.

See also Colour Display Advertisement **LOOE. Mrs N. Jenkins, Plaidy Beach Holiday Apartments, Plaidy Park Road, Looe PL13 1LG (01503 262044).** / *Approved/Commended.* Flats sleep 2/7. Situated in a commanding position on the Cornish Riviera overlooking a sheltered beach — eight completely self-contained flats varying in size accommodating from two to seven occupants. About 15 minutes' walk into Looe where shark fishing, boating, tennis are available, while riding stables, golf are about 10 minutes by car. Shops 400 yards. All flats have coastal views and are tastefully decorated. Fitted carpets, colour TV including SKY films; shower/bathroom, toilet. Kitchens have electric cooker, fridge, kettle, generous quantity of equipment. Electricity by coin meters. Blankets, pillows provided, linen by hire. Extra children's beds, cots, high chairs. Launderette/ironing facilities. Free car parking. Pets welcome. Many places of interest to visit. Discounts on golf green fees. Terms from £65 to £125 low season; £160 to £340 high season. These rates refer to minimum size up to maximum size of flats. SAE or telephone for brochure as above.

WHEN MAKING ENQUIRIES PLEASE MENTION THIS *FHG* PUBLICATION

MARAZION. Trenow Farm Cottage, Perranuthnoe, Marazion, Penzance TR20 9NW. 🔑🔑🔑 *Commended.* **Sleeps 4/5.** Commanding a superb coastal position with unrivalled views of Mount's Bay and St. Michael's Mount, this barn conversion to two character cottages provides a high standard of accommodation. There are accessible coves along the Coastal Footpath to the picturesque village of Perranuthnoe with pub, shop and post office and lovely sandy beach. The magical St. Michael's Mount can be reached from the old market town of Marazion (one mile) with a safe beach and water sports facilities. St. Ives, Penzance, Land's End and The Lizard Peninsula are all within easy reach of this ideal holiday location. Both cottages have own garden, patio, barbecue, bath, electric shower, lounge diner, fitted kitchen, electric cooker, microwave, fridge/freezer, automatic washing machine, colour TV, video, night store heaters. Linen provided. Cot and high chair available. Open all year. Sorry, no pets. Terms from £110. Members of Cornwall Tourist Board. Contact **David and Frances Phillips (01736 710421).**

MARAZION near. "Sunnyside", Perranuthnoe, Near Marazion. Sleeps 5. This fully modernised furnished cottage has superb views and is situated in the small, unspoilt village of Perranuthnoe, two miles from Marazion. The village has a pub and ancient church. Sunnyside is only five minutes' walk from the sandy family beach. There are good coastal walks and fishing from the rocks. Nearby are St. Michael's Mount and many tourist attractions, within easy reach of St. Ives, Penzance, the Land's End area, Helston and the Lizard Peninsula. The cottage has fine coastal views from livingroom and bedrooms. The livingroom has sliding glass doors on to a sheltered patio and small secluded garden. Upstairs, the bedroom verandah has a panoramic view of Mount's Bay. It sleeps four, but a fifth folding Z-bed can be supplied. Bed linen is provided but please bring your own towels, otherwise the cottage is fully equipped including TV and a modern all-electric kitchen. Also night storage heaters for winter use. "Cornwall Registered Accommodation". SAE please to **Mrs F.S. Roynon, "Treetops", Perran Downs, Goldsithney, Near Penzance TR20 9HJ (Penzance [01736] 710482).**

MEVAGISSEY. Treleaven Farm Cottages. Sleep 2/6 persons. 🔑🔑🔑🔑 *Highly Commended.* Three luxury converted barns situated close to village, harbours, shops, safe sandy beaches and coastal walks. Each cottage is equipped to a very high standard with luxury kitchens and bathrooms. Some have en suite bedrooms. Games barn and putting green available. Ample parking. Sorry no pets. Please telephone for brochure **01726 843558.**

MITHIAN, near St. Agnes. Mrs Jenny Osborne, Mellowvean, Mithian, St. Agnes TR5 0QA (01872 553274). Sleeps 4. This single caravan/chalet is situated in a peaceful spot with its own lawn and garden on a two and a half acre smallholding. Mithian's central location makes it an ideal base for touring the whole of Cornwall. St. Agnes village offers good shops, pub, restaurants, beach, etc. The accommodation comprises a caravan which has been extended to include a separate bedroom, flush toilet with handbasin and a large porch. All-electric facilities include a cooker, fridge, water heater and colour TV. A shower is available and there is ample parking. Terms £60 to £140 per week including electricity.

MULLION (near Helston). Mr and Mrs R.P. Tyler-Street, Trenance Farm, Mullion, Near Helston TR12 7HB (01326 240639). Trenance Farm Cottages are situated halfway between the village and Mullion Cove. Only half a mile to swimming/surfing beach, plus splendid coastal walks mainly over National Trust land. Golf, fishing and riding locally. The old farm outbuildings have been converted into nine comfortable two/three bedroomed cottages, all fully equipped, with colour TV, etc. Bed linen provided. Heated swimming pool, games room, laundry, children's play area, ample parking, metered electricity. Bed and Breakfast available in the farmhouse. Children and pets welcome. Registered with the Cornwall Tourist Board.

PADSTOW. Mrs Caroline Brewer, Carnevas Farm Holiday Park, Carnevas Farm, St. Merryn, Padstow PL28 8PN (01841 520230). Bungalow/Chalets sleep 4/5. ✓✓✓✓ Rose Award Park 1995. Situated only half a mile from golden sandy beach, fishing, golf, sailing etc. Quaint harbour village of Padstow only four miles. Bungalows/chalets sleep four/six, have two bedrooms, bathroom, kitchen/diner, airing cupboard, colour TV. Caravans six berth or eight, all have showers, toilets, fridge, colour TV (also separate camping and caravan facilities). Newly converted barn called the Coach House now available, sleeps six persons, furnished to a high standard, fully double glazed, some sea views upstairs. ETB & WCTB also AA three pennant site. Brochure on request.

ONE MINUTE STROLL TO THE BEACH!

MARINE COURT

SELF CATERING FAMILY LEISURE FLATS

Situated in the centre of Perranporth. Level and adjacent to the shops and three-mile sandy beach, with private car park. The flats accommodate 2-6 persons and are supervised by the owners living close by. We welcome your enquiry and will be delighted to send our Brochure.

Please state property required.

Terms: From £70 per week (including VAT) according to season. Reductions small parties. Includes colour television.

West Country Tourist Board — AA Listed

R. T. & S. PILSTONE, MARINE COURT, 7 Pentreve, Wheal Leisure, Perranporth, Cornwall TR6 0EY or Telephone Truro (01872) 572157

Extensive holiday home in the centre of Perranporth and only 50 yards from the sandy surfing beach. This spacious family flat has all the facilities for 2-8 persons to have a seaside holiday in comfort. 4 bedrooms (H&C), 2 bathrooms and separate shower room, large dining room, modern fully fitted kitchen with split level cooker, fridge etc. Large lounge. All rooms (including bedrooms) with TV sockets. Cots available. Completely self contained and boasting full central heating in every room. Supervised by owner living close by. Colour television. Secluded bungalow, centrally heated, with gardens plus garage and parking. Sleeps 2-6. From £70 (VAT inclusive). Brochure with pleasure.

Please state property required.

Mrs S. Rilstone, Seathrift Seaside Flat, 7 Pentreve, Wheal Leisure Road, Perranporth TR6 0EY.

Sea Thrift

Opposite the beach. Sleeps 2/8.

PADSTOW (one mile). Trevorrick Farm, St. Issey, Wadebridge PL27 7QH (Rumford [01841] 540574). Working farm. Sleeps 2/4. Ideal for peaceful holiday in lovely countryside, with magnificent views overlooking creek and near beautiful beaches. Superb 31 foot long caravan with dining kitchen, lounge with good put-u-up, double bedroom with dressing room, full bathroom, hot and cold water, electric light, cooker, microwave, immersion heater, colour TV, airing cupboard and fridge. Children and well-behaved dog welcome. The caravan is sited in its own fenced garden facing south. Good approach road. Shops, pubs, garages and church within one mile. English Tourist Board Approved. Weekly terms £100 to £200. Also available, quality farmhouse Bed and Breakfast (ETB Listed *Highly Commended*), and five quality cottages (ETB ♀♀♀♀ *Highly Commended*).

PENZANCE. Mrs James Curnow, Barlowenath, St. Hilary, Penzance TR20 9DQ (Penzance [01736] 710409). Working farm. Cottages sleep 4/5. These two cottages are on a dairy farm, in a little hamlet right beside St. Hilary Church, with quiet surroundings and a good road approach. A good position for touring Cornish coast and most well-known places. Beaches are two miles away; Marazion two-and-a-half miles; Penzance six miles; St. Ives eight; Land's End 16. Both cottages have fitted carpets, lounge/diner with TV; modern kitchen (fridge, electric cooker, toaster, iron); bathroom with shaver point. Electricity by £1 meter, night storage heaters extra. One cottage sleeps five in three bedrooms (one double, twin divans and one single). The second cottage sleeps four in two bedrooms (twin divans in both). Linen not supplied. Cot by arrangement. Available all year. £75 to £250 weekly, VAT exempt.

Terms quoted in this publication may be subject to increase if rises in costs necessitate

PLYMOUTH near. Belhaven, Cawsand, Near Plymouth. Overlooking Cawsand Bay and Plymouth Sound this three bedroomed detached house offers the best in self cateirng holidays. Fully equipped including hi-fi, dishwasher, colour TV, barbecue, fridge/freezer, microwave, huge bathroom with separate power shower. Call **(01752 822287)** for colour brochure.

POLPERRO

WILLY WILCOX and **QUAY**: two beautiful, spacious 400-year-old cottages, just eleven feet from the safe, sandy beach. Three miles along coast **LANLAWREN FARM**: mellow old stone barn cottages and apartments. **BLANCHES WINDSOR**: isolated coastal residence with old church organ, "minstrel's gallery", set in 3½ acres of grounds; sea views and a hidden cove below the house.

INDOOR HEATED SWIMMING POOL (85°F)

SPA, SAUNA, SOLARIUM, JET STREAM and GAMES ROOM with Table Tennis & Pool Table. Children's play room with Wendy House, dressing up clothes, sit-upon toys etc. Outside games, sandpits. Farm pets: Goats, pigs, sheep, ducks & hens. All properties fully equipped; maintained to a very high and professional standard; cleanliness guaranteed; feature exposed beams, stone walls, open log fires, full heating & cosy atmosphere. Barbecues & Sun Loungers. Personal service: tea/coffee and home made cakes welcome all guests. Terms £100 – £1200.

Short Breaks available.

Please contact FIONA and MARTIN NICOLLE (01720 423000 or 0836 58 51 58).

PORT ISAAC. Mr and Mrs R.W. Mably, Trentinney Farm, St. Endellion, Port Isaac PL29 3TS (01208 880564). These cottages sleep up to six. They are approached from St. Endellion down a winding country lane with woods on either side. These traditional listed buildings have been recently converted and provide very high standard accommodation with outstanding views of the surrounding countryside. Come and enjoy a holiday on our family run working farm which has ponies and other animals. The cottages are fully equipped with washing machine, microwave, Fastext/Nicam stereo TV, iron, etc. Cot, highchair and barbecue available. Shared dryer in utility room. Fully insulated and double glazed for Autumn and Winter use. Storage heaters, bed linen, electricity and VAT included in price. Terms from £90 to £398 per week. Bed and Breakfast available in farmhouse.

PORT ISAAC. 🔑🔑🔑🔑/🔑🔑🔑🔑🔑 Up to *Highly Commended.* Open all year. Come and enjoy being a part of a working family farm. Stay in one of our beautiful cottages with lovely countryside views, own garden and parking. Tastefully furnished, catering for your every need, each having double glazing, microwave, fridge freezer, washer-dryer, food processor, coffee maker, colour TV and video, etc. All our animals are very friendly; meet "Barney" our Vietnamese Pot-Bellied Pig and our dogs who think visitors come to entertain them! We lamb from Christmas until March and everyone enjoys feeding the lambs. We have a tennis court, games room and fitness room on the farm and acres of wildlife habitat to wander through. Sandy beaches, surfing, sailing, golf, riding, fishing, country pubs all within a three mile radius. We also have a large period house overlooking a wooded valley near Camelford, sleeping 12 plus cots. Moors and golf two miles, sea six miles. Out of season short breaks available. For details please send SAE to: **Henry and Shirley Symons, Trevathan, St. Endellion, Port Isaac PL29 3TT** or telephone **(01208 880248).**

PORT ISAAC. The Lodge, Treharrock, Port Isaac. Sleeps 6. Pleasant, south facing and convenient bungalow, set in its own small, natural garden and surrounded by fields and woodland with streams. About two miles inland from Port Isaac, a sheltered, secluded spot at the end of driveway to Treharrock Manor. Rugged North Cornish cliffs with National Trust footpaths and lovely sandy coves in the vicinity. Excellent sandy beach at Polzeath (five miles), also pony trekking, golf etc. in the area. South facing sun room leads on to terrace; TV. Accommodation for six plus baby. Bathroom, toilet; sittingroom; kitchen/diner. Open all year. Linen extra. Sorry, no pets. Car essential — parking. Terms from £150 to £300 per week (heating included). SAE to **Mrs E.A. Hambly, Home Farm House, Little Gaddesden, Berkhamsted, Hertfordshire HP4 1PN (Little Gaddesden [0144-284] 3412).**

PORT ISAAC. The Dolphin, Port Isaac. Sleeps 9. This delightful house, originally an inn, is one of the most attractive in Port Isaac. Fifty yards from the sea, shops and pub. Five bedrooms, three with washbasins. Two bathrooms and WCs. Large diningroom. Cosy sittingroom. Spacious and well-equipped kitchen with electric cooker, gas-fired Aga, dishwasher, washing machine. Sun terrace. Port Isaac is a picturesque fishing village with magnificent coastal scenery all round. Nearby attractions include surfing, sailing, fishing, golf, tennis, pony trekking. The Dolphin sleeps nine but reduced rates offered for smaller families and off-peak season. Weekly terms: £300 to £475 inclusive. SAE for details to **Mrs Thomas, 2 Stephenson Terrace, Worcester, Hereford and Worcester WR1 3EA (Worcester [01905] 20518/21967).**

PORT ISAAC. Mrs Kathy Alford, Penhill, Pendoggett, Bodmin PL30 3HJ (01208 880278; Fax: 01208 880464). Properties sleep 3/4/5. Pendoggett is a small village two miles from the north Cornwall coast and is an excellent centre for touring, walking, surfing and sea fishing. The accommodation, situated at Penhill, commands spectacular views down the valley to Port Gaverne and over Port Isaac Bay. Village stores and Egon Ronay recommended restaurant situated nearby. Available are a cottage and two flats set in large grounds with ample parking space and safe play area for children. The cottage sleeps five, one flat sleeps four and the second sleeps two/three. All are furnished to a high standard with electric cookers, fridges, storage heaters, TVs, etc. Available April to October. Children and pets welcome. Weekly terms from £75. Electricity by 50p meters. Tourist Board registered.

PORT ISAAC. Salters Cottage and Penny Cottage, Port Gaverne, Port Isaac. Sleep 4/6. On National Trust Land. Port Gaverne is a hamlet adjoining Port Isaac on an inlet in the magnificent rugged North Coast, and its shingle beach is one of the safest bathing beaches in Cornwall. Salters and Penny Cottages are about 100 yards from the sea, made from the old fishermen's netting lofts and fish "cellars", dating from the days when Port Gaverne had a flourishing herring and pilchard trade. The cottages are fully equipped and most comfortably furnished and Penny Cottage, being all on the ground floor, is most suitable for the elderly or disabled. Salters Cottage has a piano which is tuned each Spring. I will be most happy to send you full details of rents and all vacant dates on receipt of SAE. **Mrs M.M. Cook, The Beach House, Port Gaverne, Port Isaac PL29 3SQ (Bodmin [01208] 880296).**

PORT ISAAC. Carn Awn, Port Gaverne, Port Isaac. Sleeps 6. Carn Awn stands on its own in the hamlet of Port Gaverne, and overlooks the harbour and sea. Fishing, swimming, boating and delightful rock pools for the children. Magnificent coastline where you can walk for miles along coastal paths. Many beaches within reach. Plenty of shopping facilities. Car essential, parking. Accommodation for six people in three double bedrooms; bathroom, separate toilet; sitting/diningroom; kitchen. Cot available. Linen may be hired. All electric, coal fire. Well behaved dogs welcome. Open all year. For terms contact **Mrs S.A. May, Orcades House, Port Gaverne, Port Isaac PL29 3SQ (01208 880716).**

PORT ISAAC. Mrs M.E. Warne, Tresungers Farm, Port Isaac PL29 3SY (Port Isaac [01208] 880307). Working farm. Sleeps 6. Ideal spot for anyone desiring quiet holiday this farmhouse, on 160 acres of mixed farmland, offers furnished self-contained wing for self catering holidays from March to November. Approximately 400 yards from B3314 coast road, just over two miles from sea at Port Isaac. Accommodation for five/six people in two double bedrooms, one with extra single bed; also cot available; bathroom, toilet; sitting/diningroom; well equipped kitchen with electric cooker, fridge, etc. Terms include bed linen. Shops just over two miles. Car essential — parking. Electricity on meter. Golf, pony trekking, bathing and surfing within easy reach. St. Endellion Church about one and a half miles away. Terms on receipt of SAE, please.

PRAA SANDS near. Lower Kenneggy Farm, Rosudgeon, Near Praa Sands. Working farm. Sleeps 6. A comfortable, modernised cottage near the farm, with its own garden and ample parking space. The cottage accommodates six persons, has three bedrooms, fully fitted kitchen, diningroom and lounge with TV; bathroom and toilet; airing cupboard with immersion heater. Metered electricity; linen not supplied. Children are welcome, cot provided. Sorry, no pets. Lower Kenneggy is a country area with sea views, but close to Marazion (three miles) and Praa Sands (one mile) beaches; seven miles from Penzance and Helston. SAE, please, for terms to **Mrs P. Laity, Lower Kenneggy Farm, Rosudgeon, Penzance TR20 9AR (Penzance [01736] 762403).**

BOSINVER

- COTTAGES & BUNGALOWS (sleeps 2-7) one suitable for a wheelchair
- FARMHOUSE (sleeps 12)
- Quality SELF CATERING on small RURAL ESTATE
- Relax in quiet seclusion away from the crowds
- Approved by English Tourist Board and Cornwall County Council
- Well-mannered dogs welcome

Special discounts given.
"Bosinver is the best value for money"
(quote from visitor)

- Solar heated swimming pool.
- Sauna and solarium
- Tennis court
- Own private fishing
- Games room
- Children's swings and clock golf
- Free library books and puzzles
- Washing and drying machines
- Bed linen included, cots and barbecue available
- Telephone

Close to golf course, village with Post Office/Stores and Old World Pub.
Short drive to many safe beaches, town, recreation centre and horse riding.
Personally supervised by owners who are pleased to welcome many returning guests.

Colour brochure from: F. A. M. Milln, Bosinver Farm, St. Austell PL26 7DT. Telephone (01726) 72128

See also Colour Display Advertisement **ST. AUSTELL. Mrs J. King, St. Margaret's Holiday Park, Polgooth, St. Austell PL26 7AX (01726 74283).** ✓ ✓ ✓ ✓ ✓ BHP Approved. Family owned and run Holiday Park set in six acres of beautiful parkland and offering good quality accommodation of varying sizes from detached bungalows (sleep up to eight) to self contained chalets (sleep two to five people). Two bungalows suitable for disabled visitors. All the properties are well equipped with the usual facilities. Colour TV and fitted carpets. Launderette and pay phone on park. Golf course is 400 yards away and the Polgooth shops and inn are conveniently near. Well controlled pets allowed. Special rates available. Open March to December. Terms and colour brochure available.

ST. COLUMB. Mrs J.V. Thomas, Lower Trenowth Farm, St. Columb TR9 6EW (01637 880308). Sleeps 6. This accommodation is part of a large farmhouse, all rooms facing south. Situated in the beautiful Vale of Lanherne, four miles from the sea, eight miles from the holiday resort of Newquay. Golf, horse riding, etc all within easy reach. One double room, one twin-bedded room and one single room with bunk beds, all with washbasins. Bed linen provided. Bathroom. Large lounge with colour TV. Fully equipped kitchen/diner. Electricity included in tariff. Large lawn. Ample parking. Dogs accepted if kept under control. SAE for further details please.

ST. IVES. Higher Trenoweth, Carbis Bay, St. Ives. Sleeps 7 plus cot. A delightfully modernised cottage standing in large secluded garden half a mile from Carbis Bay beach and two miles from St. Ives. There is a large lounge with colour TV, night storage heater and log-burning stove; open plan stairs leading to three bedrooms — one with double bed, one with full sized bunk beds and one with a double and a single bed (a cot can be provided on request); bathroom with bath, WC and washbasin; huge well-fitted kitchen with dining area. Stable doors lead to a sun-soaked patio. There is also a downstairs cloakroom with WC, washbasin and automatic washing machine. Duvets and covers are provided and all electricity is included in the rental. Well-behaved dogs are normally allowed. Terms from £170 to £355. Contact **Mr and Mrs G.N.F. Broughton, Orchard House, Wall, Gwinear, Hayle TR27 5HA (01736 850201).**

ST. IVES. Myrtwedhen, Hellesveor, St. Ives. A country cottage and garden surrounded by farmland, one mile from St. Ives town, harbour and beaches and a short walk to the cliffs via the footpaths which pass the cottage — close to lovely countryside with plenty to see and do as well as being just a short distance from the town. A lovely house in a superb setting, comfortably equipped for four to six people, clean, warm and well maintained with every need provided for. Colour TV, central heating, automatic washing machine (a cot and high chair can be provided on request). Available all year round for full weeks in the summer of off-peak breaks of any length. We are very happy to have children and dogs stay and personal supervision assures you of a very warm welcome at any time of the year. Tourist Board Category 3. Prices from £150 — £390 (including linen and heating) dependent on season. Details from **Mrs F.H. Seabrook, 30 Newcombe Street, Market Harborough, Leicestershire LE16 9PB (01858 463723).**

ST. IVES. Trenoweth Farm, Carbis Bay. Working farm. Sleeps 6 adults; 5 children. This large attractive modernised farmhouse lies half a mile from Carbis Bay beach and two miles from St. Ives. The accommodation comprises a large lounge/diningroom with wood-burning stove and colour TV; a second small lounge; spacious kitchen; shower room with WC; utility room with washing machine. Upstairs there is one double-bedded room, two twin-bedded rooms, one large bedroom with three single beds; bathroom/WC and an unusual twin-bedded landing. A cot can also be provided Electricity is included in the rental. Duvets and duvet covers are provided, but not sheets, pillowcases and towels. A well-behaved dog is normally allowed. The farmyard offers plenty of parking space. There is a small front garden and a sun-soaked patio area at the rear. Terms from £265 to £510. **Mr and Mrs G.N.F. Broughton, Orchard House, Wall, Gwinear, Hayle TR27 5HA (01736 850201).**

Key to Tourist Board Ratings

The Crown Scheme

(England, Scotland & Wales)

Covering hotels, motels, private hotels, guesthouses, inns, bed & breakfast, farmhouses. Every Crown classified place to stay is inspected annually. *The classification:* Listed then 1-5 Crown indicates the range of facilities and services. Higher quality standards are indicated by the terms APPROVED, COMMENDED, HIGHLY COMMENDED and DELUXE.

The Key Scheme

(also operates in Scotland using a Crown symbol)

Covering self-catering in cottages, bungalows, flats, houseboats, houses, chalets, etc. Every Key classified holiday home is inspected annually. *The classification:* 1-5 Key indicates the range of facilities and equipment. Higher quality standards are indicated by the terms APPROVED, COMMENDED, HIGHLY COMMENDED and DELUXE.

The Q Scheme

(England, Scotland & Wales)

Covering holiday, caravan, chalet and camping parks. Every Q rated park is inspected annually for its quality standards. The more ✓ in the Q – up to 5 – the higher the standard of what is provided.

ST. IVES BAY. Mrs Catherine Ayris, Cove Bungalow, 33 Riviere Towans, Phillack, Hayle TR27 5AF (01736 753673). Sleeps 5. Cove holiday bungalow could not be much closer to the sea, the garden extends down to the Cornish Coastal Footpath and just below is a fine beach of golden sand. Access to the beach is by a short footpath; there are no roads to cross. The bungalow is very well furnished with fitted carpets, colour TV and it is double glazed. From the lounge window you will enjoy superb sea views to St. Ives harbour and Godrevey Lighthouse. Will sleep five maximum. Private car park. Dogs welcome. SAE or phone for letting rates and available dates. Also Bed and Breakfast accommodation available from £13.50 per night in luxury bungalow next door.

ST. KEVERNE. Mrs Rosemary Peters, Trenoweth Valley Farm Cottages, St. Keverne, Helston TR12 6QQ (01326 280910). Spacious, comfortable rural cottages, fully furnished and carpeted with well equipped kitchen, colour TV and laundry facilities. Kitchen/diner, lounge/sittingroom, shower room/toilet. Sleeping six persons, each cottage has two bedrooms with duvets and covers for each bed. Surrounded by trees and fields, there is a safe play area for young children and a barbecue. Quiet, relaxing environment, midway between St. Keverne and Porthallow. Pleasant walks; beach, village shops and inns one and a half miles. Open Easter to end October. Sorry, no pets. **Attractive early and late prices.** Cornwall Tourist Board approved. Terms from £60 to £245 per week.

ST. KEVERNE. Badger Cottage, St. Keverne. Working farm, join in. Sleeps 6. This cottage faces south overlooking its own private garden which is formed out of an old marl pit and has a lawn running through the length of it. Shrubs on the bank opposite hide the badger holes and there are attractive semi-circular steps leading up to the cottage. Downstairs is one very long (32 foot) room divided, sitting-room from kitchen/dining area, by a curtain. The accommodation is for six people in three bedrooms, cot available; bathroom and two toilets. Well-equipped with everything except linen. Colour TV. Electricity on meter. Tregellast Barton is a lovely Tudor farmstead, near St. Keverne and about one and a half miles from the sea. Cows, dogs, cats, etc. Milk is made into cream, many flavoured ice creams, fudges and chocolates. We also make jams, chutneys and mustards and have a small shop, tea rooms and salad bar on the farm. Washing machine, drying space and also use of freezer. Visitors are welcome to watch milking etc. Exclusive information on local walks and drives, etc., available. Telephone kiosk. Tourist Board registered. Long SAE, please, or stamps. **Mrs Rachel Roskilly, Tregellast Barton, St. Keverne, Helston TR12 6NX (Tel & Fax: 01326 280479).**

TRURO near. Mr Chris Warner, The Old Barn, Lower Tresithick Farm, Carnon Downs, Near Truro TR3 6JW (Truro [01872] 863687). Sleeps 4. Livery yard. The Old Barn now converted to a self-contained cottage with its own garden can accommodate four people. Simple but comfortable; full of character with exposed beams in the upstairs open-plan lounge, which also has one double bed sleeping area, colour TV, stable door onto small balcony overlooking one of the stable yards. Downstairs has a bathroom; washing machine; one bedroom with bunk beds; dining room-cum-kitchen which is large and homely with electric cooker, fridge/freezer, microwave and £1 coin meter. Linen supplied. Car not essential but parking available. Lower Tresithick is a small livery yard tucked away in a little valley above the creeks of the Fal Estuary. A long, bumpy lane leads only to the farm so peace and privacy are assured, although local shops and the main Truro/Falmouth road are reached by 10 minutes' walk. Local creek and boatyard are 20 minutes' walk away. Lots of space for children to play in surrounding woods and fields. Ducks, geese, chickens, pony, etc in residence. Available all year. SAE for terms.

TRURO near. Mrs George, Nanteague Farm, Marazanvose, Near Truro (01872 540351). Two self catering cottages set in 130 acres of beef farmland on the A30, 10 minutes from Truro and the coast. There is a cottage with kitchen, lounge, diner downstairs and en suite family bedroom will sleep two/four. Also we have a five room apartment with kitchen and lounge, two family bedrooms (one en suite), separate bathroom; will sleep four/eight. Facilities include outdoor solar heated pool; nine hole golf course; a two acre lake for coarse fishing (also canoes and rowing boats), a fly fishing pond; clay pigeon shooting by arrangement. Price, seasonally adjusted, from £195 per week.

WADEBRIDGE. Down Below. Luxury converted barn with large garden, ample parking space. Situated in its own grounds on 140 acre dairy farm in the centre of beautiful peaceful hamlet of Trewethern. Only four miles from the lovely beaches at Rock, Polzeath, Daymer Bay and Port Isaac, ideal for surfing, fishing safe bathing and golf. Two local pubs one mile either side with excellent food. Also village stores and Post Office, lovely walk to both and 15th century church of St. Kew. Furnished to a very high standard, accommodation comprises very large lounge featuring open fire with millstone hearth, colour TV and video. Fully equipped kitchen/diner including fridge, electric cooker, toaster and microwave. Three large bedrooms; two twin-bedded, one double. All bedding supplied. Electric heaters in all rooms. Shower room, separate toilet. Suitable for six people plus baby. Cot and high chair available. 50p slot meter. Laundry room available with automatic washing machine and tumble dryer. Linen on request. Pets by arrangement only; please enquire. Friday to Friday bookings. Available all year. SAE for prompt reply. Details from **Mrs V. Davey, Carns Farm, Trewethern, Amble, Wadebridge PL27 6EB (01208 880398).**

WADEBRIDGE/BODIEVE. Sleeps 6 plus cot. 300 year old farmhouse, converted in 1990, surrounded by sunny gardens, ample parking space in front of house in quiet country crescent. Only three miles from the sandy beaches at Rock and Daymer Bay, the surfing beach at Polzeath, close to the ancient fishing harbour of Padstow. Ideal for surfing, safe bathing, walking, fishing, sailing, golf, cycling (cycle hire in Wadebridge). The excellent shops, pubs, markets at Wadebridge are half a mile away. Wadebridge Leisure Centre with its brand new indoor swimming pool is only a five minute walk. The house comprises lounge with wood/coal burner in fireplace, colour TV, comfortable sofa bed (double). Large, cosy, well equipped kitchen/diner with fridge, electric cooker, microwave, double aspect windows; laundry room with automatic washing machine, tumble dryer, fridge/freezer. Three bedrooms — large master bedroom (double aspect windows) with king size bed and vanity unit, one twin bedroom and a bedroom with bunk beds (brand new beds, mattresses and bedding). Linen and towels on request at extra charge. Bathroom, shower, toilet. Night storage heaters. Pets by arrangement. Available all year. Terms from £120 to £350 per week (including electricity and cleaning). Saturday to Saturday bookings. Ring or write for further details. **Mr and Mrs Peter Simpson, 32 Wolsey Road, East Molesey, Surrey KT8 9EN (0181-979 2433).**

CUMBRIA — including "The Lakes"

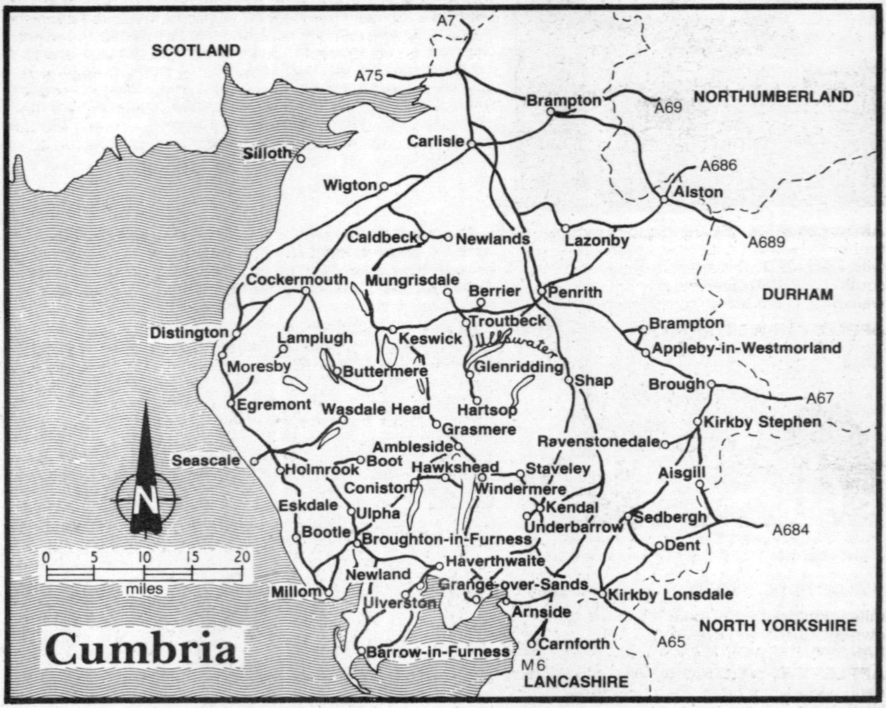

AMBLESIDE. Peter and Anne Hart, Bracken Fell Cottage, Outgate, Ambleside LA22 0NH (015394 36289). Sleeps 2/4. Bracken Fell Cottage is situated in beautiful open countryside between Ambleside and Hawkshead in the picturesque hamlet of Outgate. The two bedroomed accommodation has central heating and is immaculately furnished. Fully equipped kitchen. Linen and electricity included. Ideally positioned for exploring the Lake District. All major outdoor activities catered for nearby. Ample parking. Patio area and two acres of gardens. Open all year. Terms from £135 per week. Sorry, no pets or children under eight years. Bed and Breakfast accommodation also available (two crowns Commended). Non smoking. Write or phone for brochure and tariff.

Bracken Fell

AMBLESIDE. Sally and Anthony Marsden, Betty Fold, Hawkshead Hill, Ambleside LA22 0PS (Hawkshead [015394] 36611). 🔑🔑🔑 *Approved.* Properties sleep 4. Betty Fold is a large country house in its own spacious grounds with magnificent views and set in the heart of the Lake District National Park. The quaint village of Hawkshead is nearby and Coniston and Ambleside are within four miles; the beauty spot of Tarn Hows is 20 minutes' walk away. As well as being a Guest House, Betty Fold offers self catering accommodation for up to four persons; there is "Garden Cottage" in our grounds and a flat which is part of the main house. All accommodation is centrally heated and facilities such as linen, colour TV and cots are provided, also heating, power and lighting. Pets welcome. Terms approximately £240 to £360 per week, in main season. Special Packages from November to Easter. Dinner available in Guest House. See also advertisement in BOARD SECTION of this guide. Tourist Board registered.

AMBLESIDE. Mrs J.R. Benson, Tock How Farm, High Wray, Ambleside (015394 36481). Lakeland Cottage, once owned by Beatrix Potter, with oak beams and feature stone staircase. Set in idyllic surroundings with wonderful views of the tranquil Blelham Tarn nestled at the foot of the adjacent meadows. The accommodation consists of one double and two twin-bedded rooms, all linen provided. Large comfortable lounge with colour TV, video and Sky TV. Fitted kitchen with microwave, fridge/freezer, automatic washing machine, tumble dryer and electric cooker. Storage heating. The cottage has recently been refurbished to a very high standard. Open all year. Telephone for full details. Bed and Breakfast accommodation also available at the farmhouse.

AMBLESIDE. Mr Evans, Ramsteads Coppice, Outgate, Ambleside LA22 0NH (015394 36583). Six timber lodges of varied size and design set in 15 acres of mixed woodland with wild flowers, birds and native wild animals. There are also 11 acres of rough hill pasture with views of the surrounding fells. Three miles south west of Ambleside, it is an ideal centre for walkers, naturalists and country lovers. No pets. Children welcome. Open March to November.

APPLEBY-IN-WESTMORLAND near. Milburn Grange, Appleby-in-Westmorland CA16 6DR (Tel & Fax: 017683 61867; Vodaphone 0836 547130). 🔑🔑🔑🔑 *Commended.* **Sleeps 2/8.** Milburn Grange is a tiny hamlet nestling at the foot of the Pennines enjoying extensive views over Lakeland hills and Pennines. Six quality cottages (three beamed) equipped to highest standards set within two acres. All have colour TV, microwaves, all except smallest have washing machines, large cottages have dishwashers. Drying facilities available. All cottages have electric central heating. Linen included. Cots and high chairs available. Safe children's play area, picnic tables, barbecue. Milk may be ordered for arrival. HOME COOKING AVAILABLE. Shop, Post Office, garage close by, public house within walking distance. Well behaved pets accepted. Two other cottages available in nearby idyllic villages. Excellent walking/touring base for couples and families. Ullswater 11 miles, children's fun park 11 miles, Appleby five miles — swimming, golf, fishing, castle etc. Resident owners. BABYSITTING AVAILABLE. TOURIST BOARD MEMBERS. OPEN ALL YEAR — OFF SEASON BARGAIN BREAKS. TERMS from £80 to £350. SAE **Mrs M.J. Burke.**

APPLEBY-IN-WESTMORLAND near. "Jubilee Cottage". Sleeps 5/6. 18th century cottage, fully equipped except linen. Two bedrooms (sleep five plus small child). Bathroom, lounge with colour TV and kitchen/diner with electric cooker, automatic washing machine, fridge, iron, etc. Economy 7 storage heater. Carpeted throughout. Situated between North Lakes and the Pennines. Car essential, off road parking for two cars in front of cottage. Open March to November. Well behaved pets welcome. Terms £125 to £160 inclusive of all electricity. **Miss L.I. Basten, Daymer Cottage, Lee, Near Ilfracombe, Devon (01271 863769).**

BRAMPTON. Dorothy Potts, Chapel House Farm, Talkin, Brampton CA8 1LP (01228 70535). 🔑🔑🔑 *Approved.* **Sleeps 6.** Chapel House is a dairy farm within easy walking distance of the village of Talkin. The self catering property adjoins the farmhouse and comprises one double and one family room with cot available, sleeps five. Colour TV, electricity on meter, coal fire if necessary. Large garden with garden furniture and barbecue. Near Talkin Tarn for fishing, boating and wind surfing, Gelt Woods for beautiful walks and one mile from Brampton golf course. Ideal for touring Lakes, Scotland, Hadrian's Wall and North East Coast resorts. From £140 to £220 per week.

CARLISLE. Mrs J.T. James, Midtodhills Farm, Roadhead, Carlisle CA6 6PF (016977 48213). Up to 🔑🔑🔑🔑 *Highly Commended.* **Working farm.** Situated overlooking beautiful Lyne Valley on the Cumbria/Scottish border. On a traditional working farm guests are welcome to join in and learn about life on a farm, and may also enjoy guided walks. We are ideally situated for touring Hadrian's Wall, Kielder, Carlisle, Gretna and Lakes. Good fishing and walking area. **Arch View** sleeps eight, new sandstone barn conversion comprising kitchen/diner, shower room, lounge, twin bedroom; first floor two double rooms with vanity units, two single bedrooms and bathroom. **Riggfoot** sleeps four/five, detached cottage, open plan kitchen/lounge, log fire; one double room with four-poster bed, one twin bedroom; bathroom. Properties have dishwasher, microwave, fridge, cooker, washer/dryer, colour TV, video, radio. Storage heaters. Garden with barbecue and furniture. Prices from £120 per week. Use of swimming pool May to September.

See also Colour Display Advertisement **CARLISLE. Mrs Ivinson (FHG), Green View, Welton, Near Dalston, Carlisle CA5 7ES (016974 76230; Fax: 016974 76523). 🔑🔑🔑🔑 & 🔑🔑🔑🔑🔑 up to** *Highly Commended.* **Properties sleep 2/7.** Three superb Scandinavian pine lodges, surprisingly spacious, two 17th century oak beamed cottages, one with wood burning stove, also delightful pine panelled converted chapel for two. Tiny picturesque rural hamlet, unspoilt open views to Caldbeck Fells three miles away. Every home comfort provided for a relaxing country holiday in peaceful surroundings. Own gardens. All properties have shower/bath, colour TV, microwave, telephone, laundry, central heating, linen and towels. Second WC in three-bedroomed properties. Within half an hour's drive of Keswick, Lake Ullswater or Gretna Green. Golf five miles. Dogs permitted. Open all year. Ideal for an off season break, warm for your arrival. Resident owners. Weekly terms £135 to £440. Car essential. Accommodation is suitable for accompanied disabled visitors.

CARLISLE. Mrs Georgina Elwen, New Pallyards, Hethersgill, Carlisle CA6 6HZ (Nicholforest [01228] 577308). 🔑🔑🔑🔑 *Commended.* **Working farm, join in.** GOLD AWARD WINNER. Filmed for BBC TV. Relax and see beautiful North Cumbria and the Borders. A warm welcome awaits you on our 65 acre livestock farm tucked away in the Cumbrian countryside, yet easily accessible from M6 Junction 44. In addition to the surrounding attractions there is plenty to enjoy, including hillside walking, peaceful forests, ponies and sea trout/salmon fishing — or just nestle down and relax with nature. One comfortable well-equipped bungalow, 3/4 bedrooms. Two lovely, pleasant cottages on a working farm, 1/2 bedrooms. Terms from £80 to £295 weekly. Also Award Winning Bed and Breakfast and Half Board. HWFH, ETB, FHB.

COCKERMOUTH. Mrs J. Hope, Cornhow Farm, Loweswater, Cockermouth CA13 9UX (Lorton [01900] 85200). Working farm. Sleeps 8. Ideal for a family holiday, spacious, fully modernised house adjoining an 18th-century farmhouse on a 250-acre dairy and stock-rearing farm. Situated in the beautiful Loweswater Valley it is well-placed for all country activities and central for the coast and lakes (Crummock half-a-mile). Fully equipped for eight people, the house is quiet and comfortable and accommodation comprises four double bedrooms; two bathrooms, two toilets; sittingroom. Electric cooking facilities and solid fuel heating. Everything supplied for the ease and enjoyment of your holiday. Private fishing. Children welcome and they may bring their pets. Open all year, a car is essential and there is parking. Three miles from shops. Weekly terms £160 to £260 (inclusive of electricity). No linen supplied. Further details on request with SAE, please.

CONISTON (Lake District). Mrs M. Wilkinson, Station House and Cottage, Torver, Coniston LA21 8AZ (015394 41392). Sleeps 2. Detached property in half an acre of garden. Accommodates two people. Warm accommodation. En-suite facilities. Private parking. Low and high level walks. Coniston two miles, Lake walk 20 minutes. Dining facilities in the quiet village of Torver. Sorry, no smokers. Regret no pets. Registered with SLT Board. Rents from £120 to £190. Cheap rates off season. Open all year. Telephone or write (SAE, please) for full details.

CONISTON. Hanson Ground, Coniston. Sleeps 4. Hanson Ground is situated at the northern end of the road running along the eastern shore of Coniston Lake, two miles from Coniston Village. Set high up amidst the fields with Grizedale Forest behind, it occupies the first floor of a barn on the small agricultural holding of Knipe Ground, standing adjacent to the 16th century farmhouse. Though secluded it is ideal for exploring Lakeland. Two bedrooms, one with twin beds, one with bunk beds, cot; bathroom with toilet; sitting/diningroom with balcony overlooking lake; electric kitchen. No linen supplied. Sorry, not suitable for disabled guests. Terms from £100 to £160. Pets £20. SAE to **Mrs Mary Dutton, Knipe Ground, Coniston LA21 8AE (015394 41221).**

CONISTON. Mr E. Usher, Dixon House, Coniston LA21 8HQ (015394 41217). 🔑🔑🔑 *Commended.* "Graythorne" is a stone-built detached bungalow, set in its own garden, in the centre of Coniston village. It is ideally situated with only two minutes' level walk to the shops, whilst enjoying magnificent views of the Coniston fells. The lake is only a 15 minute walk away for sailing, rowing and the beautiful steam yacht Gondola. The accommodation comprises one double bedroom, one twin bedroom (all beds have continental quilts); lounge with stone fireplace, colour TV, video and radio; fully fitted kitchen; bathroom with shower; private parking. Linen provided; owner maintained. For terms/further details telephone or write for brochure.

CONISTON. Mrs D.A. Hall (FHG), Dow Crag House, Coniston LA21 8AT (015394 41558). Two bungalows to let as holiday chalets, sleeping two/six. One mile from Coniston village on A593. Resident owner. First bungalow has sittingroom, kitchen/diningroom, three bedrooms sleeping six; bathroom, separate toilet. Electric cooker, fridge/freezer. Night store heaters. Second bungalow comprises livingroom/kitchen, three bedrooms sleeping five, shower room. All equipped with continental quilts. Please bring own linen. Parking space. These holiday chalets are set in private garden with direct access to the Fells and Hills. Superb views overlooking Lake towards Grizedale Forest. Freedom, yet safe for children. Pets welcome by arrangement. Mountain walks, boating, fishing, tennis and bowls in village. Available March till November. Terms on application with SAE, please.

CONISTON. Mr and Mrs T. Holliday, High Arnside Farm, Coniston LA21 8DW (015394 32261). Working farm. Properties sleep 4/6/9. High Arnside is a well preserved and comfortable old Lakeland farmhouse, reputedly 16th century, but well equipped for holiday letting. Accommodation in four double bedrooms, one room with single bed and cot. Bathroom, toilet; sittingroom, diningroom; all electric kitchen, fully equipped except for linen. The house is open all year. Sorry, no pets allowed. Car is essential and there is parking for three or four cars. Shops three and a half miles. Terms include fuel. Also available is cottage to sleep six and chalet to sleep four. SAE, please, for terms.

CONISTON near. Mrs J. Halton, "Brookfield", Torver, Near Coniston LA21 8AY (Coniston [015394] 41328). ♀♀ *Approved/Commended.* This attractive, modern Bungalow property in quiet picturesque surroundings has a lovely outlook and extensive views of the Coniston mountains. It is completely detached and stands in its own half acre of level garden and grounds. The accommodation inside is in two entirely separate self-contained units. The holiday bungalow is spacious but compact, and is suitable for two-four persons (special rate for two persons). It contains large sitting/diningroom, kitchen, utility room, two double bedrooms, bathroom and toilet. Fully equipped except linen. Good parking space. Village inns are handy (300 yards). Coniston three miles. Available all year. Small dogs only, by arrangement. From £135 to £215 weekly. SAE for further details and terms stating number of persons and dates required. Tourist Board registered.

DUDDON VALLEY. Mrs M.E. Boyd, High Bigert Mire, Ulpha, Broughton-in-Furness LA20 6EY (01229 716493). This cosy flat, ideal for two, is situated in a hamlet on the western slopes of the Duddon Valley five miles from Broughton-in-Furness. Attached to the owner's house, it includes a living room/kitchen, a bedroom with double bed and en suite bathroom. There is an open fire for central heating, double glazing, colour TV, gas cooker, fridge. It provides a good base for walking, birdwatching or exploring the Lakes. Good views. Car essential, parking. No pets. Price inclusive of gas, electricity, coal, logs, linen and towels. Terms from £130 per week. Telephone for leaflet.

ENGLISH LAKES & EDEN VALLEY. Selection of fully furnished Apartments, Cottages and Houses situated in the Lake District and in the popular Eden Valley Villages, all within easy access of the M6 motorway. Pets by arrangement. For Brochure and further details contact **Lowther Scott-Harden, St Andrew's Churchyard, Penrith, Cumbria CA11 7YE (Penrith [01768] 64541) 24hrs.**

TEL. MRS J. HALL (019467) 23319

FISHERGROUND is a lovely traditional fell farm on the quieter, sunnier side of the Lakes. High quality self catering holidays are offered either in three custom built Scandinavian-style Pine Lodges or two traditional stone and slate cottages complete with coal fires. All have colour TV, fully equipped kitchens with microwave ovens and dishwashers, and bathrooms and quality fittings throughout. All have electric central heating which keeps them snug and comfortable on the coldest winter days. FISHERGROUND is a paradise for children and pets and there is an acre of orchard and a natural adventure pool plus an adventure playground.

We have our own station on the 7 mile Ravenglass and Eskdale Miniature Railway, and nearby are lakes, boating, walking, climbing, historic castles, forts, horse riding, coastal harbours, fishing and other attractions. Selection of good bar meals nearby (children welcome).

Brochure on request. 🔑🔑🔑🔑 Commended.

FISHERGROUND FARM ESKDALE CUMBRIA CA19 ITF

GRASMERE. 3,4 & 5 Field Foot, Broadgate, Grasmere. 🔑🔑🔑 *Approved.* **Properties sleep 4,7 & 8.**

Three terraced cottages situated down a private lane in the heart of Grasmere village bordering the River Rothay. Literally one minute from bus route and shops, they are convenient for those without their own transport. Built of traditional Lakeland stone, our fully equipped cottages stay cool in summer but are very cosy in winter. No. 3 sleeps eight, No. 4 sleeps four, No. 5 sleeps seven and has its own riverside patio. Cots, high chairs and extra camp beds available. Come to Grasmere, "the jewel of the Lakes", and enjoy a wonderful holiday. Contact **Mrs S.H. Brown, High Dale Park Farm, Satterthwaite, Ulverston LA12 8LJ (01229 860226).**

GRIZEDALE FOREST. High Dale Park Barn, High Dale Park, Satterthwaite, Ulverston LA12 8LJ.

Delightfully situated south-facing barn, newly converted, attached to owners' 17th century farmhouse, with wonderful views down secluded, quiet valley, surrounded by beautiful broadleaf woodland. Oak beams, log fires, full central heating, patio. Grizedale Visitor Centre (three miles) includes the indoor Theatre-in-the-Forest, award-winning sculpture trails, gallery and unique sculptured playground. Grizedale Forest is one of the Lake District's richest areas of wildlife. Accommodation in two self contained units, one sleeping eight, the other two plus baby; available separately or as one unit at a reduced rate. Hawkshead three miles, Beatrix Potter's home three miles. Contact: **Mrs S.H. Brown, High Dale Park Farm, High Dale Park, Satterthwaite, Ulverston LA12 8LJ (01229 860226).**

HAWESWATER. Goosemire Cottages. Lovely Lakeland self catering cottages for two to six people.

Furnished and equipped to a high standard, set in one of the Lake District's loveliest corners, the tranquil Lowther Valley lies between Haweswater and Ullswater. An ideal base for walking, fishing, bird watching, visiting historic sites or just relaxing in a beautiful and peaceful setting. Local pubs and post office/shop nearby. Log fires and central heating. Heating, electricity and bed linen included in the tariff. Open all year. Short Breaks available. Details and brochure from **Anne Frith, "Goosemire", The Mews, Bampton, Penrith CA10 2RE (01931 713245).**

Terms quoted in this publication may be subject to increase if rises in costs necessitate

HAWKSHEAD. Peter and Anne Hart, Bracken Fell Cottage, Outgate, Ambleside LA22 0NH (015394 36289). Sleeps 2/4. Bracken Fell Cottage is situated in beautiful open countryside between Ambleside and Hawkshead in the picturesque hamlet of Outgate. The two bedroomed accommodation has central heating and is immaculately furnished. Fully equipped kitchen. Linen and electricity included. Ideally equipped for exploring the Lake District. All major outdoor activities catered for nearby. Ample parking. Patio area, two acres of gardens. Open all year. Terms from £135 per week. Sorry, no pets or children under eight years. Bed and Breakfast accommodation also available. Non smoking. Write or phone for brochure and tariff.

KENDAL. Mrs M. Hoggarth, Low Hundhowe Farm, Burneside, Kendal LA8 9AB (01539 722060). ♛♛ Working farm. Recently converted wing of farmhouse situated between the villages of Stavely and Burneside, on the edge of the Lake District National Park. It is an ideal base for touring or walking; fishing available. The accommodation sleeps four in one double and one twin-bedded rooms; bathroom; large lounge with colour TV; kitchen/diner; utility room for wellies, etc. Open all year with Short Breaks available from November to March. Electricity and linen included in price. Sorry, no smokers. Dogs by arrangement. SAE for brochure and prices.

KENDAL. Mrs E. Barnes, Brackenfold, Whinfell, Kendal LA8 9EF (01539 824238). Working farm, join in. Sleeps 5. Brackenfold is a 147-acre dairy/sheep farm set in a quiet country area. There are beautiful scenic views from the farm and also a river running through the middle of the farm which is suitable for paddling and picnicking. Brackenfold is situated centrally for touring the Lake District and the Yorkshire Dales. All children are welcome and babysitting is available. Milk can be obtained from the farm. The accommodation is part of the farmhouse and has two double bedrooms, cot; bathroom, toilet; sitting/diningroom; fully equipped kitchen with electric cooker, fridge, etc. Shops four miles, sea 20. Sorry, no pets. Open March to November. SAE, please, for terms.

KENDAL. Mrs E. Bateman, High Underbrow Farm, Burneside, Kendal LA8 9AY (Kendal [01539] 721927). Working farm. Sleeps 4. The cottage, converted in 1985, adjoins the 17th century farmhouse in a sunny position with wonderful views. Ideal spot for touring the Lake District and Yorkshire Dales, with many pleasant walks around. There are two bedrooms (one with double bed, the other with two singles). Children are welcome and a cot is available. Bathroom with bath, shower, toilet and washbasin. Large livingroom/kitchen with fitted units, fridge and cooker. Electricity by £1 coin meter. Storage heaters 50p meter. Understairs store. Fitted carpets throughout. Own entrance porch. Sorry, no pets. Shops at Burneside two miles away, Kendal four miles, Windermere eight miles. Linen provided. Car essential — parking. Terms from £110 weekly. There is also a new six-berth holiday caravan to let from £110 per week.

KENDAL. The Barns, Field End, Patton, Kendal. ⚲⚲⚲⚲ *Commended.* Two detached barns converted into five spacious architect-designed houses. The Barns are situated on 200 acres of farmland, four miles north of Kendal. A quiet country area with River Mint passing through farmland and lovely views of Cumbrian Hills, many interesting local walks with the Dales Way Walk passing nearby. Fishing is available on the River. The Barns consist of four houses with four double bedrooms and one house with three double bedrooms. Each house fully centrally heated for early/late holidays; lounge with open fire, diningroom; kitchen with cooker, fridge, microwave and washer; bathroom, downstairs shower room and toilet. Many interesting features include oak beams, pine floors and patio doors. Central to Lakes and Yorkshire Dales, National Parks. Terms from £120 to £290. Electricity at cost. Pets welcome. For brochure of The Barns apply to **Mr and Mrs E.D. Robinson, 1 Field End, Patton, Kendal (Kendal [01539] 824220 or [01539] 721636).**

KESWICK near. Mrs A.M. Trafford, Bassenthwaite Hall Farm, Bassenthwaite Village, Near Keswick CA12 4QP (017687 76393). Working farm. Three immaculate cottages of charm and character, near a stream in this tranquil and pretty hamlet. Six miles north of Keswick, off A591 half a mile from village. Children spend many happy hours nearby playing on the swings in the wood whilst the ducks and hens roam freely. Lovely walks to the Lake, Skiddaw Dash Falls and surrounding hills. Excellent inn nearby serving good food. All cottages are situated around the farmyard. We have small properties for two and family properties sleeping four to 10. Large groups of up to 20 can also be catered for. Pets welcome. Terms from £75 to £525. Reduction off peak. Long weekends, cheap mid-week breaks from November to March. Also farmhouse Bed and Breakfast.

PLEASE SEND A STAMPED ADDRESSED ENVELOPE WITH ENQUIRIES

LAKE DISTRICT – KESWICK

HARNEY PEAK
PORTINSCALE
Nr. KESWICK, CUMBRIA

We offer you the very best in S/C accommodation in our spacious well-equipped apartments in the quiet village of Portinscale – overlooking Derwentwater yet only one mile from Keswick.

- Hot water and central heating included in rental.
- Ample off-street parking.
- Glorious Lake views.
- Open all year.
- Dogs welcome.
- Laundry facilities.

* Ideal for Couples – 6 flats designed and priced for two people – doubles & twins.
* Ideal for Families – Cots & highchairs free and plenty of free hot water included in rental.
* Ideal for Winter – Extremely efficient gas central heating included in the rental.
* Ideal for Disabled – one flat suitable for wheelchair access – others on the ground floor.
* Ideal for Short Breaks – Good value off season. Short Breaks available.

English Tourist Board UP TO COMMENDED

Cumbria Tourist Board MEMBER

For brochure please apply to:

Mrs J. Smith, 55 Blythwood Road, Pinner, Middlesex HA5 3QW
Tel: 0181 429 0402 or 0860 721270

GILL HEAD

Gill Head, a working Hill Farm, offers the perfect base for that relaxing holiday touring or walking in the beautiful Lake District. The self catering accommodation is of a high standard, with a beautifully furnished ground floor apartment overlooking the gardens (sleeps 4). Or stay in the new luxury bungalow with its own garden and panoramic views of Blencathra and the Northern Fells (sleeps 4/6). We are open all year including Christmas and New Year. Bed & Breakfast also available in the farmhouse. For further information contact:

J. A. Wilson, Gill Head Farm, Troutbeck, Penrith, Cumbria CA11 0ST. Telephone: 017687 79652.

Available from most bookshops, the 1995 edition of THE GOLF GUIDE covers details of every UK golf course – well over 2000 entries – for holiday or business golf. Hundreds of hotel entries offer convenient accommodation, accompanying details of the courses – the 'pro', par score, length etc.

Endorsed by The Professional Golfers' Association (PGA) and including Holiday Golf in Ireland, France, Portugal, Spain and the USA.

£8.50 from bookshops or £9.50 including postage (UK only) from FHG Publications, Abbey Mill Business Centre, Paisley PA1 1TJ.

KIRKBY LONSDALE near. Mrs M. Dixon, Harrison Farm, Whittington, Kirkby Lonsdale, Carnforth, Lancashire LA6 2NX (015242 71415). Properties sleep 2/8. Near Hutton Roof, three miles from Kirkby Lonsdale and central for touring Lake District and Yorkshire Dales. Coast walks on Hutton Roof Crag, famous lime stone pavings. Sleeps eight people, one room with double and single bed and one room with double and cot, while third bedroom has three single beds. Bathroom. Sittingroom, diningroom and kitchen. Everything supplied but linen. Parking space. Pets permitted. Other cottages available for two to eight people. Electric cooker, fridge, kettle, iron, immersion heaters and TV. Electricity and coal extra. Terms from £120 to £200. Registered with Cumbria Tourist Board. SAE brings quick reply.

KIRKOSWALD. Elaine and Colin Eade, Howscales, Kirkoswald, Penrith CA10 1JG (01768 898666: Fax; 01768 898710). ♀♀♀♀ *Highly Commended.* **Sleep 2/4.** COTTAGES FOR NON-SMOKERS. Howscales is a retired farmstead, in local red sandstone and with buildings grouped around a pretty courtyard located in a rural setting one and a half miles from Kirkoswald. Three cottages are two storey, with the lounge, dining area and kitchen on the first floor, and the bedrooms and bathroom on the ground floor. One is single storey at ground floor level, suitable for accompanied disabled guests, with two en suite double bedrooms. All cottages are furnished and equipped to a high standard. Bed linen, all towels and tablecoths are included in the tariff. Sorry, no pets. Children 12 years and over welcome. All cottages are notably warm and well insulated — making them a good choice for a holiday at any time of the year. Colour brochure available from **Elaine and Colin Eade.**

KIRKOSWALD. Crossfield Cottages with Leisure Fishing. ♀♀♀♀ *Commended.* Tranquil quality cottages overlooking small trout lakes amid Lakeland's beautiful Eden Valley countryside. Only 30 minutes' drive from Ullswater, North Pennines, Hadrian's Wall and Scottish Borders. You will find beds freshly made up for your arrival, tranquillity and freedom in your surroundings, and good coarse and game fishing at hand. Accommodation is guaranteed clean, well equipped and maintained; laundry area; pets welcome. Centrally located, good fishing and walking. Relax and escape to YOUR home in the country — why settle for less? No silly rules. Telephone or SAE for terms and full details: **Crossfield Cottages, Kirkoswald, Penrith CA10 1EU (01768 896275 (Fax available), answering machine only between 10pm and 8am; or 24 hour brochure telephone number 01768 898711 (manned most Saturdays)).**

LAMPLUGH. Nos 1 and 2 Hodyoad Cottages, Lamplugh. Hodyoad stands in its own private grounds with extensive views of the surrounding fells in peaceful, rural countryside. Midway between the beautiful Lakes of Loweswater and Ennerdale, six miles from Cockermouth and 17 from Keswick. Fell walking, boating, pony trekking, and trout fishing can all be enjoyed within a three and a half mile radius. Each cottage is fully centrally heated, and sleeps five persons in two bedrooms; cot provided, all linen supplied. The lounge has a colour TV, the kitchen has fitted units, cooker, fridge, etc, and the bathroom has shower, wash-basin, toilet and shaver point. Car essential, ample parking. The sea is eight miles distant Open all year. For further details contact: **Mrs J.A. Cook, Hodyoad House, Lamplugh, Workington CA14 4TT (01946 861338).**

LOWESWATER. Waterhead Cottage, Loweswater, Cockermouth. Sleeps 4. Charming country cottage, recently modernised, yet retaining many of its original features and charm. Seven miles from Cockermouth, 10 miles from Keswick. Self catering cottage comprising lounge with feature fireplace and colour TV; fully fitted kitchen/dining area including electric cooker, fridge and kettle. Shower room/WC. Two bedrooms. Cot and high chair available. All very comfortably furnished. Everything supplied except linen. Electricity payable by 50p coin meter. Children and pets welcome. Available all year. Weekly terms from £150 to £170. Booking forms, etc from: **R.F. Bell, Oakbank, Loweswater, Cockermouth CA13 0RR (01900 85227).**

Terms quoted in this publication may be subject to increase if rises in costs necessitate

MORESBY. Swallows Return and Owls Retreat, Moresby. 🔑🔑🔑🔑 *Highly Commended.* Sorry no smokers, no pets. Maintained with loving care by the owners who live within two minutes' walking distance, recently converted 19th century farm buildings tastefully furnished to a high standard in a courtyard setting within a rural hamlet. Two miles from Georgian Whitehaven with its antiquarian bookshop, half a mile from Rosehill Theatre and Restaurant. Easily reached: Ennerdale, Wastwater, Loweswater, Crummock and Buttermere, St. Bees with its red sandstone cliffs, Ravenglass and miniature railway, Muncaster Castle and Owl Centre. Full gas central heating, living flame gas fires, double glazing. Open all year. Each property sleeps four, cot available. Ample parking. Brochure available on request from **James and Joyce Moore, Moresby Hall Cottage, Moresby, Whitehaven CA28 6PJ (01946 64078).**

MUNGRISDALE. Copy Hill, Mungrisdale, Penrith. An 18th century farm cottage, recently renovated to a high standard featuring oak beams and open fireplace and oil fired central heating. Situated in the quiet and unspoilt village of Mungrisdale overlooking the fells, eight miles from Keswick and 10 miles from Penrith. It is an ideal base for touring the Lakes or for walking in the hills. Comprises comfortable lounge/diningroom, fully equipped kitchen, cloakroom with shower, three bedrooms (one family/double, one double and one twin), bathroom. Price from £160 to £300 weekly includes electricity, central heating, colour TV and bed linen. Ample parking. Sorry, no pets. Available all year. SAE or telephone for details. **Mrs Wilson, High Beckside, Mungrisdale, Penrith CA11 0XR (017687 79636).**

PATTERDALE. Parcey House Barn, Hartsop, Penrith CA11 0NZ (017684 82413). 🔑🔑🔑🔑 *Commended.* This small cottage is both off the beaten track and in the heart of the Lake District. Hartsop is a Conservation Area and the cottage part of a Grade II Listed former farmhouse. The village is quietly placed up a side road off the main A592 near Brotherswater. The cottage offers comfortable self catering accommodation for two in a beautiful location. It has all the usual facilities and suits best those who value peace and quiet, excellent walking and interesting wildlife. Gardeners find it especially attractive. Prices from £70 to £160 per week.

PENRITH. Rampshowe, Orton, Penrith. Working farm, join in. Sleeps 2/8. Rampshowe is a 150 acre fell farm with sheep, lambs, beef cattle and calves and a riding pony. Delightfully positioned in the peace and quiet of Birbeck Fells, with a river flowing through the fields, lovely waterfall and pool for bathing. Ideal area for birdwatchers. Local angling club. Shops, post office, pub serving snacks. Unspoilt, rural countryside, yet only five miles from M6 motorway. Accommodates eight people in three double bedrooms, cot; bathroom, toilet; colour TV, sittingroom, diningroom. All downstairs rooms and bathroom with night-store electric heaters and there is an open fire with back-boiler (wood and coal provided). Kitchen with fridge, cooker, electric kettle, toaster, vacuum cleaner, twin-tub washer etc., only linen required. Fitted carpets throughout. Pets and children welcome. Car essential, parking. Open all year. The house stands on its own, with garden and large farmyard. SAE to **Mrs M.E. Mawson, Sproat-Ghyll Farm, Orton, Penrith CA10 3SA (015396 24244).**

PENRITH. Westwood, Cliburn, Near Penrith. 🔑🔑🔑 *Commended.* **Sleep 8 and 2/4 respectively.** Comfortable modern bungalow with self contained flat in large private garden, with uninterrupted panoramic Lakeland views. Set within pleasant farmland on quiet village edge midway between Penrith and Appleby. Main Bungalow: one double-bedded, one twin-bedded, one family room with twin beds and two bunks; large lounge/diner with open fire; fully fitted kitchen; bath with shower. Flat: one double-bedded room; one double bed settee in lounge; fully fitted kitchen; bath with shower. Both kitchens have electric cooker, automatic washing machine, fridge/freezer and are extremely well equipped. Oil-fired central heating throughout — fuel and electricity included. Duvets and covers provided. Cot and high chair available, plus linen hire. Can be let as one unit for up to 12. Parking for four cars. Terms from £100 to £300 per week per unit. Short Breaks available. Contact: **Mrs J. Day, 7 Naddlegate, Burnbanks, Penrith CA10 2RL (01931 713376).**

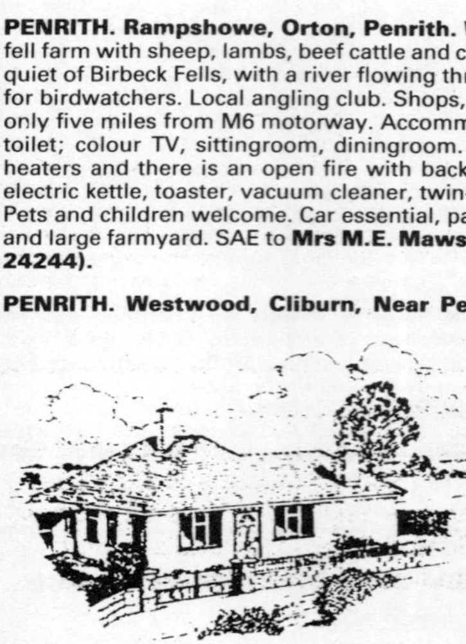

ULLSWATER. South View, Dacre, Ullswater. Working farm. Sleeps 6. The farmhouse is situated in the small village of Dacre just four miles from M6 and Penrith. There is a large walled garden and plenty of parking space. Car essential. The house is comfortable, clean and well equipped for six people including bed linen. Children welcome. Cot available on request. Well controlled pets only. One double-bedded room, two twin-bedded rooms; bathroom with toilet; diningroom, sittingroom with electric fire and colour TV. Kitchen with electric cooker and fridge. Storage heaters downstairs and in bathroom, included in rent. Other electricity on £1 meter. Weekly terms from £150. Short breaks off season. **Mrs N. Bennett, Hollins Farm, Dockray, Penrith CA11 0JY (017684 82374).**

See also Colour Display Advertisement **ULLSWATER. The Estate Office, Patterdale Hall Estate, Glenridding, Penrith CA11 0PJ (Tel & Fax: 017684 82308 24 hours). Apartments** 🔑🔑🔑🔑 *Commended;* **Cottages** 🔑🔑🔑 *Approved;* **Pine Lodges** 🔑🔑🔑 *Commended;* **Chalets** 🔑 *Commended;* **The Dairy** 🔑 *Commended;* **Bothies** (to be graded). Our range includes three very comfortable, large apartments, two stone-built cottages with open fires, two three-bedroomed pine lodges, six two-bedroomed cedar chalets, a unique, detached, converted dairy, and two converted gardeners' bothies which make ideal, low cost accommodation for two people. All set in a private 300 acre Estate between Lake Ullswater and Helvellyn and containing a working hill farm, a Victorian Waterfall Wood, private lake foreshore for guests to use for boating and fishing, and 100 acres of designated ancient woodland for you to explore. Children welcome. Dogs by appointment in some of the accommodation. Colour TV, central heating, launderette. Day time electricity metered. Linen hire available. Short Breaks and special offers available. Please phone for full brochure.

ULLSWATER. Roma Rigg, Glenridding, Penrith. 🔑🔑 *Commended.* **Sleeps 6/8.** Slate/stone bungalow in large private garden, with mountains on all sides and Lake Ullswater in front. Fishing, boating (including Lake steamer), ski-ing, fell-walking, pony trekking and sailing nearby. Good bar meals, hotels and shops within 500 yards. Well-furnished accommodation sleeping eight (six on ground floor and additional two in loft studio); cot and high chair available. Facilities for disabled. Central heating and open fire. Everything provided except linen. Pets allowed. Terms are from £180 to £375 per week, including central heating and hot water. Other electricity by coin meter. SAE please to **Mrs M. Matthews, Thornthwaite Vicarage, Keswick CA12 5RY (017687 78243).**

WASTWATER LAKE. Mrs J. Burnett, Greendale, Wasdale CA20 1EU (Wasdale [019467] 26243). Lakeland cottage-style apartments to sleep four/five people half a mile from Wastwater Lake. All apartments have one double and one twin bedded room and some have a third room with a small single bed. Bathroom with shower. Colour TV. Economy 7 electric heating and hot water. Linen supplied. Electricity included in the weekly price of £180 — £275. Fell walkers and mountaineers alike will be attracted to the impressive peaks within easy reach — Great Gable, Scafell etc. Other interests include Ravenglass Miniature Railway, Muncaster Castle. Golf, fishing and pony trekking may be enjoyed in this area. Sandy beaches eight miles away. Full details on request.

CUMBRIA – LAKELAND SPLENDOUR!

The Lake District has for long been a popular tourist destination; however, the Fells and Pennine areas are also worth exploring. The many attractions of Cumbria include the Ennerdale Forest, St. Bees Head, Langdale Pikes, Bowness-on-Solway, the market town of Alston, Lanercost Priory, Scafell Pike – England's highest mountain – and the Wordsworth country around Ambleside, Grasmere and Cockermouth.

See also Colour Display Advertisement **WINDERMERE. Birthwaite Edge Apartments.** 𝟖𝟖𝟖 *Commended.* Situated in extensive grounds in one of the most exclusive areas of Windermere, 10 minutes' walk from village and lake — the perfect all year round holiday base. Ten self catering apartments for two to six people. Resident proprietors personally ensure the highest standards of cleanliness and comfort. Swimming pool open May to September. Colour TV. Well equipped kitchens. Hot water included. Coin metered electricity for lighting, cooking and electric fires. Background central heating during winter. Duvets, linen provided. High chairs and cots extra. Ample car parking. Regret no pets. Terms from £100 to £370 per week. Brochure from **Bruce and Marsha Dodsworth, Birthwaite Edge, Birthwaite Road, Windermere LA23 1BS (015394 42861).**

WINDERMERE. Mrs R. Dodgson, Cragg Farm, Bowston, Burneside, Kendal LA8 9HH (01539 821249). *Approved.* Cragg Farm Cottage adjoins the farmhouse and is set in quiet rural surroundings with ample parking space and opportunity to walk in countryside. It is three-quarters of a mile from main Kendal to Windermere road (A591). Good position for visiting Lakes and Windermere (15 minutes away) and Kendal, a busy market town and good shopping centre, four miles. Villages of Staveley and Burneside two miles. The cottage is comfortable, clean and well equipped. One double and one twin-bedded rooms. Gas fire and central heating, electricity on 50p meter. Bed linen provided. Colour TV. Details on request.

FHG DIPLOMA WINNERS 1994

Each year we award a small number of diplomas to holiday proprietors whose services have been specially commended by our readers and the following advertisers were our FHG Diploma winners for 1994.

ENGLAND

Mrs Judith Goddard, Cherry Tree Villa, 7 Newbridge Hill, Bath, Avon
Mrs S. Briggs, High Wray Farm, High Wray, Ambleside, Cumbria
Mr & Mrs F. Cervetti, Lightwood Farmhouse, Bowland Bridge, Cumbria
Mrs Jenny Fox, Highstead Farm, Bucks Cross, Near Bideford, Devon
Mrs B. Williams, Abbots Court, Church End, Twyning, Gloucestershire
Mr & Mrs Hayward, Castlemere Hotel, 13 Shaftesbury Avenue, Blackpool
Mrs Wainwright, Homestead House, 5 Ashley Road, Medbourne, Leics
Mrs Sheila Potts, Aydon, 1 Osborne Avenue, Hexham, Northumberland
Mr & Mrs B. Joyner, Anro, 90 Kings Road, Harrogate, N. Yorks

SCOTLAND

Mr & Mrs I. Weir, Appin Holiday Homes, Appin, Argyll

WALES

Mrs J.E. Thom, The Grange, Penrose, Raglan, Gwent

DERBYSHIRE

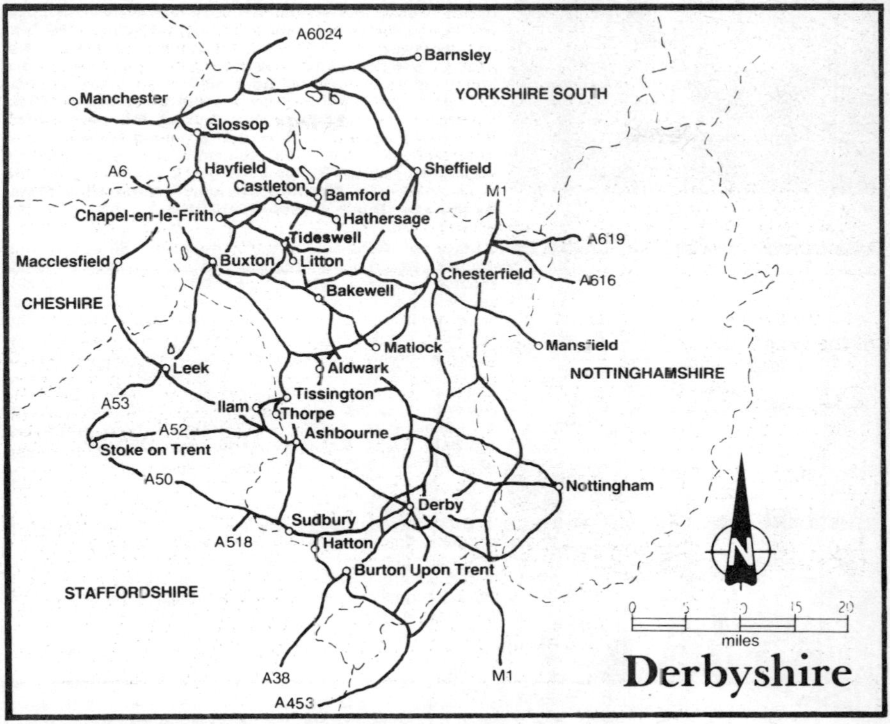

ASHBOURNE. Mrs Louie Tatlow, Ashfield Farm, Calwich, Near Ashbourne DE6 2EB (Ellastone [01335] 324279 or 324443). 🔑🔑🔑 *Approved.* **Working farm. Sleeps 5.** Ashfield Cottage is a recently renovated oak-beamed cottage on this working farm well situated for the Peak District and many other places of interest with beautiful views of Dove Valley and Weaver Hills. Accommodation is for five persons in two bedrooms (one family room and one with twin beds). Well furnished and equipped with storage heaters, colour TV, automatic washing machine, tumble dryer, fridge/freezer. Coloured bathroom suite and shower. Linen for hire. Parking space. Price and brochure on request.

ASHBOURNE. Mrs J. Audrey Gray, Hayes Farm, Biggin, Hulland Ward, Ashbourne DE6 3FJ (Ashbourne [01335] 370204). 🔑🔑🔑🔑 *Commended.* **Working farm, join in.** Relax in our peaceful valley. Superb bungalow for six on small dairy farm near Carsington Water. Panoramic views of unspoilt countryside. Join in farm activities. Accommodation includes utility room with automatic washer/tumble dryer; separate toilet. Fully fitted kitchen with microwave, split level electric cooker. Rayburn (free coal). Diningroom, lounge with colour TV. Bathroom with toilet. Two double bedrooms and one twin-bedded room. Heated throughout by storage heaters. Close to Peak District, Dovedale, Chatsworth House. Terms from £180 to £250 all year.

ASHBOURNE. 2 & 3 Trinity View, Clifton. Sleep 4/8. 🔑🔑🔑 *Commended.* These charming 300-year-old cottages, recently refurbished to the highest standards, provide every modern comfort whilst retaining their original old world cosiness and character. They are both fully equipped with lounge/diner, separate kitchens, bathrooms and two bedrooms each (a double and a twin-bedded). They have a large secure rear garden and no parking problems. The tranquil and charming village of Clifton is on the southern edge of the Peak District and is convenient for Alton Towers, Carsington Water, Chatsworth, Kedleston, etc. The cottages are situated opposite the church, overlooking the golf course to the rear, with the village pub, which serves meals, and local shop nearby. Terms £200 to £250 weekly. Leaflets available. Contact: **Mrs M.J. Davies, Clifton Hall, Clifton, Ashbourne DE6 2GL (01335 342265).**

ASHBOURNE. Dove Cottage, Church Lane, Mayfield, Ashbourne. 🔑🔑🔑 *Approved.* **Sleeps 8.** This modernised 200-year-old cottage in Mayfield village is ideally situated for shops, pubs, busy market towns, sporting facilities, lovely Dove Valley, Alton Towers, Peaks and Staffordshire Moorlands and many other places of interest. The cottage is comfortably furnished and well equipped with TV, fridge, automatic washing machine, gas central heating. The fenced garden overlooks farmland. Garage and parking. Children welcome. Pets by arrangement. Available for long and short lets, also mid-week bookings. Price and brochure on request. Further details from **Arthur Tatlow, Ashview, Ashfield Farm, Calwich, Ashbourne DE6 2EB (Ellastone [01335] 324443 or 324279).**

ASHBOURNE near. Yeldersley Hall. 🔑🔑🔑🔑 *Commended* **to** 🔑🔑🔑🔑🔑 De Luxe. We have two delightful flats (each to sleep two) in the stable block and a fabulous apartment (to sleep four) in the East Wing of our historic Georgian house, two miles from Ashbourne. This is an operational country house with horses in the stables and 12 acres of gardens and grounds to explore. Each flat is furnished and equipped to a very high standard with full heating, colour TV, microwave, payphone, etc. Use of washing machine and dryer. All linen and electricity included. Cot available. Regret no pets or children under 12 except baby in cot. Terms from £140 per week. Further details and brochure from **Mr and Mrs R. Sevier, Yeldersley Hall, Ashbourne, Derbyshire DE6 1LS (01335 343432).**

ASHBOURNE near. Tony and Linda Stoddart, Cornpark Cottage, Swinscoe, Near Ashbourne DE6 2HR (01335 345041). Adjacent to our old farmhouse, overlooking the hills of Dovedale and with extensive views over three counties, this exciting barn conversion, set beside a pond, affords privacy with easy access to all of the Derbyshire/Staffordshire attractions. Dovedale and Alton Towers 15 minutes. Converted to use all of the ground floor and part of the first, the barn sleeps four/five. All necessary modern conveniences are provided in a beamed setting. Large gardens, tennis court, barbecue all surrounded by open countryside. Well behaved pets welcome. Linen provided, electricity metered. Car essential. Open March to November, Saturday to Saturday booking. Terms from £85 to £190. Also available, static caravan (on mains services), ideal for two and Bed and Breakfast (at farmhouse) from £14.50. Phone or write for brochures.

DERBYSHIRE – PEAK DISTRICT AND DALES!

The undulating dales set against the gritstone edges of the Pennine moors give Derbyshire its scenic wealth. In the tourists' itinerary should be the prehistoric monument at Arbor Low, the canal port of Shardlow, the country parks at Elvaston and Shipley, the limestone caves at Creswell Crags and Castleton and the market towns of Ashbourne and Bakewell. For walkers this area provides many excellent opportunities.

ASHBOURNE near. Very picturesque stone holiday cottage with superb views in delightful setting by river and close to Dovedale. Ideally situated for quiet, peaceful holidays walking/touring in the Peak District with stately homes, cycling, trekking fishing and Alton Towers close by for those who seek a more active holiday. This property has been sympathetically modernised to a high standard, retaining its old beams and character. It sleeps up to six and has fitted carpets, electric cooking/heating and all modern conveniences, cots, Satellite TV, etc. Available for weekly periods at a charge of between £100 and £280 per week. Leaflet giving full information from **Mrs Y. Bailey, 4 Woodland Close, Thorpe, Ashbourne DE6 2AP (0133 529 447).**

ASHBOURNE near. Throwley Moor Farm and Throwley Cottage, Ilam, Near Ashbourne. 🔑🔑🔑🔑 **Working farm, join in. Properties sleep 7/12.** Self catering farmhouse and cottage on this beef and sheep farm near Dovedale and Manifold Valley. Approached by A52/A53 Ashbourne to Leek road, then via Calton and follow signs for Throwley and Ilam. Within easy reach of Alton Towers, cycle hire and places of historic interest. An ideal touring centre. The cottage accommodates seven people and the farmhouse 12. Ample toilet facilities; sittingrooms and diningroom (kitchen/diner in cottage). Electric cookers; fridges; washing machine and dryer. Pay phone. Pets permitted. Car essential — parking. Available all year; terms according to season. Nearest shops three miles away. Tourist Board registered. SAE, please, for further details to **Mrs M.A. Richardson, Throwley Hall Farm, Ilam, Near Ashbourne DE6 2BB (01538-308 202/243).**

ASHBOURNE near. Mount Pleasant Farm Cottage, Snelston, Near Ashbourne. Working farm. Sleeps 6. Modern self-catering farm cottage at Snelston (off the A515 Sudbury to Ashbourne road), in beautiful setting ideal for walking and touring in the Peak District. Market town of Ashbourne two miles; Alton Towers eight miles; golf course half a mile. Available all year, the cottage is fully equipped to accommodate six holidaymakers and linen is supplied. Three double bedrooms plus cot; bathroom, toilet. Large lounge with colour TV; diningroom/kitchen includes refrigerator, electric cooker. Electric heating. Pets welcome. Large garden for the children, also babysitting provided if required. Car essential, parking. Further enquiries and terms (including fuel) to **Mrs A.M. Hollingsworth, Mount Pleasant Farm, Snelston, Near Ashbourne DE6 2QJ (Ashbourne [01335] 342330).**

BELPER. Mr and Mrs C. Postles, Chevin Green Farm, Chevin Road, Belper DE56 2UN (01773 822328). One property 🔑🔑🔑 *Commended,* four properties 🔑🔑🔑🔑 *Commended.* Enjoy a holiday in one of our five attractive bungalows overlooking rolling Derbyshire countryside. The bungalows, with original beams, are fully equipped to a high standard accommodating four/six people with lounge, fully fitted kitchen, bathroom; two or three bedrooms, one has wheelchair access throughout. Ideally situated for all places of interest, Alton Towers, American Adventure, Chatsworth, Dovedale, Peak District. Terms £75 to 270. Also farmhouse Bed and Breakfast accommodation (all rooms en suite) available.

BUXTON near. Mr C. Lawrenson, Grove House, Elkstone, Longnor, Buxton SK17 0LU (01298 84223). 🔑🔑🔑 *Commended.* Stable Cottage is a delightful fully equipped, oak beamed cottage situated in small quiet village near Manifold Valley and Dovedale in the beautiful Peak District. Patio garden, parking space. Ideal for a couple plus put-u-up bed for third person. Cot available. Good walking and cycling area and convenient for National Trust properties in Derbyshire and Staffordshire. The perfect location for the true country lover. Sorry, no pets. Weekly terms from £110 to £180.

CASTLETON (Peak National Park). Sleeps 5. Seventeenth century farm cottage restored and maintained to a high standard. Central heating and double glazing. Fitted carpet in living areas, colour TV, radio. Fully equipped, including linen, for up to five persons. One double and one twin bedded room, two bathrooms, kitchen/diner, lounge. Pets by arrangement. Children welcome. Ample parking. Private terrace with view to Mam Tor — the "Shivering Mountain". Ideal for walking. Terms £150 to £290 (heating and electricity supplied at extra charge through meters). The farm lies half-mile from A625 in the beautiful Hope Valley. ETB registered. **Mrs C. Bell, Spring House Farm, Castleton S30 2WB (Hope Valley [01433] 620962).**

CUTTHORPE. Mr and Mrs D. Sutton, Cow Close Farm, Overgreen, Cutthorpe, Chesterfield S42 7BA (Chesterfield [01246] 232055). 🔑🔑🔑 A small farm dating from the 17th century, situated in the tiny hamlet of Overgreen. It lies on the B6050, four miles from Chatsworth, on the edge of the Peak. A country inn across the road serves good food and traditional ales. The two fully equipped cottages are renovations of single storey farm buildings, which surround a central courtyard and accommodate four persons. Fitted carpets, exposed timbers, central heating, separate kitchen, colour TV, garden sitting areas and ample car parking. Beds made up for your arrival; children, pets welcome. Terms from £100 to £180 per week includes heating and hot water. Brochure on request.

DOVEDALE. Mrs Beryl Howson, Hallfields Farm, Wetton, Ashbourne DE6 2AF (Alstonefield [0133-527] 282). 🔑🔑🔑🔑 *Commended.* **Properties sleep 3/5.** Recently renovated from stables, the first self-catering holiday cottage sleeps four/five, while the second cottage (suitable for the disabled) sleeps three/four. Situated in the country with panoramic views overlooking the Manifold Valley and Thor's Cave. A quarter mile from the next residence and the village of Wetton. Central heating is by storage radiators (included in the price). TV supplied. There is unlimited safe parking, an excellent choice of country pubs and inns for your evening meals, some within walking distance. Dovedale is two miles, Ashbourne, Leek and Buxton 10 miles. Open all year. Terms from £100 — £230 per week. Short stay holidays available off season. Pets and children welcome.

DOVEDALE/ASHBOURNE. Alstonefield Holiday Homes, Post Office House, Alstonefield, Ashbourne DE6 2FX (01335 310201). 🔑🔑🔑/🔑🔑🔑🔑 A choice of five properties sleeping two/six people, all situated in the quiet picturesque limestone village of Alstonefield; five times winner of the Best Kept Village award. Complete with a 13th century church, an old coaching inn and village shop. An ideal base to explore the Peak National Park situated between Dovedale and Manifold Valleys, also near the attractions of Alton Towers, Chatsworth House, etc. All accommodation recently modernised and tastefully furnished in country style to a high standard having received the Approved award by the English Tourist Board. Ideal for those Winter Breaks. Children and pets welcome. Terms from £150 to £395.

LONGNOR, Near Buxton. Mrs G.A. Lownds, Golden Green, Barrowmoor, Longnor, Near Buxton SK17 0QP (01298 83583). Sleeps 8. This stone built, double glazed farmhouse is situated two miles from Longnor Village at Barrowmoor in the centre of the Peak District National Park. Ideally placed for all types of holiday, either walking, climbing, cycling or just relaxing and enjoying the scenery. Longnor boasts three good inns, a quaint restaurant, post office, well stocked shop and a market hall craft centre. Within easy driving distance (30 minutes) of many places of interest including Alton Towers, Chatsworth House, Buxton, market towns, etc. Golden Green Farmhouse caters for every home comfort with bed linen supplied. Electricity by meter; Economy 7 heaters and immersion included in tariff. Ample parking. Terms from £130 to £350 per week. Reductions for smaller parties. Brochure sent on request.

MATLOCK. Meadow Cottage, Low Moor, Pikehall, Matlock. 🔑🔑🔑. **Working farm, join in. Sleeps 5.** This semi-detached cottage is situated on owners' 300 acre farm between four market towns in the centre of the Derbyshire Dales. Good walking area. Nature Trails half-a-mile. Many historic houses in the area including Chatsworth and Haddon Hall. The cottage has fitted carpets throughout and lawned garden with parking space. Milk and eggs may be purchased from the farm daily. Accommodation for five in two double and one single rooms, cot; bathroom, toilet; sitting/diningroom with colour TV. Kitchen has sink unit, fridge, electric cooker, kettle and water heater (£1 meter). Pets permitted. Car essential — parking. Available all year. SAE, please, for terms to **Mr W. Bunting, Low Moor, Pikehall, Matlock DE4 2PP (01335 390522).**

DEVON

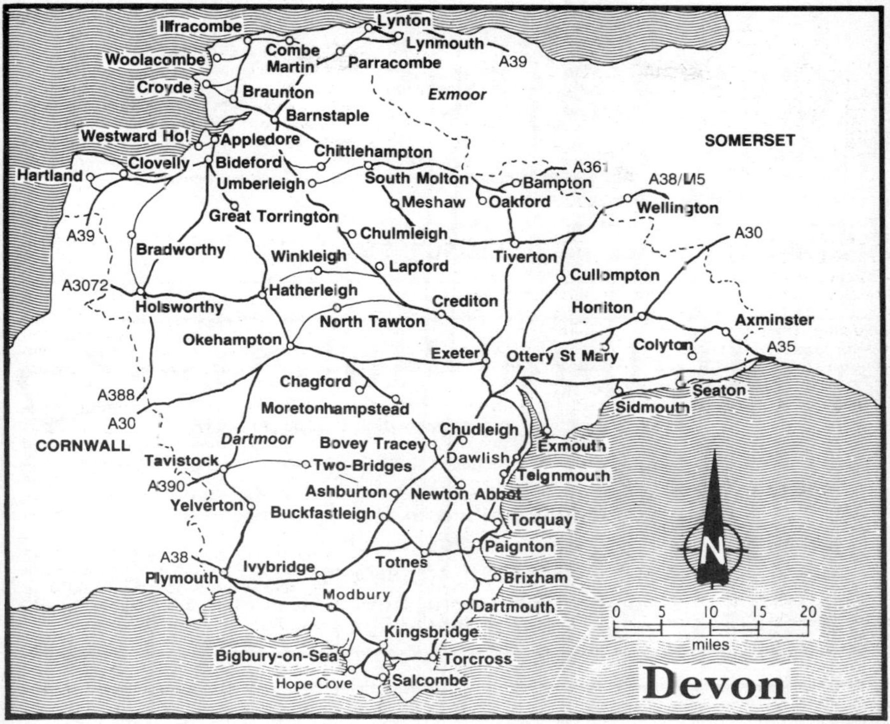

APPLEDORE. Sea Birds Cottage, Appledore. Sea edge, pretty Georgian cottage facing directly out to the open sea. Sea Birds is a spacious cottage with large lounge, colour TV; dining room with french windows onto garden; modern fitted kitchen; three double bedrooms; bathroom, second WC downstairs. Lawned garden at back overlooking the sea with garden furniture. Sea views from most rooms and the garden is magnificent; views of the open sea, boats entering the estuary, sunset, sea birds. Appledore is still a fishing village — fishing trips from the quay, restaurants by the water. Area has good cliff and coastal walks, stately homes, riding, swimming, golf, surfing, excellent beaches. Off peak heating. From £95. Other cottages available. **Ring 01237 473801** for prices and vacancies or SAE to: **F.S. Barnes, Boat Hyde, Northam, Bideford EX39 1NX.**

APPLEDORE. Mariner's Cottage, Irsha Street, Appledore. Sleeps 6. Elizabethan fisherman's cottage right at the sea edge — the high tide laps against the garden wall. Extensive open sea and estuary views of ships, lighthouses, fishing and sailing boats. The quayside, beach, ships, restaurants and fishing trips are close by. Riding, sailing, tennis, golf, sandy beaches, historic houses, beautiful coastal walks, and the Country Park are all near. Mariner's Cottage (an historic Listed building), has three bedrooms, modern bathroom, fitted kitchen with tumble dryer, dining-room and large lounge with colour TV. Children's play house. Gas central heating makes Mariner's good for winter holidays. Dog welcome. Picture shows view from back garden. From £95 per week. SAE, please, for brochure of this and other cottages to **Mrs F.A. Barnes, Boat Hyde, Northam, Bideford or telephone (Bideford [01237] 473801)** for prices and vacancies.

Key to Tourist Board Ratings

The Crown Scheme

(England, Scotland & Wales)

English Tourist Board COMMENDED

Covering hotels, motels, private hotels, guesthouses, inns, bed & breakfast, farmhouses. Every Crown classified place to stay is inspected annually. *The classification:* Listed then 1-5 Crown indicates the range of facilities and services. Higher quality standards are indicated by the terms APPROVED, COMMENDED, HIGHLY COMMENDED and DELUXE.

The Key Scheme

(also operates in Scotland using a Crown symbol)

English Tourist Board COMMENDED

Covering self-catering in cottages, bungalows, flats, houseboats, houses, chalets, etc. Every Key classified holiday home is inspected annually. *The classification:* 1-5 Key indicates the range of facilities and equipment. Higher quality standards are indicated by the terms APPROVED, COMMENDED, HIGHLY COMMENDED and DELUXE.

The Q Scheme

(England, Scotland & Wales)

Covering holiday, caravan, chalet and camping parks. Every Q rated park is inspected annually for its quality standards. The more ✓ in the Q – up to 5 – the higher the standard of what is provided.

ASHBURTON. Mrs D. Dent, Adams Hele Farm, Ashburton TQ13 7NW (01364 652525). Sleeps 6/7 plus cot. Situated in Dartmoor National Park this self catering Cottage accommodation comprises three bedrooms, large kitchen, lounge and dining area. Large conservatory with lovely views over Dart Valley. Garden. Central for exploring Dartmoor and coast. Bed linen provided. Amenities include washing machine, TV, etc. Farm stocked with cattle, sheep and ponies. Terms from £170 per week includes storage heating.

ASHBURTON. Mrs Angela Bell, Wooder Manor, Widecombe-in-the-Moor, Near Ashburton TQ13 7TR (013642 391 or 01364 621391 from July 1995). *Commended.* Modernised granite cottages and converted coach house, on 108 acre working family farm nestled in the picturesque valley of Widecombe, surrounded by unspoilt woodland, moors and granite tors. Half a mile from village with post office, general stores, inn with dining room, church and National Trust Information Centre. Excellent centre for touring Devon with a variety of places to visit and exploring Dartmoor by foot or on horseback. Accommodation is clean and well equipped with colour TV, central heating, laundry room. Children welcome. Large gardens and courtyard for easy parking. Open all year, so take advantage of off-season reduced rates. Weekend lets also available. One property suitable for disabled visitors. Brochure available.

AXMINSTER. Cider Room Cottage, Hasland Farm, Membury, Axminster. Sleeps 4. This delightfully converted, thatched cider barn, with exposed beams, adjoins main farmhouse and overlooks the outstanding beauty of the orchards, pools and pastureland, and is ideally situated for touring Devon, Dorset and Somerset. Bathing, golf and tennis at Lyme Regis and many places of interest locally, including Wildlife Park, Donkey Sanctuary and Forde Abbey. Membury Village, with its post office and stores, trout farm, church and swimming pool is one mile away. The accommodation is of the highest standard with the emphasis on comfort. Two double rooms, cot if required; shower room and toilet; sitting/diningroom with colour TV; kitchen with electric cooker, microwave, fridge, kettle and iron. Linen supplied if required. Pets by arrangement. Car essential. Open all year. Terms from £115. SAE, please to **Mrs Pat Steele, Hasland Farm, Membury, Axminster EX13 7JF (01404 881558).**

BARNSTAPLE. Mrs R. Gard, Brinscombe Farm, Arlington, Barnstaple EX31 4SW (Shirwell [01271] 850529). Working farm. Sleeps 6. An 18th century farmhouse situated on a 180-acre hill farm in a peaceful location approached by a concrete drive. It is ideally situated for touring the Exmoor National Park and North Devon beaches. Wistland Pond Reservoir for fishing two miles; Arlington Court, a National Trust property, one and a half miles; Barnstaple with its Leisure Centre nine miles. Nearest beach Combe Martin, six miles. The large self-contained wing of the farmhouse comprises one family bedroom and one double room, both with washbasins, diningroom, sittingroom with colour TV and electric fire, bathroom and fitted kitchen. Fully carpeted, night storage heaters, large lawn. No linen supplied. Shops three miles. Car essential, ample parking. Open end April to end September. No pets. Personally cleaned between each booking. A comfortable stay and a warm welcome guaranteed. From £130 to £220. SAE please.

See also Colour Display Advertisement **BARNSTAPLE. North Devon Holiday Homes, 19 Cross Street, Barnstaple EX31 1BD (01271 76322 24-hour brochure service).** With our Free Colour Guide and unbiased recommendation and booking service, we can spoil you for choice in the beautiful unspoilt region around Exmoor and the wide sandy beaches and coves of Devon's National Trust Coast. Over 500 selected properties including thatched cottages, working farms, beachside bungalows with swimming pools, luxury manor houses, etc. From only £67 per week in Spring and Autumn. First class value assured.

PLEASE SEND A STAMPED ADDRESSED ENVELOPE WITH ENQUIRIES

BARNSTAPLE. Mrs Lawrence, The Church House, Charles, Barnstaple EX32 7PX (01598 710326).

Charles, a hamlet in peaceful North Devon farmland, is within easy driving distance of Exmoor and the best beaches in the West Country for riding, fishing, swimming, walking. A safe haven from traffic and crowds, the house has changed from vicarage to schoolhouse, and is now a charming home for you to enjoy. Ideal for family (of four) or friends, it stands sheltered and secluded close by an 11th century church. One double bedroom; bathroom; two single bedrooms; living-room; well equipped kitchen. Hall, stairs, landing shared with owners. Private garden. Car parking. Shops 20 minutes. A361 15 minutes, M5 45 minutes. Further details on request.

BARNSTAPLE. Mr and Mrs C.L. Hartnoll, Little Bray House, Brayford, Barnstaple EX32 7QG (Brayford [01598] 710295). Properties sleep 2/7.

Situated nine miles east of Barnstaple, Little Bray House is ideally placed for day trips to East Devon, Somerset and Cornwall, the lovely sandy surfing beaches at Saunton Sands and Woolacombe, and many places of interest both coastal and inland. Exmoor has much charm. Lovely walks abound, and there is a large garden with lawn and woodland, small animals, fun for children. Indoor badminton and ping-pong rooms. The accommodation is in three cottages sleeping from four to seven people and a flatlet which sleeps two, all self-contained and fully furnished with well-equipped kitchens and colour TV. Cot and high chair available on request. Bring own linen and towels. Well behaved dogs allowed, on lead. Terms range from £80 to £225 per week, depending on season. Telephone or write for brochure.

BARNSTAPLE. Huish Farm, Kings Heaton, Marwood, Barnstaple. Working farm. Sleeps 10. This 17th century farmhouse, in a quiet, yet not secluded position is three-and-a-half miles from market town of Barnstaple and five miles from Saunton. A ten-minute walk takes you to Marwood Hill Gardens with lakes (open to public from March to October). Four spacious double bedrooms (one room contains four beds). Bathroom, separate toilet; sittingroom; large kitchen with all essentials. Colour TV. Cot and high chair provided. Plenty of room for children to play. Ten people accommodated. Electricity included in price. No linen supplied. Pets permitted. Car essential, parking. Open all year. Terms from £130 to £300 weekly. Out of season from £20. Fresh milk available daily. Apply to **Mrs. V.M. Chugg, Valley View, Marwood, Barnstaple EX31 4EA (Barnstaple [01271] 43458).**

BARNSTAPLE near. Mrs Veronica Ley, "Stock Farm", Brayford, Barnstaple EX32 7QQ (01598 710498). Working farm, join in. Sleeps 7. This completely self-contained part of the farmhouse is beautifully situated on 280-acre beef and sheep farm in beautiful countryside with lovely views over the moors and along the Bray Valley. Ideal for touring and walking; two miles from Exmoor and 10 miles from the sea. Visitors are welcome to join in the working life of the farm. The house has two bedrooms, sleeping seven, with sofa bed. All fully carpeted. Fitted electric kitchen/diner with microwave and washer/dryer. The oak beamed lounge is full of character. Colour TV. Own garden, lawn and drying area. Adjacent patio and barbecue area. Personally cleaned; linen/bedding and towels provided. Cot and babysitting. Separate play area where children can play safely with our own family. Pets under supervision. Terms from £100 to £240. Excellent sporting facilities in the area including windsurfing, fishing, riding and golf. SAE please.

FUN FOR ALL THE FAMILY IN DEVON

Arlington Court, near Barnstaple; Bygones Victoria Street, Torquay; Clovelly Village, near Bideford; Dartington Crystal, Great Torrington; Dartmoor Wildlife Park, Sparkwell; English Riviera Leisure Centre, Torquay; Exeter Maritime Museum; Exmoor Bird Gardens, Bratton Fleming; Kents Cavern Show Caves, Torquay; Babbacombe Model Village, Torquay; National Shire Horse Centre, Yealmpton; Paignton Zoo and Botanical Gardens; Plymouth Dome; Plym Valley Railway Steam Centre, Plymouth; Woodland Leisure Park, Blackawton.

BIDEFORD. Webbery Cottages, Webbery, Alverdiscott, Bideford. Once the home farm and stables of the old Manor of Webbery, our architect-designed conversions of farm buildings offer a high degree of modern comfort and luxury. Set in a peaceful walled garden at centre of private five acre grounds with views extending to Exmoor, Bideford Bay and Lundy Isle. Two all-electric, two-bedroomed cottages. One centrally heated three bedroomed cottage. All tastefully furnished. Colour TV, fitted carpets. Fridge, toaster, coffee maker, etc. Separate laundry room. Ample parking. Quietly situated between market towns of Bideford and Barnstaple Beaches, birdwatching, fishing, golf, riding, sailing, surfing and walks nearby. Brochure with pleasure. **Mrs B.M. Wilson, Webbery Garden Cottage, Webbery, Alverdiscott, Bideford EX39 4PU (Newton Tracey [01271] 858430).**

BIDEFORD. The Pines at Eastleigh, Near Bideford EX39 4PA (Tel & Fax: 01271 860561). Set in the grounds of a small country house hotel; seven acres of gardens, orchard and fields with glorious views to the sea at Hartland Point and Lundy Island. VINE COTTAGE: sleeps four plus cot in two bedrooms, bathroom, shower room, lounge/kitchen/diner with patio doors to garden. Woodburning stove. £137 to £310 per week. TREETOPS: sleeps two plus cot. Bedroom, shower room, lounge/kitchen/diner with super views. Patio, raised garden. £110 to £229 per week. Cooker, microwave, fridge, colour TV, direct-dial telephones (baby listening to hotel). Bed linen, towels, electricity included. Laundry room. Central heating extra.

BIGBURY near. The Bungalow, Buckleys Harraton, Modbury. Properties sleep 6/8. Small bungalow with garden situated on Plymouth/Kingsbridge main road near Modbury, five miles from sandy beaches of Bigbury Bay. Within easy reach of Cornwall (15 miles) and Dartmoor (10 miles). Sleeps six. Saturday bookings. Also main part of Bennicke Farmhouse (self contained) in peaceful situation reached by lane quarter of a mile from road. Large garden. Three bedrooms sleeping eight. Sunday bookings. Both have mains water, electricity and colour TV. Well behaved dogs allowed. Linen is not provided. SAE for details. Terms from £155 to £215 weekly. No VAT. **Miss C.M. Hodder, Bennicke Farm, Modbury, Ivybridge PL21 0SU (01548 830265).**

BRAUNTON. Mrs J.M. Barnes, Denham Farm Holidays, North Buckland, Braunton EX33 1HY (Tel & Fax: 01271 890297). 🔑🔑🔑/🔑🔑🔑🔑 *Commended.* These newly converted self-catering units are situated in a small hamlet only two miles from the golden sands of Woolacombe and Putsborough and the quaint old village of Croyde. An ideal touring base for walking, surfing, golfing and riding. One unit sleeps eight in four bedrooms; lounge with colour TV, inglenook fireplace with woodburner. The other sleeps four in one family bedroom; downstairs room with kitchen/diner and lounge area with colour TV. Both units have lovely kitchens with electric cooker, fridge, microwave. Large unit has two bathrooms, small unit has one. Barbecue area, large lawn with swings/trampoline for children. Indoor games room. Evening meals may be obtained (by arrangement) from the licensed farmhouse. Pets taken. Ample parking and some garage space. Send for colour brochure.

BRAYFORD. Mrs Shirley Barrow, Lower Hall Farm, Brayford, Barnstaple EX32 7QN (01598 710569). Working farm, join in. A peaceful scenic setting on Exmoor boundary of a 200 acre mainly dairy farm, some beef cattle and sheep. Guests are welcome to watch activities and walk on the farm. Ideal for walks — the "Tarka Trail" goes through the farm. Small river for fishing. Beaches half-hour drive. Ideal for touring local beauty spots — Tarr Steps, Dunkery, Doone Valley, etc. Market town of South Molton seven miles, Barnstaple nine miles. End of farmhouse cottage sleeps four/six in double bedroom plus cot and bunk-bedded room leading to second double, all with superb views. Comfortable lounge with stone fireplace, woodburner and colour TV. Fitted kitchen/diner. Bathroom/WC. Babysitting by arrangement. Fresh milk. Walled garden used by family, ideal for the children; tennis court, also suitable for other games. No pets. Electricity, bed linen and wood inclusive. Terms from £100 to £240 weekly. Reduced rates for two persons out of season.

BUDLEIGH SALTERTON. Lemprice Farm, Yettington, Budleigh Salterton EX9 7BW (01395 567 037; Fax: (on request) 01395 567 585). 🔑🔑🔑/🔑🔑🔑🔑 *Commended/Highly Commended.* Five south-facing self catering barn cottages, each with own patio garden. Exceptionally spacious conversion with exposed beams. Outstanding views over small lake with abundant wildlife (also home of rare Barn Owl). Peaceful rolling countryside. Close to moor and sea; ideal for walking. ETB Disabled Accessible Accommodation Grade 2/3. Suitable for small conferences/groups. OS Map Ref: SY055856. Bed and Breakfast also available at the Farmhouse.

CHULMLEIGH near. Mrs M.E. Gay, Manor Farm, Riddlecombe, Chulmleigh EX18 7NX (01769 520335). 🔑🔑🔑🔑 *Commended.* Working dairy and sheep farm. Three bedrooms sleeping seven/eight plus baby. You are assured of a friendly welcome at our lovely farmhouse which has a self catering wing with glorious views and large garden. Children can bottlefeed baby lambs, watch the milking, see baby calves, make friends with "Poppy" our tame sheep, collect eggs, etc. Superb adjoining games room with endless range of toys, games, etc for all ages including ride-on toys, snooker, table tennis, piano, Fisher Price kitchen, play cottage, swing, etc. Bed linen provided, washer/dryer, fridge freezer, microwave. Woodland walks nearby. Central heating and lovely stone fireplace with gas woodburner. Handy for sea and moors. Terms from £150 per week.

CHULMLEIGH near. Sandra Gay, Northcott Barton Farm, Ashreigney, Near Chulmleigh EX18 7PR (Ashreigney [01769] 520259). 🔑🔑🔑 *Commended.* Northcott Barton is a working farm set amidst green fields, wooded valleys and quiet country lanes where you can explore the farm and see the animals. The holiday wing of our lovely old farmhouse sleeps seven/nine plus cot and offers well equipped "home from home" comfort with oak beams, heating throughout and a log fire to welcome early and late season guests. Bed linen provided. Large south-facing garden. Golf, riding, fishing close by. Handy for sea/moors. Terms from £130 weekly. Farm Holiday Bureau Member.

PLEASE ENCLOSE A STAMPED ADDRESSED ENVELOPE WITH ENQUIRIES

COLYTON. Mrs R. Gould and Mrs S. Gould, Bonehayne Farm, Colyton EX13 6SG (01404 87396 or 87416). Working farm. Bonehayne Farm is situated in the beautiful Coly Valley amidst 250 acres working farmland on the banks of the River Coly. Daffodils are quite a feature in Springtime. Mallard Duck and Kingfishers too are a common sight. Trout fishing freely available and woodlands to explore. This is an annexe of the farmhouse, completely modernised and tastefully furnished, with fitted carpets, to accommodate up to six people. Master bedroom with double and bunk beds, also a twin-bedded room. Lounge with oak beams, inglenook fireplace, TV; fully centrally heated making it ideal for out of season holidays. Kitchen and diningroom with electric cooker, fridge/freezer; electricity by meter; bathroom and toilet; cot and babysitting available. Fully equipped except linen. Parking space. The sea four miles. Weekly terms on application. Caravan also available.

See also Colour Display Advertisement **COMBE MARTIN. Mr and Mrs T. Massey, Wheel Farm Country Cottages, Berrydown 12, Combe Martin EX34 0NT (01271 882100).** 🔑🔑🔑🔑 *Highly Commended.* Nestling at the head of a valley, with magnificent views across Exmoor, yet only 10 minutes from the beach. Watermill and traditional stone barns in eight acres of gardens and woodland, converted into 10 high quality cottages. Indoor heated swimming pool and sauna. Four poster beds, dishwashers, microwaves, central heating, woodburning stoves, home made meals service, shop, laundry, children's playground. Bed linen and maid service inclusive. Open March to November. Prices from £160 to £750 per week. Short Break holidays available off peak.

Compton Pool Farm, South Devon

★ Heated indoor swimming pool ★ Children's play area ★ Fishing lakes ★ Tennis court ★ Games barn ★ Sauna ★ Family holidays ★ Farm animals ★ Lots to do

E.T.B.

Nestling in a sheltered sunny valley, surrounded by red Devon hills, the nine tastefully converted, comfortably furnished stone cottages are grouped around a central courtyard and fish pond. All cottages are attractively decorated and fully equipped. The farm is kept tidy and the gardens colourful. Torquay and the sea are nearby and Dartmoor is close at hand.

JOHN & CATHY SONGER, COMPTON POOL FARM, COMPTON, DEVON TQ3 1TA.
Tel: 01803 872241 Fax: 01803 874012

SEE ALSO OUR COLOUR ADVERTISEMENT

CROYDE BAY. "Sandyholme". Sleeps 6. Chalet bungalow, comfortably furnished and carpeted. Lounge/diner, colour TV, good selection of books, maps and games. Bathroom with separate shower. Well equipped all electric kitchen including microwave, fridge, cooker, spin dryer. Situated on quiet private road, safe for children with enclosed garden, ample parking. Just five minutes through sand dunes leads to the superb sheltered bay with golden sands and rock pools. The olde world village with quaint cottages, pubs and restaurants five minutes' amble away. Set amidst National Trust protected countryside offering wonderful walks. Excellent base for touring beautiful North Devon. Sorry, no pets. Brochure on request from **Mrs J. Pearce, 59 Avonmead, Greenmeadow, Swindon, Wiltshire SN2 3NY (01793 723521).**

The information in the entries in this guide is presented by the publishers in good faith and after the signed acceptance by advertisers that they will uphold the high standards associated with FHG PUBLICATIONS LIMITED. The publishers do not accept responsibility for any inaccuracies or omissions or any results thereof. Before making final holiday arrangements readers should confirm the prices and facilities directly with advertisers.

DARTMOOR NATIONAL PARK. Mrs Susan Booty, Rogues Roost, Poundsgate, Ashburton TQ13 7PS (01364 631223). Properties sleep 4/8. Two self catering properties available. Off the beaten track, they are surrounded by open moorland and ideal for riding, walking, fishing. Within easy reach of many interesting places, Torbay 22 miles. The first property, part of a large house, sleeps eight and consists of four bedrooms, bathroom, two toilets, large sittingroom, dining room/kitchen. The second property is a bungalow for four comprising two double bedrooms, sittingroom, dining room, bathroom, separate toilet, kitchen with electric cooker. Open from May to end September. Car essential. Terms (from £130) inciude bed linen. SAE please.

ROGUES ROOST

DARTMOOR NATIONAL PARK. L.A. Astley, Summersbridge Cottage, Higher Coombe, Buckfastleigh (01364 642388). Self-catering old world, picturesque, detached country cottage situated in an idyllic spot, surrounded by woodlands, moorland, valleys and rivers. Ideal for walking, horse-riding, fishing and sightseeing. Within easy reach of Torbay and Plymouth for sea and shops. The cottage sleeps four/five, is well equipped, fully modernised, comfortable and has a "fairy-like magic". Pets allowed. Parking. Children over seven years welcome.

DARTMOUTH. Allan and Marcia Green, Gara Mill, Slapton, Kingsbridge TQ7 2RE (01803 770295). Sleep 1-7. We offer eight comfortable cedar lodges in idyllic setting on a sunny slope above the River Gara. Two bedrooms, fully equipped including colour TV. There are also two cosy self-contained flats within the 16th century mill building. Four acre site off quiet lane, sheltered and peaceful, yet convenient for Dartmouth and Kingsbridge. Children's play area, outdoor badminton court, games room, launderette. Cots available. Dogs welcome. Woodland walks on your doorstep. Two miles to beaches and spectacular coastline. Daily rates for Short Breaks out of season. From £120 to £275 per week including VAT. Free brochure.

DARTMOUTH. The Mates House, 17 Higher Street, Dartmouth. 🔑🔑🔑 *Approved.* **Sleeps 4/6.** The Mates House is a small cottage situated in the centre of town and originally built in 1628 in the reign of King Charles I. It is about 100 yards from the River Dart frontage. There is one double and one twin-bedded room and a double bed-settee in the lounge. Cot is also available. Colour television. Electric heating, cooking and fridge. Linen provided, towels on request. There are no extra charges except for electricity from October to May. Open all year from £130 per week. **Mr N.P. Jestico, The Captain's House, 18 Clarence Street, Dartmouth TQ6 9NW (Dartmouth [01803] 832133).**

DARTMOUTH near. Mrs B.S. Wall, Lower Fuge Farm, Strete, Near Dartmouth TQ6 0LL (Stoke Fleming [01803] 770541). Working farm. Sleeps 10. A holiday here at Fuge can be peaceful, with picturesque farm walks. We have a 240-acre dairy farm and are only one mile from Strete village, two miles from two pretty beaches, Blackpool and Slapton. This completely self-contained part of a farmhouse has two family and one double fully carpeted bedrooms (one bedroom has en suite facilities), sleeping 10 (cots available). Linen provided and beds ready made. Nice bathroom. Fitted electric kitchen/diner with fridge/freezer, automatic washing machine, dishwasher, microwave, tumble dryer, Kenwood Chef, high chairs. Lounge is large, fully carpeted, with three-piece suite, easy chairs, colour TV. Garden with spacious lawn for playing/sunbathing. Electricity metered. Car essential. Pets allowed by prior arrangement. Further details on request.

The Warmest WELCOME *in the West!*

FAMILY HOLIDAY PARK

Ever had too much to do?

- Stylish **DOLPHIN CLUB** & Entertainment Centre.
- Super Indoor Heated **NEPTUNE TROPICANA** Water Leisure complex - four Feature-packed Pools, Solarium, Sauna, spectator viewing.
- New **CRUISERS** adult Cocktail bar
- Children's **JOLLY ROGER** Club with Disco, Cinema & large Games Arcade.
- Short, level walk to safe sandy beach.
- Great ***Value - for - money*** prices
- **FREE** Electricity, Linen, Colour TV
- Welcome TV - great films, local attractions, and YOU having fun!
- 2 Shops · Cafe · 2 Takeaways
- Crazy Golf · Adventure Playground
- Laundrette · Baby Listening
- Hire Service with computer games
- Pets *Welcome* (at small charge)

You will at Welcome Family!

RESERVATIONS 01626 862070
DIAL a BROCHURE 01626 888323

See our main advert in the Colour Section

BEACH & BRACKEN EXMOOR HOLIDAYS

All E.T.B. Inspected

- Comfortable Self-Catering Cottages
- Farmhouse Accommodation with Food
- Short notice all season breaks
- Riding, Cycling, Shooting & Fishing

Beach & Bracken Holidays, Bratton Fleming, Barnstaple, Devon EX31 4TJ
Telephone anytime (01598) 710702

RECOMMENDED SHORT BREAK HOLIDAYS IN BRITAIN

Introduced by John Carter, TV Holiday Expert and Journalist

Specifically designed to cater for the most rapidly growing sector of the holiday market in the UK. Illustrated details of hotels offering special 'Bargain Breaks' throughout the year.

Available from newsagents and bookshops for £3.60 or direct from the publishers for £4.20 including postage, UK only.

FHG PUBLICATIONS LTD
Abbey Mill Business Centre, Seedhill,
Paisley, Renfrewshire PA1 1TJ

EXMOOR. Mrs C.M. Wright, Friendship Farm, Bratton Fleming, Barnstaple EX31 4SQ (015983 291 evenings). Working farm, join in. Friendship Bungalow is quietly situated down a short drive from the farmhouse, in its own garden, and surrounded by fields. There is ample parking space. The farm is situated 12 miles from Barnstaple and Ilfracombe, at the junction of roads B3226 and B3358, within easy reach of the beaches of Woolacombe and Combe Martin. Exmoor is literally on the doorstep. The accommodation comprises three bedrooms (sleep six), plus cot. Linen supplied. Lounge with colour TV. Well equipped kitchen/diningroom. Bathroom, laundry room, washing machine. Metered electricity. Weekly terms, low season from £95, high season £215.

HONITON. Francis Wigram, Riggles Farm, Upottery, Honiton EX14 0SP (01404 891229). Working farm. Caravans sleep 8. Three beautifully situated caravans on 450-acre dairy/arable farm, six miles from Honiton, with easy access to many lovely beaches, moors and local attractions. Visitors welcome on farm, well behaved pets accepted. Children's play area, table tennis, darts, fishing lake. Linen hire, washing machine and dryer. Caravans set in two peaceful acres near farmhouse. Each is fully equipped for two/eight people. Two separate bedrooms and spacious living areas. Own bathroom with shower, flush toilet, washbasin. Gas cooker, heater, colour TV, fridge. WCTB registered. Terms from £85 to £185 per week (10% reduction for couples, not school holidays). For brochure please write or telephone.

See also Colour Display Advertisement **ILFRACOMBE. Mrs F.M. Irwin, Smythen Farm Coastal Holiday Cottages, Sterridge Valley, Berrynarbor, Ilfracombe EX34 9TB (01271 883515).** 🔑🔑🔑🔑 *Commended* **and** *Highly Commended.* The cottages are set in an area of natural beauty, with unspoilt views over the beautiful Sterridge Valley to the sea and the coast of Wales beyond. Heated swimming pool in a suntrap enclosure, spacious lawns and gardens. Children's play area with treehouse, swings and slide; garden funiture, barbecues. Games room, laundry room and payphone. All cottages are well equipped and cleanliness guaranteed. Central for sandy beaches and for touring Exmoor; the village of Berrynarbor is just two miles away with stores, an inn and many good quality eating places. The area is well blessed with tourist attractions, also surfing, golf and pony trekking. Please telephone for brochure and terms.

ILFRACOMBE near. Mrs M. Cowell, Lower Campscott Farm, Lee, Near Ilfracombe EX34 8LS (Ilfracombe [01271] 863479). Four excellent holiday cottages on a 90 acre dairy farm with a delightful one mile walk down to the beach at Lee Bay. The cottages have been newly converted from the original farm buildings to a high standard. Two of the cottages will accommodate four people, one will accommodate up to six people and the large one will take eight/ten people; laundry room; linen included in the price. We also have a large, self-contained six-berth caravan to let, with Bed and Breakfast in the farmhouse. Children welcome but regret no pets. Terms from £129 weekly. Spring Mini Breaks (three nights) from £70.

KING'S NYMPTON. Venn Farm Cottages. 🔑🔑🔑🔑 *Commended.* **Sleep 2/6 adults; 2/4 children.** Delightful holiday cottages converted from old stone barn on small working farm set in beautiful Devon countryside. The children will love to feed the lambs and goat kids. Nearly 50 acres of rolling fields to wander over with views to Exmoor and Dartmoor. The cottages are furnished and equipped to a high standard and have patios with a picnic table and barbecue. Cottages have two or three bedrooms sleeping up to six persons plus cot. One cottage is suitable for disabled visitors. Bed linen provided. Laundry room and children's play area. Pets welcome. Weekly terms from £110 to £380. For brochure apply to: **Mrs Martin, Venn Farm, King's Nympton, Umberleigh EX37 9TR (01769 572448).**

KINGSBRIDGE. "Savernake," Thurlestone Sands, Kingsbridge. Sleeps 10. This substantial house, with a beautiful and unobstructed view of the sea and Thurlestone Rock, stands in its own grounds, adjoining the dunes and beach. The area is of outstanding beauty with wonderful cliff walks. Golf, tennis, quarter mile. Sailing and riding in area. Accommodation for 10 in three twin-bedded double rooms with washbasins; three single rooms (one with washbasin); cot; bathroom, three toilets; lounge and diningroom. Kitchen fully equipped with electric cooker, fridge, kettle and toaster. Linen not supplied. Regret no pets. SAE to **Mrs M.D. Horsfall, Century Cottage, Foxdon Hill, Wadeford, Chard, Somerset TA20 3AN (Chard [01460] 62475).**

KINGSBRIDGE. Mr and Mrs A.R. Wotton, "Andryl", Lower Farm, Beeson, Kingsbridge TQ7 2HW (01548 580527). Working farm. Sleeps 4 adults; 2 children. "Andryl" is situated in a sheltered sunny position on Lower Farm, Beeson. The flat is part of "Andryl", with bathroom, separate toilet, kitchen/diner/lounge with TV. Linen is optional. The garden has a swing, and there are other attractions for the children including chicks, ducks, goslings and a pony. The countryside around is very picturesque, and there are numerous walks including the very pleasant coastal paths. Beesands is half a mile away, and other beaches are very near; Kingsbridge is the nearest town, while Dartmouth and Salcombe are within easy reach. Babysitting can be arranged. Pets are not allowed. Car essential. Terms from £90 per week including domestic hot water. Reductions for two people in out of season weeks. SAE, please, for brochure.

KINGSBRIDGE. Mr and Mrs M.B. Turner, Cross Farm, East Allington, Kingsbridge TQ9 7RW (01548 521327). Working farm, join in. Sleeps 11/12. For a peaceful holiday in the heart of the South Hams, come to Cross Farm, a mixed working farm situated in beautiful countryside at the head of a valley only four miles from Kingsbridge, and within four to six miles radius of many lovely beaches, coves and coastal footpaths to explore. East Allington village is just a mile away with shops and character Inn. Good centre for visiting Plymouth, Torbay, Salcombe and Dartmoor. Lovely farm walks and riding facilities nearby. Rough shooting in season. Accommodation in lovely 17th century self-contained farmhouse wing to sleep 12 persons, plus two cots; also beautiful old barn — both have four bedrooms and are furnished and equipped to a high standard, including colour TV, showers, automatic washing machine, tumble dryer, fridge freezer, microwave, dishwasher. Duvets and linen provided. Heated for early/late holidays. Recreation barn with billiards, table tennis, etc, and a play area for children. Babysitting by arrangement. SAE for brochure please.

Beachdown

CHALLABOROUGH BAY, KINGSBRIDGE,
SOUTH DEVON TQ7 4JB
TEL: KINGSBRIDGE (01548) 810089

Delightful cedarwood chalets just 250 yards from a safe sandy beach. Gardens and children's play areas on peaceful 2½ acre site. Experience stunning cliff walks on South Devon's heritage coast. A haven for surfing, windsurfing and diving enthusiasts. Heated pool and golf nearby, Dartmoor National Park 30 minutes. Pets welcome. Colour brochure available. Contact Nicky Faulkner for details.

ETB 3 KEYS APPROVED

KINGSBRIDGE. Mrs M. Goodman, Mattiscombe Farm, Stokenham, Near Kingsbridge TQ7 2SR (Kingsbridge [01548] 581058). Working farm. Sleeps 8. Mattiscombe is a 150 acre mixed farm between the coastal towns of Kingsbridge and Dartmouth, close to the three mile stretch of Slapton Sands and the conservation area of Slapton Ley. Within easy reach are spectacular coastal footpaths, beautiful beaches and good fishing. The flat at Mattiscombe Farm offers comfortable accommodation for eight people. There are four bedrooms (two double, two twin) and a large lounge/diner with colour TV. The kitchen has electric cooker, microwave, fridge/freezer and washing machine and the bathroom has bath and shower. Children welcome, cot and high chair available. Sorry no pets. Open April to October. SAE please for details.

KINGSBRIDGE near. Mrs J. Tucker, Mount Folly Farm, Bigbury-on-Sea, Near Kingsbridge TQ7 4AR (Bigbury-on-Sea [01548] 810267). Working farm. Sleeps 6. A delightful family farm, situated on the coast, overlooking the sea and sandy beaches of Bigbury Bay. Farm adjoins golf course and River Avon. Lovely coastal walks. Ideal centre for South Hams and Dartmoor. The spacious wing comprises half of a farmhouse, self-contained with separate entrance. Large, comfortable lounge with sea views; colour TV. Well equipped kitchen/diner — all electric; metered. Sleeps six persons in three bedrooms — one family, one double and one single; two have washbasins and sea views; bathroom and toilet. All rooms attractively furnished. Visitors made most welcome. Nice garden, ideal for children. Cot and babysitting available. Car essential, ample parking. Available all year. Large SAE for terms please.

See also Colour Display Advertisement **LYNTON. Mr and Mrs Boyce, Dean Steep, Barbrook, Lynton EX35 6JS (01598 753272).** "Dean Steep" is peacefully situated in 17 acres in the Exmoor National Park and offers relaxation in a lovely natural setting close to the sea, just inland from Woody Bay and the Valley of Rocks. No commercialisation, just an opportunity to recapture (develop) lost pastimes e.g., photography, riding, fishing, birdwatching, exploring along National Trust walks, etc. Wildlife abounds. Each of the 12 stone-built bungalows has unsurpassed views. All are clean, warm and comfortably furnished including colour TV. Night storage heaters provide additional comfort for early or late holidays. Parking adjacent. Pets welcome in some bungalows. English and West Country Tourist Board registered. Terms from £120 to £340 per week per bungalow. Brochure with pleasure.

HELP IMPROVE BRITISH TOURIST STANDARDS

You are choosing holiday accommodation from our very popular FHG Publications. Whether it be a hotel, guest house, farmhouse or self-catering accommodation, we think you will find it hospitable, comfortable and clean, and your host and hostess friendly and helpful. Why not write and tell us about it?
As a recognition of the generally well-run and excellent holiday accommodation reviewed in our publications, we at FHG Publications Ltd. present a diploma to proprietors who receive the highest recommendation from their guests who are also readers of our Guides. If you care to write to us praising the holiday you have booked through FHG Publications Ltd. – whether this be board, self-catering accommodation, a sporting or a caravan holiday, what you say will be evaluated and the proprietors who reach our final list will be contacted.
The winning proprietor will receive an attractive framed diploma to display on his premises as recognition of a high standard of comfort, amenity and hospitality. FHG Publications Ltd. offer this diploma as a contribution towards the improvement of standards in tourist accommodation in Britain. Help your excellent host or hostess to win it!

FHG DIPLOMA

We nominate ....

....

Because

Name ....

Address ....

.... Telephone No. ....

LYNTON. Mrs Victoria Eveleigh, West Ilkerton Farm, Lynton EX35 6QA (01598 752310). ♀♀♀♀ *Commended.* **Sleeps 6.** Luxurious semi-detached cottage on a secluded 240 acre hill farm bordering beautiful open moorland of Exmoor. Ideal for walking, riding, fishing or a relaxed family farm holiday. Sheep, cattle and carthorses. Coast three miles, riding stables half a mile. Three bedrooms (two king size, one twin); two bathrooms; living/diningroom; kitchen (Rayburn, dishwasher, washer/dryer, microwave). Central heating, colour TV, video. Children, dogs and horses welcome. Baby equipment and babysitting. Visitors welcome to join in with farm life when possible. Special winter ' Exmoor Farmer Holidays" for those who would like to try their hand at farming. Emphasis on enjoyment. Terms from £150 to £380 weekly.

LYNTON/LYNMOUTH. Mrs J.A. King-Fretts, West Lyn Farm, Barbrook, Lynton EX35 6LD (Lynton [01598] 753618). Working farm. Farmhouse sleeping eight/ten and two Cottages sleeping four/five on traditional 134 acre working sheep farm, with Shire horses, ponies, vintage machinery, goats and poultry. Adjoining coastal footpath and National Trust woodland with breathtaking views across the Bristol Channel. Farmhouse has four bedrooms, one double, one family, one twin and one bunk bedded. Two bathrooms. Cottages have one double and one twin (plus one). Pine fitted kitchens (electric) and colour TVs in lounges, modern bathrooms. Full double glazing, part central heating. Ample gardens and parking. Shop/launderette within walking distance. WCTB registered. Long SAE for brochure and tariff for friendly farm holidays.

NEWTON ABBOT. Averil Corrick, Shippen and Dairy Cottages, c/o Lookweep Farm, Liverton, Newton Abbot TQ12 6HT (01626 833277). Sleep 1/5. Come and relax in the peace and tranquillity of these two delightful barn conversion cottages. Set within the Dartmoor National Park with easy access to the coast, golf, riding, walking and fishing locally. Sleep four/five, fully equipped and well furbished throughout. Own garden with beautiful views. Ample parking. Use of outdoor heated swimming pool. Children welcome, high chairs, cots and linen available. Pets also welcome. Terms from £115 to £375.

NEWTON ABBOT near. Mrs Y. Tully, Dunscombe Farm, Chudleigh, Near Newton Abbot TQ13 0BS (01626 853149). Working farm. A 150 acre mixed farm situated in a valley just under Haldon Moor, midway between Exeter and Newton Abbot. Chudleigh one and three-quarter miles away; main road A380. Ideal position for touring moors and also within easy reach of the sea, riding, climbing and golf. The accommodation comprises kitchen, large living/diningroom which has a bed settee, bathroom with washbasin, bedroom (large) with double bed and bunk beds. Separate toilet. TV in livingroom. Calor gas cooking and heating. Electricity metered. Linen available by arrangement. Children and pets welcome. Prices from £120 weekly. SAE or telephone for further details.

NORTH MOLTON. Mrs Gladys Ayre, Pitt Farm, North Molton EX36 3JR (01598 740285). ♀♀♀♀ *Commended.* **Sleeps 5/6.** Enjoy peaceful surroundings at our charming cottage set in lovely Exmoor countryside. One mile from village of North Molton with local pubs, shops, garage. Accommodation has recently been converted and is equipped to high standard throughout with night storage heating. Three bedrooms, woodburner, bath/shower room, beamed lounge with colour TV, oak fitted kitchen/diner with automatic washing machine, fridge, microwave, etc. Your own patio overlooking the valley with garden furniture and barbecue. There is a small pond nearby with ducks and geese. Our guests are welcome to explore our sheep farm and to observe seasonal activities. Cot and high chair available and babysitting by arrangement. Dog by arrangement. Linen available. Electricity by coin meter. Terms from £130 to £320 per week. Illustrated brochure on request.

DEVON – FROM COAST TO COAST

Dramatic cliffs, hidden coves, rolling surf and traditional family holiday resorts are some of the attractions which make holidaymakers return year after year to the unspoiled coastline of North Devon. There are unparalleled opportunities for watersports of all kinds, and, for the less energetic, picturesque fishing villages to explore and hidden coves for sunbathing.

The sheltered South Coast has been dubbed the "English Riviera", with an exceptionally mild climate and lively resorts offering amenities and attractions for all the family.

PAIGNTON. Mrs J. Smerdon, Glenside, Moles Cross, Marldon, Paignton TQ3 1SY (Kingskerswell [01803] 873222). Working farm. Self-contained, enjoying complete privacy, **The Maisonette,** — Glenside, having been the residence of the former owner of the property is modern and maintained to a high standard. Comprising three bedrooms, one with balcony; lounge/diningroom with colour TV. Beautifully fitted kitchen with breakfast bar, fridge freezer, washing machine. Bathroom, fully tiled and with shower. Open all year. 100 yards up the lane stands the Farm Bungalow **Glenside** Self-contained (owners' living accommodation to one side), well maintained — being the owners' winter residence. Comprises three bedrooms, large lounge/diningroom with colour TV. Kitchen with fridge, electric cooker and washing machine. Bathroom with separate shower. Both properties ideally located for Torbay, three miles, Dartmoor, 12 miles. Many interesting local walks. Farm shop for eggs, fruit, vegetables. Both properties sleep and are fully equipped for up to eight. Large lawn and field for children. Central heating available. Terms £100 low season to £240 high season — inclusive of electricity.

SEATON. Mrs Elsie Pady, Higher Cownhayne Farm, Cownhayne Lane, Colyton, Near Seaton EX13 6HD (01297 552267). Working farm. Properties sleep 4/8. Higher Cownhayne is a family working farm. Accommodation consists of three self catering farmhouse holiday apartments which are open all year round. Each apartment has all modern conveniences, with its own dining room, kitchen, bathroom and WC (no linen is provided). Caravan four-berth, fully equipped. Farm produce available, including milk from a brucellosis-free herd, eggs, etc. Babysitting can be arranged. Trout fly fishing on the farm. Leisure facilities available to visitors include badminton, squash, gymnasium, sauna, solarium, swimming pool and licensed restaurant one and a half miles from farm at Tower Seaton Down Hill. Air strip on farm for small plane enthusiasts. No pets. Terms on application, at a price families can afford to pay.

SEATON. Mrs E.P. Fox, West Ridge, Harepath Hill, Seaton EX12 2TA (Tel & Fax: 01297 22398). 🔑🔑🔑 *Commended.* West Ridge bungalow stands on elevated ground above the small coastal town of Seaton. It has one and a half acres of lawns and gardens and enjoys wide panoramic views of the beautiful Axe Estuary and the sea. Close by are Axmouth, Beer and Branscombe. The Lyme Bay area is an excellent centre for touring, walking, sailing, fishing, golf, etc. This comfortably furnished accommodation is ideally suited for three to five people. Cot can be provided. Available March to October. £125 to £315 weekly (fuel charges included). Full gas central heating; colour TV. SAE for brochure.

SLAPTON. The Old Chapel, Slapton, Near Kingsbridge. Sleeps 4/5. Attractive converted old chapel set in the heart of this ancient and picturesque village. Within walking distance of famous Slapton Ley Nature Reserve with its rich variety of birds and three-mile-long Slapton beach. Dartmouth, other South Hams resorts and Dartmoor within easy reach. Two bedrooms (one double, one twin), spacious lounge, fitted kitchen, bathroom. Secluded sunny garden, patio, barbecue. Parking. TV, telephone, washing machine, heating. Linen can be provided. Pets by arrangement. Terms from £125 to £285. Short out of season breaks available. Contact: **Mr and Mrs S. Garner (01752 336719).**

SOUTH MOLTON. Mike and Rose Courtney, West Millbrook, Twitchen, South Molton EX36 3LP (01598 740382). 🔑🔑🔑 *Approved.* **Working farm. Properties sleep 2/9.** Adjoining Exmoor. Three fully equipped bungalows and one farmhouse annexe at West Millbrook which is a 150 acre stock farm, partly situated in the Exmoor National Park. Ideally situated for touring North Devon and West Somerset and within easy reach of the Lorna Doone Valley. There are many peaceful walks and lovely scenery; North Molton village is only one mile away. The bungalows sleep two, six or nine people. All units are fully carpeted and have electric cookers, fridge-freezers, sink units, irons, TV, cots and high chairs. Linen extra charge. Car essential, parking. Central heating if required. Electricity metered. Beautiful lawns and gardens. Weekly prices from £55 — £220. Stamp for colour brochure.

SOUTH MOLTON near. Court Green, Bishop's Nympton, Near South Molton. Sleeps 6 adults; 2 children. This most attractive and comfortable cottage is on the edge of the unspoilt village of Bishop's Nympton eight miles south of Exmoor. South-facing with lovely views and large garden. Garage. This is an ideal holiday centre, being within easy reach of moors and coasts. Lovely places for walking, riding, fishing, driving and many places of interest to see. Sleeps eight, but cosy for two. Large kitchen, sitting and dining rooms. Wood-burning stove. Night storage heaters, electric fire. Four bedrooms, cot. Bathroom, shower room, two toilets. All well-equipped. Sea/trout fishing. From £90 to £180 weekly. Discount on fortnightly lets. **Mrs J.D. Greenwell, Tregeiriog, Near Llangollen, Clwyd LL20 7HU (01691 76672).**

TAVISTOCK. Mrs P.G.C. Quinton, Higher Quither, Milton Abbot, Tavistock PL19 0PZ (0182286 284). A modern self contained, open-plan barn conversion on the edge of Dartmoor, four miles from the ancient stannary town of Tavistock. The cottage is an ideal base for a whole variety of enjoyable holiday activities and both coasts are within easy reach. The cottage has its own private garden. Amenities include colour TV, electric cooker, microwave, washing machine, refrigerator, electric fires; coal and logs for the open fires and duvets and linen all provided. The village of Chillaton is three-quarters of a mile away with pub, village shop and post office. Children and pets welcome. Terms from £175.

TIVERTON. Mrs Anne McLean Williams, Wonham Barton, Bampton, Tiverton EX16 9JZ (01398 331312). 🔑🔑🔑 *Commended.* Welcome to our comfortable self-contained farmhouse wing and enjoy panoramic views over the beautiful Exe Valley. Close by is the scenic splendour and romance of Exmoor National Park. Country pursuits — riding, walking, fishing, swimming, golf, await you here. Ideal for touring the coasts of Devon and Somerset and discovering market towns, historic buildings and hidden gems in our tranquil countryside. The accommodation for four to six persons is Tourist Board inspected and is comprehensively equipped; has central heating and is set in its own pleasant garden. Guests are invited to explore our 300 acre working farm with pasture woodlands and abundant wildlife.

TORBAY. Honeysuckle and Horseshoe Cottages, Kingskerswell, Torbay. Sleep 2 adults, 3 children. These delightful and comfortable cottages await you at Kingskerswell, two miles from the glorious beaches of "The English Riviera", set in a quiet backwater of this charming village with local pubs, thatched restaurant and shops all nearby. Going inland Newton Abbot, Totnes, Dartmoor and South Hams all within easy reach. The cottages are fully double glazed, have gas central heating and well equipped fitted kitchen, are tastefully furnished, carpeted throughout. Lounge with colour TV. One double room, one twin-bedded (with extra bed). All linen provided. Bathroom, toilets plus downstairs toilet. Children welcome. South facing garden with patio and barbecue area. Open views of surrounding countryside. Parking beside cottages. Frequent bus service. Telephone for brochure. **Mr and Mrs F.C. Down, Ruby Farm, Abbotskerswell, Newton Abbot TQ12 5NQ (01803 812425).**

Terms quoted in this publication may be subject to increase if rises in costs necessitate

TORRINGTON. Mrs L.M. Millman, Winscott St. Giles, Torrington EX38 7JP (01805 623120). Sleeps 6. Charming country cottage with large south facing garden and driveway to door, quietly situated in peaceful countryside three and a half miles from Torrington which has Dartington Glass and RHS Rosemoor Gardens. Ideal touring base for the North Devon Coast with its miles of sandy beaches, Dartmoor and Exmoor. The well maintained and comfortable accommodation comprises three double bedrooms, bathroom and toilet, well equipped kitchen, diningroom and sittingroom with colour TV. Linen supplied. Electricity by meter. No pets. Please write or telephone for terms and brochure with colour photo.

TOTNES. Hemsford Country Holidays, Hemsford, Littlehempston, Totnes TQ9 6NE (01803 762637). HEMSFORD — THE COMPLETE COUNTRY HOLIDAY. Hemsford is ideally situated in the heart of South Devon with Torbay, Dartmoor and the excellent beaches of the South Hams only a short drive away. Our 16 comfortable and well appointed cottages (one equipped for disabled visitors) all have night storage heating and accommodate two/10 people; they are available throughout the year. Facilities include our own riding stables, heated indoor pool, sauna, solarium, games room, licensed bar, two all-weather tennis courts, 9 hole approach golf and children's play area. Terms from £90 to £1062 per week. Full colour brochure on request. Regret no pets.

TOTNES. Mr and Mrs D. Christie-Mutch, Lower Well, Broadhempston, Totnes TQ9 6BD (01803 813417). Not a working farm. Charming, comfortable, well equipped self contained one and two bedroomed cottages, formerly part of Georgian farm. Colour TV; laundry facilities; cot and high chair available. Orchard garden. Linen not provided. Lovely unspoiled Devon village with two pubs, church and shop, situated between Dartmoor and the Torbay coast with easy access to the beautiful South Hams, historic Totnes, Dartington and Exeter, etc. Telephone or write for details.

WELLINGTON. Mr and Mrs L.J. Tristram, West End, Holcombe Rogus, Wellington, Somerset TA21 0QD (01823 672384). Working farm, join in. Sleeps 6. This 16th century olde worlde farm cottage in Devon has an inglenook fireplace and bread oven. It is approached by a private tarmac road and surrounded by a large garden. Situated on 180-acre family farm, over which guests are free to wander. Half-a-mile from the small village of Holcombe Rogus which has general store with post office, garage, public house, church. Within easy reach of Exmoor, Taunton, Exeter and the coast. Excellent walks in unspoilt countryside; extensive views. Six people accommodated in three double rooms, cot; bathroom, toilet; sitting/diningroom. Kitchen with electric cooker, fridge, kettle, iron, etc.; glass conservatory at front of house. Linen by arrangement. Pets allowed. Car an advantage, ample parking. Open all year. TV provided. Tourist Board registered. SAE, please, for terms.

See also Colour Display Advertisement **WESTWARD HO! John and Gill Violet, West Pusehill Farm, Westward Ho! EX39 5AH (Bideford [01237] 475638 or 474622). Cottages sleep 2/8.** Our eleven cottages are situated in an idyllic setting in an area of "outstanding natural beauty" and only one mile from Devon's golden coast. Each stone-built cottage is equipped and furnished to a high standard. Varying in size they accommodate from two to eight people. Suitable for holidays throughout the year. Facilities include: heated swimming pool, licensed restaurant and bar, sauna, solarium, children's play area, pets corner, games room and laundry. Prices from £103 to £562. For full colour brochure phone or write to **John & Gill Violet.**

WOODY BAY, near Lynton. Gordon and Barbara McKay, Martinhoe Manor, Woody Bay, Near Lynton EX31 4QX (Parracombe [01598] 763424). Apartments sleep 1/8. "WHERE EXMOOR MEETS THE SEA". Magnificently situated Manor House set amidst spectacular coastal scenery, 26 acres of lovely grounds, including third of a mile of private coastline, jetty, swimming pool. Superb walking, riding, fishing and touring — the ultimate escape from pressures of modern living. Spacious self-contained apartments for one to eight persons, with breathtaking views and superior facilities, including full central heating and colour TV, laundry room and residents' lounge bar. Children and pets welcome. Cots and high chairs available. Open all year. Apartments from £90 per week INCLUDING central heating and colour TV. We hope to have the pleasure of welcoming you to our lovely home. Please write or telephone for colour brochure. Tourist Board registered.

WOOLACOMBE. Resthaven Holiday Flats. Situated in own grounds on the sea front with magnificent views of the glorious North Devon coast including the headlands of Morte and Baggy Point and Lundy Island on the horizon. Two spacious flats, one ground floor which sleeps five and one first floor sleeping nine. Family, double and single bedrooms, all with washbasins. Lounge furnished to high standard with colour TV and videos; fully equipped kitchens; bathrooms have bath, shower and toilet (first floor flat has extra toilet). Electricity by 50p meter, hot water free. Free car parking. Laundry and payphone. Blue Flag Beach 1992/93/94. Write or telephone **Mr B.A. Watts, Resthaven Holiday Flats, The Esplanade, Woolacombe EX34 7DJ (01271 870298 or 870248).**

YELVERTON. Mrs M. Sherrell, Hole Farm, Bere Alston, Yelverton PL20 7JE (01822 840 241). Working farm. Sleeps 4 adults; 1 child. Situated near the edge of Dartmoor and in the beautiful Tamar Valley, this working farm enjoys lovely estuary views. Walking, birdwatching, riding, golf nearby. Within easy reach of both the north and south coasts of Devon and Cornwall, half an hour's drive from Plymouth. Accommodation comprises a self contained wing of this attractive and tastefully modernised 350 year old farmhouse. One twin bedded room and one double room with washbasin; shower room and WC. Extra folding bed or cot available. Large lounge/kitchen equipped with electric cooker, fridge, spin dryer. Colour TV and electric heating. Not suitable for disabled visitors. Personally cleaned. Linen on request. Terms from £80.

FOR THE MUTUAL GUIDANCE OF GUEST AND HOST

Every year literally thousands of holidays, short-breaks and overnight stops are arranged through our guides, the vast majority without any problems at all. In a handful of cases, however, difficulties do arise about bookings, which often could have been prevented from the outset.

It is important to remember that when accommodation has been booked, both parties — guests and hosts — have entered into a form of contract. We hope that the following points will provide helpful guidance.

GUESTS: When enquiring about accommodation, be as precise as possible. Give exact dates, numbers in your party and the ages of any children. State the number and type of rooms wanted and also what catering you require — bed and breakfast, full board, etc. Make sure that the position about evening meals is clear — and about pets, reductions for children or any other special points.

Read our reviews carefully to ensure that the proprietors you are going to contact can supply what you want. Ask for a letter confirming all arrangements, if possible.

If you have to cancel, do so as soon as possible. Proprietors do have the right to retain deposits and under certain circumstances to charge for cancelled holidays if adequate notice is not given and they cannot re-let the accommodation.

HOSTS: Give details about your facilities and about any special conditions. Explain your deposit system clearly and arrangements for cancellations, charges, etc, and whether or not your terms include VAT.

If for any reason you are unable to fulfil an agreed booking without adequate notice, you may be under an obligation to arrange alternative suitable accommodation or to make some form of compensation.

While every effort is made to ensure accuracy, we regret that FHG Publications cannot accept responsibility for errors, omissions or misrepresentation in our entries or any consequences thereof. Prices in particular should be checked because we go to press early. We will follow up complaints but cannot act as arbiters or agents for either party.

DORSET

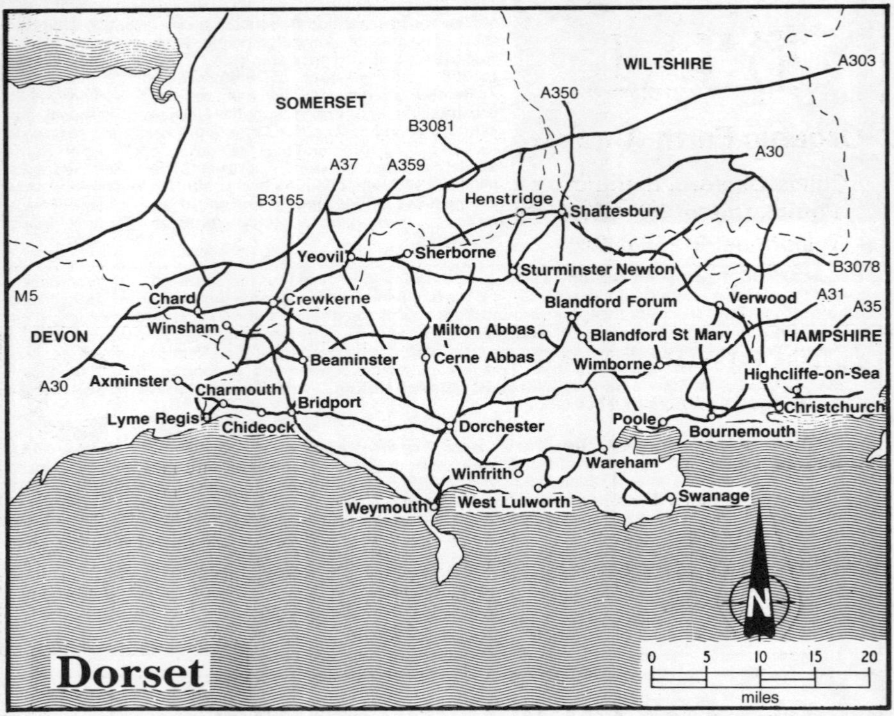

See also Colour Display Advertisement **BEAMINSTER. Mrs Jackie Spooncer, Lewesdon Farm, Stoke Abbot, Beaminster DT8 3JZ (01308 868270).** 🔑🔑🔑🔑 *Commended.* **Sleep 5/6.** Lewesdon Farm nestles in the soft rolling hills of Dorset. Beneath magnificent hill forts, in an area of outstanding natural beauty. Blissfully peaceful. An abundance of wildlife, ideal for walking. Stable and Barn Cottages offer superior accommodation, equipped to a high standard, sleeping five/six, all bedrooms en-suite. Warm and cosy, log fires if you wish. Electric blankets. Safe play area, cot, high chair and babysitting service. Bed linen available. Washer/dryer. Special Winter Breaks. Our barn conversion is designed with disabled visitors in mind. Non-smokers please. Weekly terms from £160 to £435.

BEAMINSTER near (Hooke). "Orchard End", Hooke, Beaminster. 🔑🔑🔑🔑 **Working farm. Sleeps 6.**

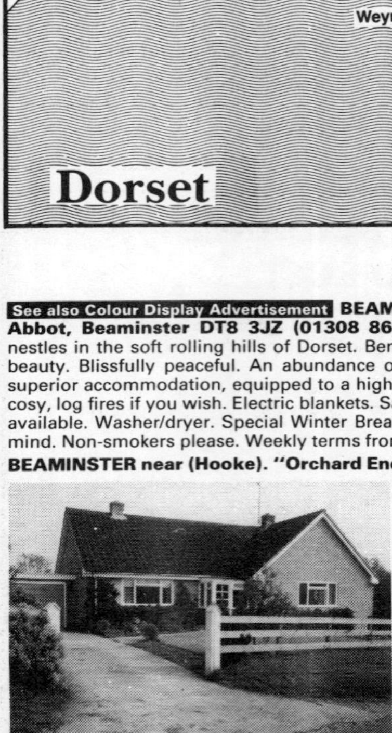

Hooke is a quiet village nine miles from coast. Good walking country and near Hooke Working Woodland with lovely woodland walks. Trout fishing nearby. Bungalow is stone built and has electric central heating, some double glazing. It is on a working dairy farm and is clean and comfortable. Three bedrooms all with duvets. Cot available. Large lounge/ dining room with colour TV. Well equipped kitchen with electric cooker, microwave, fridge/freezer and automatic washing machine. Bathroom and separate toilet. Carpeted. Payphone. Large garden and garage. Terms from £160 to £280 per week inclusive of electricity, bed linen and VAT. ETB registered. **Mrs P.M. Wallbridge, Bridge Farm, Hooke, Beaminster DT8 3PD (Beaminster [01308] 862619).**

BEXINGTON. Mrs Josephine Pearse, Tamarisk Farm, West Bexington, Dorchester DT2 9DF (01308 897784). 🔑🔑/🔑🔑🔑 On Chesil Beach between Abbotsbury and Burton Bradstock. Farm slopes down to the sea. One large and two smaller bungalows (ETB 2/3 Key Classification) and two chalets; properties sleep four/eight. Terms from £75 to £390. Each one stands in own garden. Glorious views along West Dorset and Devon coasts. Lovely walks by sea and inland. Active mixed family farm with sheep, cows, horses and organic market garden — vegetables and herbs available. Sea fishing, riding in Abbotsbury, lots of tourist attractions and good markets in Bridport (six miles), Dorchester, Weymouth and Portland, all 13 miles. Good centre for touring Thomas Hardy's Wessex. Safe for children and pets can be quite free.

GOLD HILL

Organic Farm Annexe

Childe Okeford, Blandford Forum, Dorset DT11 8HB
Telephone: 01258 860293

Self-catering ground floor flat suitable for 2 adults and child over 5 years. Light and airy, tastefully furnished and set in peaceful surroundings. Well equipped kitchen. Sitting room with colour TV. Central heating. Toilet with basin and separate shower. Prices include own linen. Gold Hill is a 30 acre working farm specialising in vegetable and salad crops, and raising rare breed British White Cattle. We also breed and work Shire Horses. Childe Okeford is in Dorset's beautiful Blackmore Vale, with its associations with Thomas Hardy and Lawrence of Arabia. Only 20 miles from the nearest coast at Poole. Ideal for walking, riding (own horses taken), National Trust Properties and places of historical interest. Short breaks available during winter. Prices from £85 to £175 per week. Contact D. N. & A. D. Cross for further details. ETB 🔑 🔑 🔑 Commended.

Luccombe Farm

🔑 🔑 🔑 COMMENDED

Milton Abbas, Blandford
Dorset DT11 0BE
Telephone: 01258 880 558

Our courtyard of traditional brick and flint barns are converted to a high standard, with disabled facilities.ETB Category 3. They lie peacefully around a pond in beautiful open countryside. Historic Milton Abbas Village, Abbey and School are nearby. Three well equipped cottages include colour TV, microwaves. Sleeping 2/5. Children and pets welcome. Our farm provides a licensed riding school, as well as sailing, clay shooting, and good walks. Most other activities can be arranged. Linen, laundry, maid service, child care, cots, high chairs, telephone, games room and ample parking are all available. From £150–£350. Brochure available.

Other specialised

FHG PUBLICATIONS

* Recommended SHORT BREAK HOLIDAYS IN BRITAIN £3.60

* Recommended COUNTRY HOTELS OF BRITAIN £3.60

* PETS WELCOME! £3.99

* BED AND BREAKFAST IN BRITAIN £2.90

Published annually. Please add 50p postage (U.K. only) when ordering from the publishers:

FHG PUBLICATIONS LTD
Abbey Mill Business Centre, Seedhill,
Paisley, Renfrewshire PA1 1TJ

BLANDFORD. Mrs M.J. Waldie, The Old Rectory, Lower Blandford St. Mary, Near Blandford Forum DT11 9ND (Blandford [01258] 453220). Sleeps 6. Completely self-contained wing of Georgian Old Rectory, one mile from the market town of Blandford Forum, within easy reach of the south coast, Poole, Bournemouth, Salisbury and Thomas Hardy country around Dorchester. Local fishing and many places of historical interest. Accommodation for six in three rooms, one double bedded, one twin bedded and smaller room with bunk beds. Large well equipped kitchen, spacious sitting/diningroom with colour TV; cloakroom downstairs; bathroom and separate toilet upstairs. All freshly decorated. Pets allowed by prior arrangement. Children welcome. Parking spaces. Use of secluded garden. Everything provided except linen and towels. Terms from £155 to £215 per week. May to September. SAE, please, for further details.

BOURNEMOUTH. Bournemouth Holiday Homes, Henbury View, Dullar Lane, Sturminster Marshall BH21 4AD (01202 518967). For more than a quarter of a century, Bournemouth's oldest self catering holiday accommodation agency has been providing a letting service for scores of privately owned houses, cottages, bungalows, flats, caravans and chalets in Bournemouth, Poole, Ringwood, Christchurch and about 20 miles around. All inspected before acceptance and accurately described. Prices to suit every pocket. Most properties welcome children and many accept pets. Colour brochure on request.

©

Happy Holidays

BRIDPORT. Mrs Sandra Huxter, Strongate Farm, Strongate Lane, Salwayash, Bridport DT6 5JD (01308 488295). A picturesque thatched cottage off the beaten track in peaceful surroundings. Situated on a small working family farm with cows, sheep, geese, ducks, pond, etc. Seaside five miles, within easy reach of charming Dorset villages, beautiful walking areas. Ideal for recharging batteries in relaxing unspoilt countryside. Families especially welcome, children can play freely. Cottage has two bedrooms, one with double bed, the other with two single beds, cot available. Secluded garden with barbecue and swings. Electricity, bedding, colour TV, automatic washing machine, fitted carpets. Dogs by arrangement only. Non smokers only. Further details on request.

BRIDPORT near. "Carinya", Marshwood, Near Bridport. 🔑🔑 *Approved.* **Sleeps 5 plus cot.** This modern well furnished bungalow has a large lawn and small field adjoining providing plenty of space. Situated in a village with National Trust land nearby and about 15 minutes' drive from the sea. The bungalow is fully equipped except for bed linen and has two bedrooms (cot and high chair available); bathroom, toilet; large lounge/dinette with colour TV; kitchen with electric cooker, automatic washing machine, fridge, toaster, iron, etc. One well behaved dog by arrangement. Car essential, garage and parking. Beautiful surrounding countryside to explore and historical landmarks. Property is well maintained and under personal supervision. Details and terms from **Mrs P.B. Bowditch, Colmer Farm, Marshwood, Bridport DT6 5QA (01297 678278).**

BRIDPORT. Mrs Carol Mansfield, Lancombes House, West Milton, Bridport DT6 3TN (01308 485375). 🔑🔑🔑🔑 *Approved.* Lancombes House is a 200 year old stone barn built 300 feet above sea level set in 10 acres; there are tame animals for children to play and help with. Farm has panoramic views to the sea only four miles away. There are four superbly converted cottages, each with its own sitting out area, barbecue and garden furniture. They have spacious open plan living areas, most with wood burning stoves. Modern fitted kitchens, double and twin-bedded rooms. Electric central heating, shared laundry. Deep in the heart of Hardy country, this is a delightful area to explore whether on foot or horseback. There is riding available locally. There are many things to do and pets and children are very welcome. Prices start at £120 for mini breaks and we are open all the year round.

BRIDPORT near. Mrs S. Norman, Frogmore Farm, Chideock, Bridport DT6 6HT (01308 456159).

Working farm, join in. Sleeps 5 adults, 1 child. Delightful farm cottage on ninety-acre grazing farm set in the rolling hills of West Dorset. Superb views over Lyme Bay, ideal base for touring Dorset and Devon or rambling the many coastal and country footpaths of the area. This fully equipped self-catering cottage sleeps six, plus cot. Bed linen supplied. Cosy lounge with woodburner and colour TV, French doors to a splendid columned sun verandah. Children and well behaved dogs welcome. Car essential. Open all year. Short Breaks available, also Bed and Breakfast in the 17th century farmhouse. Brochure and terms free on request.

CHARMOUTH. Mrs R. J. White, Little Catherston Farm, Charmouth, Bridport DT6 6LZ (Charmouth [01297] 560550). Working farm. Sleeps 4. Our self-contained holiday flat has superb views over Charmouth and the sea, where the beach is safe and sandy and is well known for its fossils. There are many coastal walks on National Trust land. Golden Cap is the highest point on the South coast. Golf at Lyme Regis and West Bay, also wildlife park near Chard. Accommodation comprises bedroom with two single beds; kitchen; bed sitting room with colour TV; bathroom. Metered electricity. Cot and high chair available. Bed linen supplied. Car parking. Dogs welcome if kept under control. SAE please for terms.

DORSET – FOLLOW THE HARDY TRAIL

The life-size statue of Thomas Hardy in Dorchester, his "Casterbridge" and home for many years, bears witness to his love for this peaceful county. Hardy enthusiasts should visit his birthplace at Higher Bockhampton; Waterston Manor, east of Puddletown – Bathsheba's home in "Far From the Madding Crowd"; Bere Regis – "Kingsbere"; Puddletown – "Weatherbury". Full details can be obtained from local Tourist Information Offices.

DORCHESTER. Kennel Cottage, Moreton, Dorchester. Quiet comfortable three bedroom cottage on working dairy farm. Equipped with colour TV, video, washing machine, microwave, central heating, and set in well fenced garden with sandpit and swing. Cot, high chair, stairgate provided. Dogs welcome. Splendid base for exploring Dorset countryside and coast. Weekly rates from £200 to £350 including electricity and linen. Open April to September inclusive. Details from: **Jim Hosford and Miranda Dicks, Broompound Dairy, Moreton, Dorchester DT2 8RL (01929 462464).**

DORCHESTER near. Old Dairy Cottage, sleeps 6; Clyffe Dairy Cottage, sleeps 4. *Commended.* Two attractively furnished, comfortable character cottages with beams and inglenook fireplaces; central heating. On mixed farm with cows, calves, horses and beautiful woodland walks; ducks and wildlife on the pond and streams nearby. Easy reach of coast, golf, trekking, tennis, fishing and leisure centre; ideal cycling location. Children welcome. Excellent value low season breaks/winter breaks. Senior Citizens' reductions. Open all year. Terms from £120 to £325 per week. Contact: **Rosemary Coleman, Clyffe Farm, Tincleton, Dorchester DT2 8QR (01305 848252).**

DORCHESTER. Mrs J.M. Morris, Huish Farm, Sydling St. Nicholas, Dorchester DT2 9NS (01300 341265). Working farm. Sleeps 2. The perfect place for a peaceful holiday for two people only, this self contained flat in thatched farmhouse is set amidst beautiful countryside, within easy reach of the coast, and near Cerne Abbas village abounding with historic interest dating back to the 14th century, including remains of the Abbey. The Cerne Giant, 180 feet high, is a curious figure cut in the chalk hillside to the north east of the village. Upstairs, one very large sunny room with twin beds, private bathroom, toilet; downstairs, large kitchen equipped with electric cooker, fridge and all utensils. Linen not supplied. No TV. Car essential, ample parking. Own entrance and sunny corner of garden. Pets are permitted. Weekly terms from £85 including fuel. SAE, please, for further details.

WHEN MAKING ENQUIRIES PLEASE MENTION *FARM HOLIDAY GUIDES*

DORCHESTER near. Pitt Cottage, Ringstead Bay, Near Dorchester. Sleeps 6. An attractive part thatched stone-built cottage, surrounded by farmland and situated on the edge of a small wood about quarter of a mile from the sea, commanding outstanding views of Ringstead Bay on the Dorset Heritage Coast. The cottage has been renovated and is equipped to sleep six; three bedrooms (two beds in each), two bathrooms, sitting room with open fire and large kitchen/dining area. Cot/high chair; washing machine; TV; electric radiators in all rooms. Car essential. Available from £85 per week. For details please send SAE (reference FHG) to: **Mrs S.H. Russell, 14 Brodrick Road, London SW17 7DZ or telephone 0181-672 2022.**

GILLINGHAM. Mrs J. Wallis, Meads Farm, Stour Provost, Gillingham SP8 5RX (01747 838265). Working farm, join in. Sleeps 6. Mead Bungalow is a superior property enjoying outstanding views over Blackmore Vale. Situated one mile from A30 at the end of the lovely village of Stour Provost. Shaftesbury with its famous Gold Hill is nearby and within easy reach are Bournemouth, Weymouth and Bath. Many attractive and interesting places lie a short car ride away. Over one mile of private coarse fishing 160 yards from bungalow. Spacious accommodation sleeps six plus cot. Large lounge with colour TV, diningroom, three double bedrooms, bathroom, luxury oak kitchen with automatic washing machine etc; all electric (no meters), full central heating; linen supplied. Quarter acre lawns. Sorry no pets.

HOLDITCH. Old Forge Cottage, Holditch, Chard. Sleeps 4. Ideal for peace and seclusion in glorious unspoilt countryside within easy reach of the sea. This delightful old world cottage with oak beams stands just outside Holditch on the Devon/Dorset/Somerset borders, affording splendid views over beautiful countryside. Charmouth and its sandy beaches seven miles distant. Lyme Regis, with safe bathing and recreational facilities eight miles. The cottage is completely modernised and tastefully furnished with fitted carpets throughout, for up to four people. One twin-bedded room and two single rooms; sittingroom with colour TV; kitchen with dining area; modern bathroom; second toilet; electric cooker, fridge, vacuum cleaner, modern sink unit, immersion heater, night storage heaters throughout (included in terms). Everything supplied except linen. Electricity charged by meter reading. Phone; walled garden; garage. Chard four and a half miles. Terms £100 to £140 weekly. Open all year. Regret no children under 12 years. No pets. All enquiries to **Mrs P.A. Spice, Orchard Cottage, Duke Street, Micheldever, Near Winchester, Hants SO21 3DF (01962 774563).**

LYME REGIS. Mrs M. Thompson, "Spinney", Rocombe, Uplyme, Lyme Regis DT7 3RR (01297 442757). Well appointed self contained flat annexed to large cottage situated in quiet rural lane. Ideally situated to explore West Dorset, East Devon, two miles from Lyme Regis and sea. Our flat enjoys panoramic views of the Uplyme Valley, designated an area of outstanding natural beauty. There are many delightful local walks through unspoilt countryside and coastline. Accommodation includes bedroom, twin beds plus folding bed; sittingroom/diningroom with colour TV; bathroom. Well equipped galley kitchen with electric cooker and fridge. Electricity inclusive. Use of large peaceful garden. Ample parking. From £100 to £190 weekly. SAE for details. Non-smokers preferred.

DORSET – RURAL SPLENDOUR!

Absorbing old towns like Dorchester and Shaftesbury, surrounded by panoramic vales, undulating chalklands and peaceful villages contribute to Dorset's great appeal. Included in any tourist's itinerary should be, Abbotsbury Village and Swannery, Ackling Dyke Roman road, Brownsea Island, Lulworth Cove and, of course, the many locations that constitute Hardy's Dorset.

MARNHULL. Mrs K. Cook and Mrs J. Williams, Walton Elm House, Marnhull, Sturminster Newton DT10 1QG (01258 820553). Situated in the heart of Thomas Hardy country, offering accommodation of one, two or three bedrooms each with colour TV, shower or bath, and usual kitchen facilities. Surrounded by countryside of outstanding natural beauty, yet within easy reach of Yeovil, Blandford and Shaftesbury with its famous Gold Hill, perfect for a relaxing holiday. Available at no extra cost is a solar heated swimming pool, tennis court, badminton room and table tennis, whilst for a small charge adults can enjoy the full size snooker table. Offering a warm family welcome — we can provide cots, high chairs and babysitting service if required. Pets welcome by prior notice. Terms from £120 to £315 per week.

MILTON ABBAS. Mrs V.O. Davey, Little Hewish Farm, Milton Abbas, Near Blandford DT11 0LH (Milton Abbas [01258] 880326). 🔑🔑🔑 *Commended.* **Cottages sleep 4/5/6.** Three modernised farm cottages at Little Hewish Farm in Hardy country, situated one mile from the unique village of Milton Abbas with its picturesque thatched cottages, lake and abbey. It is within easy driving distance of the coast with sandy beaches at Bournemouth, Studland, Swanage and Weymouth, with many coastline walks between; farm walk also. The cottages contain two and three bedrooms sleeping two to six persons. Cot if required. Sittingroom, dining/kitchen; bathroom and separate toilet. Cottages are comfortably furnished and fully equipped including fridge and hot water. Fully carpeted. Colour TV. Electricity by £1 meter. Linen extra. Nightstore heaters. Laundry room. Sorry, no pets. Car essential, parking. Available all year. Terms £90 to £235 per week. Please phone or send SAE for details.

SHAFTESBURY. Mrs Sue Smart, Hartgrove Farm, Shaftesbury SP7 0JY (01747 811830). 🔑🔑🔑🔑 *Commended.* **Working farm. Two cottages sleep 2/5; Farmhouse flat sleeps 2.** Situated in glorious countryside with panoramic views, in an area of outstanding natural beauty four miles south of Shaftesbury, our 145 acre family dairy farm is the ideal place for a relaxing holiday. The character cottages are situated in the centre of the farm and have oak fitted kitchen, close carpeted beamed lounge and private gardens. The delightful farmhouse flat has stunning views and private access from gardens. All are equipped and furnished to a very high standard with central heating and linen provided. Laundry room, cot and high chair also available. Glorious walking, pretty thatched villages and good pubs. One cottage graded Category 1 for disabled facilities. Brochure available.

STURMINSTER NEWTON. Mrs Sheila Martin, Moorcourt Farm, Moorside, Marnhull, Sturminster Newton DT10 1HH (Marnhull [01258] 820271). Working farm. Sleeps 4. Ground floor flat with own entrance and front door key. It is part of the farmhouse, kept immaculately clean and furnished to the highest order. We are a 117 acre dairy farm in the middle of the Blackmore Vale. Guests are welcome to wander round, watch the farm activities and laze in the large garden — we have some garden loungers for your use. We are very central for touring with easy access to New Forest, Longleat Wildlife Park, Cheddar, Stonehenge and the lovely Dorset coast. Accommodation for four people in two double bedrooms, one with a double bed, the other with twin beds. Bathroom, separate toilet. Sittingroom with colour TV and door leading striaght onto the back garden. Well equipped kitchen/diner. Full size cooker, fridge/freezer, microwave and washing machine; all utensils colour co-ordinated, matching crockery, etc. Beds made up with fresh linen on arrival. Towels, tea towels, etc provided. Electric heaters in all rooms; electricity payable by meter, units to be read at the start and finish of your holiday. Sheila creates a friendly atmosphere here "down on the farm" and does her best to make your holiday an enjoyable one. Open April to November. Car essential. Sorry, no pets. Weekly terms from £100 to £200. SAE please.

SWANAGE. Mrs Rosemary Dean, Quarr Farm, Valley Road, Swanage BN19 3DY (01929 480865). 🔑🔑 *Approved.* **Sleeps 10 plus cot.** Quarr Farmhouse, a 17th century stone building built in Purbeck marble quarried on farm. The farm is family managed in a close to nature way. Chickens run free and hatch eggs in barns, peacocks, cows, calves, horses are much in evidence. You will see chicks and ducks on your lawn, watch steam trains passing through our meadows. The house has four bedrooms, two double rooms (plus one single in each) and two twin rooms; bathroom with shower; large sittingroom with stone walls and 1651 built fireplace with log fire, colour TV; well-equipped kitchen including washer/dryer, dishwasher, microwave, fridge/freezer. Three miles from Swanage and five miles from Studland's sandy beach. Further details available on request.

SYDLING ST. NICHOLAS. Grace Cottage, Waterside Lane, Sydling St. Nicholas. Sleeps 4 plus cot.

Charming cottage with flint walled garden. Peaceful, secluded position in beautiful village situated in countryside made famous by Thomas Hardy. Large lounge/dining room with colour TV and video, study, two bedrooms (double and twin), two bathrooms. Modern kitchen with cooker, microwave, fridge/freezer, washing machine, tumble dryer. Good touring centre, excellent walking country, beaches 12 miles. Guide books and maps available for guests' use. Pub nearby. Non-smokers only. Pets welcome. Apply: **Mrs Willis, Lamperts Cottage, Sydling St. Nicholas DT2 9NU (01300 341659).**

WAREHAM near. Mrs M.J.M. Constantinides, "Woodlands", Hyde, Near Wareham BH20 7NT (01929 471239). THE MAISONETTE, north wing of secluded house, formerly Dower House of Hyde Estate, stands alone on a meadow of the River Piddle in four and a half acres in the midst of "Hardy Country". The Maisonette comprises upstairs lounge with colour TV; one bedroom (two single beds); downstairs large kitchen/diner, small entrance hall, bathroom; electric cooker (in addition to Aga cooker), refrigerator. Independent side entrance. Extra bedroom (two single beds) on request at £20 per week. Visitors are welcome to use house grounds; older children can fish or play in the boundary stream. Pleasant walks in woods and heath nearby. Golf course half a mile, pony trekking nearby. All linen included, beds ready made and basic shopping arranged on arrival day. Aga will be lit and maintained on request. Ideal for a quiet holiday far from the madding crowd. Cot and high chair available and children welcome to bring their pets. SAE, please, for terms and further particulars.

DURHAM

FROSTERLEY near. Rose Cottage, White Kirkley, Near Frosterley. Sleeps 4 adults, 2 children plus cot. For a peaceful retreat and walking holiday stay in our cosy Dales cottage next to a pleasant working farm, nestled in hills abover Frosterley near moors, in an area of outstanding natural beauty. Accommodation comprises three comfortable bedrooms; bathroom with shower over and toilet; good size lounge/diner with open coal/log fire; well equipped kitchen. Central heating in all rooms. Pretty rear walled garden with views. Ideal for visiting the historic City of Durham and forests, waterfalls; full leisure facilities, fishing and pony trekking nearby. Brochure available. SAE, please, to **Mrs C. Middleton, 36 Uppertown, Wolsingham DL13 3ET (01388 528927).**

STANLEY. Mrs P. Gibson, Bushblades Farm, Harperley, Stanley DH9 9UA (01207 232722). Sleeps 2/4. Comfortable wing of Georgian farmhouse. Centrally heated. Own patio and garden. Modern kitchen including automatic washing machine and fridge/freezer. Large beamed lounge/dining room with colour TV and double sofa bed. Large beamed bedroom with en suite shower room. Ample parking. Children over 12 years welcome. Electricity and heating included in price. Linen and towels not provided. Shops and supermarket two miles. Ideal base for visiting Beamish Museum (two miles), Durham City 20 minutes, Metro Centre 15 minutes, Hadrian's Wall and Northumberland coast under an hour. Walks and golfing nearby. Weekly terms from £150.

HELP IMPROVE BRITISH TOURIST STANDARDS

You are choosing holiday accommodation from our very popular FHG Publications. Whether it be a hotel, guest house, farmhouse or self-catering accommodation, we think you will find it hospitable, comfortable and clean, and your host and hostess friendly and helpful. Why not write and tell us about it?

As a recognition of the generally well-run and excellent holiday accommodation reviewed in our publications, we at FHG Publications Ltd. present a diploma to proprietors who receive the highest recommendation from their guests who are also readers of our Guides. If you care to write to us praising the holiday you have booked through FHG Publications Ltd. – whether this be board, self-catering accommodation, a sporting or a caravan holiday, what you say will be evaluated and the proprietors who reach our final list will be contacted.

The winning proprietor will receive an attractive framed diploma to display on his premises as recognition of a high standard of comfort, amenity and hospitality. FHG Publications Ltd. offer this diploma as a contribution towards the improvement of standards in tourist accommodation in Britain. Help your excellent host or hostess to win it!

FHG DIPLOMA

We nominate ....

....

Because

Name ....

Address ....

.... Telephone No. ....

GLOUCESTERSHIRE

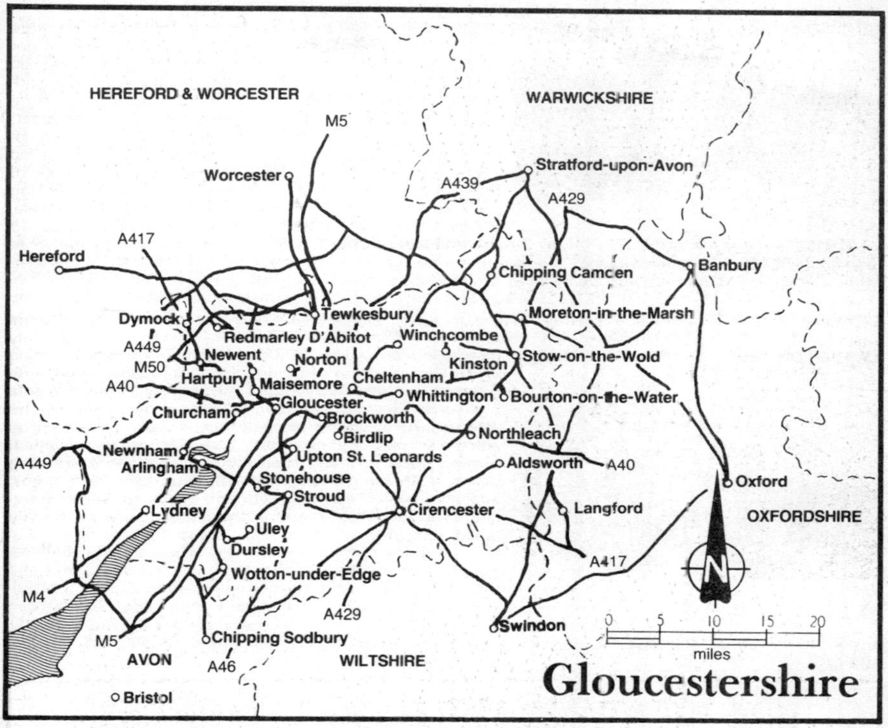

CHELTENHAM. Mr and Mrs J. Close, Coxhorne Farm, London Road, Charlton Kings, Cheltenham GL52 6UY (01242 236599). 🔑🔑🔑 *Commended.* **Sleeps 3.** Eastern outskirts of Cheltenham. Self catering in a well equipped studio apartment of Annexe adjoining farmhouse on working dairy farm. Accommodation consists of large lounge with sleeping for three plus extra bed on request. Gas fire and full central heating. Comfortable chairs and colour TV. Large fully fitted kitchen and en suite bathroom. Steps from kitchen leading to garden and plenty of parking space. Sorry, no smoking or pets. Children welcome. Electricity and linen included in rental. Ideal location for touring and walking Cotswolds. The farm is situated half a mile off the Cotswold Way with lovely views. Terms from £100 to £150 per week

COTSWOLDS. Mrs Ann Harris, Church Farmhouse, Upper Cam, Dursley GL11 5PB (Tel & Fax: 01453 543165). Sleeps 5/6. Church Farm Cottage is a converted coach-house adjacent to a listed farmhouse in the village of Upper Cam, lying between the Cotswold Escarpment and the Severn Vale in lovely countryside. The Cotswold Way runs through the village. Nearby are Slimbridge Wild Fowl Trust and Berkeley Castle. Within a wider radius are Gloucester, Bath, Cheltenham, Wye Valley and Forest of Dean. The well equipped cottage sleeps five/six in three bedrooms, with extra bed and cot available. A large comfortable sittingroom has gas fire and colour TV. Washing machine available. Bedroom on ground floor has en-suite basin and toilet. Lawn with picnic table for guests' use. Reasonable rates. Details on request.

DURSLEY. Stable Cottage, Upper Cam, Dursley. Sleeps 5. Situated in a tiny unspoilt village in the West Cotswolds, this delightful detached cottage was formerly a stable of our 17th century Cotswold farmhouse. Upper Cam is by the Cotswold Way and is surrounded by beautiful countryside for walking, picnics and scenic drives. Golf, gliding, pony trekking and water sports are available nearby and visitors can explore Slimbridge Wildfowl Trust, Berkeley Castle, Westonbirt Arboretum, Wye Valley, Bath and many more places of interest. Accommodation in this carefully converted cottage is for five people, with carpeting throughout, beamed ceilings, pine fittings, tasteful furnishings, storage heating, colour TV etc. Ample parking. Small garden. Sorry, no pets. Cot and linen available. English Tourist Board registered. Terms from £110 to £210. Brochure on request, from **Mrs J.T. Whitton, Street Farm, Upper Cam, Dursley GL11 5PG (Dursley [01453] 542837).**

GLOUCESTER near. Mrs J.P. Whitaker, Overtown Farmhouse, Cranham, Near Gloucester GL4 8HQ (01452 862573). "Shepherds Piece" is a twin unit mobile home with two double bedrooms. Lounge with colour TV; kitchen; bathroom and diningroom. Fitted carpets and double glazing. Parking and small garden. Necessary household requisites are supplied except linen; electricity is metered. Situated adjoining the Common and near the nature reserve Common Woods. There are attractive walks. Cranham is in a good position for touring the Cotswolds. Children and pets welcome. Terms from £55 to £155.

ILMINGTON (North Cotswolds). Foxglove Cottages, Ilmington. 🔑🔑🔑🔑 *Highly Commended.* Single storey Cotswold stone built country cottage accommodation. Situated in a quiet sunny spot overlooking village orchard. Two units sleeping two to five people plus cot, etc, for children. All modern conveniences including microwave, automatic washing machine; bath and shower. Central heating. Electricity and linen included. Extremely well furnished in typical cottage style with cosy fires, country pine and dried flowers and each with own private garden with sun patio and garden furniture. Easy parking. Suitable for disabled. Ilmington is a delightful Cotswold village nestling at the foot of the Campden Hills, with village shop/Post Office, pub, church, playing fields with tennis, cricket, bowls and children's playground. Ideally placed for visiting Stratford-upon-Avon or surrounding Cotswold villages. Terms from £95 to £330 per week. Mini Breaks available in Winter. **Mrs S. Lowe, Folly Farm Cottage, Ilmington, Shipston-on-Stour, Warwickshire CV36 4LJ (01608 682425).**

HAMPSHIRE

BROCKENHURST (New Forest). Mrs D.C. Korbey, New Park Farm, Brockenhurst SO42 7QH (01590 23127 or 23643; Fax: 01590 23427). 🔑🔑 Farmed by one family since 1877, this is a working farm, surrounded by the Forest and central for touring. In summer emphasis is on recreational activities including polo, youth camps, shows and fayres, etc. There are two holidays cottages sleeping six persons each. Fully furnished, each with two bathrooms; electric cooker, microwave, fridge and TV. Open all year round with storage heaters. Also mobile home sleeping four adults and a child. Available Easter to September. Milk from farm available from part-time shop stocking groceries, sweets, souvenirs, etc. Launderette. Terms from £100 for caravan and £160 to £250 for the cottages.

SWAY. Mrs H.J. Beale, Hackney Park, Mount Pleasant Lane, Sway, Lymington SO41 8LS (Lymington [01590] 682049). Properties sleep 4/6. Situated in commanding and tranquil setting two miles from Lymington and Sway village. Delightful residence in own extensive grounds adjoining New Forest Heath with superb walks, rides and drives. Apartment to sleep six (further bedrooms available). Coach House cottage to sleep four. Comfortable and modern, colour TV, bed linen and electricity included. Pets by prior arrangement. First class stables for those wishing to bring own horse and excellent riding facilities within walking distance. Many famous places of interest nearby. Close to Isle of Wight ferry and within six miles of sandy beaches, 15 miles Bournemouth and Southampton. Open all year.

HAMPSHIRE – THE NEW FOREST

One of the most extensive tracts of oak woodland in England, interspersed with heathland and modern plantations of conifers, the New Forest was used by William the Conqueror as a hunting reserve. Today it is popular with walkers and riders, and is home to deer and half-wild ponies. To find out more, call in at the Visitor Centre at Lyndhurst and learn about traditional customs.

HEREFORD & WORCESTER

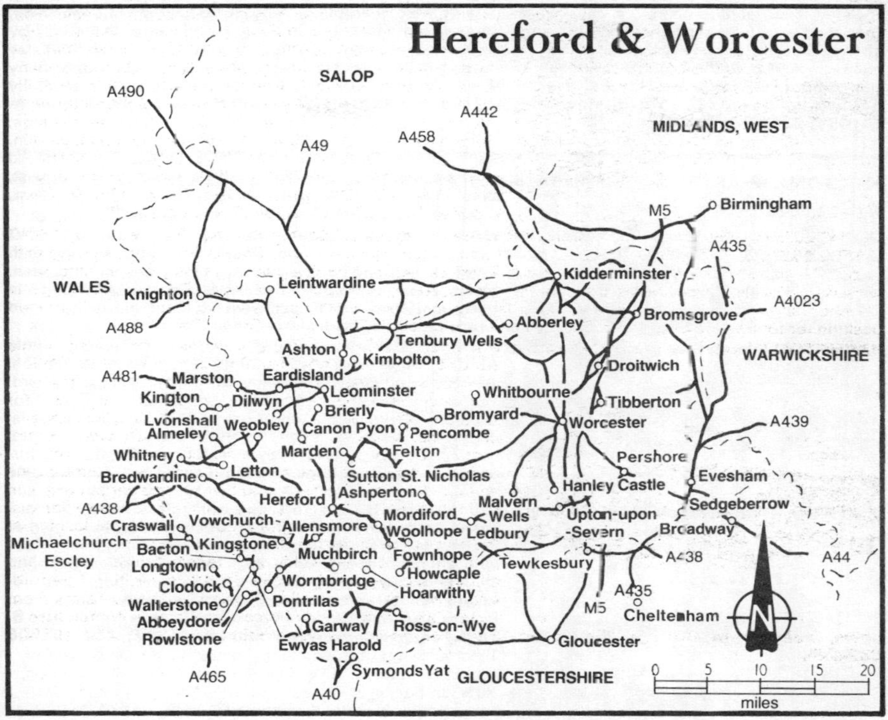

ABBEYDORE (Golden Valley). Ivy Green Cottage, Abbeydore. Sleeps 4. Traditional two bedroomed cottage painted white in pretty garden setting, sheltered but with lovely views all around. Situated on minor, quiet road two miles from A365, equidistant Hereford and Abergavenny. Close to Welsh border country. Explore North, South, East or West. The Cottage is fully equipped and has electric heaters throughout plus log fires; electric cooker, fridge, microwave and immersion heater. Bathroom with bath, heated towel rail; spin dryer, colour TV. One double bedroom and one twin-bedded room. Children and dogs welcome; fields all around. Price from £80 to £130 per week. Electricity inclusive, dogs £5 extra. Please write, or telephone, **Mrs D. Jeffreys, Wellfield, Abbeydore HR2 0AD (01981 21347).**

GREAT MALVERN. Mr and Mrs D.G. Coates, Mill House, 16 Clarence Road, Great Malvern WR14 3EH (01684 562345). Sleeps 4/6. Delightful Mill Cottage is situated at the foot of the beautiful Malvern Hills in the tranquil grounds of Mill House, a few minutes' walk from the town centre, hill walks, Malvern's leisure pool or Great Malvern station. An ideal centre for touring the Cotswolds, the Severn and Wye Valleys and Welsh Marches. Colour TV, central heating, automatic washing machine, dishwasher, microwave, linen, towels, etc. Payphone. Well behaved children and dogs welcome. Parking within grounds of Mill House. From £200 inclusive. Non-smokers preferred. SAE please.

WHEN MAKING ENQUIRIES PLEASE MENTION THIS *FHG* PUBLICATION

HEREFORD. Rose Cottage, Craswall, Hereford. 🔑🔑 *Approved.* **Sleeps 5.** Rose Cottage is a modernised stone-built cottage, retaining its original character situated at the foot of Black Mountains, on a quiet country road. Hay-on-Wye, Hereford, Abergavenny easily accessible and ideal base for walking and touring. Many churches and castles of historic interest; close to River Monnow where trout fishing is available. Pony trekking, hang gliding nearby. A car is essential and there is ample parking. Rose Cottage is comfortably furnished with full central heating and wood fire (heating and hot water included). Linen provided free of charge. Electricity by meter reading. Two bedrooms, one with double bed, one with three single beds. Cot can be provided. Bathroom, toilet. Kitchen fully equipped with electric cooker, kettle, fridge etc. Sittingroom; diningroom. TV. Dogs are allowed. Registered with the English Tourist Board. Available all year round. Terms from £120 to £130. **Mrs M. Howard, The Three Horseshoes, Craswall HR2 0PL (Michaelchurch [01981] 23631).**

HEREFORD. Mrs S. Dixon, Swayns Diggins, Harewood End, Hereford HR2 8JU (01989 730358).

This highly recommended first floor flat is completely self-contained at one end of the main house. The bedroom, sitting room and private balcony all face south with panoramic views over farmland towards Ross and Symonds Yat. The fully equipped kitchen overlooks the garden with grand views towards Orcop Hill and the Black Mountains. Open all year, rental from £110 per week includes electricity, linen, heating, colour TV. Ideal base for exploring the beautiful Wye Valley, Herefordshire, Gloucestershire and the historic Welsh Marches. There is much to see and do in the area. Write or phone for further particulars.

KINGTON. Lilwall Green, Kington. The house has rural views across unspoilt Herefordshire, where a warm welcome awaits you. The property is set in its own on an 84 acre farm, 300 yards off A411, with lawns to the front, one and a half miles from market town of Kington, and half a mile from owners' farmhouse. It has three bedrooms and sleeps six. Ideal for walking, exploring Welsh Border and scenic Black and White villages. Golf, riding, small breeds farm, working farm centre and leisure centre in the area. Electricity and central heating included. One pet and children welcome. Rates of £140 to £240 represent a saving of up to 30% on agencies' prices for this property. Contact: **Mrs J. Hughes, Oaklands, Kington HR5 3HB (01544 230500).**

KINGTON. The Harbour, Upper Hergest, Kington. Properties sleep 5/9. This bungalow is on a good second-class road facing south with beautiful views from its elevated position, across the Hergest Ridge and Offa's Dyke. The Welsh border is a mile away. Shops are two-and-a-half miles away. Kington Golf Club nearby. Accommodation for five/nine in two double rooms (one with extra single bed) downstairs and two double dormer bedrooms; two cots; bathroom, toilet; sittingroom (TV); diningroom; sun porch for relaxing; kitchen with electric cooker, fridge, food store and usual equipment. No linen. Suitable for the disabled. Children and pets welcome. Car essential — parking. Available all year. Also mobile home sleeping two with bathroom and flush toilet. SAE, please, to **Mr A.J. Welson, New House Farm, Upper Hergest, Kington, Herefordshire HR5 3EW (Kington [01544] 230533).**

LEDBURY near. High House Farmhouse, Preston Cross, Near Ledbury. 🔑🔑🔑 *Approved.* **Working farm. Properties sleep 6.** High House Farmhouse (part 13th century), is divided into two holiday houses, equipped to very good standard. Superb views towards Ross-on-Wye (eight miles) and Gloucestershire. Fully electric kitchen/diner; sittingroom; bathroom and toilet; three bedrooms, all with fitted carpets; TV; telephone. Garage (car essential). All rooms have either night storage or electric heaters. Each house sleeps six. No linen supplied. Electricity extra. Farm buildings are nearby (this is a working stock and arable farm). Dogs allowed, under strict control. Children welcome, cot. Historical market town of Ledbury three miles, Malvern eight miles. Weekly terms from £150 to £210; reductions off season. CARE Association Approved. **Mrs G.M. Thomas, White House Farm, Preston Cross, Near Ledbury HR8 2LH (01531 660231).**

FREE and REDUCED RATE Holiday Visits!
See our Readers' Offer Vouchers for details.

HELP IMPROVE BRITISH TOURIST STANDARDS

You are choosing holiday accommodation from our very popular FHG Publications. Whether it be a hotel, guest house, farmhouse or self-catering accommodation, we think you will find it hospitable, comfortable and clean, and your host and hostess friendly and helpful. Why not write and tell us about it?

As a recognition of the generally well-run and excellent holiday accommodation reviewed in our publications, we at FHG Publications Ltd. present a diploma to proprietors who receive the highest recommendation from their guests who are also readers of our Guides. If you care to write to us praising the holiday you have booked through FHG Publications Ltd. – whether this be board, self-catering accommodation, a sporting or a caravan holiday, what you say will be evaluated and the proprietors who reach our final list will be contacted.

The winning proprietor will receive an attractive framed diploma to display on his premises as recognition of a high standard of comfort, amenity and hospitality. FHG Publications Ltd. offer this diploma as a contribution towards the improvement of standards in tourist accommodation in Britain. Help your excellent host or hostess to win it!

FHG DIPLOMA

We nominate ....

....

Because

Name ....

Address ....

.... Telephone No. ....

LEOMINSTER. Mrs E.M. Thomas, Woonton Court Farm, Leysters, Leominster HR6 0HL (01568 750232). Sleeps 3/4 plus cot. 🔑🔑🔑 to 🔑🔑🔑🔑 **up to** *Commended.* Half timbered brick and stone detached mill, recently converted to provide comfortable first floor self-contained accommodation. Open plan kitchen/dining room/ spacious sitting room, electric fire, colour TV. Night store heating and fitted carpets throughout. Linen/electricity included. Telephone. Sunny patio, parking, freedom to walk on the farm and enjoy a wealth of nature. Own farm produce. Children and pets welcome. Short Breaks available. Open all year. Terms from £95 to £250 per week.

PETERCHURCH. Hinton Green, Peterchurch. Sleeps 7. 18th century stone semi-detached cottage with exposed beams. Situated in quiet hamlet in the Golden Valley, half a mile from village shop, post office, church and pubs. 12 miles from the market town of Hereford, nine miles from Hay — town of second-hand books. Close to Black Mountains and Brecon Beacons National Park. Golf courses and swimming pool within 10 miles. House sleeps seven: double brass bed, modern divan and three singles; cot available. Colour TV, washing machine, fridge. Pleasant cottage garden with garden furniture. Pets and children welcome. Linen, logs and electricity included. Open all year. £100 to £280 per week. **J.M.S. Hinton, Orchard Bungalow, Ewyas Harold, Hereford HR2 0ES (Golden Valley [01981] 240596).**

ROSS-ON-WYE. Mr and Mrs I.J. Morris, Little Wharton Farm, Weston-Under-Penyard, Ross-on-Wye HR9 5TP (01989 750221). Sleeps 4/6. Little Wharton Farm is a family owned dairy farm on the edge of the Royal Forest of Dean. Situated three miles Herefordshire/Gloucestershire border, it is ideally located for visiting the Wye Valley, Malvern Hills, Cotswolds and South Wales. The accommodation sleeps four (with the possibility of extra space for two). Comfortable sittingroom, modern bathroom, large fitted kitchen with electric cooker, fridge, kettle and iron. Colour TV. All linen provided. Children welcome, cot and high chair available on request. Well behaved pets welcome. Car parking. Public transport and public house half a mile. Weekly terms from £80.

WORMBRIDGE. Mrs J. Thomas, Granary Flat, Lower Jury Farm, Wormbridge HR2 9EE (Wormbridge [0198-121] 229). Working farm. Sleeps 5. Granary Flat is attached to the early 16th century farmhouse on Lower Jury Farm. Situated in a peaceful valley, it is close to the Black Mountains, Golden Valley, market towns and places of historic interest. The flat has a wealth of exposed beams, and the lounge (with colour TV) and bedrooms are fully carpeted. There are lovely views to the distant hills and the Grey Valley. Children are welcome to help with the farm animals and hay-making. Shooting for experienced guns. Accommodates four/five people. Usual conveniences. Kitchen with electric cooker, fridge and dining area. Slot meter (50p) for electricity. Linen supplied. Pets permitted. Car essential — parking. Open April to October. Terms from £90 per week. Registered with the English Tourist Board.

KENT

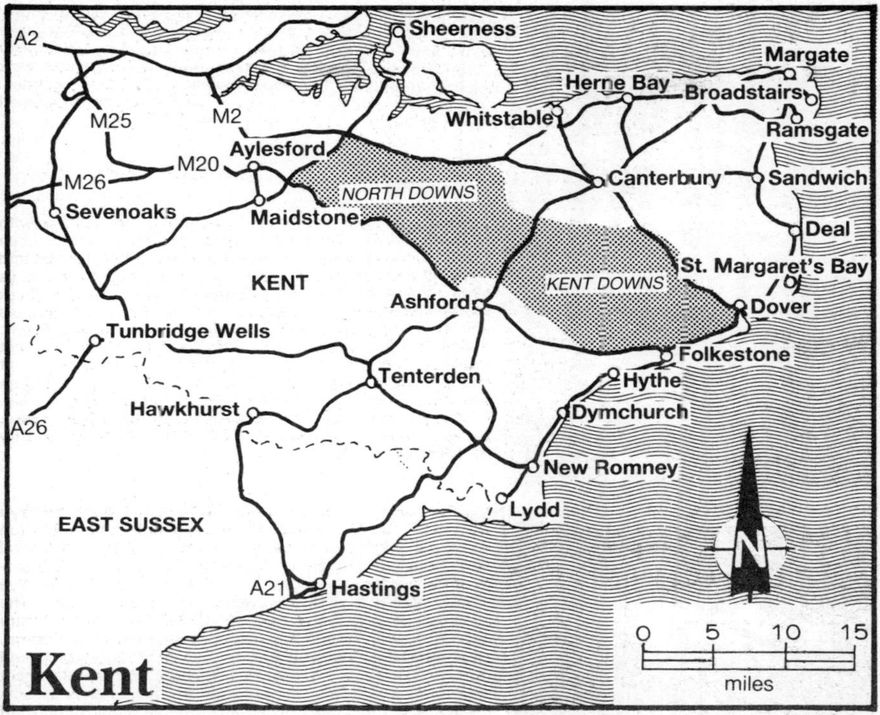

BENENDEN. Miss P.A. Cyster, Spider's Lodge, Iden Green, Benenden, Cranbrook TN17 4HH (01580 240509). Sleeps 4. Self catering accommodation is offered in this charming two-bedroomed Cottage which stands on the edge of an orchard on the outskirts of a small hamlet called Iden Green which has one shop and a pub. A car is essential here to take advantage of the many historic and interesting places to visit in this beautiful area. Children are welcome but sorry, no pets. Weekly terms from £80 to £140. Non-smokers only. SAE or phone for full details.

BENENDEN. Waggon Lodge. Working farm. Sleeps 6. The cottage is situated down a private road. Beautiful and peaceful countryside, much of historic interest in the area. Recently converted to sleep six in three double bedrooms; bathroom, shower and toilet; lounge; dining area; kitchen with electric cooker, fridge, washing machine etc. Linen supplied. Storage heaters and electric fire. Colour TV. Cleaner calls once a week. Shop half a mile. Car essential — plenty of parking space. No pets. Terms from £180 to £250. SAE to **Mrs Anne Cyster, Walkhurst Farm, New Pond Road, Benenden TN17 4EN (Cranbrook [01580] 240677).**

HAWKHURST. Mrs L.C. Johnson, Highwell, Heartenoak Road, Hawkhurst, Cranbrook TN18 5EU (01580 752152). Sleeps 3. Enjoy a peaceful holiday in the spacious self-contained annexe (own entrance) to our attractive Edwardian house. The accommodation is furnished and equipped to a very high standard and provides a large, comfortable sittingroom with delightful country views, modern kitchen, double bedroom, bathroom, plus linen, colour TV, central heating, telephone. Set in an acre of secluded gardens down a country lane yet only half a mile from Hawkhurst village, Highwell offers an ideal base for touring Kent and East Sussex with a wealth of famous gardens, castles, coastline and picturesque scenery within easy reach. Terms from £80 to £130 weekly. Sorry, no pets.

LEYSDOWN-ON-SEA. Mrs Sally Marsh, Newhouse Farm, Leysdown Road, Leysdown-on-Sea, Near Sheerness ME12 4BA (01795 510201). 𝟒𝟒𝟒𝟒 *Highly Commended.* BIRDWATCHERS COTTAGE. This idyllic, well equipped, quality cottage set on a family-run cattle, sheep and arable farm allows visitors to share in the peace of the countryside. It boasts beamed ceilings, has four bedrooms, gas central heating and is surrounded by a large garden with panoramic views. In an area free from crowds and traffic, the cottage is situated between two nature reserves near to several local places of interest, including Blue Flag Award clean beaches. It is under one hour to Canterbury, Maidstone and Rochester and by train to London. Open all year it's an ideal touring base and quiet hideaway. Prices from £160 weekly. Send SAE for a detailed leaflet.

See also Colour Display Advertisement **SOUTHERN ENGLAND. Fairhaven Holiday Cottages.** An extensive selection of personally inspected holiday homes. Various shapes, sizes and locations in southern England and Wales. Available throughout the year. Long and short winter lets. Featuring KENT and the KINGSDOWN LEISURE PARK NEAR DEAL. Contact: **Fairhaven Holiday Cottages, Derby House, 123 Watling Street, Gillingham, Kent ME7 2YY (01634 570157).**

LEICESTERSHIRE

MARKET HARBOROUGH. Mrs M.J. Hart, The Wrongs, Welford Road, Sibbertoft, Market Harborough (01858 880886). 𝟒𝟒𝟒 We are centrally placed being near to the borders of Northamptonshire, Leicestershire and Warwickshire, which makes us an ideal base for visiting Warwick, Stratford, Coventry, the battlefields of Naseby and Market Bosworth, the historic houses of Belvoir Castle, Kirby Hall, Burley House, Althorpe and Sulgrave Manor. We offer two Norwegian spruce chalets beside a peaceful five acre carp fishing lake in the middle of our 600 acre working farm. Both chalets are furnished to a high standard and equipped with shower, microwave, colour TV and all linen. Dogs welcome. Brochure available.

LINCOLNSHIRE

BOURNE near. Mrs V. Sanders, Barn Farm House, Station Street, Rippingale, Near Bourne PE10 0TD (01778 440666). Two cottages in beautiful Lincolnshire countryside within reach of Stamford, Grantham, Lincoln, Peterborough. One 400 year old cottage, low ceilings, electric heating and open fires, three bedrooms, diningroom, sittingroom, kitchen, bathroom, garden. Washing machine, tumble dryer, fridge, colour TV. Linen provided, sleeps four. Four bedroomed cottage sleeps eight people. Sittingroom, hall, diningroom, downstairs toilet, kitchen; upstairs two bedrooms with double beds, two bedrooms with twin beds and bathroom including electric shower. Washing machine, fridge, colour TV, garden, garage, central heating, linen. £100 to £225 per week.

FULSTOW, near Louth. Waingrove Farm, Fulstow, Near Louth LN11 0XQ (01507 363704). *Highly Commended.* **Farmhouse sleeps up to 6 plus nursery; Cottages sleep up to 4.** Three luxuriously equipped cottages enjoying peace and privacy of our 200 acre farm. THE OLD FARMHOUSE circa 1839, has spacious accommodation with one double, two twin rooms and nursery. BRAMBLE and HAWTHORNE are single storey cottages converted from an old barn, each having a double and twin bedroom overlooking a paved and gravelled "courtyard". All cottages have pretty furnishings, beams and pale walls setting off pine furniture. Nearby Lincolnshire Wolds are beautiful; explore Tennyson Country, Lincoln Cathedral, antique shops, Tattershall Castle. there's so much to do! Sorry, no pets. £150 to £350 per week including linen. Brochure available.

SOUTH WILLINGHAM. Lavender Cottage, South Willingham. Sleeps 4. This small country cottage is situated at the end of a short lane in the picture postcard village of South Willingham. It is an ideal base from which to explore the Lincolnshire Wolds, the historic city of Lincoln and the market towns of Louth Horncastle and Market Rasen. Accommodation is on one floor and comprises a sittingroom, kitchen, bathroom and two bedrooms (one twin room and one family room). Full central heating. Surrounded by quiet country lanes it is ideal walking country. Bed and Breakfast accommodation available at farm where fishing and our off road driving course are available (with tuition if necessary). **Kay Olivant, Skirbeck Farm, Panton Road, Benniworth, Lincoln LN3 6JM (01507 313682; Fax: 01507 313692).**

WOODHALL SPA. "Kirkstead Old Mill Cottage", Woodhall Spa. *Highly Commended.* Isolated, three-bedroomed holiday home which sleeps seven to 10 plus baby, which is only let to NON-SMOKERS. The sunny house is over a mile off the Tattershall road on the outskirts of Woodhall Spa, Lincolnshire. It is set beside the wide but quiet River Witham that is noted for its fishing. A small rowing boat is provided. There is also a large, grassy garden and a three-acre nature reserve for picnics. The house is extremely well equipped with colour TV, dishwasher, automatic washing machine, tumble dryer, fridge/freezer, microwave and piano etc. There is plenty of parking space, and a home help is provided for two hours midweek. Membership of local leisure club with swimming pool is included. Weekly rates from £99 to £400. Contact: **Mrs Barbara Hodgkinson, "Hodge's Lodges", 52 Kelso Close, Worth, Crawley, West Sussex RH10 7XH (01293 882008; Fax: 01293 883352).**

NATURELAND SEAL SANCTUARY offers free entry for one child when accompanied by a paying adult when using our READERS' OFFER VOUCHER.

NORFOLK

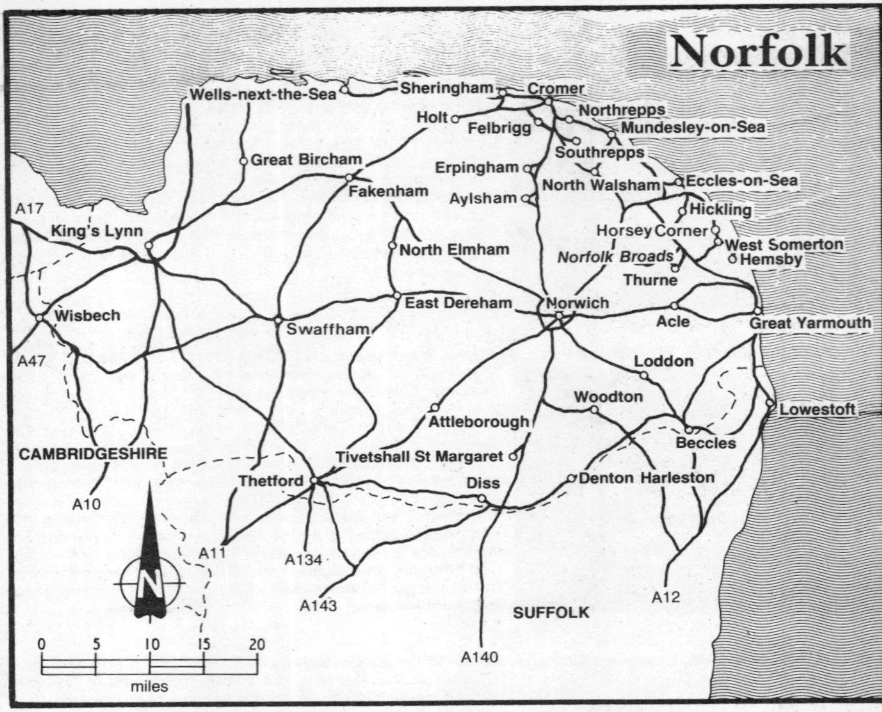

BLAKENEY. 4 Mariners Hill, Blakeney & Starlings, 82 High Street, Blakeney. Properties sleep 8/6. All year round, beautiful house and attractive cottage available to visitors hoping for a holiday that combines true relaxation, first class accommodation and splendid scenery. MARINERS HILL is a flint/brick-built house sleeping eight, with spectacular views over the quay and marsh. Small, secluded, walled garden. Extremely well furnished and equipped. Colour TV, washing machine, dishwasher and fridge/freezer. STARLINGS is a pink-washed cottage with a part covered courtyard. With accommodation for six, it provides TV and night storage heaters. Good dinghy sailing and birdwatching at hand, golf courses nearby. For further details please write to: **Mrs A. Suckling or Mrs B. Marris, The Merchants House, 86 High Street, Blakeney, Holt NR25 7AL. Telephone enquiries: Mrs A. Suckling (Holt [01263] 712636).**

BRISLEY. Church Farm Cottages, Brisley, East Dereham NR20 5LL. 🔑🔑🔑🔑 *Highly Commended.* **Properties sleep 2/5.** Situated just off the village green between East Dereham and Fakenham, these cottages are on a mixed working farm of 230 acres. Kept to a very high standard of cleanliness and comfort, they have full central heating, log fires, colour TV, video, washing machine, etc. Each has lawned garden and plenty of parking space. Open all year, Short Breaks available. Linen, logs and heating included in price. Terms from £170 to £400. Swimming pool, golf, sports and leisure centre all within easy reach. Ideal for birdwatchers and cyclists. Further details contact **Gillian Howes (01362 668332).**

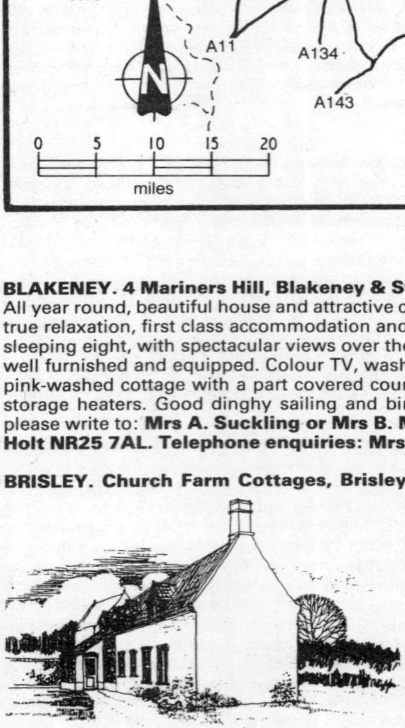

CLIPPESBY. Mrs Jean Lindsay, Clippesby Holidays, Clippesby, Near Great Yarmouth NR29 3BJ (01493 369367). 🔑🔑/🔑🔑🔑🔑 *Approved.* ✓ ✓ ✓ ✓ ✓ Excellent. IN BROADLANDS NATIONAL PARK, near nature reserves, rivers and coastal resorts. 23 Holiday Cottages and a touring park in the secluded grounds of Clippesby Hall. All "🔑🔑" cottages are simply and comfortably furnished and equipped with linen and colour TV and completely self contained. The "🔑🔑" cottages have fireplaces, dishwashers, microwave ovens and central heating. Terms from £80 to £460 per week. Available all year. In summer there is swimming, lawn tennis, a family club room and other things to do. Send for colour brochure. Finalist "Best Park in England" Calor Award.

CROMER. Beverley Holiday Flats, 17 Alfred Road, Cromer. Spacious self contained apartments for two people. NON SMOKERS only. Furnished and equipped to a high standard including microwave cookers and orthopaedic beds. No pets or young children. Ground floor accommodation available. Six times winner of Tourism Award for Excellence. Restful holiday assured in a quiet homely atmosphere. Private parking. Situated close to the seafront in a delightful part of Cromer. Convenient for town centre, shops, railway and coach stations. An excellent base for visiting the many attractions in the area including National Trust properties, Christian Shrine at Walsingham, Sandringham, City of Norwich and the Broads. Weekly terms from £140. For brochure please telephone **Mrs Marshall on 01394 450343.**

CROMER. Hobby Cottage, Driftway Farm, Felbrigg, Cromer. Sleeps 4/6 plus cot. Completely modernised, comfortable cottage at the end of a quiet farm lane. Two miles from sandy coast and within easy access of North Norfolk bird sanctuaries, stately homes and Norfolk Broads. The cottage sleeps four/six having a sitting room with TV and bed settee; two double bedrooms (one with double bed, one with twin beds); diningroom, well-equipped kitchen and bathroom. Garden and parking for two cars. Own transport essential. Available March-October. From £115 — £240 per week, including electricity. No linen. Enquiries, with SAE please, to **Mrs E. Raggatt, The Ferns, Berkley Street, Eynesbury, St. Neots, Cambs PE19 2NE (Huntingdon [01480] 213884).**

CROMER. Northrepps Holiday Properties, Cromer NR27 0JW (01263 578196 and 512236). Sleep 4/7. Our cottages are very comfortably furnished, generously equipped and very carefully maintained. All are fully electric with cooker, water heater, fridge, colour TV and electric fires. Accommodation for four to six persons. Cots available on request. Pets always welcome. Some of the cottages have their own enclosed garden, ideal for children and pets. Ample parking for cars. As well as local wonderful sandy beaches we have golf, sailing, lake fishing, bird watching and miles of good walking in lovely surroundings. Cromer has a cinema and Pier with first rate live shows. Inclusive charges from £200 to £380 per week. Detailed brochure on request.

FAKENHAM. Saddlery Cottage and Hillside Cottage, Colkirk, Fakenham. Sleep 7 and 6 respectively. Both cottages are situated near the farm on the outskirts of Colkirk village, overlooking farmland. Saddlery Cottage (shown in picture) has large and light sittingroom with beams and woodburner, fully fitted kitchen/dining room with fridge and electric cooker, utility room with automatic washing machine. Garage, parking and fenced garden. Hillside Cottage has sittingroom with colour TV, large airy kitchen/dining room with fitted units and washing machine. Fenced garden, parking. Both have central heating/Calor gas heating. Children and pets welcome. Cots available; linen supplied. Tourist Board recommended. Apply **Mrs C. Joice, Colkirk Hall, Fakenham NR21 7ND (01328 862261).**

GELDESTON. Hillside, 15 Kells Way, Geldeston, Beccles. Sleeps 4/6. This bungalow situated in small country village, very quiet and near River Waveney, is within easy reach of Great Yarmouth, Norwich, Lowestoft, Southwold and seaside. Accommodates four/six people; one double, one twin bedroom; bed settee in lounge, storage heaters, colour TV, wood burner, beams; diningroom; bathroom/shower, toilet; kitchen, electric cooker, microwave, etc. Carpets throughout. Cot available. Sorry, no pets. Bed linen supplied. Open all year. Car essential — parking. Shops nearby. Terms on request. Special winter rates. **Mrs M. Rolt, "Conifer", 17 Kells Way, Geldeston, Beccles, Suffolk NR34 0LU (01508 518689).**

PLEASE SEND A STAMPED ADDRESSED ENVELOPE WITH ENQUIRIES

MUNDESLEY-ON-SEA. 47 Seaward Crest, Mundesley-on-Sea. Sleeps 4. Mundesley-on-Sea is an attractive seaside village situated centrally on the Norfolk coast, within 10 miles of the Norfolk Broads, seven miles from Cromer and 20 miles from Norwich. The clean sandy beaches stretch for miles with safe bathing and natural paddling pools. This attractive west-facing brick-built chalet is in delightful setting with lawns, flower beds, trees and ample parking. Beach 500 yards away and shops 800 yards. There is an excellent golf course nearby and bowls and riding are within easy reach. Large lounge/diningroom tastefully furnished including easy chairs, settee and colour TV. Kitchenette with electric cooker, fridge, sink unit, etc. One double, one twin-bedded rooms. Fully carpeted. Bathroom and toilet. Lighting, hot water, heating and cooking by electricity (50p slot meter). Fully equipped except for linen. Weekly terms from £65. East Anglia Tourist Board registered. Details, SAE, please, **Mrs J. Doar, 4 Denbury Road, Ravenshead, Nottinghamshire NG15 9FQ (Mansfield [01623] 798032).**

NORWICH. Mrs G.L. Coiley, Pond Farm, Cringleford, Norwich NR4 6UE (01603 54895). 🔑🔑🔑🔑 *Highly Commended.* One mile A11/A47 intersection, excellently situated three miles south Norwich, easy access to city centre and all Norfolk. Imaginative barn conversion into two cottages, courtyard garden set in grounds of owner's picturesque, thatched 16th century farmhouse with duck pond, adjacent village green. The Old Stables (sleeps four) and Horseshoe Cottage (sleeps two), both have twin bedded rooms, cot and high chair available; bathroom; attractive beamed lounge/diner, colour TV; fully fitted kitchen. No stairs, therefore suitable for those with limited mobility. Bed linen (duvets), towels, electricity, gas central heating included in price. Telephone. Regret no smoking, nor pets. Terms: Old Stables £220 to £290, Horseshoe Cottage £160 to £230 per week. Please telephone or send for brochure.

FOR THE MUTUAL GUIDANCE OF GUEST AND HOST

Every year literally thousands of holidays, short-breaks and overnight stops are arranged through our guides, the vast majority without any problems at all. In a handful of cases, however, difficulties do arise about bookings, which often could have been prevented from the outset.

It is important to remember that when accommodation has been booked, both parties — guests and hosts — have entered into a form of contract. We hope that the following points will provide helpful guidance.

GUESTS: When enquiring about accommodation, be as precise as possible. Give exact dates, numbers in your party and the ages of any children. State the number and type of rooms wanted and also what catering you require — bed and breakfast, full board, etc. Make sure that the position about evening meals is clear — and about pets, reductions for children or any other special points.

Read our reviews carefully to ensure that the proprietors you are going to contact can supply what you want. Ask for a letter confirming all arrangements, if possible.

If you have to cancel, do so as soon as possible. Proprietors do have the right to retain deposits and under certain circumstances to charge for cancelled holidays if adequate notice is not given and they cannot re-let the accommodation.

HOSTS: Give details about your facilities and about any special conditions. Explain your deposit system clearly and arrangements for cancellations, charges, etc, and whether or not your terms include VAT.

If for any reason you are unable to fulfil an agreed booking without adequate notice, you may be under an obligation to arrange alternative suitable accommodation or to make some form of compensation.

While every effort is made to ensure accuracy, we regret that FHG Publications cannot accept responsibility for errors, omissions or misrepresentation in our entries or any consequences thereof. Prices in particular should be checked because we go to press early. We will follow up complaints but cannot act as arbiters or agents for either party.

SHERINGHAM. "High Lee", 68 Cliff Road, Sheringham. "High Lee" is a delightful detached, newly-built three bedroom (one double, two twin) chalet bungalow. It is ideal for exploring the beautiful North Norfolk coast, the Broads or enjoying the attractive family resort of Sheringham. Close to the beach, coastal path and a short walk from the town centre. "High Lee" offers comfortable accommodation for six, with one of the bedrooms, bathroom and separate shower on ground floor. Heating, electricity, fridge, colour TV, cot and high chair are all inclusive. Separate detached garage. Attractive garden with patio and barbecue. Open all year. Weekly terms £150 to £300. Sorry, no pets. **Mr and Mrs M. Nelson, 85 Hillside Grove, Chelmsford, Essex CM2 9DB (01245 262436).**

SPILSBY. Mrs C.A. Miller, Northfields Farm, Mavis Enderby, Spilsby PE23 4EN (01507 588251). 🔑🔑🔑 *Commended.* Situated in a secluded rural area and in the middle of our farm away from busy roads, are two semi-detached Victorian cottages. Very cosy and well equipped, each having three bedrooms which sleep four, cot and high chair available. The farm is three miles west of Spilsby in a lovely area for walking; Snipe Dales Country Park and Nature Reserve just one mile away and many interesting things to do in the area. An ideal base for a country holiday. Open all year. Dogs allowed. Terms from £125 to £295 per week inclusive of linen, heating, lighting, etc.

See also Colour Display Advertisement **THURNE. Hedera House and Plantation Bungalows, Thurne. Sleep up to 12.** Hedera House is a comfortably furnished Georgian-style house comprising spacious lounge and dining area with colour TV, kitchen with split level hob and double oven, breakfast bar, five double (with washbasins) and two single bedrooms, bathroom, shower and two WCs. Heating available for all seasons. Plantation Bungalows are a select group of 10 individual holiday homes, roomy and comfortably furnished and carpeted. Colour TV, fully fitted bathroom and kitchen, electric radiator heating in lounge and bedrooms. Cavity wall insulation. Electric meter. Norfolk is rich in places of historic interest, beautiful beaches, Broads, villages and countryside, all within easy motoring distance of Thurne. Fishing, boating, nearby golf course, horse riding. Free mooring and launching facilities for small craft. SAE to **Miss H.G. Delf, Thurne Cottage, The Staithe, Thurne NR29 3BU (01692 670242 or 01493 844568).**

WINTERTON-ON-SEA. Timbers, The Lane, Winterton-on-Sea. Sleeps 5. Comfortable, well furnished ground floor flat in attractive timber cottage situated in quiet seaside village just eight miles north of Great Yarmouth. Broad sandy beach and sand dunes (nature reserve) for pleasant walks. Three miles from Norfolk Broads (boating and fishing). Flat is carpeted throughout and is fully equipped for self-catering family holidays. Ideal for children, and pets are welcome. One double, one twin-bedded and one single bedroom. Sleeps five plus cot. Bed linen provided and maid service every other day for general cleaning. Beamed sittingroom with colour TV. Secluded garden. Car parking. Available May to September. Terms from £140 to £300 per week. For full details write to **Mr M.J. Isherwood, 79 Oakleigh Avenue, London N20 9JG (0181-445 2192).**

WIVETON. Laneway Cottage. This lovely flint cottage, which is all on one floor, faces south with a flint-walled garden with furniture. The large sittingroom with open fire and colour TV opens out on to a patio. It has one double and one twin bedroom with fitted carpets and cupboards, and is fully equipped for four people. Kitchen-dining room with fitted units, electric cooker, Aga and fridge. Utility room with washing machine. Cloakroom with shower, toilet and washbasin. Bathroom with washbasin and WC. Oil-fired central heating. Telephone. Garage and parking area. Suitable for disabled visitors. Contact: **Mrs C. Joice, Colkirk Hall, Fakenham NR21 7ND (01328 862261).**

NORFOLK – NOT JUST THE BROADS!

There's more to do in Norfolk than messing about in boats – pleasurable though that may be. Other places of interest include the gardens and steam museum at Bressingham, the Broadland Conservation Centre, the flint mines at Grimes Graves, The Norfolk Rural Life Museum, Sandringham – which is often open to the public – and of course Norwich itself.

NORTHUMBERLAND

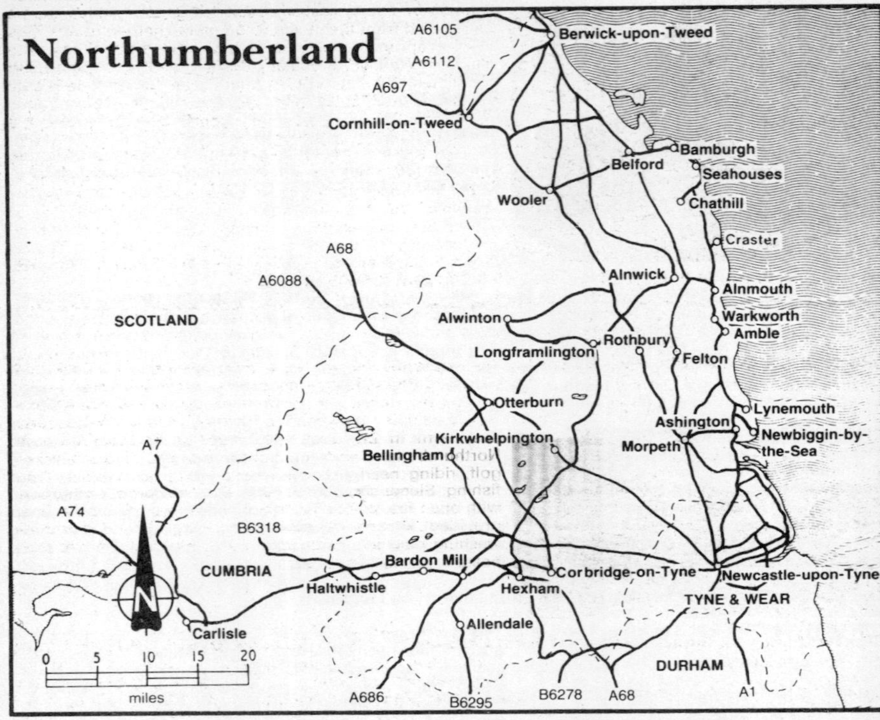

ALNWICK. Mrs V. Purvis, Titlington Hall Farm, Alnwick NE66 2EB (01665 578253). *Commended.* **Sleeps 2-10.** Two lovely country cottages available for holiday lets all year round. They are situated in a quiet and beautiful area with many interesting places just a short drive away. Facilities include central heating, TV, fridge, microwave, washing machine, tumble dryer and linen. Children welcome, pets by arrangement. Prices from £155 to £295 per week.

ALNWICK. Birling Vale, Warkworth, Alnwick. Birling Vale is an attractive stone-built, detached house standing in a very pleasant, secluded garden (which can be appreciated from the recently completed garden room). This house is approximately one-third of a mile from picturesque village of Warkworth which is beside the River Coquet and dominated by an ancient Norman Castle. Birling Vale is only half-a-mile from lovely sandy beaches; 15 minutes from trout and salmon rivers, and within a comfortable drive of many places of interest, including Hadrian's Wall, Holy Island and Scottish Borders. The house, which is tastefully furnished and fully equipped including colour TV, has two bedrooms with double beds and a third bedroom with single divans. Cot available. Oil for full central heating is provided free of charge. Well trained dogs welcome. Weekly terms from £100 low season; £210 mid-season; £325 high season. Tourist Board Commended. SAE to **Mrs Janet Brewis, Woodhouse Farm, Shilbottle, Near Alnwick NE66 2HR (01665 575222).**

BERWICK-UPON-TWEED. Mrs H. Wight, Gainslawhill Farm, Berwick-upon-Tweed TD15 1SZ (01289 386210). Well equipped cottage with own walled garden on mixed farm, three miles from Berwick-upon-Tweed, situated between the Rivers Tweed and Whiteadder (last farm in England). Ideal position for touring north Northumberland and the Border country. Good beaches, golf, riding nearby. Lovely walks along both rivers. Trout fishing. Sleeps six, cot available. Pets welcome. Livingroom with open fire, colour TV, telephone. Three bedrooms (linen provided), kitchen with dining area, fridge freezer, automatic washing machine, microwave oven. Bathroom. Night store heaters. Terms from £160

CHATHILL. Mrs M. Riddell, Newstead Farm Cottages, Chathill NE67 5LH (01665 589263). A stone built cottage to sleep five persons, situated on a working farm, half a mile from A1, four miles from sandy beaches and the Farne Islands Bird Sanctuary. Ideal for day touring to the Borders and many places of historical interest. Six coastal golf courses within easy reach. The cottage has two bedrooms, cot available; bathroom and toilet; sittingroom and kitchen with electric cooker and fridge. Night storage heating. Electricity by meter. Linen available at extra charge. A safe playing area for children and ample parking. Pets by arrangement. SAE for details. Available March to November.

CORBRIDGE. Mr F.J. Matthews, The Hayes, Newcastle Road, Corbridge NE45 5LP (Corbridge [01434] 632010). Spacious attractive stone-built guesthouse. Set in seven acres of grounds. Single, double, twin, family bedrooms; lounge and dining rooms. Open 11 months of the year. Bed and Breakfast from £16. Children's reductions. Stair lift for disabled visitors. Self catering properties — three cottages, flat and caravan. Awarded two Farm Holiday Guide Diplomas. Car parking. For brochure or booking SAE/phone. ETB registered.

Don't miss the special ENTRY OFFERS for visits to Hexham Herbs.
See our READERS' OFFER Vouchers for details.

HEXHAM (Haydon Bridge). Mrs V.R.A. Drydon, West Deanraw, Langley-on-Tyne, Haydon Bridge, Hexham NE47 5LY (Hexham [01434] 684228). Working farm. Detached bungalow situated on a farm in rural Northumberland, approximately three miles from the village of Haydon Bridge, and 10 miles from the market town of Hexham. The property enjoys delightful views of the Tyne Valley, and is an ideal touring base for Hadrian's Wall, Kielder Reservoir, Border country, the magnificent Northumbrian coastline, Cumbria and the Lake District. Accommodation comprises one double and one twin bedrooms (extra children's beds available); bathroom with electric shower; livingroom with sofa bed; colour TV; diningroom. Fully fitted kitchen, all-electric, includes microwave, fridge, washing machine, immersion heater, plus open fire-back boiler (fuel for fire provided but electricity metered). Central heating. Pets welcome but extra charge. Personally supervised by owners to ensure high standards of cleanliness and comfort. Terms and further details on request.

MORPETH. Mr & Mrs A.P. Coatsworth, Gallowhill Farm, Whalton, Morpeth, NE61 3TX (01661 881241). *Highly Commended.* **Working farm. Sleeps 4-6.** Relax in our two spacious stone-built cottages. Recently converted and modernised to give you every facility you require. Electric cooker, fridge, freezer, dishwasher, washer/dryer, microwave. Located in the heart of Northumberland on a very tidy farm with private gardens. Bolam Lake two miles, Belsay Castle four miles, coast 20 minutes, Hadrian's Wall 30 minutes, to name only a few attractions. All linen, heating, electricity included in price. Sorry, no pets. All children welcome. Brochure on request. Terms £190 to £385.

WOOLER. Mrs E. Logan, The Bungalow, Fenton Hill, Wooler NE71 6JJ (016686 200). Cottages sleep 5/6. Two traditional cottages on a working farm with quiet country road running past and overlooking the Cheviot hills. Ideal walking countryside with access to the sea, hills and the Scottish Border Country. Farne Islands and Lindisfarne within easy reach; many other places of interest in the area. Golf, fishing and pony-trekking nearby. Two bedroom cottage, one with double bed and three singles in the other. Other cottage has double bed in one room and other room has a double and a 'three-quarter' bed. Linen NOT provided. Kitchen with electric cooker and fridge. Sitting room has electric or coal fire and colour TV. Bathroom. Cot available. Pets permitted. Shop two-and-a-half/three miles. Car essential. Terms £85–£120.

NOTTINGHAMSHIRE

Sherwood Forest Farm & Country Holidays

This 17th century converted granary is situated in the heart of Robin Hood Country, close to the historic town of Southwell and Nottingham. Comfortably furnished with original beams in lounge and kitchen. Central heating, colour TV, log fire, utility room with washer/dryer. Two twin-bedded rooms, each with own bathroom. Use of heated swimming pool May/September and snooker room in walled garden. Open all year. Children welcome. Terms from £245 to £285.

HIGHLY COMMENDED

Contact: Jenny Esam, The Loft House, Criftin Farm, Epperstone, Nottingham NG14 6AT. Tel: 0115 965 2039.

OXFORDSHIRE

SWINBROOK. Hill View Cottage, Swinbrook, Oxford OX18 4EF (01993-82 3440). Sleeps 3 adults.

At village edge in the beautiful Windrush Valley this 18th century stone cottage was recently renovated providing comfortable accommodation for three people. Adjoining owner's cottage in peaceful garden setting, it is ideally situated for exploring the Cotswolds. Downstairs well equipped kitchen/dinette leading to single bedroom and bathroom; upstairs large bright double-bed/sitting room with lovely views is well furnished. Colour TV. Weekly prices include linen, but not towels. Children and pets by arrangement. Washing machine. Parking space. Heating by night store heaters; electricity paid by meter reading. Weekly terms from £135. SAE or telephone for further details.

SHROPSHIRE

BISHOP'S CASTLE. Walcot Hall, Lydbury North, Bishop's Castle. Flats sleep 4/9. Spacious flats in Stately Home. Secluded location in own grounds; splendid scenery and ideal area for peaceful holiday for young and old. All flats fully furnished and recently decorated and sleep four/nine. Larger parties by arrangement. Village shop half a mile; local market towns, castles, villages and hill country of the Border Counties provide opportunities for exploration and walking. Coarse fishing in pools and lake. Boats and bicycles available, and riding locally. Terms from £147 to £285 weekly. **Mrs M. Smith, 41 Cheval Place, London SW7 1EW (0171-581 2782)**.

CLUN VALLEY. Mrs P.E. North, The Old Shop, Clunton, Craven Arms SY7 0HP (Little Brampton [0158-87] 327). On B4368 Craven Arms to Clun road. Self-contained, centrally heated, single storey ground floor flat in centre of the small village of Clunton on the River Clun, within six miles of the Welsh Border. Superb walking country with relatively quiet roads and much of historic interest. Sandy beaches within 90 minutes' drive. Entrance hall; comfortable lounge with double bed settee, fitted carpets, central heating, double glazing and open fire; dining kitchen with pine units, electric cooker, kettle, fridge and constant hot water. Shower room with WC and washbasin. Bedroom with two single beds, plus camp bed if required. Cot available, babysitting by arrangement. Bed linen can be supplied. Attractive cottage-style garden. Pets welcome. Car essential, parking. Village shops one-and-three-quarter miles. Fishing and riding locally. Terms from £95 to £110 per week. Ideal for winter breaks.

CLUN VALLEY (South Shropshire). Mrs Sue Wheeler, Brynmawr, Newcastle-on-Clun, Craven Arms SY7 8QU (01588 640298). Sleeps 5.

Self catering mobile home on busy stock rearing farm overlooking the Clun Valley. On the mid-Wales Border in easy reach of Snowdonia National Park, Brecon Beacons, Ironbridge Gorge Museum, Shrewsbury, etc. Beautiful touring/walking area along "Offa's Dyke". The mobile home stands in its own garden. Lovely views from lounge overlooking valley and hills. Kitchen, double bedroom, single, double bunk room and bathroom. Central heating from Parkray fire. Immersion heater. Babysitting available. Sorry, no pets. Disabled persons welcome if facilities are suitable. 35 miles to Hereford, Shrewsbury and 12 miles to Newtown. Warm welcome assured. Terms from £90 to £120.

CRAVEN ARMS. Mrs B. Freeman, Upper House, Clunbury, Craven Arms SY7 0HG (015887 629 or 203).

Welcome to Horseshoe Cottage which is situated in the beautiful gardens of Upper House (17th century Listed) in Clunbury, a village of archaeological interest in a designated area of outstanding natural beauty — A.E. Housman countryside. This self catering cottage is completely furnished and equipped; being on one level the accommodation is suitable for elderly and disabled persons. Colour TV. Sleeps four; cot available. Children and pets welcome. Ample parking. This Welsh Border countryside is rich in medieval history, unspoilt villages and natural beauty. Enjoy walking on the Long Mynd and Offa's Dyke, or explore Ludlow and Ironbridge. £125 to £150 per week. Please write or phone for further details.

LUDLOW. Hazel Cottage, Duxmoor, Onibury, Craven Arms. 🔑🔑🔑🔑 *Highly Commended.* **Sleeps 4.**

Beautifully restored, semi-detached, yet private, period cottage, set in its own extensive "cottage" garden with drive and ample parking space. It has panoramic views of the surrounding countryside and is situated five miles north of historic Ludlow. The cottage comprises a comfortable livingroom with colour TV, radio and telephone, diningroom; fully equipped kitchen; hall; bathroom; two bedrooms (one double and one with twin beds) with washbasins. Electric central heating throughout. All linen included. No pets. The cottage retains all the original features having been decorated traditionally and furnished with antiques throughout. Tourist information. Winter breaks. Terms from £130 to £300 per week. **Mrs Rachel Sanders, Duxmoor Farm, Onibury, Craven Arms SY7 9BQ (01584 77 342 or from June 1995 01584 856342).**

NEWCASTLE ON CLUN. Mr and Mrs J.K. Goslin, The Riddings Firs, Crossways, Newcastle-on-Clun, Craven Arms SY7 8OT (Kerry [01686] 670467). Sleeps 2 adults, 3 children. Ideal holiday location on the Welsh Borders, at 1300 feet, in an area designated as being of outstanding natural beauty. For those seeking complete peace and relaxation, this attractive self-catering family accommodation, for four to five people, is in a self-contained traditional farmhouse annexe with own private entrance. Fully equipped and attractively furnished including colour TV, wood burning stove. Open plan arrangement comprises one double, two bunk beds and bed settee; electric cooker, fridge etc.; shower, toilet, washbasin. Children especially welcome. Pleasantly situated in excellent walking country; several interesting market towns, hospitable inns with dining facilities, Castle within easy reach. Pony trekking and trout fishing can be arranged; area is suitable for mountain bikes. Grazing available for visitors' ponies. Babysitting available. Self-catering terms from £80 per week. Linen supplied at extra cost if required. Out of season and week-end visitors welcome.

OSWESTRY. Mrs Glenice Jones, Lloran Ganol Farm, Llansilin, Oswestry SY10 7OX (Llansilin [0169-170] 287). Working farm. Sleeps 5.

A luxury self-catering bungalow on mixed farm in quiet valley. Farm and bungalow are situated over the border in the Welsh hills in Clwyd. Five people accommodated in two double and one single bedrooms; bathroom, toilet; sittingroom, diningroom; colour TV; long kitchen with dining area; automatic washing machine and fridge. Linen supplied. Extra charge for pets. Two and a half miles from the shops. Car essential — parking. Shooting, horse riding and trout fishing on farm; fishing, golf and trekking in surrounding area. Open all year round, the bungalow is suitable for disabled guests. Storage heaters, fitted carpets and garden furniture provided. Glass conservatory. Weekly terms from £80. Bed and Breakfast also available with family in house adjoining from £12.50 per night, Bed, Breakfast and Evening Meal from £24 per night.

OSWESTRY near. Mrs P. Jackson, Lloran Isaf, Llansilin, Near Oswestry SY10 7QX (0169-170 253). Working farm.

This beautiful bungalow is set on a working farm in its own valley which has wonderful scenery, walks, trout fishing and shooting. Accommodation comprises fitted kitchen; large lounge and dining area with colour TV and wood-burning stove; three bedrooms — one twin, one double and one single (cot available); separate toilet and bathroom. Fitted carpets and electric heating; barbecue area and garden furniture in enclosed garden. One and a half miles from the village, in a wonderful touring area with lots of attractions without the crowds. Open all year. Pets by request only. Prices from £80. Tourist Board registered.

SHREWSBURY near. Mr T.W.E. Corbett, Dower House, Longnor, Shrewsbury SY5 7PR (01743 718628). 🔑🔑🔑 *Approved.*

Property is a modernised stone cottage in a magnificent position with extensive views at the foot of Lawley Hill, five miles from Church Stretton, nine miles from Shrewsbury and one mile from the village of Longnor. It is set in one third of an acre of garden and orchard, and offers excellent facilities for walking, riding, golf, tennis and swimming. There are two double bedrooms, with two fold-down beds in addition. Downstairs there is a bathroom, kitchen/diningroom and sittingroom with TV; electric cooker, fridge. Weekly terms include off peak electricity and wood for open fire. Open season from May to October. Weekly terms from £150. SAE for full details please.

SOMERSET

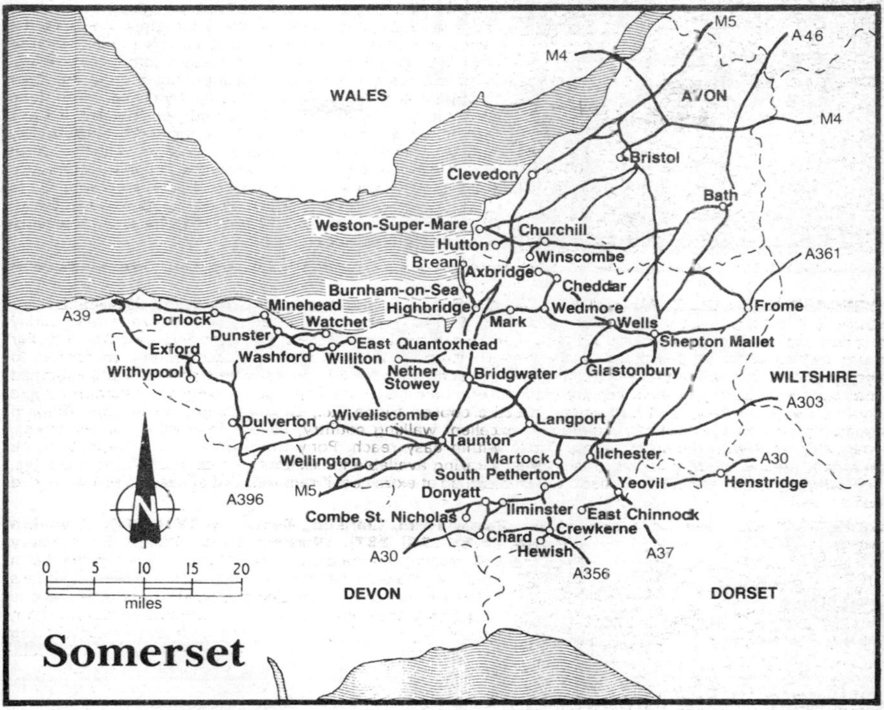

BATH near. Mrs Audrey Rich, Whitnell Farm, Binegar, Emborough, Near Bath BA3 4UF (Oakhill [01749] 840277). Working farm. Holiday home sleeping two, four, six, eight. A mixed farm in picturesque setting of peaceful countryside, relaxed friendly atmosphere. Lawns leading to open fields. Enjoy pleasant walks across the farmland or stroll to country pubs. Excellent base for touring the beautiful unspoilt Mendip Hills and its towns, villages, caves, castles, stately homes. 20 miles to the coast. All properties fully equipped. Electric cookers, fridges, fires, colour TV. Oil central heating. Forecourt all on one level, suitable for disabled people. Just off B3139 Bath to Wells. Bus service passes the gate every hour. Short Breaks available out of season. Discount of 5% on bookings confirmed before 1st March. Ample parking. Open all year. Terms from £90. Farmhouse Bed and Breakfast also available.

See also Colour Display Advertisement **BURNHAM-ON-SEA near. Mrs W. Baker, Withy Grove Farm, East Huntspill, Near Burnham-on-Sea TA9 3NP (Burnham-on-Sea [01278] 784471). Properties sleep 4/6.** Come and enjoy a relaxing and friendly holiday "Down on the Farm" set in beautiful Somerset countryside. Peaceful rural setting adjoining River Huntspill, famed for its coarse fishing and close to Burnham-on-Sea and other beauty spots. Self catering barns and cottages are tastefully converted, sleeping four/six. Fully equipped with colour TV. Facilities include heated swimming pool, licensed bar and entertainment (in high season), games room, skittle alley. Reasonable rates. For more information please do not hesitate to contact us.

Take a child free to RODE BIRD GARDENS, near BATH, Somerset – use our READERS' OFFER VOUCHER.

classic cottages

Goose Barn
Watchet Somerset

Choose your cottage from 300 of the finest coastal and country cottages throughout the West Country.

Classic Cottages (25) Helston Cornwall TR13 8NA

24 hour dial a brochure 01326 565555

Helpful Holidays

MANY ARE ON FARMS

for West Country self-catering

We have a wonderful variety of cottages, houses, apartments all over the West Country - seaside, moorland, farmland or villages. All, and their surroundings, are **very fully described** and **star rated by us in our free colour brochure.**

English Tourist Board REGISTERED AGENCY

CORNWALL REGISTERED ACCOMMODATION

WEST COUNTRY TOURIST BOARD MEMBER

HELPFUL HOLIDAYS,
Coombe 1, Chagford, Devon TQ13 8DF
Tel: (01647) 433593 (24 Hours)

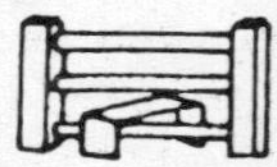

Other specialised

FHG PUBLICATIONS

* Recommended SHORT BREAK HOLIDAYS IN BRITAIN £3.60

* Recommended COUNTRY HOTELS OF BRITAIN £3.60

* PETS WELCOME! £3.99

* BED AND BREAKFAST IN BRITAIN £2.90

Published annually. Please add 50p postage (U.K. only) when ordering from the publishers:

FHG PUBLICATIONS LTD
Abbey Mill Business Centre, Seedhill,
Paisley, Renfrewshire PA1 1TJ

CHARD. Andrew and Kay Clegg, Pulleys Barn, Wambrook, Near Chard TA20 3DF (01460 62583).

This delightful Victorian Barn is situated in an area of outstanding natural beauty. The tiny hamlet of Wambrook is two miles from Chard, 14 miles from Lyme Regis with its beach and picturesque harbour. The accommodation adjoins the main barn and comprises double gallery bedroom, twin bedroom, bathroom, fully fitted kitchen, sittingroom with woodburning stove; french doors to patio; garden furniture for guests to relax and enjoy views of hills and countryside. The pub with its excellent food is within walking distance. Prices from £145 to £235 inclusive of bed linen, electricity. Out of season Short Breaks Regret no pets.

CHARD. Mrs P.P. Maidment, Manor Farm, Knowle St Giles, Chard TA20 3DA (Chard [01460] 63102). 🔑🔑🔑 *Approved.* **Working farm. Sleeps 5.** Manor Farm is situated half-a-mile from main A358 road, two miles from Chard and three miles from Ilminster. This is a modernised self-contained farmhouse, dating from 15th century. It is a dairy farm of 100 acres, with a Friesian herd of cows. The spacious lounge has colour TV; sun lounge; bathroom upstairs and cloakroom downstairs; sleeps five plus cot in two bedrooms; babysitting by arrangement. Modern fully equipped kitchen with electric cooker, microwave and fridge. Bed linen supplied. Pets permitted. Car essential — ample parking. Open all year. Terms from £100 to £250 per week. Owner supervised. It is an ideal centre for touring Somerset, Devon and Dorset. Coast 15 miles. Wildlife Park four miles away; Arts and Crafts Museum half-a-mile.

CHARD near. Mrs Susan J. Adams, Manor Farm, Forton, Near Chard TA20 2LZ (01460 63240). Working farm, join in. Part of 16th century farmhouse (self-contained) of historic importance. Interesting wood structure with murals on walls of large bedroom which will sleep up to three persons. Cot supplied if desired. One medium bedroom with double bed; fully equipped kitchen; separate shower room, toilet; large sitting/diningroom; Super-Ser gas heater. Children can play in safe garden and observe life on this Somerset Dairy Farm set in beautiful countryside. Special attractions of the area include Cricket St Thomas Wildlife Park with its new attraction, "World of Noel Edmonds' Crinkley Bottom" and Mr Blobby; Forde Abbey and many different seaside resorts easily accessible. Members of the West Country Tourist Board. No dogs allowed. Shops one mile. There is also a badminton court; rackets provided for grown-ups. Car essential. Weekly terms from £150 to £200; all electricity and linen included.

CHEDDAR. Mrs K. Thompson, Hillside, Venns Gate, Cheddar BS27 3LW (01934 742493). Sleeps 2/4. 🔑🔑🔑 *Commended.* Four comfortable, well maintained, holiday cottages in converted barn and farmhouse, on southern slopes of the Mendips. Sleep two/four persons in one/two bedrooms, some en-suite (extra sofa bed and cot available). All fully equipped including linen, central heating, colour TV and garden furniture. Cheddar with its famous Gorge, caves and many tourist attractions is within walking distance. Ideally situated for touring West Country, with Bath, Wells, Weston-super-Mare, Bristol and coast all within easy travelling distance. Nearby activities include walking, golfing, fishing, swimming, sailing, riding and caving. Prices from £115 per week Low Season to £250 per week High Season.

SOMERSET HAS IT ALL!

Peaceful thatched cottages, stately homes, sandy beaches, breathtaking caves, churches and cathedrals, romantic legends, heather-covered moorland — Somerset has something for everyone! Much of West Somerset lies within Exmoor National Park, and the county's many areas of upland make it ideal for a walking or nature-study holiday.

DULVERTON. Mrs Strong, Lower Chilcott Farm, Dulverton TA22 9QQ (01398 23439). Sleep 4-7. A friendly, relaxed atmosphere and warm welcome are the top priority at Lower Chilcott Farm. We offer two luxury self catering cottages carefully converted from stone barns and nestling at the end of a quiet lane close to the River Barle Valley on the edge of the Exmoor National Park. It is also within easy reach of North Devon's spectacular coastline, the wild open moors and pretty, thatched villages. Both cottages are well equipped and comfortably furnished. Electricity is by meter reading. Children, pets, horses and mothers-in-law welcome. Bed and Breakfast accommodation can also be enjoyed in our historic, centrally heated farmhouse. Lower Chilcott is an ideal place to stay in an area that offers so much for the country lover and once discovered, you will find it hard to say goodbye! Further details and terms on request.

DULVERTON. Mr and Mrs F.A. Heywood, South Greenslade Farmhouse, Brompton Regis, Dulverton TA22 9NU (Brompton Regis [0139-87] 207). Keens Cottage and Little Harewoods Cottage, South Greenslade Farm: in quiet countryside 200 yards from Wimbleball Lake. Two clean and comfortable holiday houses. Keens Cottage takes six adults plus one or two children; Little Harewoods Cottage takes four adults and baby (cot available), reduced terms for fewer occupants. Both with oil-fired cookers, electric storage heaters, fridge/freezers, automatic washing machines, colour TV and microwave ovens. Situated beside Wimbleball Lake and near open moorland of Haddon Hill, on the eastern side of Exmoor National Park. Ideal for walking, fishing and countryside activities holidays. Terms from £185 — £270 per week (price includes heating, lighting and electricity). Pets allowed, under control. We aim to make your holiday a success. Please phone for details.

DUNSTER. Mrs Sue Gould, Old Cleeve Farm, Old Cleeve, Dunster TA24 6HU (01984 40321). Working farm. Lovely self-contained twin-bedroomed flat, adjoining Old Cleeve Farmhouse in the pretty thatched village of Old Cleeve. Own entrance from the garden and own garage. Accommodation comprises living/diningroom; kitchen; bathroom/toilet; one double and one twin-bedded rooms. Fully equipped with colour TV; all bedlinen and towels supplied. Children welcome, cot provided. Ideally situated for the beautiful scenery of the Quantocks and Exmoor; pony trekking, walking, golf, etc. The farm is three-quarters of a mile from the sea; the seaside resort of Minehead is five miles away with the National Trust's Dunster Castle three miles distant. The West Somerset Steam Railway runs through the farm grounds. Open all year.

EXMOOR. Mrs Jones, Higher Town, Dulverton TA22 9RX (013984 272). Our property is set on 80 acres of parkland, half a mile from open moorland and visitors are welcome to walk over our beef and sheep farm. The bungalow is situated on its own with lovely views, lawn and parking space. It sleeps six with one bunk-bedded room, double bedroom and one bedroom with two single beds. Bedding, linen and electricity are provided. The bathroom and toilet are separate and the bath also has a shower over. The lounge has an open fire and colour TV, the kitchen has electric cooker, fridge freezer and washer dryer. Centrally heated and double glazed. SAE please for further information.

GLASTONBURY. Mrs M. Moon, West Town Farm, Baltonsborough, Glastonbury BA6 8QX (01458 50217). Spacious, fully furnished flat in wing of 17th century farmhouse, situated in lovely Somerset countryside. Ideal for touring — Glastonbury, Wells, Cheddar, Wookey, Longleat — and midway between south and north coast seaside resorts. Self contained with own bathroom/toilet. Lounge/diner with TV and electric fire; fitted kitchen with electric cooker, fridge and breakfast bar. One bedroom with double and single beds, washbasin; second bedroom with two single beds, washbasin; cot. Central heating. Large walled garden with lawns. Visitors must supply own linen. Children most welcome. Sorry, no pets. Holder of FHG Diploma. SAE for full details, terms and dates available.

GLASTONBURY near. Mrs P. Creed, South Town Farm, West Pennard, Glastonbury BA6 8NS (01458 51127). Working farm. Detached stone cottage in a quiet situation, four miles from Glastonbury in village with Post Office, Store and Pub. Three bedrooms: a family room with double and single beds, a twin-bedded room and a twin-bedded landing room with steep staircase. Lounge with colour TV and open fire; diningroom; kitchen and bathroom downstairs. Electricity for cooking, heating, hot water, etc by £1 coin meter. Small lawn front and rear. Off road parking. Pets welcome. A cot and high chair available by prior request. Beds have pillows, blankets and bedspreads. Linen hire extra £2.50 per person per week. Terms from £80 to £130 per week; Dogs £5.

MONTACUTE. Woodhouse Cottage. 🔑🔑🔑 *Commended.* **Sleeps 4/6 plus baby.** Peacefully situated, spacious, centrally heated, hamstone cottage on outskirts of historic village of Montacute, four miles from Yeovil. Ideal centre for walking, cycling, sightseeing and Dorset coast. Many local attractions to suit all tastes including several National Trust properties. Cottage is luxuriously furnished with large lounge, log fire, colour TV (teletext), two comfortable double (one en suite) and one twin-bedded rooms, whirlpool bath, shower, well equipped kitchen with microwave and attractive enclosed garden with furniture. All bed linen supplied. Ample parking space. Brochure available with full details. Inclusive prices. Children and one pet welcome. Open all year. **Mr and Mrs G. Baggesen, Woodhouse Cottage, Montacute TA15 6XL (01935 824487).**

PORLOCK. Lucott Farm, Porlock, Minehead. Sleeps 2/10. Isolated farmhouse on Exmoor, with wood burning fireplaces and all modern conveniences. It lies at the head of Horner Valley and guests will delight in the wonderful scenery. Plenty of pony trekking in the area. Ten people accommodated in four double and two single bedrooms, cot; bathroom, two toilets; sittingroom; diningroom. Kitchen has oil-fired Aga and water heater. No linen supplied. Shops three miles; sea four miles. Car essential — parking. Open all year. Terms (including fuel) on application with SAE please to **Mrs E.A. Tucker, West Luccombe Cottage, Porlock, Minehead TA24 8MT (Porlock [01643] 862810).**

SHEPTON MALLET. Mrs J.A. Boyce, Knowle Farm, West Compton, Shepton Mallet BA4 4PD (01749 890482; Fax: 01749 890405). 🔑🔑🔑🔑 *Approved.* **Working farm. Cottages sleep 2/5/8.** Knowle Farm Cottages are converted from the old cowstall and stables, set around the old farmyard now laid out as a pleasant garden. Quiet location at the end of a private drive. Excellent views and plenty of wildlife. All cottages furnished to a high standard — bathroom (bath, shower, toilet, wash-basin); fully fitted kitchen (automatic washing machine, fridge/freezer, full size gas cooker). Two cottages have kitchen/diner, separate lounge, colour TV, the other two have kitchen, lounge/diner, colour TV. Cot, high chair by prior arrangement. Bed linen supplied, towels by request. Surrounding area full of interesting places to visit. Good golf courses, fishing, selection of pubs and restaurants. Around the farm plenty of walks, play area for children. Sorry, no pets. Terms: low season £145 to £230; high season £160 to £360. Car essential, ample parking. Payphone for guests. Open all year. WCTB.

SIMONSBATH. Jane and Barry Styles, Wintershead Farm, Simonsbath, Exmoor TA24 7LF (0164 383 222). 🔑🔑/🔑🔑🔑🔑 *Highly Commended.* Three tastefully furnished and well equipped spacious cottages offering all the comforts of home, situated in the midst of beautiful Exmoor with panoramic views. The area is ideal for enjoying the country pursuits of walking, riding, fishing or just relaxing while taking in the spectacular scenery. A safe place for children and pets, with a recreation room for those not so sunny days. The cottages sleep from two to six people plus cots. There is also a small bedsit flat for one or two people. All are centrally heated, two also have open fires. Situated 10 miles from Lynmouth, Wintershead and makes an ideal base to explore North Devon and Exmoor. From £105 weekly. Short Breaks out of season. Please telephone or write for a colour brochure.

WIVELISCOMBE near. Oddwell and Cridland Cottages, Brompton Ralph, Near Wiveliscombe. 🔑🔑🔑 *Commended.* **Cottages each sleep 7.** Charming 300-year-old cottages with beamed ceilings and inglenook fireplaces for cosy open fires, standing in peaceful and unspoilt countryside at foot of Brendon Hills. Equipped for seven, plus a cot in each. Two bedrooms, one with three single beds, other with double bed; bed/sitting room with double bed/settee; bathroom, toilet, with extra toilet/wash-room upstairs in Oddwell and downstairs in Cridland; dining/living room; kitchen with oil-fired Rayburn (in Oddwell only), both with electric cooker, fridge, iron, toaster, spin-dryer etc; separate larder in Oddwell. Available all year, indoor games and books provided. Cot, high chair. Trout fishing, riding, walking, pony trekking. Nine miles to sea and half mile to shop/post office. Car essential, ample parking; garage in keeping with character of cottage. Pets by arrangement. Weekly terms from £120 to £260. ETB and WCTB approved. **Adrian and Pippa Blizzard, Talgarth, Bentley, Near Farnham, Surrey GU10 5LN (01420 23839).**

STAFFORDSHIRE

ABBOTS BROMLEY. John Myatt, Priory Farm Fishing House, Priory Farm, Blithbury, Rugeley WS15 3JA (0188922 269). 🔑🔑🔑 Working farm.

Tastefully converted, Listed 18th century fishing house overlooking the picturesque River Blithe, offers unique accommodation for up to four persons on secluded dairy farm. Ideal for lovers of the countryside and wildlife. Badger watching can usually be arranged as well as bird watching on the beautiful Blithfield Reservoir. The farm is convenient for visitors to Cannock Chase, Lichfield, Alton Towers and the Peak District. Comfortable accommodation includes large bed-sitting room with colour TV, modern kitchen and shower room. Terms from £65 to £110 per week. Open all year. Well behaved pets welcome. Brochure on request.

LEEK. Edith and Alwyn Mycock, Lower Berkhamsytch Farm, Bottom House, Near Leek ST13 7QP (01538 308213). 🔑🔑🔑 *Approved.* **Sleep 6 plus cot.** Two tastefully converted flats with their own private entrance, each sleeping six plus cot, on traditional family-run dairy and pig farm, within walking distance of two pubs serving meals and a "Little Chef" restaurant. Central to Alton Towers, Potteries and Peak District. One double bedroom, one twin-bedded room and double bed settee in lounge. Colour TV. Shower room and toilet. Sitting area. Children welcome, cot and high chair available; children's play area. Well behaved pets welcome. Visitors can walk in the fields, watch cows being milked and maybe see piglets born. Guests are offered a warm welcome by the owners who are on hand to help in any way. Terms from £100 to £195 per week, electricity included.

HELP IMPROVE BRITISH TOURIST STANDARDS

You are choosing holiday accommodation from our very popular FHG Publications. Whether it be a hotel, guest house, farmhouse or self-catering accommodation, we think you will find it hospitable, comfortable and clean, and your host and hostess friendly and helpful. Why not write and tell us about it?

As a recognition of the generally well-run and excellent holiday accommodation reviewed in our publications, we at FHG Publications Ltd. present a diploma to proprietors who receive the highest recommendation from their guests who are also readers of our Guides. If you care to write to us praising the holiday you have booked through FHG Publications Ltd. – whether this be board, self-catering accommodation, a sporting or a caravan holiday, what you say will be evaluated and the proprietors who reach our final list will be contacted.

The winning proprietor will receive an attractive framed diploma to display on his premises as recognition of a high standard of comfort, amenity and hospitality. FHG Publications Ltd. offer this diploma as a contribution towards the improvement of standards in tourist accommodation in Britain. Help your excellent host or hostess to win it!

FHG DIPLOMA

We nominate ....

....

Because

Name ....

Address ....

.... Telephone No. ....

STAFFORDSHIRE'S
Farm & Country Holidays
SELF-CATERING

DAIRY HOUSE FARM, Alkmonton, Derby. (A. & D. Harris) 01335 330 359. 🔑🔑🔑🔑 Highly Commended. Converted Victorian Pigsty and Looseboxes tastefully furnished and finished retaining beams and other original features. No smokers, No pets. **From £120.**

ELMHURST DAIRY FARM, Lichfield, Staffs. (Mrs J. Hollinshead) 01543 262 595. Four cottages. Barn conversions. Max. occupancy 6. Bed linen provided. Laundry room. Pets by arrangement. Ideal base for holidays or business. **From £145.**

GORTON LODGE FARM, Longdon, Lichfield. (Mrs L. Hammersley) 01543 682 248. Superior standard cottages in listed courtyard buildings. Beautiful countryside. Lichfield 3 miles. Excellent base for Midlands attractions, holiday or business. Fully equipped. **From £90 + electricity.**

NOTHILL FARM, Crakemarsh, Uttoxeter, Staffs. (Mrs M. Brookes) 01889 26 210. Comfortable, spacious 3 bedroomed cottages for 6 + cot. Convenient for Alton Towers, Potteries and Peak District. Ample parking space and garden.

OFFLEY GROVE FARM, Adbaston, Staffs. (Mr & Mrs F. Hiscoe-James) 01785 280 205. The Old Brew House: Newly converted barn with original features. Fully equipped to high standard. Sleep 6/8 plus cot(s). One bedroom ensuite. Convenient for many attractions.

OLD HAYBARN APARTMENTS, Corporation Farm, Lichfield. (Mrs M. Lees) 01543 263 095. Attractive old barn converted into 3 luxury apartments. Sleep 2–6. **From £100 per week inclusive of electricity and bedding etc.** Convenient for many Midland attractions.

OULTON ROCK COTTAGE, near Norbury, Stafford. (Mrs G. Palmer) 01785 284 405. 🔑🔑🔑🔑 Commended. Fully equipped 3 bedroomed country cottage. Peacefully situated, south facing. Own large garden. One mile Norbury Junction Canal Basin. Ideal for touring Shropshire/Staffordshire.

OWSLOW FARM, Carsington, Matlock, Derby DE4 4DD. (Mr P. Oldfield) 01629 540 510. Overlooking Carsington Water on working dairy farm. Sleeps 8 plus cot(s). Recently refurbished. 2 baths, 1 ensuite shower. **From £334 per week.**

PRIORY FARM, Blithbury, Rugeley, Staffs. (Mrs J. Myatt) 01889 22 269. Secluded and picturesque accommodation on a working dairy farm. Includes large bedsitting room, modern kitchen and shower room. Suitable for up to four persons. **From £110.**

ROOKERY FARM, Canwell, Sutton Coldfield, W. Midlands. (Mrs L. Packwood) 0121 308 1039. Barn Owl and Little Owl, 2-bedroomed bungalows. Suitable for disabled. 🔑🔑🔑🔑 Approved. Lounge, dining, kitchen, bathroom, fridge-freezer, microwave and washer-dryer in each. Close Lichfield, Tamworth, Sutton Coldfield. No pets.

UPPER CADLOW FARM, Winkhill, Leek, Staffs. (Mrs S. Plant) 01538 266 243. Beautiful farm cottage. ETB 🔑🔑🔑🔑 Commended. Sleeps 5 + cot. Set in a superb position with magnificent views. Close to Alton Towers (3 miles).

WINDMILL COTTAGE, Essington, Wolverhampton. (Mrs V. M. Simkin) 01902 732166. Country location. 1 Bedroom, Lounge, Dining/Kitchen, Bathroom. Central heating. Electricity by 50p meter. No children or pets. **From £90.**

SEE ALSO FULL PAGE BED & BREAKFAST ADVERTISEMENT UNDER STAFFORDSHIRE.

Phone or send a 9" × 4" SAE to any member of our group for their own individual or the group brochure.

SUFFOLK

HALESWORTH. Beck's End Cottage, Westhall, Halesworth. 𝕜𝕜𝕜 *Commended.* This delightful red-brick house, converted from the one-time village school, with landscaped gardens and lawns, set on the hillside of a charming Suffolk village overlooking a valley of quiet countryside, is available for holiday letting all year round. Westhall is an interesting village with its 12th century Norman Church, typical village pub and shop and rolling farmlands. Only seven miles from Southwold and Suffolk's Heritage coastline, this is an excellent base from which to tour Norfolk and Suffolk. Many places of interest, both historical and scenic, within easy driving distance. Lovely walking terrain. The accommodation comprises large lounge/diner, entrance hall, two large bedrooms, cot for baby; bathroom, toilet. Modern fitted kitchen with electric cooker, fridge, kettle, toaster, cutlery, crockery and cooking utensils. Electric heating. Car essential, parking. Children welcome. Pets permitted. Bargain breaks November to April. SAE, please, or telephone (evenings) to **O.A. Johnson, Beck's End Farm, Westhall, Halesworth IP19 8QZ (01502 575239).**

KESSINGLAND. Kessingland Cottages, Rider Haggard Lane, Kessingland. Sleeps 6. An exciting three-bedroom recently built semi-detached cottage situated on the beach, three miles south of sandy beach at Lowestoft. Fully and attractively furnished with colour TV and delightful sea and lawn views from floor to ceiling windows of lounge. Accommodation for up to six people. Well-equipped kitchen with electric cooker, fridge, electric immersion heater. Electricity by 50p meter. Luxurious bathroom with coloured suite. No linen or towels provided. Only a few yards to beach and sea fishing. One mile to wildlife country park with mini-train. Buses quarter-of-a-mile and shopping centre half-a-mile. Parking, but car not essential. Children and disabled persons welcome. Available 1st March to 7th January. Weekly terms from £50 in early March and late December to £245 in peak season. SAE to **Mr S. Mahmood, 156 Bromley Road, Beckenham, Kent BR3 2PG (0181-650 0539).**

SAXMUNDHAM. Mrs Mary Kitson, White House Farm, Sibton, Saxmundham IP17 2NE (Peasenhall [0172-879] 260). Working farm. Sleeps 4/6 adults; 2/4 children. The flat is a self-contained part of late Georgian farmhouse standing in 130 acres of quiet farmland with a variety of livestock. Fishing on farm. Accommodation in three double bedrooms (two double/two single beds) plus cot; livingroom with TV; shower/toilet on first floor. Entrance hall, kitchen/diner on ground floor. Full central heating. Situated one-and-a-half miles from village shops, etc. Ten miles from coast at Dunwich, Minsmere Bird Sanctuary, Snape Maltings. Linen optional. Pets permitted. Car essential — parking. Available all year. Terms from £130 to £180 per week. SAE, please, for further details. Cottage also available.

SOUTHWOLD. 4 Marlborough Road, Southwold. Two modern well equipped self contained flats, close to sea front and shopping centre of this charming unspoilt seaside town. Well situated for Minsmere Bird Sanctuary and Festival town of Aldeburgh. First floor flat has large lounge, kitchen, one bedroom with double and one single beds. Separate toilet and bathroom. Ground floor flat has two bedrooms — one double and one twin. Lounge, kitchen, separate toilet and bathroom. Both flats have well equipped kitchens with cooker, fridge, microwave, etc. Fully double glazed and both have night storage heaters. TV aerial. Small dogs welcome, by arrangement. Further details please contact **H.A. Adnams, High Street, Southwold (01502 723292) or Mr and Mrs Collett on (01728 724036).**

STANSFIELD. Plough Hill Bungalow, Stansfield, Sudbury. Sleeps 4. Plough Hill Bungalow, with attractive garden to front, is situated in a small village with pub, within 15 miles of Sudbury, Gainsborough's birthplace, Newmarket Racecourse and historic Bury St. Edmunds, Long Melford and Lavenham. At picturesque Clare, five miles distant, there are good shopping facilities. The Bungalow, suitable for disabled visitors, is well equipped to accommodate four people in two twin-bedded rooms, sittingroom, kitchen/diner with electric cooker, fridge, cutlery and crockery. Colour TV. Bathroom, toilet. Car essential, parking. Children and pets welcome; cot available. Solid fuel heating or electric fires. Linen supplied on request. Open all year round at very reasonable rates. Terms from £48 to £97 per week. For further details send SAE to **Mrs M. Winch, Plough House, Stansfield, Sudbury CO10 8LT (01284 89253).**

WALSHAM-LE-WILLOWS. Bridge Cottage, Walsham-le-Willows, Near Bury St. Edmunds. Sleeps 5. Bridge Cottage is illustrated in the book "English Cottages", with introduction by John Betjeman. Built in the 17th century it has been attractively modernised. There are fitted carpets and comfortable beds; centrally heated and well furnished. The kitchen is well equipped with electric cooker and fridge. Plenty of hot water. Children and well behaved pets are welcome. Electricity and heating included in rent. Colour TV. Tennis court and swimming pool available in summer by arrangement. Walsham-le-Willows is in the centre of East Anglia (11 miles from Bury St. Edmunds) and has shops and post office. Available all year. Terms from £160 to £220. **Mrs H.M. Russell, The Beeches, Walsham-le-Willows, Near Bury St. Edmunds IP31 3AD (Walsham-le-Willows [01359] 259227; Fax: 01359 258206).**

SUSSEX

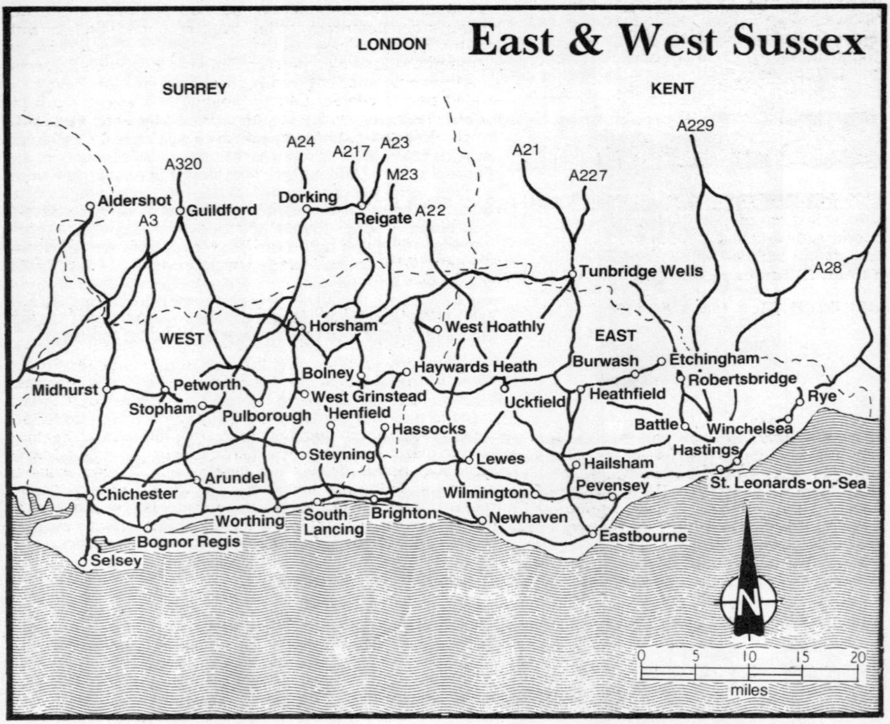

EAST SUSSEX

NUTLEY. 2 Victoria Cottage, c/o Hole and Alchorne Farm, Bell Lane, Nutley TN22 3PD (01825 712 475). 🔑🔑🔑🔑 *Highly Commended.* **Sleeps 5 plus baby.** A warm welcome awaits you at our comfortable, well appointed semi-detached cottage, with lovely garden, on our dairy farm. Near Ashdown Forest. Comprises three bedrooms (one double, one twin and one single); bathroom and separate WC; sittingroom with TV and telephone; diningroom; kitchen with electric cooker, microwave, fridge, washing machine and tumble dryer. Beds made up. Ideal base for visiting South Downs, castles and coast. Children welcome. Terms from £145 to £250 per week.

EAST SUSSEX – A POPULAR DESTINATION!

Apart from its famous resorts East Sussex has many attractions, such as, Ashdown Forest, Ditchling Common Country Park, Lullington Heath Wildlife Refuge, the Medieval town of Rye and Hastings Country Park.

POLEGATE, near Alfriston. Lakeside Farm Holiday Bungalows. Sleeps 4 to 6. Lakeside Farm is situated on the edge of Arlington Reservoir, with views of the South Downs. Eastbourne, Brighton and Lewes within 15 miles, Drusillas Zoo two miles, shopping half a mile. Modern comfortable accommodation, two double rooms, lounge, dining area, bathroom, toilet. Well equipped kitchen with electric cooker, fridge. Duvets on all beds. Open April to October. Car essential, parking. Suitable for disabled guests. Children welcome, cot and high chair available. Well controlled pets accepted. Electric heating. Weekly terms from £140. Electricity included. **Mrs P. Boniface, Lakeside Farm, Arlington, Polegate BN26 6SB (01323 870111).**

See also Colour Display Advertisement **SOUTHERN ENGLAND. Fairhaven Holiday Cottages.** An extensive selection of personally inspected holiday homes. Various shapes, sizes and locations — coast, countryside and town, in Southern England and Wales. Available throughout the year. Long and short winter lets. Many situated in SUSSEX. Contact: **Fairhaven Holiday Cottages, Derby House, 123 Watling Street, Gillingham, Kent ME7 2YY (01634 570157).**

UCKFIELD. Mr & Mrs L.A. Arnold, Whitehouse Farm, Horney Common, Nutley, Uckfield TN22 3EE (Nutley [0182571] 2377). 🔑🔑🔑 *Commended.* **Sleep 4.** Whitehouse Farm Holiday Homes are situated on a small working farm overlooking the beautiful Ashdown Forest, home of that fictional bear Winnie the Pooh. An ideal place for a varied holiday. National Trust properties, castles and gardens abound, and London, Brighton and the coast are within easy reach. Sleeping four with full central heating, double glazing and showers. Large lounge/diners leading to individual patios. Newly installed colour TV and cassette recorders. Full pine kitchens with washer/dryers, fridge/freezers, slow cookers and coffeemakers. Personalised parking. Pets welcome. Full linen supplied. Heating and cots free. Weekly terms from £206 to £314. Brochure on request.

WEST SUSSEX

HENFIELD. The Holiday Flat, New Hall, Small Dole, Henfield BN5 9YJ (Henfield [01273] 492546). 🔑🔑🔑 *Commended.* Situated just 11 miles north of Brighton, New Hall, the manor house of Henfield, one wing of which dates back to 1600, stands in three-and-a-half acres of mature gardens, surrounded by farmland with abundant footpaths. The holiday flat is completely self-contained being the upper part of the 18th century dairy wing of the house. Its own front door opens from the Georgian Courtyard. Accommodation comprises three bedrooms, one double, one single, one twin-bedded; lounge/diner; newly fitted kitchen with microwave; bathroom; comfortably furnished, carpeted throughout; central heating; free hot water and electricity; children welcome. Open all year. Terms from £100 to £235 per week. Apply to **Mrs M.W. Carreck.**

HENFIELD. The Granary, Great Betley Farm, Henfield. Sleeps 6. Detached period Granary lovingly restored to a high standard providing comfortable and spacious accommodation of great character with superb views of the Downs. Set in a secluded 200 acre working farm near the River Adur. Coarse fishing permits available. Ample parking. Facilities include fitted kitchen/diner, washer/dryer, colour TV/video, gramophone, selection of videos/records old and new, piano, payphone. 50p electric meter. Duvets provided, linen, cot and high chair available. Terms from £105 low season to £230 high season. Short breaks by arrangement. Details from **John How, Weppons, Wiston, Steyning BN4 3DN (01903 813270).**

RUSTINGTON. Sleeps 3/4. Ground floor flat in modern block, 100 yards from the beach. All beds have blankets or duvets; living room with door to balcony; TV and telephone; kitchen with electric cooker, fridge/freezer and washing machine; bathroom with WC and electric shower. Communal gardens. On street parking. Children welcome. Sorry no pets. Contact **Mr P. Paganuzzi, Willow End, 66 Quinta Drive, Arkley, Herts. EN5 3BE (0181-441 3925).**

STORRINGTON. Byre Cottages. Sleep 2/6. New conversion of farm buildings into four self-contained cottages, situated in rural location on working farm. Good walking district with South Downs Way going through farm one and a half miles from Storrington and eight miles from Worthing. Each cottage has central heating and is well equipped; use of outdoor swimming pool in summer. Laundry/drying room and payphone. Gas and electricity charges extra. Prices range from £90 per week in winter for the one bedroomed cottage to £220 per week in July/August for the three bedroomed cottage. No pets but kennels are available for dogs. Contact: **Mr and Mrs Kittle, Sullington Manor Farm, Storrington RH20 4AE (01903 742469).**

WARWICKSHIRE

Warwickshire Farm Holidays

Warwickshire farming families welcome guests into their homes to enjoy the comforts of a traditional English farmhouse and discover the peace of the English countryside. Each home listed has it own unique character and differs in size, style, and price, but all offer a high standard of accommodation, good food, a warm welcome and excellent value for money to holidaymakers and business travellers. All owners are members of the Farm Holiday Bureau, all properties are inspected and classified by the English Tourist Board, some also participate in the ETB grading scheme. Warwickshire, in the heart of England, provides the perfect setting for the perfect holiday. Mile upon mile of rolling countryside, picturesque villages and meandering waterways. There are castles, stately homes, theatres, country gardens and some of the prettiest villages to be found.

Places to visit within easy reach include Stratford-upon-Avon, Warwick, Royal Leamington Spa, The Cotswolds, Oxford, Coventry. National Exhibition Centre and National Agricultural Centre.

For further details about Bed & Breakfast or Self-catering cottages, please write or telephone for a free brochure to: Warwickshire Farm Holidays (FHG), Crandon House, Avon Dassett, Leamington Spa CV33 0AA. Telephone: (01295) 770652.

FARM HOLIDAY BUREAU

WILTSHIRE

ROWDE. Miss M.I. Marks, Mulberry Lodge House, Rowde, Devizes SN10 2QQ (Devizes [01380] 723056). 𝔊𝔊 Sleeps 5/6. Come and relax in "GLORIOUS WILTSHIRE, PEACEFUL COUNTRYSIDE", Devizes two miles. Self contained, fully equipped furnished flat in wing of Georgian house (own entrance). Children welcome. Large bedroom, double and single beds (first floor), second bedroom (curtain divided, with two windows), three single beds, cot; bathroom, toilet; sitting/dining room; TV; electric fires; three night storage heaters; kitchen, electric cooker, fridge, spin dryer; £1 meter. This seven acre farm is on the fringe of village. Ideal touring centre for historic places — Avebury, Longleat, Salisbury, Stonehenge. Fishing, shops and village. Canal trips. Ample parking. Weekly terms from £65 to £155 April to September (book by April 30th — 10% discount). Weekend Breaks. SAE, please, for colour brochure.

YORKSHIRE

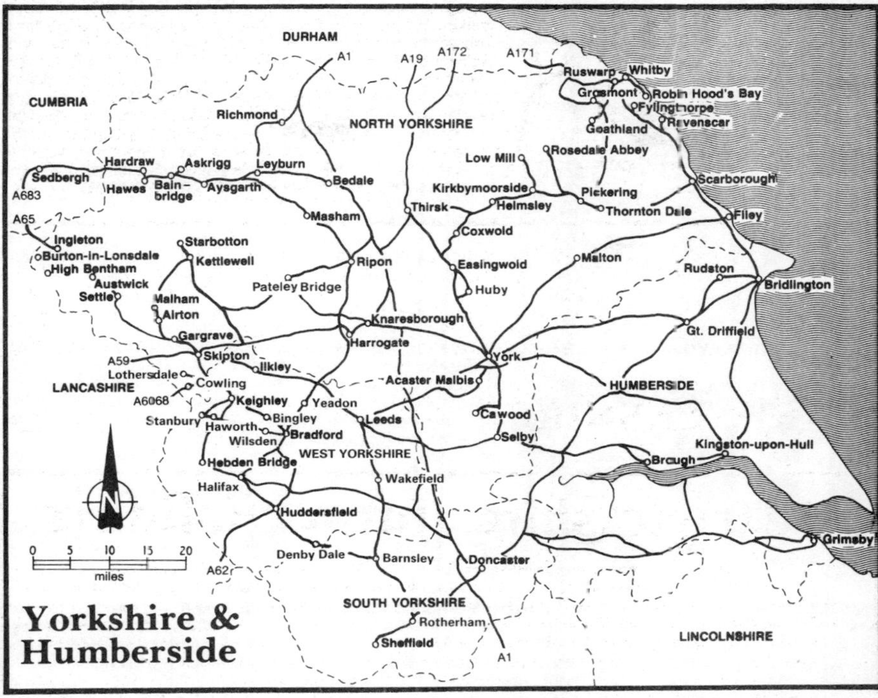

EAST YORKSHIRE

DRIFFIELD near. Manor Farm Cottage, Foxholes, Near Driffield. 🔑🔑🔑🔑 *Commended.* **Working farm. Sleeps 7.** Manor Farm Cottage is a detached brick cottage with garage and enclosed garden in small Wolds village 12 miles from East Coast and within easy drive to Yorkshire Moors and York. Three double bedrooms accommodating seven. Bathroom, toilet, sittingroom with colour TV and open fireplace with electric fire. Diningroom. Fully equipped electric kitchen. Immersion heater in bathroom. Economy 7 heating. Open from May to October. Pets welcome. Terms from £170 to £200 per week. SAE, please, for terms and further details to **Mrs M. Lamplough, Manor Farm, Foxholes, Near Driffield YO25 0QH (01262 470255).**

FORDON. Mr and Mrs J.S. Marshall, High Fordon Farm, Fordon, Near Driffield YO25 0HU (01262 470276). Adjoining the farmhouse, this luxury cottage is located in a peaceful setting on a 108 acre working farm with outstanding views over the surrounding Wolds. Furnished to highest standards, with beamed ceilings. An idyllic rural cottage central for country, coast, National Parks, stately homes; shop, pub three miles. Car essential. Accommodation comprises lounge, kitchen, dining room, conservatory; one double and one twin-bedded room with vanity units; bathroom with bath, shower and toilet. Oil central heating (free), open fire. Electric meter. Fully equipped electric kitchen. Colour TV, cot, duvets. Lawned garden. Ample parking. Sorry, no pets. Please supply own linen. Terms from £140 weekly. Brochure.

NORTH YORKSHIRE

ASKRIGG. Fern Croft, 2 Mill Lane, Askrigg. Sleeps 4. A modern cottage enjoying quiet location on edge of village with open fields rising immediately behind. Attractive and compact, this Wensleydale village is an ideal centre for Dales, with facilities for everyday needs, including two shops, post office, restaurant and a couple of pubs. Furnished to a high standard for four, ground floor accommodation comprises large comfortable lounge/diner with colour TV and well equipped kitchen. Upstairs there are two double bedrooms with a double and twin beds respectively, and modern bathroom. Storage heating included, other electricity by meter. Regret no pets. Terms from £90 to £195 weekly. Brochure: **Mr and Mrs K. Dobson (01689 838450 or 01423 868710).**

ASKRIGG/WENSLEYDALE. Mrs E. Scarr, Coleby Hall, Askrigg, Leyburn DL8 3DX (01969 650216). Working farm. Sleeps 5 plus cot. Situated in Wensleydale, half a mile from Bainbridge and one mile from Askrigg, Coleby Hall is a 17th century gabled farmhouse with stone mullioned windows, the west end being to let. A stone spiral staircase leads to two bedrooms; linen provided. The kitchen is equipped with electric cooker, fridge, crockery, etc., and coal fire. The lounge has an inglenook coal fire and metered TV. There are night storage heaters in each room. Coleby has lovely views and is an ideal situation for walking, fishing and driving round the Yorkshire Dales. Children and pets welcome. Terms from £130 to £140 per week.

AUSTWICK. Blythesgarth Cottage, Eldroth, Austwick. Working farm. Sleeps 6. Detached cottage on a farm two miles from Austwick and six from Settle. Peaceful location with lovely views. Ideal for walking or exploring Yorkshire Dales. Easy reach Lake District and west coast. Three bedrooms, two with double beds, one with two singles. Cot available. Three piece bathroom suite; lounge with colour TV; kitchen/diner. All electric, with electricity extra. Comfortably furnished and fully equipped (except linen). Garage and parking. Car essential. Part central heating included in rent October to May. Pets by arrangement. Open all year. Personally supervised by owner for 16 successful years. Stamp only please for brochure and terms to **Mrs M. Booth, Slated House, Eldroth, Austwick, Lancaster LA2 8AG (015242 51365).**

COVERDALE. Mrs Caroline Harrison, Hill Top Farm, West Scrafton, Leyburn DL8 4RU (01969 640663). 🔑🔑🔑 *Highly Commended.* **Working farm. Properties sleep 4/6.** Relax in our recently converted traditional Dales stone barns with panoramic views of Rova Crag and open moorland. This peaceful hamlet nestles in the heart of the Yorkshire Dales National Park, Herriot country. The properties' fully equipped kitchens and modern bathrooms retain much character with original exposed beams and open fireplaces. Facilities include en suite bathrooms, central heating, log fires, colour TVs, dishwashers, automatic washing machines, fridges, deep freeze facilities, microwaves, electric cookers, fitted carpets throughout. Linen provided. Games room. Pets corner, ideal for the children and pets. Rough shooting, fishing and riding school on farm — qualified instructors, special holiday courses, liveries available. Comprehensive brochure available.

NORTH YORKSHIRE – RICH IN TOURIST ATTRACTIONS!

Dales, moors, castles, abbeys, cathedrals – you name it and you're almost sure to find it in North Yorkshire. Leading attractions include Castle Howard, the moorlands walks at Goathland, the Waterfalls at Falling Foss, Skipton, Richmond, Wensleydale, Bridestones Moor, Ripon Cathedral, Whitby, Settle and, of course, York itself.

EASINGWOLD. Mrs Rachel Ritchie, The Old Rectory, Thormanby, Easingwold, York YO6 3NN (01845 501417). The Old Rectory's Coach House and Stable have been lovingly converted into two holiday cottages and enjoy a delightful setting in a quiet country lane, just out of the small village of Thormanby (three miles north of Easingwold). It is an excellent base for visiting York (17 miles), the North Yorkshire Moors to the east and Dales to the west. There are many country houses, abbeys and castles in the area. Stable Cottage has one double and one twin-bedded rooms plus cot. The Coach House has one double and two twin rooms plus cot. They are fully equipped. All linen and towels provided. Colour TV, open fires (fuel supplied). Night storage heaters when required. Children and well behaved pets welcome. Electricity by meter reading. Open all year. From £130 weekly. SAE for brochure.

GRASSINGTON near. Mrs Judith M. Joy, Jerry and Ben's, Hebden, Skipton BD23 5DL (01756 752369; Fax: 01756 753370). Properties sleep 3/6/8/9. Jerry and Ben's stands in two acres of grounds in one of the most attractive parts of the Yorkshire Dales National Park. Seven properties; Ghyll Cottage (sleeps eight); Mamie's Cottage (sleeps eight); Paradise End (sleeps six); Robin Middle (sleeps six); High Close (sleeps nine); Cruck Rise (sleeps six); Raikes Side (sleeps two/three). All have parking, electric cooker, fridge, colour TV, electric heating and immersion heater; lounge, dining area, bathroom with shower; cots if required. Fully equipped, including linen if requested. Washing machine and telephone available. Well behaved pets accepted. Open all year. Fishing and bathing close by. Terms from £65. SAE, please for detailed brochure. Suitable for disabled.

HARDRAW. Cissy's Cottage, Hardraw, Hawes. Sleeps 4. A delightful 18th century cottage of outstanding character. Situated in the village of Hardraw with its spectacular waterfall and Pennine Way. Market town of Hawes one mile. This traditional stone built cottage retains many original features including beamed ceilings and an open fire. Sleeping four in comfort, it has been furnished and equipped to a high standard using antique pine and Laura Ashley prints. Equipped with dishwasher, microwave and tumble dryer. Outside, a south-facing garden, sun patio with garden furniture, and a large enclosed paddock make it ideal for children. Cot and high chair if required. Open all year. Terms £95-£250 include coal, electricity and trout fishing. For brochure, contact **Mrs Belinda Metcalfe, Southolme Farm, Little Smeaton, Northallerton DL6 2HJ (01609 881302).**

HARROGATE. Mrs Janet Hollings, Dougill Hall, Summerbridge, Harrogate HG3 4JR (Harrogate [01423] 780277). 🔑🔑🔑/🔑🔑🔑🔑 Working farm. Sleeps 4. Dougill Hall Flat occupies the top floor of the Hall, which is of Georgian design, built in 1722 by the Dougill family who lived on this farm from 1496 to 1803. It is in Nidderdale, half a mile from the village of Summerbridge, just by the River Nidd, where there is fishing available for visitors. There are good facilities for horse riding, tennis, swimming, squash, etc. Well situated for the walking enthusiast and within easy reach of the Dales, the beautiful and ancient city of York, Fountains Abbey, How Stean Gorge and many other places of interest. The flat sleeps up to four people. Well equipped, with electric cooker and fridge, iron, vacuum cleaner. Linen by arrangement. Pets permitted. Car essential, parking. The old Cooling House flat attached to the house is now available and sleeps four. Terms £109 — £190. Bring your own horse — stables, hay and grazing available. SAE, please, for details.

HAWES. River View, Dyers Garth, Hawes. Sleeps 6. A spacious three-bedroomed terraced cottage, River View is situated in a cul-de-sac overlooking "Duerley Beck" an attractive trout stream which runs through Hawes, a market town in the centre of Yorkshire Dales National Park and on the Pennine Way. The cottage has the benefit of storage heaters and also an open coal fire for out of season lets which is an attraction. An ideal situation for walking, fishing and visits to local scenic attractions which include Hardrow Scar, Aysgarth Falls and National Carriage Museum, Castle Bolton; the Lake District is approximately 30 miles away. The cottage accommodates six plus baby (cot); three double bedrooms, bathroom, lounge with colour TV and fully equipped kitchen/diner. Shops 30 yards. Parking space for one car. SAE, please, for terms to **Mrs Sheila Alderson, "Inverdene", Hawes DL8 2NJ (Wensleydale [01969] 667408).**

HELMSLEY near. Mrs Rickatson, Summerfield Farm, Harome, Near Helmsley, York YO6 5JJ (01439 748238). Working farm, join in. Sleeps 6. Enjoy walking or touring in North Yorkshire Moors National Park. Lovely area 20 miles north of historic city of York. Modernised, comfortable and well equipped farmhouse wing; sleeps four/six plus cot. Kitchen equipped with electric cooker, fridge and automatic washing machine. Sit beside a log fire in the evenings. Linen supplied to overseas visitors. Weekly terms from £75 to £190. Open all year. Mid-week and weekend bookings are possible in winter. For further information send SAE, or phone.

ETB 🔑🔑🔑🔑 Highly Commended

Henley Award

SPROXTON HALL

Farm Cottages

Enquiries and brochure: Mr & Mrs Wainwright,
Sproxton Hall, Sproxton, Helmsley, N. Yorkshire YO6 5EQ
Telephone: 01439 770225 Fax: 01439 771373

Award-winning conversions of 17th century stone barns, providing 5 self-contained cottages, accommodating 4-8 people. Lovingly and imaginatively restored and furnished to an exceptionally high standard, whilst retaining an atmosphere of character and charm. A haven of peace and tranquillity amidst idyllic countryside with superb views. On family farm, one and a half miles south of Helmsley on edge of North Yorkshire Moors. Central heating, log fires, linen and towels, colour TV, laundry facilities, payphone. South-facing gardens with barbecue area. Regret no dogs.

Cottage suitable for disabled.

Bed and Breakfast accommodation also available at Sproxton Hall (non-smoking). See separate entry under N. Yorkshire, Board section of the guide.

NIDDERDALE. Mr and Mrs C.D. Huby, Dodd Hill, Dyke Lane, Heysham Road, Dacre, Near Harrogate HG3 4EY (01423 780643). Two recent barn conversions adjoining owner's home in superb setting overlooking beautiful Dales countryside. Mistal Cottage has three bedrooms (one double en suite and two twin), bathroom, and sleeps six/eight. Spinney Cottage has one double and one twin-bedded rooms sleeping four/six. Both fully centrally heated, very comfortably equipped with cooker, fridge/freezer, automatic washer/dryer, colour TV and gas fires in sittingrooms. All services and linen included. Garden and extensive grounds including small wood. Garden furniture and barbecue available. Children welcome, cot provided. Pets by arrangement. Open all year. Central for touring Dales. Weekly terms from £130 to £330.

MISTAL SPINNEY

PICKERING. Mrs Livesey, Sands Farm Country Hotel Cottages, Wilton, Pickering YO18 7JY (01751 474405). Quietly secluded in 15 acres of fields, gardens and a wildlife pond, the delightfully renovated four/five/six and eight bedded cottages are grouped round an attractive courtyard amidst shrubs, roses and honeysuckle. They are individually designed, luxuriously decorated in Laura Ashley style, with exposed beams; some four-poster beds; colour TV, gas central heating, log fires and farmhouse style kitchens. Bed linen provided and beds are made up for your arrival. All the cottages have private parking. Also adjacent to the cottages stands a converted chapel with four bedrooms, each with en-suite facilities. Bed and Breakfast with Evening Meal is also available from the main guest house. NO SMOKING. No pets. Wilton is an ideal base for visiting the Moors, coast, stately homes, North York Moors Railway and the ancient attractive city of York. Fishing, riding, swimming is less than five miles away. No children under 10 years. Special low season breaks. SAE for brochure.

PICKERING. Town End Farm Cottage, Pickering. A well appointed south-facing Cottage on the outskirts of Pickering, with large garden and secluded paved area with garden furniture. Ample parking space and field at the side of the house for games or exercising the dog. Dining kitchen, sittingroom with colour TV and bedsitting room on the ground floor, three bedrooms and bathroom on first floor. Central heating and automatic washing machine available. Shop and telephone kiosk nearby. The property is thoroughly checked before arrival of visitors as our aim is to cater for those who wish for the best. House trained pets welcome. Pickering is a good centre for touring the North Yorks Moors, Forestry and is 24 miles from York, the ancient capital of the North, dominated by the Minster and steeped in history. Flamingo Park Zoo, riding, fishing and swimming pool in the vicinity. 18 miles to the coast. Another self catering property is available, send SAE, or telephone for enquiries. Terms from £60 to £250. Apply **Mr P.R. Holmes, Town End Farm, Pickering YO18 7HU (Pickering [01751] 472713/473983).**

RICHMOND. Mrs F. Turnbull, Whashton Springs Farm, Richmond DL11 7JS (01748 822884). 🔑🔑🔑🔑 *Highly Commended.* **Working farm, join in.** This beautifully furnished cosy coach house is situated on a 600 acre mixed farm in the heart of Herriot country, three miles north of Richmond, only an hour's drive from Durham, York and the Lake District — wonderful walking country. Bed linen is provided in the double and twin-bedded rooms (sleeps four/five plus cot). The large beamed sittingroom looks out over a small patio adjoining the kitchen/diningroom which is fully fitted with microwave, washing machine, fridge, freezer, etc. Children welcome. Sorry no pets. Open all year. From £150 to £255 per week inclusive of VAT, bed linen and heating.

RICHMOND. Mrs Kathleen Hird, Smarber, Low Road, Richmond DL11 6PX (Richmond [01748] 86243). Working farm. Sleeps 7. Splendid views south over Swaledale. Spacious stone-built farmhouse set along a private road high over Low Row. Beautiful walking country in most interesting area of the Dales, convenient to all highpoints of Yorkshire and Durham. Accommodating seven people in three double bedrooms; cot provided; bathroom, shower; sittingroom. Fully equipped electric kitchen with cooker and fridge. No linen supplied. Part central heating. Sorry, no pets. The cottage has a private garden and is ideal for children. Babysitter available Car essential — ample parking, plus garage. Available year round. Weekly terms from £130 (fuel not included).

RIPON. May Cottage & Braeside Cottage, Kirkby Malzeard; Rose Cottage, Winksley. 🔑🔑🔑/🔑🔑🔑🔑 *Approved/Commended.* Stone cottages, very cosy and full of character. Bedrooms — two double, one double and folding beds. Lovely walking, riding, pony trekking, golf, tennis, swimming, fishing nearby. Excellent touring area, 25 miles York. Many local houses of historic interest. Fully equipped, colour TV, central heating. Pets not allowed in May Cottage. Off road parking. Cot available. Bed linen. May Cottage only: washing machine, tumble dryer, phone for incoming calls, barbecue, garage. TOURIST BOARD INSPECTED. Weekly terms from £110 to £285 includes log fire in winter. Stamp for brochure please. **Mrs K. Bailey, Owster Hill, Galphay, Ripon HG4 3NE (01765 658338 [Ansaphone] or 658801).**

ROBIN HOOD'S BAY. Working farm. Near Robin Hood's Bay at Boggle Hole. Five minutes' walk to beach. Between Whitby and Scarborough. Super detached stone cottages and bungalow on dairy farm. Two and three bedrooms and cot. Fully equipped with central heating, fitted carpets, colour TV, fridge, washbasins in bedrooms. Own garden and car parking. North York Moors all around. Pony trekking nearby. Open all year. Sorry, no pets. Terms from £70 to £300. **Mrs N. Pattinson, South House Farm, Robin Hood's Bay, Whitby YO22 4UQ (Whitby [01947] 880243).**

SCARBOROUGH. Peter and Maggie Martin, Gowland Farm, Gowland Lane, Cloughton, Scarborough YO13 0DU (01723 870924). 🔑🔑🔑/🔑🔑🔑🔑 *Highly Commended.* **Sleep 2/7.** Four charming converted stone barns situated within the beautiful North Yorkshire Moors National Park enjoying wonderful views of Harwood Dale and only two miles from the coast. The cottages have been sympathetically converted from traditional farm buildings, furnished and fitted to a very high standard, retaining the old features as well as having modern comforts. They are fully carpeted, warm and cosy with central heating and double glazing. Electric fires and colour TVs in all lounges. Well equipped kitchens. All linen and bedding provided (duvets). Large garden with plenty of car parking space. Garden furniture and laundry facilities. Sorry, no pets. Open all year. From £80 to £350 per week. Bed, Breakfast and Evening Meal also available from April to October. White Rose Award Self Catering Holiday of the Year runner-up 1993.

SCARBOROUGH. Mrs R. Pickering, Keasbeck Cottage, Harwood Dale, Scarborough YO13 0LA (Scarborough [01723] 870311). Sleeps 7. The cottage is situated among the glorious unspoilt countryside which surrounds Scarborough with forest walks and trails nearby. It sleeps seven people comfortably and has been modernised. Three double bedrooms, one single and cot; bathroom with toilet; sittingroom with colour TV; large kitchen with electric cooker, fridge freezer; automatic washing machine; oil central heating. Linen not supplied. Pets are permitted, if kept under strict control. Seven miles from the sea. Stabling can be provided. Car essential, parking. Open May to September. For terms and further details please send SAE.

SKIPTON. Mrs Brenda Jones, New Close Farm, Kirkby Malham, Skipton BD23 4DP (01729 830240). A supa dupa cottage on New Close Farm in the heart of Craven Dales with panoramic views over the Aire Valley. Excellent area for walking, cycling, fishing, golf and touring. Two double and one single bedrooms; bathroom. Colour TV. Full central heating and double glazing. Bed linen and all amenities included in the price. Low Season £165, High Season £200; deposit required. Sorry, no young children. Non-smokers preferred. The weather can't be guaranteed but your comfort can.

SLINGSBY. The Barn, Banchory Cottage, Railway Street, Slingsby, York YO6 7AH (01653 628409). This lovely little cottage has recently been converted from an old barn adjacent to the owners' house. The well equipped accommodation comprises two bedrooms (one double, one twin); shower room with washbasin and WC; kitchen and lounge/diner with colour TV. Linen provided, electricity on £1 coin meter. Short Breaks available. Sorry no pets. Ideal base for York, East Coast, North York Moors, Flamingoland and many other interesting places. Pub, shop, post office and children's playground/sports field in village. Fishing, pony trekking, swimming and lovely walks nearby. Please write or phone for details, SAE appreciated.

STOCKTON-ON-FOREST. Orillia Cottages, Stockton-on-Forest, York. Three converted farmworkers' cottages in a courtyard setting at the rear of the 300 year old farmhouse in Stockton-on-Forest; three miles from York. Golf course nearby, pub 200 yards away serves food. Post office, newsagents and general stores within easy reach. Convenient half-hourly bus service to York and the coast. Fully furnished and equipped for four, the cottages comprise lounge with sofa bed, colour TV, etc; kitchen area with microwave oven, grill and hob. Bedroom has double bed and single bed. Gas central heating. Non-smokers preferred. Children and pets welcome. Available Easter to October. Short Breaks may be available. Terms from £150 to £200 weekly includes heating, linen, etc. Contact: **Jackie Cundall, Orillia House, 89 The Village, Stockton-on-Forest, York YO3 9UP (01904 738595).**

HOLIDAY ACCOMMODATION
Classification Schemes in England, Scotland and Wales

The National Tourist Boards for England, Scotland and Wales have agreed a common 'Crown Classification' scheme for **serviced (Board)** accommodation. All establishments are inspected regularly and are given a classification indicating their level of facilities and services.

There are six grades ranging from 'Listed' to 'Five Crowns'. The higher the classification, the more facilities and services offered. Crown classification is a measure of *facilities* not *quality*. A common quality grading scheme grades the quality of establishments as 'Approved', 'Commended', 'Highly Commended' or 'Deluxe' according to the accommodation, welcome and service they provide.

For **Self-Catering**, holiday homes in England are awarded 'Keys' after inspection and can also be 'Approved', 'Commended', 'Highly Commended' or 'Deluxe' according to the facilities available. In Scotland the Crown scheme includes self-catering accommodation and Wales also has a voluntary inspection scheme for self-catering grading from '1 (Standard)' to '5 (Excellent)'.

Caravan and Camping Parks can participate in the British Holiday Parks grading scheme from 'Approved (✓)' to 'Excellent (✓ ✓ ✓ ✓ ✓)'. In addition, each National Tourist Board has an annual award for high-quality caravan accommodation: in England – Rose Awards; in Scotland – Thistle Commendations; in Wales – Dragon Awards.

When advertisers supply us with the information, FHG Publications show Crowns and other awards or gradings, including AA, RAC, Egon Ronay etc. We also award a small number of Farm Holiday Guide Diplomas every year, based on readers' recommendations.

YORKSHIRE DALES NATIONAL PARK

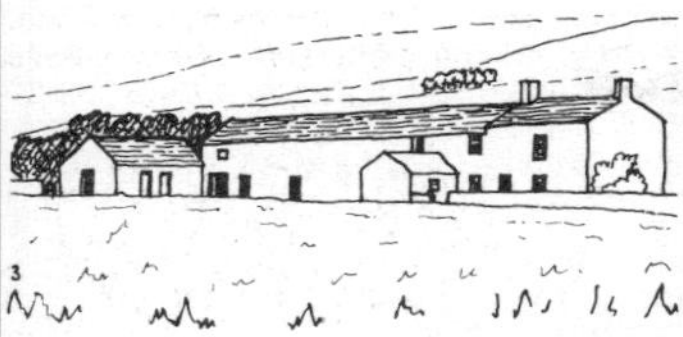

Enjoy panoramic views over secluded Coverdale from this traditional stone farmhouse (Herriot's house "Rowangarth" on TV). Quiet road, near hamlet. Three bedrooms sleeping six/eight, spacious living and dining rooms with traditional fireplaces. Unobtrusively modernised, storage heating. Ground floor bathroom etc., useful for elderly/disabled. Telephone; colour TV. Large barn/playroom and a garden. New conservatory, glazed for sunshine and views, due for completion early 1995. Pets welcome. Ideal for families/walkers. Self-catering from £180 pw.

Adrian Cave, Westclose House, West Scrafton, near Middleham, North Yorkshire DL8 4RM Telephone: 0181-567 4862 for bookings.

See also Colour Display Advertisement **WHITBY.** Cliff House — for non-smokers, a house of character with spectacular views of harbour, town and sea; all holiday amenities within a short walk. Two separate apartments: Cliff Haven — ground floor with patio, one bedroom (sleeps two/three persons); Overcliff — first/second floor, three bedrooms (sleeps four/five persons). Each apartment is well equipped with kitchen, bath/shower, central heating, colour TV, double glazing, fridge, microwave, spin/tumble dryer, superb views. Available all year. From £84 to £240 per week. Christmas/New Year and Winter/Spring breaks. Weekly bookings only May to October. Telephone enquiries welcome or send stamp and details of party and dates required; early booking advised. Contact: **Mrs P. Beale, Ref CH, 156 Coach Road, Sleights, Near Whitby YO22 5EQ (01947 810534).** See also our advertisement in Board Section of this Guide.

WHITBY. Mrs K. Wilkinson, Mickleby Moorside Farm, Ugthorpe, Whitby YO21 2BL (01947 840333). Sleeps 2/3. This comfortable cottage is a self contained annexe of the main farmhouse. Situated one mile outside Ugthorpe it is in easy reach of Staithes, Runswick Bay, Sandsend, Whitby and the Moors. The cottage comprises a fitted kitchen with electric cooker, fridge/freezer, washing machine and radio; bedroom with double bed and adjoining shower room comfortable lounge cum dining room with colour TV and open fire, fuel provided. A folding bed and cot are also available. Car space and garden for guests' use. Highly Commended. Children welcome. Non-smokers preferred. Terms from £80 to £160 weekly. SAE, or telephone, for brochure.

WHITBY near. Mr and Mrs Geoffrey Hepworth, Land of Nod Farm, Near Whitby YO21 2BL (01947 840325). Sleeps 6 plus cot. Attached sandstone bungalow, situated in the clear air, carefree part of North Yorkshire Moors National Park. All five windows face south across pastures, the sittingroom window also faces east across six miles of widening valley to Whitby Abbey Headland. Runswick Bay is three miles northward. The holiday property is separated from the farm house by a dividing passage. There are three compact bedrooms, one of which has two single beds. Modern toilet facilities and shower. Kitchen/diner fully equipped with electric cooker, microwave, fridge; spin dryer, colour TV. Bed linen, electricity included in hire. Only extra charge is for pets! No telephone bookings. Owner attended. For availability, enquiries, brochure phone (01947 840325). Rates from £69 Low Season to £159 High Season per week.

YORK. Mrs M.S.A. Woodliffe, Mill Farm, Yapham, Pocklington, York YO4 2PH (01759 302172). Three attractive self-catering choices on the farm. 12 miles from York with fine views of the Yorkshire Wolds. WOODLEA, detached house, sleeping five/six people, with fully equipped kitchen, dining area, large lounge with colour TV, bathroom, downstairs cloakroom and three bedrooms. BUNGALOW adjacent to farmhouse sleeps two/four with kitchen, bathroom, lounge/diningroom with colour TV and double bed settee, twin room with cot. Children and pets welcome. STUDIO adjacent to farmhouse, sleeps two. Modern kitchen, lounge/diningroom with colour TV, twin bedroom, bathroom/toilet. Parking for all. Open all year. Shopping and other amenities at Pocklington (two miles). Eating out, stately homes, a variety of activities available locally; coast 28 miles. SAE for details.

NORTH YORKSHIRE – SCENIC COASTLINE!

Three of England's most popular East Coast resorts sparkle along the dramatic cliffs and bays of the North Yorkshire coast. Filey, Scarborough and Whitby remain popular touring and holiday centres.

YORK. Sunset Cottages, Grimston Manor Farm, Gilling East, York. ♀♀♀♀ *Commended.* **Working farm.** Six beautiful cottages lovingly converted from the granaries of our family farm. Superbly situated in the heart of the Howardian Hills, on the outskirts of the National Park and only 17 miles north of the historic City of York, in Herriot Country. With panoramic views, these warm and comfortable cottages retain their original mellow beams and interesting stonework while still providing all the modern comforts you rightfully expect in a well-designed self-catering cottage. Full central heating. Personally supervised by the resident owners Heather and Richard Kelsey. Sorry, no pets (sheep country). Prices from £150 per week. Please phone or write for brochure **Mr and Mrs R.J. Kelsey, Grimston Manor Farm, Gilling East, York YO6 4HR (01347 888654; Fax: 01347 888347).**

YORKSHIRE DALES. Mrs E. Lodge, High Croft, Burnsall, Skipton BD23 6BP (01756 720668 or 720264). Located near the centre of this loveliest of Yorkshire Dales villages, the two 17th century cottages enjoy a large shared garden extending to the bank of the sparkling River Wharfe where there is a short stretch of private fishing for trout and grayling. This is an ideal centre for exploring the Dales by car or walking the moors, fells and riverside paths of Upper Wharfedale. Both cottages sleep up to five (double and triple bedrooms). Private parking. Shop two miles. Controlled pets acceptable. Rates from £120 to £300 per week (no VAT). SAE for brochure.

WEST YORKSHIRE

HAWORTH. 7 Upper Marsh, Oxenhope. A small stone cottage and garden on the edge of moorland, one mile from Haworth, well maintained and cared for. Sleeps six in two bedrooms and the lounge. The cottage has sunny rooms, lovely views, colour TV, gas central heating, well equipped kitchen including washing machine. Waymarked walks to miles of moorland start near the cottage. Spectacular countryside close by and you are within easy driving distance of the beautiful Yorkshire Dales with Skipton, Bolton Abbey, Burnsall and Malham as well as many other places of interest — not forgetting the historic and popular village of Haworth. We are pleased to have children and dogs to stay and personal supervision assures you of a very warm welcome at any time of year. Tourist Board Category 3. Prices £150 to £200 (winter) and £200 to £280 (summer) including linen and heating. Details from **Mrs F.M. Seabrook, 30 Newcombe Street, Market Harborough, Leicestershire LE16 9PB (01858 463723).**

ISLES OF SCILLY

ST. MARY'S. Mrs Rosemary May, Seaways Flower Farm Holiday Flats, Grenofen, St. Mary's, Isles of Scilly TR21 0NE (Tel & Fax: 01720 422398). ♀♀♀ *Approved.* Two self-contained units in converted farm buildings and one chalet in its own grounds. All enjoy magnificent views of St. Mary's Harbour as shown. A pleasant 20 minutes coastal walk into Hugh Town, passing three beaches. The Patio, Summerhouse and Chalet each sleep up to five in two bedrooms and are adjacent to Juliet's Garden Restaurant and the Island's Golf Course. All have fully equipped kitchens, bathrooms (with showers), livingrooms with colour TV and electric heaters. Linen and towels supplied. Children welcome. Cots available. Boat trips to other islands with magical white sand beaches. See seals, puffins and much more! Prices range from £185 to £505 weekly.

ISLE OF WIGHT

TOTLAND BAY. 3 Seaview Cottages, Broadway, Totland Bay. Sleeps 5. ♀♀ This well-modernised cosy old coastguard cottage holds the Farm Holiday Guide Diploma for the highest standard of accommodation. It is warm and popular throughout the year. Four day winter break — £35; a week in summer £220. Located close to two beaches in beautiful walking country near mainland links. It comprises lounge/dinette/kitchenette; two bedrooms (sleeping five); bathroom/toilet. Well furnished, fully heated, TV, selection of books and other considerations. Another cottage is also available at Cowes, Isle of Wight. Non-smokers only. **Mrs C. Pitts, 11 York Avenue, New Milton, Hampshire BH25 6BT (New Milton [01425] 615215).**

WROXALL. Mrs Jane Owen, Appuldurcombe Farm, Wroxall PO38 3EW (01983 840188). Working farm, join in. This is the gateway to the idyllic historic estate where our well-furnished holiday cottages with nice gardens are situated around the estate, now a large family-run dairy farm. Children love to watch the milking and young animals. Two miles from the sea. A very good area for cycling and walking especially in Spring and Autumn. Short Breaks and special ferry prices available. Free access to Appuldurcombe House. Sorry no dogs. Weekly terms from £120 to £450.

CHANNEL ISLANDS

HOLIDAY

• JERSEY •

BUNGALOWS

3 bungalows, all near beach, at Grouville. In quiet countryside but close to bus stop, shops and golf course. Accommodates 2-8 people, also suitable for disabled. Livingroom, bathroom and toilet, fully equipped kitchen. Everything supplied including linen. Cot. Children and pets welcome.

Open all year. Reduced rates out of season.

Terms from £80 to £290 per week all told.

Jersey is a beautiful place to visit all year round. Excellent restaurants, shops (no VAT) and entertainment. Trips to France or other Channel Islands easily arranged. Write for further details from:

Mrs. P. Johnson, 'Mon Repos', Coast Road, Grouville, Jersey JE3 9BA (01534) 853333

CARAVAN AND CAMPING HOLIDAYS

CORNWALL

BUDEMEADOWS

Touring Holiday Park, Bude, Cornwall

100 pitches in 9.5 acres of landscaped grounds. **NO OVERCROWDING.** One mile from renowned surfing beach of Widemouth Bay. Heated outdoor pool and separate heated toddler pool, TV lounge and games room. Giant chess, barbecues, logland playground. Award-winning loos. Dishwashing, shop, laundry. We charge per person – no additional charges for what you bring. No charge for hot water, showers, hairdryers, swimming pool. The spectacular scenery within easy reach is also free. Large holiday chalet – well equipped – sleeps 6. Prices on application.

AA "Excellent" ►►►►

Easily accessible 3 miles south of Bude on A39.

Please write or phone 01288 361646 for free brochure.

ETB "Excellent" ✓✓✓✓✓

RAC LISTED · ANWB · ALAN ROGERS · CARAVAN & CAMPING CLUB

PLEASE ENCLOSE A STAMPED ADDRESSED ENVELOPE WITH ENQUIRIES

MITHIAN, near St. Agnes. J. Thorley, Treleaver, Mithian Downs, Near St. Agnes TR5 0PY (St. Agnes [0187255] 2486.) Sleeps 6. This modern caravan is situated on a 20 acre smallholding set in sheltered valley two miles from the coast and one mile from the village. A 25 foot BK Bluebird caravan, with fully fitted and equipped kitchen; shower and flush toilet. Accommodation is suitable for six people in one double bedroom, one bunk bedroom and a pull-down bed in the lounge; mains electricity with Calor gas cooker and heater; television socket. Various farm animals including pony; pets welcome if safe with farm animals. Terms from £100 to £150 weekly (inclusive of gas and electricity used). Further details on request.

PENZANCE. C. Hichens, Carne Cottage, Morvah, Pendeen, Penzance TR19 7TT (01736 788309). Carne Farm is a working dairy farm situated on the North Cornish coast, one mile from the nearest beach at Portherras Cove. It is an excellent walking area with breathtaking views of fields, moorlands and sea, yet visitors are only six miles from the lovely town of Penzance and two miles from the nearest village shops, pubs and restaurants at Pendeen. The spacious eight berth caravan with double bedroom, bunkroom, shower and toilet is located in the field beside the farmhouse. It is fully supplied with electricity, fridge, full-size electric cooker, electric fire, duvets, utensils and hot and cold water. Car parking nearby. Linen not provided. Visitors welcome on the farm. Pets by arrangement. Babysitter usually available. Rates from £100 to £160 plus electricity. Available all year round. Please ring of send SAE.

ST. AGNES near. Mr Anthony Harper, Fern Hill, Barkla Shop, St. Agnes TR5 0XN (01872 553371). Sleeps 4/5. Comfortable 26′ caravan with own garden. Colour TV, fridge, gas, electricity and bedding included. Flush toilet in caravan. Washroom, shower and toilet by caravan door. The caravan is situated in an interesting position on a smallholding down a lane, well away from the road next to woods and farmland. There is a streamside footpath through wooded valleys to Trevellasporth beach (one mile). Goats and chickens kept. Regret no dogs. Cooking camp fires allowed. Suit country/wildlife lovers. Surfing beaches of St. Agnes two miles, Perranporth three miles. Terms from £70 to £125 per week.

CUMBRIA — including "The Lakes"

APPLEBY-IN-WESTMORLAND. Mrs L.M. Watson, Whygill Head Farm, Little Asby, Appleby-in-Westmorland (017683 71531). Two six-berth caravans on their own private site in two and a half acre sheltered copse near the farm. Fully equipped except for bed linen. Electricity and running water in both vans. Heating and cooking by Calor gas (no extra charge). Flush toilet and hot water a few yards away, also shower and telephone. Children welcome and pets kept under control. An ideal centre for walkers and naturalists — rare plants and wildlife near at hand. Golf, fishing, swimming and pony trekking; interesting market towns, villages, craft workshops and artists' studios in the surrounding area. Price from £70 per week; weekends £10 per night. £30 deposit payable on booking.

BROUGHTON-IN-FURNESS. Mrs H. Glessal, Whineray Ground, Broughton-in-Furness LA20 6DS (Broughton-in-Furness [01229] 716500). Working farm. Private, sheltered yet within easy reach of a whole host of facilities — miniature railway, castles, gardens, beach, museum, fishing, bird watching, fell walking — attractive six-berth, 30′ modern static caravan set in its own half acre on a working fell farm. Marvellous views and absolute seclusion can be guaranteed. Two bedrooms (one with bunks, one with double bed), spacious living area and separate kitchen; shower and toilet. Fridge, gas fire and cooker — no additional charge for electricity and gas. Hot and cold water. River Duddon close by, indoor swimming pool, village, shops, pub, restaurant and golfing within two miles. Ulverston market town about ten miles. Further details on request. Terms from £80 weekly.

CARLISLE. Mrs P.E. Johnston, Yeast Hall, New House Farm, Newby West, Carlisle CA2 6QZ (Carlisle [01228] 23545). Two attractive caravans on private farm site — 28 foot Fairview five-berth, 30 foot Willerby six-berth, both with lounge, kitchen, bedroom, bathroom and each completely private in own enclosure. Situated three and a half miles west of Carlisle, a quarter-mile from road down private lane. It is ideally situated for visiting Lake District, Solway coast, Scottish Borders, Roman Wall, Eden Valley, etc. Vans are very well equipped, with everything supplied except linen, and thoroughly cleaned between visitors. Electric lighting, heating. Calor gas/electric cooker, water heater. Terms from £48. Further details with pleasure. Phone or write (SAE please).

CONISTON. Mrs E. Johnson, Spoon Hall, Coniston LA21 8AW (015394 41391). Caravans sleep 6. Three 33ft caravans situated on a 50 acre working hill farm one mile from Coniston, overlooking Coniston Lake. All have flush toilet, shower, gas cookers, fires and water heaters, electric lighting and fridge. All have colour TV. Children are welcome. Pets are allowed free. Available all year round. Pony trekking arranged from farm. Weekly terms on request.

DERBYSHIRE

ASHBOURNE. Mrs Louie Tatlow, Ashfield Farm, Calwich, Near Ashbourne DE6 2EB (Ellastone [01335] 324279 or 324443) Working farm. Five modern six-berth caravans, fully equipped, each with gas cooker, fridge, TV; shower and flush toilet; mains electricity. Ashfield Farm overlooks the peaceful Dove Valley and is convenient for the Peak District. The old market town of Ashbourne only two miles away with golf course, swimming pool, squash and bowling. Within easy reach of stately homes like Haddon Hall and Chatsworth, with the Potteries and Lichfield 25 miles distant, Uttoxeter 10 miles, while Alton Towers Theme Park is under five miles away. Prices and brochure on request. Write or telephone for further information.

BUXTON near. Mr and Mrs J. Melland, The Pomeroy Caravan Park, Street House Farm, Flagg, Near Buxton SK17 9QG (Longnor [0129883] 259). √ √ √ Working farm. Sleeps 6. This newly developed site for 30 caravans is situated five miles from Buxton, in heart of Peak District National Park. Ideal base for touring by car or walking. Site adjoins northern end of now famous Tissington and High Peak Trail. Only nine miles from Haddon Hall and ten from Chatsworth House. Landscaped to the latest model standards for caravan sites; tourers and campers will find high standards here. New toilet block with showers, washing facilities and laundry; mains electric hook-up points. Back-packers welcome. Large rally field available. Tourist Board registered. Children welcome; dogs on lead. We now have six-berth 28ft x 10ft Holiday Van with separate end bedroom; hot and cold water; WC and shower. Fridge, full size gas cooker and fire, TV. Weekly rates only. Fully equipped except linen. Open Easter to end of October. SAE, please, for weekly and nightly rates.

DEVON

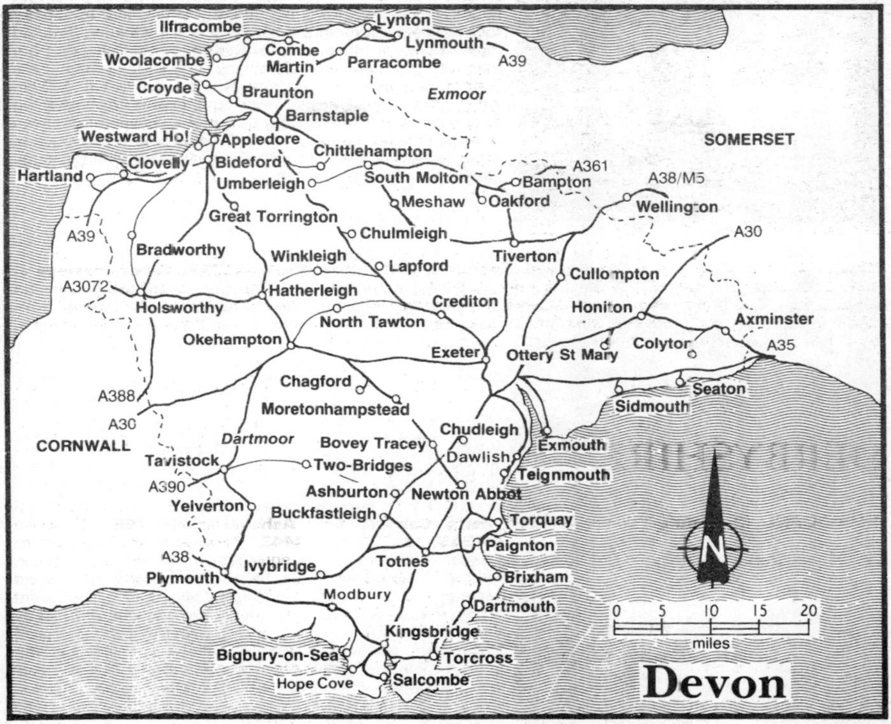

ASHBURTON. Mrs Rhona Parker, Higher Mead Farm, Ashburton TQ13 7LJ (Ashburton [01364] 652598). A friendly, family run farm site, set in 400 acres and surrounded by beautiful countryside. 12 miles to the sea and close to Dartmoor National Park. Ideal for touring Devon/ Cornwall. Perfect for children and pets with all farm animals, play area and plenty of space to roam, also large area for dogs. Holiday cottages and caravans fully equipped except for linen. Level touring site with some hard standings. Electric hook-up. Free showers in fully tiled block, laundry room and games room. Small family bar, shop and phone. Good discounts for couples. To find us: From Exeter take A38 to Plymouth till you see "26 miles Plymouth" sign; take second left at Alston Cross signposted to Woodland and Denbury.

BIDEFORD. Mrs Sarah Hunt, Greencliff Farm, Abbotsham, Bideford EX39 1JL (01237 424674). Only one caravan, peaceful situation, panoramic sea views, beautiful North Devon coastline. Mixed farm, Tudor farmhouse, easy access cliffs (Coastal Footpath) and rocky shore (prawning and surfing — for the experienced). Sleeps six in one double plus bunks. Gas cooker, fridge, hot and cold water, flush toilet, colour TV and fan heater. Separate building with toilet plus shower. Village amenities one mile, sandy beach at Westward Ho! three miles; water sports on Taw/ Torridge estuary. Historic market town of Bideford two miles and convenient for Clovelly, Exmoor, Lundy. Price from £90 to £120 per week.

BIDEFORD. Mrs J.A. Fox, Highstead Farm, Bucks Cross, Bideford EX39 5DX (01237 431201).

Large and attractive modern caravan on a private farm site with fine sea views nearby. Just off the A39 Bideford/Bude road close to the coast of North Devon and convenient for Clovelly, Bideford and Westward Ho! Luxury accommodation for six adults (sleeping accommodation for up to 11 at extra charge) with bath/shower, separate toilet, fully equipped kitchen including microwave, gas fire and colour TV. Babysitting also available. Pets welcome by arrangement. Linen supplied as extra. Shopping, beaches, local attractions and Moors within easy reach. Car essential but good walking country. Open March to October from £90 weekly low season.

CHITTLEHAMHOLT (North Devon). Snapdown Farm Caravans, Chittlehamholt. Caravans sleep 6.

Twelve only, six berth caravans, in two sheltered paddocks in lovely unspoilt countryside, down a quiet lane on a farm, sheltered by trees and well away from busy roads. Each caravan has hard standing for a car. Caravans are equipped with flush toilet, shower, fridge, colour TV, gas cooker and fire. Outside seats, picnic tables, barbecue. Table tennis. Children's play area in small wood adjoining. Laundry room with spin dryer, tumble dryer, iron, etc. Plenty of space — field and woodland walks. No commercialism. Within easy reach of sea and moors. Well behaved pets welcome. Two types of caravan available. Terms: £70 to £180 and £75 to £195 including gas and electricity in caravans. REDUCTIONS FOR COUPLES, EARLY AND LATE SEASON. Illustrated brochure from **Mrs M. Bowen, Snapdown, Chittlehamholt, Umberleigh EX37 9PF (01769 540708).**

COLYTON. Mrs S. Gould and Mrs R. Gould, Bonehayne Farm, Colyton EX13 6SG (01404 87416 or 87396). Working farm.

Six-berth luxury caravan in secluded spot on farmhouse lawn, overlooking the river, fields and woodlands where wildlife is a common sight. Many animals to make friends with on this 250 acre farm. Good trout fishing available. Caravan contains well fitted master bedroom, twin bedded room with cot rail available, and convertible double in lounge. Kitchen with cooker and fridge freezer. Spacious lounge and dining area. Colour TV. Bathroom with toilet, washbasin, shower and bath, heated towel rail. Fully equipped except linen. All rooms with plenty of cupboard space. Built-in radiators, fully insulated, making it ideal for out of season holidays. Milk and eggs obtainable from farmhouse. Colyton two miles, sea four and and a half miles. Brochure available.

CULLOMPTON. Mrs J. Davey, Pound Farm, Butterleigh, Cullompton EX15 1PH (01884 855 208). Working farm. Sleeps 6. A Pound Farm holiday combines finest English scenery with traditional beauty of village of Butterleigh, half a mile away. Enjoy family break from April to November on this 80-acre sheep and beef farm. Spacious comfortable caravan accommodation for six, in grass paddock with paths and parking for two cars. Enter by road. Well-equipped; linen hire by arrangement. Hot and cold water, shower. Electric cooker, kettle, iron (plus ironing board), toaster, fridge, heater, electric blanket, colour TV, lights, several power points (8). All cutlery, utensils, blankets and pillows. Washroom/Utility room. Adjoining caravan has flush toilet, double drainer stainless steel sink unit in utility room with shaving point, hot/cold water, electric light and two-bar heater. Farmstead within sight of caravans. Visitors free to walk over the farm. South and North coast 45 to 60 minutes' drive. Four miles from M5, Cullompton, North Devon Link road (A361), Tiverton, Silverton, Bickleigh thatched olde worlde village in heart of beautiful Exe Valley. Pets allowed. Free coarse fishing, no closed season — carp, tench, perch, roach, rudd. Terms from £90 to £160. FHG Diploma Winner. Also separate small site suitable for a few tents or caravanettes.

FUN FOR ALL THE FAMILY IN DEVON

Arlington Court, near Barnstaple; Bygones Victoria Street, Torquay; Clovelly Village, near Bideford; Dartington Crystal, Great Torrington; Dartmoor Wildlife Park, Sparkwell; English Riviera Leisure Centre, Torquay; Exeter Maritime Museum; Exmoor Bird Gardens, Bratton Fleming; Kents Cavern Show Caves, Torquay; Babbacombe Model Village, Torquay; National Shire Horse Centre, Yealmpton; Paignton Zoo and Botanical Gardens; Plymouth Dome; Plym Valley Railway Steam Centre, Plymouth; Woodland Leisure Park, Blackawton.

EXETER near. Mr D.L. Salter, Haldon Lodge Farm, Kennford, Near Exeter EX6 7YG (Exeter [01392] 832312). Working farm. Peace and seclusion are assured on this private residential site. The Salters offer a family holiday for all ages, with a special invitation to younger members to join in pony riding and enjoy a free and easy farm holiday with them. Exeter four and a half miles, Dawlish (short car drive away) ideal centre for touring all South Devon resorts and Dartmoor. The two luxury six-berth residential holiday caravans adjoin a large lawn with a background of fields, pine trees and rhododendrons. Six comfortable beds, blankets, pillows. Fully equipped kitchen, carpeted lounge with TV, bathroom (hot and cold), flush toilet, electricity and mains connected. Horses and ponies nearby are an interest to everyone. Horse lovers and children are invited to explore the beautiful Teign Valley Forest on horseback. Day pony treks are arranged for small parties. The well-known Nobody Inn is one of the attractive country inns where you can have a drink and a meal in a friendly atmosphere. Pets allowed. Riding and Trekking Holidays can be arranged. Three well stocked fishing lakes. Caravans can be hired from March to December from £70 to £160 per week. Tourers and campers at very reasonable daily charge. No extra charge for pets etc.

ILFRACOMBE. Mrs A.R. Burge, Outer Narracott Farm, Bittadon, Barnstaple EX31 4HN (01271 862951). A warm welcome, cream tea and flowers on the table await you in a spacious mobile home on our working farm, set amidst unspoilt countryside midway between coast and moor. We have sheep, some cattle, and ducks and chickens in the paddock! Guests are welcome to enjoy the farming activities in season. Traditional Devonshire cream teas can be provided on the lawn occasionally if required. All facilities in mobile home — fridge freezer, shower, toilet, two separate bedrooms. Laundry room nearby. Beautiful secluded gardens. Very peaceful. Beautiful beaches within four to six miles approximately, Exmoor 15 to 20 miles. SAE for further details.

PLEASE ENCLOSE A STAMPED ADDRESSED ENVELOPE WITH ENQUIRIES

TEIGN VALLEY. S. and G. Harrison-Crawford, Silver Birches, Teign Valley, Trusham, Newton Abbot TQ13 0NJ (01626 852172). Two luxury 23ft and 29 ft four-berth caravans in an attractive two acre garden on the bank of the River Teign. Each has mains water, electricity, shower/bath, flush toilet, washbasin, immersion heater, Calor gas cooker, fridge; TV available. Ideally situated two miles from A38 on B3193. Dartmoor, Exeter, Torquay easily accessible. Sea 12 miles. Car essential, ample parking. Excellent centre for fishing (river and reservoir), bird watching, forest walks; 70 yards private salmon and trout fishing. Golf courses and horse riding within easy reach. Shops two and a half miles. Milk delivered. We personally clean caravans and ensure your comfort. Pets by arrangement. ETB registered. Open March to October. Terms from £80 to £145. Breakfast available in bungalow from £20 per person per night and £140 weekly per person.

TOTNES. J. and E. Ball, Higher Well Farm and Holiday Park, Stoke Gabriel, Totnes TQ9 6RN (01803 782289). ✓ ✓ ✓ A quiet secluded farm park welcoming tents, motor caravans and touring caravans. It is less than one mile from the riverside village of Stoke Gabriel and within four miles of Torbay beaches. Central for touring South Devon. Facilities include toilets, showers, launderette, shop, payphone and electric hook-ups. There are also static caravans to let. Enjoy a delightful relaxing holiday in the beautiful Devonshire countryside. Static caravans from £85 per week.

WOOLACOMBE. Twitchen House and Mortehoe Caravan Park, Woolacombe. ✓ ✓ ✓ ✓ LUXURY CARAVANS AT WOOLACOMBE. Have a carefree and comfortable holiday in one of our Executive, luxury or modern caravans on this attractive, well equipped Rose Award Park. Park facilities include heated pool, licensed club with two bars, snooker, activities room, games and family areas, free entertainment, shop, launderette, putting green, etc. We offer a wide selection of caravans all on concrete bases, with mains water and drainage, flush toilets, hot and cold water to sinks/shower, refrigerators, heating, TV, etc. Fully inclusive terms from £95 per week, with special low rates/Senior Citizen discounts out of season. For colour brochure and tariff, SAE or phone **Woolacombe Caravan Hirers, Dept FHG, Garden Cottage, 27 East Street, Braunton EX33 2EA (01271 816580).**

WOOLACOMBE SANDS. CARAVANS TO LET. Farm site above Rockham Beach (only 500 yards). Delightful situation in the heart of National Trust land, magnificent sea views. Famous three miles of Woolacombe Sands only one mile away. Marvellous walking, surfing. Magnificent coast for lovers of unspoilt beauty. Wide choice of new king-size caravans (33ft.) with toilet, shower, hot water, fridge, TV etc. Very well equipped, parking beside caravan. On site shop, laundry, showers etc. Rates from £99 to £299. SAE please. **Morte Point Caravans, 23 Brooks Road, Wylde Green, Sutton Coldfield B72 1HP (Tel & Fax: 0121-354 1551).**

PUBLISHER'S NOTE

While every effort is made to ensure accuracy, we regret that FHG Publications cannot accept responsibility for errors, omissions or misrepresentation in our entries or any consequences thereof. Prices in particular should be checked because we go to press early. We will follow up complaints but cannot act as arbiters or agents for either party.

DORSET

MANOR FARM HOLIDAY CENTRE

Charmouth, Bridport, Dorset

Situated in a rural valley. Charmouth beach a level ten minutes' walk away.

Luxury 6-berth Caravans for Hire with toilet/shower, refrigerator, full cooker, colour TV, gas fire.

30-acre Tourist Park for touring caravans, dormobiles and tents.

Centre facilities include * Toilets; * Hot showers; * Fish and chip takeaway; * Licensed bar with family room; * Amusement room; * Launderette; * Shop and off-licence; * Swimming pool; * Electric hook-up points; * Calor gas and Camping Gaz; * Ice pack service; * Chemical disposal unit.

Send SAE for colour brochure to Mr R. B. Loosmore or Tel: 01297 560226

See also Colour Display Advertisement in this Guide.

CHARMOUTH. Mrs Axman, Monkton Wylde Farm, Charmouth DT6 6DB (01297 34525). Come and stay and enjoy your holiday in our one luxury six-berth static caravan. Fully equipped and serviced with colour TV, garden furniture, shed for bikes, outdoor coats etc. South-facing overlooking paddock on working farm with large woods to explore and plenty of space for children to play. Historic and busy Lyme Regis three miles. Safe beaches nearby. Many and varied tourist attractions for all ages with golf, National Trust, Heritage Coast walks and fishing by arrangement. From £70 to £150 per week. Railway (Axminster) three miles, bus stop one mile.

LYME REGIS. Mrs C. Grymonprez, Beechfield Cottage, Yawl Hill Lane, Uplyme, Lyme Regis DT7 3RW (Lyme Regis [01297] 443216). Caravans sleep 4/6. Beechfield is a four-acre smallholding situated on Yawl Hill, commanding a truly scenic outlook over Lyme's countryside and the sea. It is conveniently located on the borders of Devon, Somerset and Dorset. To ensure utmost privacy we have a well-kept one acre field, hedge-screened and peaceful, set aside for only two modern caravans. Both are fully equipped (except linen), with fridge, mains electricity and water, inside flush toilet, shower, gas cooker and fire, colour TV. Cleanliness guaranteed. Lyme Regis is only two and a half miles away. Organically grown vegetables according to season, home made bread, some herbs and free-range eggs available. SAE appreciated.

LYME REGIS. Mrs J. Tedbury, Little Paddocks, Yawl Hill Lane, Lyme Regis DT7 3RW (Lyme Regis [01297] 443085). Sleeps 6. A six-berth caravan on Devon/Dorset border in a well-kept paddock overlooking Lyme Bay and surrounding countryside. Situated on a smallholding with animals, for perfect peace and quiet. Lyme Regis two-and-a-half miles, Charmouth three-and-a-half miles. Both have safe beaches for children. Easy driving distance to resorts of Seaton, Beer and Sidmouth. The caravan is fully equipped except linen. It has shower room with handbasin and toilet inside as well as flush toilet just outside. Electric light, fridge and TV. Calor gas cooker and fire. Car can be parked alongside. Dogs welcome. Terms from £80. Also fully equipped chalet for two from £65. SAE, please.

HAMPSHIRE

HAYLING ISLAND. Lower Tye Camp Site, Copse Lane, Hayling Island PO11 0QR (01705 462479), The Oven Camp Site, Manor Road, Hayling Island PO11 0QX (01705 464695) and Fleet Farm Camp Site, Yew Tree Road, Hayling Island PO11 0QB (01705 463684). Sites from £6 per unit per night. Parking by unit. Safe beaches, windsurfing, golf, horse riding, etc. Ideal touring area for Portsmouth, Isle of Wight, New Forest. Follow A3023 from Havant, turn left into Copse Lane where indicated for Fleet and Lower Tye; for Oven Camp Site continue on main A3023 until roundabout, bear right, site 200 yards on left. Caravans permanently sited (£10 per week plus VAT) or stored (£3.50 plus vat) if required. Rallies catered for. RAC and AA registered.

HEREFORD & WORCESTER

LEOMINSTER. Miss P. Moore, Meadow Bank, Hamnish, Leominster HR6 0QN (01568 760267). There are eight-berth caravans for hire on this farm. They have mains water, colour TV, gas cooker, microwave, all necessary utensils, etc., fridge and everything except personal linen. Flush toilets in all vans and all now have showers. Small pony usually available and fishing, riding, hacking and driving as well on the farm; golf locally. Children welcome. Pets allowed under proper control. Phone on site. The only site rules are for reasonable peace and quiet, with friendly atmosphere. Facilities for touring vans and campers. Shops in Leominster, two miles, also swimming pool. Miss Moore enjoys people coming to stay at her caravans and helps in every way she can with information about interesting places to visit. Self-catering Riding Holidays are available most of the year, unaccompanied children catered for. Touring caravans and tents welcome. Terms according to season. Touring caravans also available.

LEOMINSTER. Mrs E.M. Thomas, Woonton Court Farm, Leysters, Leominster HR6 0HL (01568 750232). We have two acres of secluded grass field for camping and touring caravans on our small mixed farm in rural Herefordshire. We can accommodate 10 tents, five caravans. Our facilities include toilet, shower, hot water, washing machine and dryer, fridge, payphone. Electric hook-up. Farm produce available. Dogs welcome under control. Good walks with abundance of wildlife to watch. Situated in the Heart of England and Welsh Border area with lots of tourist attractions to visit. Caravan Club Site nearby and farmhouse Bed and Breakfast accommodation available.

NORTHUMBERLAND

ALNWICK. Mrs J.W. Bowden, "Anvil-Kirk", 8 South Charlton Village, Alnwick NE66 2NA (01665 579324). One six-berth caravan on single private site. Hard standing and lovely spacious surroundings. Three-quarters of a mile from the A1; six miles north of Alnwick and six miles also from the lovely clean beaches of Beadnell, Seahouses, Craster Village; nine miles from the Cheviot Hills. Many castles nearby — Bamburgh and Alnwick being the largest; wild cattle and bird sanctuaries; Ingram Valley for the hill walker, Berwick and Morpeth markets. Holy Island is a must with its tiny castle and harbour with fishing boats. Many places to eat out within a radius of 10 miles. The caravan has mains water and electricity; electric cooker, fridge, microwave, TV. End bedroom (bunk beds); flush toilet in bathroom. Open Easter to October. Children and pets welcome. Milk and bread delivered, papers and greengrocery daily. Terms from £120 to £170 per week. Tourist Board Commended; one Rose Award. SAE, please. Also Bed and Breakfast available in house from £13.50 per night.

SHROPSHIRE

BRIDGNORTH. Carol Skinner, Park Grange, Morville, Bridgnorth WV16 4RN (01746 714285). ✓ ✓ ✓ Experience country living in luxury holiday caravans on our small, quiet family park set in 12 acres. Panoramic views of Shropshire's hills. Children's play area, picnic area, fishing and wildlife pools, see our goats, pony and poultry. Ideal location for visiting Ironbridge Gorge, Ludlow, Severn Valley Railway, Jack Mytton Way, and for walking, cycling or horse riding holidays. Guests' horses stabled. Each caravan is fully equipped with fridge, cooker, microwave and has mains water, electricity, drainage, etc. Situated quietly off the A458 midway between Bridgnorth and Much Wenlock — look for holiday caravan sign. From £90 to £200 per week based on six people. No smoking or pets in caravans. Bed and Breakfast also available. SAE, please, for brochure.

SOMERSET

AA

RAC appointed

CHEDDAR GORGE

"ENGLAND'S GRAND CANYON"

A TOTALLY UNIQUE 5 STAR CARAVAN AND CAMPING FAMILY EXPERIENCE

One of the most interesting inland parks in the West Country. A family business specialising in family holidays. A free cuddle with the Llamas a speciality. Prices include the use of the heated outdoor swimming pool, and entrance to the Bar/Family room. Activities on the park include Archery, Abseiling and Shooting. Mountain bike/Tandem hire. Table Tennis, Crazy Golf, Boule, Croquet, Skate-board ramps.

BROADWAY HOUSE HOLIDAY

Touring Caravan and Camping Park, Cheddar, Somerset.
Tel: (01934) 742610
Fax: (01934) 744950
Stamp for details.

Rose award park

British Graded Holiday Parks ✓✓✓✓

If you've found FARM HOLIDAY GUIDES of service please tell your friends

DULVERTON. Mrs M.M. Jones, Higher Town, Dulverton TA22 9RX (Anstey Mills [0139-84] 272). Working farm. Caravans sleep 8. Our farm is situated half a mile from open moorland, one mile from the Devon/Somerset border and four miles from Dulverton. 80 acres of the farm is in the Exmoor National Park. We let **two caravans** which are quarter of a mile apart and do not overlook each other, and have lovely views, situated in lawns with parking space. Both are eight berth, with a double end bedroom, bunk bedroom, shower, flush toilet, hot/cold water and colour TV. The caravans are modern and fully equipped except linen. Cot and high chair available. Visitors are welcome to watch the milking or walk over our beef and sheep farm. Riding and fishing nearby. Open May to October. Price from £70, includes gas and electricity.

WIVELISCOMBE. Richard and Marion Rottenbury, Oxenleaze Farm Caravans, Chipstable, Wiveliscombe TA4 2QH (Wiveliscombe [01984] 623427). √ √ √ √ This exceptional site is set in the peace and tranquillity of the Devon/Somerset borders close to Exmoor known for its beautiful countryside. Super Luxury and luxury caravans on a working hill farm. Each caravan has its own shower and flush toilet, hot and cold water, cooker, fridge, fire and colour TV. Parking is available beside each caravan; car is essential. The site, ideal for the "away from it all" holiday, offers a games room, children's play area, sandpit, swings, barbecue, indoor swimming pool, laundry and telephone. A fisherman's paradise for those keen on coarse angling — free fishing on one and a half acre ponds stocked with large carp and tench. No closed season. Early booking advised. Strictly no pets. Open Easter to end October. Prices from £105 weekly. SAE for colour brochure.

NORTH YORKSHIRE

WHITBY. Mrs A.G. Shardlow, Beckside Farm, Sneatonthorpe, Whitby YO22 5JG (01947 880550 and 880213). One 25ft luxury two-bedroomed static caravan, accommodating six persons, plus cot, situated on small livestock farm on edge of North Yorkshire Moors, overlooking small beck and wooded area, five miles from the sea. The beautiful coastline, with sandy beaches and rocky coves, is an ideal location for fishing, riding, boating on river; visiting tea gardens, craft centres, steam railway, zoo and enjoying many lovely walks. The caravan is equipped with cooker, fridge, colour TV, hot and cold water, mains sanitation, gas heater and all necessary utensils. Shower on site. Everything supplied for your holiday requirements, except linen. Children's play area and parking space. Available April to October. SAE, for weekly terms.

WHITBY near. Mrs M. Cana, Partridge Nest Farm, Eskdaleside, Sleights, Whitby YO22 5ES (01947 810450). Set in beautiful Esk Valley, six caravans on secluded site in 45 acres of interesting land reaching up to the moors. Just five minutes from the sea and the ancient fishing town of Whitby. The North Yorkshire Moors Steam Railway starts two miles away at Grosmont. Ideal for children, birdwatchers and all country lovers. Each caravan has mains electricity, gas cooker, fire, colour TV, fridge and shower/WC. Ideal touring centre. Riding lessons available on our own horses/ponies. Terms from £115. Telephone or write with SAE, please.

Please mention this guide when you write or phone to enquire about accommodation.

If you are writing, a stamped, addressed envelope is always appreciated.

ACTIVITY HOLIDAYS

DEVON, ASHBURTON. Mrs Rhona Parker, Higher Mead Farm, Ashburton TQ13 7LJ (Ashburton [01364] 652598). SELF CATERING: GENERAL. A friendly, family-run farm site set in 400 acres and surrounded by beautiful countryside. 12 miles from the sea and close to Dartmoor National Park; ideal for touring Devon/Cornwall. Perfect for children and pets with all farm animals, play area and plenty of space to roam, also large area for dogs. Holiday cottages and caravans, fully equipped except for linen. Level touring site with some hard standings. Free showers in fully tiled block, laundry room and games room. Small family bar, shop and phone. Good discounts for couples. From Exeter take A38 to Plymouth till you see "26 miles Plymouth" sign; take second left at Alston Cross signposted to Woodland and Denbury.

DEVON, EXETER near. Mr D.L. Salter, Haldon Lodge Farm, Kennford, Near Exeter EX6 7YG (01392 832312). Working farm. SELF CATERING: RIDING & TREKKING. Peace and seclusion are assured on this private residential site. The Salters offer a family holiday for all ages, with a special invitation to younger members to join in pony riding and enjoy a free and easy farm holiday with them. Exeter four and a half miles. Dawlish (short car drive away) ideal centre for touring all South Devon resorts and Dartmoor. The three six-berth residential holiday caravans adjoin a large lawn with background of fields, pine trees, rhododendrons. Six comfortable beds, blankets, pillows. Fully equipped kitchen, carpeted lounge (TV), bathroom (H/C), flush toilet, electricity and mains connected. Horses and ponies nearby are an interest to everyone. Horse lovers and children we invite to explore the beautiful Teign Valley Forest on horseback. Day pony treks arranged for small parties. The well-known Nobody Inn is one of the many attractive country inns where you can have a drink and a meal in the midst of a friendly atmosphere. Pets allowed. Three well stocked fishing lakes. Riding and Trekking Holidays from £55 per week. Caravans March to December from £70 to £160 per week. Tourers and campers from £4 per day. No extra charge for pets, etc.

HEREFORD & WORCESTER, LONGTOWN. Trewern Farm Park Holidays (0187 387615). CAMPING: GENERAL. Seven day camping holidays on a traditional working farm with panoramic views of the Black Mountains. Perfect quiet family holiday with many friendly farm animals. Also available, orienteering and assault course. We provide all you need for a camping holiday. Fully equipped seven berth frame tent includes sleeping bags, gas cookers, etc. On site facilities include toilet block. Also space for 10 tent pitches. For further information please ring **Nigel or Sue.**

SOMERSET, CHEDDAR. Broadway House Holiday Touring Caravan and Camping Park, Cheddar (01934 742610; Fax: 01934 744950). ✓ ✓ ✓ ✓ Cheddar Gorge — "England's Grand Canyon". A totally unique five star caravan and camping family experience. One of the most interesting inland parks in the West Country. A family business specialising in family holidays. A free cuddle with the Llamas a speciality. Prices include the use of the heated outdoor swimming pool and entrance to the Bar/Family room. Activities on the park include archery, abseiling and shooting; mountain bike/tandem hire; table tennis, crazy golf, boules, croquet, skate-board ramps. AA 4 Pennants, RAC Appointed, Rose Award Park.

WALES

BOARD ACCOMMODATION

CLWYD

DENBIGH. Mrs Helen Parry, College Farm, Peniel, Denbigh LL16 4TT (01745 550276). ♛ *Highly Commended.* **Working farm, join in.** Situated in a quiet and peaceful area of the Vale of Clwyd nine miles from the A55, three miles from the market town of Denbigh with its ancient castle, wide high street and colonnades. We are central for the coast, Snowdonia and Chester. Nearby Brenig Reservoir has facilities for fishing, sailing and surfing. Our bungalow has one double and one family room with washbasins, hospitality trays and full central heating. Spacious lounge with separate dining room. Farmhouse fare is served with free-range eggs and vegetables from our organic garden. Children welcome at reduced rates. Bed and Breakfast from £15. Evening Meal by arrangement. No smoking. You are assured of a Warm Welsh Welcome by the bilingual Parry family. Open March to October. Wales farmhouse Award.

LLANSILIN. Mrs G. Jones, Lloran Ganol Farm, Llansilin, Oswestry, Shropshire SY10 7QX (0169170 287). ♛ **Working farm, join in.** A friendly welcome is assured at this modern farm set in 300 acres in Welsh valley. A busy working farm of dairy, sheep and cattle, it has surrounding garden and lawns. Fly fishing, rough shooting and horse riding on farm. Tastefully furnished farmhouse has two bedrooms (one double, one twin), both have washbasins and tea-making facilities; modern bathroom; large lounge and dining room; colour TV. Bed and Breakfast from £12.50; Dinner, Bed and Breakfast from £24. Weekly self catering from £80. WTB inspected.

RUTHIN. Mrs E.O. Jones, Llanbenwch Farm, Llanfair D.C., Ruthin LL15 2SH (0182-470 2340). Working farm. ♛ *Highly Commended.* Situated three miles south from Ruthin, on the main (A525) Wrexham road, this is a 40-acre working farm amidst beautiful scenery. The old house, oak-beamed and modernised without spoiling its character, is conveniently situated for travelling throughout North Wales. There is a nice garden and quiet roads for evening walks and mountain roads for driving. Good food is assured, with personal attention. One family, two double bedrooms, all with washbasins, TV and tea-making facilities; bathroom, two toilets; diningroom with separate tables, sittingroom with TV. Central heating. Sorry, no dogs in house and no children under five years. Ample parking. Open February to November for Evening Dinner/Meal, Bed and Breakfast from £16 daily; Bed and Breakfast from £12 to £15 daily. SAE, please, for reply. Awarded and Commended farmhouse.

ST. ASAPH. Mrs Eirlys Jones, Rhewl Farm, Waen, St. Asaph LL17 0DT (01745 582287). 👑👑 Enjoy Welsh hospitality on our 180 acre farm, conveniently situated half a mile from A55 expressway in peaceful and beautiful setting. Comfortable bedrooms with radiators and tea/coffee making facilities. Double room has en suite facilities, twin and family rooms have washbasins. Spacious lounge with inglenook fireplace and colour TV. Evening Meal by arrangement. Convenient for Chester, coast and Snowdonia. Free fishing. Games room. Reductions for children. Bed and Breakfast from £13.50 to £15. This is a non-smoking household. Please send SAE for brochure.

WREXHAM. Pat Thompson, Saith Daran Farm, Llandegla, Wrexham LL11 3BA (01978 790685). 👑👑 Beautifully situated near the top of the breathtaking Horseshoe Pass at the junction of the A5104 and A542, near Llangollen and medieval Ruthin. Ideal for touring the North Wales coast, Snowdonia and Chester. 85 acre dairy/beef farm. Conservatory to relax and enjoy the lovely views. Bedrooms en suite with tea/coffee making facilities, electric blankets, radio and TV. Riding nearby. Children welcome. Open March to November. Bed and Breakfast from £17 to £19. Caravan and camping site available.

WALES

FOR THE MUTUAL GUIDANCE OF GUEST AND HOST

Every year literally thousands of holidays, short-breaks and overnight stops are arranged through our guides, the vast majority without any problems at all. In a handful of cases, however, difficulties do arise about bookings, which often could have been prevented from the outset.

It is important to remember that when accommodation has been booked, both parties — guests and hosts — have entered into a form of contract. We hope that the following points will provide helpful guidance.

GUESTS: When enquiring about accommodation, be as precise as possible. Give exact dates, numbers in your party and the ages of any children. State the number and type of rooms wanted and also what catering you require — bed and breakfast, full board, etc. Make sure that the position about evening meals is clear — and about pets, reductions for children or any other special points.

Read our reviews carefully to ensure that the proprietors you are going to contact can supply what you want. Ask for a letter confirming all arrangements, if possible.

If you have to cancel, do so as soon as possible. Proprietors do have the right to retain deposits and under certain circumstances to charge for cancelled holidays if adequate notice is not given and they cannot re-let the accommodation.

HOSTS: Give details about your facilities and about any special conditions. Explain your deposit system clearly and arrangements for cancellations, charges, etc, and whether or not your terms include VAT.

If for any reason you are unable to fulfil an agreed booking without adequate notice, you may be under an obligation to arrange alternative suitable accommodation or to make some form of compensation.

While every effort is made to ensure accuracy, we regret that FHG Publications cannot accept responsibility for errors, omissions or misrepresentation in our entries or any consequences thereof. Prices in particular should be checked because we go to press early. We will follow up complaints but cannot act as arbiters or agents for either party.

DYFED

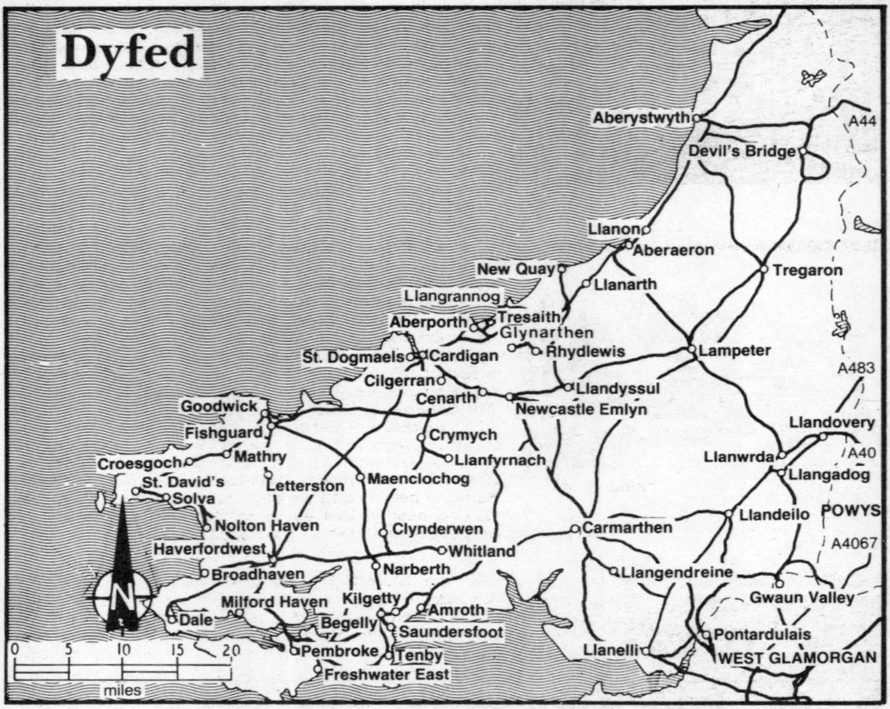

ABERPORTH. Peter and Olwen Duckworth, Ffynonwen Country Guest House, Aberporth, Cardigan SA43 2HT (01239 810312). *Highly Commended.* This is a 300 year old farmhouse brought thoroughly up to date with the addition of a new extension of six bedrooms, five of which are en-suite and one which is specially adapted for use by disabled visitors. It is set in its own 20 acres with its own trout lakes and is within easy reach of one of the last unspoilt coastlines in Wales. It excels in home-cooked food and friendly atmosphere and has a cosy little olde-worlde bar. The nearby village of Aberporth has safe bathing and Cardigan is seven miles away. Bed and Breakfast from £20; reductions for children and pets welcome. Brochure and full tariff by return post.

ABERPORTH. Mr and Mrs A.J. Davis, Glandwr Manor Hotel, Tresaith, Aberporth, Cardigan SA43 2JH (Aberporth [01239] 810197). *Highly Commended.* Standing proudly within its own five acres of secluded grounds, Glandwr Manor Hotel in Tresaith offers a tranquil, rather luxurious base just five minutes from the sandy beach. This Grade II Listed Georgian building has been gradually refurbished since 1978 to very high standards by the current owners, Janet and Arthur Davies. Attractive from the outside, inside it offers a warm and homely atmosphere. Exposed beams and open fires enhance the building's original character, whilst every modern facility is provided. Add to this the first class cuisine provided by the extensive restaurant menu and you really have all you need under one roof. Most bedrooms are en-suite; family suites consist of a large double bedroom, with a small room off the main bedroom in which there are two bunk beds, and en-suite bathroom.

PLEASE ENCLOSE A STAMPED ADDRESSED ENVELOPE WITH ENQUIRIES

ABERYSTWYTH. Miss Ann J. Evans, Glynwern Guest House, Llanilar, Aberystwyth SY23 4NY (01974 247203). Drift off to sleep to the sound of the River Ystwyth which flows directly past "Glynwern", a Victorian house in its own grounds, and backing onto the hills. Half a mile from the village of Llanilar (pub/free house), and five miles south of Aberystwyth. "Glynwern" has two double rooms (washbasins) and one single room. Guests have exclusive use of TV lounge and a separate dining room. Local amenities include 9 hole golf course, riding school/pony trekking, free fishing, any number of pleasant walks; varied wild life. "Glynwern" is open all year, guarantees a warm welcome and is recommended by the Welsh Tourist Board. Sorry, no pets. Bed and Breakfast £20 per person per night; Bed, Breakfast and Evening Meal £25 per person per night. Croeso Cynnes.

CLYNDERWEN. Brian and Ann Barney, Yethen Isaf, Mynachlogddu, Clynderwen, Pembrokeshire SA66 7SN (01437 532256). Yethen Isaf is situated a short distance from Foel Cwm Cerwyn, the highest peak in the Preseli Mountains, enjoying superb views, surrounded by common land, interspersed with bubbling streams and grazed by ponies and sheep. The walking and scenery are some of the finest in the British Isles and the coast is reached in about 20 minutes by car, via beautiful lanes with hedgerows carpeted in wild flowers. Our farm is accessible to our visitors at all times and supports a herd of Pedigree Welsh Black Cattle and a flock of Beulah Speckleface Sheep. Come and relax with us in our 250 year old farmhouse and get to know Pembrokeshire. Three double/twin rooms (one en suite) with tea making facilities; central heating, log fires. Sorry no pets. Ample parking. Pony trekking, fishing, golf, walking nearby. Bed and Breakfast from £16 to £18 per person per night. Dinner on request.

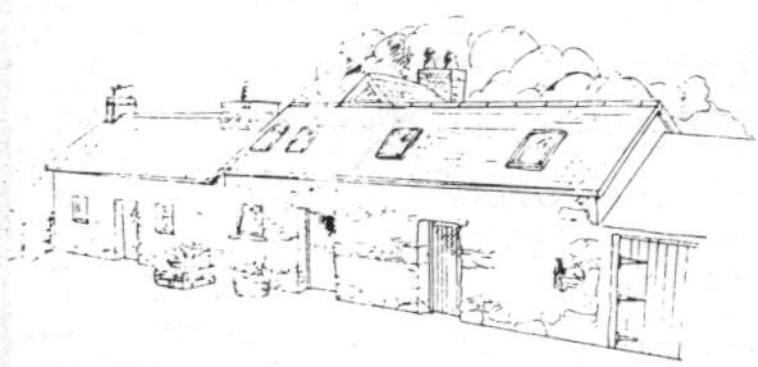

Yethen Isaf

FISHGUARD near. Heathfield Mansion, Letterston, Near Fishguard SA62 5EG (01348 840263). A Grade II listed Georgian country house in 16 acres of pasture and woodland, Heathfield is the home of former Welsh rugby international, Clive Rees, and his wife Angelica. This is an ideal location for the appreciation of Pembrokeshire's many natural attractions. There is excellent golf, riding and trout fishing in the vicinity and the coast is only a few minutes' drive away. The accommodation is very comfortable, two of the three bedrooms have private bathrooms, and the cuisine and wines are well above average. This is a most refreshing venue for a tranquil and wholesome holiday. Children and pets welcome. Bed and Breakfast from £15 — £18 per person; Dinner by prior arrangement.

HAVERFORDWEST. Joyce Canton, Nolton Haven Farm, Nolton Haven, Haverfordwest SA62 1NH (01437 710263). The farmhouse is beside the beach on a 200 acre mixed farm, with cattle calves and lots of show ponies. It has a large lounge which is open to guests all day as are all the bedrooms. Single, double and family rooms; two family rooms en suite, four other bathrooms. Pets and children most welcome babysitting free of charge. 50 yards to the beach, 75 yards to the local inn/restaurant. Pony trekking, surfing, fishing, excellent cliff walks, boating and canoeing are all available nearby. Riding holidays and short breaks all year a speciality. Colour brochure on request.

HAVERFORDWEST. Mrs M.E. Davies, Cuckoo Mill Farm, Pelcomb Bridge, St. David's Road, Haverfordwest SA62 6EA (01437-76 2139). Working farm. This farm is situated in central Pembrokeshire, two miles out of Haverfordwest on St. David's road. It is within easy reach of many beaches and coastline walks. There are peaceful country walks on the farm, also a small trout stream. Children are welcome at reduced rates and cot, high chair and babysitting provided. The house is cosy with open fires and welcomes guests from January to December. Car is not essential, but parking available. Home-produced dairy products; poultry and meats all home-cooked. Mealtimes arranged to suit guests. Two family, one double, one twin-bedded and one single bedrooms, each with washbasin and tea-making facilities. Two bathrooms. Sittingroom, two diningrooms. Pets permitted. Evening Dinner/Meal, Bed and Breakfast or Bed and Breakfast only. Rates also reduced for Senior Citizens. Tourist Board Listed.

HAVERFORDWEST. John Birt-Llewellin, The Bower Farm, Little Haven, Haverfordwest SA62 3TY (01437 781554). *Commended.* An extensively modernised traditional farmhouse on working sheep farm offering peace, warmth, comfort and friendliness to the casual or longer stay visitor. Dogs, horses (livery available) and children welcome. Walking distance of Broadhaven beach and coast path. Impressive sea views over St. Brides Bay and islands. All rooms en suite. Open all year except Christmas. Bed and Breakfast from £18 to £22.

HAVERFORDWEST. Mrs Judith Williams, Knock Farm, Camrose, Haverfordwest SA62 6HW (01437 762208). Knock Farm is a 275 acre working dairy farm, situated in a scenic valley, 10 minutes' drive from Pembrokeshire's sandy beaches and coastline walks; two miles from Haverfordwest. Good home cooking using home produce. All rooms have tea/coffee making facilities; family room en suite; TV lounge with log fire available all day. Children welcome at reduced rates. Reductions for Senior Citizens. Wales Tourist Board registered. Terms on request.

HAVERFORDWEST. Mrs Susan Evans, Spittal Cross Farm, Spittal, Haverfordwest SA62 5DB (01437 741206). Come to our family-run 200 acre dairy farm in the heart of the beautiful Pembrokeshire countryside, making it a convenient touring base for the many attractions we have on offer in the county. In the dining room we serve hearty breakfasts and good traditional home cooked dinners, all on separate "family" tables. The lounge area has a colour TV, plenty of books and board games for our guests' use. The two bedrooms have washbasins, beverage trays and radio/clock alarms. Children of all ages welcomed; cot, high chair and babysitting by arrangement. Comfort, cleanliness and personal attention assured. Pets by arrangement. Brochure on request. Basic Food Hygiene Certificate, Wales Tourist Board Member, "Welcome Host" Award.

HAVERFORDWEST. Mrs Nesta Thomas, Lower Haythog Farm, Spittal, Haverfordwest SA62 5QL (01437 731 279). *Highly Commended.* **Working farm, join in.** Peace and relaxation can be enjoyed at our old farmhouse, set in 250 acres of picturesque, unspoilt countryside five miles north of Haverfordwest. Centrally situated for all the beauty spots, on a dairy farm where home cooking, warm hospitality and laughter are assured. Comfortable lounge heated by log fire, with colour TV, books, games for guests' use; separate diningroom. Two family, one double, one single bedrooms with en suite facilities. Cot, high chair, washing and drying facilities for guests with small children and babies. Fish for trout in the brook or ponds — abundance of wild life — pony rides. Pets by arrangement. Bed, Breakfast and Evening Meal. Open all year. AA Listed, WTB Award. Fire Certificate. Brochure on request.

HAVERFORDWEST. Mrs A.M. Roberts, Haroldston Tongues Farm, Portfield Gate, Haverfordwest SA62 3LE (Broad Haven [01437] 781287). Working farm, join in. This comfortable farmhouse on a working dairy farm with lovely views of the Prescelly Hills is excellently situated being near the sandy beaches; Broad Haven two miles, Newgale three, St. David's 13. Island of Skomer worth visiting especially in May and June. Riding for novice or expert one mile away. Two double rooms and two single rooms, all with washbasins; bathroom, shower room and three toilets; TV lounge; quiet sitting area in large L-shaped diningroom. Children welcome, cot and babysitting. Sorry, no pets and no smoking. Open March to November with central heating. Car essential, parking. Evening Dinner, Bed and Breakfast; Bed and Breakfast. Rates reduced for children, and for Senior Citizens in low season. Terms on request. SAE, please.

LLANELLI. Jackie and John Rawlings, Dan-y-Cwarre Farm, Five Roads, Llanelli SA15 5JA (01269 860187). Working farm, join in. This large 200 year old farmhouse supporting cattle, pigs and sheep provides superb views across Carmarthen Bay. Ideal centre for touring Gower, Brecon Beacons and Pembrokeshire. A wealth of fine beaches are easily accessible as is Swansea with its Marina, theatres and Leisure Centres. Nearby are riding stables, golf courses and local establishments which serve superb value evening meals. Family horse for children to ride. Cooked breakfasts served in diningroom with panoramic views. Accommodation comprises guests' bedrooms all with own bathroom and tea making facilities. Separate lounge with colour TV. Central heating throughout. Children very welcome, cot, high chair, babysitting. Open all year for Bed and Breakfast only, £15 per person per night, reduced rates for children. Evening Meals available if requested. For further information please write or telephone.

Terms quoted in this publication may be subject to increase if rises in costs necessitate

LLANGRANNOG. Mr and Mrs Painting, Morfa Isaf, Llangrannog SA44 6RS (Tel/Fax:01239 654282). In 1763 the farmhouse was built from stone quarried on the farm. Oak beams from ships' timbers and three foot thick walls retain the character of that period. Central heating has been added and modern conveniences. There is a private tarmac road to the farm and 106 acres of grassland running spectacularly to the cliff edge, with a steep winding footpath down to a sandy cove. With safe bathing, this is an outstandingly secluded, scenic beach. A warm, friendly atmosphere ensures a relaxing holiday. Tea/coffee making facilities in all rooms. Varied breakfast and dinner menu. Bed and Breakfast from £16. Evening meal optional on a daily basis. Brochure and tariff on request. Luxury caravan, only one on site, also available.

LLANTOOD. Andy and Sylvie Gow, Croft Farm, Llantood, Cardigan SA43 3NT (01239 615179). *Highly Commended.* **Working farm, join in. Sleeps 2/7.** We welcome you to stay in our lovingly renovated farmhouse with two double rooms and one twin-bedded room, all en suite. Each has colour TV and tea/coffee facilities. There is a comfortable sittingroom with fireplace and fully equipped kitchen for your use. Full cooked breakfasts are provided and home cooked, three course evening meals are available five nights per week. Our smallholding, set amidst beautiful North Pembrokeshire countryside, has a variety of animals which children may help feed, and lovely garden, patio, barbecue and play area. We are near beaches and Preseli National Park. Bed and Breakfast from £14. Children half price.

MARTINS HAVEN/MARLOES. Mrs Christina Chetwynd, East Hook Farm, Marloes, Haverfordwest SA62 3BJ (01646 636291). Farm on Pembrokeshire Coast Path offering Bed and Breakfast, camping, caravans, horse and pony riding, cycle hire, sea fishing, bird watching and walking. Convenient for boat trips to Skomer and Skokholm Islands and next to Marloes Mere Nature Reserve. 110 acres of natural unspoilt beauty. Bedrooms with washbasins, TVs and tea/coffee making facilities. Reception room on site. Collection service offered from Haverfordwest. Also transport to Martins Haven for boat trips, diving and Marine Nature Reserve. Bed and Breakfast from £12 to £13 per person per night. Children and pets welcome.

NARBERTH. Mrs Naomi Jones, Highland Grange Farm, Robeston Wathen, Narberth, Pembrokeshire SA67 8EP (01834 860952; Fax: 01834 860952). This lovely modern family home is set in a location you will find hard to beat. Panoramic views. An ideal base on the A40 for your holiday in central Pembrokeshire; yet only 8 miles from safe, sandy beaches. Good farmhouse cooking, ground floor accommodation. Small library, pool, darts, table-tennis, barbecue. Numerous amenities in area, many waymarked walks. Coarse fishing lakes abound, cycling routes available, horse riding arranged. Country Inn nearby, also water mill and tea room in a tranquil setting. Open all year. Sorry, no pets. Finally, we wish it to be known our house is a home where you will always be most welcome. WTB Welcome Host Certificate.

PEMBROKE. Mrs Ruth Smith, Chapel Farm, Castlemartin, Pembroke SA71 5HW (01646 661312). 17th century farmhouse offers comfortable accommodation for a relaxing holiday. The 260 acre dairy farm is a mile from the coast in Pembrokeshire Coast National Park and has splendid views out to sea. The large bedrooms are equipped with radios and tea making facilities. The TV lounge with its inglenook fireplace has a grand piano for guests to enjoy. Good tasty farmhouse food is prepared. Packed lunches on request. The long distance footpath passes the farm and within five miles are wild surfing beaches, quiet bathing coves, riding and fishing. Bed and Breakfast from £15; Dinner, Bed and Breakfast £135 to £145 per week. Reductions for children sharing.

The information in the entries in this guide is presented by the publishers in good faith and after the signed acceptance by advertisers that they will uphold the high standards associated with FHG PUBLICATIONS LIMITED. The publishers do not accept responsibility for any inaccuracies or omissions or any results thereof.
Before making final holiday arrangements readers should confirm the prices and facilities directly with advertisers.

PENUWCH. Mr and Mrs Ken Nicholls, "The Edelweiss", Penuwch, Near Tregaron SY25 6QZ (01974 821601). ♛♛ Small beamed country guest house set in two acres of gardens, surrounded by beautiful countryside and farmland. Pony trekking and horse riding nearby, lovely walks, wonderful wild flowers and birds to see (red kites, hawks, kestrels breed locally). Situated eight miles inland from unspoilt Cardigan Bay (B4577). Aberaeron, Aberystwyth, Lampeter and Tregaron are nearby, also local beauty spots and National Trust houses. The Edelweiss offers comfortable accommodation for non-smokers throughout the year. All bedrooms have central heating, H&C vanity unit and colour TV. Home cooking with full Breakfast, Sunday lunch and Evening Dinner available. Morning coffees, afternoon teas served. Single, twin or double rooms, one ground floor en suite studio available. Bed and Breakfast £12 to £15 daily, £73 to £80 weekly; Bed, Breakfast and Evening Meal £18.50 to £20.50 daily, £111 to £118 weekly. No VAT. Full Hygiene Certificate. Special discounts for long stay guests. Open Christmas.

A.A. QQQ W.T.B. 3 Crowns

VINE FARM

The Ridgeway
Saundersfoot
Pembrokeshire
SA69 9LA
Telephone 813543

Just half mile from the village centre and beaches. Our delightful former farmhouse has been sympathetically modernised whilst retaining its charm, including beamed dining room and large comfortable lounge with log fires early and late season. Central heating throughout, licensed, ample parking and grounds extending to approximately one acre, including an exercise paddock for dogs. All five bedrooms are ensuite with colour TV, tea/coffee tray and clock/radio. We take great pride in the quality of our food, with choices on all menus, including a five course dinner. All our meat and fish is bought locally, most vegetables are grown in our garden and of course all soups, desserts and ices are home made. B&B from £20 per person; D,B&B from £180 weekly per person. Special three day breaks throughout the season. Bargain four day breaks late May/early June and late August. Also one bedroom self-catering flat for two from £120 per week.

The Ridgeway, Saundersfoot, Pembrokeshire SA69 9LA. Telephone 01834 813543

SAUNDERSFOOT. Mrs Joy Holgate, Carne Mountain Farm, Reynalton, Kilgetty SA68 0PD (01834 860546). Working farm. A warm welcome awaits you at our lovely 200 year old farmhouse set amidst the peace and tranquillity of the beautiful Pembrokeshire countryside. Distant views of Preseli Hills, yet only three and a half miles from Saundersfoot. Pretty, picturesque bedrooms with TV, washbasins, tea/coffee tray, central heating. Separate dining room with interesting plate collection, books and maps. Delicious farmhouse cooking using local produce, free range eggs and meat whenever possible. Let the strain and stress slip away as you enjoy the peaceful atmosphere and friendly farmyard animals. Bed and Breakfast from £13. Wales Tourist Board Listed and Commended. Welcome Host Award. Comfortable six-berth caravan also available in pretty, peaceful setting £75 to £85 per week. SAE please.

SOLVA. Mrs Sarah C. Griffiths, Llanddinog Old Farmhouse, Solva, Haverfordwest SA62 6NA (01348 831224). ♛♛♛ Reached by peaceful flowery lanes, this 16th century farmhouse offers warm, friendly accommodation in two family bedrooms, both with private bathing facilities, teatrays, clock radios, etc. The cosy sitting-room with inglenook fireplace and roaring fire on chilly nights has a colour TV, books and games and leads into the diningroom with separate tables overlooking the extensive garden, reached through French windows. Children enjoy the rope swings and variety of small animals. Good country cooking from local foodstuffs is offered, and picnics, laundry services and hairdryer can all be provided. Close to Solva Harbour and St. David's. Child reductions. Holder of Hygiene Certificate and "Welcome Host" award. SAE please.

See also Colour Display Advertisement

SOLVA. Mrs M. Jones, Lochmeyler Farm, Llandeloy, Pen-y-Cwm, near Solva, Haverfordwest SA62 6LL (Tel & Fax: 01348 837724). ♛♛♛♛ *De Luxe.* A 220 acre dairy farm situated in centre of St. David's Peninsula, two and a half miles from coastal path, four miles from Solva Harbour, six miles from St. David's. The 16th century farmhouse has been modernised but still retains its olde worlde character with beams and open fires in early and late season. 10 en-suite bedrooms with colour TV. Video library available. Tea making facilities, electric blankets, clock/radios, hair dryers and telephones. Some rooms have four-poster beds. No smoking in bedrooms. Two lounges (one for smokers). Spacious diningroom with separate tables. Traditional farmhouse fare with vegetarians catered for. Plenty of wildlife trails, pond and streams. Children over 10 years welcome. Dogs accepted FREE. Outside kennels available. Bed and Breakfast £20; Dinner £10. Evening Dinner, Bed and Breakfast £200 weekly. Credit cards accepted. Open all year round, including Christmas and New Year Breaks. AA Selected, RAC Highly Acclaimed. RAC Guest House of the Year 1993. Brochure available.

WALES

WHITLAND. Mrs Brenda Worthing, Maencochyrwyn Farm, Login, Whitland SA34 0TN (Hebron [01994] 419283). Working farm. This attractive, well situated farm is located in a quiet, rural area, within two and a half miles of the quaint little village of Llanboidy. Accommodation consists of one double, one family and one single rooms, all with washbasin; bathroom, separate shower, toilet; sittingroom and diningroom. The farm has every modern amenity the discerning visitor could wish, including fitted carpets, colour TV. Children are very welcome and babysitting available. Open April to October. Ample parking. Enjoy the best of Wales — Tenby, Pendine Sands, Saundersfoot, Pembrokeshire coast and the picturesque Prescelly Mountains — from a most comfortable, friendly base. Bed and Breakfast from £14. Reduced weekly rates. Tourist Board listed. SAE, please, for brochure.

HELP IMPROVE BRITISH TOURIST STANDARDS

You are choosing holiday accommodation from our very popular FHG Publications. Whether it be a hotel, guest house, farmhouse or self-catering accommodation, we think you will find it hospitable, comfortable and clean, and your host and hostess friendly and helpful. Why not write and tell us about it?

As a recognition of the generally well-run and excellent holiday accommodation reviewed in our publications, we at FHG Publications Ltd. present a diploma to proprietors who receive the highest recommendation from their guests who are also readers of our Guides. If you care to write to us praising the holiday you have booked through FHG Publications Ltd. – whether this be board, self-catering accommodation, a sporting or a caravan holiday, what you say will be evaluated and the proprietors who reach our final list will be contacted.

The winning proprietor will receive an attractive framed diploma to display on his premises as recognition of a high standard of comfort, amenity and hospitality. FHG Publications Ltd. offer this diploma as a contribution towards the improvement of standards in tourist accommodation in Britain. Help your excellent host or hostess to win it!

FHG DIPLOMA

We nominate ....

....

Because

Name ....

Address ....

.... Telephone No. ....

GLAMORGAN

SOUTH GLAMORGAN

CARDIFF. Ace House, 154 The Philog, Whitchurch, Cardiff CF4 1ED (01222 627850). A small, friendly, privately run guesthouse offering full cooked breakfast or continental. Central heating throughout. One family room, one twin and one double, each with its own washbasin, shaver point, tea/coffee making facilities and TV; duvets on all beds. Ace House is situated approximately two miles from Cardiff City Centre with its beautiful Castle and noted peacocks which roam freely around the flower-filled gardens. Five miles to Caerphilly Castle, three miles to Castle Coch (The Fairy Castle). Ideally situated for all tourist attractions and nearby seaside resorts. Buses 24 and 35 from Central Rail Station. Car parking opposite premises. Terms from £25 per double. Reductions for under 14-year-olds sharing with two adults.

WEST GLAMORGAN

SWANSEA. Winston Private Hotel, 11 Church Lane, Bishopston, Swansea SA3 3JT (01792 232074). ♛♛ This medium-sized, comfortable hotel is set in quiet wooded surroundings at the entrance to a National Trust Valley. Convenient for the beautiful beaches of Gower, it is just six miles from Swansea and three-and-a-half from Mumbles with its watersports, dancing etc. Most bedrooms have showers, some have en suite facilities and all have washbasins. Two lounges (one with TV). Indoor heated swimming pool. Billiards room, sauna and solarium. Residential licence. Excellent Welsh cooking. AA Listed, RAC Acclaimed. SAE please, for terms.

Key to Tourist Board Ratings

The Crown Scheme

(England, Scotland & Wales)

Covering hotels, motels, private hotels, guesthouses, inns, bed & breakfast, farmhouses. Every Crown classified place to stay is inspected annually. *The classification:* Listed then 1-5 Crown indicates the range of facilities and services. Higher quality standards are indicated by the terms APPROVED, COMMENDED, HIGHLY COMMENDED and DELUXE.

The Key Scheme

(also operates in Scotland using a Crown symbol)

Covering self-catering in cottages, bungalows, flats, houseboats, houses, chalets, etc. Every Key classified holiday home is inspected annually. *The classification:* 1-5 Key indicates the range of facilities and equipment. Higher quality standards are indicated by the terms APPROVED, COMMENDED, HIGHLY COMMENDED and DELUXE.

The Q Scheme

(England, Scotland & Wales)

Covering holiday, caravan, chalet and camping parks. Every Q rated park is inspected annually for its quality standards. The more ✓ in the Q – up to 5 – the higher the standard of what is provided.

GWENT

ABERGAVENNY. Mr and Mrs S. Watkins, Treloyvan Farm, Llantilio, Crossenny, Abergavenny NP7 8UE (0160085 478). Friendly family-run 113 acre working farm in beautiful rural setting mid-way between Abergavenny and Monmouth on B4233. Within walking distance of White Castle: Offa's Dyke, the long distance footpath, runs by the castle, also three Castles of Gwent — White, Skenfrith and Grosmont, another nice long walk. Nearby you will find golf, fishing and canoeing. Magnificent views. Children welcome, lots of farm animals and pets to see. Bed and Breakfast from £13 to £14; weekly from £84, from £140 with Evening Meal. Good home cooking with a Swiss cook. Cot and high chair available. Reductions for children. Bedrooms with shower and washbasin. Family speaks German and a little French. Wales Tourist Board registered. For further details write or phone **Mrs S. Watkins.**

WALES

BLAINA. Malcolm and Betty Hancocks, Chapel Farm, Blaina NP3 3DJ (01495 290888). *Commended.* Guests are assured of a warm welcome when they visit this 15th century renovated farmhouse and many return each year. A good base for touring Big Pit, Blaenavon; Bryn-Bach Park, Brecon Beacons, Abergavenny. Family and double rooms; one bedroom has shower en suite. Packed lunches available; Evening Meal on request. There is a drinks licence but no bar, though there is an unusual drinks cupboard. No smoking in bedrooms. Bed and Breakfast from £16. WTB Merit Award. Full details available.

CHEPSTOW. Mrs M. Newman, The Old Rectory, Tintern, Chepstow NP6 6SG (01291 689519). A warm welcome awaits the visitor to this fine old 18th/19th century house, which with its beautiful views and own spring water, is situated exactly between England and Wales. Ideally suited for exploring the Border country or the Forest of Dean and Brecon Beacons; nearby facilities include fishing, riding, golf, Chepstow racecourse; excellent walking from the house. Most rooms have washbasins. Guests have separate sitting and dining rooms with central heating and log fires in winter. Pets by arrangement. Enjoy home comfort and cooking in a relaxed friendly atmosphere. Bed and Breakfast £14.50 per person; Evening Meal £7.50. Reduced rates for children sharing room with adults. Vegetarian meals by arrangement.

MONMOUTH. Rosemary and Derek Ringer, Church Farm Guest House, Mitchel Troy, Monmouth NP5 4HZ (01600 712176). *Commended.* A spacious and homely 16th century former farmhouse with oak beams and inglenook fireplaces, set in large attractive garden with stream. An excellent base for visiting the Wye Valley, Forest of Dean and Black Mountains. All bedrooms have washbasins, tea/coffee making facilities and central heating; some are en-suite. Own car park. Colour TV. Non-smoking. Terrace and barbecue area. Bed and Breakfast from £16.50 per person. Evening Meal by arrangement. We also offer a programme of guided and self-guided Walking Holidays and Short Breaks. Separate "Wysk Walks" brochure on request.

GWENT – BORDER COUNTY

Nestling in the south-east corner of Wales, Gwent is an undulating county which includes the ever popular Wye Valley. Other attractions are Chepstow, Abergavenny, Tintern Forest and Tredegar.

MONMOUTH near. Solveig Preece, Grange Farm, Newcastle, Near Monmouth NP5 4NX (01600 712636). Stock rearing farm in the Wye Valley district. The farmhouse is 16th century and peacefully situated in quiet countryside within easy reach of Forest of Dean, the ancient border town of Monmouth and South Wales. Farming family welcomes children and pets. Open March to November. Bed and Breakfast from £13; Evening Meal from £8. Non-smokers preferred. Tourist Board Listed.

MONMOUTH near. Mrs K. Anders, Mill House Farm, Llanvihangel-Ystern-Llewern, Near Monmouth NP5 4HN (01600 85468). A comfortable and homely 17th century Welsh farmhouse set between Monmouth and Abergavenny. An excellent base for visiting the Usk and Wye Valleys, Offa's Dyke, Forest of Dean, Black Mountains and Hay-on-Wye. Activities in the area include golfing, fishing, canoeing, walking and pony trekking. All bedrooms have washbasins, tea/coffee making facilities; one room en suite. Bed and Breakfast from £16 per person; Evening Meal by arrangement. Wales Tourist Board Listed and registered. Please write or telephone for further details.

TINTERN. Anne and Peter Howe, Valley House, Raglan Road, Tintern, Near Chepstow NP6 6TH (01291 689652). ♛♛ Valley House is a fine Georgian residence situated in the tranquil Angidy Valley 800 yards from the A466 Chepstow to Monmouth road and within a mile of Tintern Abbey. Numerous walks through picturesque woods and valleys right from our doorstep. The accommodation is of a very high standard; all rooms are en-suite, have tea/coffee making facilities and colour TV. The guests' lounge has a wealth of exposed beams and a working range whilst the diningroom has an arched stone ceiling. Numerous places to eat nearby. Bed and Breakfast from £17.50 per person. Open all year. Non-smokers preferred. AA QQQ, RAC Acclaimed.

USK. Mrs Ann Bradley, Pentwyn Farm, Little Mill, Pontypool NP4 0HQ (Tel & Fax: 01495 785249). ♛♛♛ *Highly Commended.* Pentwyn is a 120 acre stock farm on the edge of the Brecon Beacons National Park where good food and hospitality are of prime importance and the reason why so many guests return. The 16th century Welsh Longhouse, with 20th century comforts, has a beamed dining room and sitting room with log fires. Swimming pool and large garden. Three bedrooms (two en suite). Restaurant licence. Rough shooting. Bed and Breakfast from £14 to £18. WTB Farmhouse Award. Also two charming single-storey converted self catering stable cottages adjoining the house where guests can choose to be independent or join house guests for dinner in season. All linen and electricity included. WTB 🔑🔑🔑🔑. From £160 to £230 per week.

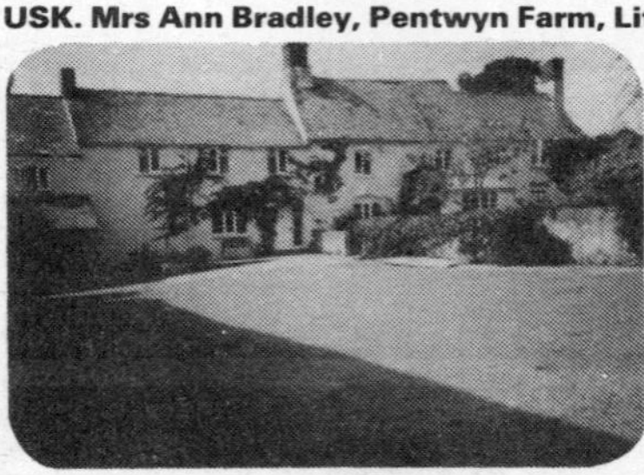

GWYNEDD

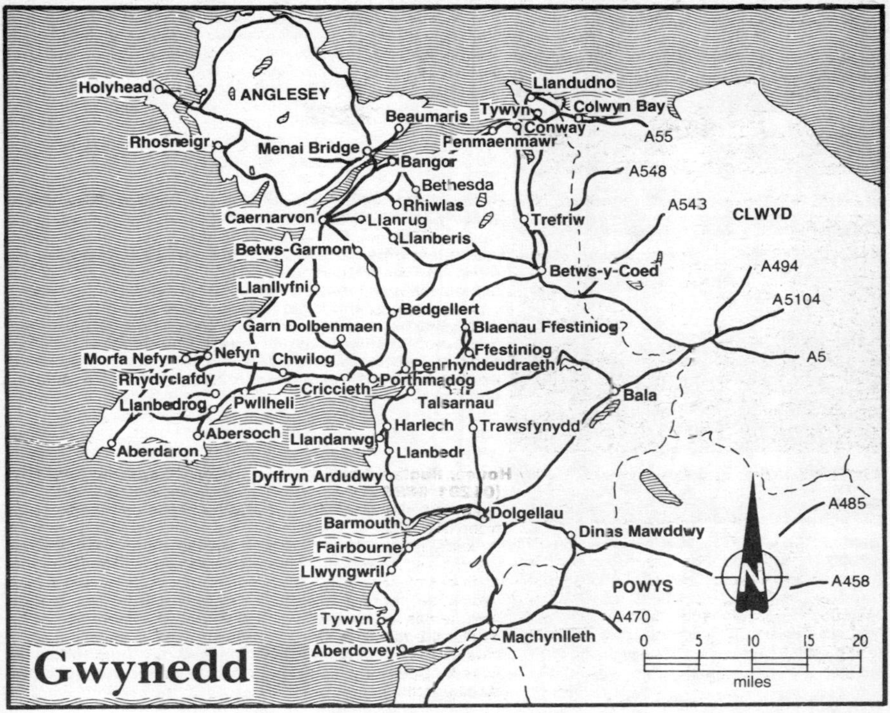

ABERDARON. Barbara and David Marshallsay, Carreg Plas, Aberdaron, Pwllheli LL53 8LH (Aberdaron [0175886] 308). 17th century manor house of historic interest in sheltered position on west side of Lleyn Peninsula, set in five acres of secluded wooded grounds, surrounded by National Trust land. Only half a mile from the well-known Whistling Sands Beach, and two miles from the picturesque village of Aberdaron. Lovely coastal scenery and sandy beaches nearby. Seven bedrooms available with washbasins and tea-making facilities, five en-suite or with private bath/shower room. Large lounge; separate TV lounge; two diningrooms. Cots, high chairs provided, children especially welcome (reduced rates). Pets by arrangement. Ample car parking. Open all year. Bed and Breakfast from £17; Evening Meal Bed and Breakfast from £25. Guests requested not to smoke in house.

ANGLESEY. Mrs M.E. Williams, Llanerch, Pendref Street, Newborough, Anglesey LL61 6SY (01248 440235). Llanerch is situated in a quiet part of a country village. It used to be the village rectory and stands in an acre of ground with excellent panoramic views of Snowdonia Mountain Range and the Menai Straits and has plenty of room for children to play in. It is only minutes from Llanddwyn beach which has over four miles of golden sands, is close to forest walks, picnic areas and nature reserves and is ideal for fishing and birdwatching. Llanerch has one double and three family bedrooms, all with washbasins; two bathrooms and toilets; TV lounge; diningroom; central heating throughout. Children welcome, cot, high chair and babysitting offered. Small pets permitted. Plenty of parking space. Bed and Breakfast from £11. Late night cup of tea and packed lunches available on request. Reduced rates for children. SAE brings prompt reply.

ANGLESEY. Mrs Rosemary A. Abas, Bwthyn, Brynafon, Menai Bridge, Isle of Anglesey LL59 5AH (01248 713119). Warm, welcoming Bed and Breakfast in pretty Victorian terrace, half-a-minute from the sparkling Menai Straits, conveniently located 1 mile from A5/A55 expressway, 2 miles rail/coaches, 5 minutes level walk buses/village centre, 15 minutes drive beautiful beaches/ countryside/Snowdonia National Park. Bwthyn offers a degree of comfort and hospitality rarely experienced in so modestly-priced a guest house, in 2 warm, comfortable and beautifully fitted en-suite double rooms, full/varied country breakfasts or "healthy" alternative — fresh fruit, yoghurt, wholegrain bread/cereals, luscious Welsh preserves and REAL coffee (or selection of quality teas). NB: wholly non-smoking. WTB Highly Commended — de luxe grading. Come as guests — leave as friends.

ANGLESEY. Mrs J. Bown, Drws-y-Coed, Llannerch-y-Medd, Isle of Anglesey LL71 3AD (01248 470473). ♛♛♛ *Highly Commended.* Drws-y-Coed, a beautifully appointed farmhouse on 550 acres of beef, sheep and arable farmland is set in beautiful wooded countryside with panoramic views of Snowdonia, near to picturesque Bodafon Mountain. Centrally located for beaches, fishing, golf, riding, leisure centres. Tarmac drives. A warm welcome awaits our guests who are accommodated in well-appointed bedrooms, all en-suite with colour TVs, tea-making facilities and clock radios. Full central heating. Spacious lounge with log fire. Diningroom with separate tables. Good home cooking with ample portions. Games room. Free pony rides. Lovely walks in vicinity. WTB Rural Tourism Award. Farm Holiday Guide Diploma Award. Reductions for children. Bed and Breakfast (Evening Meal optional). Open all year. Brochure available.

ANGLESEY SOUTH. Mrs Naylor, Bryntirion Working Farm, Dwyran, Anglesey LL61 6BQ (01248 430232). ♛ Bryntirion is situated just off the A4080 midway between Brynsiencyn and picturesque Newborough beach. The farmhouse is pleasant with guests' TV lounge, tea making facilities and dining room. A Fire Certificate is held. Bed and full Breakfast from £12.50. Children's play area. The farm is open to the public for guided tours from May to September. There is a tea room with home made cakes and scones and an interesting exhibition plus antique farm machinery; wood turning, fishing. Our farm tours are a fascinating experience, which children enjoy particularly. Large car park. WTB Member. Brochure available.

BALA. Mr T.G. Jones, Frondderw Private Hotel, Stryd-y-Fron, Bala LL23 7YD (Bala [01678] 520301). ♛♛♛ *Commended.* Delightful period mansion on the hillside five minutes from the town of Bala and within the boundaries of Snowdonia National Park. There are lovely walks, boating, swimming, fishing and picnic facilities, golf and magnificent scenery. The accommodation is well maintained and consists of eight bedrooms, four en-suite, two with showers, all with washbasins, central heating and tea/ coffee making facilities. Guests' lounge, separate TV lounge and diningroom. Non-smoking accommodation available. Residential licence. Free parking. Sorry, no pets in the house. Open March to November inclusive. Bed and Breakfast from £14 to £19 daily, £94 to £129 per week; Dinner optional £8.50. Dinner, Bed and Breakfast from £150.50 to £185.50 per person per week. AA QQ.

BALA. Mrs S.E. Edwards, Bryn Melyn, Rhyduchaf, Bala LL23 7PG (01678 520376). ♛ *Commended.* **Working farm.** Bryn Melyn, Rhyduchaf is situated in the beautiful countryside of Bala, and offers accommodation all year. The house is stone-built and stands on 35 acres of mixed farmland. Home cooking and home produced food makes this a real home from home. Two double and one twin bedroom (two with washbasins); two bathrooms, toilet; sittingroom; diningroom; central heating. Children welcome at reduced rates. Sorry, no pets. A car is necessary to ensure that visitors derive all the pleasure that this region offers. Parking space. Sea 28 miles. Good recreation facilities in the area. Evening Dinner, Bed and Breakfast from £134 weekly or Bed and Breakfast £13 per person, with Dinner £21. Mrs Edwards is a Farm Holiday Guide Diploma winner. Six-berth caravan also available from £80 per week.

GWYNEDD – OUTSTANDING NATURAL BEAUTY!

With Snowdonia National Park and the Lleyn Peninsula, Gwynedd well deserves its designation as an 'Area of Outstanding Natural Beauty'. The tourist is spoiled for choice in this county but should endeavour to visit the hill-fort at Tre'r Ceiri, the Llugwy Valley, Cwm Pennant, Dinas Dinlle hill-fort, the gold mine at Clogau and the railways and quarries at Blaenau Ffestiniog.

BALA near. Mrs J. Best, Cwm Hwylfod, Cefn-Ddwysarn, Bala LL23 7LN (016783 310). *Commended.* **Working farm.** Remote, peaceful 400 year old farmhouse on working sheep farm. Beautiful countryside and wonderful views. Two double rooms, one large family room, all with washbasins and tea making facilities. Two bathrooms, clothes washing and drying machines. Guest lounge with colour TV. Full central heating. Cot, high chair available. Parking space. All meals are home cooked. Special diets catered for. Ideal centre for touring, walking, fishing, pony trekking and watersports. Bala Lake 10 minutes by car. Snowdon and many beaches can be reached in 40 minutes. Bed and Breakfast from £13.50 to £15.50; Evening Meal optional from £9.50. Reductions for long stays and children under 10 years. Brochure available. Children most welcome.

BARMOUTH. Mr & Mrs T.L. & S.L. Dyer, Hendreclochydd Hall, Llanaber, Barmouth LL42 1RR (Barmouth [01341] 280242). Situated about two miles from Barmouth on the coast road to Harlech, with superb views of Cardigan Bay and the Lleyn Peninsula. We are practically surrounded by the Snowdonia National Park with Narrow Gauge Steam Railways being only a short drive away. Accommodation is offered in rooms overlooking the sea, all with colour TV, easy chairs and beverage facilities; en suite rooms available. Excellent parking and pleasant garden for our guests' pleasure. Golden sands and safe bathing are not many minutes' walk away. Children welcome at reduced rates. Pets accepted by prior arrangement. Bed and Breakfast from £15. Our aim is to give you a holiday to cherish!

BEAUMARIS. Mrs E. Roberts, Plas Cichle, Beaumaris LL58 8PS (01248 810488). *Highly Commended.* **Working farm, join in.** Here on this 200 acre working farm only one and a half miles from Beaumaris and its historic Edwardian castle guests can relax in spacious well-appointed rooms. All rooms have hospitality tray, colour TV, clock/radio and hair dryer and most are en suite. Then look out of your bedroom window at the sheep and cattle peacefully grazing and gaze in awe at the majestic mountains of Snowdonia beyond. Enjoy the fresh home-cooked, generous portions we serve in the dining room for breakfast; dinner by arrangement. Bed and Breakfast from £19. Non-smoking accommodation available. Children welcome. Golf, riding, fishing, sandy beaches and other major attractions nearby. A warm Welsh welcome assured. CROESO! Brochure available.

BEDDGELERT. Joan Williams, Colwyn, Beddgelert (01766 890276). Welcome to Colwyn. Warm, small and friendly, our 18th century cottage guesthouse, with its original stone fireplace in the low beamed lounge, is restful and unpretentious. Old-fashioned (but modernised of course), most rooms en suite with white linen, warm duvets, Welsh tapestry covers and central heating. Colwyn overlooks the river in the centre of picturesque Beddgelert, probably the most popular and unspoiled village in the area, lying in a National Trust valley right at the foot of Snowdon with lakes, streams and forests all round. Spectacular scenery both winter and summer, a perfect central base for the whole National Park. There are small shops, inns, cafes in the village. Walkers, muddy boots and exhausted dogs welcome. Dinner, Bed and Breakfast four nights (Monday — Friday) Low Season £112. Bed and Breakfast from £17. Booking usually advisable. Also tiny cottage, sleeps two, £150.

WALES

BETWS-Y-COED. Arthur and Ann Eaton, Crafnant Guest House, Trefriw LL27 0JH (01492 640809).

♛♛ *Commended.* Crafnant is a 100 year old farmhouse, comfortably refurbished as small guest house. It nestles in pretty village of Trefriw between Betws-y-Coed and Conwy, beneath some of the most beautiful lakes and scenery of Snowdonia. Superbly located for tourist attractions, walking, climbing, fishing, golf. No smoking. En suite facilities available; TV and drinks in rooms. Children's rates. Parking. Dogs by arrangement. Traditional and vegetarian menus; packed lunches. Bed and Breakfast from £13 to £16 per person; Dinner (optional) from £6.50 to £8.50. Midweek Mini Breaks — double room, Dinner, Bed and Breakfast two nights £59, three nights £85. Open all year. A non returnable £20 deposit required.

BETWS-Y-COED. Mrs M. Jones, Tyddyn Gethin Farm, Penmachno, Betws-y-Coed LL24 0PS (01690 760392). Working farm. 80 acre mixed farm situated 200 yards off B4406 half a mile from Penmachno Village, one mile from Woollen Mills, near to Falls and very central for touring. Within easy reach of sea and mountains. Pony trekking nearby. Three and a half miles from Betws-y-Coed. Clean and comfortable, always a welcome and good home cooking. Bathroom with shower and shower room; washbasins in all bedrooms, shaving points; separate shower room. Two lounges, one with colour TV. Separate tables in diningroom. Lovely views from the house. Ample parking. Bed and Breakfast from £13; Bed, Breakfast and Evening Meal from £19. SAE brings a prompt reply. Also comfortable well-equipped holiday cottage — two bedrooms sleeping four/five.

BETWS-Y-COED. Mrs Meryl Metcalfe, Tan Yr Eglwys, Llanrhychwyn, Trefriw, Llanrwst LL27 0YJ (Llanrwst [01492] 640547). ♛♛ 'Tan Yr Eglwys' is a modernised farmhouse where some of the walls are a yard thick! Llanrhychwyn is a little hamlet, conveniently situated above the Conwy Valley between the market town of Llanrwst and Trefriw village. A car is essential, unless very energetic! Ideal haven for country lovers and hill walkers. Central for mountains and lakes of Snowdonia and also the coast. The farmhouse is surrounded by fields and woods. The ancient Church at St. Rhychwyn is about 800 yards up a path leading from the farm. Places of interest include Betws-y-Coed (golf) four miles; Trefriw (Woollen Mill) one mile; Llanrwst two miles, Geirionnydd Lake two miles, Llanberis (Snowdon) 17 miles, Llandudno 10 miles. A homely welcome with log fires available on chilly evenings, and good home cooking is assured. All rooms have washbasins. Open Easter to October. Terms on application. Reduction for children in family rooms. SAE for prompt reply and directions from main road. OS Grid Reference 777616. We also have a static caravan in a lawned garden backed by forest.

BETWS-Y-COED. Mrs E. Jones, Maes-y-Garnedd, Capel Garmon, Llanrwst, Betws-y-Coed (01690 710 428). Working farm. This 140-acre mixed farm is superbly situated on the Rooftop of Wales as Capel Garmon has been called, and the Snowdonia Range, known to the Welsh as the "Eyri", is visible from the land. Two miles from A5. Surrounding area provides beautiful country scenery and excellent walks. Safe, sandy beaches at Llandudno and Colwyn Bay. Salmon and trout fishing (permit required). Mrs Jones serves excellent home produced meals with generous portions including Welsh Lamb and Roast Beef. Gluten-free diets can be arranged. Packed lunches, with flask of coffee or tea. One double and one family bedrooms with washbasins; bathroom, toilet; sittingroom and diningroom. Children welcome, cot, high chair and babysitting available. Regret, no pets. Car essential, ample parking. Open all year. Bed and Breakfast, Evening Meal optional. SAE brings prompt reply with details and terms. Reductions for children. Bala Lakes, Bodnant Gardens, Ffestiniog Railway, slate quarries, Trefriw Woollen Mills nearby. Member of AA, Tourist Board Approved.

Purchase two adult tickets to the Museum of Childhood, 1 Castle Street, Beaumaris, Anglesey, with our READERS' OFFER VOUCHER and take grandad or his grandson for FREE.

WALES

BETWS-Y-COED. Mr and Mrs M. Fakhri, Bryn Bella Guest House, Llanrwst Road, Betws-y-Coed LL24 0HD (01690 710627). ♛♛ *Highly Commended.*

Bryn Bella is a small Victorian guest house noted for its caring and friendly atmosphere, situated in a quiet elevated position overlooking Betws-y-Coed, in the Snowdonia National Park. Five recently refurbished rooms (three with en-suite), each having tea/coffee making facilities and colour TV. Guests' lounge and patio from which to enjoy the glorious views. Private parking. Superb breakfast; packed lunches on request. Ideal centre for touring, climbing, riding, fishing and golf and within easy reach of Holyhead Ferry. Bed and Breakfast from £13.50. Reduced rates for children sharing parents' room. Special weekly rates. Open all year.

BETWS-Y-COED. Jim and Lilian Boughton, Bron Celyn Guest House, Llanrwst Road, Betws-y-Coed LL24 0HD (01690 710333). ♛♛♛ *Highly Commended.*

A warm welcome awaits you at this delightful guest house overlooking the Gwydyr Forest and Llugwy/Conwy Valleys and village of Betws-y-Coed in Snowdonia National Park. Ideal centre for touring, walking, climbing, fishing and golf. Also excellent overnight stop en-route for Holyhead ferries. Easy walk into village and close to Conwy/Swallow Falls and Fairy Glen. Most rooms en-suite, all with colour TV and beverage makers. Lounge. Full central heating. Garden. Car park. Open all year. Full hearty breakfast, packed meals, snacks, evening meals — special diets catered for. Bed and Breakfast from £16 to £19, reduced rates for children under 12 years.

BETWS-Y-COED near. Mrs Eleanore Roberts, Awelon, Plas Isa, Llanrwst LL26 0EE (Llanrwst [01492] 640 047). ♛ Awelon once formed part of the estate of William Salisbury, translator of the New Testament into Welsh during the 16th century. It has three foot thick outer walls, and now modernised, is an attractive small guesthouse. Three bedrooms are tastefully furnished, have washbasins, tea-makers, colour TVs and new beds. A cosy lounge and central heating throughout ensures a comfortable stay. Llanrwst is a busy market town at the centre of the beautiful Conway Valley, with Bodnant Gardens, Snowdonia and the North Wales Coast easily reached. Central for walking and touring. Pets welcome. Plenty of parking available. Mr and Mrs Roberts have been welcoming guests to their Welsh home for over 20 years. Bed and Breakfast with varied menus £12.50 to £13.50; optional four-course Dinner £6.50. Children welcome, reduced rates. Open March to November. Brochure on request.

Terms quoted in this publication may be subject to increase if rises in costs necessitate

BLAENAU FFESTINIOG. Mrs G.E. Hughes, Bryn Celynog Farm, Cwm Prysor, Trawsfynydd, Blaenau Ffestiniog LL41 4TR (01766 540378). A true Welsh welcome awaits you, where you can relax and unwind after a day out on this working beef/sheep farm, set amidst beautiful mountains in the centre of Snowdonia National Park, three miles from Trawsfynydd village. Stonebuilt farmhouse, centrally heated throughout, choice of twin, double or family bedrooms, one en-suite, all with washbasins, tea/coffee making facilities. Lounge with colour TV and log fire. Separate tables in dining room. Reputation for excellent food and friendliness. Optional evening meal. Open all year. Bed and Breakfast from £15 to £18; Bed, Breakfast and Evening Meal from £23 to £25.50. SAE please for brochure. Farm House Award.

BLAENAU FFESTINIOG. Keith and Liz Lethbridge, Cae Du Guest House, Manod, Blaenau Ffestiniog LL41 4BB (01766 830847). *Highly Commended.* Cae Du is a part 16th century farmhouse in the heart of Snowdonia. It is no longer a working farm but is quiet and peaceful whilst central to most of Snowdonia's varied attractions. There are wonderfully scenic walks direct from the house which is set up on a mountain looking down the beautiful Vale of Ffestiniog. Also available in the area: fishing, canoeing, climbing, birdwatching, pony trekking and dry ski slope, as well as old castles, mines, and steam railway. Keith and Liz run Cae Du as their own home to which you are given a warm welcome as guests or friends; they provide home cooking with a vegetarian menu too. Terms from £18. Brochure available.

CAERNARVON. Mrs B. Cartwright, "Tan Dinas", Llanddeiniolen, Caernarvon LL55 3AR (Port Dinorwic [01248] 670098). A modernised stone farmhouse situated in a picturesque, secluded, yet very central location and surrounded by typical Welsh scenic beauty and with a pleasant garden sloping down to a small stream running alongside the woods. Guests have their own private and centrally-heated lounge and diningroom. The area is ideal for touring, also all types of fishing, walking and pony trekking. Caernarvon, Bangor, Anglesey and Snowdon itself are all within very easy reach. Take the B4366 out of Caernarvon. One mile through Bethel come to the "Gors Bach Inn". Turn into lane by side of Inn and travel on for half a mile. Children welcome, cot, high chair, babysitting available. Car essential — parking. Open March to October with central heating and open fires. Pets accepted. Bed and Breakfast from £14, with Evening Dinner from £17. Reductions for children. Tourist Board Listed.

CAERNARVON. Mrs Audrey Pierce, "Caer Siddi", Llanddeiniolen, Caernarvon LL55 3AD (01248 670462). *Highly Commended.* An old Georgian vicarage, now in use as a private residence, in peaceful and attractive rural setting surrounded by trees and enjoying glorious views towards Snowdon, the Rivals and Caernarvon Bay. Ideally and centrally located only four miles from Caernarvon on the B4366, for all outdoor activities and places of interest in Gwynedd and Snowdonia. A large Ordnance Survey Map of North Wales and plentiful brochures available to help plan your daily outings. Fully modernised and spacious accommodation coupled with warm, friendly atmosphere and good wholesome food. Variety of Breakfasts; three course Dinner. Tea making facilities in bedrooms. Children welcome. Colour TV lounge. Private parking. Fire Certificate. Wales Tourist Board — Rural Tourism Award.

Please mention this guide when you write or phone to enquire about accommodation.

If you are writing, a stamped, addressed envelope is always appreciated.

CONWY. Mrs C. Roberts, Henllys Farm, Llechwedd, Conwy LL32 8DJ (01492 593269). ♛♛♛ *Highly Commended.* **Working farm.** This 140 acre working sheep and cattle farm is situated one and a half miles from Conwy in the heart of beautiful countryside. Accommodation comprises one double and one family room, both en suite with tea/coffee making facilities; colour TV lounge; diningroom. Ideally placed for touring Snowdonia and the North Wales coast. Conwy Castle, town walls and fish quay are within easy reach, as are Llandudno, Betws-y-Coed, Caernarvon and Bodnant Gardens. Pony trekking nearby. Good home cooking. Children welcome. Bed and Breakfast from £15; Bed, Breakfast and Evening Meal from £22 daily, from £140 weekly. Farm House Award.

CONWY. Mrs Sylvia Baxter, Glyn Uchaf, Conwy Old Road, Dwygyfylchi, Penmaenmawr, Conwy LL34 6YS (01492 623737). ♛♛♛ Enjoy a quiet, peaceful holiday at this old mill house set in 11 acres of National Parkland in beautiful mountainous countryside. Ideal touring centre for Snowdonia. Accommodation comprises three bedrooms, all en-suite and having lovely views. Lounge with colour TV; diningroom. Excellent cuisine with varied menus and home produce. Tea/coffee making facilities available. Children welcome. Two-and-a-half miles to Conwy, five to Llandudno and Colwyn Bay — three minutes' walk to village. Pony trekking and fishing locally. Also stabling available for those wishing to bring their own horses. Ample parking. Guests have access to house at all times. Bed and Breakfast from £17 to £20, or Bed, Breakfast and Evening Meal. Moderate terms, reductions for children under 12. WTB registered. Highly recommended. SAE or phone please.

CRICCIETH. Mrs S.A. Reynolds, Glyn-y-Coed, Porthmadoc Road, Criccieth LL52 0HL (01766 522870; Fax: 01766 523341). ♛♛♛ *Highly Commended.* Lovely Victorian family Hotel facing sea, mountains and two castles. Full central heating, cosy bar, private parking. Highly recommended home cooking with most diets catered for. All bedrooms en suite (one ground floor bedroom) with colour TV and tea-making facilities. Moderate rates with good reductions for children. Also available for self catering, dormer four-bedroomed bungalow sleeping eight plus cot. In own grounds with parking, just two minutes from beach and four minutes from shop and pub. Terms: Bed and Breakfast from £18 to £21 per person per night; Self Catering accommodation from £80 to £450 per week.

DOLGELLAU. Mrs D.M. Rowlands, Tanyfron, Arran Road, Dolgellau LL40 2AA (Tel & Fax: 01341 422638). ♛♛ *Highly Commended.* Situated half a mile from Dolgellau in a quiet setting with lovely views. All rooms are en suite and have colour TV, hair dryers and tea making facilities. Central heating. Public telephone and laundry available. Children welcome. Sorry, no pets. Ample private parking. Open February to November. Bed and Breakfast from £16 to £18 per person per night (no single rooms). Non-smokers please.

DOLGELLAU. Mrs Griffiths, Llwyn Talcen, Brithdir, Dolgellau LL40 2RY (01341 450276). Situated in an acre of rhododendron and azalea gardens, Llwyn Talcen offers a warm welcome, outstanding views, together with peace and quiet. Our location, about four miles east of Dolgellau, makes an ideal centre for hill walkers and nature lovers. We offer good fresh food, organic whenever possible. Traditional and vegetarian fare are both available. Bed and Breakfast from £14 to £16; Evening Meal £7. Reduced rates are available for children. Ample parking. WTB listed. To find us take narrow lane from the centre of the village of Brithdir (telephone box) past the village hall and wooden houses for about half a mile until you reach a crossroads, turn right, Llwyn Talcen is on the right in the trees after about 200 yards.

DOLGELLAU. Mrs Margaret E. Roberts, Tan-y-Foel, Llanfachreth, Dolgellau LL40 2NA (Dolgellau [01341] 423074). Working farm. Beautifully situated on a 500-acre hill farm, carrying Pedigree Welsh Black cattle and Welsh Mountain sheep, this farmhouse enjoys unrestricted views of Cader Idris and Aran Mountain ranges, and is within walking distance of famous Precipice and Torrent walks. Nearest beaches are at Barmouth and Fairbourne. Pony trekking, fishing, golf courses, old mines, slate caverns, narrow gauge railways, all within driving distance. One double and one family bedrooms; bathroom, toilet; sittingroom; diningroom. Cot, babysitting, reduced rates for children. Sorry, no pets. Car essential — parking. Open from April to November for Evening Meal, Bed and Breakfast, or Bed and Breakfast. SAE, please, for terms.

FFESTINIOG. Mrs R. Lethbridge, Morannedd Guest House, Ffestiniog LL41 4LG (01766 762734). Modernised Victorian Guesthouse situated in the centre of Snowdonia National Park enjoying spectacular views over Vale of Ffestiniog and Moelwyn Mountains. Most of the five bedrooms are en suite and all have tea making facilities. The dining room with its log fires and exposed beams has a large picture window allowing food with a view. We provide scrumptious home cooked food and excellent choices for vegetarians; the 21 breakfast options include many local dishes. An ideal base for touring, walking, beaches and tourist attractions including slate caverns, Portmeirion, Ffestiniog and other narrow gauge railways. Non-smoking. Bed and Breakfast from £15.50; four-course Dinner £11.

HARLECH. Mrs G.M. Evans, Glanygors, Llandanwg, Harlech LL46 2SD (01341 241410). This detached house with two acres of land is situated 400 yards from sandy beach, and has beautiful views of the mountains. It is one and a half miles from Harlech Castle, golf club and swimming pool, and within a quarter mile of train station. Ideal place for bird watching. Presenting good home cooking in a homely and relaxed atmosphere and run by a Welsh speaking family. Open all year. Central heating and electric blankets for Winter months. Accommodation comprises two double, one twin and one family bedrooms, all with washbasins, TV and tea-making facilities; bathroom, toilet; TV lounge and diningroom. Reduced rates for children and Senior Citizens. WTB Member. Bed and Breakfast from £13; Evening Meal optional.

LLANBERIS. Geoff and Babs Hall, Dolafon Hotel, High Street, Llanberis LL55 4SU (01286 870993). ♛♛♛ Enjoy an "away from it all" holiday in Snowdonia National Park. Dolafon Hotel is a residentially licensed hotel, which offers all amenities to make your stay pleasurable. The hotel stands in its own grounds with ample parking and is ideally situated to take full advantage of Snowdonia for fell or mountain walking, pony trekking, etc. Just three minutes' walk to the Mountain Railway and the twin lakes of Padarn and Peris. All rooms have tea/coffee facilities, six en suite with TV. Open all year. Children welcome, also groups (rates on application). Bed and breakfast from £14.50; Evening Meal optional. Traditional or vegetarian cooking. Canoe hire.

LLANFACHRAETH. Mrs Joyce A. Roberts, Penyrorsedd Farm, Llanfachraeth, Holyhead LL65 4YB (01407 730630). A 17th century 400 acre working farm just off the A5025 outside the village of Llanfachraeth, ideally situated for overnight stops when travelling to Ireland. Two miles from sandy beach, other beaches close by. The farm is full of character and has a home from home atmosphere. Traditional English breakfast served to guests' own requirements. Central heating. Accommodation comprises double en suite, double room and twin room with private bathroom. Separate lounge with TV. Reductions for children; travelling cot available. Open all year. Bed and Breakfast from £16. Further details gladly provided on application.

MACHYNLLETH. Mrs Lynwen Edwards, Bryn Sion Farm, Cwm Cywarch, Dinas Mawddwy, Machynlleth SY20 9JG (01650 531251). A very warm welcome awaits you when you visit Bryn Sion Farm which is situated in the quiet, unspoilt valley of Cywarch at the foot of Arran Fawddwy (3,000ft), within easy reach of the beach. Fishing and shooting available on farm. Bryn Sion is a mixed farm of 700 acres offering a variety of good farmhouse meals and bed-time tea/coffee. Log fire in sittingroom in evening. Two double rooms, both with tea making facilities, shaving point, washbasin; bathroom. Cot and high chair available. Car essential — parking. Open all year for Bed, Breakfast and Evening Meal (from £19.50 to £21.50 per person) or Bed and Breakfast (from £12 to £14 per person). Reductions for children under nine years. SAE, please, with enquiries.

NEFYN near. Mrs Jean Coker, Mathan Farm, Boduan, Pwllheli LL53 8TU (01758 720487). ♛ **Working farm, join in.** We offer a warm welcome on a working dairy farm where guests can help feed the calves and collect the eggs. Large garden for children to play. Double and family rooms with washbasins, shaver point and tea-making facilities, lounge with TV and separate dining room. Good home cooking. Central heating. Bed and Breakfast from £15. Reductions for children. SAE, please, for brochure.

PENGWERN. Gwyndaf and Jane Lloyd Rowlands, Pengwern, Saron, Llanwnda, Caernarfon LL54 5UH (01286 830717). ♛♛♛ *De Luxe.* Charming, spacious farmhouse of character, situated between mountains and sea. Unobstructed views of Snowdonia. Well appointed bedrooms, all en suite. Set in 130 acres of land which runs down to Foryd Bay. Jane has a cookery diploma and provides excellent meals with farmhouse fresh food, including home-produced beef and lamb. Excellent access. Children welcome. Open February to November. Bed and Breakfast from £16; Evening Meal from £8.50.

See also Colour Display Advertisement **PORTHMADOG. Tyddyn Du Farm, Gellilydan, Near Ffestiniog LL41 4RB (01766 590281).** ♛♛♛ *Highly Commended.* This beautiful 17th century historic farmhouse is situated amidst spectacular scenery in the heart of the Snowdonia National Park. It is an excellent central location base for the numerous attractions, beaches and walks of North Wales. The farmhouse has a relaxed homely atmosphere, charm and character, with a massive stone inglenook fireplace, antique furniture, exposed beams and stonework. We also have a superb private ground floor cottage suite, with a solid fuel stove which sleeps up to four (meals served in farmhouse). All rooms have remote-control colour TV, tea/coffee/drinking chocolate trays; most are en suite. Payphone for guests' use. Candlelit dinners are served using fresh local produce with home-made soup, buns, etc. Vegetarians welcome. Packed lunches available. Breakfast menu with seven choices, plus porridge! Non-smoking area in farmhouse. You are welcome to bottle feed pet lambs, collect the eggs, feed ducks on our mill pond and fuss over Polly the pony. We are easy to find, 300 yards off the A470 near the village of Gellilydan. Open all year. Bed and Breakfast from £16; Dinner £9. Weekly Dinner, Bed and Breakfast from £150. Stamp for brochure please to Mrs P. Williams.

CORBETT ARMS HOTEL

CORBETT SQUARE, TYWYN LL36 9DG
Tel: 01654 710264

On the Welsh Cambrian coastline at Tywyn and on the edge of Snowdonia National Park, this 42 bedroom former coaching inn is a delightful find. A traditional warm and friendly welcome is assured. Here one finds all the services of a hotel at bed and breakfast prices of £16 p.p. except June–September when £18 p.p. applies. Superb bar food is served in our real ale pub with a full restaurant service for more substantial meals. A supplement of £8 applies for half board. All rooms naturally are with private bath and/or shower and WC, have colour television, direct dial telephone and beverage making facilities. Lift.

Welsh Tourist Board ♛♛♛ and AA/RAC ★★ rating.

IMPORTANT ... PRICES QUOTED ONLY APPLY IN REFERENCE TO THIS PUBLICATION. PLEASE MENTION AT THE TIME OF BOOKING.

Available from most bookshops, the 1995 edition of THE GOLF GUIDE covers details of every UK golf course – well over 2000 entries – for holiday or business golf. Hundreds of hotel entries offer convenient accommodation, accompanying details of the courses – the 'pro', par score, length etc.

Endorsed by The Professional Golfers' Association (PGA) and including Holiday Golf in Ireland, France, Portugal, Spain and the USA.

£8.50 from bookshops or £9.50 including postage (UK only) from FHG Publications, Abbey Mill Business Centre, Paisley PA1 1TJ.

WALES

POWYS

BRECON. Mrs Ray M. Roderick, Pwllaca Farm, Soar, Llanfihangel-Nant-Bran, Brecon LD3 9LY (01874 636255). ♛♛ Working farm. Situated four miles from A40 between Sennybridge and Brecon in beautiful rural countryside within easy reach of Brecon Beacons and Black Mountains. Lovely 18th century character beamed farmhouse furnished in true country style. Double/twin bedroom has own bath/shower room; family/double and single en suite. All rooms with washbasins, shaver points and tea-making facilities. Large comfortable lounge with log fire in original stone fireplace, colour TV and piano. Numerous maps and brochures available. Dining room with separate tables. Good parking, also large gardens with swing. Good home cooking, Evening Meal on request. Dogs by arrangement. Open February to November.

BRECON. Mrs M.E. Williams, Lower Rhydness Bungalow, Llyswen, Brecon LD3 0AZ (01874 754264 or 01874 85264). Working farm. Lower Rhydness is on a 150-acre farm with beef cows and sheep. It is a very comfortable fully centrally heated bungalow with views across open fields to the Wye Valley. There are two bedrooms, one with single bed and one with a single bed and a double bed; both rooms with washbasins and close to bathroom with shower. Colour TV in lounge. Bed, Breakfast and Evening Meal or Bed and Breakfast only. Home produce served in season. SAE for brochure.

BRECON. Mrs Eileen Williams, Upper Farm, Llechfaen, Brecon LD3 7SP (01874 665269). Working farm. A modernised farmhouse offering Bed and Breakfast only, situated just off the A40 Brecon to Abergavenny road, two miles from Brecon town. A 64-acre dairy farm in the heart of the National Park directly facing Brecon Beacons. Ideal for touring, with golf, trekking and fishing nearby and many Welsh craft shops to visit. Two double and one family bedrooms with washbasins and tea/coffee facilities; bathroom, toilet; sittingroom; diningroom. Cot, babysitting, reduced rates for children. Open all year. Bed and Breakfast from £13.50 per person. Car essential — parking. No pets.

BRECON. Mrs Pamela Boxhall, The Old Mill, Felinfach, Brecon LD3 0UB (01874 625385). ♛♛ Peacefully situated in its own grounds in the village of Felinfach just 50 metres off A470 Brecon to Hereford Road. The Old Mill has a wealth of character with original features being retained. Friendly atmosphere, large garden. Two bedrooms, one double and one twin (en-suite), TV lounge, tea/coffee facilities. Within easy reach of Brecon Beacons, Black Mountains, Hay-on-Wye. Pony trekking nearby. Local pubs within walking distance. Packed lunches by arrangement. Children and pets welcome. Bed and Breakfast from £13.50 to £16. Reductions for weekly stays.

BRECON near. Mrs Sue Morgan, Maes-y-Coed Farm, Llandefalle, Brecon LD3 0WD (01874 754211). ♛♛♛ Working farm, join in. A comfortable friendly 17th century farmhouse with oak beams, panelling and inglenook fireplace offers you a warm welcome. Lovely views of the Black Mountains. We are 10 miles from Hay-on-Wye, eight miles from Brecon and 15 from Builth Wells. Ideal centre for touring and walking. Accommodation is in one family and one double bedded room en suite and one twin-bedded room with washbasin, all with tea making facilities. Bathroom with WC. Large dining/sitting room with colour TV. Bed and Breakfast from £14; Evening Dinner by arrangement. Children welcome.

POWYS – MOUNTAINOUS AND LANDLOCKED

With many border castles and the Brecon Beacons, which cover the south of the county, Powys can be very spectacular. You will also find the best stretches of Offa's Dyke, Hay-On-Wye, the steam railway at Llanfair Caereinion, Radnor Forest, the fortified house of Tretower, the farming centre at Builth Wells and the abandoned medieval town of Cefnllys.

BRECON near. Gwyn and Hazel Davies, Caebetran Farm, Felinfach, Brecon LD3 0UL (01874 754460). ♛♛♛ Working farm, join in. "Welcome Host". A warm welcome, a cup of tea and home-made cakes await you when you arrive at Caebetran. Visitors are welcome to see the cattle and sheep on the farm. There are breathtaking views of the Brecon Beacons and the Black Mountains and just across a field is a 400 acre Common, ideal for walking, bird watching or just relaxing. Ponies and sheep graze undisturbed, while buzzards soar above you. The farmhouse dates back to the 17th century and has been recently modernised to give the quality and comfort visitors expect today. There are many extras in the rooms to give that special feel to your holiday. The rooms, a twin and two doubles, are all en suite and have colour TV and tea making facilities. Comfortable lounge with colour TV. Caebetran is an ideal base for exploring this beautiful, unspoilt part of the country with pony trekking, walking, birdwatching, wildlife, hang gliding and so much more. For more details, a brochure and terms please write or telephone. "Arrive as visitors and leave as our friends".

BUILTH WELLS. Mrs P.A. Evans, Llwyn Farm, Aberedw, Builth Wells LD2 3YD (01982 570328). Take a break. Superb en suite Bed and Breakfast with optional Evening Meal in idyllic rural setting with panoramic views on working mixed farm. Spacious 15th century farmhouse recently refurbished with oak beams and log fires. Home cooking with own produce. Own lounge/dining room. Open all year. Terms on request.

GLADESTRY. Mrs M.E. Hughes, Stonehouse Farm, Gladestry, Kington, Herefordshire HR5 3NU (Gladestry [0154-422] 651). Working farm. Large Georgian farmhouse, modernised whilst retaining its character, situated on Welsh border with Offa's Dyke Footpath going through its 380 acres of mixed farming. Beautiful unspoiled area for walking. Many places of interest within driving distance such as Elan Valley Dams, Devil's Bridge, Llangorse Lake, Kington golf course. Guests are accommodated in one double and one twin-bedded rooms, with washbasins; bathroom, two toilets; sitting and diningroom. TV. Homely informal atmosphere with home produced food and home cooking. Vegetarian meals on request. Children welcome. Babysitting available. Bed and Breakfast from £12.50; Evening Meals by arrangement. No pets.

LLANDRINDOD WELLS. Mrs Ceinwen Nixon, Brynhir Farm, Chapel Road, Howey, Llandrindod Wells LD1 5PB (01597 822425). ♛♛♛ *Highly Commended* Charming olde worlde farmhouse on working hill farm situated in magnificent mountain setting. One mile off the A483, an ideal place for a getaway and relaxing holiday. Good walking area, trout fishing lake; wonderful area for wildlife, with pied flycatchers, redstarts, buzzards and owls commonly seen; conducted badger sett tours. The house is well away from crowds yet it provides an excellent centre for seeing Llandrindod Wells, the Elan Valley Dams, Hay-on-Wye, Brecon Beacons and Powis Castle. A car is essential. All double/twin and family rooms en suite; lounge available at all times — traditional inglenook fireplace. Beverage tray. Delicious cuisine. Bed and Breakfast from £16.50, with Evening Meal if required. Conservation and Rural Tourism Award, Hygiene and Fire Certificates held. Brochure available.

MACHYNLLETH. Mrs R.J. Hughes, Mathafarn, Llanwrin, Machynlleth SY20 8QJ (01650 511226). ♛♛ *Highly Commended.* Henry VII is reputed to have stayed here en-route to the Battle of Bosworth. Now this elegant 16th century country house is part of a working farm. Inglenook fires, central heating, TV lounge; one double room en suite, one twin with private bathroom, one single room. Tea/coffee making facilities. Close to Machynlleth and beautiful coastline of Aberdovey. Price £17 per person. AA Listed.

MACHYNLLETH. Mrs E.O. Harris, Cefn Coch Uchaf, Cemmaes Road, Machynlleth SY20 8LH (01650 511 552). 16th century farmhouse in the Welsh hills. Excellent country for bird watching, walking, golfing and fishing. Easy access to beaches. Good home cooking — vegetarians catered for. One en-suite bedroom available. Central heating. Bed and Breakfast from £14; Evening Meal £7.50. Open April to October. Children and pets welcome. Babysitting offered. WTB Merit Award.

MONTGOMERY. Mrs G.M. Bright, Little Brompton Farm, Montgomery SY15 6HY (01686 668371).

Highly Commended. **Working farm.** Robert and Gaynor warmly welcome you to their charming 17th century farmhouse on a working farm situated on B4385 two miles east of the Georgian town of Montgomery. Many rooms have a wealth of oak beams. Family, double or twin bedrooms, some en suite. Good traditional cooking. An ideal place to explore Mid Wales and the Border country. Offa's Dyke passes through the farm. AA Selected QQQQ. Open all year. Bed and Breakfast from £16; Evening Meal from £8.

MONTGOMERY. Ceinwen Richards, The Drewin Farm, Churchstoke, Montgomery SY15 6TW (01588 620325). *Highly Commended.* A family-run mixed farm set on hillside overlooking panoramic views of the most beautiful countryside. The Drewin is a charming 17th century farmhouse retaining much of its original character with oak beams and large inglenook fireplace, separate lounge; two well furnished and pretty bedrooms, one en-suite, and all modern amenities with colour TV. Fully centrally heated. A games room with snooker table in converted granary for guests' use. Offa's Dyke footpath runs through the farm. Ideal base for touring the many beauty spots around. Good home cooking and a very warm welcome await our visitors. Bed and Breakfast from £15; Bed, Breakfast and Evening Meal from £22. AA Selected QQQQ and featured in The Travel Show 1993. Holder of Essential Food Hygiene Certificate and Farmhouse Award from Wales Tourist Board. Open (Easter) April to November.

PENYBONT-FAWR. Mrs Anne Evans, Glanhafon, Penybont-Fawr, Oswestry SY10 0EW (0169174 377). *Commended.* **Working farm, join in.** Glanhafon is a working sheep farm situated in the heart of the magnificent Tanat Valley. The traditional Welsh farmhouse offers good home cooking with fresh farm produce which makes it attractive to families or those who seek the peace and quiet of the countryside. Bordering the Berwyn Mountains with easy access to Lake Vyrnwy and Bala Lake, both offering water sports. You may wish to spend a day browsing in the old market towns of Oswestry and Welshpool. Accommodation comprises three bedrooms, all en-suite, with own sittingroom. Tea making facilities in bedrooms. Full central heating. Ample parking. Children and pets welcome. Open Easter till October. Bed and Breakfast from £14.

HOLIDAY ACCOMMODATION
Classification Schemes in England, Scotland and Wales

The National Tourist Boards for England, Scotland and Wales have agreed a common 'Crown Classification' scheme for **serviced (Board)** accommodation. All establishments are inspected regularly and are given a classification indicating their level of facilities and services.

There are six grades ranging from 'Listed' to 'Five Crowns'. The higher the classification, the more facilities and services offered. Crown classification is a measure of *facilities* not *quality*. A common quality grading scheme grades the quality of establishments as 'Approved', 'Commended', 'Highly Commended' or 'Deluxe' according to the accommodation, welcome and service they provide.

For **Self-Catering**, holiday homes in England are awarded 'Keys' after inspection and can also be 'Approved', 'Commended', 'Highly Commended' or 'Deluxe' according to the facilities available. In Scotland the Crown scheme includes self-catering accommodation and Wales also has a voluntary inspection scheme for self-catering grading from '1 (Standard)' to '5 (Excellent)'.

Caravan and Camping Parks can participate in the British Holiday Parks grading scheme from 'Approved (✓)' to 'Excellent (✓ ✓ ✓ ✓ ✓)'. In addition, each National Tourist Board has an annual award for high-quality caravan accommodation: in England – Rose Awards; in Scotland – Thistle Commendations; in Wales – Dragon Awards.

When advertisers supply us with the information, FHG Publications show Crowns and other awards or gradings, including AA, RAC, Egon Ronay etc. We also award a small number of Farm Holiday Guide Diplomas every year, based on readers' recommendations.

SELF-CATERING HOLIDAYS

CLWYD

LLANGOLLEN. Min-yr-afon, Llanarmon Dyffryn Ceiriog, Llangollen. Llanarmon Dyffryn Ceiriog is a beautiful village set in breathtaking countryside, with the Berwyn Mountains rising to almost 3,000ft to the west. Not only famous for fishing, shooting and walking, it was the home of Welsh lyric poet John Ceiriog Hughes, born about 150 years ago. Nestling in this haven of Welsh beauty is Min-yr-afon, a three-bedroomed cottage. Carpeted throughout. Accommodation for six in one double, one single and one family bedrooms, with cot. Separate lounge with colour TV, downstairs bathroom and shower; diningroom. Fully equipped kitchen (electric cooker, fridge, toaster, kettle, cooking utensils, crockery, cutlery). Also spin dryer, iron and ironing board. Linen not provided. Car parking available. Weekly terms from £70 to £165. Available January to December. Enquiries to **Mrs C. Edmonds, 7 Keymer Parade, Burgess Hill, West Sussex RH15 0AB (01444 236367 day; 01342 810908 evening).**

RUTHIN. Mrs E. Jones, Tyddyn Isaf, Rhewl, Ruthin LL15 1UH (01824 703367). Sleeps 6 + cot. A warm welcome is assured on this 80 acre mixed farm, three miles from market town of Ruthin, within easy reach of Chester, the coast, Llangollen, Betws-y-Coed and Snowdonia. The accommodation in the spacious self contained part of farmhouse with oak beams has one double and one family bedroom (one double and two single beds); bathroom with shower over bath, separate toilet; kitchen with microwave and washing facilities; lounge/diner with colour TV, radio, high chair; cot available. Bed linen inclusive. Central heating during winter months. Sorry, no pets. Open all year. Three Dragons Award. One static caravan sleeping six also available. Weekly terms from £90 to 220.

CLWYD – MOUNTAINS, RESORTS AND CASTLES

A mountainous county with pleasant resorts such as Colwyn Bay and Rhyl on its north coast and a number of castles, including Chirk, Denbigh, Ewloe, Flint, Hawarden and Ruthin. Gresford parish church, Corwen, Ruthin, the church at Llanrhaeadr and the Pontcysyllte aqueduct are also worth visiting.

DYFED

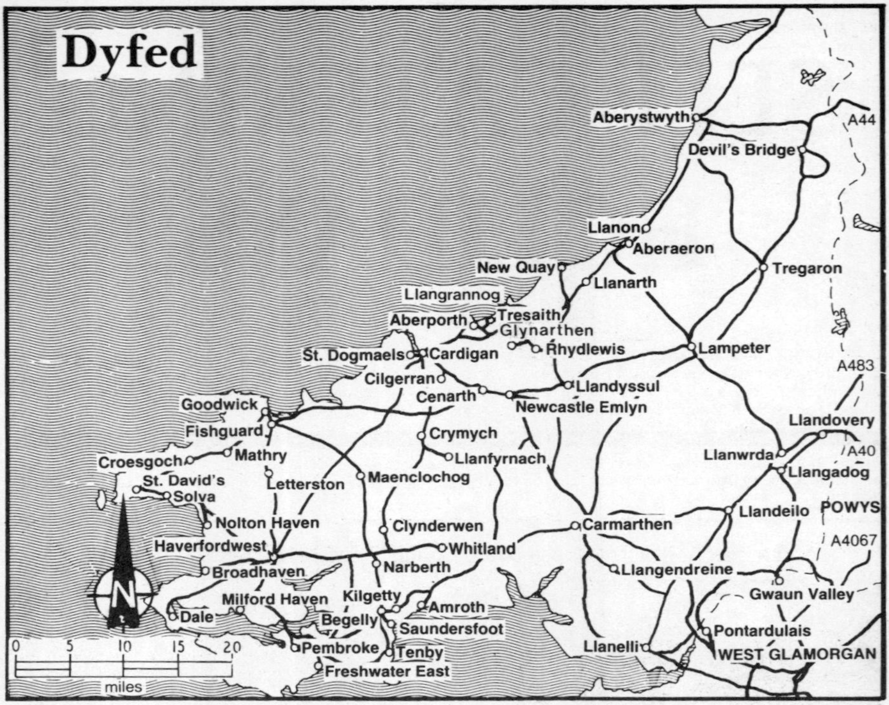

ABERPORTH. Mr and Mrs T. Williams, Ffrwdwenith-Uchaf Farm, Aberporth, Cardigan SA43 1RW (01239 810 209). Sleeps 6. Furnished farm cottage situated on the Cardiganshire coast in a beautiful spot overlooking Cardigan Bay and within easy reach of many lovely sandy beaches. Two double bedrooms with three double beds and cot for child. Bathroom, sittingroom with colour TV, diningroom, kitchen with cooker and fridge. Hot and cold running water. Ideal for a quiet and away-from-it-all holiday. Cardigan five and a half miles, village shop one mile. SAE brings brochure giving full particulars. Visitors are requested to bring their own sheets, pillowcases and towels. Children welcome. Fresh milk daily. Weekly terms from £150 to £200.

ABERPORTH. Neuadd-Wen Holiday Bungalows, Aberporth, Cardigan. Sleep 4/5/6. Neuadd-Wen has six holiday bungalows peacefully situated just off the sea-front in the picturesque coastal village of Aberporth, and only 250 yards from sandy beach. Modern brick-built construction and fully equipped for up to six (except linen). Lounge, kitchenette, two bedrooms, bathroom with WC. Fridge, electric cooker, electric fires and colour TV. Cleanliness assured. Private parking. Shops, restaurant, cafe and hotel only three minutes' walk. Golf, squash, fishing, pony trekking/riding within easy reach. These bungalows are also ideal for early/late holidays, for the beach, coastal walks or for touring the surrounding areas of outstanding natural beauty. Terms from £80 to £200 per week. SAE for brochure to **Mr and Mrs A. Phillips, Orchard House, Aberporth SA43 2HG (01239 811167).**

ABERPORTH. Quality Cottages. Around the magnificent Welsh coast. Away from the madding crowd. Near safe, sandy beaches. A small specialist agency offering privacy, peace and unashamed luxury. Wales Tourist Board 1989 Award Winner. Residential standards — dishwashers, microwaves, washing machines, central heating, log fires, no slot meters. Linen provided. Pets welcome free. All in coastal areas famed for scenery, walks, wild flowers, birds, badgers and foxes. Free colour brochure. **S.C. Rees, Quality Cottages, Cerbid, Solva, Haverfordwest, Pembrokeshire SA62 6YE (01348 837871).**

BOSHERTON. Quality Cottages. Around the magnificent Welsh coast. Away from the madding crowd. Near safe sandy beaches. A small specialist agency offering privacy, peace and unashamed luxury. Wales Tourist Board 1989 Award Winner. Residential standards — dishwashers, microwaves, washing machines, central heating, log fires, no slot meters. Linen provided. Pets welcome. All in coastal areas famed for scenery, walks, wild flowers, birds, badgers and foxes. Free colour brochure. **S.C. Rees, Quality Cottages, Cerbid, Solva, Haverfordwest, Pembrokeshire SA62 6YE (01348 837871).**

CARDIGAN. Mrs J. Young, Cryngae Mawr, Blaenannerch, Cardigan SA43 2BQ (01239 811286). Working farm, join in. Converted barn retaining many original period features. Secluded position surrounded by trees in peaceful setting with views of surrounding countryside. Situated on small quiet 30 acre smallholding with Jersey cows, donkey and tame sheep. Two storey barn has one double bedroom and two single bedrooms; bathroom upstairs and separate shower room; well fitted kitchen with cooker and microwave; comfortable lounge with heating and colour TV. Two miles from beaches at Aberporth. Linen provided at small extra charge. Sorry, no pets. Further details available on request.

CARDIGAN. Llantood Farm Cottages. Sleep 4/6. Situated on 200-acre working farm, three miles south of Cardigan, three miles coast, the Cottages are ideal for exploring Pembrokeshire National Park. The three cottages which sleep four, five and six have been carefully renovated to the highest standards and provide luxury accommodation including central heating, woodburning stoves, colour TV, washing machine, microwave, fridge/freezer, inglenook and exposed beams. Each cottage has its own secluded fenced garden with patio table. Visitors welcome to explore the farm and our 30 acres of unspoilt woodland bordered by a small stream and observe wildlife. Pets welcome. Linen provided. Open all year. Terms from £130 to £330. WTB Award 4 Dragons. Brochure: **Mrs G. Evans, Llantood Farm, Llantood, Cardigan SA43 3NU (01239 612537).**

CARDIGAN. Mrs B. Davies, Nantycroy Farm, Verwig, Cardigan SA43 1PU (Cardigan [01239] 612506). Working farm. Accommodation for self-catering holidaymakers in a house on a 191-acre working farm off the main road between Gwbert-on-Sea and Mwnt Beach, overlooking the sea and Cardigan Island. Footpath to Mwnt Beach. Delightful cliff walks and seals can sometimes be seen at play. Golf, fishing, sailing, pony riding and many lovely beaches, woollen and flour mills to visit, all within easy reach. Three double bedrooms; bathroom, toilets; sittingroom with colour TV; fully equipped kitchen with electric cooker, fridge, hot and cold water. Immersion heater. No linen supplied. Children welcome, cot and high chair available. Pets by prior arrangement. Car essential — parking. Available March to December. Terms from £75 weekly.

CARDIGAN. Andy and Sylvie Gow, Croft Farm, Llantood, Cardigan SA43 3NT (Tel & Fax: 01239 615179). Sleep 2/7. WTB 5 Dragons Award. We warmly welcome you to stay in one of our recently converted slate farm cottages, situated in unspoilt countryside three miles from the market town of Cardigan. Croft is a working smallholding with a variety of farm animals, a pets corner and child's play area. Each cottage is carpeted throughout and furnished to high standard with colour TV, flowers and bottle of wine to welcome you. The beautiful farmhouse makes a luxury self catering let with en suite facilities, freezer, dishwasher, etc. Self Catering Short Breaks from £40 and weekly from £105. Pets welcome.

CARDIGAN near. Quality Cottages. Around the magnificent Welsh coast. Away from the madding crowd. Near safe sandy beaches. A small specialist agency offering privacy, peace and unashamed luxury. Wales Tourist Board 1989 Award Winner. Residential standards — dishwashers, microwaves, washing machines, central heating, log fires, no slot meters. Linen provided. Pets welcome free. All in coastal areas famed for scenery, walks, wild flowers, birds, badgers and foxes. Free colour brochure. **S.C. Rees, Quality Cottages, Cerbid, Solva, Haverfordwest, Pembrokeshire SA62 6YE (01348 837871).**

CARDIGAN COAST (Tresaith/Llangrannog). Mrs C. Davies, Brynarthen, Glynarthen, Llandysul SA44 6PG (Rhydlewis [01239] 851783). Cottages sleep 6; Caravan sleeps 4. Brynarthen is a small working farm delightfully situated amidst beautiful unspoilt countryside, minutes from sandy beaches, one mile off the A487 Cardigan/Aberaeron coastal road. Within the grounds are two charming traditional stone cottages and one caravan, each surrounded by pleasant lawns and gardens, ideal for those just wishing to relax and take it easy. The superb cottages are personally maintained to a high standard and whilst retaining all their charm and character, are comfortably furnished to meet family needs. One is also ideal for the elderly or disabled. Each cottage sleeps six with three bedrooms, bathroom, fully equipped kitchen/diner, lounge with colour TV and fitted carpets throughout. The modern 28' caravan sleeps four with a double bedroom, bathroom, bunk bedroom, shower room with instant hot water, fully equipped kitchen/diner and spacious lounge with colour TV and fitted carpets throughout. Open all year. Brochure on request.

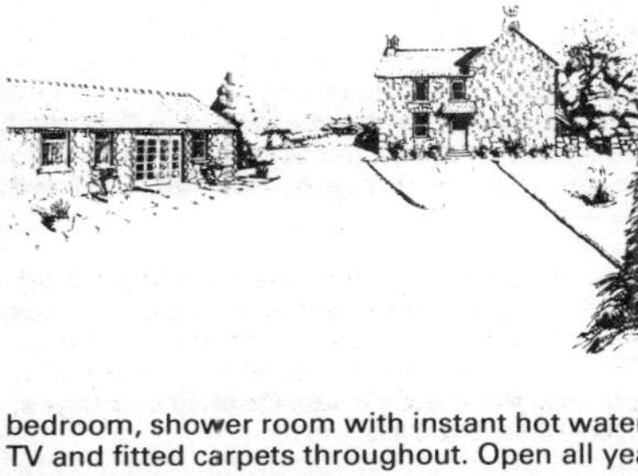

CRICCIETH. Quality Cottages. Around the magnificent Welsh coast. Away from the madding crowd. Near safe sandy beaches. A small specialist agency offering privacy, peace and unashamed luxury. Wales Tourist Board 1989 Award Winner. Residential standards — dishwashers, microwaves, washing machines, central heating, log fires, no slot meters. Linen provided. Pets welcome free. All in coastal areas famed for scenery, walks, wild flowers, birds, badgers and foxes. Free colour brochure. **S.C. Rees, Quality Cottages, Cerbid, Solva, Haverfordwest, Pembrokeshire SA62 6YE (01348 837871).**

WALES

FISHGUARD. Garden Farm, Tufton, Haverfordwest. Working farm, join in. Situated in the Preseli Hills only nine miles from coast at Fishguard and nine miles from Haverfordwest, this is a tranquil 160 acre working beef and sheep farm. Two self catering houses available, both with modern kitchen facilities and bed linen provided. "The Farmhouse" — an attractively restored Victorian farmhouse, warm and comfortable, with heating, log fires, TV, etc. Three/four bedrooms. "The Granary" — an interestingly converted farm building with unusual lounge and kitchen upstairs enjoying magnificent views of the surrounding countryside. Two bedrooms. Both properties ideal for country lovers. Sorry, no pets. Stabling and facilities for horses available. Terms from £100 to £350 per week. Contact: **Mrs Ann and Miss Jennifer Barney, Yethen Isaf, Mynachlogddu, Clynderwen SA66 7SN (Tel & Fax: 01437 532256).**

FISHGUARD. Hendrewen Farm, Manorowen, Fishguard. Working farm. Sleeps 12. Hendrewen is a spacious comfortable modernised self-contained wing of the farmhouse on a working farm of 300 acres. Four bedrooms with good comfortable beds, bed linen provided. Rural views from each window. Sleeps 12 people. Full central heating, fitted carpets, double glazing, lounge with log fire, colour TV, games room with pool table. Modern kitchen with electric cooking. Garden with barbecue. Open all year. Visitors allowed to walk the farm and moorland to see the animals. Near to many beaches. Wales Tourist Board Approved Grade 3. Apply: **Mrs C. James, Hendrewen, Manorowen, Fishguard SA65 9QD (013485 242).**

GOODWICK. Mrs Rosemary Johns, Carne, Goodwick SA64 0LB (St. Nicholas [013485] 665). Working farm, join in. Sleeps 6. Part of old stone farmhouse in peaceful surroundings on 200 acre dairy and sheep farm. The self catering accommodation which sleeps six comprises three bedrooms; large living/diningroom with colour TV; bathroom and fitted kitchen including washing machine. No linen supplied. Children are welcome and there is fenced garden where they can play safely. Cots, high chairs and babysitting available. The farm is three miles from Fishguard, two miles from the sea and within easy reach of many beaches by car. You can be sure of a warm welcome and visitors are invited to join in farm activities. Pets welcome if under control. Open all year.

HAVERFORDWEST. Nolton Haven Farm Cottages in the Pembrokeshire National Park. Situated beside Nolton Haven's sandy beach which they overlook, these six stone, slate and pine cottages offer discerning guests the ideal situation to enjoy the superb Pembrokeshire coastline. The cottages are fully equipped with colour TV, microwave, fridge/freezer, etc. 30 yards to the beach, 75 yards to the local inn/restaurant. Pony trekking, surfing, fishing, excellent cliff walks, boating and canoeing are all available nearby. Contact **Jim Canton, Nolton Haven Farm, Nolton Haven, Haverfordwest SA62 1NH (01437 710263).** Colour brochure on request.

HAVERFORDWEST. Mrs E.M. Thomas, Trewilym Farm, Hayscastle, Haverfordwest SA62 5AA (01348 831381). Sleeps 5. Nicely situated self catering accommodation for five people on this 400 acre farm where visitors and their children are welcome to walk around. The farm is near Newgale beach and many other beautiful sandy beaches. There are lovely country walks along the coastal path. Accommodation comprises double bedroom and singles, bathroom, sitting room with TV. Well equipped kitchen/diningroom. Car essential — ample parking. Market town of Haverfordwest, Cathedral City of St David's and many other places of interest within easy reach. Open all year. Linen provided, cot and high chair available. Sorry no pets. Terms from £100 to £240.

HAVERFORDWEST. Mrs E.M. Mathias, Court House Cottages, Wolfsdale, Camrose, Near Haverfordwest SA62 6JJ (Camrose [01437] 710310). Cottages sleep 6. Centrally situated for all St. Bride's Bay and close to Prescelli Hills, three homely, stone-built cottages, each sleeping six in three double rooms, plus cots. Well-equipped kitchen area, lounge/diner, colour TV, shower room and toilet. Electricity by 50p meter. Situated in quiet, unspoilt hamlet of Wolfsdale, the owners' 300-acre farm is nearby, and through it flows the Western Cleddau with good trout, sewin and salmon fishing. Lovely country walks, near beautiful sandy beaches and coastal paths. Car essential — ample parking. Shops half-a-mile. Open all year — weekly terms from £100. The market town of Haverfordwest, Cathedral City of St. David's, popular seaside resorts and many places of historic and geological interest within easy driving distance. Further details on request.

HAVERFORDWEST. Charles and Joy Spiers, West Lambston, Portfield Gate, Haverfordwest SA62 3LG (01437 710038). Delightfully restored cottage in 200 year old farmhouse. No early morning tractors to disturb peacefulness. Beach within three miles. Many delightful walks (maps provided). Fitted kitchen with automatic washing machine, ironing equipment, fridge, electric and microwave cookers. Shower and toilet room. Sleeps four in two bedrooms. Gas cast-iron stove set in charming oak-beamed inglenook, colour TV and cosy window seat. Children welcome. Highchair, cot and babysitter available. Swings and climbing frame. Pets by arrangement. Bed linen, beach, bath, hand and tea towels provided inclusive. Electricity by meter. Terms from £90 to £270 per week.

HAVERFORDWEST. Curlew Cottage, Haverfordwest. Luxury cottage set in large private grounds in the heart of the Pembrokeshire National Park, overlooking sea and open countryside. Five minutes' walk to clean, sandy beach and spectacular coastal path scenery. Modern pine kitchen has fridge/freezer, dishwasher, washing machine and microwave. Sleeps four/five people in two large bedrooms (linen and electric blankets supplied). Swing provided, and games room with table-tennis and darts. Delicious home-cooked meals delivered to your table. Double glazing and heating ensure all year round comfort. Doorstep parking for cars and boats. Weekly terms; £100 to £370. Three night mini-breaks from October to April: £65. Linen, heating, electricity, colour TV etc. inclusive. Telephone bookings recommended. Wales Tourist Board 4 Dragons Award. SAE appreciated. **Capt. R.W.D. Kenyon, Folkeston Hill Farm, Nolton Haven, Haverfordwest SA62 3NL (01437 710621).**

LLANDOVERY. Tyncoed Farm, Myddfai Road, Llandovery. Sleeps 7+. This spacious and very comfortable old farmhouse is beautifully set overlooking the Towy Valley, with magnificent views from the house. Tyncoed is in a secluded and private position, yet very conveniently situated just off the A4069 Llandovery/Llangadog road. The farmhouse retains much character and charm with its original stone fireplace and oak beams. As it is on the fringe of the Brecon Beacons National Park, it makes a perfect base for touring this delightful rural area. Log fires and storage heaters. Fully equipped. Cot and high chair available. Terms from £120 to £220 per week. SAE, please for further details to **Mrs Lewis Jones, Llwynmeredydd Farm, Myddfai, Llandovery SA20 0JE (Llandovery [01550] 20450).**

LLANGADOG (Brecon Beacons). Mrs D.J. Price, Gwydre Farm, Llanddeusant, Llangadog SA19 9YS (Gwynfe [015504] 242). Working farm. Sleeps 6 adults. Gwydre is a comfortable, spacious and well equipped cottage on a working beef and sheep farm situated at 900 feet in the peaceful, beautiful Black Mountain area of the Brecon Beacons National Park. There are extensive views of farmland and mountains. Superb walking, from gentle strolls on country lanes to strenuous climbs on the Black Mountain. Fishing in nearby lakes and reservoirs and birdwatching. The cottage has an original inglenook fireplace and woodburner and consists of three bedrooms; two double beds, two single and a cot; portable TV. Bathroom with hot shower; separate toilet. Fully fitted kitchen with microwave. Large lounge with colour TV and snooker table. Carpeted throughout. Full central heating. Electricity by 50p meter. Small pets allowed. Linen is supplied. Wales Tourist Board registered. Open April — October from £140 to £240 weekly.

LLANGOEDMOR. Glandwr, Llangoedmor, Near Cardigan. Glandwr Holiday House is in the Parish of Llangoedmor near Cardigan. Situated on the B4570, one mile from market town of Cardigan. Glandwr is a charming, well-equippped semi-detached holiday house in its own grounds with a small drive. Ample parking space. Sunny position with lawn front and back. Lovely countryside views and walks. Comprising fitted kitchen/dining area, fully equipped with full size electric stove, microwave oven, all utensils etc., two fridges; comfortable sittingroom has 20" colour TV. Two double bedrooms (double bed in each), single bedroom, all well equipped. Bathroom with over bath electric shower, washbasin, toilet; downstairs toilet. Fitted carpets. Central heating, electricity inclusive in charge. Available all year from £90 inclusive per week. Mini Breaks from £65. One well-trained pet £8 per week extra. Sandy beaches two to eight miles; fishing on River Teifi. High standard of comfort, service and heating. SAE to **Mrs B. Evans, Rhydyfuwch Dairy Farm, Near Cardigan SA43 2LB (Cardigan [01239] 612064).**

WALES

LLANGRANNOG. Quality Cottages. Around the magnificent Welsh coast. Away from the madding crowd. Near safe, sandy beaches. A small specialist agency offering privacy, peace and unashamed luxury. Wales Tourist Board 1989 Award Winner. Residential standards — dishwashers, microwaves, washing machines, central heating, log fires, no slot meters. Linen provided. Pets welcome free. All in coastal areas famed for scenery, walks, wild flowers, birds, badgers and foxes. Free colour brochure. **S.C. Rees, Quality Cottages, Cerbid, Solva, Haverfordwest, Pembrokeshire SA62 6YE (01348 837871).**

See also Colour Display Advertisement **MYDROILYN. Blaenllanarth Holiday Cottages, Mydroilyn, Lampeter SA48 7RJ (Lampeter [01570] 470374).** Stone farm buildings, recently converted into four cottages, providing a modern standard of comfort in a traditional setting. Sleep two/three (terms £80-£160) or four/eight (terms £140-£280). Gas, electricity and linen included in price. All have shower room and fully equipped kitchen. Colour TV; shared laundry room; facilities for children. Open Easter to October. Situated in a secluded rural area, with abundant wildlife and flowers, and only five miles from sandy beaches and picturesque harbours of Cardigan Bay. Within easy reach of National Trust coastal footpaths, sites of historic and cultural interest, steam railways, castles and breathtaking mountain scenery. Bird watching, fishing and pony trekking nearby. Wales Tourist Board and AA Approved. Full details from **Gil and Mike Kearney**.

NEW QUAY. Mrs Catherine Davies, Cwmcynon Farm, Llwyndafydd, New Quay SA44 6LE (New Quay [01545] 560426). Working farm, join in. Sleeps 6 adults, 1 child. Cwmcynon is a working family farm with a milking herd and a flock of sheep, guests being welcome to watch or take part in farm activities! Llwyndafydd one-quarter-of-a-mile with village pub. Accommodation comprising a self-contained part of the owner's farmhouse (private and separate front and back door) includes: Four bedrooms — one with double and single bed, one with single bed, one with single bed with washbasin and one with double bed with washbasin; large sittingroom with colour TV, electric or open fire; kitchen/diner with electric cooker, fridge/freezer, washing machine, tumble dryer; large private bathroom. Central heating throughout. Cot, high chair and baby bath available, babysitting by arrangement. Large lawn where children can play. Ample parking. Pets welcome. Open March to October. Places of interest, recreation/leisure facilities accommodated nearby. From £160 to £280 weekly, including bed linen and electricity.

FOR THE MUTUAL GUIDANCE OF GUEST AND HOST

Every year literally thousands of holidays, short-breaks and overnight stops are arranged through our guides, the vast majority without any problems at all. In a handful of cases, however, difficulties do arise about bookings, which often could have been prevented from the outset.

It is important to remember that when accommodation has been booked, both parties — guests and hosts — have entered into a form of contract. We hope that the following points will provide helpful guidance.

GUESTS: When enquiring about accommodation, be as precise as possible. Give exact dates, numbers in your party and the ages of any children. State the number and type of rooms wanted and also what catering you require — bed and breakfast, full board, etc. Make sure that the position about evening meals is clear — and about pets, reductions for children or any other special points.

Read our reviews carefully to ensure that the proprietors you are going to contact can supply what you want. Ask for a letter confirming all arrangements, if possible.

If you have to cancel, do so as soon as possible. Proprietors do have the right to retain deposits and under certain circumstances to charge for cancelled holidays if adequate notice is not given and they cannot re-let the accommodation.

HOSTS: Give details about your facilities and about any special conditions. Explain your deposit system clearly and arrangements for cancellations, charges, etc, and whether or not your terms include VAT.

If for any reason you are unable to fulfil an agreed booking without adequate notice, you may be under an obligation to arrange alternative suitable accommodation or to make some form of compensation.

While every effort is made to ensure accuracy, we regret that FHG Publications cannot accept responsibility for errors, omissions or misrepresentation in our entries or any consequences thereof. Prices in particular should be checked because we go to press early. We will follow up complaints but cannot act as arbiters or agents for either party.

B&B or self-catering on beautiful Pembrokeshire coast

Close to a major horseriding centre, fabulous sandy beaches, watersports, miles of scenic coastal paths, and our own well-stocked trout lakes. Farmhouse B&B serves traditional home cooking, or choose self-catering in spacious, well-equipped cottages (sleep 6 to 8, include colour TV, washing machines and made-up beds)

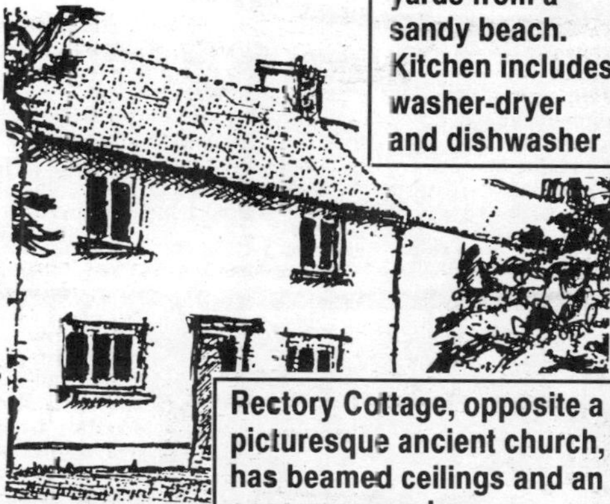

Beach Cottage is yards from a sandy beach. Kitchen includes washer-dryer and dishwasher

Rectory Cottage, opposite a picturesque ancient church, has beamed ceilings and an enormous garden

Hillside Cottage has a peaceful secluded garden that's a real sun-trap. Handy for horse-riding and trout fishing

Phone or fax **(01437) 710360** for details, or write to Mrs Owen at:
East Nolton Farm, Nolton, Nr. Haverfordwest, Pembrokeshire SA62 3NW

WALES

NEWGALE. Quality Cottages. Around the magnificent Welsh coast. Away from the madding crowd. Near safe, sandy beaches. A small specialist agency offering privacy, peace and unashamed luxury. Wales Tourist Board 1989 Award Winner. Residential standards — dishwashers, microwaves, washing machines, central heating, log fires, no slot meters. Linen provided. Pets welcome free. All in coastal areas famed for scenery, walks, wild flowers, birds, badgers and foxes. Free colour brochure. **S.C. Rees, Quality Cottages, Cerbid, Solva, Haverfordwest, Pembrokeshire SA62 6YE (01348 837871).**

NORTH PEMBROKESHIRE. Mrs T. Jones, Penbanc, Tegryn, Llanfyrnach SA35 0BP (0123-977 279/666). Working family farm with sheep, cows, calves, ponies, free range hens, ducks and geese; sometimes pigs. Traditional stone-built farmhouse accommodation sleeps six plus cot; bathroom; kitchen; sittingroom with colour TV and woodburner, dining room. Small garden with picnic table. Plenty of books and games for wet days, also old piano. Petrol, stamps, milk and pub meals one mile; village store two miles. Centrally based for trekking, walking, touring, swimming, golf; coast 20 minutes' by car (essential). Fishing — river, reservoir, sea or farm pool. Sandy beaches, rocky coves, coastal path. Island to visit. Plenty to do — castles, woollen mills, nature reserves, museums, crafts, leisure centres, theme park, zoo. Available May to September. Also eight-berth caravan available.

PENUWCH. Mr and Mrs Ken Nicholls, The Edelweiss, Penuwch, Near Tregaron SY25 6QZ (01974 821601). En suite garden studio for two adults (plus child). Ground floor, every comfort, everything provided including linen and colour TV. Fully inclusive. Ideal for non-smoking guests, available throughout the year. Long lets at favourable terms. Weekly £118 to £120. Situated in beautiful position overlooking Ceredigian countryside, eight miles from the Cardigan Bay coastline near Aberaeron. Also caravan in private ground adjacent to house, sleeps one to five. Mains services. Non-smoking guests only. Every comfort. From £85 to £110 weekly including linen. Meals and groceries available if required.

SOLVA. Quality Cottages. Around the magnificent Welsh Coast. Away from the madding crowd. Near safe, sandy beaches. A small specialist agency offering privacy, peace and unashamed luxury. Wales Tourist Board 1989 Award Winner. Residential standards — dishwashers, microwaves, washing machines, central heating, log fires, no slot meters. Linen provided. Pets welcome free. All in coastal areas famed for scenery, walks, wild flowers, birds, badgers and foxes. Free colour brochure. **S.C. Rees, Quality Cottages, Cerbid, Solva, Haverfordwest, Pembrokeshire SA62 6YE (01348 837871).**

ST. DAVID'S. Quality Cottages. Around the magnificent Welsh coast. Away from the madding crowd. Near safe sandy beaches. A small specialist agency offering privacy, peace and unashamed luxury. Wales Tourist Board 1989 Award Winner. Residential standards — dishwashers, microwaves, washing machines, central heating, log fires, no slot meters. Linen provided. Pets welcome free. All in coastal areas famed for scenery, walks, wild flowers, birds, badgers and foxes. Free colour brochure. **S.C. Rees, Quality Cottages, Cerbid, Solva, Haverfordwest, Pembrokeshire SA62 6YE (01348 837871).**

QUALITY COTTAGES

AROUND THE MAGNIFICENT WELSH COAST

Away from the Madding Crowd · Near safe sandy beaches

A small specialist agency with over 32 years experience of providing quality self-catering offers privacy, peace and unashamed luxury.

The first Wales Tourist Board Self-Catering Award Winner. Highest residential standards.

Dishwashers, Microwaves, Washing Machines, Central Heating. No slot meters.

LOG FIRES LINEN PROVIDED PETS WELCOME FREE!

All in coastal areas famed for scenery, walks, wild-flowers, birds, badgers and foxes.

Away from the madding crowd.

Free colour Brochure: F.G. Rees, "Quality Cottages", Cerbid, Solva, Haverfordwest, Pembrokeshire SA62 6YE. Telephone: (01348) 837871.

ST. DAVID'S. Ffynnon Ddofn, Llanon, Llanrhian, Haverfordwest. Luxury cottage in quiet lane between St. David's and Fishguard, with panoramic views over many miles of this spectacular coastline. Ideal for walking; rocky coves and safe sandy beaches nearby. The cottage is fully carpeted, warm, comfortable and very well equipped, sleeping six in three bedrooms, plus cot. Washing machine, tumble dryer, freezer. Games room with table tennis and snooker, children's toys, lovely garden with swing. Perfect for early or late holidays, with central heating and double glazing. Parking beside cottage. Shop one mile. Footpath to beach. Pets welcome. Open all year. WTB Approved Four Dragons Award. Terms from £195, including heating and electricity. Brochure on request. **Mrs T.A. Rees White, Brickhouse Farm, Burnham Road, Woodham Mortimer, Maldon, Essex CM9 6SR (01245 224611).**

TENBY. Quality Cottages. Around the magnificent Welsh coast. Away from the madding crowd. Near safe, sandy beaches. A small specialist agency offering privacy, peace and unashamed luxury. Wales Tourist Board 1989 Award Winner. Residential standards — dishwashers, microwaves, washing machines, central heating, log fires, no slot meters. Linen provided. Pets welcome free. All in coastal areas famed for scenery, walks, wild flowers, birds, badgers and foxes. Free colour brochure. **S.C. Rees, Quality Cottages, Cerbid, Solva, Haverfordwest, Pembrokeshire SA62 6YE (01348 837871).**

WHITLAND. Mrs Angela Colledge, Gwarmacwydd, Llanfallteg, Whitland SA34 0XH (01437 563260). Gwarmacwydd is a country estate of over 450 acres, including two miles of riverbank. Come and see a real farm in action, the hustle and bustle of harvest, cows being milked, newborn calves and lambs. Children are welcomed. On the estate are five character stone cottages, Tourist Board Grade 4. Each cottage has been lovingly converted from traditional farm buildings, parts of which are over 200 years old. Each cottage is fully furnished and equipped with all modern conveniences. All electricity and linen included. All cottages are heated for year-round use. Colour brochure available.

DYFED – MANY TOURIST ATTRACTIONS!

Dyfed, the largest county in Wales, has for a long time been a popular tourist destination. This is due to the fact that it contains such attractions as Aberystwyth, Cardigan, Carmarthen, Haverfordwest, Pembroke, St. David's and Tenby. The enterprising tourist should also head for the monastery on Caldy Island, the village of Llangrannog, Hafod, the wool museum at Dre-fach Felindre and the village of Laugharne – Dylan Thomas's Wales.

GWENT

ABERGAVENNY. Ann Ball, Granary and Coach House, Upper Cwm Farm, Llantilio Crossenny, Abergavenny NP7 8TG (01873 821236). Holidays and short breaks in beautifully converted old barn on working sheep farm. Family accommodation with central heating, TV, electricity, bed linen, towels included. Peaceful superb views, ideal for walking, birdwatching, exploring Welsh castles, Brecon Beacons, Wye and Usk Valleys. The Granary (upper) and Coach House (ground) each have three double bedrooms, lounge/dining/kitchen, bathroom with shower. Children and pets welcome. Open all year. Terms from £170 to £330 per week. Brochure available. WTB 4 Dragon Award.

RAGLAN. Mrs V. Jones, Worcester House, Castle Farm, Raglan NP5 2BT (01291 690492). Sleeps 6/8. Part of a 17th century manor house, the oldest building in Gwent, on a 200 acre dairy/arable farm. Accessible to main roads leading to Wye Valley, Brecon Beacons, Forest of Dean; Raglan Castle 20 yards away. Fully furnished and centrally heated, the property has separate modern kitchen with electric cooker, fridge and automatic washing machine; diningroom, sittingroom with french windows leading to large lawn; shower room, toilet. Upstairs there is a large bedroom with double bed and bed settee, second bedroom containing two single beds, the third small room has two bunk beds; large bathroom with toilet. Children welcome, cot, etc available. Pets accepted. WTB Grade 3 Dragons.

WALES

GWYNEDD

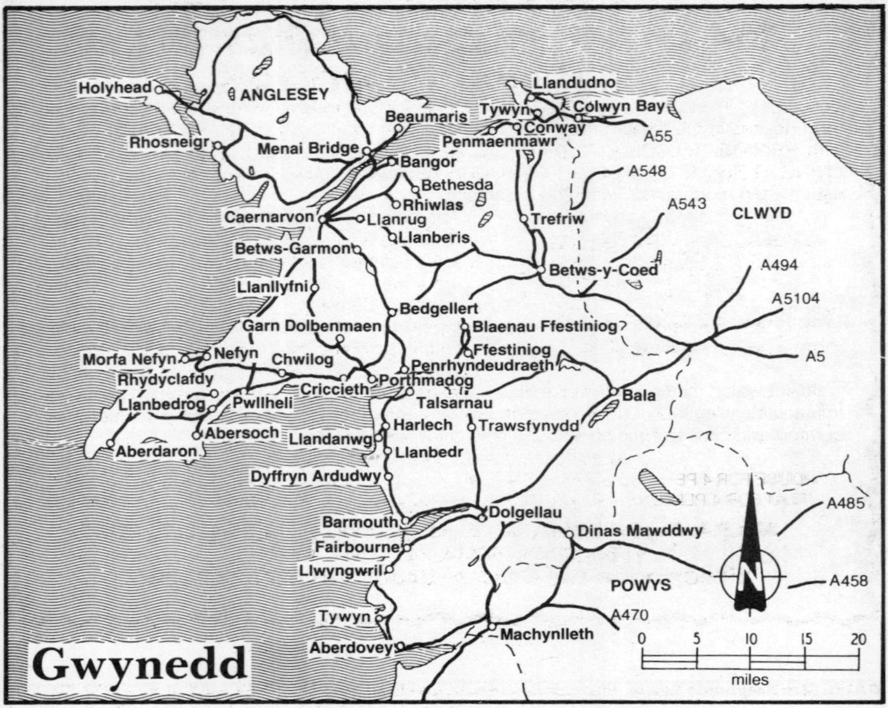

ABERDARON. Mrs J.J. Evans, Bodrydd, Rhoshirwaun, Pwllheli LL53 8HR (Rhiw [0175-888] 257). Accommodation for six in self-contained farmhouse, Bodrydd Farm, centrally situated near tip of Lleyn Peninsula, standing back from main road, in lovely Welsh countryside and peaceful surroundings with open view of hills and fields. Within easy reach of Whistling Sands, numerous picturesque sandy beaches. Riding stables at nearby farm. Licensed hotels in Aberdaron (two miles). Small river running through farmland for trout fishing. Small working farm with plenty going on to interest all ages. Comfort and cleanliness guaranteed. Three double bedrooms; cot, high chair; bathroom, toilet; sittingroom with colour TV; diningroom with electric fire; kitchen all electric with all utensils, etc. No linen. Shop 10 minutes' walk. Sea one and a half miles. Sorry, no pets. Car essential, ample parking. May to September. SAE please for terms and brochure.

ABERDARON. Mrs M.P. Roberts and Mrs A. Jones, "Ty Fry", Aberdaron, Pwllheli LL53 8BY (Aberdaron [0175-886] 274). Sleeps 5. Completely modernised and fully furnished with linen supplied, this Welsh cottage has exclusive views over Aberdaron Bay. Few minutes' walk from the local grocery shop. Private drive from main road and ample parking space. Convenient for many sandy beaches and coves, including the famous Whistling Sands. Mountain walks where the sea views literally surround you on the extreme tip of the Lleyn Peninsula. Accommodation to let furnished without attendance. Two bedrooms, sleeping five, cot available; bathroom; immerser; large lounge (TV); kitchen/diner with electric cooker, fridge; metered electricity. Pets welcome. Bookings from March to October. For prompt reply SAE, please.

ABERSOCH. Quality Cottages. Around the magnificent Welsh coast. Away from the madding crowd. Near safe sandy beaches. A small specialist agency offering privacy, peace and unashamed luxury. Wales Tourist Board 1989 Award Winner. Residential standards — dishwashers, microwaves, washing machines, central heating, log fires, no slot meters. Linen provided. Pets welcome free. All in coastal areas famed for scenery, walks, wild flowers, birds, badgers and foxes. Free colour brochure. **S.C. Rees, Quality Cottages, Cerbid, Solva, Haverfordwest, Pembrokeshire SA62 6YE (01348 837871).**

Terms quoted in this publication may be subject to increase if rises in costs necessitate

FOR THE PERFECT HOLIDAY

Aberdovey, House and Flats To Let
. . . Beach 10 seconds

Beautifully furnished and equipped, superb conversions to Maisonettes and flats of old sea front houses in the lovely Snowdonia National Park, also luxury BUNGALOW AND HOUSE with PRIVATE BALCONY, TERRACES even a JACUZZI, on the hillside above. LUXURY LIVING AT REALISTIC PRICES, TOP TOURIST BOARD GRADE 5. All have stunning views of estuary and mountains. Sleep 2 to 8 persons.

Aberdovey is a picturesque village (the jewel of Cardigan Bay), which visitors say has a SPECIAL MAGIC, there is something for every member of the family – sailing (hire and instruction), windsurfing, golf, fishing (river and sea – regular boat trips, catch shrimps to sharks!), pony trekking, tennis, bowls; climb, walk in fantastic scenery, canoe, laze on the miles of quiet dune backed sands or watch the children on the beach and boats from your own very comfortable lounge. Immaculately maintained by resident owners, launderette, central heating, in fact every comfort and convenience so that you may enjoy your holiday to the full.

EXAMPLES OF PRICES PER UNIT, PER WEEK

HOUSE FOR 4 PERSONS – MAY FROM £195 FLAT FOR 6 PERSONS – SEPT FROM £115
FLAT FOR 4 PERSONS – AUG FROM £199 BUNGALOW FOR 4 PERSONS – JULY FROM £260

Mrs P.A. Bendall, Hafod, Sea Front, Aberdovey, Gwynedd LL35 0EB
Tel. 01654 767418, Fax 01654 767418

"Freephone for Colour Brochure 0800 212305"

BALA. Mrs Stephanie Lewis, Maesafallen, Rhosygwaliau, Bala LL23 7EY (01678 520373). Ty-Ucha is a 33 acre sheep farm. It is combined with a 1000 acre sheep farm which is in the next valley. Bala, three miles away, is famous for its Lake which is the largest natural lake in Wales. You can sail, fish, windsurf and swim in the lake. There are two golf courses and pony trekking near by. Ideal touring centre for Snowdonia. The farmhouse has a self contained flat which accommodates two. Fully equipped and all bed linen provided. Colour TV, central heating, microwave. Open Easter to the end of October. SAE for brochure.

BEDDGELERT. Beudy Coed, Oerddwr, Beddgelert. Sleeps 6. Beautifully renovated shepherd's cottage, one mile from Aberglaslyn Pass and situated on wooded hillside overlooking the Glaslyn River and the Cnicht and Moelwyn Mountain Ranges. Ideal central location for walking, climbing, fishing, yet only four miles from Porthmadog's lovely beaches. The cottage can accommodate six people. Two double bedrooms. Dining/sittingroom with stone fireplace; fully equipped kitchen; shower room. Patio area in the garden with table and benches. Eat out and enjoy the magnificent scenery. Open March to October. Children and pets welcome. Contact **Ann Jones, Frondeg, Llanfair, Harlech LL46 2RE (01766 780448).**

BEDDGELERT. Bron Eifion, Rhyd Ddu, Beddgelert. Sleeps 6. Attractive semi-detached house on edge of small village in National Park at foot of Snowdon. Splendid mountain, valley and Pass walks from village including path up Snowdon. Lakes nearby. Excellent centre for seaside, historic castles and houses, riding, fishing and touring. Three bedrooms; two living rooms; bathroom; modern kitchen, fridge, airing cupboard, heaters. Well equipped. Mountain view, terrace, rough garden. Inn (serving meals) nearby. Cot. Sorry, no pets. High season £150 to £240 per week; low season £55 to £140 per week. Short Breaks by arrangement. Open all year. Apply: **Davies, 218 Clive Road, London SE21 8BS (0181-670 2756).**

QUALITY COTTAGES

AROUND THE MAGNIFICENT WELSH COAST

Away from the Madding Crowd · Near safe sandy beaches

A small specialist agency with over 32 years experience of providing quality self-catering offers privacy, peace and unashamed luxury.

The first Wales Tourist Board Self-Catering Award Winner. Highest residential standards.

Dishwashers, Microwaves, Washing Machines, Central Heating. No slot meters.

LOG FIRES LINEN PROVIDED PETS WELCOME FREE!

All in coastal areas famed for scenery, walks, wild-flowers, birds, badgers and foxes.

Away from the madding crowd.

Free colour Brochure: F.G. Rees, "Quality Cottages", Cerbid, Solva, Haverfordwest, Pembrokeshire SA62 6YE. Telephone: (01348) 837871.

BEDDGELERT. Meillionen, Beddgelert. Farmhouse situated in the heart of Snowdonia within one mile of picturesque village. Large house divided into two separate units. One consists of large kitchen/livingroom with colour TV, electric cooker, fridge and Rayburn; stone staircase leading to two double bedrooms and bathroom. Other unit consists of sittingroom, open fireplace; colour TV; kitchen with fridge and electric cooker; downstairs bathroom; three double bedrooms and single bed; cot and high chair also available. Bed and table linen not provided. Storage heaters in winter. Electricity on meter. Fishing, pony trekking and sports facilities nearby, also beaches within easy reach. SAE to **Mrs S.H. Owen, Cwm Cloch, Beddgelert, Caernarfon (0176-686 241).**

BEDDGELERT. 2 Glanfa, Rhyd Ddu, Near Beddgelert. 150 year old, well-equipped stone cottage in the centre of a pretty village at the foot of Snowdon. In the heart of the National Park, it is an ideal centre for mountains or sea. Suitable for two families, sleeps eight in three bedrooms (two double and four single beds). Large livingroom with exposed beams, Welsh dresser, storage heater, radio and colour TV. Good-sized kitchen with fridge, electric cooker. Bathroom with electric shower. Cot and high chair available. Metered electricity. No pets. Near pub. Terms high season from £160 to £270; low season £70 to £120, with Short Breaks by arrangement in low season. Open all year. Apply **Mr and Mrs C.R. Vernon, 166 Court Lane, Dulwich, London SE21 7ED (0181-693 3971).**

BETWS-Y-COED. Jim and Lilian Boughton, Bron Celyn, Llanrwst Road, Betws-y-Coed LL24 0HD (01690 710333). Our cosy 200-year-old converted coach house has beeen tastefully refurbished and offers accommodation for up to four persons. Upstairs: one double room with space for a cot, and one bunk-bedded room with full length/width bunk beds. All bed linen is provided but not towels. Downstairs: lounge with colour TV and wood-burning stove (ample supply of chopped timber available). Kitchen with fridge, electric cooker, toaster and water heater. Shower room and toilet. Electric storage heaters fitted throughout. Metered electricity (read arrival/departure). Open all year. Ideal centre for walking, climbing, fishing or simply just relaxing! Terms £120 to £300 per week. Short Breaks available.

BETWS-Y-COED (6 miles). Two detached cottages. Sleep 5/6. Situated a quarter of a mile apart in a farming area with panoramic views of Snowdonia and the Conwy Valley, the accommodation is of a high standard and under the owners' personal supervision. Welsh Tourist Board Grade 4. Centrally heated, open fire with fuel and electricity supplied free. Colour TV. Modern well equipped kitchen with automatic washing machine. Bed linen supplied. Ideal location for touring North Wales — within easy reach of sea, lakes, mountains and castles. Ideal for two families holidaying together. Available all year from £135 weekly. Details from **Mrs N. Evans, Pen y Bryn Bach, Maenan, Llanrwst LL26 0UR (01492 640438/640768).**

See also Colour Display Advertisement **CAERNARFON. Mrs M. Gray-Parry, Bryn Bras Castle, Llanrug, Near Caernarfon LL55 4RE (Tel & Fax: 01286 870210). Sleep 2-4.** Welcome to beautiful Bryn Bras Castle — enchanting castle Apartments, elegant Tower House and cosy mini-cottage, within unique romantic turreted Regency Castle (Listed Building) in the gentle foothills of Snowdonia. Centrally situated, amidst breathtaking scenery, for exploring North Wales' magnificent mountains, beaches, resorts, heritage and history. Near local country inns, restaurants and shops. Each spacious apartment is fully self contained, gracious, peaceful, clean with distinctive individual character, comfortable furnishings, generously and conveniently appointed from dishwasher to fresh flowers. Free central heating, hot water, duvets and bed linen. All highest WTB grade (except one). 32 acres tranquil landscaped gardens, sweeping lawns, woodland walks of natural beauty, panoramic hill walk overlooking the sea, Anglesey and Mount Snowdon. Mild climate. Enjoy the comfort, warmth, privacy and relaxation of this Castle of timeless charm in truly serene surroundings. Open all year (including for Short Breaks). Brochure sent with pleasure.

CAERNARVON. Mrs M. Hughes, Glan Llyn, Llanfaglan, Caernarvon LL54 5RD (01286 674700). Sleeps 4. Glan Llyn is a two bedroomed semi-detached cottage situated in a quiet area, yet only two miles from historic town of Caernarvon and within easy distance of Caernarvon golf course and Caernarvon Bay for sea fishing. Ideally situated for touring North Wales, just seven miles from Snowdon and Anglesey and within easy reach of many seaside resorts. Accommodation comprises two double-bedded rooms; bathroom; lounge with TV; kitchen/diner with fridge, electric stove, electric fires or open fire. Bed linen supplied. Parking space. Cottage available all year round. Mid-week Breaks and Weekend Breaks available during off season. Reduction for winter breaks and weekend bookings during off season period; summer terms and full details on request.

CAERNARVON. Mrs Ivy Atkin, Cwm Farm, Clynnogfawr, Caernarvon LL54 5DW (01286 660244). 300 acre mountain farm with private two acre fishing lake with islands and rowing boat. In elevated position overlooking Cardigan Bay with views of the Snowdon Mountains in the distance. Eight miles from Pwllheli and Criccieth, four miles from Clynnog and Bryncir. Large safe garden, plenty of parking space. House sleeps eight plus cot and high chair. Sittingroom with colour TV, inglenook fireplace and exposed beams; kitchen-cum-diner with oil-fired Rayburn cooker, microwave, fridge freezer and Calor gas cooker. Sun lounge with children's play area. Large downstairs bathroom; two double bedrooms and small bedroom with two single beds on main landing. Loft bedroom over bathroom, separate from main landing, with two single beds. Terms from £150 to £225 per week. No pets.

See also Colour Display Advertisement **CAERNARVON. Beach Holiday Homes, West Point, The Beach, Pontllyfni, Caernarvon LL54 5ET (01286 660400).** ✓ ✓ ✓ ✓ and ✓ ✓ ✓ ✓ ✓. Beach Holiday Homes offers bungalow, chalet and caravan accommodation in areas of outstanding natural beauty, all with sea views. Nearby restaurants, bar snacks, takeaways, most leisure activities including sea/river fishing, golf, rambling, pony trekking. Ideal for touring Snowdonia. Personal attention. Brochure available.

CHURCH BAY. Mrs Lindy Wood, The Lobster Pot Cottage, Church Bay, Holyhead, Anglesey LL65 4EY (01407 730241/730588). 3 Dragons Award. 11 miles from Holyhead, the ferry port to Ireland, The Lobster Pot cottage/flat is above a renowned seafood restaurant in picturesque Church Bay, with working lobster tanks in the garden. The flat is small but cosy, well equipped with electric cooker, microwave, fridge, percolator, etc. It sleeps four in one double and one twin-bedded rooms. Gas wall fires, use of washing machine and tumble dryer and all linen included in tariff. Lawned gardens with barbecue. Well behaved pets welcome. Ideal for coastal walks, boating, bathing, bird watching. Nearby trout fishing, horse riding and golf. Within easy reach of beautiful Snowdonia. Terms from £110 to £240. SAE, please.

CRICCIETH. Betws-Bach & Rhos-Dhu, Ynys, Criccieth LL52 0PB (Tel & Fax: 01758 720047; 01766 810295). Wales Tourist Board Grade 5. A truly romantic, memorable and special place to stay and relax in comfort. Old world farmhouse and period country cottage. Situated just off the B4411 road in tranquil surroundings. Equipped to Wales Tourist Board Grade 5 with washing/drying machines, dishwashers, microwaves, freezers, colour TV, old oak beams, inglenook with log fires, full central heating. Snooker table, pitch 'n' putt, romantic four-poster bed, sauna and jacuzzi. Open all year — Winter Weekends welcomed. Ideal for couples. Sleep two — six plus cot. Own fishing and shooting rights, wonderful walks, peace and quiet with Snowdonia and unspoilt beaches on our doorstep. For friendly personal service please phone, Fax or write to **Mrs Anwen Jones.**

CRICCIETH. Mrs H.E. Jones, Bryn Dewin Farm, Chwilog, Pwllheli LL53 6LQ (01766 810468). Criccieth four miles — furnished farmhouse near Chwilog between Criccieth and Pwllheli. Sleeps seven plus cot. A very comfortable furnished farmhouse on a working farm. Centrally situated in a rural area and enjoying panoramic views of Snowdonia and across the sea to the North Wales coastline. Nearest beach is one and a half miles away, shop and pub one mile. Golf, riding and Leisure Centre nearby. Parking for two cars. Children welcome. Accommodation comprises four bedrooms, all modern conveniences, lounge with TV, piano; kitchen/diner, scullery with cooker, fridge, microwave, automatic washing machine, iron. Children welcome, sorry no pets. High chair available. SAE for further details or telephone evenings after 6pm.

CRICCIETH. Mrs E.W. Roberts, Cae Canol Farm, Criccieth LL52 0NB (01766 522351). Sleeps 2 adults; 3 children. Pleasantly situated with lovely mountain views, this country cottage has two bedrooms sleeping four/five plus cot. Bathroom, toilet; spacious kitchen/diner, fully equipped with fridge, etc. Sittingroom with TV. Everything supplied except linen. Garden in front of cottage with plenty of parking space. Golf, tennis, boating, walks, shooting, fishing and horse riding all within easy reach of cottage. FREE fishing on private river — salmon and trout. Terms on request with SAE, please. Open all months of the year.

GWYNEDD – OUTSTANDING NATURAL BEAUTY!
With Snowdonia National Park and the Lleyn Peninsula, Gwynedd well deserves its designation as an 'Area of Outstanding Natural Beauty'. The tourist is spoiled for choice in this county but should endeavour to visit the hill-fort at Tre'r Ceiri, the Llugwy Valley, Cwm Pennant, Dinas Dinlle hill-fort, the gold mine at Clogau and the railways and quarries at Blaenau Ffestiniog.

CRICCIETH. Mrs B. Williams, Gaerwen Farm, Ynys, Criccieth LL52 0NU (01766 810324). Sleeps 7.

This 200 acre dairy/mixed farm is situated four-and-a-half miles inland from Criccieth and beaches. An ideal centre for enjoying climbing, fishing, pony trekking and quiet country walks with extensive views of Snowdonia and Cardigan Bay. Within easy reach of various historic places nearby. Accommodation is self-contained in furnished farmhouse, comprising TV lounge with inglenook fireplace and oak beams, electric fire; fitted kitchen with electric cooker, automatic washing machine, fridge/freezer and microwave; dining room; two double bedrooms, one twin-bedded room and one single bedroom, with duvets and bed linen; bathroom/shower with washbasin and toilet. Children most welcome, cot and babysitting available. Pets welcome. Car essential. Electricity provided. Weekly terms from £125 to £260. Short Breaks offered. SAE, please, for more details.

CRICCIETH. Tyddyn Madyn, Golan, Garndolbenmaen LL51 9YY (01766 75605). Sleeps 4 adults; 2 children plus cot. Semi detached stone built farm house with traditional beams. It is set within a 35 acre working farm and has a panoramic view of the beautiful Pennant Valley, situated at the edge of the Snowdonia National Park and five miles easy motoring to Porthmadog and beaches at Criccieth. Ideal for mountain walking, fishing, mountain railways, Llyn Peninsula and the famous Italianate village of Portmeirion. Farmhouse has three bedrooms; one with double bed, one with two single beds and one with bunk beds. Downstairs lounge with colour TV, electric fire, central heating; kitchen with gas cooker, fridge, microwave. Back hall toilet, bathroom with shower above bath. Linen not provided. Terms on request.

CRICCIETH. Mrs L. Hughes Jones, Tyddyn Heilyn, Chwilog LL53 6SW (01766 810441). Freshly renovated but keeping its antique features, charming farm cottage in tranquil, unspoilt countryside with sea on either side, sheltered by Snowdonia Mountain in distant background. Comfortably sized kitchen full of electrical gadgets, spacious lounge with colour TV. Capricorn bathroom suite has full size Twingrip bath and shower. Victorian furnished bedrooms have Continental quilts. As well as flower and shrub beds, there is an olde worlde character to the front and back courtyards — ample parking space here. Also, but not in cottage vicinity, furnished home sleeping up to six persons. Passing through this farmland, the renowned Lon Goed walk has six mile roadway of oak and ash trees and in the flowered hedgerows too there are species of rare birds. Llanystumdwy, the home village of Earl Lloyd George with its commemorative museum, two fishing rivers, riding school, pets and rabbit farm, the church, cafes and a pub is one mile away. Write or phone for the moderate terms of the two holiday accommodation properties.

DOLGELLAU. Cefn Clawdd, Cross Foxes, Dolgellau. Farm cottage in open valley situated on A470 out of Dolgellau. Very accessible, 200 yards from main road, with hard road to farm. At foot of Cader Idris with panoramic views, little way along mountain path; Tal-y-Llyn Lake and Pass can be seen below. Tiny stream with trout fishing. Low beamed, low ceilinged old world cottage, solidly furnished, accommodates nine in three double bedrooms; cot; bathroom, toilet; sittingroom; dining-kitchen with electric cooker, fridge, vacuum, twin-tub washing machine, clothes dryer. Shops five miles, sea eight miles. Car essential, parking. Pets by arrangement. Terms from £60 to £250 per week. Also converted wing attached to house, a separate unit sleeping four/five persons. Available all year. SAE, please, to **Mrs E. Wyn Price, Glyn Farm, Dolgellau LL40 1YA (01341 422286).**

DYFFRYN ARDUDWY. Mrs Jane Williams, Ynys, Ystumgwern Hall Farm, Dyffryn Ardudwy LL44 2DD (01341 247249; Fax: 01341 247171). Working farm. Sleep 1-8. Situated in Snowdonia National Park on 1000 acre working farm. Beautifully renovated 16th century cottages and barn conversions sleeping one to eight people in one, two, three and four bedroomed units. Within six miles there is pony trekking, bird watching, golf, walks, rivers, lakes, mountains, steam trains, castle and sandy beaches. De Luxe grade Bed and Breakfast also available from same units. Equipped to the highest of standards. On site payphone, play area, games room, barbecue and picnic area. Children welcome, pets by arrangement. Terms from £140 to £420 per week. All properties Grade 5. A warm welcome to all. Colour brochure available on request.

DYFFRYN ARDUDWY. Mr O.G. Thomas, Bron Foel Uchaf, Dyffryn Ardudwy LL44 2HZ (01341 247570). Bron Foel is a spacious 18th century farmhouse full of character with outstanding views of Cardigan Bay and beyond. The lounge is spacious with oak beams and inglenook fireplace with wood supplied. Modern fitted kitchen with oil-fired Aga; three bedrooms — a double, a twin and a family room, all tastefully decorated. The house is set amidst ample grounds, in an elevated position to give privacy from the working farm. We are one and a half miles from the village of Dyffryn with Barmouth and Harlech a short distance away. Small pets and children welcome. Terms from £150.

WALES

LLANBEDR. Mrs Moira Holland-Jones, Graig Isaf, Cwm Nantcol, Llanbedr LL45 2PL (01341 23341). Working farm, join in. Sleeps 6. Graig Isaf is four miles from the village of Llanbedr. The cottage is a renovated stable with all modern conveniences, built in traditional stone architecture. All electric and fully equipped to accommodate six people. Full central heating. Situated amongst the Rhinog Mountains and with a view of the sea, it enjoys splendid scenery and is ideally placed for walking, fishing and bird watching. Beautiful beaches within easy reach. Places of historic interest include Harlech Castle, slate mines and miniature railway — just some of the attractions of this picturesque area. SAE for terms.

LLANBEDR. Mrs L. Howie, Gwyn Fryn Farm, Llanbedr LL45 2NY (01341 23381). Stone built farm cottages set in 20 peaceful acres of beautiful scenery half a mile outside the village of Llanbedr. Our three bedroomed cottage has one double bedroom en suite and two twin rooms plus cot. The other cottage has a double bedroom. Both properties have oak beams, are warm, comfortable and of a high standard. Fully equipped fitted kitchens with microwaves and washing machines; colour TV, heating; parking. Children will love the animals — friendly ponies, goat, hens and ducks. Bed and Breakfast is also available in the farmhouse. Rooms with en suite facilities. Warm and welcoming.

LLANBEDR. Mrs O. Evans, Werngron Farm, Llanbedr, Merioneth LL45 2PF (Llanbedr [0134-123] 274). Pleasant bungalow on working farm, set in own grounds and enjoying open views of unspoilt countryside. Llanbedr two miles, Harlech three, Barmouth 10. Good touring centre for north and mid Wales; within easy reach of sandy beaches, golf course, indoor swimming pool, pony trekking, freshwater coarse fishing, sea fishing, boat trips and lovely country and mountain walks. Sleeps six, plus cot, in three bedrooms — double, twin and bunks — all with own washbasins. Sittingroom with colour TV; diningroom; well equipped all electric fitted kitchen; spacious sun lounge; bathroom/shower. Fitted carpets throughout, electric fires, oil central heating. Bed linen provided. Open all year. Terms from £140 to £175 per week.

LLANBEDR. Mrs G.P. Jones, Alltgoch, Llanbedr LL45 2NA (01341 241229). Sleeps 5 adults plus cot. Sheep farm situated two miles from Llanbedr village. Llanbedr is on the A496 between BARMOUTH and HARLECH. The house faces the Lleyn Peninsula in a quiet position with garden and plenty of parking space. Ideally situated for walking the Rhinog range, and paths to woodlands and moorlands for nature lovers. Good trout fishing and private lake. Three miles from the beach. The house sleeps five persons with modern conveniences including microwave, new kitchen units, large lounge with colour TV, central heating. Bed linen extra; cot and high chair available. Terms from £95 to £225 per week.

MACHYNLLETH. Tyhymaes, Dinas Mawddwy, Machynlleth. Holiday cottage in Cywarch Valley at the foot of Aran Fawddwy, near Cader Idris, not far from Aberystwyth and Barmouth. Ideal for walking, peaceful and safe for children to play. Centrally situated for Snowdonia National Park. Well behaved house-trained dogs are welcome. Plenty of space for car parking. Everything supplied except linen and coal for fire. Electricity for light, cooking and hot water. Cottage sleeps six people comfortably. Send SAE for prompt reply with full details: **Mrs Betty Humphreys, Pencae, Dinas Mawddwy, Machynlieth SY20 9JG (01650 531427).**

CHOOSE FROM 200 SEASIDE & MOUNTAIN COTTAGES etc.

in superb locations in and around the beautiful Snowdonia National Park. Available all year round. Sleep 1 to 14 persons from as little as £95 per cottage per week in the low Season.

Central Reservations: SNOWDONIA TOURIST SERVICES, PORTHMADOG, GWYNEDD, LL49 9PG. Telephone 01766 513829 or 513837 or 512660.

Please send me your FREE brochure

Name .... **Address** ....

.... **Postcode** ....

PORTHMADOG (Snowdonia). Felin Parc Cottages. Discover this idyllic 17th century riverside millhouse and charming wool manager's cottage in superb waterfall valley between Porthmadog and Beddgelert. Mill with large character beamed livingroom, period furnishings, open fire, central heating, colour TV. Luxury kitchen, modernised bathroom/cloakroom. Sleeps eight/10 in four bedrooms and overflow ping-pong annexe. Secluded terraces (barbecue/floodlighting) adjoin Mill pool and falls. Cottage sleeping four/six in two bedrooms, and self-contained gable annexe with similar facilities, is delightfully situated overlooking ancient fording bridge. Superb local scenery with Snowdon, Portmeirion, Ffestiniog Railway all nearby. Terms £150 to £500 weekly. Brochure, photographs:- **Williams-Ellis, 4 Sylvan Road, London SE19 2RX (0181-653 3118).**

PORTHMADOG. "Alderley", Borth-y-Gest, Porthmadog LL49 9TP (Porthmadog [01766] 512118). "Alderley" is situated on the shore of the beautiful Glaslyn Estuary with superb mountain views. There are good, sandy beaches in small coves a short distance away. There are many other resorts and excursions in the area as well as many beautiful walks. The ground floor flat comprises two twin bedded rooms, bathroom with WC and washbasin. Modern kitchen with electric cooker and stainless steel sink and fridge. The lounge/diningroom with TV faces the harbour and estuary. There is also a twin bedded room on the first floor available if required, at a small extra charge. Children over five welcome. There is a village shop selling groceries, newspapers etc., also post office, and in Porthmadog (about one mile away) there are usual shops and supermarkets for other items not available in the village. Linen not supplied. Sorry, no pets. SAE for brochure. WTB Approved, two Dragons.

PORTHMADOG. Mrs A.E. Pugh, Farmyard Cottage, Tremadog, Porthmadog LL49 9PP (Porthmadog [01766] 512338). Working farm, join in. Sleeps 4 adults plus cot. Farmyard Cottage, which adjoins farmhouse, is situated on a working farm one mile from the village of Tremadog. Black Rock Sands are only three miles away and Snowdonia is within easy reach. The farm is an deal centre for railway enthusiasts, rock climbers and walkers. The cottage itself has two bedrooms: one double, one double and single beds (cot and high chair available); bathroom; fully equipped kitchen; sittingroom with colour TV. Electrically heated, 50p coin meter. Ample parking space. Children welcome. Sorry, no pets. Terms from £75 to £175, with Short Breaks offered during off-peak season. WTB Verified.

PWLLHELI. Mrs M. Adams, Cae'r Ferch Uchaf, Pencaenewydd, Pwllheli LL53 6DJ (01766 810660). Cedarwood Chalet on a secluded working 24 acre smallholding; consists of three bedrooms, all with fitted wardrobes; large lounge with colour TV; luxury shower room with WC, additional WC in boiler room; fully fitted kitchen/diner. The chalet is double glazed and centrally heated enabling us to open all year. The area is superb for walking and photography, etc, particularly in early spring or late autumn. We are also central for all beaches and just a few miles from Snowdon. Charges are from £135 to £210 according to season. Dogs by arrangement. Please write or ring for details.

PWLLHELI. Mrs C.A. Jones, Rhedyn, Mynytho, Pwllheli LL53 7PS (Llanbedrog [01758] 740669). Working farm, join in. Sleeps 6. Rhedyn is a small dairy farm overlooking the beautiful Nanhoran Valley, and the farm cottage, accommodating six people, is offered for hire between April and November. It is two miles from Llanbedrog and Abersoch, both noted for their safe bathing. Children will enjoy watching the animals, and are made especially welcome. The house has two double bedrooms and one twin with cot available. Bathroom and toilet; combined sitting/diningroom with TV; kitchen with immersion heater, washing machine, microwave oven. Calor gas stove and fridge. Linen supplied. Pets permitted. One mile from shops and two from the sea. Car essential, ample parking. SAE, for further details and terms.

TALSARNAU. Mrs A.M. Wells, Yr-Ogof, Ynys, Talsarnau LL47 6TL (Harlech [01766] 780058). Sleeps 4/5. This comfortable, old fashioned cottage is three miles from Harlech and just five minutes' walk to Ynys Beach. Convenient for shops. Lovely mountain views from cottage windows. Swimming pool at Harlech. Very attractive area with lovely walks. Also fishing nearby. All modern conveniences. Accommodation to sleep four/five persons in double and twin-bedded rooms; bathroom, toilet, also downstairs toilet; lounge with oak beams and colour TV; kitchen/diner with electric cooker, microwave, fridge etc. Everything supplied except linen. Extra charge for electricity used. Economy 7 central heating. Parking. Guaranteed clean home from home. Vacant May to September. Lower charges May to June. SAE, please for terms and further details or phone.

TAL-Y-BONT. "Saronfa", Tal-y-Bont, Near Conwy. Sleeps 4. This stone built cottage on the edge of the National Park is comfortably furnished and modernised yet retaining old world charm. Inglenook fireplace; log or electric fire, storage heaters. Two bedrooms (one double, one twin), kitchen, lounge, bathroom with shower. Secluded rear garden with views of mountains. Parking for two cars. Situated in the beautiful Conwy Valley it provides an ideal base for walking or touring the National Park. Short distance from coastal resorts, the historic town of Conwy, Roman spa, Woollen Mill, and the famous Bodnant Gardens. Shop, inn and country restaurant within walking distance. Weekly terms from £95 to £195. Pets taken. Winter Breaks £14 per night including logs. **Mrs M.C. Waddingham, "Cefn", Tyn-y-Groes, Conwy LL32 8TA (01492 650233).**

TYWYN. Coastal House, 35 Corbett Close, Tywyn. Lovely three bedroomed coastal house with garage, very close to the sea with easy access to sandy beach. Accommodation in one double, one bunk-bedded and one single rooms, blankets provided. Equipped as if it were your own home — new furnishings, washing machine, cooker, microwave, crockery, colour TV and stereo. Large bathroom with additional built-in shower room. Sole use of garden front and rear, patio set provided. Ten minutes' walk from Tywyn centre, within walking distance of Tal-y-Llyn Steam Railway, two minutes from pub with excellent meals, and eight doors from shop selling home-baked bread, pies, pasties etc. Very good walks in this beautiful area close to Snowdonia National Park. Pets are most welcome free of charge. Terms from £130 to £199 weekly. Further details from **Mr and Mrs Ian Weston, 18 Elizabeth Road, Basingstoke, Hampshire RG22 6AX (01256 52364).**

PUBLISHER'S NOTE

While every effort is made to ensure accuracy, we regret that FHG Publications cannot accept responsibility for errors, omissions or misrepresentation in our entries or any consequences thereof. Prices in particular should be checked because we go to press early. We will follow up complaints but cannot act as arbiters or agents for either party.

WALES

POWYS

BRECON. Lower Penllanafal, Llangorse, Near Brecon. Sleeps 6 plus cot. Lower Penllanafal is a superbly furnished cottage situated in beautiful countryside in National Park with views of Brecon Beacons. 50 yards off the road with its own private tarmac road leading up to a large yard by cottage for parking. It has its own garden with lawn and orchard with stream. Sleeps six in two bedrooms; upstairs bathroom with toilet; comfortable lounge with easy chairs and colour TV; dining room with large table; fully equipped kitchen with electric cooker, fridge freezer. Heating by storage heaters, electric fires, open fires (logs provided). Wales Tourist Board Grade 3. SAE for brochure. **Mrs S. Hamer, Middle-Penllanafal, Llangorse, Brecon LD3 7UN (01874 84307).**

BRECON. Wern-y-marchog, Cantref, Brecon. WTB Grade 4. The perfect setting for a relaxing peaceful holiday situated amongst spectacular scenery in the Brecon Beacons. Bungalow accommodation comprises well equipped fitted kitchen, spacious lounge, shower room, three bedrooms. Storage heaters. Also available, beautiful recently renovated farmhouse sleeping two to seven persons, which is very comfortably furnished and equipped to a high standard with all modern conveniences including colour TV, shower, automatic washing machine, fridge/freezer, dishwasher and microwave. This can be hired as one unit or two individual apartments. Well maintained grounds. Children's play area. Barbecue and garden furniture. Ample parking. Personally supervised to ensure complete comfort and cleanliness. Pets by arrangement. Open all year from £100 to £260 weekly. Short Breaks available. A warm welcome awaits you. Colour brochure on request to: **Mrs Ann Phillips, Tylebrythos Farm, Cantref, Brecon LD3 8LR (01874 86 329).**

BRECON near (Bwlch). Mrs Iris Lloyd, Talybryn, Bwlch, Near Brecon LD3 7LQ (Talybont-on-Usk [0187-487] 278). Sleeps 4. This luxury flat stands in 60 acres of farmland, situated off the A40, looking down on the River Usk. The hills hug the lovely old farmhouse, secluded and "away from it all". Available all year and always warm and comfortable with central heating. This is an area of natural loveliness with green meadows and lush pastures. Nature excels herself at every season here. There is accommodation for four in one double bedroom and one twin bedroom; bathroom and toilet; large sittingroom, colour TV; diningroom; fully fitted all-electric kitchen with all utensils etc.; sink unit and fridge. No meters. Regret no pets. Shops one mile, the beautiful Gower coast 38 miles. Car not essential (on bus route), though plenty of parking space. A warm welcome awaits you here and brochure gladly sent on request with SAE, please. Weekly terms from £95 to £200. WTB registered, Farm Holiday Guide Diploma.

See also Colour Display Advertisement **CAERSWS. Mrs Gwyneth Williams, Red House, Trefeglwys, Caersws, Montgomeryshire SY17 5PN (01686 430285).** A highly furnished, self contained part of the farmhouse, situated on a mixed working family farm with panoramic views, unspoilt scenery and the tranquillity of the Trannon valley it makes an ideal, convenient base for Llanidloes (six miles) and Clywedog Reservoir, Powys Castle and the coast which are all close at hand. A fully equipped kitchen with washing machine, a refurbished bathroom and tea served on arrival all ensure guests' comfort, which is a priority; other facilities include log fire, bed linen, garden furniture and ample parking. Lots of wildlife. So come to Red House and enjoy a refreshing change. Open all year. SAE for brochure. WTB 4 Dragons Award. OS Map Ref SN992 899.

CRICKHOWELL. Mrs B. Broyd, Penrhiw Farm, Llangenny, Crickhowell NP8 1HD (Crickhowell [01873] 810130). Teg Fan is a modern bungalow situated beside a quiet country lane on the 112-acre farm (beef, sheep, horses), in a beautiful setting at the foot of the Black Mountains in Brecon Beacons National Park. Pony trekking, fishing, hang gliding, lovely walks and 10 acres of woodland to hand. Homely village pub serving meals, half a mile away. Crickhowell (one and a half miles) has good shops and the busy market town of Abergavenny is six miles; Brecon 16 miles. Old industrial sites, castles, abbeys, caves to visit. Very good eating places nearby. The bungalow affords every comfort with fitted carpets throughout, colour TV, large livingroom with superb views and three bedrooms (one double, two twin) sleeping six people. Accommodation all on one level so suitable for partially disabled guests, though not wheelchairs. Gas central heating, immersion heater, electric fires; fully fitted kitchen and bathroom. Pleasant garden. Milk delivered. Well controlled pets allowed. Bargain Breaks Spring/Autumn. Terms from £120 to £220.

LLANDINAM. Cwm y Gath. Sleeps 4. Enjoy a welcome on the hillside at the cosy shepherd's cottage which is situated central to three villages all within three miles. Overlooking the beef and sheep farm of Trewythen in the renowned Trannon Valley, it offers peace and tranquillity with magnificent views, an ideal spot for those who enjoy outdoor activities and an abundance of wildlife. The cottage has a wealth of oak beams and inglenook fireplace with woodburner, its unique feature being the different floor levels. Cwm y Gath sleeps four in one twin and one double bedroom, both with washbasins. Bed linen provided. Well equipped kitchen with electric cooker, fridge, washing machine, iron, vacuum cleaner. Children and pets welcome. Weekly rates from £80 to £250. WTB Approved. **Miss A. Davies, Trewythen, Llandinam SY17 5BQ (Tel and Fax: 01686 688444).**

LLANDRINDOD WELLS. Mr and Mrs M.H. Kendrick, Cwmbirth Farm, Penybont, Llandrindod Wells LD1 5SR (01597 822391). Delightful modern bungalow built of red brick with green tiled roof, situated on 600 acre hill farm rearing sheep and cattle. Comprises lounge-cum-dining room, three double bedrooms, two with twin beds; bathroom; kitchen with electric cooker, fridge, stainless steel sink, etc. Storage heaters. No linen supplied. Children welcome. Car essential, parking. Three miles from shops and public transport. One and a half miles of fishing. Three miles from old spa town of Llandrindod Wells with all amenities, golf, lake fishing, two trout pools, bowling, tennis, pony rides, etc. Seaside Aberystwyth 40 miles. Available all year round except Christmas. Terms from £95 weekly.

LLANRHAEADR-YM-MOCHNANT. Aber-Rhaeadr Cottages, Llanrhaeadr-Ym-Mochnant. Two riverside cottages in the heart of the Welsh Uplands (renowned for mountain views, lakes, forests and waterfalls) having traditional Welsh cottage charm with pointed riverstone walls, each with beamed inglenook fireplace, open beam ceiling, winding staircase, low doors and sun-trap patio overlooking the riverside lawn and hills to the south. Superbly furnished, carpeted and equipped, including cot, TV, radio, fridge, washing machine, spin-dryer, airing cupboards etc. (Also sandpit under the damson tree in the riverside garden.) Local attractions include Pistyll Rhaeadr Waterfall, Lake Vyrnwy, Little Trains of Wales, pony trekking, Powys Castle, local markets and character pubs. Associate Members of the Welsh Tourist Board and complying with their standards. Just write for illustrated brochure and terms to **Mr Mark Lucas, 69 Grasmere Avenue, Whitton, Twickenham, Middlesex TW3 2JG (0181-898 8728).**

LLANSANTFFRAID-YM-MECHAIN. Tanybryn, Deytheur, Llansantffraid-ym-Mechain. Tanybryn is a quality, detached cottage maintained throughout to a high standard, personally supervised by Mrs Mary Jones and family who have extended warm hospitality to discerning guests for over 30 years. Situated in its own enclosed grounds of lawns and gardens in peaceful countryside with glorious views. Ideal for a relaxing holiday, and an ideal base for exploring many interesting and magical areas of Wales. One and a quarter miles from nearest village, close to Powis and Chirk Castles, Pistyll Rhayader, Lakes Vyrnwy and Bala, also the medieval town of Shrewsbury. Close to Offa's Dyke. Three bedrooms, bathroom with bath and shower, attractive lounge with open fire and colour TV; spacious kitchen/diner with cooker, microwave, fridge/freezer, automatic washing machine, etc. All rooms have electric heaters. AA QQQ Recommended. SAE appreciated for full details and terms to **Mrs M.E. Jones, Glanvyrnwy Farm, Llansantffraid-ym-Mechain SY22 6SU (Llansantffraid [01691] 828258).**

WALES

MACHYNLLETH. Penygraean, Llanymawddwy, Machynlleth. Sleeps 6 plus cot. Situated on the upper part of the Dovey Valley, five miles from the Montgomeryshire Border, this cottage is to let from March to November. Surrounded by farms and mountains, it is a haven for walkers and climbers. Sleeps six in three double bedrooms; cot; lounge with black and white TV, diningroom; bathroom, toilet; kitchen with electric cooker, fridge, kettle, immerser, all utensils and hot and cold water. Storage heaters extra. Fully equipped except linen. Pets allowed if under control. Car essential, parking. Fishing by permit. Excellent for touring North and South Wales. Dolgellau 15 miles, Bala Lake 10 miles. Terms from £85 to £115 per week. SAE please to **Mrs Catherine Roberts, Cerdinn, Llanymawddwy, Near Machynlleth SY20 9AJ (01650 531234).**

NEWTOWN. Mrs D. Pryce, Aberbechan Farm, Newtown SY16 3BJ (01686 630675). Working farm, join in. Sleeps 10. This part of quaint Tudor farmhouse with its lovely oak beams is situated in picturesque countryside on a mixed farm with trout fishing and shooting in season. Newtown three miles, Welshpool, Powis Castle and Llanfair Light Railway, 14 miles; 45 miles to coast. The sleeping accommodation is for 10 people in four double and two single bedrooms, also cot. Two bathrooms, two toilets. Sitting/diningroom with colour TV. Fully fitted kitchen with fridge, electric cooker, washing machine and dishwasher. Log fires and off-peak heaters. Electricity on meter. Large lawn with swing. Everything supplied for visitors' comfort. Linen available for overseas guests at extra cost. Car essential to obtain the best from the holiday. Farm produce available in season. Village shop one and a half miles away. Open all year. SAE please.

See also Colour Display Advertisement **TALGARTH. Mrs Bronwen Prosser, Upper Genfford Farm Guest House, Talgarth, Brecon LD7 0EN (01874 711360).** AA QQQ Recommended. Situated in the Brecon Beacons National Park, two cosy single storey farm cottages. The cottages accommodate five/six people in two bedrooms including one family room. Both are beautifully furnished with fitted carpets throughout. Oak beamed lounges, log fires, Calor gas heaters, central heating, colour TV. Terms from £90 to £150. The BED AND BREAKFAST COTTAGE has two en-suite bedrooms with tea-making facilities, and one room also has a shower. From £14.

TALGARTH. Genffordd Cottage, Talgarth. Working farm, join in. Sleeps 9. Wales Tourist Board Grade 3. Set in the Brecon Beacons National Park, the cottage is ideal for hill walkers and ramblers. Pony trekking, sailing, canoeing, boating and gliding nearby. The cottage is beautifully furnished with fitted carpets throughout and has double glazing and central heating. Very large lounge with oak beams, open log fires and colour TV. Modern fitted kitchen/diner, fully equipped including microwave; bathroom, toilet; three double bedrooms, plus cot (sleeps nine). Linen supplied by request. Children welcome. Pets allowed. Car essential, ample parking. Shop two miles. Available all year. Suitable for disabled guests. Weekly terms from approximately £120 to £285 per week. Short Breaks out of season available. SAE, please, to **Mrs Susan Prosser, Genffordd Farm, Talgarth LD3 0EN (01874 711014).**

CARAVAN AND CAMPING HOLIDAYS

CLWYD

CARAVANS

ABERGELE. Mr and Mrs T.P. Williams, Pen Isaf Caravan Park, Llangernyw, Abergele LL22 8RN (01745 860276). This small caravan site in beautiful unspoilt countryside is ideal for touring North Wales and is situated 10 miles from the coast and 12 miles from Betws-y-Coed. The eight-berth caravans are fully equipped except for linen and towels and have showers, flush toilet, hot and cold water, Calor gas cooker, electric light and fridge. Fresh eggs and milk can be obtained from the farm on which this 20 caravan site is situated. Children especially will enjoy a holiday here, there being ample space and facilities for fishing and pony riding. Pets are allowed but must be kept under control. Open March to October. Terms on application with SAE, please.

DYFED

CARAVANS

ABERPORTH. Mrs C. Jones, Manorafon, Sarnau, Llandyssul SA44 6QH (Aberporth [01239] 810564). Sleeps 6. Quiet, peaceful site of 11 caravans, fully equipped except linen, all six-berth with end bedrooms. All essential facilities provided. Bathroom facilities with hot water on tap in each van; Calor gas cooker, electric lighting and heating. Toilets and washbasins, showers, shaving points and electric clothes dryer on site. Calor and camping gaz sold. Available Easter to October. Children welcome. Dogs must be kept on lead. Dairy produce available. Only half a mile from the pleasant Penbryn beach and nine miles from the market towns of Cardigan and Newcastle Emlyn. One and a half acres for campers and tourers. SAE for further particulars.

ABERYSTWYTH. Mrs Anne Bunton, Cwmergyr Farm, Ponterwyd, Aberystwyth SY23 3LB (01970 890301). This luxury six-berth caravan is sited in its own enclosure on a 250-acre sheep farm in the beautiful Cambrian Mountains, 16 miles east of Aberystwyth, off the A44. Accommodation consists of two bedrooms, bathroom (flush toilet, vanity unit and shower); kitchen (fridge and gas cooker); spacious lounge with colour TV and spectacular views; gas fire and hot and cold water throughout. Linen not supplied. No pets allowed. Car essential with ample parking. Within 15 mile radius there are sandy beaches, fishing, golf, pony trekking, steam railway, scenic drives and walks. An ideal location to explore mid-Wales. A stream and the farm animals await the children. Open 1st April to 31st October. Terms £100–£125 per week (all gas and electricity included).

HAVERFORDWEST. Scamford Caravan Park, Keeston, Haverfordwest SA62 6HN (01437 710304).

✓ ✓ ✓ ✓ ✓ 25 Dragon Award luxury holiday caravans on peaceful park in attractive countryside, near Pembrokeshire Coastal Path and many lovely beaches. Every caravan has all mains services, fridge, gas fire, shower and colour TV. Also five touring pitches with electric hook-ups, free hot showers. Excellent children's playground — swings, sand pit, climbing frame and trampoline. Dog welcome. Some caravans "dog-free" for the sake of children with allergies. Telephone. Launderette, with ironing facilities. Plenty to do in the area — castle, farm parks, craft shops, boat trips, island bird sanctuaries, surfing, golfing, riding, etc., or spend a day at Oakwood Leisure Park. Weekly from £90. Colour brochure from resident owners **Jean and Maurice Gould.**

HAVERFORDWEST near. Charles and Joy Spiers, West Lambston, Portfield Gate, Haverfordwest SA62 3LG (Camrose [01437] 710038). Well equipped six-berth caravan in half acre of well mown paddock. Two end bedrooms (one double, the other with bunks); immersion heater for kitchen and bathroom — yes, it does have a bath and flush toilet! Gas cooker, gas fire, colour TV. Bed linen, beach, bath, hand and tea towels provided. Peace and quiet on non-working farm. Beach three miles. Delightful walks (maps provided). Children welcome, pets by arrangement. Electricity by meter. Prices £80 to £220 inclusive per week.

TENBY. Mrs J.N. Frazer, Highlands Farm, Manorbier-Newton, Tenby SA70 8PX (Manorbier [01834] 871446). A spacious six-berth caravan situated in a quiet three-acre meadow. The caravan is fully serviced with electric lighting and TV, also gas cooker and room heater. There are two separate end bedrooms, fully fitted shower room, kitchen/diner and a lounge with panoramic views. The caravan is sited a couple of hundred yards from the main road providing a peaceful countryside setting ideal for children or a well behaved pet. A car is essential. Shopping facilities can be found in nearby Tenby or Pembroke. Please write or phone for details.

TENBY/SAUNDERSFOOT. Mr W.H. Davies, Masterland Farm Touring Caravan and Tent Park, Broadmoor, Kilgetty SA68 0RH (Saundersfoot [01834] 813298). ✓ ✓ ✓ ✓ "Wales in Bloom" award. Tourist Board registered. Masterland is a perfect spot for a "get away from it all" summer holiday, approximately two miles from Saundersfoot and four miles from Tenby. Both resorts have beautiful beaches. It makes an ideal centre for touring Pembrokeshire and the area's many places of historic interest. It is a small, friendly site for ten touring caravans and ten tents on a private working farm where visitors are made welcome. The proprietor is in attendance to ensure a carefree and enjoyable holiday. Children are welcome and pets are permitted if kept under control. All amenities. Shop on site. Fresh milk daily. Booking essential for July and August. Terms from £4 to £9.50 per night approximately. SAE, please. Also two 6-berth caravans available.

GWYNEDD

CARAVANS

BALA. Mrs S.E. Edwards, Bryn Melyn, Rhyduchaf, Bala LL23 7PG (01678 520376). Sleeps 6. One six-berth caravan available on Bryn Melyn, a 56 acre mixed farm in the village of Rhyduchaf, two miles from Bala situated in beautiful countryside. The caravan has a bathroom, inside flush toilet, hot and cold water, electric light, gas cooker, gas heater, fridge, colour TV. Fully equipped with blankets, etc. Children welcome. Sorry, no pets allowed. Open from April to September. Electricity on slot meter (10p). SAE please for further details.

CRICCIETH. Mrs Margaret Roberts, Ynys-Wen, Llangybi, Pwllheli LL53 6TB (01766 810294). One only spacious six-berth caravan for hire on mixed working farm situated in its own private garden with beautiful views of Snowdonia and its majestic scenery. The caravan has a large double bedroom with fitted wardrobes and separate bedroom with twin bunks. All bedding and bed linen is supplied. Large lounge area has a convertible bed settee. Separate bathroom with shower, toilet and washbasin. The Lleyn Peninsula, where we are situated, has many different beaches and coves. River and sea fishing, golf, horse riding, walking, etc., all close by. Rent includes electricity and gas. Terms from £80 per week. Further details sent on receipt of SAE.

PORTHMADOG. Mrs E.M. Pritchard, Llys, Derwin Bach, Garn Dolbenmaen, Porthmadog LL51 9LX (01766 530616). Modern Lynton six-berth caravan on private site on an 80 acre farm. Three separate bedrooms, diningroom, lounge area, inside flush toilet. Equipped with electric lights and points; gas fire and cooker; good sized fridge; colour TV and cooking utensils. Children and pets welcome. Good shops in nearby towns, trout and salmon fishing on own river. Within easy reach of numerous beaches and plenty of scenic walks on the western perimeter of Snowdonia National Park. Rates from £60 weekly inclusive of gas used. SAE for further details.

PORTHMADOG. Mrs E.A.J. Williams, Tyddyn Deucwm Isaf, Penmorfa, Porthmadog LL49 9SD (01766 513683). Luxurious six-berth leisure home, between Porthmadog and Criccieth. Only one on quiet working farm in Snowdonia National Park. Magnificent views of Cardigan Bay from the lounge, also Porthmadog Estuary and Criccieth Castle. Sunny position. Black Rock Sands (two miles of golden sands) approximately 10 minutes away; three minutes from shops; five minutes from Ffestiniog Narrow Gauge Railway at Porthmadog. Fishing and riding nearby. Walking and climbing on farm (famous rocks shelter behind the farm). Three separate bedrooms; electricity and gas; fridge, hot and cold water, shower and toilet; colour TV. Pets by arrangement. Meets Wales Tourist Board standard. SAE or telephone.

ACTIVITY HOLIDAYS

DYFED, MARTINS HAVEN/MARLOES. Mrs Christina Chetwynd, East Hook Farm, Marloes, Haverfordwest SA62 3BJ (01646 636291). BOARD: GENERAL. Farm on Pembrokeshire Coast Path offering Bed and Breakfast, camping, caravans, horse and pony riding, cycle hire, sea fishing, bird watching and walking. Convenient for boat trips to Skomer and Skokholm Islands and next to Marloes Mere Nature Reserve. 110 acres of natural unspoilt beauty. Bedrooms with washbasins, TVs and tea/coffee making facilities. Reception room on site. Collection service offered from Haverfordwest. Also transport to Martins Haven for boat trips, diving and Marine Nature Reserve. Bed and Breakfast from £10 to £13 per person per night. Children and pets welcome.

GWYNEDD, CRICCIETH. Betws-Bach & Rhos-Dhu, Ynys, Criccieth LL52 0PB (Tel & Fax: 01758 720047; 0766 810295). Wales Tourist Board Grade 5.

SELF CATERING: FISHING/SHOOTING. A truly romantic, memorable and special place to stay and relax in comfort. Old World farmhouse and period country cottage. Situated just off the B4411 road in tranquil surroundings. Equipped to Wales Tourist Board Grade 5 standard with washing/drying machines, dishwashers, microwaves, freezers, colour TV, old oak beams, inglenook with log fires, full central heating. Snooker table, pitch 'n' putt; romantic four-poster bed, sauna and jacuzzi. Open all year — Winter Weekends welcomed. Ideal for couples. Sleep two to six plus cot. Own fishing and shooting rights, wonderful walks, peace and quiet with Snowdonia and unspoilt beaches on our doorstep. For friendly personal service please phone, Fax or write to Mrs Anwen Jones.

GWYNEDD, LLANBEDROG. Mrs L.O. Williams, Bodwrog Farm, Llanbedrog, Pwllheli LL53 7RE (01758 740341). SELF CATERING: GENERAL. One well equipped Pemberton Cresta Villa 32 foot six-berth luxury caravan to let, Easter to end of October. The only static on mixed farm with stupendous coastal and mountain views. Sandy beach, one and a half miles. Clean and well-aired, the caravan is fully equipped with shower, washbasin, flush toilet, fridge, colour TV Plenty of clean bedding; cot available (free occasional babysitting). Terms from £80 to £100 per week according to season INCLUDE electricity, gas and pillowcases. Sheets can be hired but are free for FORTNIGHTLY lets. One house-trained pet allowed. Free rough shooting on request for static caravan guests. "Special Breaks" available in April, early May and October. Also campsite with shower and toilet facilities, mains water and superb sea views; no overcrowding. Pub three-quarters of a mile. Family tents £2.50 per night; caravanette £2.50; tourer caravan £2.50 to £3 per night.

COUNTRY INNS

DYFED, LLANDOVERY. The Royal Oak Inn, Rhandirmwyn, Llandovery SA20 0NY (015506 201; Fax: 015506 332 — from June 1995 Tel: 01550 760201 and Fax: 01550 760332). "Free and Easy" can sometimes by synonymous with slapdash and badly run, but one need have no such fears at the Royal Oak. The proprietors here have managed to combine informality with efficiency, and friendliness with courteous good service. Spacious rooms offer comfort as well as attractive decor and most have colour TV and private facilities. The very full menu presented in the restaurant caters for most tastes, and bar snacks are available together with a nice range of local beer. Dinner is from 6pm to 10pm and sleepyheads will be pleased to note that breakfast will be served right up till 9.30 in the morning.

DYFED, TALGARTH. Castle Inn, Pengenffordd, Near Talgarth LD3 0EP (01874 711353). *Commended.* The name "Castle Inn" derives from the ancient fortress of Castle Dinas which was at one time both Iron Age Fort and Norman Castle. It lies a short walk behind the Inn, which is situated in the rural heart of the Black Mountains in the Brecon Beacons National Park. This is an area very popular with those who love the great outdoors, with many activities available. The Inn offers accommodation in prettily decorated bedrooms, all with colour TV and washbasins. In the evenings guests can relax by the log fire, perhaps with a choice from the economically priced menu of home-cooked dishes or from the selection of real ales. Children welcome.

Key to Tourist Board Ratings

The Crown Scheme

(England, Scotland & Wales)

Covering hotels, motels, private hotels, guesthouses, inns, bed & breakfast, farmhouses. Every Crown classified place to stay is inspected annually. *The classification:* Listed then 1-5 Crown indicates the range of facilities and services. Higher quality standards are indicated by the terms APPROVED, COMMENDED, HIGHLY COMMENDED and DELUXE.

The Key Scheme

(also operates in Scotland using a Crown symbol)

Covering self-catering in cottages, bungalows, flats, houseboats, houses, chalets, etc. Every Key classified holiday home is inspected annually. *The classification:* 1-5 Key indicates the range of facilities and equipment. Higher quality standards are indicated by the terms APPROVED, COMMENDED, HIGHLY COMMENDED and DELUXE.

The Q Scheme

(England, Scotland & Wales)

Covering holiday, caravan, chalet and camping parks. Every Q rated park is inspected annually for its quality standards. The more ✓ in the Q – up to 5 – the higher the standard of what is provided.

IRELAND

BOARD ACCOMMODATION

CLARE

QUILTY. Mrs T. Donnellan, "Fionnuaire", Mullagh, Quilty (00 353 65 87179). Working dairy farm in quiet location with sweeping views of scenic countryside and Atlantic Ocean. Fitted leisure room and gym for fitness enthusiasts, well equipped angling room — we offer organised angling holidays. Also available, guided walks, cycle tours (bicycle hire arranged). Guests welcome to participate in farm work. Music in village pubs within walking distance. Families especially welcome. Children catered for — pony rides, play area. Bed and Breakfast per person with en-suite room £15, without en-suite £13.50. Evening Meal £11. Reductions for children sharing with parents. Self catering accommodation also available. Brochure and full tariff on request.

CORK

BANTRY. Mrs Agnes Hegarty, Hillcrest Farm, Ahakista, Durrus, Bantry (00 353 27 67045). Seaside dairy farm. Charming old-style farmhouse, newly renovated, retaining traditional character. Situated in picturesque peaceful setting overlooking harbour and Dunmanus Bay, quarter of a mile from Ahakista village on the Sheep's Head Peninsula. Magnificent sea and mountain scenery; swimming, fishing, boating and five minutes' walk to the sea. Irish pubs and restaurants close by. Bantry 12 miles, Durrus six miles. Ideal centre for touring the Peninsulas of West Cork and Kerry. Signposted in Durrus. Four guest bedrooms, three with bath/shower en suite, one with washbasin; two are family rooms. Ground floor room available. Tea/coffee making faciltiies and electric blankets in all bedrooms. Bathroom; spacious dining room with stone walls; sittingroom with old world fireplace and log fire. Play/games room, antiques, swing, lovely garden with mature trees. Warm hospitality. Fresh farm vegetables and home baking. Babysitting. Irish Tourist Board Approved. Bed and Breakfast from (Ir)£14.50; Dinner (Ir)£12; Evening Meal (Ir)£9. Reductions for one week's stay, 25% reductions for children. Light meals also available. Award Winner of Farmhouse of the Year 1991/2. Also to let, modern seaside bungalow for self catering. Fully equipped and in superb location, from (Ir)£100 to (Ir)£220.

KERRY

KILLARNEY VILLA

This is an elegant purpose-built family-run establishment in a rural setting, adjacent to the Lake District of Killarney and convenient to all holiday amenities. Information booklets and maps available to our guests on arrival. Four-course Evening Dinner (choice of menu) arranged. Guided coach tours depart daily from the premises for the Ring of Kerry/Dingle Peninsula. Jaunting car trips around the Killarney Lakes and through the National Park of 25,000 acres. Pony trekking, hill walking, nature trails, golfing on two 18-hole courses, fishing, bicycles for hire daily – all available locally. There is a wide choice of first class restaurants and good pubs with prices to suit everybody. At night Killarney has established itself as Ireland's top free entertainment centre, with a wide range of lounge bars, singing pubs, traditional music, etc. It's all here waiting for you!

For bookings, contact either P.J. or Rosaleen O'Sullivan, KILLARNEY VILLA, WATERFORD ROAD (N72), KILLARNEY Telephone: 00 353 64 31878 **See also our Colour Display on page 20.**

TRALEE. William and Helen O'Connor, El Rancho Farmhouse and Riding Stables, Ballyard, Tralee (Phone/Fax: 00 353 66 21840). Situated in the Vale of Tralee, viewing the Slieve Mish Mountains, Blennerville Windmill and Tralee Bay, one mile south of Tralee town off Ballyard road. Horse riding available on site to Queen Scotia's Glen, also special one week and three-day post to post trail riding on the magnificent Dingle Peninsula where "Ryan's Daughter" was filmed. Brochure and/or video available on request.

TIPPERARAY

LIMERICK near. Mrs Mary Sheary, "Eagles Nest", Greenhills, Birdhill, Near Limerick (00 353 61 379178). "Eagles Nest" farmhouse is situated one km off the N7 in peaceful surroundings in an area of great scenic beauty. Killaloe (3km) is well known for its water sports and scenery. There are many country pubs within easy reach. Matt the Thrasher situated in the village of Birdhill is well known for its fine food and drink. Good golf and pitch and putt courses nearby. The farm is mainly dairy and also has a Charolais breeding herd. There are many pets on the farm. Guests may wander freely on the farmland. Supervised pony rides for children. Good old-fashioned cooking with ample portions, all freshly prepared with own organic produce used; no microwave cooking. Choice of breakfast menu. Complimentary tea/coffee, scones and home made jam on arrival. Bed and Breakfast £10.50; Evening Dinner £10; Evening Meal £6. 50% reduction for children. Open all year.

SELF-CATERING HOLIDAYS

CORK

IRELAND

BANTRY. Mrs Agnes Hegarty, Ahakista, Durrus, Bantry (00 353 27 67045). Working farm. Sleeps 6 adults; 2 children. Charming seaside bungalow overlooking harbour and Dunmanus Bay in the "Sheep's Head" Peninsula. Magnificent scenery. Excellent bathing, fishing, boating and mountain climbing within 10 minutes' walk. Shops, Irish pubs and restaurants locally. Bantry 12 miles. Durrus six miles, Kilcrochane three miles. Ideal centre for touring West Cork and Kerry. Accommodation comprises three bedrooms (two double and one twin), all with washbasins; bathroom, shower room; large lounge with studio couch, open fireplace and colour TV; spacious fitted kitchen cum diningroom. Solid fuel cooker, electric cooker, fridge, kettle, toaster, fire, etc. Fully equipped for six people. Central heating. Bed linen provided Donkey on farm. Car park and lovely garden. Irish Tourist Board Approved. Terms: April and May IR£140 per week; June and September IR£170 per week; July and August IR£220 per week; rest of the year IR£90 per week. Also available Bed and Breakfast in family farmhouse plus Evening Meals. Superb hospitality, en-suite rooms. Award Winner of Farmhouse of Year 1991/92.

BANTRY. Mrs Sheila O'Shea, Ard-na-Greine, Adrigole, Bantry (00 353 27 60018). Ard-na-Greine is a furnished holiday house to let on private ground including a field suitable as children's playground. Situated in the Beara Peninsula overlooking Bantry Bay and within 200 yards of the shore of the peaceful sea inlet of Adrigole Harbour. Adrigole is adjacent to the Healy Pass on the Ring of Beara and is an ideal centre for touring; it is within easy reach of Gougane Barra, Glengarriff, the Lakes of Killarney, Ring of Kerry and the fishing town of Castletownbere. Adrigole lies at the foot of Hungry Hill (highest peak in the Caha Mountains) with their fishing lakes, waterfall and numerous walks. Accommodation consists of five bedrooms, bathroom with electric shower, sittingroom with colour TV, dining room, modern kitchen/breakfast room with electric cooker, fridge, automatic washing machine. Open fire, electric fires and off peak storage heating. Meter read. Linen not supplied. Terms from £150 to £200. Reply coupon please.

CASTLETOWNBERE. Mrs Margaret O'Dwyer, Toormore Bungalow, Toormore, Castletownbere (00 353 27 70598). Luxury double glazed bungalow in West Cork overlooking the fishing port of Castletownbere, Bere Island and Bantry Bay. Situated amongst peaceful surroundings with superb views of sea and mountains. One mile from town and sea. Ideal base for touring around the scenic Ring of Beara, Ring of Kerry, Killarney, Blarney, Glengarriff, etc. Golf, fishing, boating, sailing, swimming, cycling, horse riding, mountain climbing, water sports and shooting available locally. Four double rooms, one room with double and single beds; sittingroom with open fire, living room with colour TV, bed settee; bathroom with shower; oak kitchen with all modern conveniences. Cot, high chair and baby-sitting available. Oil and solid fuel central heating. Weekly from £150 to £250. Telephone or write for brochure. International Reply coupon please.

KERRY

ANNASCAUL. Mrs M. Sayers, Kilmurry Farm, Minard Castle, Annascaul (066 57173; from UK 00 353 6657173). Are you looking for a nice, peaceful holiday? All year round self catering accommodation is offered in the heart of Dingle Peninsula. One property accommodates six people (three double beds), the other sleeps four people (two double and one single beds). Fully equipped and carpeted. Bathroom, sittingroom, diningroom, kitchen with electric cooker, fridge, immersion heater. Linen at extra charge. Ideally situated, you can enjoy your meals looking out over Dingle Bay; also magnificent views of mountains all round. Beach within walking distance (safe for children). Minard Castle (famous for its part in "Ryan's Daughter"), and local pub and shops add enjoyment to your holiday. Car essential, parking. Suitable for disabled visitors. Weekly terms: March-April £100; May £120; June £150; July-August £200; September £120; pets £5. Rest of the year £80 per week. Electricity extra. Farmhouse also available, sleeps eight. International Reply coupon please.

KILLARNEY. Mrs Mary Horgan, Eden Villa Farm, Loreto Road, Killarney (064 31138; from UK 00 353 64 31138). Lovely old country house in extensive gardens overlooking the lakes, mountains and town. Semi-detached from owners' residence. National Park with forest walks, mountain climbing, pony trekking, boating, fishing nearby. Accommodation comprises one double room and one twin-bedded room and bathroom upstairs; downstairs modern kitchen, sittingroom-cum-dining area with open fire and TV. Hallway and washroom with shower and toilet and washing machine. Storage heaters thoughout. Linen and cot supplied. Electricity extra. Moderate terms. Town centre three miles, shop one mile.

See also Colour Display Advertisement **KILLARNEY. Killarney Lakeland Cottages, Muckross, Killarney (00 353 6431538; Fax: 00 353 6434113).** Superb complex of traditional and modern cottages situated on O'Shea's Farm on 12 acres of landscaped parkland on the edge of the Killarney National Park, providing an ideal base for touring in South-West Ireland. Two, three and four bedroomed cottages, (sleep 4/8), colour/multi-channel TV, direct-dial telephone, dishwasher, laundry service, full central heating. Brochure available.

LAURAGH. Mrs M. Moriarty, Creveen Lodge, Healy Pass Road, Lauragh (064 83131; from UK 00 353 64 83131) Sleeps 6/8. Attractive two-storey dormer-style farmhouse attached to proprietors' residence, 200 yards from roadside, with magnificent views of sea and country-side. The 80-acre mixed farm is conveniently situated for fishing, mountain climbing, Derreen Gardens, shops and old Irish pub: 16 miles south of Kenmare. Accommodation for five/six persons in three double and one twin-bedded rooms, all with washbasins; cot. Sittingroom with large stone fire-place, TV; separate diningroom. Kitchen has gas and solid fuel cooker; solid fuel central heating and storage heating; washing machine and dryer. Everything supplied including linen. Solid fuel on sale. Children and pets welcome; high chair, and babysitting arranged. Car essential — parking. Available all year. April, May, June and September £130 to £140 per week; July and August £175 per week; rest of the year by arrangement. Gas and electricity extra. Irish Tourist Board Approved.

PUBLISHER'S NOTE

While every effort is made to ensure accuracy, we regret that FHG Publications cannot accept responsibility for errors, omissions or mis-representation in our entries or any consequences thereof. Prices in particular should be checked because we go to press early. We will follow up complaints but cannot act as arbiters or agents for either party.

TRALEE. Mrs Mary O'Connor, The Abbey Tavern, Abbeydorney, Tralee (066 35145 or (from Britain) 00 353 6635145). Self catering flats, with optional Evening Meal, clean and reasonably priced, available from March to December, at this country village inn five miles from Tralee and five miles from Banna Beach; also within easy reach of Ballyheigue, Killarney, Dingle, Ring of Kerry. The flats have shower, toilet, livingroom/kitchenette with electric cooker, fridge, heater, etc. Linen and towels supplied. Cot on request. Also four bedroomed house available. Car essential, parking. Overnight stops welcome. Meals served all day. Also Bed and Breakfast and partial Board. Terms on request.

TRALEE. Mr G. Doyle, 46 Cloondara, Oakpark, Tralee (066 26261). Modern two-storey detached house in quiet residential area of Tralee town, County Kerry. Within walking distance of town, ideally located for golfing, fishing, boating, mountain walks and touring the Ring of Kerry, Killarney 20 miles and Dingle 25 miles away. Also convenient for beautiful beaches. Ideal base from which to explore Kerry's awe-inspiring landscape. The house has five bedrooms sleeping up to 10 people, one room en suite. Bed linen supplied. Weekly rate (Saturday to Saturday) £280. Bord Failte (Irish Tourist Board) Approved.

CARAVAN AND CAMPING HOLIDAYS

IRELAND

KERRY

See also Colour Display Advertisement

KILLORGLIN. West's Holiday Park, Killarney Road, Killorglin (066 61240; from UK 00 353 66 61240). Caravan holiday homes to hire. Situated on the Killorglin/Killarney road, one mile from Killorglin on Ring of Kerry with Ireland's highest mountain in background, on the banks of River Laune renowned for trout and salmon fishing. On park facilities include circular indoor heated children's swimming pool, tennis court, river fishing (racquets and rods for hire), hairdryers, children's play area, table tennis, pool table, colour TV lounge, babysitting service, shop, payphone, etc. Central site for touring Kerry. Open Easter to end October. Further details on request.

ENGLAND WALES & IRELAND
FARMS HOTELS
GUESTHOUSES
SELF-CATERING
CARAVANS
& CAMPING
'95
FREE VISITS!

SCOTLAND
FARMS HOTELS
GUESTHOUSES
SELF-CATERING
CARAVANS
& CAMPING
'95
FREE VISITS!

Recommended
SHORT
BREAK
HOLIDAYS
in
BRITAIN
1995
WITH MAPS

Self-Catering
& Furnished
Holidays '95
ENGLAND
SCOTLAND
WALES
FREE VISITS!

Bed & Breakfast
Stops '95
ENGLAND
SCOTLAND
WALES
IRELAND
and the
ISLE OF MAN
FREE VISITS!
Non-smokers, Disabled & Special Diets
plus CAMPUS HOLIDAYS

BRITAIN'S
HOLIDAYS
1995

GOLF GUIDE
OVER 2000 COURSES
HUNDREDS OF HOTELS
FRANCE • PORTUGAL • SPAIN • USA

RECOMMENDED
COUNTRY
HOTELS
OF BRITAIN
1995
Country Hotels
& Country House
Hospitality
WITH MAPS

RECOMMENDED
WAYSIDE
INNS
OF BRITAIN
1995

GÎTES
GUIDE

THE ORIGINAL & UNIQUE
£ 3.99
PETS
WELCOME!
1995
HOLIDAYS
FOR
OWNERS
& PETS
WITH
MAPS

CHILDREN
WELCOME!
Family Holiday Guide
95
FREE VISITS!

ONE FOR YOUR FRIEND 1995

FHG Publications have a large range of attractive holiday accommodation guides for all kinds of holiday opportunities throughout Britain. They also make useful gifts at any time of year. Our guides are available in most bookshops and larger newsagents but we will be happy to post you a copy direct if you have any difficulty. We will also post abroad but have to charge separately for post or freight. The inclusive cost of posting and packing the guides to you or your friends in the UK is as follows:

Farm Holiday Guide ENGLAND, WALES and IRELAND
Board, Self-catering, Caravans/Camping, Activity Holidays. Over 400 pages. **£4.80**

Farm Holiday Guide SCOTLAND
All kinds of holiday accommodation. **£3.00**

SELF-CATERING & FURNISHED HOLIDAYS
Over 1000 addresses throughout for Self-catering and caravans in Britain. **£4.20**

BRITAIN'S BEST HOLIDAYS
A quick-reference general guide for all kinds of holidays. **£3.30**

The FHG Guide to CARAVAN & CAMPING HOLIDAYS
Caravans for hire, sites and holiday parks and centres. **£3.30**

BED AND BREAKFAST STOPS
Over 1000 friendly and comfortable overnight stops. Non-smoking, The Disabled and Special Diets Supplements. **£4.40**

CHILDREN WELCOME! FAMILY HOLIDAY GUIDE
Family holidays with details of amenities for children and babies. **£4.40**

Recommended SHORT BREAK HOLIDAYS IN BRITAIN
'Approved' accommodation for quality bargain breaks. Introduced by John Carter. **£4.20**

Recommended COUNTRY HOTELS OF BRITAIN
Including Country Houses, for the discriminating. **£4.20**

Recommended WAYSIDE INNS OF BRITAIN
Pubs, Inns and small hotels. **£4.20**

PGA GOLF GUIDE Where to play and where to stay
Over 2000 golf courses in Britain with convenient accommodation. Endorsed by the PGA. Holiday Golf in France, Portugal, Spain and USA. **£9.50**

PETS WELCOME!
The unique guide for holidays for pet owners and their pets. **£4.60**

BED AND BREAKFAST IN BRITAIN
Over 1000 choices for touring and holidays throughout Britain. Airports and Ferries Supplement. **£3.30**

THE FRENCH FARM AND VILLAGE HOLIDAY GUIDE
The official guide to self-catering holidays in the 'Gîtes de France'. **£9.50**

Tick your choice and send your order and payment to FHG PUBLICATIONS, ABBEY MILL BUSINESS CENTRE, SEEDHILL, PAISLEY PA1 1TJ (TEL: 0141-887 0428. FAX: 0141-889 7204). **Deduct** 10% for 2/3 titles or copies; 20% for 4 or more.

Send to: NAME ....

ADDRESS ....

....

.... POST CODE ....

I enclose Cheque/Postal Order for £ ....

SIGNATURE .... DATE ....

Please complete the following to help us improve the service we provide. How did you find out about our guides:

☐ Press ☐ Magazines ☐ TV ☐ Radio ☐ Family/Friend ☐ Other.